D1692876

Gutenberg-Jahrbuch

86. Jahrgang des Gutenberg-Jahrbuchs. Begründet 1926
von ALOYS RUPPEL

GUTENBERG-JAHRBUCH 2011

Im Auftrag der Gutenberg-Gesellschaft herausgegeben
von STEPHAN FÜSSEL

Grußwort zum Gutenberg-Jahrbuch 2011

Das *Times Literary Supplement* stellte seinen Leserinnen und Lesern im Dezember das Gutenberg-Jahrbuch 2010 als ein "rich feast for bibliophiles" vor. Rezensent John L. Flood bezog diese Bemerkung nicht nur auf die ertragreichen Artikel, die sich über 1000 Jahre Buchforschung erstreckten, sondern zudem explizit auf die neue Satzschrift LT Malabar von Dan Reynolds, die auch in diesem Jahrgang wiederum Verwendung findet. Qualitätsvolle buchwissenschaftliche Beiträge und gediegene typografische Gestaltung gehören nach unserem Verständnis zum Wesen von Publikationen der Internationalen Gutenberg-Gesellschaft. Wir haben uns daher auch gefreut, dass das Gutenberg-Jahrbuch durch Nennung auf der Short-List des Wettbewerbs »Die schönsten deutschen Bücher 2010« in der Gruppe 2 (Wissenschaftliche Bücher, Fachbücher) wieder einmal ausgezeichnet wurde.

Ebenfalls war es eine große Freude, im Jahr 2010 den führenden indischen Typografen Prof. Mahendra Patel mit dem Preis der Internationalen Gutenberg-Gesellschaft und der Stadt Mainz, dem Gutenberg-Preis, auszeichnen zu können. Er ist ein Schüler von Adrian Frutiger und entwickelte mit ihm bereits in den 1970er Jahren eine moderne Typengestaltung einer der indischen Schriften, Devanagari. In Indien, einem Land mit großer Sprachen- und Schriftenvielfalt, sind 11 Schriftsysteme für 13 offizielle indische Sprachen in Gebrauch. Für 8 dieser Schriftsysteme entwarf Patel nun die Gestaltung der Schriftzeichen, die kongenial aufeinander abgestimmt sind, und trug so wesentlich zur Entwicklung der modernen Typografie in Indien bei. Aus diesem Grunde wird man gleich bei der Ankunft im Land auf den Schrifttafeln der Flughäfen vielsprachig, aber »wie aus einem Guss« mit den Schriften Patels geleitet.

Das vorliegende Gutenberg-Jahrbuch dokumentiert nicht nur die Preisverleihung an Mahendra Patel, sondern bietet wie in jedem Jahr Beiträge zur Geschichte des Buchdrucks seit der Frühdruckzeit von Autoren aus Frankreich, Großbritannien, Italien, den Niederlanden, Spanien, Deutschland, den USA, Ungarn und Indien, und in diesem Jahr einen besonderen Schwerpunkt mit Berichten über die aktuelle Entwicklung der Bücher im Umbruch zur digitalen Information. Katharina Ebenau berichtet über eine neue Form von Buchwerbung, die sich über YouTube rasch verbreitet: nämlich Buchwerbefilme, sogenannte *booktrailer*, als gern gesehene Marketinginstrumente für die Verlagsbranche. Christoph Kochhan hat für den Börsenverein des Deutschen Buchhandels eine Studie über Kinder- und Jugendliteratur erstellt, die einen hochinteressanten Einblick in die Chancen der E-Books im Markt für junge Leser bietet.

Ein aktueller Tagungsbericht referiert über den momentanen Stand von digitalen Editionen und der Einrichtung von virtuellen Forschungsumgebungen; die Tagung wurde im Januar 2011 vom Forschungsschwerpunkt Medienkonvergenz der Johannes Gutenberg-Universität unter Leitung von Prof. Dr. Elmar Mittler durchgeführt. Im Jahr 2011 zeigt sich ein Durchbruch der E-Books in erheblichem Umfang, der weltweite Vertrieb von ca. 20 Millionen iPads der Firma Apple in nur einem Jahr, der Vertrieb von Amazons Kindle nun auch in Europa – seit Ostern 2011 in Deutschland – und die zunehmende Ausrichtung wissenschaftlicher und belletristischer Verlage auf den elektronischen Markt sprechen eine eindeutige Sprache: Der größte geisteswissenschaftliche Verlag Europas, DeGruyter in Berlin, stellt seine gedruckten Produkte vollständig auch als

E-Books zur Verfügung; der größte Publikumsverlag der Welt, Random House, New York und Gütersloh, meldet für 2010 eine 250-prozentige Steigerung der Absatzzahlen von elektronischen Publikationen. Das Gutenberg-Jahrbuch wird seine Mittlerposition der Akzentuierung buchhistorischer und buch-kulturwissenschaftlicher Fragestellungen der letzten Jahrhunderte beibehalten, selbstverständlich aber auch die Umbruchsituation begleiten und die sich dadurch ergebenden Fragen für die Lesefähigkeit, für die Vermittlung von Information etc. analysieren.

Die Internationale Gutenberg-Gesellschaft mit Sitz in Mainz hat im zurückliegenden Jahr einen spürbaren Aufschwung erleben können. Erstmals wurde ein qualitativ hoch stehendes Jahresprogramm angeboten, das mit zahlreichen Exkursionen (Weimar, Antwerpen, Karlsruhe, Basel), Vortragsveranstaltungen zu Themen der Typografie oder der Verlagsarchive in Mainz, in Offenbach oder in Essen einlud, dazu Vorbesichtigungen speziell für die Mitglieder der Gesellschaft von Ausstellungen im Gutenberg-Museum. Die neu gestaltete Homepage www.gutenberg-gesellschaft.de lädt aktuell und optisch ansprechend zu den zahlreichen Aktivitäten ein. Unser Dank gilt der neuen Geschäftsführerin Christina Schmitz MA und zahlreichen Praktikantinnen aus dem Institut für Buchwissenschaft, die diese vielfältigen Aktivitäten kompetent managen. Beim Gutenberg-Jahrbuch sorgen sich dankenswerterweise Corinna Norrick MA um die Redaktion und Prof. Ralf de Jong um die Gestaltung.

Die Gesellschaft trauert um zwei geschätzte Mitglieder, die langjährige Schatzmeisterin und Vorsitzende des Senatorenrates Frau Hannetraud Schultheiß, die am 31. Januar 2011 verstarb, und um das langjährige Vorstandsmitglied und den verdienten Mainzer Ehrenbürger, den gelernten Schriftsetzer Karl Delorme, der am 12. März 2011 verstarb. Wir werden beiden ein ehrendes Angedenken bewahren. Das Gutenberg-Jahrbuch gedenkt seines Autors, Pfarrer i. R. Siegfried Risse, einem anerkannten Psalmenforscher, von dem wir im vorliegenden Band noch einen Artikel »Zwei Auflagen von Michael Furters Psalterium im Jahr 1503« veröffentlichen können.

Jens Beutel
Präsident der Int. Gutenberg-Gesellschaft

Univ.-Prof. Dr. Stephan Füssel
Herausgeber des Gutenberg-Jahrbuchs

INHALT

Gutenberg-Preis 2010

MAHENDRA PATEL
My Journey into Type Design and Typography 11

BRUNO PFÄFFLI
Laudation 19

15. Jahrhundert

FRANCISCO J. CORNEJO
Iconografía de las ilustraciones del *Fasciculus temporum*,
de Werner Rolevinck 27

RANDALL HERZ
Three Fifteenth Century Proof Sheets with Manuscript Corrections
from Nuremberg presses 56

ADOLFO TURA
Edizioni quattrocentine delle *Facezie* di Poggio in volgare
(ed una postilla su Leonardo lettore) 77

ANETTE LÖFFLER
Neue Fragmente mit der Postilla des Nikolaus von Lyra
aus dem Duisburger Stadtarchiv 81

HANS-WALTER STORK
»Hier hefft an dat Landrecht aver Ditmarschen.«
Neue Fragmente des gedruckten Dithmarscher Landrechts
(Lübeck: Steffen Arndes, 1487/88) 85

16. Jahrhundert

SIEGFRIED RISSE †
Zwei Auflagen von Michael Furters Psalterium im Jahr 1503 102

FEDERICA FABBRI
Tridenti: per Mapheum de Fraçacinis, M.ccccxj 110

GISELA MÖNCKE
Ein wieder aufgefundener Erfurter Lutherdruck von 1523
mit einem Bildnis des Reformators 127

H. GEORGE FLETCHER
A Manuscript Aldine Catalogue from the Mid-Sixteenth Century 131

ANDRÁS NÉMETH
Willibald Pirckheimer and his Greek codices from Buda 175

HERMANN BAUMEISTER
Universalis Cosmographiae descriptio 199

ANNELIESE SCHMITT
Alexius Bresnicer – Humanist, Dramatiker, Theologe und Reformer.
Eine Bibliothek gibt Auskunft über ein Leben   216

17. & 18. Jahrhundert

DAPHNE HOOGENBOEZEM
Madame D'Aulnoy en Angleterre: La réception des *Contes des fées*   247

DENNIS E. RHODES
Biblioteca Windhagiana. Part II.   261

WILLIAM A. KELLY
Survey of pre-1801 Low Countries Imprints
in Scottish Research Libraries   264

MARVIN J. HELLER
On the Identity of the First Printers in Slavuta   269

STEVEN VAN IMPE
The Social and Geographical Repositioning of a Minor Printer
in Eighteenth Century Antwerp   282

21. Jahrhundert

KATHARINA EBENAU
»Als die Bücher laufen lernten...« Buchtrailer als Marketing-
instrument in der Verlagsbranche   290

CHRISTOPH KOCHHAN
Kinder- und Jugendliteratur   299

ELMAR MITTLER / CHRISTINA SCHMITZ
Digitale Edition und Forschungsbibliothek   306

Zur Diskussion gestellt

ANNIKA ROCKENBERGER
Albrecht Dürer, Sebastian Brant und die Holzschnitte
des *Narrenschiff*-Erstdrucks (Basel 1494)   312

FRIEDER SCHMIDT
Überlegungen zu einer Klassifikation
der Aufzeichnungs-, Speicher-, Kopier- und Vervielfältigungssysteme
aus fertigungstechnischer Sicht   330

WOLFGANG SCHMITZ *Nachruf*
Der Bucharchivar. Nachruf auf Ludwig Delp
(1921–2010)   342

Abkürzungsverzeichnisse   348
Autorenanschriften   353
Ehrentafel der Gutenberg-Gesellschaft   354
Präsidium und Vorstand der Gutenberg-Gesellschaft   355
Jahresbericht der Gutenberg-Gesellschaft   356
Jahresbericht des Gutenberg-Museums   360
Jahresbericht des Instituts für Buchwissenschaft   365
Verzeichnis der Webseiten   374
Impressum

Gutenberg-Preis 2010

MAHENDRA PATEL

My Journey into Type Design and Typography*

INDIA IS THE COUNTRY FULL OF DIVERSITIES of cultures, religions, languages and also of scripts. It has many states; the respective identities of these states are differentiated by the language the people of the region speak and most of these languages have their own scripts [fig. 1]. All these languages derive from the Sanskrit language that has a phonetic structure; Sanskrit has Devanagari as a script. Devanagari script is used for Hindi, which is one of the national languages of India. Hindi is the language of the states Uttar Pradesh and Madhya Pradesh. The Haryanvi language of the state Haryana, the Rajasthani language of the state Rajasthan and the Marathi language of the state Maharashtra also use Devanagari script. *Shiro-Rekha* (head-line) is a typical characteristic of the Devanagari script, where the characters are drawn below the *Shiro-Rekha* connected by a vertical stoke. The vowels have characters as well as vowelization *Matras* (signs) that connect to consonant characters to give pronounceable sounds to the consonants. The *Matras* are written at the top, bottom, left or right side of the consonant characters. The Bengali language, spoken in the state of Bengal, uses Bengali script. Bengali also has *Shiro-Rekha* and a system of vowelization similar to that of Devanagari script. But its characters are different than Devanagari. The Assames language of the state of Assam also uses Bengali script; however, a few consonants are modified. The Gurumukhi script of the Punjabi language, which is spoken in the state of Punjab, has the *Shiro-Rekha* integrated into characters; its vowelization is carried out with modified *Matras* than those of Devanagari. The Gujarati script of the Gujarati language, which is spoken in the state of Gujarat, on the other hand, is a reformed developed script from Devanagari, where the *Shiro-Rekha* has merged as an integral part of the main characters. It follows a vowelization system similar to that of Devanagari but without *Shiro-Rekha*. The Oriya script of the Oriya language, spoken in the Orissa state, has a typical depiction of *Shiro-Rekha* as a curvilinear arch integrated on the top of the characters, giving it its relation with south Indian script forms. Most of the north Indian scripts, on the other hand, have forms which are based on reed pen with a 45 degree cut flat nib, giving a typical stress on the top left and bottom right at 45 degrees – in writing as well as in type designs.

While the south Indian scripts (Tamil, Malayalam, Telugu and Kannada) have the same phonetic structure of Sanskrit, they are based on stylus writing and tend to be of mono-line thickness with curvilinear and circular strokes. Most of the time, the *Matras* are extended strokes on right, left,

India, a country with diversity, aspiring for unity

* This is a transcript of Mahendra Patel's presentation on Friday, June 25, 2010 and his acceptance speech, held on June 26, 2010. We have respected the oral style of delivery.

top or bottom from the main characters. The Tamil script of the Tamil language, spoken in the state of Tamilnadu, only has Ousthya and nasal consonants, which are pronounced differently in different contexts. Tamil has more nasal consonants and an extended vowelization system. The vowel *Matras* extends as the integral part of consonants. The Malayalam script of the language Malayalam from the state of Kerala has the same consonants and vowels as Devanagari but its letter forms are more similar to some of the Tamil characters. The Kannada script of the Kannada language, spoken in the state of Karnataka, has a typical *Shiro-Rekha* that has a semicircular turn on the right side. The letter forms are curvilinear and more symmetrical or balanced on a vertical axis. It has *Vottus* (half letter forms in smaller proportion at the bottom right side of the main characters). The Telugu script of the Telugu language from the state of Andhra Pradesh has very similar letter forms as the Kannada script with one major difference in *Shiro-Rekha* which is like a tick sign.

The type designs in most of the Indian scripts evolved regionally, influenced by local individual initiatives and efforts producing varied and diversified designs in terms of styles, proportions and structures. In today's era of nationalization and globalization, harmony and unity in this diversity is felt to be a necessity while retaining regional identity is central as well.

My educational background
My early childhood and school education were spent at a village in Gujarat. Though I was excellent in science and mathematics, I was most inspired, influenced and motivated by my drawing teacher, Nathubhai, and I used to thoroughly enjoy painting floors, walls and pots in school. Against the expectations of my teachers and friends that I would go into engineering, I decided to graduate in Painting/Fine Arts (1960–64). My Fine Arts education at Maharaja Sayajirao University, Baroda, gave me good sensitivity and understanding of the life around me.

But my logical and business-oriented mindset (my father was a tobacco businessman) led me to the National Institute of Design (NID), Ahmedabad, to do my Post-Graduation in Graphic Design (1964–67). I became extremely interested in hot-metal typography at NID and Peter Teubner and Hans Christian Pulver taught me the skills and design principles of typography at NID (1965/66), leading me to the School of Design, Basle (1967/68) to learn Type & Typography extensively. In Basle, Armin Hofmann gave me good grounding in graphic design, and Andre Gurtler gave me in-depth insight to and the skills of Sans-Serif letterforms. Then in 1971 I had my breakthrough at the Atelier Frutiger (Paris) in the area of type design development of Indian scripts. Adrian Frutiger took a keen interest and shared his type design knowledge and skills; I acquired expertise, focus and a mission of type designing to follow back at NID in India.

My type design development projects
In the following, I would like to present some examples of my type design development projects:

– Devanagari type design in linear style, 1971: I commenced my first type design exploration with Devanagari script under the mentorship of Adrian Frutiger in 1971 at Atelier Frutiger (Paris). It was based on design principles of his type design "Univers". This type design was based on the structure of vertical and horizontal axis and stroke endings either in vertical or horizontal as well as strong visual corrections in the joints. Monotype Corporation did a test trial 36 pt hot metal type in 1972. This design was perceived as an adoption of Univers to Devanagari and was resisted in India as a design which was seen as westernized during public presentations to designers, type foundry and printing personnel. [Fig. 2]

– Devanagari type design based on reed pen writing in contemporary style, 1972: I developed a new type design in reed pen form with a simplified, structural and graphical treatment to the joints, endings and loops. It can be considered a transitional design between type designs of linear style and existing traditional reed pen type designs. [Fig. 3]

– Devanagari type design for stencil writing, 1974: I was commissioned by ISI (Indian Standardization Institute) to design the Devanagari letterforms for stencil writing to be used by architects and engineers. I designed form, structure, joints and endings considering the constraints of stencil grove and pen (techno-graph/rapido-graph). [Figs. 4a and 4b]

– Devanagari type design for display/exhibition text, 1979: NID took on the theme pavilion exhibition project from the government of India. I made a new type design that is humanistic as well as graphic in style, that goes well with Frutiger bold, a typeface selected by NID.

– Devanagari, Tamil & Bengali type designs for signage, 1976: NID Airport Authority of India had commissioned NID to prepare type designs in Devanagari, Tamil & Bengali scripts to be used on their then international airports (Delhi, Mumbai, Chennai and Kolkatta). I made Devanagari, Tamil and Bengali type designs in humanistic style in bold weight for this purpose. [Figs. 5a and 5b]

– Gujarati type design for phototypesetting, 1981: Gopal krishna Modi of Gujarati Type Foundry, Mumbai, asked me to develop a linear type design in Gujarati to be executed by ITR, Pune. I made the master design in normal weight for text in humanistic style. [Fig. 6]

– Kannada type design for body text, 1982: Deccan Herald, a publishing house from Bangalore, asked me to develop a contemporary design in Kannada script for body text use in their publications. I designed the bottom stroke heavy type design in linear style for them. [Fig. 7]

– Malayalam type design for body text, 1985: Malayalam Manorama, Cochin, the most popular publishing house from South India, asked me to develop a new design in Malyalam script for body text use in their publications. I made a type design based on rational writing with a quill pen nib in normal and bold weights. [Figs. 8a and 8b]

My signage design projects
These are some of my signage design projects:

– Logo name design for SBI in different Indian languages, 1989: I developed a matching logo name design in 13 major languages with 11 different scripts including English for the State Bank of India. The design is harmonious, matching visually in term of style, size and weight. The logo name is used in tri-lingual (regional, national and international) configuration all over India. [Fig. 9]

– Signage design for Ahmedabad city in two Indian languages, 1998: I did an explorative workshop with NID students on signage design for Ahmedabad city and presented it to the Municipal Commissioner of the city, who commissioned the project to me. The design distinguishes the bilingual comprehension of Gujarati and English by colors: white and yellow.

– Signage design system for Tirumala in five Indian languages, 2000: Tirupati is the richest temple and most visited pilgrimage place of India. Tirumala and Tirupati Devasthanam commissioned NID to design the signage system in five languages (Telugu, Kannada, Tamil, Hindi and English), all of them having their own script. I designed location, direction and orientation signage as well as road signage and bus-stop signage. I developed the series of pictograms and arrow signs especially for this project. It was executed on RCC pillars clad with ceramic tiles with graphics printed in ceramic ink and third-fired.

– Signage design system for Hyderabad city for international tourists, 2003: The tourism department of Andhra Pradesh approached NID for a tourism signage design for Hyderabad city to match their international tourism aspiration. We short-listed around 50 touristic sights and worked out a total direction signage plan on 70 major cross roads indicating the distance of travel to each tourist spot. We also promoted these spots with key information on the back side of the signage units and proposed orientation maps at major public and key places.

My map design projects

I would like to share some of my map design experience:

– Tourist Maps of Ahmedabad city, 1974: I was excited by the use of a map to get around the city of Basle, and on my return I ventured into making a similar map for Ahmedabad city, but without any knowledge of map designing. My first map design was almost similar in graphics to the one I used in Basle. NID sold the design and print copies to the government of Gujarat. It received a Directorate of Advertising and Visual Publicity (DAVP) award for best design and printing in 1974. When Ahmedabad Municipal Corporation approached NID for a reprint of the map, I developed a completely new design based on my experiences from the first version. I designed it in both English and Gujarati languages. I also introduced the pictograms as location marks in the maps.

– Bus route map of Ahmedabad city, 1978: Having now been recognized as a good map designer, Ahmedabad Municipal Transport Service approached me for a bus route map for their complex net of about 600 bus routes. I created a map folder with a very user-friendly presentation of the information categorized, e.g. with a route index, a bus stops index, a frequency index, a tourist places index, an outskirts route map etc. The map was produced both in English and Gujarati languages.

– Guide map of Gujarat, 1974: Soon after my first map, the Gujarat government commissioned NID to make a road map of Gujarat. It was a complex and versatile project to plot, verify and present the extensive information in the most readable format possible. My graphic and typographic choices were most critical during the manual paste-up artworks (there was no computer). The map was an accompanying folder to a booklet giving tourist information on the city and including an abridged map.

– Irrigation map of Gujarat, 1974: The irrigation department of the Gujarat government commissioned NID to design the map for their major, medium and small irrigation schemes with details of their status (proposed, in progress or completed) and including the catchments, irrigation area and power generation plant information. The map is used as a reference map for their engineers and administrative staff. It was designed to be folded and filed as well as for easy retrieval of information. The map is updated at the end of every five year plan.

– Tourist map of Goa, 1978: There was the CHOGAM meeting of the prime ministers in Goa and the governor asked NID to design a tourist map of Goa district on this occasion. I designed the tourist map of Goa with all of the tourist spots and special icons for location signs. It also included a city map of the Panjim, the most important and popular city in Goa.

– Cultural map of India, 1994: On occasion of the Festival of India in the USA, this map was designed for the government of India. It had a visual map with an overview of all artistic and archaeological monuments with a chronological index as well as brief cultural information with some visuals for each state of India.

– Industrial map of India, 1978: The Prime Minister's office commissioned NID to design an industrial map of India for the industry ministers as communication aids to interact with investors. I developed an alphanumeric color, shapes for visual codes and a supportive reference directory for more details. To cope with the complexity and multitude of information, it was divided into six individual zonal maps.

My aspiration and gratitude

With my education, training and design experience at National Institute of Design in Ahmedabad over 40 years (1964–2003), I have a mindset of evolving harmony among the type designs for different Indian scripts. I also have an inclination to explore and design in linear or mono-line style and I also aspire to work on a type design system matching different Indian scripts amongst one another as well as English as one of the Indian scripts. During the last seven years, after having retired from NID in 2003, I have imparted my experience in Letter Design, Type Design and Typography by teaching workshops at some of the leading institutes of design in India. It is my privilege that the International Gutenberg Society has appreciated my work in India and bestowed the Gutenberg Award 2010 on me. It makes me, my teachers in India and Europe, my parent institute NID and my design community in India very proud.

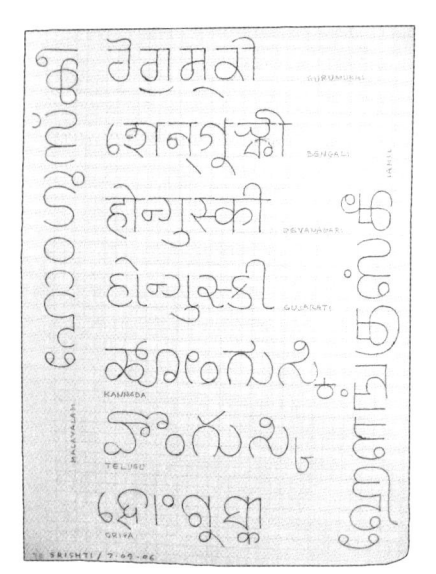

[Fig. 1]

हिंदी भाषा की पसार-वृद्धि करना उसका विकास
करना ताकि वह भारत की सामाजिक संस्कृति के
तत्वों की अभिव्यक्ति का माध्यम हो सके
तथा उसकी आत्मीयता में हस्तक्षेप किए बिना
हिंदुस्तानी और अष्टम अनुसूची में उल्लिखित अन्य
भारतीय भाषाओं के रूप
शैली और पदावली को आत्मसात् करते

[Fig. 2]

घ

अनायडी छ ढ

हिंदी भाषा की प्रसार-वृद्धि करना उसका विकास
करना ताकि वह भारत की सामाजिक संस्कृति के सब
तत्वों की अभिव्यक्ति का माध्यम हो सके
तथा उसकी आत्मीयता में हस्तक्षेप किए बिना
हिंदुस्तानी और अष्टम अनुसूची में उल्लिखित अन्य
भारतीय भाषाओं के रूप
शैली और पदावली को आत्मसात करते हुए
कखगघङ चछजझञ टठडढण तथदधन पफबभम
यरलव शषसह क्षत्रज्ञ अइईउऊए
क का कि की कु कू के कै को कौ कं कः

[Fig. 4b]

New tamil in lineal style

ஹிந்தி பாஷை பரவுவதற்கு ஆவன செய்தலும்,
இந்தியாவின் பலகூறுடைய பண்பாட்டின்
சகல அம்சங்களையும் வெளியிடுவதற்கேற்ற
கருவியாகப்பயன்படுமாறு அதை அபிவிருத்தி
செய்தலும், அதனுடைய தனிப்பண்பிற்கு
இடையூறின்றி ஹிந்துஸ்தானியிலும் எட்டாவது
• துபசிலில் குறிப்பிட்ட மற்றைய இந்திய
பாஷைகளிலும் வழங்கும் வடிவங்களையும்
நடையையும் சொற்றொடர்களையும்
கைக்கொள்வதின் மூலமாகவும்,
கங சஞ டண தந பம யரலவ ழளாறன ஷஸஹஜக்ஷ்
அஆ ஃஈ உஊ எஏஐ ஒஓஔ ∴
க கா கி கீ கு கூ கெ கே கை கொ கோ கௌ க்

• துபசிலில் குறிப்பிட்ட மற்றைய இந்திய
• **துபசிலில் குறிப்பிட்ட மற்றைய இந்திய**

இ

[Fig. 5a]

[Fig. 7]

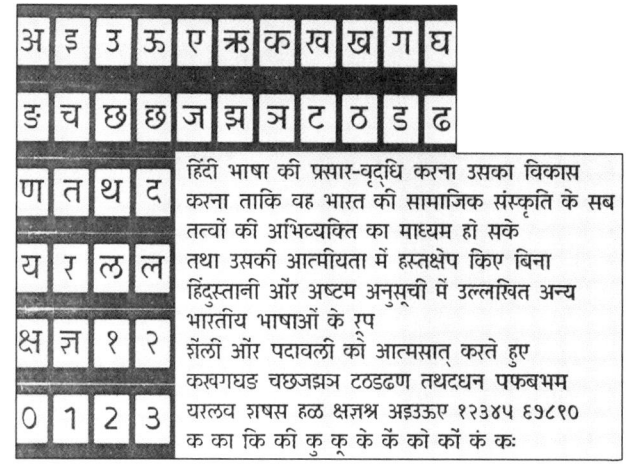

[Fig. 3]

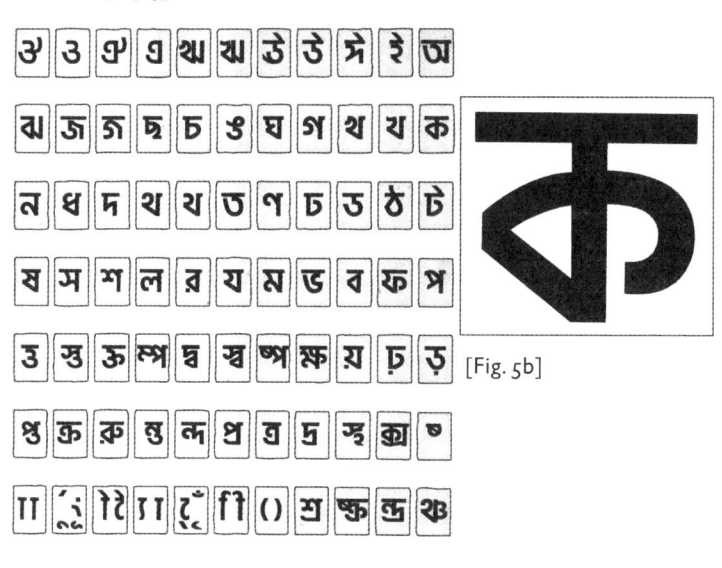

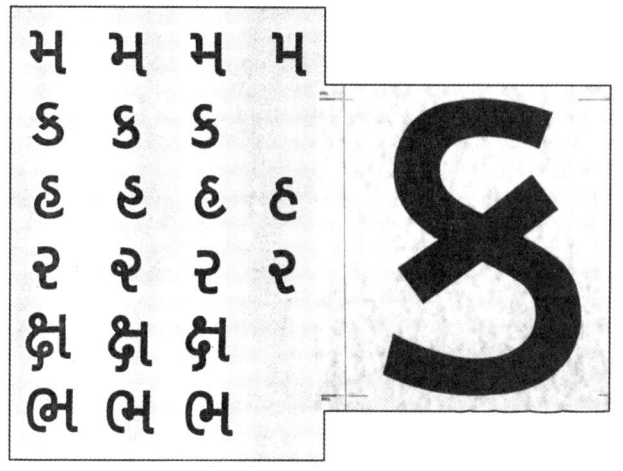

[Fig. 4a]

[Fig. 5b]

[Fig. 6]

[Fig. 8a]

ഇന്ത്യൻ പ്രധാനമന്ത്രി ഇന്ദിരാഗാദ്ധ്നീ
അആ ഇഈ ഉഊ എഏഐ ഒഓഔ
അംഅഃഴ കഖഗഘങ ചഛജഝഞ
ടഠഡഢണ തഥദധന പഫബഭമ യരലവ
ശഷസ ഹളഴറ ക്ഷങ്കക്കങ്ങ ച്ചചരഞ്ചഞ്ചേര
ഞ്ഞട്ടണ്ടണ്ണ ത്തന്തന്ദന്ന പ്പമ്പമ്മ യ്യല്ലവ്വ
ൻൽൾർൺ ഗ്ഗദ്ദബ്ബശ്ശസ്റ്റ ന്ത
ാ ീ ൂ ൈൊ ഃ ൃ ൂ
12345 67890 ½¼¾ ⅓⅔ ⅛⅜
+−×÷= %()[] .,:; "«»" !? ...·— / ●○∗

ഞ്ച

[Fig. 8b]

ഭാർതീയ സ്റ്റേറ്റ് ബ്യാംഗ്
भारतीय स्टेट बैंक
State Bank of India

ദാരതീയ സ്റ്റേററ് ബാങ്ക
भारतीय स्टेट बैंक
State Bank of India

भारतीय स्टेट बँक
भारतीय स्टेट बँक
State Bank of India

ഖാരഡീവൃ ഒ്ഷേറ്റ ഠഘാങ്ങ
भारतीय स्टेट बैंक
State Bank of India

[Fig. 9]

BRUNO PFÄFFLI

Laudation*

Ladies and Gentlemen,
Namaste Smitaben, namaste Mahendrabhai,

I CONGRATULATE THE MEMBERS OF THE COMMITTEE for having chosen Professor Mahendra Patel as the awardee of the Gutenberg Prize. This award will certainly contribute to Mahendra Patel being acknowledged in India as the man who, as a type designer and teacher, is more responsible than anybody else for the fact that some of the most important Indian scripts have discarded their antiquated appearance and obtained a modern expression. The second thing I want to mention is that I am speaking to you here as a replacement. The man most suitable to give the encomium of Mahendra Patel would have been the world-famous type designer Adrian Frutiger, the man who had a decisive influence on Mahendra Patel's professional career. Unfortunately, his state of health did not allow him to be present here.

Before I come to speak of Mahendra Patel's professional life and some of his most important works, I would like to read excerpts from a quotation by him to you. To me, these seem symbolic for his philosophy of life and work. He writes: "When I look at the complexity of my country, with its numerous states and the different languages, scripts and cultures, I am for the most part amazed and bewildered. At the same time, however, this inspires my thirst for new knowledge. That keeps me alive and active. And I must always work on one or the other challenge, or on some problem until satisfaction arises within me that I have been able to contribute something to the needs of this country so full of diversity that is striving for harmony among its people. There is always someone who needs me and a place where work is waiting for me. I feel it a privilege to live in such a country with my family and friends, with my fellow human beings and the general public around me with their sincere and human expressions of welcome and gratitude."

Mahendra Patel, as I have known and held him in high regard for over 40 years, is a rather shy, but approachable and adaptable man. All those who have had the good fortune to enter into closer contact with him think highly of his warm-heartedness, his honesty, and his untiring commitment to be of assistance to his fellow beings. He was born in Ahmedabad in the northwestern state of Gujarat in 1943. At school, his preferred subjects were mathematics, geometry, and drawing. Towards the end of his time at school, the question arose of his further education: the study of engineering, architecture or painting? The latter was finally given

* This is the English translation of the laudation for Mahendra Patel, as held by Bruno Pfäffli in Mainz in June of 2010. The text at hand respects the oral style of delivery.

Due to technical constraints, not all of the images and figures spoken about in this text have been reproduced here.

preference. This is a picture from those student days in the mid-sixties: Sketches of Ganesha, the god of happiness and prosperity [fig. 1]. Because his studies of painting did not completely satisfy him, his teacher gave him a piece of advice the consequences of which were to gain seminal significance in a vocational respect: he sent him to Gira Sarabhai, the co-foundress of the National Institute of Design in Ahmedabad. After looking through his paintings, that good lady advised him to join the newly established specialist class for graphic design. In the sixties and seventies, internationally acknowledged designers and graphic artists lectured at this institution, among others, the husband and wife team Hofmann from Basle in 1966 and, somewhat later, Adrian Frutiger from Paris.

In the classes given by Dorothea and Armin Hofmann, Mahendra Patel had his very first contact with type design. According to his own comments, he felt that the letters were like sculptures; in their composition and construction he saw parallels to the logical thinking that had fascinated him in earlier years in mathematics and geometry. Armin Hofmann's influence on his professional career was considerable, says Mahendra Patel. Discipline, analytical thinking, the endeavour to find the simple form, stylized to the extreme, and its best possible execution: those are qualities which were later in demand in his work on the various Indian scripts.

From Adrian Frutiger he learned that a type is not designed in accordance with mathematical rules, but that it is based on calligraphic forms written with a wide quill. That means: To create something new, in keeping with the times, by taking the basic rules of earlier times into consideration. In 1967, Adrian Frutiger came to NID for five weeks. At that time, the Indian types, which have beautiful calligraphic models, were in a poor state. An example is this beautiful calligraphy in Sanskrit, an excerpt from the Veda, the holy book of the Indians [fig. 2]. India's printed text script (example from the nineteen-sixties) is comparable with that of western prints from the fifteenth century [fig. 3].

Adrian Frutiger set himself the task, with the collaboration of some students, of achieving something useful from normal Devanagari, the script used for the national language Hindi. Its aesthetics, its legibility, were intended to be renewed in the sense of the development of European types. After the first script design exercises, Mahendra Patel turned out to be the most talented student. Frutiger decided to continue to work with him on the project. Of this collaboration, Frutiger said: "Sometimes I had difficulties in teaching with my poor school English. Some students accordingly made their difficulties known, but not Mahendra. Before I would come to an end with my remarks, he had already understood what I wanted to explain. His extremely rapid power of comprehension of things impressed me. He was in every respect an intelligent, industrious and gifted student."

To make Devanagari legible in small type sizes, the letters had to undergo a simplification of form. Mahendra Patel alone had to decide where the limit lay. A great degree of responsibility thus lay on his shoulders. Here is an example of the very first attempts: on the outside left the original calligraphic form of a letter, next to it the various working steps towards simplification of the form, first in old style, then in linear style and finally the definitive form [fig. 4].

The people in charge at NID were enthusiastic about the result of the first type matter samples, but they were of the opinion that there would be no sense in continuing with the work without the blessing of a special research committee at the University of Benares. Among other things, the following documents prepared by Frutiger and Mahendra Patel were submitted to this committee for evaluation: the simplified character of the letter *ka* in old style was brought into relation with a picture of a historic ruin in Central India, that in linear style with a picture of modern architecture by Louis Kahn in Ahmedabad; the revised and simplified script in old style and the script with linear strokes [fig. 5, top to bottom]; a script pattern comparison of the traditional text script cut out of a newspaper (at the limit of legibility) compared to the same text set in a significantly smaller type size from the proposed linear style version. The gain in space is considerable, the legibility guaranteed [fig. 6, from left to right]. After a lengthier discussion, the committee gave its go-ahead and the tandem Frutiger-Patel undertook the schematic design of the different widths and bold faces [fig. 7].

Frutiger asked the administration of NID to send Mahendra Patel to him to Paris so he could continue the work there. In 1968, Mahendra Patel spent a year studying at the College of Design in Basle. During the four-week summer holidays, he went to Frutiger, in order to push ahead with the conceptual layout of Devanagari. I recall that Mahendra Patel lived and worked in an annex to our studio. He got to see almost nothing of Paris and its sights as he worked almost without a break. What impressed us all was, on the one hand, the enthusiasm with which went about his work, his diligence, his perseverance and, on the other hand, his remark that he had come to Basle and Paris to acquire as much knowledge as possible so he would be able to pass it on later to his students. Because, he said, it was his duty to contribute something for the progress of his country.

A brief anecdote: during his stay in Paris the entire staff of the studio, including their families, were twice able to enjoy delicious Indian food, prepared by our friend Mahendra. To the astonishment of us all, we heard that he was an absolute novice at cooking. He told us that he had learned cooking by looking over his wife Smita's shoulder now and again when she was engaged in this activity!

In 1971, Mahendra Patel came to Paris once again, this time for 13 months in order to complete the Devanagari. He had to draw all the letters and adapt them to the special system of units of the English Monotype company which had secured the distribution rights for itself. Unfortunately, it did not come onto the market. Nowadays, it is often used for road sign systems and title types. In addition, if you take a somewhat closer look at contemporary Indian publications, you can find that various type manufacturers in India have let themselves be greatly inspired by the project prepared by Frutiger and Patel.

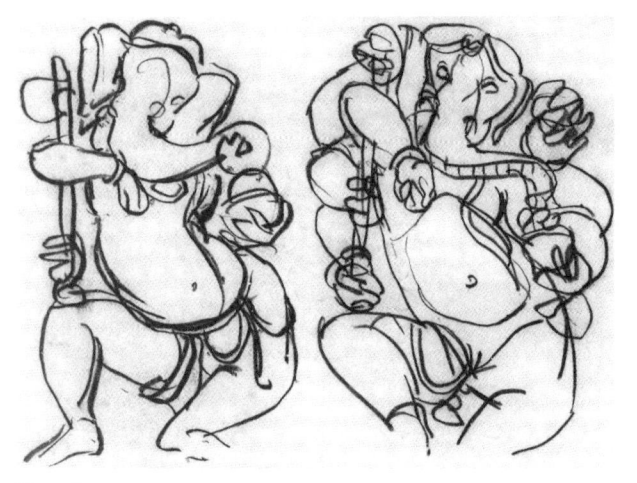

[Fig. 1]

[Fig. 2]

हिंदी भाषा की प्रसार-वृद्धि करना उसका विकास
करना ताकि वह भारत की सामाजिक संस्कृति के सब
तत्वों की अभिव्यक्ति का माध्यम हो सके
तथा उसकी आत्मीयता में हस्तक्षेप किए बिना

हिंदी भाषा की प्रसार-वृद्धि करना उसका विकास
करना ताकि वह भारत की सामाजिक संस्कृति के सब
तत्वों की अभिव्यक्ति का माध्यम हो सके
तथा उसकी आत्मीयता में हस्तक्षेप किए बिना

[Fig. 5]

अले भी पडने का समाचार प्राप्त
हुए ६ । इस देवी प्रकाश का प्रभाव
तो सम्पर्ण क्षेत्र पर पड़ा है किन्तु
बेलवार रामपर, दान, मकरा
तथा उनक अन्य समीपस्थ ग्रामा
मे तो खडी फसल पर्णतया ध्वस्त
हो गई है । मकान तथा मवेशियां
को भी काफी क्षति पहुची है ।

हिंदी भाषा की पसार-वृद्धि करना उसका विकास
करना ताकि वह भारत की सामाजिक संस्
तत्वों की अभिव्यक्ति का माध्यम हो सके
तथा उसकी आत्मीयता में हस्तक्षेप किए
हिंदुस्तानी और अष्टम अनुसूची में उल्लिखित
भारतीय भाषाओं के रूप
शैली और पदावली को आत्मसात करते हुए

[Fig. 6]

देवनागरी देवनागरी देवनागरी देवनागरी
देवनागरी देवनागरी देवनागरी देवनागरी
देवनागरी देवनागरी देवनागरी देवनागरी
देवनागरी देवनागरी देवनागरी देवनागरी
देवनागरी

[Fig. 7]

தபசிலில் குறிப்பிட்ட மற்றைய இந்திய
பாஷைகளிலும் வழங்கும் வடிவங்களாயும்

தபசிலில் குறிப்பிட்ட மற்றைய இந்திய
தபசிலில் குறிப்பிட்ட மற்றைய இந்திய

[Fig. 11]

[Fig. 10]

कांग्रेसी नेताओंपर
आचरणसंहिताके
उल्लंघनका आरोप

cū rege rex te capiet
Bohemi ergo sicut
solith laudauerat z

[Fig. 3]

ड़ ऱ ज़ ऩ

[Fig. 4]

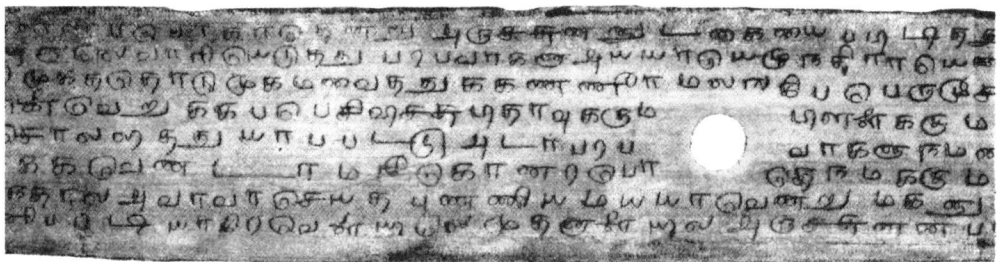

[Fig. 8]

ஸ்ரீ
ஸ்ரீ
ஸ்ரீ
ஸ்ரீ

[Fig. 9]

ভারতীয় স্টেট বেঙ্ক
ভারতীয় স্টেট ব্যাঙ্ক
State Bank of India
ભારતીય સ્ટેટ બેંક
भारतीय स्टेट बैंक
ಭಾರತೀಯ ಸ್ಟೇಟ್ ಬ್ಯಾಂಕ್
ഭാരതീയ സ്റ്റേറ്റ് ബാങ്ക്
भारतीय स्टेट बैंक
ଭାରତୀୟ ଷ୍ଟେଟ ବ୍ୟାଙ୍କ
ਭਾਰਤੀਆ ਸਟੇਟ ਬੈਂਕ
பாரதீய ஸ்டேட் பாங்கு
భారతీయ స్టేట్ బ్యాంక్
بھارتیہ اسٹیٹ بینک

[Fig. 12]

[Fig. 13]

During this second stay, Mahendra Patel worked with Adrian Frutiger on a further plan for the Tamil script used in southern India. The characters were originally scratched out on palm leaves and made visible by being sprinkled with black powder, as in this detail of an inscribed palm leaf [fig. 8]. As Frutiger described: "Mahendra drew the script from the enlargement of such a palm leaf [fig. 9]. At the top the scratched, then the written form, then the skeleton and the linear form of a letter. We made a study beforehand of how one draws a fine skeleton script from a palm script and then thickens it, without changing its style [fig. 10]. I just gave instructions, Mahendra was responsible for implementing them." This then is a typesetting specimen of the light-faced and bold font of the Tamil drawn by Mahendra Patel [fig. 11].

I quote Frutiger again: "When his time at our studio was over, he went back to India, to teach there and to develop his own types […] It was claimed that I had designed a new Indian script and it had been carried out – that is wrong! I made the first attempts at a renewal and then I was a consultant, who had created the starting point from which Mahendra himself continued the work. I am happy with the result." This concludes the part of my laudation regarding Mahendra Patel's professional development and activity until 1972.

Back at the National Institute of Design, Mahendra Patel taught script and typography. He worked on development projects for Indian scripts, prepared tourist maps and maps of towns and cities. Later lettering and signposting systems came into being in collaboration with Leaf Design, an agency run by his son Sumit in Mumbai. For a better understanding of the different Indian scripts, here is a picture of the most important language zones on the basis of the letter *ka* [fig. 12]. Please note the great extent of the Devanagari area at the centre of the map.

The specimen sets of some of his types give evidence of Mahendra Patel's contribution in being the first Indian designer to have made the attempt not only to modernize the country's types, but at the same time to design them to be more legible. He performed great pioneering work in this field. You have already seen the Devanagari and the Tamil, there are: Bengali, created in 1976 for the International Airport Authority of India; Kannada, year of origin 1981, an order from the Deccan Herald Publishing House; Gujarati, 1981 drawn for the Gujarati Type Foundry in Mumbai; study for Malayalam, drawn in 1982 for Malayalam Manorama Publishers in Cochin; and, finally, simply on account of the beauty of the drawing, two letters of Kannada which in my opinion best confirm what Mahendra Patel felt at the time of his first contact with characters: letters look similar to sculptures. The interiors catch the light, they are of the same importance as the external forms.

Here are some examples of the use of the various scripts for signposting systems: Firstly, logotypes for the State Bank of India in the twelve most important scripts [fig. 13], from the year 1989. Secondly, a design for trilingual use for house signs. The first line is in the language of the state concerned, below is Devanagari. Thirdly, this is a further example of use at one of the branches with Gujarati. These are sign boards in the south

Indian town of Tirumala-Tirupati in Telugu and Devanagari scripts from 1998. In comparison, these are sign boards in Ujjain, one of the largest and best known places of pilgrimage in India from 2004; the script is Devanagari. Here are two further photos of the signposting system of Mumbai International Airport, completed in 2008. And finally, here is a section of a sign board in Ujjain and part of a town and street map of Tirupati.

With regard to a further, very important aspect of our Gutenberg Prize-winner's professional career, his teaching activity, I can make use of comments by some of his former students. Apart from his teaching at NID and subsequently at various colleges in India, he has taught in the USA, in Canada, in New Zealand and in Pakistan. His former students all bore unanimous witness: Mahendra Patel was a highly respected teacher. His ability to empathize and his capacity to accept the cultural background of each individual were particularly emphasized as special characteristics. The influence on the renewal of Indian types through Mahendra Patel's teaching has been visible for some years, among other things in newspapers and magazines, but also in the street scene in various towns and cities. Former Indian students have entered into his inheritance, actively propagating his ideas for improving the typographical appearance.

To conclude my comments, I would like to mention the "Type Design Development Project" brought into being by Mahendra Patel in 2003. I quote some extracts from the introductory text in the brochure that was published at that time: "In our age of globalisation, harmony and uniformity within a great variety of scripts are felt as being a necessity, and this under the aspect of preserving national and regional identity. [...] What is common to India's most important scripts is their origin in Sanskrit. The types for these scripts should be developed regionally, influenced by local, individual initiatives and efforts. [...] With my training, my teaching and design experience from my 39 years working at the National Institute of Design, I have the desire to harmonise the design of the type for the different Indian scripts. It is a matter of importance for me to prepare a 'system of types' which can be used for different Indian scripts. Various projects at the National Institute of Design offered me the opportunity to work on different Indian scripts. I was able to teach letter design at several institutes, and research into the respective linguistic peculiarities which are also reflected in the script. I would like to continue this project in future."

The initial financial support from the NID was withdrawn when Mahendra Patel retired at the end of 2003. Now he has decided to continue the project, to finance it himself. He will use the prize money awarded by the Gutenberg Society for this purpose. This is in keeping with the remark made by young Mahendra Patel over 40 years ago: "My task lies in contributing something to the progress of my country."

I thank you for your attention.

15. Jahrhundert

FRANCISCO J. CORNEJO
Iconografía de las ilustraciones del *Fasciculus temporum*, de Werner Rolevinck

LAS ILUSTRACIONES DE LAS SUCESIVAS EDICIONES del *Fasciculus temporum* fueron estudiadas ampliamente hace más de un siglo por Leo Baer en su *Die illustrierten Historienbücher des 15. Jahrhunderts*, principalmente desde un punto de vista formal y estilístico.[1] Si hoy merece la pena tratar de nuevo este tema, es para desarrollar algunos aspectos relativos a la iconografía y su relación con los textos, o al uso propagandístico de determinadas ilustraciones, y, por qué no, para llamar de nuevo la atención sobre este importante fenómeno editorial de ámbito europeo, en el que ya se manifestaron con claridad algunas de las características que afectarían a la ilustración de libros y a la difusión de estampas en los siglos posteriores.[2] También la utilización de referencias a documentos electrónicos sitos en Internet, permitirá al lector interesado acceder a las páginas citadas de la mayor parte de los incunables, materia de este trabajo.

Hacia 1474, cuando vio la luz el *Fasciculus* de Arnold Ther Hoernen, la edición de textos impresos con ilustraciones xilográficas ya contaba con importantes antecedentes, sobre todo en los territorios germánicos.[3] En menos de dos décadas se habían publicado una serie de obras que, compartiendo una vocación divulgativa y de búsqueda de un nuevo público al que incorporar al mercado de la demanda de libros, utilizaban las novedades del uso de la lengua vernácula, el alemán, y de la presencia de un importante aparato de llamativas imágenes. Algunas de estas obras ilustradas plasmaron un repertorio iconográfico que, no sólo fue imitado por ediciones posteriores, sino que sirvió de modelo a seguir por las ilustraciones de los diferentes géneros librescos. Las *Biblia pauperum*, de Bamberg (Albrecht Pfister, h. 1462, h. 1463 y 1464); las *Leben der Heiligen* (Vidas de Santos) de Jacobus de Voragine (Augsburg: Günther Zainer, 1471 y 1472); o el *Speculum humanae salvationis* (Augsburg: Günther Zainer, h. 1473), incluyen más de un centenar de xilografías de tema religioso. También se da un fenómeno semejante en los de temática profana, como en *Der edelstein* (La piedra preciosa), de Ulrich Boner (Bamberg: Albrecht Pfister, 1461); *Alexander*, de Jordanus de Quedlinburg (Augsburg: Johann Bämler, 1473); *De claris mulieribus*, de Giovanni Boccaccio (Ulm: Johannes Zainer, 1473); la *Hystori wie Troya die kostlich stat erstored Ward*, Historia troyana (Augsburg: Johann Bämler, 1474).

El *Fasciculus temporum* será también un modelo a seguir, a pesar de sus relativamente pocas ilustraciones, y pondrá los cimientos de un nuevo género de libros ilustrados: los de vistas de ciudades. El manuscrito de la obra existente en la Biblioteca de Arnhem (1473) incluye algunas ilustra-

[1] LEO BAER: *Die illustrierten Historienbücher des 15. Jahrhunderts*. Straßburg 1903, pp. 58–82 y XV–XXIV.
[2] Sobre la importancia y gestación del *Fasciculus temporum* véanse: ALBRECHT CLASSEN: Werner Rolevinck's fasciculus temporum. En: GJ 2006, pp. 227–9. – JOHAN C. MARTENS: The dating of the *Fasciculus temporum* manuscript in Arnhem Public Library. En: *Quaerendo* 21/1 (1991), pp. 3–10. – JOHAN C. MARTENS: The *Fasciculus temporum* of 1474. On form and content of the incunable. En: *Quaerendo* 22/3 (1992), pp. 198–204. – EVERADUS A. OVERGAAUW: Observations on the manuscripts of Werner Rolevinck's *Fasciculus Temporum*. En: *Quaerendo*, 22/4, 1992, pp. 292–300.
[3] Existe otra edición impresa, también en Colonia [no antes de 1474], de Nicolaus Götz, que pudiera ser anterior a la de Arnold Ther Hoernen, ya que la última noticia que incluye es de octubre de 1473. La mal resuelta composición de sus contenidos indica que no copia al libro de Ther Hoernen; en cualquier caso, ni el diseño de sus páginas ni sus ilustraciones influyeron en las ediciones posteriores de la obra.

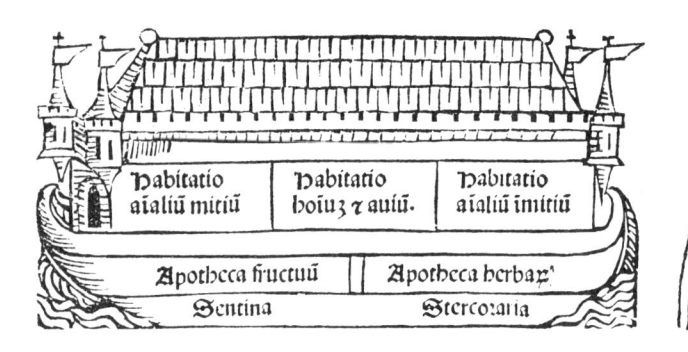

[Fig. 1] Arca de Noé
(Venecia 1479, f. 3ᵛ), UB Sevilla

[Fig. 2] Arco Iris
(Venecia, 1479, f. 3ᵛ),
UB Sevilla

4 MARTENS: The dating of the *Fasciculus temporum* manuscript (véase nota 2), p. 4. Coinciden temáticamente las ilustraciones de: Arca, Arco Iris, Torre de Babel, Nínive, Jerusalén, Roma, Salvador y Crucifixión; además, en el manuscrito aparecen la Creación de Eva, el Templo de Salomón, Natividad de Cristo y Muerte de Juan Bautista.

5 Para facilitar la consulta de las imágenes citadas a lo largo del texto se incluye al final del mismo una relación de «Ejemplares del *Fasciculus temporum* consultados» con sus correspondientes referencias de documento electrónico, siempre que exista, para su consulta virtual.

6 *The Illustrated Bartsch*. Ed. WALTHER L. STRAUSS. New York 1978. 80 Supp., 1464/27 y 1473/122.

7 Las citas utilizadas en el presente trabajo se refieren a la edición facsímil, transcripción y traducción del texto de la edición de Venecia, Erhard Ratdolt, 1481 de [WERNERIUS ROLEWINCK]: *Fasciculus temporum. Compendio cronológico*. Ed. coord. José Manuel Martínez Rodríguez. León 1993. La foliación de esta edición, como todas las venecianas, coincide con la de Arnold Ther Hoernen en Colonia (1474).

8 MARTENS: The *Fasciculus Temporum* of 1474 (véase nota 2), p. 203.

9 Las excepciones están en la edición de Memmingen (Albrecht Kune, 1482, f. 3ʳ), donde no hay textos con las partes del Arca; la de Colonia (Ludwig von Renchen, h. 1483, f. 3ᵛ), en la que, además, el Arca aparece situada sobre un monte –Ararat–; y la de Ginebra ([Jean Belot], 1495, f. 4ᵛ), la única que repite la tipología tradicional con la escena de la llegada de la paloma. En la edición de Nicolaus Götz ([Colonia, no antes de 1474], f. 11) la imagen del Arca, y del Arco Iris sobre ella, ocupa toda la página.

ciones que, sin ser copiadas exactamente por la edición impresa de Arnold Ther Hoernen, representan buena parte de sus temas.⁴ Frente a las detalladas miniaturas del manuscrito, las xilografías de la edición de Ther Hoernen (también las de casi todas las posteriores), poseen un carácter muy sintético, casi jeroglífico, subrayando lo simbólico más que lo descriptivo. Es verdad que la técnica lineal del grabado en madera requiere una mayor simplicidad de la imagen a reproducir que la realizada a pincel por el miniaturista; sin embargo, también lo es que dicha forma sintética converge con las cualidades de sobriedad y simplicidad de diseño de las páginas y de los contenidos del *Fasciculum temporum* de Rolevinck. El caso es que las ilustraciones de la edición de Ther Hoernen se consolidarían como parte sustancial del mismo, abriendo el camino a otras nuevas ilustraciones de características semejantes, que fueron enriqueciendo progresivamente las posteriores ediciones de la obra.⁵ Las imágenes de esta edición original son:

El Arca de Noé

Las primeras imágenes del libro son el Arca de Noé y el Arco Iris (f. 3ᵛ). Hasta entonces, el Arca había sido representada en el contexto de su historia bíblica; los manuscritos miniados anteriores a la invención de la imprenta, así como el libro tabelario *Biblia pauperum* (Bamberg, Albrecht Pfister, h. 1464) y el tipográfico *Speculum humanae salvationis* (Augsburg, Günter Zainer, h. 1473) muestran un barco navegando, normalmente pequeño y rudimentario, con una figura que asoma de un pequeño habitáculo en la cubierta para recibir a la paloma con la rama de olivo en su pico.⁶ En cambio, en el *Fasciculus temporum* solo se muestra un sencillo y amplio edificio cubierto a dos aguas sobre un casco en forma de artesa, acompañando a un breve y objetivo texto que dice: «El Arca de Noé medía 300 codos de largo, 50 codos de ancho, 30 codos de profundidad y un codo de altura: Génesis 6»; y, además, en el interior de la xilografía, se explicitan tipográficamente las partes del Arca: «Estancia de los animales mansos – Estancia de los hombres y las aves – Estancia de los animales salvajes / Almacén de frutos – Almacén de hierbas / Sentina – Estercoleros».⁷ Esta forma, escueta y didáctica, de presentar el Arca no se correspondía, tampoco, con la ilustración del citado manuscrito de 1473.⁸ Este esquematismo, una nave más o menos ornamentada y, a veces, de hasta tres cubiertas, se mantendrá mayoritariamente en las sucesivas ediciones del libro que, siempre, incluirán la imagen del Arca de Noé [fig. 1].⁹

El Arco Iris

El Arco Iris, que en la iconografía cristiana aparece, sobre todo, representado como asiento divino en la escena del Juicio Final, se muestra en este caso como un elemento aislado, aunque siempre próximo al Arca, y está resuelto con cinco semicírculos concéntricos en cuyo interior se puede leer el siguiente texto:

> El arco pluvial o iris tiene principalmente dos colores, dado que representa dos juicios: el color acuoso representa el diluvio ya pasado, para que no se lo tema más; el color ígneo representa el juicio que ha de venir, en la idea de que se espere con certeza.

Esta imagen se usa en casi todas las ediciones del libro [fig. 2] con el mismo tipo de línea que los círculos de las bandas cronológicas a los que se asemeja más que al resto de ilustraciones; algo que se hace más patente por su vecindad con el Arca de Noé.[10]

La Torre de Babel

La erección de la Torre de Babel es una escena habitual de las miniaturas medievales. Grúas, obreros con sus herramientas, o el rey dirigiendo la obra, son los atributos de esta iconografía; también lo son en la xilografía que ilustra el *Speculum humanae salvationis* (Augsburg: Günter Zainer, h. 1473).[11] Sin embargo, la Torre del *Fasciculus temporum* de Ther Hoernen, como en ediciones sucesivas [fig. 3], representa el puro edificio, sin personajes humanos, a veces en proceso de construcción (con grúa), otras con las grietas de su desmoronamiento. El texto que la acompaña dice (f. 4^v):

> Estos tres príncipes [de Cam, de Set y de Jafet], con sus parientes, se reunieron en territorio de Sennaar temiendo que el diluvio podía volver a inundar la tierra, y dijeron: «Construyamos una torre cuya altura llegue hasta el cielo», etc., tal como cuenta el *Génesis* en el capítulo 11. Pero Dios, viendo la insensatez que aquellos cometían, cayendo extrañamente en el pecado, confundió sus lenguas, y así se dispersaron por todo el mundo.

La única xilografía que recoge la actividad constructiva, y de manera muy detallada, es la que ilustra el f. 5^v de las ediciones S. n. 1495; Ginebra, Louis Cruse 1495; y Lyon, Mathie Husz 1498. Excepcionalmente, la Torre de Babel en la edición de [Colonia], Nicolaus Götz, [después de 1474], f. 14, es un esquema, casi infantil, de torre almenada.

Las vistas de ciudades: vistas convencionales

Las ciudades de Nínive, Tréveris, Roma, Jerusalén y Colonia poseen una xilografía propia en el *Fasciculum temporum*, de 1474. Hasta entonces no existía un género iconográfico propio para la representación de vistas de ciudades. En todo caso, la ciudad, con sus murallas y torres, podía aparecer como fondo escenográfico secundario de algún episodio histórico (batalla, cerco, entrada real, torneo, etc.) o, como ocurría con la frecuente representación de Jerusalén, la fuerte carga simbólica de la tradición bíblica conseguía que la ciudad representada poco tuviera que ver con la real.[12] Poseen estas características algunas ilustraciones xilográficas anteriores, presentes en el *Speculum humanae salvationis* o en la *Hystori wie Troya ...*[13] En cambio, las ciudades figuradas en el *Fasciculus temporum*

[Fig. 3] Torre de Babel (Sevilla, 1480, f. 4^v), UB Sevilla

10 No aparece el Arco Iris, aunque sí su texto, en la edición S. n. 1495. El único Arco Iris que supera la escueta geometría semicircular, se incluye en la edición de Ginebra ([Jean Belot], 1495, f. 4^v).
11 *Bartsch* (véase nota 6), 80 Supp., 1473/122
12 Sobre el origen de las vistas de ciudades, véase FRANCISCO J. CORNEJO: Cuando la vista engaña: Los grabados de vistas de ciudades en los primeros tiempos de la imprenta. En: *Cartografía histórica en la Biblioteca de la Universidad de Sevilla*. Sevilla 2010, pp. 148–63. Véase también en la relación de páginas web en p. 374.
13 *Bartsch* (véase nota 6), 80 Supp., 1473/122 y 1474/147.

[Fig. 4] Vista convencional (Venecia 1484, f. 14ᵛ), UB Sevilla

[Fig. 5] Vista convencional compuesta (Venecia 1484, f. 38ʳ), UB Sevilla

son ya, por primera vez, las protagonistas absolutas de la ilustración, sin ninguna otra servidumbre narrativa.

Nínive, la ciudad asiria, acompaña al texto (f. 5ʳ): «Nino amplió esta gran ciudad, la cual, tomándolo del suyo, recibió el nombre de Nínive», y se la representa como ciudad amurallada en torno a un gran edificio de planta central, que sirve de eje de simetría de toda la composición. Los remates cónicos y piramidales de los edificios sugieren la imagen de una ciudad medieval del Occidente europeo más que una de la antigua Mesopotamia. En el f. 5ᵛ se dice: «Se levanta sobre el Mosella la ciudad de Tréveris, una ciudad antigua que contaba ya mil trescientos años cuando se fundó Roma»; y se la representa amurallada, en este caso con edificios sugeridos por una menuda trama geométrica, casi cubista, de la que surgen cinco esbeltas torres. También aquí su aspecto es el de una urbe occidental.[14]

La ciudad de Roma aparece bajo el texto (f. 13ᵛ): «Se funda la ciudad de Roma, en el año 4484 del comienzo del mundo», y junto al párrafo: «Tú, romano recuerda que debes gobernar los pueblos con tu imperio, – que estas sean tus artes –, imponer las leyes de la paz, perdonar a los vencidos y reducir a los pueblos orgullosos». Lo interesante de esta ilustración es que utiliza el mismo bloque xilográfico que, ocho folios antes, se había usado para la ciudad de Tréveris, pero después de haber sido modificado: los pináculos y chapiteles de las torres han sido eliminados haciéndoles perder a éstas su esbeltez. Todo lo demás permanece igual. La representación de Jerusalén (f. 17ᵛ) también reutiliza la xilografía de Nínive, en este caso sin cambios. El párrafo descriptivo de la urbe poco tiene que ver con la imagen que lo ilustra:

> Jerusalén es reedificada por Nehemías y por otros hijos de Israel, y tiene tres habitaciones. La primera habitación es la del pueblo llano es decir, la de los operarios que trabajan en las máquinas. La segunda es la habitación de los nobles y de los profetas. La tercera es la habitación de los reyes y de los sacerdotes. Así mismo, tiene seis puertas, la primera de las cuales se llama Puerta del Valle o de Josafat; la segunda, Puerta Esterquilina; la tercera, Puerta Vieja o Judiciaria; la cuarta, Puerta de los Peces o de David; la cuarta, Puerta de la Fuente de Siloe o de las Aguas; la sexta, Puerta de los Griegos o Probática Piscina.

No deja de ser curioso que esta descripción de la Jerusalén reconstruida fuese poco después traducida a imagen en la edición del *Rudimentum novitiorum* (Lübeck 5 agosto 1475), de donde sería copiada solo en la del *Fasciculus temporum* de Utrecht (Johan Veldener, 1480); mientras que al resto de los editores no parece que les preocupara este asunto, puesto que se limitaron a ilustrar el texto con una vista convencional de ciudad.

14 Atención: las descripciones que se hacen de las ciudades de Nínive y Tréveris se corresponden sólo a cierto número de ejemplares de la edición; en los demás, las xilografías se encuentran intercambiadas.

Por lo visto hasta ahora, las ilustraciones de las ciudades de Nínive, Tréveris, Roma y Jerusalén poseen una serie de cualidades comunes: presentan un tipo de urbe medieval occidental (aunque simbolicen ciudades orientales como Nínive o Jerusalén), con murallas y torres como elementos básicos, y sirven para representar ciudades muy diferentes (Nínive-Jerusalén, Tréveris-Roma). Por lo tanto son intercambiables entre sí, puesto que ninguna posee los rasgos singulares de una sola ciudad, a la vez que todas tienen las características de cualquier ciudad de su época [fig. 4].[15] Hasta tal punto es así, que existe una variante de la edición de Ther Hoernen en la que se han trocado los tacos xilográficos de Nínive y Tréveris (ff. 5r y 5r). Esta situación – con otras que se verán más adelante – puede comprobarse comparando los dos ejemplares existentes en la Biblioteca de la Universidad de Colonia (ENNE 53 y ENNE 70).

Este tipo de imagen simbólica polivalente se corresponde a las llamadas vistas de ciudad «genéricas» o «convencionales», presentes en todas las ediciones del *Fasciculus temporum*; opuestas a las vistas «reales» que buscan plasmar los rasgos más característicos (edificios, ríos, puertos, etc.) de una ciudad contemporánea concreta, que, como se verá, también aparecen en algunas ediciones del *Fasciculus temporum*.[16]

Las vistas convencionales de las ediciones iniciales (en Colonia, Lovaina, Espira, Rougemont, Basilea, etc.) son poco numerosas, aunque repitan las tres o cuatro xilografías que utilizan; el total de urbes representadas por este tipo de vistas oscila entre cuatro y nueve. En cambio, en las ediciones venecianas de Ratdolt (1480, 1481, 1484 y 1485) las planchas de vistas convencionales, no solo aumentan – entre trece y diecinueve –, sino que se multiplican gracias a la invención de una nueva fórmula: las vistas «compuestas», surgidas de la yuxtaposición de dos o más matrices simples, de modo que, con un número limitado de imágenes, se consigue una gran variedad de ilustraciones [fig. 5]. La edición de 1484, por ejemplo, usa 16 matrices convencionales diferentes que sirven para representar a 51 ciudades o países, siete de las cuales emplean el recurso de las vistas compuestas. Porque el uso de vistas convencionales permite que una

[Fig. 6] Vista convencional (Venecia 1479, f. 14v), UB Sevilla
[Fig. 7] Vista convencional (Sevilla 1480, f. 13v), UB Sevilla

15 La edición de [Colonia], Nicolaus Götz, [no antes de 1474], también en esto es excepcional: repite el sencillo esquema de la Torre de Babel para representar a la ciudad de Nínive (f. 14) y utiliza una sola vista de ciudad convencional para Roma, que incluye la inscripción de «Remo-Romolo» (f. 60).
16 Sobre las tipologías de vistas de ciudad, en CORNEJO (véase nota 12).

[Fig. 8] Vista de Venecia
(Venecia 1479, f. 37ᵛ), UB Sevilla
[Fig. 9] Vista de Venecia
(Venecia 1484, f. 37ᵛ), UB Sevilla
[Fig. 10] Vista de Venecia
(Sevilla 1480, f. 37ᵛ), UB Sevilla

misma ilustración sirva tanto para representar a una ciudad como a un país o lugar; o, por el contrario, que una misma ciudad se ilustre con dos imágenes diferentes.

Las vistas convencionales de ciudades, que comparten función y atributos iconográficos en todas las ediciones del *Fasciculus temporum*, reflejan, además de un sello formal y estilístico propio, fruto de la técnica de los diferentes talleres de grabado, las características de la arquitectura o el clima de los países de edición. Así, en los grabados realizados en Alemania o en los Países Bajos aparecen edificios con fachadas de perfil escalonado y abundancia de remates puntiagudos; mientras que en las ediciones de Venecia predominan las bóvedas de cañón y las cúpulas bulbosas o de media naranja, e, incluso, hay góndolas, lo que no es óbice para que algunos elementos puramente nórdicos de sus modelos, como las fachadas escalonadas, convivan con el sabor bizantino de la arquitectura veneciana [fig. 6]. Las ilustraciones de la edición de Sevilla – primer libro impreso ilustrado español –, a pesar de copiar el modelo de la veneciana de 1479, incorpora una serie de novedades: la presencia de palmeras, algo inusual en las imágenes realizadas en otras latitudes; el uso de arcos de herradura en determinadas arquitecturas – elemento formal puramente hispánico –; y, en general, un aspecto de urbanismo mediterráneo, arábigo, más que nórdico, que refleja el mundo estético de aquel primer taller de grabado sevillano [fig. 7].

Las vistas de ciudades: vistas «reales»
La edición del *Fasciculus temporum* de Ther Hoernen incluyó una de estas vistas que pretendían representar a una ciudad contemporánea con sus principales elementos distintivos. Es el caso de la xilografía de Colonia, la ciudad donde el monje cartujo Werner Rolevinck escribió la obra y, sobre todo, la ciudad donde fue impresa por Ther Hoernen; sería la primera vista de ciudad «real» estampada en un libro.[17] A diferencia de las otras ilustraciones de vistas convencionales, la de Colonia recoge los elementos más notables y reconocibles de la urbe en el momento de realización de la imagen; aunque, en una primera impresión, pudieran primar las semejanzas con la xilografía usada para Tréveris y Roma (punto de vista bajo, muralla, torres). Sin embargo, para los habitantes de la ciudad, sería fácil identificar algunos elementos arquitectónicos de la misma que un lector

17 BAER (véase nota 1), p. 61. – A.G.W. MURRAY: The Edition of the *Fasciculus temporum* printed by Arnold ther Hoernen in 1474. In: *The Library*. 3rd Series, 4 (1913), p. 57–71.

foráneo podría tomar por convencionales: la mole en construcción de la catedral, con su gran grúa; el chapitel afilado de la torre del ayuntamiento, a su izquierda; las torres pareadas de las fundaciones conventuales; la característica torre octogonal (*Bayenturm Koeln*) en el extremo sur de la muralla; y el río.[18] El río Rin, al que cuesta trabajo reconocer en esa estrecha franja rectangular en la que descansa la línea de murallas pero que será un elemento imprescindible en todas las posteriores vistas de la ciudad. La ilustración complementa el texto (f. 24ʳ): «Marco Agripa, yerno de Octaviano, funda a orillas del Rin la ciudad de Agripina, que hoy se llama Colonia».

El carácter singular de la representación de Colonia en comparación con otras ciudades que aparecen en el libro, de la misma o mayor importancia histórica, se basa en esa cualidad de vista «real» de la ciudad, pero también en el propio tamaño de la imagen: si las vistas convencionales de otras ciudades tienen de anchura un tercio de la página, la de Colonia ocupa todo su ancho. Su excepcionalidad se refuerza cuando se comprueba que, al parecer, esta vista de Colonia fue un grabado que se incorporó a la edición en el último momento del proceso de impresión; de hecho hay ejemplares que no incluyen esta imagen, y entre los que la incluyen hay notables diferencias de colocación respecto a la tipografía.[19] Idéntica situación ocurre con la imagen del Crucificado. Este último hecho llevó a Leo Baer a creer que las ilustraciones se habrían estampado manualmente una vez realizada la impresión tipográfica; sin embargo, en el resto de las estampaciones no se encuentran diferencias de colocación entre las diversas variantes de la edición.[20]

La presencia de la imagen de Colonia en el contexto de una historia mundial, subrayada por su búsqueda de verosimilitud formal y por su destacado tamaño, son indicios claros de una intencionalidad propagandística por parte del editor y/o el autor del libro. Se inicia de esta forma no solo el género de las vistas de ciudades impresas sino, también, el uso de este tipo de imágenes al servicio de intereses particulares. Casi todas las ediciones de la obra impresas en Colonia incluirán una vista «real» de la ciudad.[21] La que aparece en las impresiones de Heinrich Quentell (1479, 1480 y 1481) es mucho más detallada que la de Ther Hoernen y reincide en su voluntad de propaganda: se aprecia el escudo de la ciudad en la torre defensiva y, sobre todo, desarrolla toda la zona fluvial y portuaria (barca, molino, grúa, personajes en el muelle, etc.), inexistente en la primera imagen de la ciudad. Por el contrario, en otras ediciones foráneas que copian a las de Colonia, incluida su vista – Basilea (Bernhard Richel, 1481, f. 45ʳ) y Memmingen (Albrecht Kune, 1482, f. 23ᵛ) –, se pierde buena parte de la fidelidad de los originales e, incluso, se olvida la necesidad de invertir el dibujo del grabado para que su correspondiente estampación respete el sentido de la realidad.

La otra ciudad representada de forma ‹real› en las ediciones incunables del *Fasciculus temporum* es Venecia. Aparece en la primera edición veneciana (Georgius Walch, 1479) y no faltará en ninguna de las siguientes [fig. 8]; como en el caso de Colonia, será la primera imagen impresa de la capital del Véneto.[22] Su texto dice (f. 37ᵛ):

18 La Colonia medieval creció como ciudad conventual – 14 fundaciones – sobre otra, romana, a las orillas del Rin. El desarrollo del Barrio de los Comerciantes, junto al río, anunciaba el poder que este grupo social alcanzaría ya en el siglo XII. La catedral, comenzada en 1248 y destinada a albergar las reliquias de los Reyes Magos, se convirtió muy pronto en el centro y símbolo del esfuerzo ciudadano; véase WOLFGANG BRAUNFELS: *Urbanismo occidental*. Madrid 1976, pp. 24–8.
19 Compárense los respectivos ff. 24ʳ de los dos ejemplares en la UB Colonia.
20 BAER (véase nota 1), p. 61.
21 La excepción es la edición de [Colonia], Nicolaus Götz, [no antes de 1474].
22 MAX SANDER: *Le livre à figures italien depuis 1467 jusqu'à 1530*. Milán 1969, t. III, p. 1133.

[Fig. 11] Salvador (Venecia 1479, f. 26ʳ), UB Sevilla

Por esta época, año 450, es fundada (o mejor, ampliada) la ínclita ciudad de Venecia, pero no por pastores, como Roma, sino por gentes poderosas y ricas, no oriundas de la región, pero llegadas a ella huyendo de la persecución de Atila. Es digno de admiración y hay que ensalzarlo con el mayor encomio el que una ciudad fundada por tantas y tan diversas gentes venidas de otras ciudades y pueblos haya podido conservarse durante mil años con tal incremento, tal esplendor de gloria y tan unánime sagacidad.

La singularidad de la vista de Venecia es notable, la ciudad formada por islas, canales, palafitos y puentes nunca necesitó murallas; tampoco tenía piedra para construirlas; su defensa había de basarse en su propia disposición geográfica y en su poderío naval. La primera vista de Venecia presenta, desde la laguna de su entrada, una fachada monumental compuesta por dos grandes columnas que abren paso a la plaza de la basílica de San Marcos, la torre del campanile, el palacio del Dux y el puente de la Paglia; en lugar de un frente amurallado, como cualquier otra ciudad. Estos elementos, más la ya entonces inevitable góndola con su gondolero, aparecen dispuestos en apretada síntesis en los 4,5 × 6,8 cm del grabado. La fidelidad de lo representado frente a la realidad es importante, a pesar de su carácter sintético y condensado: sobre las dos columnas se aprecian las esculturas de San Teodoro y del león alado que simboliza al evangelista San Marcos, el palacio ducal diferencia sus tres niveles de arcos, galería y ventanales (aunque sus 17 arcos se hayan reducido a siete); se aprecian las cúpulas bulbosas de la basílica y el arranque del puente sobre el canal. Sin embargo, todo este «realismo» sufre un golpe importante cuando se percibe que la imagen está invertida respecto de la vista verdadera: el inexperto grabador no tuvo en cuenta que es necesario invertir el dibujo original si se quiere que la estampación respete su sentido. Los lectores de la edición veneciana del *Fasciculus temporum*, que incluía la primera vista impresa de la ciudad de Venecia, tan ambiciosa en sus detalles, tuvieron que conformarse con una imagen especular de la misma. Lo representado no coincidía con la vista que se podía contemplar desde la laguna veneciana.

Las sucesivas ediciones venecianas, todas impresas por Erhardus Ratdolt (1480, 1481, 1484 y 1485), usaron un grabado, copia a mayor tamaño del de 1479 (4,6 × 9,7 cm), pero con su sentido invertido y, por tanto, haciendo coincidir las ilustraciones con la vista auténtica [fig. 9]. La edición de Sevilla, en 1480, incluye una reproducción del grabado veneciano de 1479 (5,5 × 7,7 cm), pero queriendo ser tan fiel al original que repite su carácter invertido [fig. 10]. En la otra ilustración no veneciana de la ciudad –Adam (de Rottweil?) Alamanus (s. l. 1486, f. 37ᵛ) –, el autor del grabado presenta a una Venecia invertida y rodeada de unas murallas que nunca tuvo. Sin duda, la asociación simbólica que por entonces se daba entre «ciudad» y «muralla» llevó al autor a «corregir» en su dibujo la supuesta deficiencia defensiva de la capital del Véneto.

Considera razonablemente Laviece Cox Ward, refiriéndose a la ilustración de Colonia en el *Fasciculus temporum*, que «La idea de representar la ciudad en la que era impreso el libro fue adoptada como un elemento importante para la venta del libro».[23] Sin embargo, es discutible lo que

23 "The idea of representing the city in which the book was printed was inmediately recognized as a selling point by others printers, for in later editions recognizable views of Lyon, Louvain, and Venice appear." LAVIECE COX WARD: Early Italian Printing and the Carthusian History. *Fasciculus Temporum*. En: *San Bruno e la Certosa di Calabria: Atti del convegno internazionale di studi per il IX centenario della Certosa di Serra S. Bruno*. Soveria Mannelli 1995, p. 113.

Ɨ Þane p̄dixerūt ꝓphete.hāc sīmul ois illa veteris testamēti laboriosa seruilisꝗ obsuantia:domīnā recognoscit.Et quid vltra?Celū terra marecꝗ cū oībus q̄ in eis sunt:nō huic famulant mysterio?Igitur gloriosa dicta sūt de te o cī vitas dei.Beata tu hierusalē quis similis tui:q̄ saluaris in dn̄o?Negabūt te inimici tui:⁊ tu eoꝝ colla calcabis. Pro pribus tuis nascent tibi fily:nec deficies in sempitna secula:Benedic dn̄e fortitudini eiꝰ:⁊ opera manuū eius suscī pe.Percute dorsa inimicoꝝ eius:⁊ q̄ oderāt eā nō ꝯsurgant.Audi dn̄e vocē eius:⁊ ad populū suū introduc eā. Deꝰ virtutum ꝗuertere respice de celo:⁊ vide:⁊ visita vineam istā:⁊ pfice cam:quam plātauit dextera tua. Fiat manus tua sup virū dextere tue:⁊ sup filiū homīs quē ꝯfirmasti tibi ih̄m xp̄m dn̄m nostrū:qui tecū viuit ⁊ regnat ī vnitate spiritus sancti deus in omnia secula benedictus.Amen.

— Johānes — Lucas — Marcus — Matheꝰ —

scripsit ī asia greco sermone. Jn p̄nciplo erat verbum.

Ɛ Ego sū lux mūdi:q̄ seq̄t me nō ābulat ī tēbris: sꝫ hēbit lumē vite.Ego sū q̄ testimoniū phibeo de meipo:⁊ testīoniū phibet de me pr̄. Ego sū pastor bonꝰ:⁊ cognosco meas:⁊ cognoscūt me mee.Ego sum via:vitas:⁊ vita:neꝰ venit ad patrez nisi per me.Ego sum vitis vera:⁊ pr̄ meꝰ agricola est.

scripsit ingrecia sermone greco. Fuit in diebꝰ herodis regis iu dee sacerdos ⁊c.

Ɛ Amen amen dico vobis celū ⁊ terra trāsibūt:verba aūt mea nō trāsibunt.Qui crediderit ⁊ baptisatꝰ fuerit:saluꝰ erit:q̄ vero nō crediderit ꝯdemnabit.Quod vobis:oībus dico.Uigilate: nescitis eni quando dn̄s veniet:Sol ꝑtenebrabit:⁊ luna dabit splendorem suum.Et tunc videbunt filium hominis venientes in nubibus ⁊c.

Ɛ Data ē mihi omnis potestas ⁊ ī celo ī terra. Ite in orbem vniuersū:⁊ p̄dicate euangelium omni creaturae.Et ecce ego vobiscum sum vsꝗ ad consūmationem seculi.

Ɛ Ego rogaui ꝑ te petre vt nō deficiat fides tua:⁊ tu aliqn̄ ꝯuersus cōfirma fratres tuos.Qui maior est in vobis:fiat sicut minor.Ego aūt in medio vestrū sum:sicut q̄ ministrat.Uide te ne seducamini.Multi eni venient in noīe meo dicentes:qꝰ ego sum.Nolite ergo ire post illos. In patientia vestra possidē bitis animas vestras.

Ɛ Ecce ego mitto vos sicut oues in medio luporū.Estote ergo pudētes sicut serpētes:⁊ simplices sic colūbe. Nolite timere eos q̄ occidūt corpꝰ:aiaz aūt nō pnt occidere:sed potius eū timete:q̄ pōt ⁊ aiaz ⁊ corpus pdere ī gehēnā. Omnis q̄ ꝯfitet me cora hoībus:⁊ ficebor:⁊ ego eū cora p̄re meo.

scripsit in italia sermone tn̄ greco. Inicium euāgely ih̄u xp̄i.

scripsit in iudea hebraice. Liber generatiōis xp̄i

Ɨ pphete sancti. Hic elegit discipulos 72:quos misit ante faciē suā:⁊ 12 āp̄los quos misit in orbē vniuersū ad p̄dicā dū euangeliū:nec amplius q̄ hos duos ordines inter discipulos dn̄i ꝯe cognouimus:quoꝝ formā nūc in ecclesia te nent presbyteri ⁊ epī. Nam apostolis succedūt epī:⁊ 62 discipulis presbyteri:quibus duobus ordinibus tota ecclesia ē cōmissa:tanꝗ gerarchis:vt pꝫ in decreto damasi pape habet̄.lxviy.di.c.coꝛ epī. Tandem pius dn̄s p grege suo mo rit acerbissima passione ꝯsūmatus omniū martyrū caput:⁊ ipse martyr. Postꝗ aūt a mortuis resurrexit:in celū ascen dit:⁊ spiritū sanctum misit.Et tunc primū cultus xp̄iani nominis incepit:qui ad finē vsꝗ durabit.

[Fig. 12] Salvador con Tetramorfos (Sevilla 1480, f. 26ʳ), UB Sevilla

afirma a continuación: «puesto que en ediciones posteriores aparecen vistas reconocibles de Lyon, Lovaina y Venecia». Es necesario puntualizar que esto no es cierto para los casos de Lovaina y Lyon. La única edición del *Fasciculus temporum* impresa en Lovaina (Johan Veldener, 1475) no incluye ninguna vista de esta ciudad, ni «real» ni convencional; tampoco he encontrado representaciones de la misma en ninguna otra edición incunable del libro. En cuanto a Lyon, su primera imagen aparece en la edición veneciana de 1481 (Erhardus Ratdolt, f. 23ᵛ) y es una vista convencional que acompaña al texto: «El orador Minacio Plauto, que fue discípulo de Cicerón, funda Lyon». A partir de este momento es habitual encontrarla, siempre como vista convencional, en otras ediciones, incluidas las realizadas en la propia Lyon. En la primera edición lionesa (Mathias Huss, 1483) el grabado correspondiente a Lyon (f. 34ʳ) es el mismo que en páginas anteriores ilustraba a Nínive, Tréveris y Atenas.

La vinculación de la presencia de las vistas «reales» de ciudad con los intereses —económicos y propagandísticos— de los impresores locales se ve confirmada también por otros hechos. Las vistas «reales» de Colonia, salvo las excepciones ya citadas, fueron incluidas en ediciones autóctonas; en cambio, las publicaciones de otras ciudades utilizan para Colonia una vista convencional. Por supuesto, las ediciones venecianas usarán una imagen convencional para Colonia mientras que incorporan una vista «real» para ilustrar su propia ciudad; vista que tan solo se copió en dos ediciones foráneas, ya citadas, porque en el resto no tuvo la suerte de gozar siquiera de una vista convencional.

Cristo crucificado

La ilustración de Cristo crucificado aparece en el f. 25^r, sobre el año 33 del nacimiento de Jesús: «Poncio Pilato. Bajo su gobierno Juan el bautista comenzó a predicar y el Señor padeció la Pasión, pues por temor al César lo condenó injustamente a morir en la cruz». Este tema iconográfico no gozará del mismo éxito que los demás, pues solamente vuelve a estar presente en las ediciones del libro publicadas en la propia ciudad de Colonia y en otra más de su área de influencia.[24] El hecho de que la imagen, al igual que la vista real de Colonia, no esté presente en algunos ejemplares de la edición de Ther Hoernen – y en los que aparece, hay diferencias de colocación respecto al texto –, puede ser la razón de que no fuese copiado por otros editores ajenos a la ciudad de Colonia, como sí lo fueron las demás ilustraciones y el texto.[25]

Cristo Salvador

Todo lo contrario ocurre con la imagen de Cristo como Salvador que, en el folio siguiente (26^r), forma parte de una composición a página completa muy especial. Su peculiar configuración tipográfica, incluida la ilustración [fig. 11], estará presente en todas las ediciones posteriores.[26] Esta página, junto a la anterior (25^v), supone una pausa en la linealidad cronológica que preside la organización del libro. La muerte de Cristo significa para la concepción ideológica del autor una transformación esencial en el devenir histórico de la humanidad que debe quedar debidamente señalada en la propia estructura del libro. En la página izquierda, sólo de texto, se visualizan verticalmente los doce artículos de la nueva fe (el *Credo*), relacionados a su izquierda con los doce apóstoles y, a su derecha, con otros tantos textos de profetas. La derecha está presidida por la imagen central del Salvador a la que rodea una línea de texto, que dice: «Me ha sido dada toda potestad en el cielo y en la tierra. Id por todo el mundo y predicad el Evangelio a toda criatura. He aquí que yo estoy con vosotros hasta la consumación de los siglos». Imagen y texto que, a su vez, están incluidos en un marco lineal con cuatro círculos en sus esquinas con los nombre de los cuatro evangelistas, mientras que cuatro textos evangélicos, uno de cada evangelista, rellenan los lados del marco. Junto al medallón de cada evangelista, ya fuera del marco, hay unos pequeños bloques de texto relativos a sus correspondientes datos biográficos. Dos amplios párrafos, en la cabecera y el pie de la página respectivamente, aluden al proceso de nacimiento, desarrollo y difusión del culto cristiano por parte de los doce apóstoles y los setenta y dos discípulos. La ilustración del Salvador se convierte, con su excepcional marco tipográfico, en la más importante y significativa de todo el libro.

24 También falta en la edición de [Colonia]: Nicolaus Götz, [no antes de 1474]; y, por el contrario, aparece en la de Memmingen, Albrecht Kune, 1482, f. 24^v.
25 Compárense los dos ejemplares de la UB Colonia, f. 25^r.
26 En [Colonia]: Nicolaus Götz, [no antes de 1474], f. 112, la página se compone de forma diferente: un diagrama circular, sin imagen del Salvador, con tres círculos concéntricos, el central representa a la Iglesia, el siguiente incluye cuatro marcos circulares con los nombres de los evangelistas, y el exterior, otros doce para los apóstoles, debajo de los cuales aparecen los nombre de otros tantos profetas.

[Fig. 13 a–d] Detalles del Tetramorfos (Sevilla 1480), UB Sevilla

Los antecedentes iconográficos de Cristo como Salvador se remontan a los iconos «no pintados por mano humana» bizantinos y a su evolución como paño de la Verónica y ‹pantocrator›; aunque su concreción formal definitiva no llegase hasta que el papa Calixto III proclamó en 1457 la Fiesta universal del Santísimo Salvador o de la Transfiguración, a través de la constitución titulada: *Interdivinae despentationas arcana*, con la que celebró la victoria que, a las puertas de Belgrado, hubieron los ejércitos cristianos sobre las fuerzas musulmanas capitaneadas por Mahomet II, el reciente conquistador de Constantinopla.[27] Una de las primeras representaciones del Salvador fue la que se puede ver en la estampa calcográfica suelta que el conocido como «Maestro E. S.» fechó y firmó en 1467, incluyendo la inscripción «sanctus salffidor» (buril, 14,9 × 12 cm); la imagen es, excepcionalmente, de medio cuerpo, con su mano derecha bendiciendo y su izquierda con un orbe rematado en cruz, como atributos señalados de esta iconografía. Del mismo autor, sin fechar, es un Salvador de cuerpo entero que forma parte de un Apostolado.[28] La serie de las ilustraciones xilográficas de libros se inició con la magnífica del Salvador, ya de cuerpo entero y a toda página, que encabeza las ediciones en Augsburgo del *Plenarium*, en alemán y con 55 estampas sobre la vida de Cristo, (Günter Zainer, 1473; y Johann Bämler, 1474).[29] El Salvador del primer *Fasciculus temporum* es mucho más modesto: sobre un fondo liso y sin adorno repite el tipo iconográfico, bendice y sostiene el orbe, aunque, como novedad, la parte superior de su figura está enmarcada por una larga, y muda, filacteria. Un Salvador muy semejante (en vez del orbe, sujeta la filacteria con la mano izquierda), incluso en tamaño (buril, 8,5 × 5,9 cm), aparece en un estampa de Martin Schogauer (¿Colmar? h. 1450 – Breisach 1491); al no estar fechada no es posible determinar cuál pueda ser original y cuál la copia.[30]

Todas las ediciones de Colonia, Venecia y sus zonas de influencia mantienen esencialmente la misma iconografía de la edición de Arnold Ther Hoernen. En otras ediciones se pueden ver algunas variantes, incluso notables. La xilografía empleada en las ediciones de Johan Veldener (Lovaina 29 diciembre 1475, f. 26^r, y Utrecht 1480, f. 75^v) muestra un Salvador que bendice, muestra un libro abierto con la mano izquierda, mientras pisa el orbe. El Salvador de las ediciones de Rougemont (Henricus Wirtzburg, 1481) y de Lyon (Mathie Husz, 1483), que copia a la anterior, aparece flanqueado por los apóstoles en un interior arquitectónico, aproximando así el contenido de la imagen al de los textos – que tratan del proceso fundacional eclesiástico – de la página en la que está insertada.[31] La mayor diferencia se encuentra en la edición ginebrina de Jean Belot, 1495, f. 37^r; aquí Cristo, entre los apóstoles, se muestra en un espacio abierto, flotando en el aire y rodeado de una nube resplandeciente, pero sin bendecir y sin el orbe: es decir, se muestra como en el episodio evangélico de la Transfiguración. Para entender esta evolución iconográfica hay que recordar que Calixto III creó la festividad universal de San Salvador a partir de cultos locales dedicados al episodio de la Transfiguración, por lo que la relación entre los dos temas tenía una justificación litúrgica.

Otra novedad en la ilustración de esta página será la sustitución de los

---

27 Hechos recogidos por Rolevinck en un párrafo sobre el medallón correspondiente a Calixto III en el f. 64^r del *Fasciculus temporum*.
28 Bartsch (véase nota 6), 8, 84-I y 50 (21).
29 Ibid., 80 Supp., 1473/63 y 1474/1.
30 Ibid., 8, 68 (150)
31 A. CLAUDIN: *Histoire de l'imprimerie en France au XVe et au XVIe siècle*. III. París 1904, p. 251.

medallones con los nombres de los evangelistas por sus correspondientes imágenes simbólicas o Tetramorfos. A partir de la edición de Sevilla (Bartholomaeus Segura et Alfonsus de Portu, 1480) [fig. 12], esta fórmula será adoptada por diversas ediciones posteriores.[32] Las figuras de los evangelistas en la edición sevillana muestran bien a las claras la bisoñez de su grabador. Por una parte, hay un error de atribución simbólica: el hombre alado de San Mateo dice en su filacteria «S·LVCAS», y el toro de San Lucas, otra que dice «S·MATEVS»; pero, aparte de este desliz que puede no ser del tallista, se aprecia en la filacteria de San Marcos, bajo su correspondiente león alado, como aparece invertido el texto «S·MARCVS», a diferencia de los otros tres. Lo que quiere decir que fue éste el primero que realizó el grabador, todavía desconocedor de que había que tallar los textos en sentido inverso para su posterior visión correcta tras la estampación; y que esta experiencia le sirvió de lección para los posteriores grabados [fig. 13].

A las ilustraciones incluidas en la edición del *Fasciculus temporum* de 1474, que hasta aquí se han analizado, hay que sumar las añadidas en posteriores impresiones; que, casi todas, se incorporaron al diseño de las ediciones sucesivas. La de Lovaina (Johan Veldener, 1475) incorporó dos: el Templo de Salomón y la ciudad destruida.

El Templo de Salomón

«La era principal de esta historia sagrada es la de la fundación del templo. Es el cuarto año del reinado de Salomón, 480 después de la salida de Egipto, tal como se dice en el tercer libro de los *Reyes*, capítulo 6». Éste es el texto que genera la imagen del Templo de Salomón incorporado a los *Fasciculus temporum*, aunque no en todas las ediciones.[33] En este caso, las diferencias formales entre las xilografías de distintas ediciones son notables. En Colonia, Nicolaus Götz, [después de 1474], aparece como un edificio sencillo compuesto por una nave rectangular cubierta a dos aguas — coronada por una cruz — y una torre cuadrada rematada con un chapitel piramidal; y la inscripción «Templvm Domini».[34] A esta imagen del templo salomónico como edificio cristiano occidental y medieval hay que añadir otra de la edición de Sevilla (Bartholomaeus Segura et Alfonsus de Portu, 1480), pero, aquí, con toda la riqueza del estilo gótico: una magnífica portada ojival, rematada por una gran cúpula semiesférica, y flanqueadas por altas torres de tres cuerpos, sostenidas por otros tantos cuerpos de arbotantes [fig. 14]. Todo ello configura una fantástica fachada inspirada en alguna de las grandes catedrales que se construían por aquellas fechas; por ejemplo, la de la propia Sevilla.

Frente a estas imágenes, basadas exclusivamente en formas contemporáneas, la de la edición de Lovaina (Johan Veldener, 1475, f. 9ᵛ) recrea, a su manera, el antiguo templo judío. Para ello combina en una vista, a la vez interior y exterior, tabernáculo y templo: un espacio centrado en torno a un altar cilíndrico rodeado por arcos con columnas torsas — las famosas columnas salomónicas — que sostienen una cúpula rematada por un tambor. Al fondo, dos torreones cupulados flanquean este espacio principal. De este grabado deriva el de Espira (Peter Drach, 1477); en él

32 Concretamente, las de Rougemont (Henricus Wirtzburg, 1481), Lyon (Mathie Husz, 1483 y 1498), S. l. (Adam [de Rottweil?] Alamanus, 1486), [S. n.], 1495 y Ginebra ([Jean Belot], 1495 y Louis Cruse, 1495).

33 No hay Templo en Rougemont (Henricus Wirtzburg, 1481), en las de Estrasburgo (Johann Prüss, 1487, 1488, y [después de 6 abril 1490]), ni en [S. n.] 1495.

34 *Bartsch* (véase nota 6), 80 Supp., 1474/177.

[Fig. 14] Templo
(Sevilla 1480, f. 9ᵛ), UB Sevilla

[Fig. 15] Templo
(Venecia 1479, f. 9ᵛ), UB Sevilla

[Fig. 16] Templo
(Ginebra LC 1495, f. 14ʳ),
UB Heidelberg,
B 1551 A Folio INC

ya sólo hay un espacio interior, el tabernáculo, de planta octogonal, con columnas lisas que soportan un friso y, al fondo, un muro con ventanas; en el centro, cuelga una cúpula sobre un altar rectangular en el que descansa el Arca de la Alianza.[35] En la edición S. l. (Adam [de Rottweil?] Alamanus, 1486, f. 9ᵛ), es así mismo un espacio interior, pero plenamente gótico: una capilla central, de elevadas proporciones, con su altar y retablito al fondo, y flanqueada por dos naves con complejos ventanales de arcos conopiales.

La mayoría de las ediciones utilizaron, sin embargo, un modelo de templo basado en una sencilla vista exterior. Se trata de un edificio cilíndrico, con dos niveles – el superior más estrecho que el inferior – y rematado con una cubierta cónica (en las ediciones germánicas) o semiesférica (en las venecianas). Su carácter almenado y con saeteras lo hace parecer a veces más una torre defensiva que un templo; de hecho, la misma matriz del Templo se usa para representar la Torre de Babel en las ediciones de [Colonia] (Heinrich Quentell, 1480); Memmingen (Albrecht Kune, 1482); y Colonia (Ludwig von Renchen, c. 1483). Lo habitual es su presentación aislada, aunque en las ediciones venecianas este templo-torre aparezca inserto en un paisaje [fig. 15].

El libro de Bernhard von Breydenbach, *Peregrinatio in terram sanctam* (Mainz: Erhard Reuwich, 1486), publicó una vista de Jerusalén a partir de un dibujo de Erhard Reuwich incorporando elementos de la arquitectura de la ciudad según los vio su autor. Esto tuvo como insólita consecuencia que la imagen de la mezquita de la Roca situada en la explanada del antiguo Templo, con su cúpula bulbosa y su media luna islámica, viniese a ser utilizada como la de un Templo de Salomón de planta central.[36] Así aparece fielmente copiado en una de las ilustraciones del *Liber chronicarum*, de Hartmann Schedel (1493, ed. latina, f. 48ʳ) con la inscripción «Templum Salomonis» y, lo que aquí interesa, en la bella xilografía que ilustra las ediciones del *Fasciculus temporum* de Ginebra (Louis Cruse, 1495) y Lyon (Mathie Husz, 1498) [fig. 16]. Las coincidencias formales entre las imágenes de la mezquita de la Roca y de los templos-torre (carácter centralizado, dos niveles y cúpula) sugieren que la tipología de estos

35 Ibid., 1477/252.
36 Sobre la transformación de la imagen de la mezquita de la Roca en Templo de Salomón, véase JUAN ANTONIO RAMÍREZ: *Construcciones ilusorias (Arquitecturas descritas, arquitecturas pintadas)*. Madrid 1983, pp. 144–78. Las distintas reconstrucciones ideales del Templo han sido estudiadas por JUAN A. RAMÍREZ y otros: *Dios, arquitecto. J.B. Villalpando y el templo de Salomón*. Madrid 1991.

últimos proviene de alguna descripción o miniatura de anteriores viajeros a Tierra Santa en donde ya se identificaría la mezquita con el del antiguo Templo salomónico.

Finalmente, y a modo de resumen y mixtura de las tipologías vistas anteriormente, hay un hermoso Templo en la edición de Ginebra ([Jean Belot], 1495, f. 14r) que, con unas proporciones parecidas a la de la mezquita de la Roca, presenta un primer cuerpo circular con galería de columnas, un segundo cuerpo hexagonal con ventanales góticos, y una cúpula gallonada orientalizante como remate. Además, cuatro estilizados pináculos sobresalen de los dos cuerpos del edificio. Es en definitiva, una curiosa mezcla estilística que cumple perfectamente el papel simbólico que como ilustración se le pide.

La ciudad destruida
También en la edición de Lovaina (Johan Veldener, 1475) se incorpora el tema de la ciudad destruida. Esta era una iconografía con una amplia tradición, primero en miniaturas de códices y, luego, en ilustraciones de libros tabelarios como la *Biblia pauperum* (Países Bajos o Bajo Rin h. 1460/65) y el *Apocalypsis Sancti Johannis* (Alemania h. 1470); o el impreso *Speculum humanae salvationis*, (Augsburg: Günther Zainer, h. 1473). Existe en dos variantes: por un lado, la ciudad bajo lluvia de fuego; por otro, edificios en ruinas, según representaran, por ejemplo, la destrucción de Babilonia o el castigo a Sodoma y Gomorra. En las diversas ediciones del *Fasciculus temporum* estas vistas convencionales de ciudades destruidas, en sus dos variantes tradicionales, sirvieron de ilustración a textos sobre muy variados acontecimientos.

La edición de Lovaina utiliza una ciudad en ruinas para simbolizar la destrucción de Nínive (f. 5r). La misma tipología se usa en la edición de Espira (Peter Drach, 1477, f. 5r) y, sobre todo, en las venecianas de Erhardus Ratdolt. La de 1480 utiliza dos xilografías diferentes de ciudad destruida: una apaisada de poderoso expresionismo cercano a la abstracción, y otra cuadrada, de estilo semejante, que describe una explosión [fig. 17]; con ellas ilustra, respectivamente, los textos «Nabuconodosor arrasa Jerusalén» (f. 14r) y «En esta época fue tomada y destruida la gran Babilonia» (f. 16r). Ambos grabados se usan por separado o creando una vista compuesta al combinarse con ciudades convencionales. Esta fórmula resuelve el problema de la ilustración del castigo divino a la ciudad de Antioquia:

[Fig. 17] Ciudad destruida (Venecia 1484, f. 16r), UB Sevilla
[Fig. 18] Ciudad semidestruida (Venecia 1484, f. 40v), UB Sevilla

«Antioquía es destruida por un ángel de Dios, que se apareció vestido de blanco, y sólo se salvó un hombre que daba limosnas. Algunos dicen que la mitad de la ciudad fue arrasada y que la otra mitad la salvó aquel hombre con sus plegarias» (f. 40ᵛ) [fig. 18]. En la edición de 1481, Ratdolt incorporó una nueva ciudad ruinosa, de formato cuadrado y más realista, y, además, utilizó un nuevo grabado de un campamento militar con artillería para combinar con cualquier vista de ciudad, destruida o no [fig. 19]. De esta forma, con estas cuatro xilografías, más el resto de vistas convencionales, Ratdolt consiguió en sus ediciones una gran cantidad de variantes para ilustrar los abundantes acontecimientos bélicos recogidos en el libro.

La edición de Rougemont (Henricus Wirtzburg, 1481) utiliza la tipología de ciudad en ruinas para ilustrar estas historias: el castigo a Sodoma y Gomorra, la caída de Troya y la destrucción de Babilonia; los dos primeras no aparecían ilustradas en ediciones anteriores. La edición de Lyon (Mathie Husz, 1483) sigue el modelo de Rougemont al copiar exactamente la ilustración y sus aplicaciones.

También copian a Rougemont otras ediciones en el hecho de que una sola imagen acompañe a esas tres mismas historias; sin embargo, hay en todas ellas un cambio en la tipología de la ciudad destruida: ahora es una ciudad bajo la lluvia de fuego, tema muy adecuado para el castigo a Sodoma y Gomorra, pero poco pertinente para la guerra de Troya o la destrucción babilónica. Al modelo usado en Basilea (Bernhard Richel, 1482) le seguirán tres copias grabadas, muy semejantes a él a pesar de que alguna esté invertida, que ilustran un total de nueve ediciones del *Fasciculus temporum*, las de Estrasburgo (1487–92), Ginebra (1495), S. n. (1495) y Lyon (1498) [fig. 20].

En su edición de Utrecht (1480), Veldener repitió muchas de las xilografías que cinco años antes había usado en Lovaina. Sin embargo, no lo hizo con la de la ciudad destruida; aquí ilustran las respectivas caídas de Nínive (f. 9ʳ) y Babilonia (f. 38ᵛ) dos grabados de un tercer tipo, el del asedio a una ciudad: ante las murallas hay un grupo de soldados con armadura, uno de ellos, arrodillado, dispara un cañón, mientras otro sujeta una escalera de mano. Los dos copian ilustraciones del *Rudimentum novitiorum* (Lübeck 5 agosto 1475). Esta iconografía no volvería a ser utilizada en posteriores *Fasciculus temporum*.

Los Reyes Magos

Las ediciones que Heinrich Quentell publicó en Colonia (1479, 1480 y 1481) tienen un interesante grabado que representa la Adoración de los Reyes Magos en el centro de un cortejo cívico (f. 24ʳ). Sus integrantes llevan diversos gallardetes y dos escudos: el de la derecha es el de la propia ciudad de Colonia, que incluye las tres coronas alusivas a los propios Magos, sus patronos, cuyas reliquias se veneraban en su catedral. El escudo en blanco de la figura de la izquierda cumple la función –como en algunas estampas sueltas y en portadas de libros de su época– de facilitar al comprador del libro un espacio privilegiado para poner su propio escudo de armas; no se debe olvidar que durante las primeras décadas de la historia del libro impreso las ilustraciones xilográficas estaban concebidas para ser coloreadas posteriormente. Sobre la imagen se despliega el siguiente texto alusivo: »Celeberrimo cultu sa[ncti] tres reges munera p[re]ciosa regi celi xpto nato: deuotiss[i]me offer[un]t · aurum sczthus et mirram« (f. [24ʳ]), que, lo mismo que el grabado, se ha añadido exclusivamente en estas ediciones.

La ilustración, situada en la parte inferior de la página, ocupa casi el mismo ancho que el texto, exactamente con la misma disposición y tamaño que, en la página opuesta (f. [23ᵛ]) tiene la vista de Colonia. Las imágenes de la ciudad y la de sus santos patronos, simétricamente dispuestas, configuran un mensaje propagandístico en el que se puede apreciar un contenido cuidadosamente elaborado en honor a la propia ciudad. La vista de Colonia en Quentell, además, despliega un desarrollo notable de lo civil (el puerto comercial, el escudo de la ciudad, los ciudadanos) en comparación con el carácter monástico de la de Ther Hoernen.³⁷ El Ayuntamiento de Colonia, presente en la vista con su gran pináculo arquitectónico, poseía en su sede un altar, un tríptico, dedicado a sus patronos, los Reyes Magos (*Altar der Kölner Stadtpatrone* o *Kölner Dombild*).³⁸ La tabla principal del retablo, pintado por Stephan Lochner h. 1445, sirvió de modelo al grabado utilizado por el impresor Heinrich Quentell en varias de sus producciones, incluidas las del *Fasciculus temporus*.³⁹ Se copian la escena de la Virgen sedente presentando al Niño a los Reyes y el detalle de las tres banderolas con sus emblemas que llevan los servidores de los Reyes, aunque el resultado estampado aparezca invertido con respecto al sentido de la pintura original.

La presencia de esta ilustración en el contexto de la sobriedad de contenidos del *Fasciculus temporum* sólo es explicable en las ediciones impresas en Colonia y debido a un afán de promoción de la obra para que fuese más atractiva a sus conciudadanos, y sirviese de propaganda de la urbe a los lectores foráneos. Dicho lo cual, hay que señalar que la edición estampada en Memmingen (Albrecht Kune, 1482), que sigue bastante fielmente las ilustraciones de las ediciones de Colonia, incluye una copia del grabado de los Reyes Magos, eso sí, simplificada, invertida y también propagandística (f. 24ʳ), ya que sustituye el escudo de armas de Colonia por el de Memmingen, así mismo invertido, y añade en el escudo opuesto lo que parece ser la marca del impresor.⁴⁰

Temas bíblicos

Las ilustraciones de otros temas de la historia bíblica – distintos del Arca de Noé o la Torre de Babel – fueron apareciendo esporádicamente en algunas, pocas, ediciones del *Fasciculus temporum*. En su edición de Utrecht, Veldener (1480) añadió varias.

Al comienzo del libro (f. 1ʳ) aparece, con alusiones al libro del *Génesis* I, Dios creando el sol, la luna y las estrellas, y poniéndolas en el cielo. El grabado, como otros de esta edición, se inspira en los del *Rudimentum novitiorum* (Lübeck 5 agosto 1475). Sólo se repite este tema en las tres últimas ediciones venecianas de Erhardus Ratdolt (1481–85) y su derivada de Adam [de Rottweil?] Alamanus (S. l. 1486), aunque con un grabado de formato y disposición muy diferentes. Si en la estampa de Veldener, cuadrada, Dios está de pie sobre un sencillo paisaje y los astros aparecen

37 BRAUNFELS (véase nota 18), pp. 24–9.
38 El altar fue trasladado en 1810 a la catedral de Colonia, donde permanece.
39 Por ejemplo, en su: *Biblia*. Colonia, Heinrich Quentell, c. 1478 y TOMÁS DE AQUINO: *Opus quarti scripti*. Colonia: Heinrich Quentell, 2. 2. 1480.
40 No se le conoce marca tipográfica a Albrecht Kune; véase ERNST WEIL: *Die deutchen Druckerzeichen des XV. Jahrhunderts*. Hildesheim, New York 1970.

[Fig. 19] Ciudad destruida (Venecia 1484, f. 65ʳ), UB Sevilla
[Fig. 20] Ciudad bajo lluvia de fuego (Ginebra LC 1495, f. 7ʳ), UB Heidelberg, B 1551 A Folio INC

encerrados en un círculo; en las venecianas, y en un largo rectángulo vertical, Dios flota rodeado de nubes, cabezas de angelitos, estrellas, sol y luna, sobre un orbe rodeado de aguas [fig. 21]. En la edición de Ginebra (Louis Cruse, 1495) la escena representada, en formato cuadrado, será la del sexto día de la creación, Dios sacando a Eva del costado de Adán.

Temas exclusivos de la edición de Utrecht son el Arca de la Alianza, las Tablas de la Ley y el candelabro de siete brazos (los tres en f. 14ᵛ), que ilustran textos sobre Moisés, los mandamientos y el Tabernáculo. También son únicas las imágenes — de nuevo sacadas del *Rudimentum novitiorum* — que muestran la construcción de Roma y Jerusalén, bajo la dirección de un rey, en lugar de las vistas genéricas de otras ediciones (ff. 32ʳ y 44ʳ). Así como, finalmente, una interesante composición que representa una alegoría de la Iglesia con San Pedro (f. 71ᵛ), que acompaña al texto siguiente:

> La santa madre Iglesia es comparada a una ciudad, calificada de gloriosa, como se dice en el salmo 86. ¿Qué puede ser más gloriosa que aquella a la que glorificó por entero la Santa Trinidad; a la que defendió la majestad divina; a la que ilumina la divina claridad; a la que gobierna la divina bondad; cuya cabeza es Jesucristo, verdadero Dios y hombre; cuyos ciudadanos son todos selectos; cuyos ministros son los ángeles, aquellos espíritus bienaventurados que están día y noche de guardia sobre sus muros? Esta es la que edificó el unigénito de Dios sobre una firme piedra, y las puertas del infierno no prevalecerán contra ella.

San Pedro abre con su llave la puerta de un torreón hexagonal de grandes sillares para que entren las almas de los justos que, en forma de figuras desnudas, suben por sendas escaleras laterales. Arriba, la fortificación se transforma en un espacio cupulado en el que se abren tres arcos: en el central se ve a Dios con atributos imperiales, adorado por los justos; y, en los laterales, dos ángeles músicos tocan la trompa y el laúd. La estampa recuerda a los edículos que, como templo o como paraíso, se usaban en los misterios de origen medieval, como el famoso de Valenciennes.

Johannes Prüss incorporó cuatro temas nuevos, pero sólo en la edición de 1492, de Estrasburgo. El primero trata de la idolatría (f. 7ʳ), y muestra, sobre un pedestal, la imagen de un rey de la cual salen volando dos demonios; a ambos lados, varios hombres la contemplan, entre ellos los operarios que la han levantado. Su texto dice así:

Nace la idolatría. Téngase en cuenta que quien rebusque bien en las historias, encontrará que fueron principalmente tres las causas que empujaron al hombre a la idolatría: el afecto a los moribundos, el temor y la adulación a los reyes, y la escrupulosidad de los artistas en su obra escultórica. Los demonios, escondiéndose en los ídolos y dando respuestas, fortalecieron de tal forma este engaño que quien no se mostrase de acuerdo con él era castigado con la pena capital. Por si fuera poco, vino a añadirse la falaz alabanza de los poetas, que escribiendo poesías elevaron al cielo a los desgraciados y condenados, y como por esta misma época comenzaban los demonios a hablar bien a los hombres, el Señor, haciendo gala de su clemencia, envió a sus ángeles para que hablasen públicamente a algunos a los que había elegido, intentando evitar que toda la humanidad pereciese a la vez por causa de aquel pésimo engaño.

El segundo tema (f. 9ʳ) muestra como José es empujado por dos de sus hermanos hacia un pozo cuadrado, mientras un barco con las velas desplegadas espera en la costa:

> José, hombre santo. José fue vendido cuando tenía 16 años. Cuando contaba treinta años se estableció en el palacio del faraón Ecrán como intérprete de sus sueños, y el faraón lo glorificó. Dada su castidad y su respeto a Dios, el señor lo orientaba continuamente.

Con el mismo formato, Prüss introduce la ilustración de la Apoteosis de Hércules (f. 12ᵛ) entre los temas bíblicos, donde el héroe, de pie sobre una hoguera encendida y con armadura medieval, está rodeado de figuras que lo veneran arrodilladas:

> Hércules, junto con Jasón, devasta Ilión, es decir, Troya, ciudad que Príamo reconstruye inmediatamente; por su parte, Hércules continúa con sus doce trabajos: funda los juegos Olímpicos, lleva a cabo muchas guerras; sobre él se han elaborado otras muchas mentiras: al final, después de haber vencido a muchos, no siendo capaz de soportar una enfermedad que padecía, vencido por ella, se arrojó a las llamas y, una vez muerto, pasó a ocupar un lugar entre los dioses.

Finalmente (f. 20ʳ), se muestra la lapidación de Zacarías, de pie, en el interior de una ciudad amurallada:

> Zacarías, hijo de Joyada, es lapidado por orden del rey Joás entre el altar y el templo, y es coronado con un martirio glorioso (2 *Paralipómenos*, 24). Reprendió a Joás porque había abandonado totalmente al Señor.

La tardía edición de Ginebra, [Jean Belot], 1495, es la más profusamente ilustrada de todas; en ella abundan los temas bíblicos. Las escenas aparecen dentro de unos pequeños marcos circulares insertos en cuadrados. Comienza el libro con una xilografía que está formada por una tira de siete de estos marcos, aquí todavía más pequeños, que presentan de forma muy sucinta los siete días de la creación (f. 1ᵛ). El centro de la misma página acoge la escena de la Caída del hombre, con Adán y Eva comiendo de la fruta prohibida. Las otras escenas con este formato son: Noé dormido con sus hijos (f. 3ʳ), el sacrificio de Isaac (f. 6ʳ), David arrepentido (f. 12ᵛ) y la transmigración de Babilonia (f. 20ᵛ). A estas imágenes hay que añadir, en formato rectangular, las escenas del Nacimiento y Calvario de Cristo que, juntas y con textos de tipografía especial, crean un espacio singular señalando el comienzo de la era cristiana (f. 34ʳ).

[Fig. 21] Creador (Venecia 1484, f. 2ʳ), UB Sevilla

[Fig. 22] Panteón (Venecia 1484, f. 41ᵛ), UB Sevilla

El Panteón de Roma

Las ediciones venecianas de Ratdolt (1480–85) incluyen la imagen del templo romano conocido como el Panteón [fig. 22], acompañando un curioso texto explicativo de cómo este edificio de la antigüedad romana fue consagrado como iglesia cristiana. Dice así:

> Panteón, en latín «templo de todos los dioses» / Este Bonifacio [IV, papa] consagró el Panteón, es decir, el templo de todos los dioses, donde los cristianos eran puestos en peligro por los demonios. Y la similitud es hermosa, ya que el Espíritu Santo sabe elegir de entre las malvadas prácticas de los paganos el santo ejercicio de la devoción, del mismo modo que del veneno se elabora una medicina: donde los impíos rendían culto a todos los demonios, allí los cristianos honran a todos los santos, y de este modo el arte es burlado con arte (f. 41ᵛ).

La imagen, sin embargo, no hace justicia a la realidad arquitectónica del templo. Si bien conserva sus rasgos esenciales, la circularidad de su planta y su monumental cúpula, añade una irreal galería de columnas a su alrededor y suprime su pórtico de frontón triangular sobre columnas. Está claro que el autor del grabado jamás estuvo en Roma.

La única edición no veneciana que incorpora una copia de esta imagen es la de Adam [de Rottweil?] Alamanus (S. l. 1486, f. 41ᵛ) que, como se ha visto, es fiel a las venecianas – aunque añadiendo sobre la entrada al templo una escultura pagana desnuda. En la última de las ediciones que Johann Prüss publicó en Estrasburgo (1492) aparece una ilustración como Panteón (f. 81ʳ); sin embargo, la imagen es la misma que Prüss empleó en todas sus ediciones para la Torre de Babel. Además, en esa misma edición se vuelve a usar como Templo de Salomón (f. 15ᵛ).

Esquemas simbólicos

Otra de las aportaciones de las ediciones venecianas de Erhardus Ratdolt es la presencia en un novedoso anexo al final del libro con esquemas simbólicos sobre cuestiones relativas al Antiguo Testamento. En la edición de 1480 hay cinco diagramas; en el f. 67ʳ, se muestra la división del mundo: Jerusalén en el centro de un orbe con los cuatro puntos cardinales, cuyo interior está dividido en tres partes: Asia, África y Europa vinculadas respectivamente a Sem, Cam y Jafet, los descendientes de Noé. Un esquema semejante al publicado en las *Etimologías* de San Isidoro de Sevilla, en Ausgburgo (Günter Zainer, noviembre 1472), libro que junto a *De responsione mundi et de astrorum ordinatione*, del mismo autor y editor (Augsburgo 7 diciembre 1472) fue un adelantado en el uso de diagramas impresos, algunos de gran belleza.[41]

El f. 67ᵛ tiene tres esquemas. Dos del arca de Noé en forma de A mayúscula: uno con la distribución de espacios y medidas en el Arca según San Agustín, y otro con los espacios según Josefo. Bajo ellos, una serie de círculos concéntricos simbolizan la Jerusalén reedificada por Nehemías con sus tres habitaciones y las seis puertas de la ciudad según el texto, ya citado, del f. 17ᵛ y al que suele acompañar una vista convencional como Jerusalén. En realidad, un diagrama de este mismo tema – y otro sustituyendo la imagen del Salvador – habían aparecido con anterioridad en la

---

41 *Bartsch* (véase nota 6), 80 Supp., 1472/156–67; el diagrama de las partes del mundo es el 1472/159.

Iconografía de las ilustraciones del Fasciculus temporum

edición de Nicolaus Götz ([Colonia] [después de 1474], f. 78); edición que, a diferencia de la de Ther Hoerner (Colonia 1474), no influyó directamente en otras ediciones de la obra.

Finalmente, en el f. 68ʳ, un nuevo círculo, en cuyo interior hay un arco sobre dos columnas, representa esquemáticamente la creación del mundo y sus siete días descritos en el Génesis [fig. 23]. Este esquema es el único que aparece en el resto de las ediciones venecianas – también en la de Adam [de Rottweil?] Alamanus (S. l. 1486) – ; porque de los otros, sólo el orbe con sus tres partes volverá a ilustrar la edición de 1484.

Santos fundadores de órdenes monásticas

La edición del *Fasciculus temporum*, en Rougemont (1481), por Henricus Wirtzburg, monje del Priorato Cluniacense de esta ciudad suiza, incorporó nuevas ilustraciones, que se añadirían a ediciones posteriores. Aportó las imágenes de los fundadores de órdenes monásticas, la de la Abadía de Cluny, y la de seres monstruosos y fenómenos astronómicos. Aparte de las citadas modificaciones del Salvador o la ilustración de Sodoma y Gomorra y la caída de Troya.

Wirtzburg ilustró los textos originales de Rolevinck relativos a las órdenes monásticas y, además, desarrolló sus noticias. San Benito (f. 54ᵛ) se muestra de cuerpo entero, con su hábito monacal, un libro, un báculo abacial y una orla de santidad tras su cabeza. El grabado acompaña a un párrafo que describe las características del hábito benedictino y cuenta detalladamente cómo el santo creó una Regla bajo la que reunió a cenobitas y anacoretas, para después fundar el monasterio de Monte Casino y otros muchos, entre los cuales se cita al de Cluny; párrafo que sustituye ampliamente al texto de la edición original, que decía:

> Sobresale San Benito, padre supremo, apoyo de toda la Iglesia y regla de la religión. Este venerable varón tuvo destacadísimos y numerosos discípulos, y conquistó el orbe de las tierras, etc. San Gregorio escribió su vida en el segundo de los Diálogos (f. 39ʳ).

A San Bruno (f. 74ʳ) se le representa con el hábito de su orden, cubierto por su característica capucha picuda, y leyendo un libro. En este caso se conserva íntegramente el texto original, aunque con algún cambio en el orden de los párrafos (f. 54ᵛ):

> Sabemos que en esta época tiene sus inicios la Orden de los Cartujos, que – de acuerdo con San Bernardo – ocupa la primacía entre todas las órdenes eclesiásticas, no por razón de antigüedad, sino por su rigor, motivo este por el cual el propio santo le da el nombre de «hermosísima columna de la Iglesia». Pero dado que por la excesiva abstinencia que propugnaba era soportable para muy pocos y para evitar que fuera exigua durante mucho tiempo, fue moderada más tarde por la Iglesia, y jamás decayó de su santo propósito, singularmente preservada hasta hoy por el Espíritu Santo / Bruno, hombre santo de Colonia y maestro en teología, se hace famoso junto con otros seis hombres venerables, porque echaron las raíces de la Orden de los Cartujos en la diócesis de Gratianópolis.

Aprovechando la biografía del papa Urbano II, que fue monje cisterciense, y del que se cita su relación con el cartujo San Bruno, Wirtzburg añade

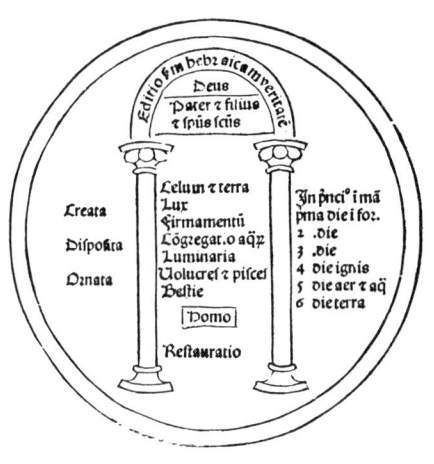

[Fig. 23] Esquema de la creación del mundo (Venecia 1484, f. 68ʳ), UB Sevilla

[Fig. 24] San Bernardo
(Ginebra LC 1495, f. 74ᵛ), UB Heidelberg,
B 1551 A Folio INC

[Fig. 25] San Benito
(Ginebra LC 1495, f. 54ᵛ), UB Heidelberg,
B 1551 A Folio INC

[Fig. 26] San Bruno
(Ginebra LC 1495, f. 74ʳ), UB Heidelberg,
B 1551 A Folio INC

un nuevo párrafo que alude a la creación de la orden del Cister por el abad Roberto y Alberico, tras reformar la Regla benedictina; así como la imagen de otro santo monje (f. 74ᵛ). El bloque xilográfico es el mismo de San Benito, al que ahora cubre una parte superior del hábito cerrada y blanca – en San Benito, abierta y rayada – gracias a que han sido eliminadas, retalladas, las líneas de esa zona. Aunque no se cite en el texto, es de suponer que el santo abad cisterciense de la imagen se corresponde con la figura de San Bernardo de Claraval, auténtico configurador e impulsor de la orden en toda Europa.

En el f. 79ᵛ se insertan las figuras de Santo Domingo y San Francisco para ilustrar unos nuevos textos. Los dos tienen orla de santidad y libro en la mano derecha; el primero, con el blanco y negro de su hábito diferenciados; el segundo, con su largo cordón y mostrando sus estigmas. La letra explica cómo Domingo, español, se dedicó a perseguir herejes e instituyó la orden de los frailes predicadores; mientras que Francisco, italiano, con un grado de amor, fervor y pobreza que lo condujo a realizar muchos milagros, fue el fundador de la orden de los frailes menores.

Hay un antecedente de ilustraciones de monjes y santos fundadores de órdenes monásticas en el *Rudimentum novitiorum* (Lübeck 5 agosto 1475), donde junto a hechos relativos a diferentes instituciones monásticas se incluyen las imágenes de hasta cuatro modelos de medio cuerpo de monjes de orden indeterminada. Son figuras convencionales que se repiten para diferentes hechos y personajes: entre ellos San Bernardo y San Benito.

Los santos monjes fueron copiados, junto a los textos añadidos o modificados por Wirtzburg, en la edición de Lyon (Mathie Husz, 1483): fielmente San Benito (f. 54ᵛ) y San Bernardo (74ᵛ) – ambos con el mismo grabado –; mientras que los demás (ff. 74ʳ y 79ᵛ) lo fueron con el sentido invertido. En la edición ginebrina de Jean Belot, 1495, están inscritos bajo arcos (ff. 54ᵛ, 74ʳ, 74ᵛ y 79ᵛ), y presentan añadidos en los atributos de Santo Domingo (una palma) y San Francisco (un crucifijo). La otra edición de Ginebra (Louis Cruse, 1495) incluye una xilografía diferenciada para San Bernardo de Claraval [fig. 24]; éste, junto a San Benito [fig. 25] y San Bruno [fig. 26] son situados junto a plantas o flores. Mientras que Santo Domingo y San Francisco comparten un mismo taco xilográfico en el que se representa un suelo liso [fig. 27]. Estas mismas xilografías fueron reutilizadas en la edición de Lyon (Mathie Husz, 1498).

Iconografía de las ilustraciones del Fasciculus temporum

Laviece Cox Ward destaca el esfuerzo de Henric Wirtzburg, el editor cisterciense, por dirigirse al mercado específico de las comunidades monacales incorporando a su edición del *Fasciculus temporum* el atractivo de las imágenes de los santos fundadores de órdenes y la vista «real» del monasterio de Cluny, del que se hablará a continuación.[42]

Abadía de Cluny

La edición de Rougemont incluye la primera representación impresa del famoso monasterio de Cluny (f. 68r), acompañando a un texto que refunde otros del original (f. 50r). En él se alude a la creación de este «famosísimo y santísimo» monasterio benedictino gracias a una donación de Guillermo I de Aquitania, duque de Aquitania y conde de Auvernia, llamado «el piadoso», y a su primer abad, Bernón. El profesor John Cowdrey identificó la imagen con el llamado Cluny III, es decir, el estado de la abadía tras su segunda reconstrucción, convertido en el mayor monasterio de la cristiandad gracias al ambicioso proyecto del abad Pons de Melgueil (1109–22).[43] La imagen refleja la singularidad del edificio; su planta de cruz latina, los tres niveles de altura de sus naves, el atrio con sus torres laterales, su compleja cabecera, etc., son fácilmente reconocibles gracias a una perspectiva bastante correcta para lo que se suele ver en las ilustraciones de la época. El valor histórico de la imagen es grande ya que el edificio representado no existe hoy: tras la Revolución Francesa, los propios habitantes de la zona fueron desmantelando el monasterio, y es muy poco lo que queda del mismo.

Ninguna de las ediciones posteriores que incorporan las novedades de Rougemont copia la imagen del monasterio de Cluny, aunque sí incluyen una imagen convencional de vista de ciudad con esa atribución; en estos casos no se copió la imagen original, como sí se hizo en las xilografías de los monjes fundadores.

Seres monstruosos y cometas

Otra aportación de la edición de Rougemont es la ilustración de casos extraordinarios, relacionados con fenómenos astronómicos como la aparición de cometas o los eclipses. Aquí, el editor ilustra los textos originales, sin modificarlos; con lo cual otorga a estos fenómenos una importancia similar a la de otros acontecimientos ilustrados en el libro (hechos

[Fig. 27] Santo Domingo y San Francisco de Asís (Ginebra LC 1495, f. 79v), UB Heidelberg, B 1551 A Folio INC
[Fig. 28] Seres monstruosos y cometa (Ginebra LC 1495, f. 57r), UB Heidelberg, B 1551 A Folio INC
[Fig. 29] Licántropo (Ginebra LC 1495, f. 68v), UB Heidelberg, B 1551 A Folio INC

42 WARD (véase nota 23), p. 110.
43 Citado por WARD (véase nota 23), p. 109.

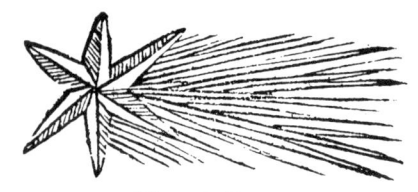

[Fig. 30] Cometa (Ginebra LC 1495, f. 47ᵛ), UB Heidelberg, B 1551 A Folio INC

bíblicos, fundación de ciudades o de órdenes religiosas) y añade de esta forma un nuevo atractivo basado en el morbo de lo raro, lo fantástico y lo inverosímil.

Hay dos grabados llamativos de seres extraordinarios, más tres de fenómenos astronómicos. La primera imagen (f. 57ʳ) recoge en su composición la presencia de un cometa y un eclipse solar sobre dos figuras: en vertical, el niño sin ojos ni manos con el cuerpo inferior de un pez, y, a cuatro patas, el niño bizantino cuadrúpedo:

> Se cuenta que en estos tiempos sucedieron hechos maravillosos. Apareció un cometa; en Bizancio nació un niño con cuatro pies y otro con dos cabezas; lanzas ensangrentadas y una luz clarísima se veían durante toda la noche; nace un niño sin ojos ni manos, y que de la cintura hacia abajo tenía forma de pez; en el Nilo, en Egipto, aparecieron dos animales de apariencia humana, hombre y mujer, de un horrible aspecto; durante el transcurso de un día, de la mañana a la noche, el sol se redujo a una tercera parte. Todas estas cosas suelen anunciar algo nuevo. Algunos piensan que prefiguran la bestial y monstruosa secta de los sarracenos, que en breve tiempo corrompió casi a la tercera parte del cristianismo, y que hizo su aparición no mucho después de esta época.

La segunda imagen (f. 68ᵛ) representa a un hombre desnudo con una feroz cabeza de lobo, dando un paso al frente y con las manos en actitud gesticulante. El texto, inquietante, que le acompaña dice:

> Un hombre monstruoso, con cabeza de perro y los restantes miembros como un hombre, es presentado a Ludovico [III, emperador], y puede muy bien representar el monstruoso estado de aquella época, en que los hombres sin cabeza y ladrando como perros iban vacilantes de un lado a otro (f. 68ᵛ).

Estos dos grabados extraordinarios, que tienen como antecedente la tradición medieval de representar a bestias y seres monstruosos, son, a su vez, la avanzadilla en el mundo de la imprenta del género específico de los «casos espantosos»; que, dentro del más amplio de las noticias y relaciones de sucesos notables o extraordinarios, fue durante siglos del gusto popular, entre otros motivos porque se incluían este tipo de estampas tan llamativas.[44] He aquí, de nuevo, el uso de las ilustraciones como reclamo que busca hacer más atractivo el libro a sus potenciales compradores. Si antes se dirigía a los ciudadanos locales, o a los miembros de las comunidades religiosas, ahora busca cualquier lector curioso o apasionado por este género de temas morbosos e inquietantes.

Por esta razón, en la mayor parte de las ediciones posteriores a 1481 se incluyen copias de estas dos imágenes fantásticas.[45] Copias que mantienen lo esencial de su modelo, aunque no les preocupe el sentido de la imagen [fig. 28 y 29].

Los cometas, eclipses y otros raros fenómenos celestes, que ya estaban presentes en el texto original de Rolenvick, se hicieron visibles a través de pequeños grabados en la edición de Rougemont. Y a partir de entonces, estas pequeñas figuras pasaron a formar parte de la iconografía de las ediciones posteriores del *Fasciculus temporum*.[46] Los textos que ilustran estas figuras celestes, repetidas en las distintas ediciones con pequeñas diferencias de calidad, son diez. El primer cometa (f. 47ᵛ) aparece junto a un texto, que comienza con la repetida fórmula *Cometa*

44 FRANCISCO BAENA SÁNCHEZ: Entre *quality papers* y prensa amarilla: los «casos espantosos». En *Relaciones de sucesos en la Biblioteca de la Universidad de Sevilla, antes de que existiera la prensa …* Sevilla 2008, pp. 72–81.

45 No están en: Memmingen (Albrecht Kune 1482); Colonia (Ludwig von Renchen h. 1483); Venecia (Erhardus Ratdolt 1484 y 1485); y Adam [de Rottweil?] Alamanus (S.l. 1486).

46 Con la excepción de las citadas en la nota anterior.

apparuit ..., en el que se explica cómo la muerte del emperador Constantino, ocurrida poco después de la presencia visible de un cometa, fue causada por su influencia negativa [fig. 30]. El texto del (f. 52ʳ) es mucho más tremendo: cuenta cómo se vio que el cielo se volvía de fuego; cómo la luna se oscureció y hubo un temblor de tierra. Apareció un cometa y, en Toulouse, un río de sangre fluyó desde el cielo hasta la tierra. En el (f. 64ʳ) cuenta cómo el sol se oscureció durante diez y siete días, el signo de la cruz apareció marcando las ropas de los hombres y, de nuevo, la sangre cayó del cielo; junto a este párrafo se incluye una nueva imagen del sol oscurecido con la lluvia de sangre [fig. 31]. Un folio después (65ʳ) una estrella cruciforme ilustra la noticia de la aparición celeste un gran signo rojo, como una cruz, rodeado de lanzas, tras lo que hubo una gran mortandad de cristianos. Y así, con estos grabados y otro de un sol oscurecido, se ilustran textos muy semejantes (de guerras, terremotos, ahogados, muertes) en los folios [65ᵛ], [77ᵛ], [82ᵛ], [83ʳ], [87ʳ] y [90ʳ]. La última de estas noticias describe la aparición de un cometa sobre Colonia en el año 1472; parece que el monje Rolenvick vivió apasionadamente esa experiencia que le movió a recoger en su libro todas estas noticias astronómicas que, por otra parte, amenizan notablemente el frío rigor cronológico de la sucesión de personajes y acontecimientos históricos que exige el contenido de su obra.

Otros grabados
Hay un último grupo de grabados que aparecen sólo en la última década del siglo XV. En la edición de Ginebra ([Jean Belot], 1495), las imágenes ilustran los contenidos del libro, ya que son retratos de los principales personajes que se suceden a lo largo de la primera parte de la obra. Los retratos sustituyen a los marcos circulares que en las demás ediciones incluyen los nombres de los personajes. Son de formato rectangular, con un arco de medio punto rebajado, bajo el cual aparece el busto del retratado, a veces de perfil, otras de tres cuartos; un fondo rayado crea sensación de profundidad. El nombre correspondiente a cada imagen está escrito dentro de la línea cronológica inferior, la relativa al nacimiento de Cristo. Son quince tipos de retratos convencionales que representan a reyes, profetas, sacerdotes y, sólo una mujer (Athalia); con ellos se ilustra a un total de ochenta personajes, desde Set, hijo de Adán y Eva, hasta San José. Después de Cristo ya no hay más retratos; tan sólo, en la línea de los papas, hay dos casos en los que estos se representan con una tiara dentro del marco circular.

Estos retratos tienen su antecedente en la publicación, un par de años antes, del famoso *Liber chronicarum* o *Crónica de Nurembreg*, de Antón Koberger, en 1493; obra del mismo género literario que, si bien incorporó el sistema de vistas convencionales de ciudades iniciado por el *Fasciculus temporum*, desarrolló su propio sistema de retratos, también convencionales, de personajes históricos con el que ilustra profusamente su amplio texto.[47]

El resto de las xilografías que se encuentran en las ediciones del *Fasciculus temporum*, aparte de las marcas tipográficas y letras ornamentadas que no serán consideradas aquí, son imágenes, hasta cierto punto también

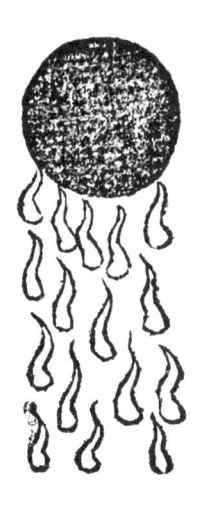

[Fig. 31] Lluvia de sangre (Ginebra LC 1495, f. 64ʳ), UB Heidelberg, B 1551 A Folio INC

[47] HARTMANN SCHEDEL: *Liber chronicarum*. Norimbergae: Antonius Koberger, 1493.

convencionales, que usan los editores para adornar diferentes obras y que, por tanto, no tienen relación directa con el contenido del libro. Son los casos de tres atractivos grabados, que se usan a página completa en los principios del libro – en el verso de la portada –, que los editores utilizaron como reclamo en diferentes obras.

Una imagen muy utilizada para encabezar los libros realizados en las primeras décadas de la imprenta es la del autor entregando un libro a su rey, emperador o señor. Ésta es la imagen (19,2 × 12,2 cm) que aparece en la edición del *Fasciculus* ... que Johannes Prüss publicó en Estrasburgo (después de 6 abril 1490/1). El taco xilográfico empleado se usó antes en la obra de Johannes de Capua, *Das buoch der weyßheyt der altten weysen*, por Conrad Feyner (Urach h. 1481), y en Augsburgo 1484, así como en el *Directorium humanae vitae*, del mismo autor y por el propio Johannes Prüss (Estrasburgo h. 1488); después de lo cual aparecería en España, utilizado por el impresor alemán Paulus Horus, afincado en Zaragoza, en [Aristóteles], *Ethica ad Nicomachum Leonardo Aretino interprete* (1492) y *Epistolae ad Lucillium* de Lucio Anneo Séneca (1496). Un grabado viajero y que tuvo un éxito notable como muestra el hecho de que se realizaran copias del mismo.[48]

En otras dos ediciones del *Fasciculus* ..., que también publicó Prüss en Estrasburgo ([después de 6 abril 1490/1] y [después de 7 noviembre 1492]) la imagen que aparece es la de un anciano caminando con un bastón (17,8 × 12,7 cm), bajo un arco de arbustos y mirando hacia arriba – pudiera ser ciego. No he visto este grabado en otros libros, pero su significación no está relacionada con el contenido del libro de Rolenvick.

La tercera imagen vuelve a ser otra muy utilizada en la portada o principios de muchos libros: la del autor en su escritorio. La usa [Jean Belot] (Ginebra 1495) en el verso de la portada, y es una cuidada xilografía (20,5 × 15,3 cm) en la que, bajo un arco de ramas y guirnaldas sostenidas por *putti*, se muestra al escritor en su estudio, sentado en su cátedra ante una mesa copiando un libro; mientras, cuatro personajes entran por una puerta que hay en el fondo. El mismo impresor, también en Ginebra, la reutiliza tras la portada de nuevos libros, como *Les sept sages de Rome* (21 julio 1498) y el *Compost et kalendrier des bergers*, ([entre 5 febrero 1498 y 1500] y 1500).

Una imagen semejante (16,5 × 14,3 cm) se encuentra en la edición de Lyon (Mathie Husz, 1498), aunque aquí el protagonista, que también está sentado en una lujosa cátedra, lee un libro rodeado de otros siete personajes, bajo una arquitectura gótica abovedada. Esta xilografía ya había sido utilizada anteriormente por el editor en sus dos ediciones de *Valère Maxime* (Lyon 23 junio 1485 y 23 de junio de 1489).[49]

---

48 Hay una copia fiel en JOHANNES DE CAPUA: *Exemplario contra los engaños y peligros del mundo*, Burgos: Juan de Burgos, 1498.

49 CLAUDIN (véase nota 31), pp. 269/270 y 282.

Ejemplares del *Fasciculus temporum* consultados[50]

1. Rolevinck, Werner: *Fasciculus temporum*. Colonia: Arnold Ther Hoerner, 1474. En: Rolewinck, Wernerus: *Fasciculum temporum* (1474). UB Bielefeld, N 32676. En línea: Digitale Sammlungen der UB Bielefeld.
2. Rolewinck, Werner: *Fasciculus temporum*. Cologne: Arnold Ther Hoernen, 1474. UB Colonia, ENNE 53. En línea: Verteilte Digitale Inkunabelbibliothek.
3. Rolewinck, Werner: Fasciculus temporum. Cologne: Arnold Ther Hoernen, 1474. UB Colonia, ENNE 70. En línea: Verteilte Digitale Inkunabelbibliothek.
4. Rolevinck, Werner: *Fasciculus temporum*. [Colonia]: Nicolaus Götz, [después de 1474]. En: Rolewinck, Werner: *Fasciculus temporum*. [Cologne]: Nicolaus Götz, [después de 1474]. UB Colonia, ENNE 138. En línea: Verteilte Digitale Inkunabelbibliothek.
5. Rolevinck, Werner: *Fasciculus temporum*. Lovaina: Johan Veldener, 29 diciembre [1475]. En: Rolevinck, Werner: *Fasciculus temporum*. Löwen 29 diciembre 1475. BSB-Ink R-233,1. En línea: DFG-*Viewer*.
6. Rolevinck, Werner: *Fasciculus temporum*. Colonia: Conrad Winters, 8 noviembre 1476. En: Rolevinck, Werner: *Fasciculus temporum*. [Köln] 8 noviembre 1476. BSB-Ink R-234,1. En línea: DFG-*Viewer*.
7. Rolevinck, Werner: *Fasciculus temporum*. [Espira]: Peter Drach, 24 noviembre 1477. En: Rolevinck, Werner: *Fasciculus temporum mit Fortsetzung bis 1476*. [Speyer] 24 noviembre 1477. BSB-Ink R-235,1. En línea: DFG-*Viewer*.
8. Rolevinck, Werner: *Fasciculus temporum*. [Colonia]: Nicolaus Götz, [1478]. Solo las ilustraciones: *The Illustrated Barstch*. 80 (Supplement). New York 1981, 1478/152.
9. Rolevinck, Werner: *Fasciculus temporum*. [Colonia]: Heinrich Quentell, 1479. En: Rolevinck, Werner: *Fasciculus temporum*. [Köln] 1479. BSB-Ink R-237,1. En línea: DFG-*Viewer*.
10. Rolevinck, Werner: *Fasciculus temporum* ... Venecia: Georgius Walch, 1479. En: Rolevinck, Werner: *Fasciculus temporum mit Fortsetzung bis 1477*. Venedig 1479. BSB-Ink R-238,1. En línea: DFG-*Viewer*.
11. Rolevinck, Werner: *Fasciculus temporum*. Utrecht: Johan Veldener, 14 febrero 1480. En: Rolevinck, Werner: *Dat boeck dat men hiet fasciculus temporum* ... Utrecht: 14 febrero 1480. BSB-Ink R-256,1. En línea: DFG-*Viewer*.
12. Rolevinck, Werner: *Fasciculus temporum, vel Chronica ab initio mundi. Auctoritates de vita et moribus philosophorum ex Laertio extractae/Diogenes Laercio*. Hispali [Sevilla]: Bartholomaeus Segura et Alfonsus de Portu, 1480. En: Rolewinck, Werner: *Fasciculus temporum, vel Chronica ab initio mundi*. Sevilla 1480. U de Sevilla, A 335/082. En línea: U de Sevilla, Fondo Antiguo.
13. Rolevinck, Werner: *Fasciculus temporum omnes antiquorum cronicas complectens*. Venecia: Erhardus Ratdolt, 24 noviembre 1480. En: Rolevinck, Werner: *Fasciculus temporum, mit Fortsetzung bis 1480*. Venedig 24 noviembre 1480. BSB-Ink R-240,2. En línea: DFG-*Viewer*.

[50] Véase también la relación de páginas en línea en p. 374.

14. Rolevinck, Werner: *Fasciculus temporum*. [Colonia]: Heinrich Quentell, 1480. En: Rolevinck, Werner: [G]*Eneratio et generatio* ... [Köln] 1480. BSB-Ink R-239, 2. En línea: DFG-*Viewer*.

15. Rolevinck, Werner: *Fasciculus temporum*. [Colonia], Heinrich Quentell, 1481. En: Rolevinck, Werner: [G]*Eneratio et generatio* ... [Köln] 1481. BSB-Ink R-241, 1. En línea: DFG-*Viewer*.

16. Rolevinck, Werner: *Fasciculus temporum*. Rougemont: Henricus Wirtzburg, 1481. En: *Fasciculus temporum* [auctore W. Rolevinck, cum additionibus fratris Henrici Wirzburg de Vach]. BNF, IFN-7300074, En línea: Gallica.

17. Rolevinck, Werner: *Fasciculus temporum*. Basilea: Bernhard Richel, 31 agosto 1481. En: Rolevinck, Werner: *Die Cronick die man nempt eyn bürdin oder versamlung der zyt* [mit Fortsetzung bis 1480]. Basel 31 agosto 1481. BSB-Ink R-253, 2. En línea: DFG-*Viewer*.

18. Rolevinck, Werner: *Fasciculus temporum, vel Chronica ab initio mundi*. [Venecia]: Erhardus Ratdolt, 21 diciembre 1481. En: *Fasciculus temporum, vel Chronica ab initio mundi*. Rolevinck, Wernerius. [Venetiis]: Erhardus Ratdolt, [21 diciembre 1481]. B Provincial de Córdoba, I-43. En En línea: B Virtual de Andalucía.

19. Rolevinck, Werner: *Fasciculus temporum*. Basilea: Bernhard Richel, 20 febrero 1482. En: Rolevinck, Werner: *Fasciculus temporum*, mit Fortsetzung bis 1475. [Basel] 20 febrero 1482. BSB-Ink R-243,2. En línea: DFG-*Viewer*.

20. Rolevinck, Werner: *Fasciculus temporum*. Memmingen: Albrecht Kunne, 1482. En: Rolevinck, Werner: [G]*Eneratio et g[e]n[er]atio* ... Memmingen 1482 [no posterior a 8 septiembre]. BSB-Ink R-244,2. En línea: DFG-*Viewer*.

21. Rolevinck, Werner: *Fasciculus temporum*. [Colonia: ¿Ludwig von Renchen?, no posterior a 1483]. En: Rolevinck, Werner, [G]*Eneratio et generatio* ..., [Köln] [no posterior a 1483]. BSB-Ink R-245, 1. En línea: DFG-*Viewer*.

22. Rolevinck, Werner: *Fardelet des temps*. Lyon: Mathie Husz, 1483. BNF, Microfilm R 102708.

23. Rolevinck, Werner: *Fasciculus temporum*. Venecia: Erhardus Ratdolt, 28 mayo 1484. En: Rolevinck, Werner: *Generatio [et] generatio* ... Venetiis 28 mayo 1484. BSB-Ink R-246,5. En línea: DFG-*Viewer*.

24. Rolevinck, Werner: *Fasciculus temporum*. Venecia: Erhardus Ratdolt, 1485. En: Rolevinck, Werner: *Fasciculus temporum* ... Venedig 8 septiembre 1485. BSB-Ink R-247, 2. En línea: DFG-*Viewer*.

25. Rolevinck, Werner: *Fasciculus temporum vel Chronica ab initio mundi*. [S. l., Francia meridional?; Aquila?]: Adam [de Rottweil?] [Steinschaber, Geneve?] Alamanus, 2 diciembre 1486. Médiathèque de Troyes Troyes-Patrimoine incunable 221.

26. Rolevinck, Werner: *Fasciculus temporum*. Estrasburgo: Johann Prüss, 1487. En: Rolevinck, Werner: *Fasciculus tempo[rum]*. Argentine: Pryss, 1487. HAB, A: 154.3 Quod. 2º (2). En linéa: Wolfenbütteler Digitale B.

27. Rolevinck, Werner: *Fasciculus temporum*. Estrasburgo: Johann Prüss, 1488. En: Rolevinck, Werner: *Fasciculus temporum*. Straßburg 1488. BSB-Ink R-249, 4. En línea: DFG-*Viewer*.

28. Rolevinck, Werner: *Fasciculus temporum*. [Estrasburgo]: [Johann Prüss], [después de 6 abril 1490]. 1: con grabado de entrega de libro. En: *Fasciculus te[m]porum omnes antiquorum cronicas complecte[n]s*. [Estrasburgo]: [Prüss], [después de 6 abril 1490]. HAB, A: 151 Quod. 2º (3). En línea: Wolfenbütteler Digitale B.
29. Rolevinck, Werner: *Fasciculus temporum*. [Estrasburgo]: [Johann Prüss], [después de 6 abril 1490]. 2: con grabado de peregrino. En: Rolevinck, Werner: *Fasciculus temporum* [después de 6 abril 1490]. BSB-Ink R-250. En línea: DFG-*Viewer*.
30. Rolewinck, Werner: *Fasciculus temporum. Eyn burdlin der zeyt*. [Estrasburgo]: [Johann Prüss], [después de 7 noviembre 1492]. En: *Ein Cronica von anfang der welt ... Genant Fasciculus temporum ...* [Estrasburgo]: [Prüss], [después de 7 noviembre 1492]. HAB, A: 288.13 Hist. 2º (1). En línea: Wolfenbütteler Digitale B.
31. Rolevinck, Werner: *Fasciculus temporum. Le fardelet hystorial*. Ginebra: Louis Cruse, 28 abril 1495. En: DVD de la UB Heidelberg, nº D047/10.
32. Rolevinck, Werner: *Fasciculus temporum en francois*. Ginebra: [Jean Belot], 1495. En: Rolevinck, Werner: *Le fardelet hystorial mit Fortsetzung bis 1495*. Genf [después de 12 mayo 1495]. BSB-Ink R-255, 1. En línea: DFG-*Viewer*.
33. Rolevinck, Werner: *Fasciculus temporum omnes antiquorum hystorias complectens*. [S. n.] 1495. En: Rolevinck, Werner: *Fasciculus temporum* [mit Fortsetzung bis 1495]. [Lyon] [no autes de 1495]. BSB-Ink R-252, 1. En línea: DFG-*Viewer*.
34. Rolevinck, Werner: *Fasciculus temporum en françoys, les fleurs et manieres de temps passe: et des faits merveilleux de Dieu tant en lancien testament ...* Lyon: Mathie Husz, 1498. En: *Fasciculus temporum en françoys ...* [authore Wermer Rolevinck]. [s. n.] 1498. BNF, NUMM-52191. En línea: Gallica.

RANDALL HERZ

Three Fifteenth Century Proof Sheets with Manuscript Corrections from Nuremberg Presses

With a Note on a Book with Correction Slips

TO SAY THAT PRE-PRESS WORK is an integral part of publishing is to state the obvious. Before a book goes to press, modern publishing houses take great pains to ensure that it is attractively designed, carefully edited, and free of all typographical errors. In the fifteenth century, printer-publishers were equally keen to produce attractive and well-edited books. Lacking the computer-aided procedures of today, compositors and house correctors carried out the tasks of copy-setting, proofreading, and lay-outing manually. Pre-press work (here perhaps an anomaly) was done by review of proof or trial sheets. This paper will look at three such sheets kept in the Handschriftenabteilung of the University of Erlangen and also in the Library of the Hungarian Academy of Sciences (HAS) in Budapest. In addition, an interesting case will be treated in which corrections were made to a book after completion of the full run.

In the hand-press era, a book was set and printed forme by forme. Before the full run was made, a proof sheet was first pulled for each forme and corrected by hand. By the seventeenth century, printing houses routinely pulled as many as three proofs per forme, made, as Philip Gaskell has noted, for the house corrector, the author and as final revise proof.[1]

Surviving historical sources and printers' manuals give us a detailed picture of pre-press work in printing houses from the late sixteenth century on. Due to a lack of source materials, our knowledge of the procedures before then is based largely on conjecture. Surviving fifteenth century proof sheets suggest that the procedure was established from early on. The oldest surviving sheets date from the 1450s and 1460s. Among them are proofs of a 40-line bible (Mainz, c. 1458), the Mentelin bible of 1460, and the Fust-Schoeffer bible of 1462, thus providing evidence that proofreading procedures were in use in the earliest presses located at Mainz and Strasbourg.[2]

However, this does not tell us how many proof sheets were made before the full run. Ongoing research in Erlangen suggests that early printing houses routinely made two trial sheets. As in seventeenth century practice, the first was made for use by the corrector in proofreading the standing type against the manuscript model (printer's copy). He entered the corrections directly onto the proof sheet in silver point or ink, and then returned it to the compositor who made the correction to the standing type. Then the press crew pulled another proof. This sheet, called the revise or "review", was to ensure that the revisions had been

---

[1] Cf. PHILIP GASKELL: *A New Introduction to Bibliography*. Winchester, Delaware 1995, pp. 110–6.

[2] A single trial sheet of a 40-line Biblia latina (Mainz: Type of the 36-line Bible, c. 1458) is preserved in Krákau, B Jagiellonska (ISTC ib00526500. IBP 983. Facsimile by CARL WEHMER: *Mainzer Probedrucke in der Type des sogenannten Astronomischen Kalenders für 1448. Ein Beitrag zur Gutenberg-Forschung*. Munich 1948, pl. 5). – For Mentelin's Biblia latina of 1460 (ISTC ib00528000. GW 4203) cf. PAUL NEEDHAM: The Cambridge Proof sheets of Mentelin's Latin Bible. In: *Transactions of the Cambridge Bibliographical Society*. 9 (1986), pp. 1–35. – For the Fust-Schoeffer bible of 1462 cf. PAUL NEEDHAM: The 1462 Bible of Johann Fust and Peter Schöffer (GW 4204): A Survey of its Variants. In: GJ 2006, pp. 19–49.

carried out properly.³ If this was the case, the press crew could proceed to print the full run. Given the predominance of older texts published in the late fifteenth century, the third type of proof mentioned above, made for author review, was rarely done, if at all, in the incunabula period.

Having served their purpose, the trial sheets were not discarded, but instead were passed on to bookbinders for use as binding material. Probably several thousand revise sheets have survived as pastedowns in the covers of fifteenth century books. Since they are identical in wording to the final printed product, they tell us little about pre-press procedures. By the same token, sheets marked with handwritten corrections by proofreaders are very rare. The three which have survived in Erlangen and in Budapest provide us with many insights into fifteenth century proofreading procedures.

The oldest one dates from the earliest years of book production in Nuremberg. It was produced in 1471 on the press run by Johann Sensenschmidt, the city's first printer.⁴ The second sheet was made by Anton Koberger, the city's third and most successful printer.⁵ The third was pulled on the press run by Georg (Jörg) Stuchs in 1496. Stuchs had received his training in the 1480s from Koberger and eventually became one of the city's leading printers.⁶

The title and place of publication of the sheets are as follows:

1. GREGORIUS I, PONT. MAX: *Moralia, sive expositio in Job*.⁷
   Nuremberg: [Johann Sensenschmidt of Eger], 11 September 1471.
2. ANTONINUS FLORENTINUS: *Summa theologica*,
   pars secunda.⁸ Nuremberg: Anton Koberger, 28 August 1486.
3. GUILLERMUS ALVERNUS, EPISCOPUS PARISIENSIS:
   Opera. Ed. PETER DANHAUSER. Nuremberg: Georg Stuchs,
   after 31 March 1496.

See appendix 4 for full bibliographical details of the sheets.

A proof sheet from Johann Sensenschmidt's press in Nuremberg (1471)
The Sensenschmidt proof sheet contains a page from the printed edition of *Moralia, sive expositio in Job*, the magnum opus of Saint Gregory the Great (c. 540–604). It provides us with an example of Sensenschmidt's early innovative and enterprising book projects: the publication, completed on 10 September 1471, was an *editio princeps*. The volume was printed in imperial folio and with a type used solely in the years 1470–72.⁹ It has a total of 406 folios. The page on the trial sheet is from book nine (*Jncipit nonus libri moralium*) and corresponds to folio l[7]ʳ (= fol. 109ʳ) of the printed edition.¹⁰

At first glance, the trial sheet and the corresponding page of the printed edition appear to be identical [fig. 1]. The page layout is the same, and each column begins with the same words, as do almost all lines within the columns. But changes are present in passages where corrections were made, involving mostly small modifications to compensate for added text or deletions. It is probably fair to say that the trial sheet provides us with an example of routine pre-press work in the printing house. This is borne out by the moderate number of correction markings noted there.

---

3 GASKELL (see note 1), pp. 114/5 and 351–7.

4 Cf. RANDALL HERZ: Sensenschmidt, Johann. In: LGB², vol. 7 p. 59. – RANDALL HERZ: Sensenschmidt, Johann. In: NDB, vol. 24 pp. 264/5. – Geldner, p. 161. – *Nürnberger Künstlerlexikon*. Ed. MANFRED H. GRIEB et alia. Vol. 3. Munich 2007, p. 1430.

5 Cf. OTTO VON HASE: *Die Koberger. Eine Darstellung des buchhändlerischen Geschäftsbetriebes in der Zeit des Übergangs vom Mittelalter zur Neuzeit*. 2ⁿᵈ ed. Leipzig 1885. – SEVERIN CORSTEN: Koberger, Anton. In: LGB², vol. 4 p. 256. – HANS-OTTO KEUNECKE: Anton Koberger (ca. 1440–1513). In: *Fränkische Lebensbilder. Neue Folge der Lebensläufe aus Franken*. Ed. ALFRED WENDEHORST and GERHARD PFEIFFER. Neustadt a. d. Aisch 1982 (*Veröffentlichungen der Gesellschaft für fränkische Geschichte*. 10), pp. 38–56. RANDALL HERZ: Buchmalerei in der Offizin Anton Kobergers. In: Dürer und die Mathematik. Neues aus der Dürerforschung. Buchmalerei der Dürerzeit. Nuremberg 2010 (*Dürerforschungen*. 2), pp. 39–64.

6 Cf. Geldner, pp. 176–80. – Cf. also WALTER BAUMANN: Die Druckerei Stuchs in Nürnberg (1484–1537). In: GJ 1954, pp. 122–32. – *Nürnberger Künstlerlexikon* (see note 4), vol. 3, pp. 1516/7.

7 Taken from shelfmark Inc. 193, now shelfmark Inc. 1940 (formerly in the collection Graphik UB, Restbestand Einblattdrucke, shelfmark II.12).

8 Cf. MARIANNE ROZSONDAI: Drei Kobergersche Makulaturblätter. In: GJ 1977, pp. 345–7.

9 Cf. BMC II, Plate 38, 114.

10 GREGORIUS I, PONT. MAX: *Moralia, sive exposition in Job*. Nuremberg: [Johann Sensenschmidt], 10./11. 9. 1471. 2º. [ISTC ig000427000. GW 11429. Hain *7928]; the proof sheet is not among GW's location copies. Copy consulted: Erlangen, UB, Inc. 1350; the page contains chapters 94–8.

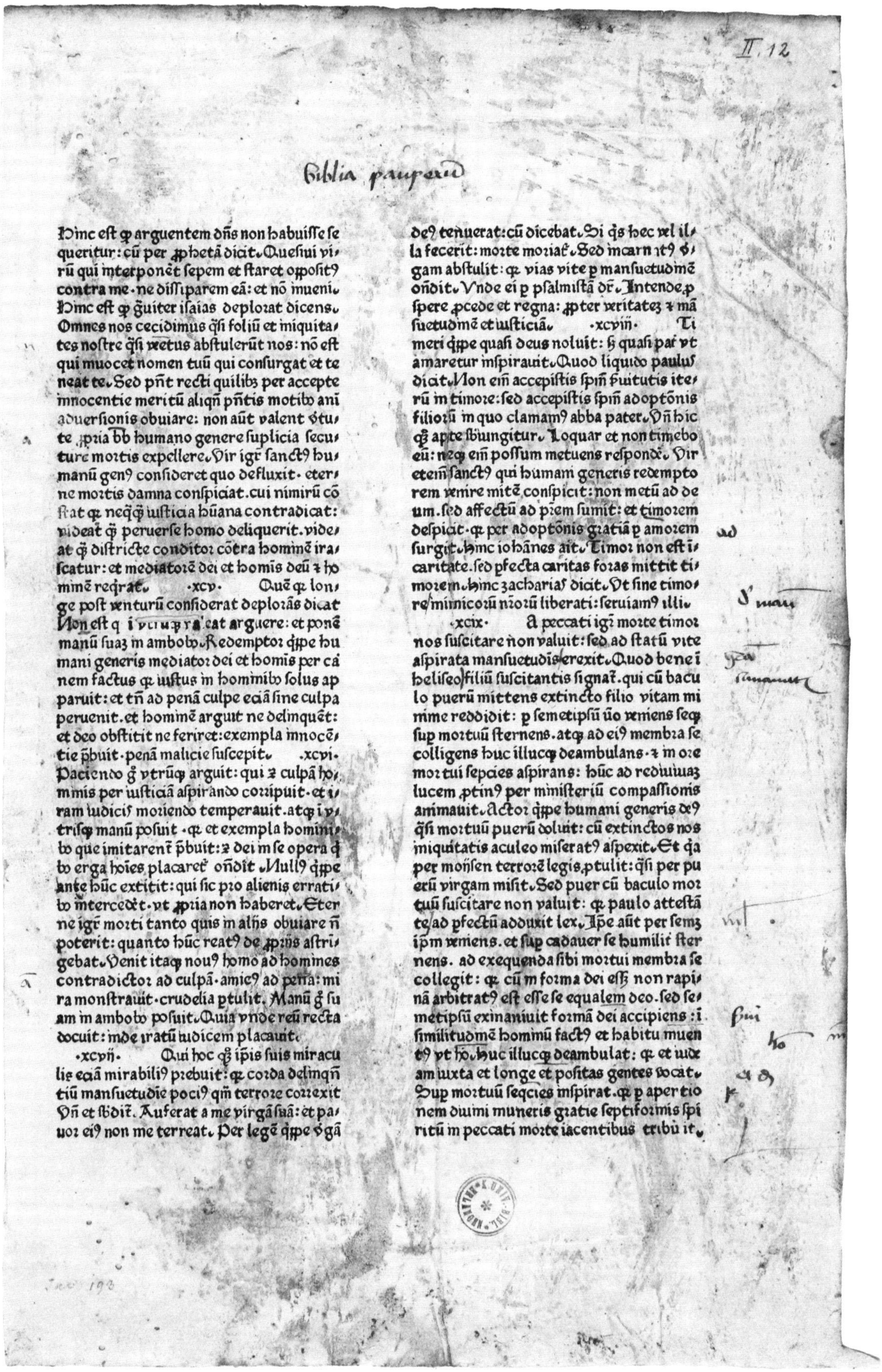

[Figs. 1a and 1b] Proof sheet with corrector's markings and corresponding page in final printed edition.
GREGORIUS MAGNUS: *Moralia*, fol. l[7]r = fol. 109r. Erlangen UB, Inc. 1940 [1a] and Inc. 1350 [1b]

Hinc est ϙ arguentem dñs non habuisse se
queritur: cū per ꝓphetā dicit. Quesiui virū qui interponēt sepem et staret oppositꝰ
contra me. ne dissiparem eā: et nō mueni.
Hinc est ϙ ꝫuiter isaias deplorat dicens.
Omnes nos cecidimus ꝗsi foliū et iniquita-
tes nostre ꝗsi ventus abstulerūt nos: nō est
qui inuocet nomen tuū qui consurgat et te-
neat te. Sed pñt recti quilibꝫ per accepte
innocentie meritū aliꝗ pñtis motibꝰ ani-
aduersionis obuiare: non aūt valent ꝫtus-
te ꝓpria ab humano genere suplicia secu-
ture mortis expellere. Vir igr̄ sanctꝰ humani genꝰ consideret quo defluxit. eter-
ne mortis damna conspiciat. cui nimirū cō-
stat ꝙ neꝗ iustitia hūana contradicat.
videat ꝙ peruerse homo deliquerit. videat ꝙ districte conditor cōtra hominem ira-
scatur: et mediatorē dei et hominis deū ⁊ hominē reꝗrat. ꝙ xcv. ꝙ Que ꝗ lon-
ge post venturū considerat deplorās dicat
Non est qui vtrūꝗ valeat arguere: et ponē
manū suaꝫ in ambobꝰ. Redemptor ꝙꝑe humani generis mediator dei et hominis per cā-
nem factus ꝙ iustus in hominibꝰ solus apparuit: et tñ ad penā culpe etiā sine culpa
peruenit. et hominē arguit ne delinquēt:
et deo obstitit ne feriret: exempla innocē-
tie ꝓbuit·penā malicie suscepit. ꝙ xcvi.
Paciendo g̃ vtrūꝗ arguit: qui ⁊ culpā hominis per iusticiā aspirando corripuit. et i-
ram iudicis moriendo temperauit. atꝗ ꝑ v-
trūꝗ manū posuit · ꝙ et exempla homini-
bꝫ que imitarenᵗ ꝓbuit: ⁊ dei in se opera ꝗ-
bꝫ erga hoies placaretᵿ oñdit. Mullꝰ ꝙꝑe
ante hūc extitit: qui sic pro alienis errati-
bꝫ intercedet: vt ꝓpria non haberet. Eter-
ne igr̄ morti tanto quis in alijs obuiare ñ
poterit: quanto hūc reatꝰ de ꝓpꝝs astri-
gebat. Venit itaꝙ nouꝰ homo ad homines
contradictor: ad culpā. amicꝰ ad penā: mi-
ra monstrauit. crudelia ptulit. Manū g̃ suam in ambobꝰ posuit. Quia vnde reū recta
docuit: inde iratū iudicem placauit.
ꝙ xcvii. ꝙ Qui hoc ꝙ ipis suis miracu-
lis etiā mirabiliꝰ ꝓbuit: ꝙ corda delinꝗn-
tiū mansuetudie pociꝰ ꝗm terrore conexit
Vñ et stdit. Auferat a me virgā suā: et pa-
uor eiꝰ non me terreat. Per legē ꝗꝑe vgā

deꝰ tenuerat: cū dicebat. Si ꝗs hec vel illa fecerit: morte moriaᵗ. Sed incarnatꝰ ꝓ-
gam abstulit: ꝙ vias vite p mansuetudinē
oñdit. Vnde ei p psalmistā dr̄. Intende ꝓ-
spere ꝓcede et regna: ꝓpter veritatē ⁊ mā-
suetudinē et iusticiā. ꝙ xcviii. ꝙ Ti-
meri ꝗꝑe quasi deus noluit: sꝫ quasi paᵗ vt
amaretur inspirauit. Quod liquido paulus
dicit. Non eñ accepistis spm̄ ꝼututis ite-
rū in timore: sed accepistis spm̄ adopt̃onis
filiorū in quo clamamꝰ abba pater. Vñ hic
ꝙ apte sꝫ iungitur. Loquar et non timebo
eū: neꝗ eñ possum metuens responde. Vir
eteñ sanctꝰ qui humani generis redempto-
rem venire mitē conspicit: non metū ad deum. sed affectū ad pietm sumit: et timorem
despicit. ꝙ per adoptōis gratia ad amorem
surgit. hinc iohānes ait. Timor non est i
caritate. sed perfecta caritas foras mittit timorem. hinc zacharias dicit. Vt sine timore d maū inimicorū nr̄ōꝝ liberati: ꝼuiamꝰ illi
ꝙ xcix. ꝙ A peccati igr̄ morte timor
nos suscitare non valuit: sed ad statū vite
aspirata mansuetudis gra erexit. Q̃d bn̄ in he-
liseo sunaitis filiū sulcitātis signaᵗ. ꝗ cū baculo puerū mittēs extincto filio vitam mi-
nime reddidit: p semetipsū ūo veniens seꝗ
sup mortuū sternens. atꝗ ad eiꝰ membra se
colligens huc illucꝗ deambulans · ⁊ in ore
mortui sepcies aspirans: hūc ad reuiuiuaꝫ
lucem ꝓtinꝰ per ministeriū compassionis
animauit. Auctor ꝙꝑe humani genēis deꝰ
ꝗsi mortuū puerū doluit: cū extinctos nos
iniquitatis aculeo miserꝰ aspexit. Et qa
per moysen terrorē legis. ptulit: ꝗsi per puerū virgam misit. Sed puer cū baculo mortuū suscitare ñ valuit. ꝙ paulo attestāte
nihil ad perfctū adduxit lex. Ipse aūt p semꝫ
ipm̄ veniens. et sup cadauer se humiliᵗ sternens. ad exequenda sibi mortui membra se
collegit: ꝙ cū in forma dei essᵗ non rapi-
nā arbitratꝰ est esse se equalem deo. sed semetipsū exinaniuit formā serui accipiens ⁊ i
similitudinē hominū factꝰ et habitu inuen-
tꝰ vt hō. huc illucꝗ deambulat: ꝙ et iude-
am iuxta et longe positas gentes vocat.
Sup mortuū sepcies inspirat. ꝙ p apertio-
nem diuini muneris gratie septiformis spiritū in peccati morte iacentibus tribuiᵗ.

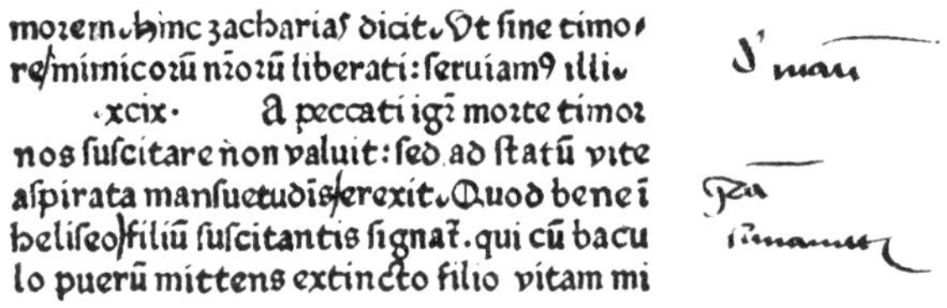

[Figs. 2a and 2b] Handwritten corrections in Sensenschmidt's edition of GREGORIUS MAGNUS: *Moralia*, fol. L [7]ʳ = fol. 72ʳ. Erlangen UB, Inc. 1940 [2a] and Inc. 1350 [2b]

[Figs. 3a and 3b] Handwritten corrections in Sensenschmidt's edition of GREGORIUS MAGNUS: *Moralia*, fol. L [7]ʳ = fol. 72ʳ. Erlangen UB, Inc. 1940 [3a] and Inc. 1350 [3b]

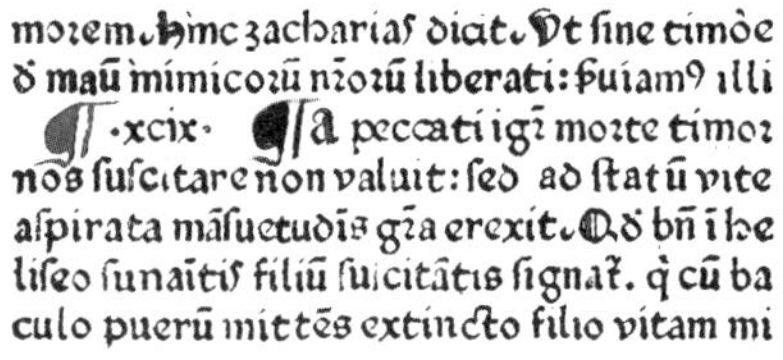

[Figs. 4a and 4b] Deletion symbol and same passage in printed edition. GREGORIUS MAGNUS: *Moralia*, fol. L [7]ʳ = fol. 72ʳ. Erlangen UB, Inc. 1940 [4a] and Inc. 1350 [4b]

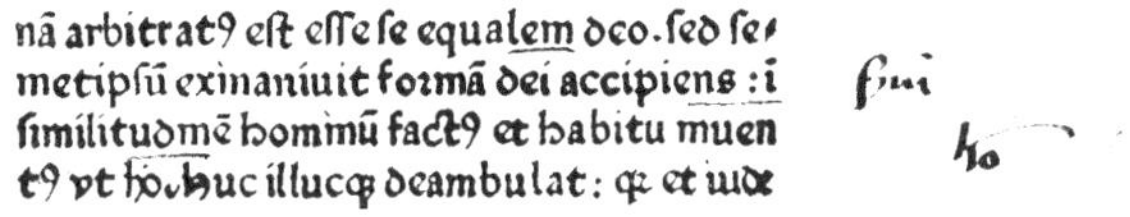

The corrections were made in a neat late 15th century *bastarda* in the margins of the sheet. Centered at the top of the page the same hand wrote the heading *Biblia pauperu(m)*. As there are no headings or running titles in the printed edition, the heading must have served as a finding aid for the house corrector, or castigator, as he was called in the 15th century, to find the passage in the model (printer's copy) quickly and check for accuracy and fidelity in the trial sheet.

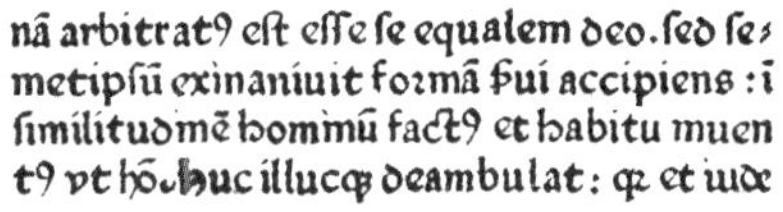

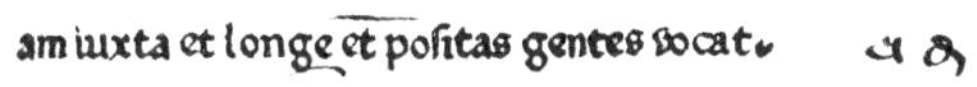

Similar to modern editorial practice, the corrections were noted in the outside margins adjacent to the line to which they referred. An insertion marking was also put at the corresponding spot in the text. The corrector made use of two different markings to indicate different kinds of corrections. A vertical line drawn between two words, for instance, indicates where a word or phrase was to be inserted into a line of text [fig. 2]. On the other hand, if any part of a word or phrase needed to be altered or replaced, or if a missing letter was to be added, the corrector made a horizontal line above the text in question [fig. 3]. The markings seem idiosyncratic to the corrector (especially the latter which is not very precise), but for both him and the compositor, who also knew Latin, they were obviously clear, easy to understand and efficient in actual practice. Lines of continuity to the present are also apparent. An editorial marking well known today was already in common use at that time: the familiar symbol ∂ (*deleatur*) to delete words. An example appears adjacent to the fourth but last line of column b, where the corrector has noted *et* ∂[*eleatur*] in the outer margin [fig. 4]. It instructed the compositor to remove the spurious *et* appearing before *positas*.

Further examples of corrections are listed in table 1:

Col. a, l. 12–4	in margin: *a*	v'tu= | te ͺppria bb humano genere suplicia secu= | ture mortis
Col. b, l. 21/2	in margin: *d' maū*	Vt sine timo= | re / (= insertion mark) inimicorū nrorū libertati :
Col. b, l. 46	*et* ∂(*eleatur*)	| am iuxto et longe et positas gentes vocat. |

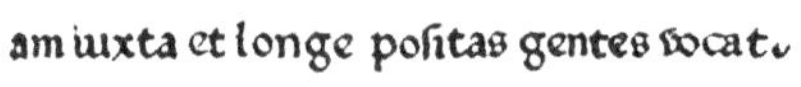

These have been changed to:

Col. a, l. 12–4	v'tuꝫ | te ꝓpria ab humano genere suplicia
	secuꝫ | ture mortis
Col. b, l. 21/2	Vt sine timo'e | d' maū inimicorū
	nostro rum libertati : [...]
Col. b, l. 46	| am iuxto et longe positas gentes vocat. |

All the other corrections have been carried out as indicated by the corrector. This is a tribute to the compositor who obviously performed his work with much care and diligence, traits by no means shared equally by all members of his trade. It also lends credence to claims of painstaking editorial revision typically made by Sensenschmidt in his colophons. For a full list of the corrections see appendix 1.

A trial sheet from Anton Koberger's press in Nuremberg (1486)
The second of the three proof sheets was used as a pastedown in shelfmark Inc. 805 (H *3994) of the Library of the Hungarian Academy of Sciences in Budapest. Attention was first drawn to the sheet in a publication by Marianne Rozsondai (Head of Manuscripts and Rare Books, L of the HAS) entitled *Über die »Koberger Einbände«* (1974).[11] It was one of several proof sheets from Koberger's press found by Rozsondai in editions by that printer, thus lending support to her thesis that the characteristic late fifteenth century Nuremberg binding (*Buchführereinband*) had originated in Koberger's printing house and was in part produced there. A picture of the sheet showing the corrections is included in the article, although they are not treated there.

The sheet is from Koberger's 1486 edition of the *Summa Theologica* of Antoninus Florentinus (GW 2189. H*1246).[12] The Dominican friar Antoninus (1389–1459; canonization in 1526) was a model reformer who became Archbishop of Florence in 1446. His *Summa*, written in the last years of his life, marked a new and significant development in moral theology, and was soon made available to a wide audience after his death. The *editio princeps* (1477–79), published by Anton Koberger,[13] a parallel publication by the Venice printer Nicolaus Jenson (1477–80), and seven other full editions of this work by 1500 are witness to the widespread interest in the *Summa*.[14] The advertisement published c. 1480 by Koberger for his own edition (BMC II 417/8) was likely the response to competition posed by Jenson's publication.[15]

The sheet was found in an exemplar of Koberger's 1485 edition of Bromyard's *Summa praedicantium* (GW M 13116. H*3994 = Inc. 805, L of the HAS),[16] in which it served as the front pastedown. Another sheet from the same edition served as pastedown in the lower cover. The sheets correspond to fol. K2ʳ (fol. 196ʳ) and fol. 16ᵛ (fol. 194ᵛ) respectively, representing non-consecutive pages from *pars secunda* of the *Summa* (completed 28 August 1486).

The proof sheet contains a number of correction markings in the gutter and outside margin of the page [fig. 5]. Unlike the Sensenschmidt sheet, Koberger's expurgator clearly indicated the line of text in which

11 Cf. MARIANNE ROZSONDAI: Über die »Koberger Einbände«. In: GJ 1974, pp. 311–23, here p. 316 nº 12. I would like to express my gratitude to Dr. Rozsondai for proofreading my manuscript and for kindly granting permission to publish images of the proof sheets.
12 ANTONINUS FLORENTINUS: *Summa theologica*, partes I–IV. Nuremberg: Anton Koberger, 1486–87. 2º [ISTC ia00875000. GW 2189. H *1249. Sajó / Soltész 253].
13 ANTONINUS FLORENTINUS: *Summa theologica*, partes I–IV. Nuremberg: Anton Koberger, 1477–79. 2º [ISTC ia00871000. GW 2186. HC *1242].
14 ANTONINUS FLORENTINUS: *Summa theologica*, partes I–IV. With additions of Franciscus Moneliensis. Venice: Nicolaus Jenson, 1477–80. 2º [ISTC ia00873000. GW 2185. HC *1243. H 1259 (IV)]. Bibliographers often falsely date Jenson's edition before Koberger's, although only one volume of his edition (*pars* III) ever appeared before Koberger completed printing of his complete edition.
15 Cf. BL, shelfmark IC. 7195 [ISTC ik00028500. GW M16361. VE 15 K-18. BMC II, 417/8 BSB-Ink K-36]. Cf. also KONRAD BURGER: *Buchhändleranzeigen des 15. Jahrhunderts*. Leipzig 1907, nº 22 and fig. 22.
16 JOHANNES DE BROMYARD: *Summa praedicantium*. Nuremberg: Anton Koberger, 29.6.1485. 2º [ISTC ij00261000. GW M13116. H *3994. Sajó / Soltész 1884].

Capitulum .VII.

riam vtrū sciens petm̄ primi et referēs illm̄ statim
plato suo an̄ facta admonitiōem secretā peccet mor
taliter. Elidet q̄ sic. q̄ cōtra ordinē datu9 a x̄po de
fraterna correctiōe agit. Rn̄.fm Tho. in quolibet.
In his distinguedū e de coditione subditi et plati.
Nā si ego scio q̄ frater p me corrigētī tunc nō debeo
denūciare plato. Si aūt hoc melius fiat per platuz
7 platus nihilomin9 sit pius et discretus et spualis
non habēs odiuz vel racolē ad illū subditū tūc pōt
denūciare sibi: nec tunc dicit ecclesie. q̄ non dicit ei
vt platus ecclesie sed vt puate persone, pficiētī ad cor
rectiōem primi et emēdatiōem. Sz ,ppter cōditiōes
diūersas platoz̄ et subditorū nō pōt in hoc dari iudi
ciū generale. vel q̄ plat9 mouet odio ad subditū. vl̄
q̄ subdit9 nō recipet bene vba plati. et io in omnib9
bis hoc ē tenendū p regula q̄ in his scruāda ē chari
tas. z qō meius et pōtecī9 videt̄. et si hoc intēdat.ſ.
emendatiōe fratris: vel cautelā in futurū z seruet
c̄tus pōt bonū charitatis non peccat denūciando
Si aūt denūciat vel plato vel amico suo vel cuicū
q̄ ex malicia vt cōfundatur z repximat: peccat mor
taliter. si autez ex incautela hoc alicui dicit. ita tn̄ q̄
in deno aliud vel infamia vel vituperiū eueniat de
linquētī non est mortale lz incaute agat. hec Tho.
Dicit etiā Ricar. in q̄to dis.xix. q̄ ,ppter fratris cor
rectione facta p admonitōem secretā nō tenetor reli
stere a secreta denūciatione prelato fienda. quia
valet ad p̄cauenduz fratri a recidiuo: nec ē in p̄iudi
ciū fame fratris si talis ē platus qualis esse debz.
Si tn̄ p signa valde ,pbabilia crederet q̄ ex illa denū
ciatione fratrē correctum infamare vell3. tunc crimē
fratris veraciter correctī sibi denūciari nō debet.
hec Ricar. Sed si ille nec illū infamaret sed d in
quens ita videtur emēdatus q̄ nulli dubiū est de re
cidiuo nō videtur q̄ debeat dicere erq̄ nil fructus
sequitur immo male faceret denūciādo eti9 p̄ela
ro fm Ũmbertū. Notādū etiā fm Ricar. in q̄to.
Q̄ in peccatis denūciandis cōsiderandū vtrū pec
catū sit oīno occultū aut ad noticiā alioz̄ puenerit
aut in prōptu sit vt ueniat. Si aūt peccatū iam
ad alioz̄ noticiā ruenit tūc debz denūciare ei qui
habz p̄atem corrigendi. vt q̄ sunt scādalisatī z cul
pa edificēnt de pena. si aūt nōdum in publicū uene
nit: sed est in via denuēdi tunc ē denūciādū de
scādalo futuro occurrat. Si aūt sit oīno occultū
tunc cōsiderādū est vtrū emendatio peccati expec
tari probabiliter pōt aut nō. qō quide refacili de
uerti pōt si cōsideret vtz aliq9 ex leui de vel passio
ne peccauerīt siue ex malicia vel infirmitate. qō idē
est dicere. Quod q̄dē q̄pendi pōt ex ꝑditione pecca
tis et z iteratione actus. quia si aliquis freq̄nt er
sine freno in aliq̄ peccm̄ lapsus est. signū ē q̄ ex mali
cia peccat et nō facile emēdet. Si aūt semel occasi
one peccati oblata in peccatū ruit. et postea tristi
ciā z verecundiā ostendit de peccato. signū ē q̄ pec
catū sit ex passione z q̄ de facili emēdetur. Si ergo
emendatio speretur: debet p̄cedere admonitio z di
ferri denūciatio quousq̄ videat admonitiōis effe
ctus. p̄cipue si in emēdatiōem obm̄tit. Si aūt est infe
ctiuū aliorum q̄ non emendet nisi immineret occa
sio similis in peccatū ruendi quā declinare nō vell3
admonitus. tunc nn̄ debz p̄lato denūciari ne in p̄
cipitium ruat. Si autē nō speret emēdatio. tunc cō
siderādum ē an illud petm̄ sit alioz̄ infectiuū. sicut
heresis. fornicatio et hm̄oi aut cedat in damnuz ali
quod alteri9. sicut furtuz. homicidiū. et hm̄oi. Si
autē peccatū non est infectiuū alioz̄ vel damnifi
ciuū. potest denūciatio differri quousq̄ videat̄ an
admonitiōis effectus, p̄cipue si in emēdatione p̄mit
tit. si aūt est infectiuū alioz̄ debet denūciari pla

ro vt gregi suo caueat. Semp em̄ bonum multor̄ de
bet p̄poni bono vnius vnde z fama vnius negligi de
bet vt innocētia vel fama multitudinis cōseruetur
Si aūt vergat in damnū corpale alterius debz fieri
compario damni illius tempalis ad damnuz fame
istius z illi damno qō p̄ponderat magis obuiandū
Dicit etiā Ricar. q̄ nisi certitissimis signis appare
at incorrigibilitas vel exasperatio .i. turbatio futu
ra corrigendi. nō debet fraterna correctio p̄ermitti
Et si cum q̄s corrigit turbari videt̄ aliq̄tulus po
stea in se reuersus se corrigit. Sz q̄d si quis sciat pec
catum aliquod alterius vl̄ impedimētuz matrimo
nij. aut irregularitate. aut aliq̄ hm̄oi: q̄ ille igno
rat. puta sit aliq̄ nō rite ordinatuz vl̄ nō baptiza
tum. et videt eum ministrare in sacris vel scit illū ex
cōmunicatū. aut scit aliquē vxorez habere quam
de iure non potest propter impedimētuz ꝯsanguini
tati vl̄ affinitatis et hm̄oi. aut etiā retinē rē alienā z
hm̄oi. Quid in hm̄oi. casib9 fieri nūq̄d illum
ignorantes auisare debz z admonere de defectu suo.
Rn̄. fm Guil. Si comode pōt euz admonere de tali
defectu et credit psonā illā ,pua sibile esse et corrigi
bile inde. debet manifestare sibi alias peccaret quia si
laborat habens talē defectū ignorātia crassa et supi
na nō excusatur. Si ignorantia probabili adhuc de
bet ei dicere. nazeris inde nō peccat exculsatus igno
rantia facti. tn̄ inde sequit̄ periculū vel damnū alie
nuz z iniuria sacramentoz̄. Sz si sit psona impsua
sibilis euin corrigibilis et tunc ē de scandalo. ius suf
ficit si dicat plato nō ex cusando nec denūciando. S̄
simpliciter significando. Et si ē tale qō vbi sit picu
lum alioz̄ vl̄ damnum et potest probare in iudicio
tenetur si credit iudicē exhibiturus iusticiā. secus
vbi nō est picu lum vel damnum aliorum. vel si est ,p
bare nō potest ar. q̄. q. vij. pleriq̄. vl̄ etiam si ,proba
ret nō fieret iustitia nec adhiberetur remedium ar.
ij. q. iij. Qn̄. Idem videtur de denūciatione fiēda
plato super crimine quando est ita malus vel negli
gens q̄ nihil ex hoc faciet ad p̄ouidendū. Inutilis
em̄ videt. et frustra.

¶Capitulum septimus de negligentia circa obser
uationem festoz̄ vbi agitur quomodo festa debeāt
celebrari.

Ertinet ad negligētiā

seu torpore3 circa p̄cepta omissio celebra
tionis festoz̄. ¶Terciuz em̄ preceptuz deca
logi est illud. Memēto vt diem sabbati sanctifices.
Expō. xx. quod preceptum litteraliter intellectum
fm Tho. schā. schē. q̄. cxij. articu. iij. est partis mo
rale et partim ceremoniale. Morale quidē q̄tū ad
hoc q̄ homo reputet aliquod tp̄s vite sue ad vacan
dū diuinis. Inest. n. homini naturalis iclinatio ad
hoc q̄ cuilib3 rei necessarie reputet aliq̄ tp̄s sicut
corpali refectioni. somno z alijs hm̄oi. vn̄ etiā z spi
rituali refectioni qua mēs hominis in deo reficitur
fm dictamē naturalis rōnis aliq̄ tp̄s reputatū ad
vacādū diuinis cadit sub p̄cepto morali. Sz inq̄tū
ī hoc p̄cepto determinatur speciale tp̄s in signuz
creationis mundi sic ē p̄ceptum ceremoniale. Simi
liter ceremoniale ē fm allegoricā significatiōes, put
fuit figura future quietis x̄pi in die sabbati in sepul
chro. Et similiter fm morale significatiōem, put si
gnificat cessatione ab oīi actu peccati. z q̄tem me
nig in deo z fm hoc ē q̄dāmo w generale p̄ceptus
Similiter etiā3 ceremoniale ē fm significationem
anagogicā, put .s. figurat futurā q̄ete3 fruitionis in
deo q̄ ē in patria. Preceptuz g̃ de sanctificatione

[Figs. 5a and 5b] Proof sheet with corrector's markings and corresponding page in final printed edition. ANTONINUS FLORENTINUS: *Summa, pars 2*, fol. [k2]r = fol. 196r. Budapest, HAS, ad Inc. 805 [5a] and Erlangen UB, Inc. 1329

Capitulum .VII.

riam vtrū sciens pctm̄ primi et referēs illud statim plato suo aū factā admonitiōem secretā peccet mortaliter. Tidetŕ q̇ sic.q̇ cōtra ordinē datuȝ a ȝp̄o de fraterna correctiōe agit. Rn̄.fm̄ Tho.in quolibet. In his distinguēdū ē de cōditione subditi et plati. Nā si ego scio q̇ frater p̄ me corrigetŕ tunc nō debeo renūciare plato. Si aūt hoc melius fiat per platuȝ ⁊ platus nihil omin⁹ sit pius et discretus et spūalis nō habes odiuȝ vel rācorē ad illū subditū tūc pōt renunciare sibi:nec tunc dicit ecclesie.qȝ nō dicit ei vŕ plato ecclesie sed vt puate persone officiēti ad correctionē.primi et emēdatiōem. Sȝ ppter cōditiōes diuersas platoȝ et subditoȝ nō pōt in hoc dari iudiciū generale .vel qȝ plat⁹ mouet odio ad subditū.vŕ q̇ subdit⁹ nō recipet bene v̄ba plati.et iō in omnibus hoc ē tenendū p̄ regula q̇ in his seruāda ē charitas. ⁊ qd̄ melius ex p̄dictis videŕ.et si hoc intēdat.s. emendationē fratris: vel cautelā in futurū ⁊ seruet ǭtuȝ pōt bonū charitatis non peccat renunciando. Si aūt renunciat vel plato vel amico suo vel cuicūq̇ ex malicia vt cōfundatur ⁊ repriāt:peccat mortaliter.si autȝ ex incautela hoc alicui dicit.ita tn̄ q̇ inde nō aliud vel infamia vel vituperiū eueniat delinquēti non est mortale lȝ incaute agat. hec Tho. Dicit etiā Ricar.in q̇to dis.xix.q̇ ppter fratris correctionē factā p̄ admonitionē secretā nō tenoȝ desistere a secreta renunciatione p̄elato fienda. quia valet ad p̄cauendum fratri a recidiuo:nec ē in p̄iudicium fame fratris si talis ē platus qualis esse debȝ. Si tn̄ p̄ signa valde pbabilia crederet q̇ ex illa renūciatione fratrē correctum infamare vellȝ tunc crimē fratris veraciter correcti sibi renunciari nō debet. hec Ricar. Sed si ille nec illum infamaret sed relinquens ita videretur emēdatus q̇ nulli dubiū est de recidiuo nō videtur q̇ debeat dicere ex quo nil fructus sequitur immo male faceret renunciado letiā p̄elato fm̄ Umbertū. Notādū etiā fm̄ Ricar. in q̇to. Q̇ in peccatis renunciandis cōsiderandū vtrū peccatū sit oino occultū aut ad noticiā alioȝ deuenerit aut in promptu sit vt deueniat. Si aūt peccatū iam ad alioȝ noticiā deuenit tūc debȝ renunciare ei qui habȝ p̄atem corrigendi.vt q̄ sunt scādalizati de culpa edificent de pena.si aūt nōdum in publicū deuenit:sed est in via deueniēdi tunc ē renunciādum vt scādalo futuro occurraŕ .Si aūt sit oino occultū tunc cōsiderādū est vtrū emendatio peccati expectari probabiliter pōt aut nō. qd̄ quidē de facili aduerti pōt si cōsideret vtrȝ aliq̄s ex elatiōe vel passiōe peccauerit siue ex malicia vel infirmitate qd̄ idē est dicere. Quod qd̄e p̄pendi pōt ex p̄ditione peccatis et ex iteratione actus.quia si aliquis freq̄nter et sine freno in aliq̄ pctm̄ lapsus est.signū ē q̇ ex malicia peccat et nō facile emendeŕ .si autē semel occasione peccati oblata in peccatū ruit.et postea tristiciam ⁊ verecundiā ostendit de peccato.signū ē q̇ peccatū sit ex passione ⁊ q̇ de facili emēdetur. Si ergo emendatio speretur: debet p̄cedere admonitio ⁊ differri renunciatio quousq̇ videat admonitiōis effectus.p̄cipue si emēdatiōem p̄mittit. Si aūt est infectiuū alioȝ q̇ non emendet nisi immineret occasio similis in peccatū ruendi quā declinare nō vellȝ admonitus.tunc em̄ debȝ plato renunciari ne in p̄cipitium ruat. Si autē nō speret emēdatio. tunc cōsiderādum ē an illud pctm̄ sit alioȝ infectiuū.sicut heresis.fornicatio et hm̄oi aut cedat in damnuȝ aliquod alteri⁹.sicut furtuȝ. homicidiuȝ. et hm̄oi. Si autē peccatū non est infectiuū alioȝ vel damnificatiuuȝ.potest renunciatio differri quousq̇ videatur admonitiōis effectus.p̄cipue si emendationē p̄mittit.si aūt est infectiuuȝ alioȝ debet renunciari pla

to vt gregi suo caueat. Semp em̄ bonum multoȝ de bet p̄poni bono vnius vnde ⁊ fama vnius negligi debet vt innocētia vel fama multitudinis cōseruetur Si aūt vergat in damnū corpale alterius tebȝ fieri compatio damni illius temporalis ad damnuȝ fame istius ⁊ illi damno qd̄ p̄ponderat magis obuiādū Dicit etiā Ricar.q̇ nisi certissimis signis appareat incorrigibilitas vel exasperatio.i. turbatio futura corrigendi.nō debet fraterna correctio p̄termitti Et si cum q̄s corrigit turbari videŕ aliquātuluȝ postea in se reuersus se corrigit. Sȝ qd̄ si quis sciat peccatum aliquod alterius.vŕ impedimētuȝ matrimonū.aut irregularitatē.aut aliqd̄ hm̄oi:qd̄ ille ignorat.puta scit aliquē nō rite ordinatuȝ vŕ nō baptizatum.et videt eum ministrare in sacris vel scit illū excōmunicatuȝ. aut scit aliquē vxorē habere quam de iure non potest propter impedimētuȝ consanguinitatis vŕ affinitatē. et hm̄oi. aut etiā retinē rē alienā ⁊ hm̄oi. Quid in hm̄oi.casibȝ fieri debȝ.nunqd̄ illum ignorantez auisare debȝ ⁊ admonere de defectu suo. Rn̄.fm̄ Guil. Si comode pōt eum admonere de tali defectu et credit p̄sona illā p̄suasibilē esse et corrigibilē inde. debet manifestare sibi aƚ𝑠 peccaret quia si laborat habens talē defectū ignorātia crassa et supina nō excusatur. Si ignorātia probabili adhuc debet ei dicere. naȝetin inde nō peccat excusatus ignorantia facti.tn̄ inde sequiŕ periculū vel damnū alienum ⁊ iniuria sacramentoȝ. Sȝ si sit p̄sona impsuasibilis et incorrigibilis et tunc est de scandalo eius sufficit si dicat plato nō accusando nec renunciando.ꝼ simpliciter significando. Et si ē tale qd̄ vbi sit piculum alioȝ vŕ damnum et potest probare in iuditio tenetur si credit iudice exhibiturū iusticiam .secus vbi nō est piculum vel damnum alioȝ.vel si est p̄bare nō potest.ar.ij.q. vij.pleriq̇. vŕ etiam si probaret nō fieret iusticia nec adhiberetur remedium ar. xi.q.iij. Qñ. Jdem videtur de renunciatione fiēda plato super crimine quando est ita malus vel negligens q̇ nihil ex hoc faciet ad p̄uidendū. Jnutilis em̄ videŕ et frustra.

Capitulum septimuȝ de negligentia circa obseruationem festoȝ vbi agitur quomodo festa debeāt celebrari.

Ertinet ad negligētiā seu torporez circa p̄cepta omissio celebrationis festoȝ. Tercius em̄ p̄ceptuȝ decalogi est illud. Memēto vt diem sabbati sanctifices. Exod.xx.quod p̄ceptum litteraliter intellectum fm̄ Tho.scd̄a scd̄e.q.cxxij.articu.iij.est partiȝ morale et partim ceremoniale. Morale quidē q̇tuȝ ad hoc q̇ homo reputet aliquod tps vite sue ad vacandū diuinis. Jn est.n.homini naturalis iclinatio ad hoc q̇ cuilibȝ rei necessarie reputeŕ aliq̇d tps sicut corpali refectioni.somno ⁊ aliȝs hm̄oi. vn̄ etiā ⁊ spirituali refectioni qua mēs hominis in deo reficitur fm̄ dictamē naturalis rōnis aliq̇d tps reputatū ad vacādū diuinis cadit sub p̄cepto morali. Sȝ inq̇tu̇ in hoc p̄cepto determinatur speciale tps in signuȝ creationis mundi sic ē p̄ceptum ceremoniale. Similiter ceremoniale ē fm̄ allegorizā significatiōes put fuit figura future quietis χp̄i in die sabbati in sepulchro. Et similiter fm̄ moralē significatiōem put significat cessationē ab om̄i actu peccati. ⁊ q̇etem mētis in deo ⁊ fm̄ hoc est qd̄āmō generale p̄cep tuȝ Similiter etiā ceremoniale ē fm̄ signification em anagogicā put.s.figurat futurā q̇etez fruitionis in deo:q̇ erit in patrįs. P̄ceptuȝ ḡ de sanctificatio ne

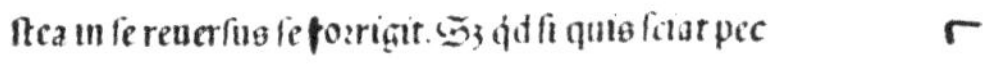

[Figs. 6a and 6b] Correction markings for changing letter t to c (*torrigit* to *corrigit*). ANTONINUS FLORENTINUS: *Summa*, pars 2, fol. [k2]ʳ = fol. 196ʳ. Budapest, HAS, ad Inc. 805 [6a] and Erlangen UB, Inc. 1329 [6b]

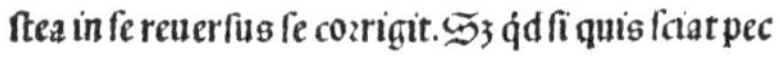

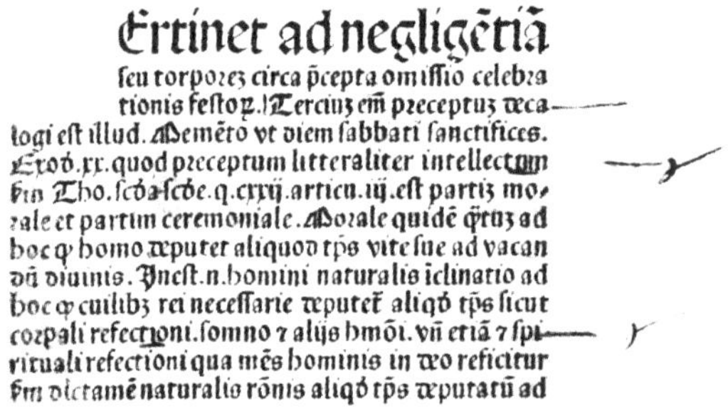

[Figs. 7a and 7b] Markings indicating turned letters and traces of lead spacing. ANTONINUS FLORENTINUS: *Summa*, pars 2, fol. [k2]ʳ = fol. 196ʳ. Budapest, HAS, ad Inc. 805 [7a] and Erlangen UB, Inc. 1329 [7b]

a correction was to be made. He drew a line c. 5–10 mm in length from the correction noted in the margin to the line of text affected. If it was a single letter which was to be changed, it was written in the margin, and at the corresponding spot in the text the letter was highlighted by a vertical mark. This is the case in col. a line 9, where the letter *r* is noted in the margin and a vertical line marks the corresponding letter in the text (emendated from *rācōne* to *rācōrē*). In col. b line 11, the expurgator noted that *torrigit* was to be corrected to *corrigit* [fig. 6].

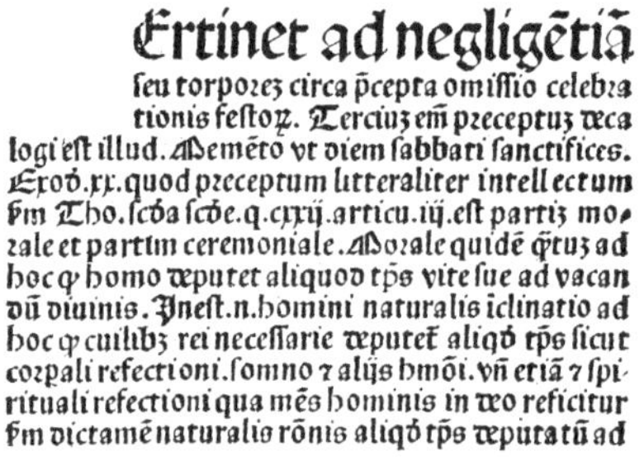

Turned letters were a persistent and common mistake made by compositors. No fewer than four instances of it occur on this page. The expurgator has marked each instance by a letter *j* with a high crossing loop and also highlighted it in the text by underlining the turned letter. A third type or class of correction was related to a special problem of the early hand press. Frequently the lead used for spacing purposes left unsightly traces of vertical lines between words. These occurrences are marked by a line in ink extending c. 10/16 mm from the line of print into the margin. Like the symbol *j*, it is another instance of the use of a set symbol to indicate a specific type of mistake [fig. 7]. As can be seen here, removing typographical blemishes was an integral part of this phase of "proofreading". All eleven corrections noted on the sheet were carried out in full.

A trial sheet from Georg Stuchs' press in Nuremberg (1496)

In 1496 a three-volume edition of the writings of William of Auvergne[17] was published by the Nuremberg printer Georg Stuchs (1484/88–1513).[18] William, a theologian, canon at the cathedral of Notre Dame in Paris and later bishop of the city from 1228–49, was the first scholastic philosopher to treat the writings of Aristotle and Platonic philosophers, which had become available in Latin translation at that time, and to attempt to reconcile them with Christian doctrine. Before the *Opera* was published, few of his works had appeared in print. His theological-philosophical opus *Magisterium divinale et sapientiale* had been largely ignored by printers; solely the tract *De fide et legibus* had been published from it in a unique Augsburg edition of 1475/6.[19] The Stuchs edition, edited by the Nuremberg humanist Peter Danhauser (d. after 1513), was the first effort to compile a near complete edition of his main work.

17 Also known under the variant Latin names Guillermus Alvernus or Guilielmus Parisiensis.

18 a) GUILLERMUS ALVERNUS, EPISCOPUS PARISIENSIS: *Opera*. Ed. PETRUS DANHAUSER. Contents: *De fide et legibus; Summa de virtutibus et vitiis; De immortalitate animae*. With table by JOHANN ROSENBACH [Nuremberg: Georg Stuchs, after 31. 3. 1496]. 2° [ISTC ig00708000. GW 11862. HC *8300]. b) GUILLERMUS ALVERNUS, EPISCOPUS PARISIENSIS: *De sacramentis*. Add: *Cur deus homo; De poenitentia*. [Nuremberg: Georg Stuchs, not after 1497]. 2° [ISTC ig00716500. GW 11869. HC *8316]. c) GUILLERMUS ALVERNUS, EPISCOPUS PARISIENSIS: *De universo*. [Nuremberg: Georg Stuchs, not after 1497]. 2° [ISTC ig00717000. GW 11870. HC *8319].

19 GUILLERMUS ALVERNUS, EPISCOPUS PARISIENSIS: *De fide et legibus*. [Augsburg: Günther Zainer, 1475/6]. 2° [ISTC ig00711O. GW 11863. H *8317].

A trial sheet of this edition has survived as binding waste in Inc. 1246. One half still serves as a pastedown inside the upper cover, while the other half of the sheet was lifted in 1909 and re-attached as a flyleaf [fig. 8]. The folios contain the pages of the outer sheet of quire h (volume 1, fol. 61ʳ): fol. h1ʳ (flyleaf) and [h6]ᵛ (pastedown). The text derives from the chapter *De legibus*. The manuscript that served as printer's copy for *pars una* has also been preserved (see below).[20]

The sheet shows numerous correction markings made in ink in the margins. Four of them concern a problem already encountered in the Koberger sheet – unsightly vertical black lines left by lead spacing between words [fig. 9]. They were removed and in the final printed edition they no longer appear. Other corrections concerned misspelled words and, on two occasions, a falsely placed letter in the margin.

One of these letters, a majuscule S, is found in the left-hand margin. A line drawn in silver point leads downward from the letter S to a spot two lines below, indicating that the letter had to be moved to that position [fig. 10]. An *j* is also noted in the margin within the curve of the line, indicating that the typesetting error *l* in *vlctoria* was to be corrected to *j* (i.e. *victoria*); a corresponding vertical line marks the spot in the text. Further below, the corrector has written the letter *u* in the margin, correcting the typesetting mistake *sertitute(m)* (i.e. *seruitutem*). Turning to the right-hand margin, we find a dash in combination with the symbol 9, designating the Latin abbreviation for *us*. The markings were to correct a mishap that had occurred during presswork. A black letter majuscule Q had come loose and fallen out of the composition during the pull, leaving two unsightly vertical black lines at the edges of the hole. In the edition, the Q was restored, but the compositor did not find it necessary to abbreviate the syllable *mus* as *m⁹* as noted [fig. 11]. Several other corrections were not carried out as well. These include the re-positioning of the majuscule U in the upper right-hand margin. Nor was the correction of the word *victoria* carried out as indicated, leaving the mistake *vlctoria* as it stood. Although the printer Georg Stuchs was never shy about praising the care with which his editions were prepared, the sheet shows us that despite best efforts to the contrary many typographical errors went uncorrected.

Brief mention should be made of the book's history. Its editor, Peter Danhauser, was presumably born in Nuremberg. After finishing his law studies in Ingolstadt and Tübingen, he returned to the city around 1489 and established contacts with its circle of humanists.[21] He was supported in many of his endeavors, financially and otherwise, by Sebald Schreyer (d. 1520), churchwarden of St. Sebald and the mentor and center of the Nuremberg humanist circle. Danhauser was a close friend of the humanist and *poeta laureatus* Conrad Celtis.[22]

Surviving poems bear witness to Danhauser's literary interests. Perhaps his most remarkable literary effort, however, lay in his activity as editor. From 1489 to 1496 he edited and published no less than seven books,[23] not to mention an illustrated work which had been commissioned by Sebald Schreyer, the *Archetypus triumphantis Romae*.[24] Its program of Roman mythology and history make it a quintessential humanist book.

20 StB Nuremberg, Cent. III, 65 (completed in 1435, with a register completed in 1440 by friar Johannes Rosenbach, OP); the manuscript served as printer's copy for pars 1 [ISTC ig00708000. GW 11862. HC *8300].

21 For a study of Peter Danhauser, his role in the circle of Nuremberg humanists, and editorial activity see ARNOLD REIMANN: *Die Älteren Pirckheimer. Geschichte eines Nürnberger Patriziergeschlechtes im Zeitalter des Frühhumanismus (bis 1501)*. Ed. HANS RUPPRICH. Leipzig 1944, pp. 160–96, esp. pp. 164/5 and 193/4.

22 Cf. HANS RUPPRICH: *Der Briefwechsel des Konrad Celtis*. Munich 1934 (*Humanistenbriefe*. 3). Danhauser's book projects are mentioned in several letters to and from Celtis: see letter 12 of 10. 9. 1491, pp. 23–5; in letter 114 of 10. 6. 1496 Schreyer reports on Danhauser's melancholy and work on William of Auvergne, p. 190; see also letter 132, of 17. 10. 1496, in which Schreyer writes about the *Archetypus triumphantis Romae*, pp. 215–7.

23 Cf. a) FIDELIS, CASSANDRA: *Oratio pro Bertucio Lamberto* (and other works). [Nuremberg: Peter Wagner, after 22. 11. 1489]. 4⁰ [ISTC if00164000. GW 9889. H *4553]. b) BARBARUS, HERMOLAUS: *Oratio ad Fridericum III Imperatorem et Maximilianum I Regem Romanorum*. Ed. PETRUS DANHAUSER. [Nuremberg: Peter Wagner, after 2. 4. 1490]. 4⁰ [ISTC ib00106000. GW 3346. H *2419]. c) *Repertorium auctoritatum Aristotelis et aliorum philosophorum*. Ed. PETRUS DANHAUSER. Nuremberg: Peter Wagner, [c. 1491/2]. 4⁰ [ISTC ib00294000. GW 3757. H 1926 = HC 2733]. d) ANSELMUS: *Opera*. Ed. PETRUS DANHAUSER. Nuremberg: Caspar Hochfeder, 27. 3. 1491. 2⁰ [ISTC ia00759000. GW 2032. HC *1134]. e) THOMAS ⟨A KEMPIS⟩: *Opera*. Nürnberg: Kaspar Hochfeder, 29. 11. 1494. 2⁰ [HC (+ Add.) 9769. Vekene, Hochfeder 17]. f) DIONYSIUS CARTHUSIENSIS: *Specula omnis status vitae humanae*. Ed: PETRUS DANHAUSER. Nuremberg: Peter Wagner, 28. 1. 1495. 4⁰ [ISTC id00248000. GW 8419. HC *6246 = H 6245]. g) GUILLERMUS ALVERNUS, EPISCOPUS PARISIENSIS: *Opera*. Ed: PETRUS DANHAUSER. [Nuremberg: Georg Stuchs, after 31. 3. 1496]. 2⁰ [ISTC ig00708000. GW 11862. HC *8300]. Cf. also REIMANN (see note 21), pp. 160–96.

24 Cf. RAINER SCHOCH: »Archetypus triumphantis Romae«. Zu einem gescheiterten Buchprojekt des Nürnberger Frühhmanismus. In: *50 Jahre Sammler und Mäzen*. Ed. UWE MÜLLER. Schweinfurt 2001, pp. 261–98.

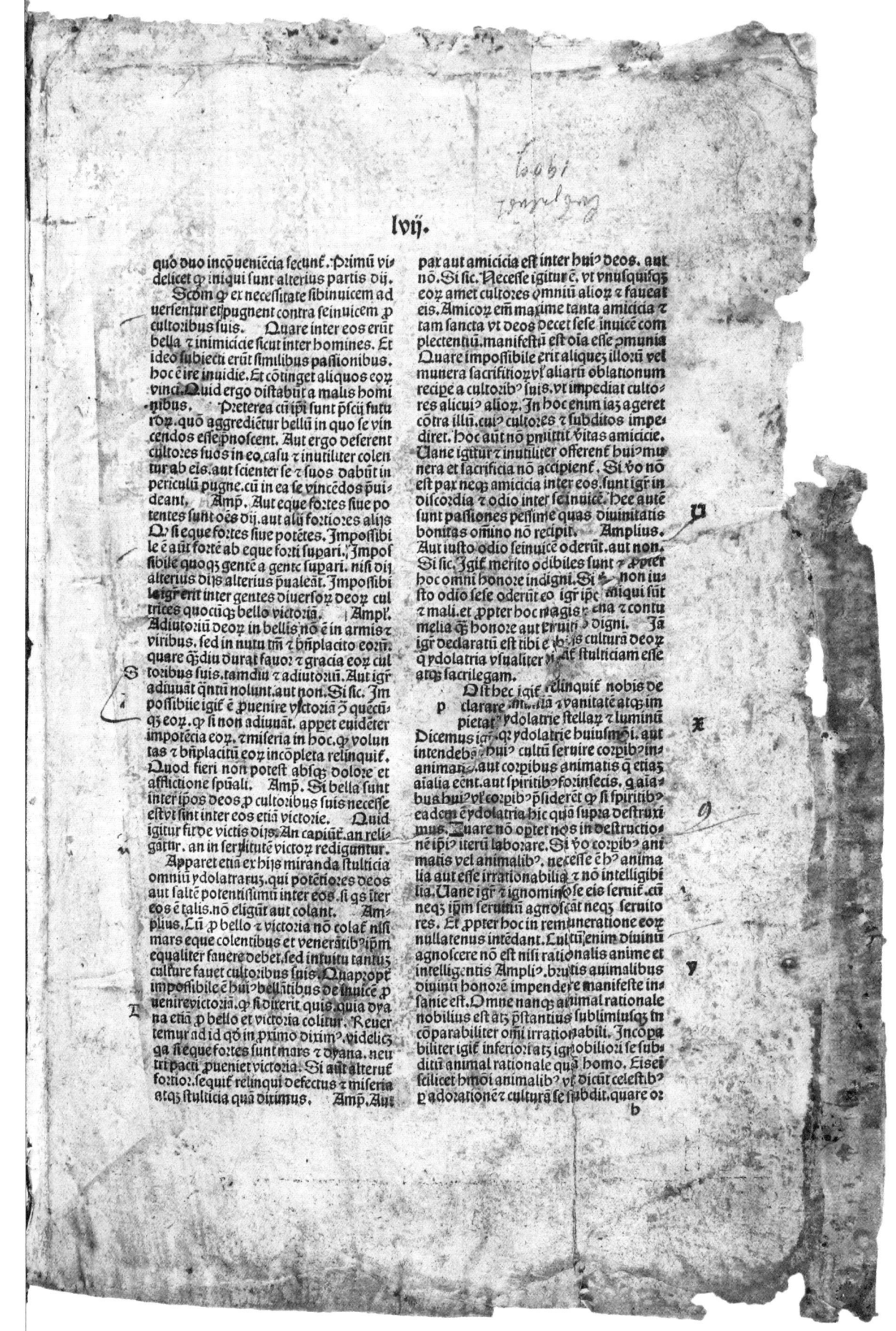

[Figs. 8a and 8b] Proof sheet with corrector's markings and corresponding page in final printed edition.
GUILLERMUS ALVERNUS: *Opera, pars 1*, fol. h^r = fol. 61^r. Erlangen UB, Inc. 1246 [8a] and Inc. 450 [8b]

quo duo incouenieciā secunt̃. Primũ vi
delicet q̃ iniqui sunt alterius partis dij.

Scōm q̃ ex necessitate sibinuicem ad
uersentur et pugnent contra seinuicem p
cultoribus suis. Quare inter eos erũt
bella τ inimicicie sicut inter homines. Et
ideo subiecti erũt similibus passionibus.
hoc ē ire inuidie. Et cōtinget aliquos eo?
vinci. Quid ergo distabũt a malis homi
nibus. Preterea cũ ipi sunt p̄scij futu
ro?. quō aggredietũr bellũ in quo se vin
cendos esse p̄noscent. Aut ergo deserent
cultores suos in eo casu τ inutiliter colen
tur ab eis. aut scienter se τ suos, dabũt in
periculũ pugne. cũ in ea se vincēdos p̄ui
deant. Amp̃. Aut eque fortes siue po
tentes sunt oēs dij. aut alij fortiores alijs.
Q̃ si eque fortes siue potētes. Impossibi
le ē aũt forte ab eque forti sup̃ari. Impos
sibile quoq̃ gentē a gente sup̃ari. nisi dij
alterius dijs alterius p̃ualeāt. Impossibi
le igĩt erit inter gentes diuerso? deo? cul
trices quocũq̃ bello victoriā. Ampl̃.
Adiutoriũ deo? in bellis nō ē in armis τ
viribus. sed in nutu tm̃ τ bn̄placito eo?.
quare q̃diu durat fauo? τ gracia eo? cul
toribus suis. tamdiu τ adiutorũ. Aut igĩt
adiuuãt q̃ntũ nolunt. aut non. Si sic. Im
possibĩle igĩt ē p̄uenire victoriā q̃ quecũ
q̃ eo?. q̃ si non adiuuãt. appet euidēter
impotēcia eo?. τ miseria in hoc. q̃ volun
tas τ bn̄placitũ eo? incōpleta relinquif
Quod fieri non potest absq̃ dolore et
afflictione sp̃uali. Amp̃. Si bella sunt
inter ipos deos p cultoribus suis necesse
ē st vt sint inter eos etiã victorie. Quid
igitur fit de victis dijs. An capiũt. an reli
gatũr. an in seruitutē victo? rediguntur.

Apparet etiã ex bijs miranda stulticia
omniũ ydolatraru?. qui potētiores deos
aut saltē potentissimũ inter eos. si qs itr̃
eos ē talis. nō eligũt aut colant. Am
plius. Lũ p bello τ victoria nō colat̃ nisi
mars eque colentibus et veneratib? ipm
equaliter fauere debet. sed intuitu tantũ
culture fauet cultoribus suis. Quaprop̃
impossibile ē hui? bellātibus de inuice p
uenire victoriā. q̃ si dixerit quis. quia dya
na etiã p bello et victoria colitur. Reuer
temur ad id q̃d in primo dixim?. videlic̃
q̃a si eque fortes sunt mars τ dyana. neu
tri pacti p̃ueniet victoria. Si aũt alteru?
fortior. sequif relinqui defectus τ miseria
atq̃ stulticia quā diximus. Amp̃. Aut

par aut amicicia est inter hui? deos. aut
nō. Si sic. Necesse igitur ē. vt vnusquisq̃
eo? amet cultores omniũ alio? τ faueat
eis. Amico? ēm maxime tanta amicicia τ
tam sancta vt deos decet sese inuice com
plectentiũ. manifestũ est oĩa esse p̃munia
Quare impossibile erit aliquē illo? vel
munera sacrifitio? vl' aliaru oblationum
recipe a cultorib? suis. vt impediat culto
res alicui? alio?. In hoc enim iaz ageret
cōtra illũ. cui? cultores τ subditos impe
diret. hoc aũt nō p̃mittit vitas amicicie.
Uane igitur τ inutiliter offerent̃ hui? mu
nera et sacrificia nō accipient̃. Si v̄o nō
est par neq̃ amicicia inter eos. sunt igĩt in
discordia τ odio inter se inuice. hee autē
sunt passiones pessime quas diuinitatis
bonitas omīno nō recipit. Amplius.
Aut iusto odio seinuice oderũt. aut non.
Si sic. Igĩt merito odibiles sunt τ p̃pter
hoc omni honore indigni. Si v̄o non iu
sto odio sese oderũt eo igĩt ipo iniqui sũt
τ mali. et p̃pter hoc magis pena τ contu
melia q̃ honore aut seruitio digni. Ia
igĩt declaratũ est tibi ex bijs cultura deo?
q̃ ydolatria vsualiter dicit̃ stulticiam esse
atq̃ sacrilegam.

Ost hec igĩt relinquit̃ nobis de
p clarare insaniã τ vanitatē atq̃ im
pietatē ydolatrie stella? τ luminũ
Dicemus igĩt. q̃ ydolatrie huiusmōi. aut
intendebãt hui? cultũ seruire corpib? in
animatis. aut corpibus animatis q̃ etiã
aialia eēnt. aut spiritib? forinsecis. q aĩa
bus hui? vl' corpib? p̃sideret q̃ si spiritib?
eadem ē ydolatria hic quā supra destrui
mus. Quare nō optet nos in destructio
ne ipi? iterũ laborare. Si v̄o corpib? ani
matis vel animalib?. necesse ē b? anima
lia aut esse irrationabilia q̃ nō intelligibi
lia. Uane igĩt τ ignominiose eis seruit̃ cũ
neq̃ ipm seruitiũ agnoscãt neq̃ seruito
res. Et p̃pter hoc in remuneratione eo?
nullatenus intēdant. Cultũ enim diuinũ
agnoscere nō est nisi rationalis anime et
intelligentis Ampli?. brutis auimalibus
diuinũ honore impendere manifeste in
sanie est. Omne nanq̃ animal rationale
nobilius est atq̃ p̃stantius sublimiusq̃ in
cōparabiliter oĩi irrationabili. Incōpa
biliter igĩt inferiori atq̃ ignobiliori se sub
ditũ animal rationale quā homo. Ei sci
scilicet hmōi animalib? vt dicit̃ celestib?
p adorationē τ culturā se subdit. quare o?
b

[Figs. 9a and 9b]   Q̃ ſi eque fortes ſiue potétes. Jmpoſſibi
le é aũt forté ab eque forti ſupari. Jmpoſ
ſibile quoqȝ genté a gente ſupari. niſi oi

Q̃ ſi eque fortes ſiue potétes. Jmpoſſibi
le é aũt forté ab eque forti ſupari. Jmpoſ
ſibile quoqȝ genté a gente ſupari. niſi oi

[Figs. 10a and 10b]   S toribus ſuis. tamdiu ⁊ adiutoriũ. Aut igĩ
adiuuãt qntũ nolunt. aut non. Si ſic. Jm
poſſibile igiť é puenire victoria ȝ quecũ
qȝ eoꝛ. ꝙ ſi non adiuuãt. appet euidéter

toribus ſuis. tamdiu ⁊ adiutoriũ. Aut igĩ
S adiuuãt qntũ nolunt. aut non. Si ſic. Jm
poſſibile igiť é puenire victoria ȝ quecũ
qȝ eoꝛ. ꝙ ſi non adiuuãt. appet euidéter

[Figs. 11a and 11b]   eadem é ydolatria hic qua ſupra deſtruxi
mus. uare nõ optet nos in deſtructio
né ipĩ? iterũ laboꝛare. Si vo corpib? ani

eadem é ydolatria hic qua ſupra deſtruxi
mus. Quare nõ optet nos in deſtructio
né ipĩ? iterũ laboꝛare. Si vo corpib? ani

[Figs. 9a and 9b] Visible spacing lines in composition. Corrector's marking on left-hand side. GUILLERMUS ALVERNUS: *Opera, pars 1*, fol. h^r = fol. 61^r. Erlangen UB, former rear pastedown, Inc. 1246 [9b] and Inc. 450 [9b]

[Figs. 10a and 10b] Corrector's marking indicating new position for majuscule and another indicating correction of letter. GUILLERMUS ALVERNUS: *Opera, pars 1*, fol. h^r = fol. 61^r. Erlangen UB, Inc. 1246 [10a] and Inc. 450 [10b]

[Figs. 11a and 11b] Letter Q lost during printing. Error noted in left-hand margin. GUILLERMUS ALVERNUS: *Opera, pars 1*. Nuremberg: Jörg Stuchs, after 31 March 1496, fol. h^r = 61^r. Erlangen UB, Inc. 1246 [11a] and Inc. 450 [11b]

Despite the advanced state of work, however, it remained unpublished.

The publication of William's *Opera* was Danhauser's last completed project before his departure to Vienna in 1497.[25] The idea for the book goes back to the year 1495 and the death of his mother. Deeply affected by her death, Danhauser turned for solace and spiritual guidance to Jörg Pirckheimer, the prior of the charterhouse in Nuremberg. It was he who proposed the publication, seeing in it a way for his friend to overcome his sorrow and at the same time for the humanist to become familiar with the works of the Christian theologian William of Auvergne.[26] As the Pirckheimer scholar Arnold Reimann has noted, the book is a monument of how humanism and scholasticism could meet in a joint project whose common ground rested on a shared interest in eloquent Latin expression and in moral and natural philosophy.[27]

Three manuscripts were used to print the anthology. Two have survived, both written on vellum and completed in or by the year 1435.[28] In 1495 all three were present in the library of the Nuremberg Dominican friars and lent to Danhauser for the publication. Each codex served as the basis for one of the three volumes of the anthology, the texts being printed as they appeared in the manuscript copy. The surviving codices were used for volume one (*ex Magisterio divinale et sapientiale*) and volume three (*De universo*).[29] Danhauser's editorial work focused on preparing each for publication, reading through the texts and making corrections. Once this task had been completed, the codices were handed over to the printer Georg Stuchs and printing could begin. Today 190 copies of Stuch's edition survive.[30] The text was never reprinted.

Let us turn now to another highly interesting case of fifteenth century correcting in which a book was corrected after the full run had been completed.

Corrections printed on paper slips and pasted in the edition (Erlangen UB, Inc. 497a)

On occasion typographical mistakes went unnoticed during the proof revisions, and the press crew went on to print the full run of an edition. Even at this late stage it was still possible to make corrections, with printers showing a remarkable inventiveness. A case in point is the edition of Michael Lochmaier's *Parochiale curatorium*, published c. 1493/4 by Friedrich Creussner.[31]

Due to an oversight during imposition, the wrong chapter headings were printed on several pages in three quires. The mishap occurred at the point when the headlines, signatures and typeset page were assembled and locked in the chase and then sent to the pressroom for printing. Although proof sheets were certainly made, the chapter headings went unchecked and the mistakes were overlooked, and the sheets were subsequently printed in a full run: a nightmare for any cost-conscious publisher trying to keep to schedule! Instead of reprinting the sheets with increased production costs and delay, Creussner solved the problem by having the correct headlines printed on separate paper, arranged so that they could be cut into narrow slips and pasted over the faulty running titles [fig. 12].[32]

It is not surprising that mistakes like these could occur when one considers the non-sequential arrangement of typeset pages used for imposition. A quire in quarto, as was used here, consists of sixteen pages and is printed on a two-pull press in four steps using two sheets [fig. 13]. Pages 1–4 and 13–6 were printed on sheet one (forme 1), pages 5–12 on sheet two (forme 2). If a new chapter started on one of the pages appearing on sheet two (e.g. pages 5–12), there was a considerable risk that a compositor would forget to change the headline for the subsequent pages on sheet one. Thus, in many cases, the column titles for pages 1–4 also appear on pages 13–16.

This is indeed what happened in quire d. The chapter headings for *Capitulum tercium* were used throughout sheet one, although the last four pages, pages 13–16, belong to chapter four.[33] When the mistake was noticed, the entire run had already been completed. To remedy the problem, headings were printed on separate paper and glued over the faulty column titles as narrow paper slips [fig. 14; headlines *Quartum* and *de penitenijs recipiendi*].

In other instances, in quires r and a, the chapter title appears at the top of the left-hand page and the general heading at the top of the right-hand page, contrary to the layout of the rest of the edition and contrary to established typographical practice. Like the mishap in quire d, the mistake came about due to faulty imposition. In quire r, the headings are reversed on pages 6 and 11 (*Capitulum Nonum*), both of which are imposed on sheet two,[34] where they form one side of a bifolium, i.e. the inner sheet of forme 2. This kind of mistake should normally never happen. The rule is that in quarto the even-numbered page is always imposed to the left and the odd-numbered page to the right, thus providing a convenient rule of thumb for the compositor when setting the headlines. This compositor simply got it wrong.

The rule should also have helped him avoid the mistake in quire a. In this instance the headlines are reversed on pages 15 and 16.[35] Looking at the diagram [fig. 13], one can see that pages 15 and 2 form one side of a bifolium, and page 16 matches with page 1 to form the other. The compositor

25 Danhauser left Nuremberg to become professor of Roman law at the University of Vienna in 1497.

26 See Sebald Schreyer's letter of 10 June 1496, in which he wrote to Conrad Celtis that the book project was helping Danhauser overcome his grief; in the same letter he mentions Celtis's desire to acquire a copy of the work: *Wilhelmus Parisiensis Danusio melancoliam ingerit; mihi rarus est, quem coram te mox comparere intelligo.* Cf. RUPPRICH (see note 21), p. 190.

27 REIMANN (see note 21), pp. 193/4.

28 The manuscripts are Cent. III, 65 and Cent. IV, 70 of the StB Nuremberg; both contain markings for page breaks made by the printer and other signs of use as printer's copy. Cf. KAREN SCHNEIDER: Die lateinischen mittelalterlichen Handschriften: Teil 1. Theologische Handschriften. Wiesbaden 1967 (*Die Handschriften der Stadtbibliothek Nürnberg*. 2,1), pp. 212/3 and 271. A paper analyzing the manuscript and the markings will appear shortly.

29 An interesting footnote to the codices is that the binding of volume three, i.e. shelfmark Cent. IV, 70, was made by Conrad Forster (d. 1463), a Dominican friar and master bookbinder at the convent (Kyriss 21.1; EBDB w000081). The other codex, shelfmark Cent. III, 65, has a binding made by the workshop attached to the Nuremberg Charterhouse (Kyriss 23; EBDB w000085), replacing the original. It was likely rebound at the time of publication.

30 As based on the ISTC data base, February 2010.

31 MICHAEL LOCHMAIER: *Parochiale curatorum*. [Nuremberg: Friedrich Creussner, not before 1493] 4° [ISTC il00267000. GW M18666. HC *10167. BMC II 455. BSB-Ink L-210. Cf. also the digital edition (DFG-Viewer).

32 Cf. GASKELL (see note 1), pp. 134/5.

33 Chapter four begins on p. 8 (fol. diiijv) of sheet two, and continues on pp. 13–6 of sheet one. The incorrect headlines (*De oblationibus* and *Capitulum tercium*) appear on pp. 13–6 (= fol. [d7]r–[d8]v). Pages 16 and 13 were imposed and printed on the outer side of sheet one; pp. 15 and 14 were printed on the inner side of sheet one; see diagram.

34 The chapter title *De collatione sacramentorum* should have been printed on p. 6 (= fol. riijv), but the general heading *Capitulum Nonum* appears there instead. The heading *Capitulum Nonum* should have been printed on p. 11 (= fol. [r6]r), but the chapter title *De collatione sacramentorum* appears there instead.

35 The chapter title *De iuribus parrochialibus* should have been printed on p. 15 (= fol. [a8]r), but the general heading *Capitulum primum* appears there instead. The heading *De iuribus parrochialibus* should have been printed on p. 16 (= fol. [a8]v), but the chapter title *Capitulum primum* appears there instead.

[Fig. 12]

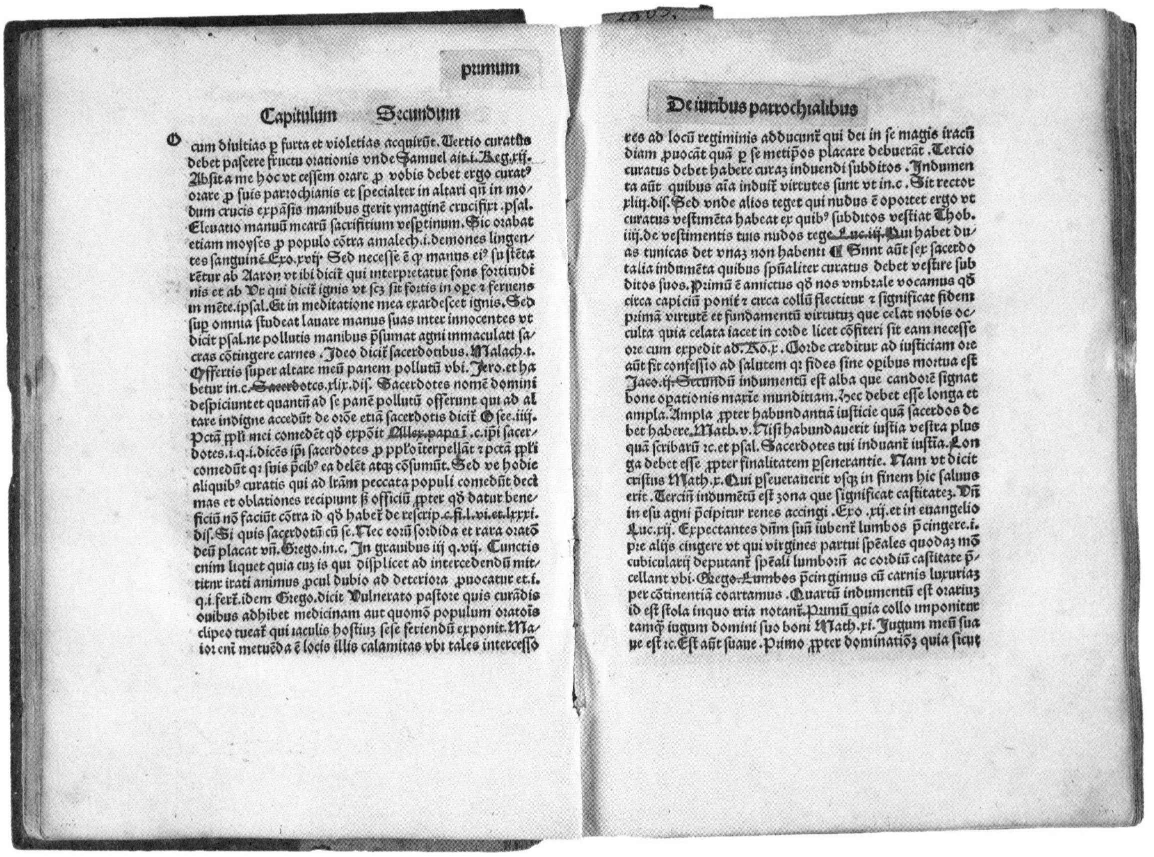

[Fig. 14]

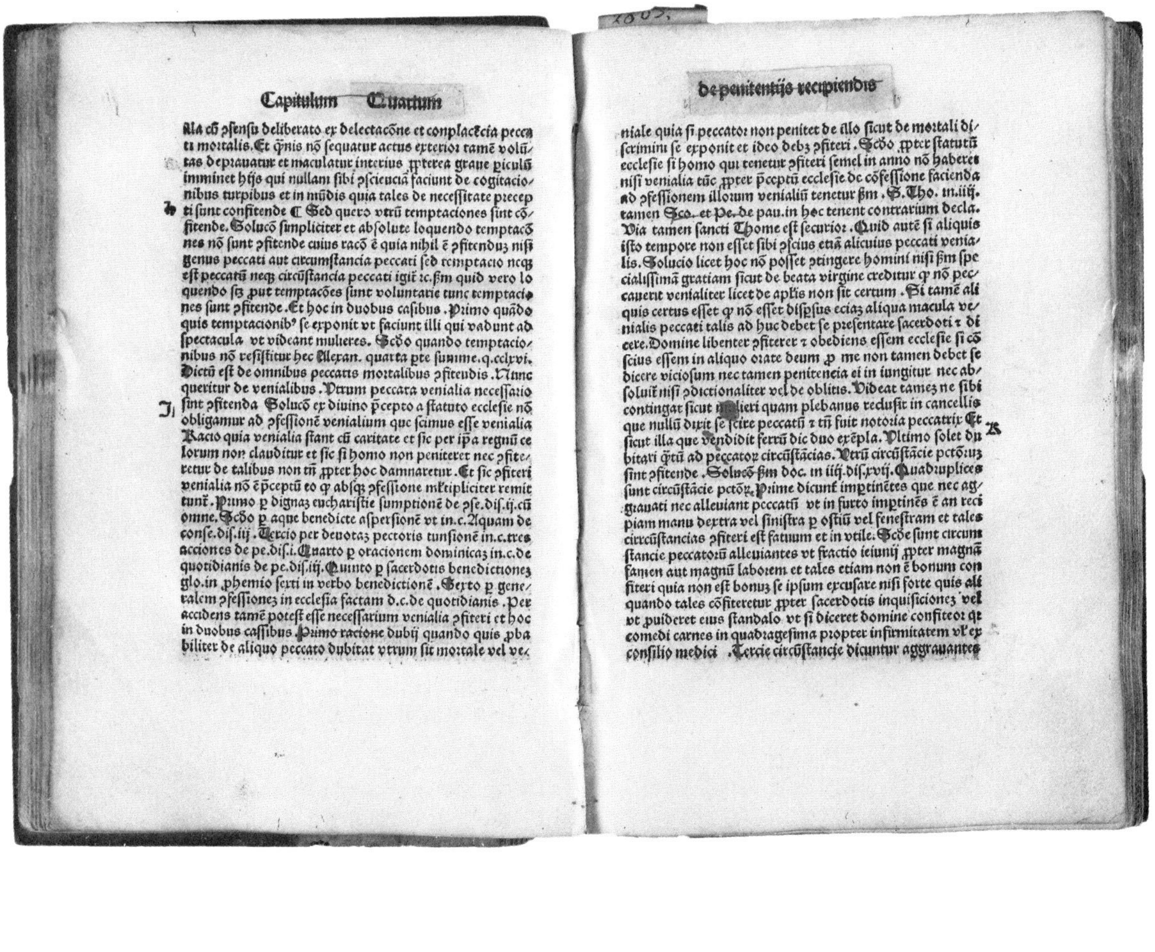

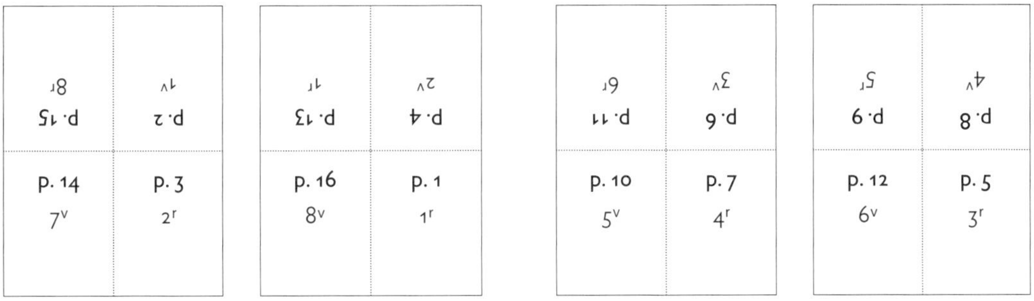

p. 2	p. 15	p. 4	p. 13	p. 6	p. 11	p. 8	p. 9
7ᵛ	8ʳ	5ᵛ	1ʳ				

[Fig. 13]

(The imposition diagram shows eight page cells arranged in four two-page units, with the top row of each unit printed upside-down.)

likely reversed them because he lacked an immediate point of reference when setting the headlines on pages 15 and 16. Pages 1 and 2, being the title-page and a blank, do not have headings.

Finally an observation which may provide a clue to the order in which quires a and b were set and printed. In quire a the heading *Capitulum Secundam* was printed mistakenly on p. 14 (= fol. [a7]ᵛ). A heading for chapter two at this point is unusual, to say the least, as the chapter does not begin until the first page of quire b. Was the compositor reusing parts of quire b, the so-called skeleton forme, for quire a, forgetting to change the headline? If so, it means that the second quire must have been printed and the type redistributed before the first quire was set.

Whether it was a brief lapse of concentration that led to these mistakes or inexperience, the responsibility must be shared equally by the compositor and house corrector. The mistakes should have been noticed by one of them and corrected. The breakdown in routine procedure on three occasions undoubtedly led to production delay and cost overruns for the printer. To prevent them from becoming even greater, Friedrich Creussner found an inexpensive solution by pasting paper slips with the correct headings over the faulty ones.

Conclusion

As we have seen, proof sheets and corrected books provide many insights into fifteenth century correction procedures. Whereas Friedrich Creussner's edition with correction slips allows the student of typography to analyze common mishaps that occurred in imposition and presswork, proof sheets with handwritten corrections offer a view of pre-press procedures in fifteenth century printing houses, though for this practice the body of evidence is small. In contrast to the masses of clean revise sheets that have survived, proof sheets used by house correctors are very rare. They are modest objects of research, but they are nevertheless an important source of information about pre-press correcting in the fifteenth century. They show us how a text was edited, and they provide a means for us to assess how thoroughly correction procedures were done. Furthermore, they provide us with a list of editorial symbols and show us how they were used. Although the way a house corrector edited a text may not have changed significantly over the centuries – a general editor still makes corrections by hand in the margins of a proof –, the documentary value of early proof sheets is obvious.

[Fig. 12] Facing pages with correction slips. Correction slip *primum* pasted over original chapter number *Secundum*. MICHAEL LOCHMAIR: *Parochiale curatorum*. Erlangen UB, Inc. 497a, fol. a[7]ᵛ–a[8]ʳ

[Fig. 13] An example of page imposition used for a quaternion in quarto (two formes)

[Fig. 14] Correction slips with correct chapter number (*Quartum*) and title (*De penitentijs recipiendis*) pasted over incorrect chapter numbers. MICHAEL LOCHMAIR: *Parochiale curatorum*. Erlangen UB, Inc. 497a, fol. d[7]ᵛ–d[8]ʳ

Appendix 1: Table of Corrections

Heading: Biblia pauperū (centered)

Left-hand margin (column a)

Line	Correction	Synopsis of trial sheet and printed edition
l. 6/7	N	et iniquita꞊ | tes noſtre q̄ſi veetus abſtulerūt nos : nō eſt
		et iniquita꞊ | tes noſtre q̄ſi ventus abſtulerūt nos : nō eſt
l. 11–3	A	x̄tu꞊ | te ꝓpria bb humano genere ſuplicia ſecu꞊ | ture mortis
		x̄tu꞊ | te ꝓpria ab humano genere ſuplicia ſecu꞊ | ture mortis
l. 41	ā	| contradictor ad culpā · amic⁹ ad pena : mi | ra
		| contradictor ad culpā · amic⁹ ad penā : mi | ra

Right-hand margin (column b)

Line	Correction	Synopsis of trial sheet and printed edition
l. 17/8	Ad	| deſpicit · qz per adoptōnis gratiā p amorem | ſurgit.
		| deſpicit · qz per adoptōis gratiā ad amorem | ſurgit.
l. 21–3	D' maū	Vt ſine timo꞊ | re / inimicorū nrorū liberati : ſeruiam⁹ illi. |
		Vt ſine timo'e | d' maū inimicorū nrorū liberati | ßuiam⁹ illi|
l. 24/5	grā	| aſpirata manſuetudīs / erexit. Quod bene ī | heliſeo
		| aſpirata māſuetudīs gr̄a erexit. Qd' bn ī he | liſeo
l. 25/6	sunanitt	heliſeo / filiū ſuſcitantis ſignat' · qui cū bacu | lo
		he | liſeo ſunaītis filiū ſuſcitātis ſignat' · ů̊ cū ba | culo
l. 37–9	ni(hi)l	qz paulo atteſtā | te / ad pfectū adduxit lex. Iꝑe aūt per ſem₃ | ipm
		qz paulo atteſtāte | nihil ad pf̄ctū adduxit lex. Iꝑe aūt p ſem₃ | ipm
l. 42/3	ßui	ſed ſe꞊ | metipſū exinaniuit formā dei accipiens : ī |
		ſed ſe꞊ | metipſū exinaniuit formā ßui accipiens : ī |
l. 44	M [...]	| ſimilitudinē hominū fact⁹ et habitu muen | t⁹ vt ho. [...]
		ſimilitudinē hominū fact⁹ et habitu muen | t⁹ vt hō. [...]
l. 45	Hō	| t⁹ vt ho. Huc illucqȝ deambulat : qz et iude |
		| t⁹ vt hō. Huc illucqȝ deambulat : qz et iude |
l. 46	et ð(*eletio*)	| am iuxto et longe et poſitas gentes vocat. |
		| am iuxto et longe poſitas gentes vocat. |
l. 47	P	Suꝑ mortuū ſeqcies inſpirat. qz p apertio | nem [...]
		Suꝑ mortuū ſepcies inſpirat. qz p apertio | nem [...]

Appendix 2: Table of Corrections

Left-hand margin (column a)

Line	Correction	Synopsis of trial sheet and printed edition
l. 1	d + (scratched)	[…] et referēs illnd ſtatim |
		[…] et referēs illud ſtatim |
l. 9	r + (scratched)	| non habēs odiuȝ vel rācōnē ad illū ſubditū tūc pōt |
		| non habēs odiuȝ vel rācōrē ad illū ſubditū tūc pōt |
l. 17	j – (ink)	chari | tas. (et) qd' mejius ex p̄dictis videt(ur).et ſi hoc intēdat.ſ. |
		chari | tas. (et) qd' melius ex p̄dictis videt(ur).et ſi hoc intēdat.ſ. |
l. 48	a – (scratched)	ad- | uerti pōt ſi cōſideret(ur) vt(rum) aliǫs et el […]tiōe vel paſſi o | ne
		ad- | uerti pōt ſi cōſideret(ur) vt(rum) aliǫs et elatiōe vel paſſi o | ne
l. 49	j – (ink)	| ne peccauerit ſiue ǝx malicia vel infirmitate qd' idē | eſt
		| ne peccauerit ſiue ex malicia vel infirmitate qd' idē | eſt

Right-hand margin (column b)

Line	Correction	Synopsis of trial sheet and printed edition
l. 11	c – (scratched)	po | ſtea in ſe reuerſus ſe torrigit. Sȝ qd ſi ǫuis ſciat pec | catum
		po | ſtea in ſe reuerſus ſe corrigit. Sȝ qd ſi ǫuis ſciat pec | catum
l. 21	(ink)	| Kn̄.ßm Guil.Si comode pōt euȝ admonere|de tali |
		| Kn̄.ßm Guil.Si comode pōt euȝ admonere de tali |
l. 30	ac – (scratched)	ſuf | ficit ſi dicat p̄lato nō // cuſando nec denunciando.ſȝ |
		ſuf | ficit ſi dicat p̄lato nō accuſando nec denunciando.ſȝ |
l. 49	(ink)	celebra | tionis feſtor(um).|Terciuȝ em̄ preceptuȝ deca | logi …
		celebra | tionis feſtor(um). Terciuȝ em̄ preceptuȝ deca | logi …
l. 51	j – + (scratched)	| Exod'.xx.quod preceptum litteraliter intellectnm |
		| Exod'.xx.quod preceptum litteraliter intellectum |
l. 57	j – (ink)	| corpali refectioni.somno (et) alijs hmōi. vn̄ etiā (et) ſpi- | rituali …
		| corpali refectioni.somno (et) alijs hmōi. vn̄ etiā (et) ſpi- | rituali …
l. 70	(ink)	| deo:q̄ erit in patria. Preceptuȝ ġ | de ſanctificatione | …
		| deo:q̄ erit in patria. Preceptuȝ ġ de ſanctificatione | …

Appendix 3: Table of Corrections

Left-hand margin (column a)

Line	Correction	Trial sheet	Printed edition
l. 4	–	et | pugnent	et pugnent
l. 19	–	ſup(er)ari. | Jmpoſſi bile	ſup(er)ari. Jmpoſſi bile
l. 27	S in margin	*to be repositioned two printed lines underneath*	*between* adiuuāt *and* poſſi bile
l. 29	i	vlctoriā	vlctoriā (uncorrected)
l. 38	u	ſernitutē	ſeruitutē

Right-hand margin (column b)

Line	Correction	Trial sheet	Printed edition
l. 17	U in margin	*to be repositioned one printed line below*	(unchanged)
l. 37	9	| mus. uare	| mus.Quare (mus *not changed to* m⁹)
l. 41	i	ignomin / oſe	Ignominioſe
l. 44		intēdant. Cultū | enim	intēdant. Cultū enim (*traces of line remain*)

Appendix 4: Descriptions of Proof Sheets

I. *One proof sheet from*
GREGORIUS MAGNUS, PAPA: *Moralia, sive expositio in Job.*[36]
Nuremberg: Johannes Sensenschmist, 1471. 2°.
    ISTC ig00427000. GW 11429. H* 7928 (var). HC 7928. GfT 2405.
    Shelfmark: UB Erlangen, Inc. 1940 (formerly II.12).

One proof sheet. Formerly a pastedown in the inside of the upper cover of Erlangen UB, Inc. 193 (see below); text: long lines; without a column title or signature; the sheet contains fol. l[7]^r (= fol. 109^r) and is well-preserved, with many handwritten corrections by the house corrector, c. 1470/71. The page contains capituli 94–99 from chapter nine.
    (410 × 262 mm); printed area: 276 × 200 mm; 49 lines; two columns.

Incipit, fol. [l 7]^r, col. a, l. 1 f.: »Hinc est qz arguentem dn̄s non habuisse se | queritur : cū per ͺpphetā dicit.« [...]. Explicit, col. a, l. 49^r: »uor ei⁹ non me terreat. Per legē q̊ppe ν̀ gā.« |
    Incipit, col. b, l. 1^r: »de⁹ tenuerat : cū dicebat . Si q̊s hec vel il⸗ | la [...]«.
    Explicit, fol. [l 7]^r, col. b, l. 48 f.: »[...] | nem diuini muneris gratie septiformis spi | ritū in peccati morte iacentibus tribuit. |«

Trial sheet was removed from the binding of UB Erlangen, Inc. 193:
NICOLAUS PANORMITANUS DE TUDESCHIS: *Lectura super primo et secundo Decretalium*. [Venice]: Vindelinus de Spira, 1471–73. 2°. In three volumes, dated: I) 1 April 1473; II) 8 July 1472; III) 1471, 1472.
    ISTC ip00058000. GW M47951. HR 12322 (R II and III.2 only).
    Provenance: [Redorf, Augustinian Canons Regular].[37]
    Bindery: EBDB w000066 (Kyriss 28.1): Rebdorf, Augustinian monastery, workshop c. 1474–1517; late fifteenth century half alum-tawed pigskin binding over wooden boards (446 × 285 × 78 mm), with blind tooling;[38] sewn on four raised double cords; endbands present; no furniture; two hook-clasp fasteners preserved.

II. *Two proof sheets from*
ANTONINUS FLORENTINUS: *Summa theologica*, pars 2.[39]
Nuremberg: Anton Koberger, 28 August 1486. 2°.
    ISTC ia00875000. GW 2189. H* 1246. Sajó/Soltész 253.

Two non-consecutive sheet halves.
    Fol. [K2]^r: The proof sheet was formerly a pastedown in the inside upper cover; text: two columns; the running chapter title *Capitulum*.VII. appears centered above the columns; without a signature. The proof formed part of the second folio of quire K (= fol. 196^r); its other side is blank. The location of the other half of the sheet (= fol. K5^v) is unknown.
    398 × 266 mm; printed area: 294 [307] × 84 [182/3] mm; 54 lines; two columns.

---

[36] Copy inspected: UB Erlangen, Inc. 1350.

[37] The binding was made in the bindery attached to Rebdorf monastery. The upper cover has a parchment station label, showing a brown Lombard E (?) as the former location; the former horn window with all metal parts has been removed; the former title label survives in part; for a possible reference to this book see *Mittelalterliche Bibliothekskataloge Deutschlands und der Schweiz. Dritter Band, Zweiter Teil: Bistum Eichstätt*. Bearbeitet von PAUL RUF. München 1969 [reprint of the first edition 1932], pp. 256,24/25.

[38] Tooling: a pomegranate tool in lozenge (EBDB s004394: Granatapfel, ohne Hüllblättern) is stamped 13 times in a vertical row on both the upper and lower covers; where the points of the lozenges meet a small diamond-shaped tool (EBDB s004393: Eichelzweig, mit Eichenblättern) is stamped horizontally on each side; no tools are visible on the spine. – Cf. KYRISS, p. 29.

[39] Copy inspected: UB Erlangen, Inc. 1329 (pars secunda).

Fol. [16]ᵛ: The proof sheet was formerly a pastedown in the inside lower cover; text: two columns; the running title *Titulus .IX.* appears centered above the columns. The other side of the folio is blank. The location of the other half of the sheet (= fol. 11ʳ) is unknown.

Measurements: 396 × 267 mm; printed area:
294 [307] × 84 [182/3] mm; 70 lines; two columns.

Fol. [K2]ʳ, heading: *Capitulum .VII.*

Incipit, fol. [K2]ʳ, col. a, l. 1 f.: »riam vtrū sciens pctm̄ ₚximi et referēs illud' statim | p̄lato [...].« Explicit, col. a, l. 69 f.: »ₚpmit꞊ | tit.si aūt est infectiuu3 alior(um) debet denunciari pla- |«

Incipit, col. b, l. 1 f.: »to vt gregi suo caueat.Semp em̄ bonum multor-(um) de | bet ₚpponi [...].«

Explicit, col. b, l. 69 f.: »[...] in | deo:q̄ erit in patria. Preceptu3 ġ de sanctificatio ne |«

The trial sheets were removed from the binding of L of the HAS, Inc. 805: JOHANNES DE BROMYARD: *Summa praedicantium*. Nuremberg: Anton Koberger, 29 June 1485. 2°.

ISTC ij00261000. H* 3994. BMC II 427. BSB-Ink I-374.

Provenance: L of Count Vigyázó, nº 1264. According to a note on the fly leaf written by Count Alexander Vigyázó, his wife »Zsuzsi« (= Susanna Podmaniczky) bought the book as a present for him, purchasing it from [Karl Wilhelm] Hiersemann for 550 ℳ [in Leipzig] on 9 May 1911.[40] – Budapest, L of the HAS.

Bindery: EBDB w000917 (Kyriss 120), Nuremberg, c. 1473–1503 (Madonna/S-S: Maria); late fifteenth century full leather binding over wooden boards (412 × 263 × 109 mm), with binder's title: *Sūm predicantiū*.[41]

III. *One proof sheet from*
GUILLERMUS ALVERNUS, EPISCOPUS PARISIENSIS: *Opera* (pars I). Ed. PETER DANHAUSER.[42] Nuremberg: Georg Stuchs, after 31 May 1496. 2°.

ISTC ig00708000. GW 11862. HC* 8300.

In two halves. One half was formerly a pastedown in the inside upper cover, which was removed in 1909 and re-attached as one of two front flyleaves; text: two columns; the foliation *lvij* appears centered above the columns; with the signature *h* (lower right-hand corner). The other half of the sheet is still attached as pastedown in the inside lower cover. The complete sheet contains fol. h1ʳ and [h6]ᵛ = fol. 61 and 66.

295 × 205 mm; printed area: 192 [202] × 122 [135/6] mm; 54 lines; two columns.

Heading: *lvij.*

Incipit, fol. [h1]ʳ, col. a, l. 1 f.: *quo duo incōueniēcia secunt'.Primū vi=| delicet* [...].

Explicit, col. a, l. 54ʳ: »atq3 stulticia quā diximus. Amp̄.Aut. |«

Incipit, col. b, l. 1ʳ: »par aut amicicia est inter hui} deos. aut | [...].«

40 I am indebted to Dr. Rozsondai (Head of Manuscripts and Rare Books, L of the HAS) for this information.
41 Cf. ROZSONDAI (see note 11), p. 316 nº 12. The tools used are:
 4 = EBDB s014132 (Greif);
 13 = EBDB s014136 (Rosette);
 22 = EBDB s028433 (Blumenstrauß);
 33 = EBDB s014153 (Laubstab);
 46 = EBDB s014146 (Blattwerk);
 55 = EBDB s010278 (Rundbogenfries);
 72 = EBDB s010274 (Blatt, einteilig).
42 Copy inspected: UB Erlangen, Inc. 450-1.

Explicit, fol. [h1]ʳ, col. b, l. 53 f.: »[...] | vl' dicūt celestib⁹ | p adoratiōnē (et) culturā se subdit.quare or |«

The trial sheet is found in UB Erlangen, Inc. 1246:
JOHANNES DE VERDENA: *Sermones ›Dormi secure‹ de sanctis*, Nuremberg: Anton Koberger, 5 January 1494. 2°.
ISTC ij00465500. GW M 14945. HC* 15979.

Provenance: L[ukas] W[eydner] (monogram on title-page); the full written form of the name appears in a crossed out price annotation on fol. [i8]ʳ, above heading (*Sermo* LVIII): *Jste liber e(st) luce weydner pl(e)b(anu) m jn gelhsee* [Gelbelsee (?), Pfarrei St. Hippolyt, Diocese Eichstätt] *et (con)stat 7 ß d* IX (?). – *Johannes Wild* (early sixteenth century, pen trial on lower pastedown). – Ansbach, Hochfürstliche Markgräfische B (see former shelfmarks in upper cover: 270 (sixteenth century), 5 and 151 (both seventeenth/eighteenth century).

Bindery: EBDB w000917 (Kyriss 120), Nuremberg, c. 1473–1503 (Madonna/S-S: Maria); late fifteenth century full calf leather binding over wooden boards (310 × 210 × 49 mm), with binder's title: *Sermones dormi secure*;⁴³ sewn on 3 raised double cords; endbands lost; middle piece present on upper and lower covers, four corner pieces lost on both; two hook-clasp fasteners lost.

IV. *Correction slips on paper pasted into*:
MICHAEL LOCHMAIR: *Parochiale curatorum*.⁴⁴
Nuremberg: Friedrich Creussner, [not before 1493]. 4°.
ISTC il00267000. GW M 18666. HC* 10167. GfT 1127.

Narrow slips with corrected running headlines on fol. [a7]ʳ, [a8]ʳ⁻ᵛ, [d7]ʳ⁻ᵛ, [d8]ʳ⁻ᵛ, r iijʳ and [r6]ʳ.
217/8 × 150 mm; printed area: 143 (152) × 98 mm.
Copy inspected: UB Erlangen, Inc. 497a.

---

43 Cf. EBDB w000917. Upper cover, centre panel: floral diaper with a pomegranate fleuron (five impressions), with two concentric frames and a binder's title at top; centre panel: Knospenstaude (EBDB s014119 = K 120.01), Rautengerank (EBDB s014120 = K 120.02); inner border: Wellenranke (EBDB r000747 = K 120.09); outer border, sides: Wellenranke (EBDB s014141); bottom: Herz von Pfeil durchbohrt (EBDB s014126 = K 120.08); lower cover, panel design X with one border: two Knospenstauden in each of the four triangles (K 120.01); a Wellenranke tool (EBDB s014141) spine: leather flaking off, no stamps visible. – Cf. KYRISS, p. 99.

44 Copies inspected to date: UB Erlangen, Inc. 497a; BL I.A. 7812; BSB 4 Inc. s.a. 1179a.

ADOLFO TURA

Edizioni quattrocentine delle *Facezie* di Poggio in volgare (ed una postilla su Leonardo lettore)

«AUCUN PAR EXEMPLE ne s'est vraiment occupé de la traduction italienne»:[1] se non fosse per lo studio, sotto più rispetti pregevole, di Olimpia Cirielli apparso una trentina di anni fa,[2] potrebbe oggi ripetersi la considerazione che, con riguardo alla versione volgare delle *confabulationes* braccioliniane, faceva nel 1878 Anatole de Montaiglon. Quello studio, tuttavia, non sembra essere servito ad assicurare alla traduzione un posto riconosciuto nella storia della novellistica italiana, quasi la versione fosse sussumibile *tout court* ed anzi già compresa nel capitolo della fortuna delle *Facetiae* come sua estrema ed estenuata propaggine. È bensì chiaro che la traduzione rappresenta un'entità letteraria del tutto irriducibile all'opera di Poggio, nella quale la scrittura latina non è meramente veste linguistica. Le *Facetiae* non sono già un'articolazione di brevi narrazioni in latino, ma la stessa esibizione dell'idoneità del latino a sostituirsi alla lingua italiana in un àmbito che questa si era appropriato. Un esempio del tutto diverso può riuscir utile a spiegare il proposito. Accennando, in un saggio del 1977, alle tarsie quattrocentesche, Carlo Del Bravo commenta: «Non sembra quindi che i cori intarsiati permettano letture iconologiche. Vi compaiono infatti oggetti la cui presenza è ammissibile in luogo sacro solo per una forte astrazione dai contenuti.»[3] A ben vedere, l'ammissibilità di tali oggetti non dipende tanto da uno sforzo astrattivo,[4] quanto dall'integrazione del *modo* in cui essi si trovano rappresentati alla definizione stessa del contenuto raffigurato: non si deve prescindere dalla considerazione che nelle tarsie i più disparati oggetti appaiono ridotti a «figure quadrate» (per usare una locuzione del Lomazzo), alla stregua di pure schematizzazioni volumetriche. Per sottile che possa sembrare la distinzione, ciò che viene rappresentato nelle tarsie non è questo o quell'oggetto, sia pure *quadrato*, ma la quadratura come tale. Similmente per il *Facetiarum liber*: se è vero, come scrisse acutamente Terracini, che l'uomo cólto «personifica la lingua»,[5] l'opera di Poggio è propriamente una messa in scena, con riguardo al latino, di tale personificazione. Messa in scena non palese se non agli occhi di uomini parimenti cólti e che per di più condividessero la stessa cultura, e dunque di nessun ingombro per i molti lettori i quali, siccome a quella cultura affatto estranei o appartenenti ad altre età, profittarono lietamente del libro senza vedervi che una raccolta di narrazioni e di motti; e si capisce che questo genere di godimento fu alla base della larghissima diffusione a stampa del testo.[6] Anziché spegnersi, la fortuna del *Facetiarum liber* sopravvisse alla rarefazione del pubblico cui l'opera era intesa. Non c'è dunque discontinuità

[1] ANATOLE DE MONTAIGLON: Préface. In: *Les Facécies de Poge* [...]. Traduction française de Guillaume Tardif [...] réimprimée pour la première fois sur les éditions gothiques. Paris 1878, p. VIII.

[2] Cfr. OLIMPIA CIRIELLI: I primi volgarizzamenti italiani delle *Facezie* di Poggio. In: *Annali della Facoltà di Lettere e Filosofia* (Università degli studi – Bari). XXV–XXVI (1982/3), pp. 201–90.

[3] CARLO DEL BRAVO: La dolcezza dell'immaginazione. In: *Annali della Scuola Normale Superiore di Pisa*. Ser. 3ª, VII (1977), p. 780.

[4] Si pone la questione dell'ammissibilità, piuttosto che della sacralità stessa, giacché si tratta di arredi, non di oggetti propriamente investiti di un carattere sacro; ma rispetto alla stessa sacralizzazione si è più volte constatata la neutralità dell'oggetto. Cfr. PASCAL VERNUS: Supports d'écriture et fonction sacralisante dans l'Égypte pharaonique. In: *Le texte et son inscription*. Ed. ROGER LAUFER. Paris 1989, p. 23: «D'emblée, soulignons que cette opposition [sacralisé/non sacralisé] est morphologique et non intrinsèque au contenu des textes ou à la nature des objets inscrits. Car nature ou contenu ne suffisent pas à préjuger, à priori, de la sacralisation ou de la non-sacralisation».

[5] BENVENUTO TERRACINI: *Lingua libera e libertà linguistica*. Torino 1970, p. 74.

[6] Cfr. LOTTE HELLINGA: The Dissemination of a Text in Print: Early Editions of Poggio Bracciolini's *Facetiae*. In: *Trasmissione dei testi a stampa nel periodo moderno*. Ed. Giovanni Crapulli. Roma 1988, pp. 85–106.

[Tav. 1]

| | f. 5ᵛ | f. 2ʳ |
| | f. 1ᵛ | f. 6ʳ |

tra la versione italiana e la fortuna del libro, ma una più riposta e remota frattura tra questa fortuna e l'opera stessa. Piuttosto che l'estenuazione della fortuna del *Facetiarum liber*, la traduzione ne rappresenta la verità. Di ciò si potrebbe avere ulteriore riscontro ponendo attenzione alla scelta delle facezie che la versione volgare accoglie (fino ad un numero di 179), ma è discorso che non può essere qui svolto.[7] Di fatto, se mutare la lingua delle *Facetiae* comportava mutarne il contenuto, ciò non poteva essere avvertito, poiché quella dimensione di contenuto che dileguava si era intanto nascosta (o nascosta era stata fin dall'inizio) a larga parte dei lettori. Era perciò ovvio che una trasposizione in italiano del sodo delle narrazioni fosse finalmente gradita (tale fu, per esempio, a Leonardo, che possedette tra i suoi libri la traduzione).[8] Per grossa che sia la pietra gettata, la superficie dell'acqua immancabilmente finisce per quetarsi: l'acqua è qui la tradizione linguistica italiana, la pietra la virtuosistica opera braccioliniana. Non c'è da meravigliarsi che la figura del traduttore non abbia avuto in questa vicenda alcun rilievo e che i testimoni a stampa (altri non si posseggono) ci consegnino la versione col semplice titolo *Facetie de Pogio florentino traducte de latino in vulgare ornatissimo*, quasi si fossero tradotte da sé. Uno sforzo rimane da compiere nel tentativo di appurare attorno a quale data la versione venne composta. Alcune manifestazioni, quali il condizionale in *-eve* (mantenuto nella sola edizione milanese) o la costruzione del passivo mediante **fire* (*fixeva*, *fixean*), dovrebbero per lo meno indurre a domandarsi se la traduzione non preceda di qualche decennio le prime stampe. Anche la massiccia univerbazione e la punteggiatura oltremodo scarsa (mancante spessissimo a segnare lo stacco di un periodo dal seguente) sembrano indicare l'uso in tipografia di manoscritti non recenti.

Nel pubblicare il suo studio Olimpia Cirielli non conosceva che due edizioni del XV secolo, forse perché le sole rintracciabili in Italia, l'una e l'altra stampate a Venezia: quella sottoscritta da Bernardino Celerio nel 1483 (R 684 = V₁) e quella di Ottino de Luna che reca la data del 13 novembre 1500 (HR 13202 = V₃). Della prima è unicamente noto l'esemplare della Biblioteca Nazionale di Napoli (IGI 7938).[9] La stampa è in 4° e si compone di 50 carte segnate a⁸ b⁶ c⁸ d⁶ e⁸ f–g⁶ (a1, g6 bianche). Si può incidentalmente notare che l'ordine in cui si segue il testo nel fascicolo f appare turbato: ciò che dovrebbe leggersi a pagina f1ᵛ si trova a pagina f5ᵛ e viceversa; così come ciò che dovrebbe seguire a pagina f2ʳ è da cercarsi a pagina f6ʳ e viceversa. Causa dello spostamento non è un errore d'imposizione, ma propriamente un errore di stampa: la forma interna del foglio esterno del fascicolo, debitamente composta [vedi tav. 1], venne fissata capovolta al torchio. Prova ne sia che pagina f6ʳ porta la segnatura f2. Dell'edizione di Ottino de Luna si conservano esemplari nella Biblioteca Comunale Augusta di Perugia (IGI 7939), nella BnF (CIBN P-530) e nella Pierpont Morgan Library (Goff Suppl. P-872a).[10] Essa è pure in 4° e si compone di 42 carte segnate a–d⁸ e⁶ f⁴ (a1 bianca). Una terza edizione veneziana (H 13201 = V₂) sopravvive oggi in un unico esemplare in una raccolta privata: senza note tipografiche, è assegnata dubitativamente a Matteo Capcasa in una scheda provvisoria del GW.[11] È anch'essa in 4°

---

[7] Si veda tuttavia CIRIELLI (vedi nota 2).

[8] Ciò è noto grazie ad una lista di alcuni dei suoi libri redatta da Leonardo durante il soggiorno milanese attorno al 1495. Cfr. CARLO VECCE: *Leonardo*. Roma 1998, p. 158.

[9] L'esemplare, recante segnatura S.Q. VIII. B. 44, è privo di c. g1.

[10] Si tratta dell'esemplare Murray. Cfr. *Catalogo dei libri posseduti da Charles Fairfax Murray*. Londra [ma Roma] 1899, t. I, n° 1567. Non sembra da identificare coll'esemplare appartenuto a Guglielmo Libri, descritto in una legatura di Bauzonnet: cfr. *Catalogue de la bibliothèque de M. L****. Paris 1847, n° 2208.

[11] Accessibile in linea (GW online). Non avendo potuto esaminare il libro se non attraverso una riproduzione (che nemmeno mi ha permesso di misurare il carattere), non mi posso esprimere sull'assegnazione tipografica.

e conta 36 carte segnate a–d⁸ e⁴ (a1, e4 bianche). Una sola edizione si conosce non prodotta a Venezia: senza note, Giuseppe Martini seppe correttamente assegnarla all'officina milanese di Cristoforo Valdarfer attorno al 1483 (H 13200 = M). In 4°, è composta da 48 carte segnate a–f⁸. Di questa si conservano due esemplari: uno a Bryn Mawr (Goff P-866), proveniente da Phyllis Gordan,[12] e l'esemplare Hibbert, tuttora in mano privata.[13]

Va fatto qui luogo ad alcune considerazioni conseguenti al raffronto del testo in M, V_1 e V_2. Per cominciare sia detto che V_2 condivide tutti gli errori e le interpolazioni di V_1, cui ne aggiunge di proprî: non par dubbio che ne discenda. In particolare, V_2 segue V_1 anche in errori manifesti e rimediabilissimi, che in V_1 hanno natura di refusi (per esempio *cuartione* per *curatione* nella facezia 128 – numerata 126 in MV_1V_2 – o *nauscante* per *nauseante* nella facezia 149 – numerata 147 in MV_1V_2). Una prova della discendenza di V_2 da V_1 si ha nella facezia 16 (numerata 15 in MV_1V_2): M legge *gli vitiosi costumi de la corte*, come sostanzialmente anche V_1, con lezione che aderisce al latino (*curiae vitia*). Diversamente V_2: *gli vici o li costumi de la corte*. Se si guarda da presso V_1, si può osservare che la parola *viciosi* è spezzata *vici osi* (c. a7ʳ, l. 6): ciò che dà bene conto dell'errore in V_2. Simile caso si ha nella facezia 88 (numerata 87 in MV_1V_2): M legge *schifare tal spesa*, V_2 *schifare ala spesa*, che è la forma innovata, cioè erronea (*eam impensam vitaret*); guardando a V_1 si trova *schifare al spesa* e la spaziatura suggerisce che appunto la *t* di *tal* sia caduta nella stampa (c. d2ʳ, l. 26). Nella facezia 139 (numerata 137 in MV_1V_2), a *piacevole homo* MV_1 si oppone *piacevole bon* V_2: in V_1 si ha l'abbreviazione *hō* (c. f6ʳ, l. 17; nel carattere impiegato a stampare V_1 la *h* si connota per una pancia pressoché chiusa che facilmente può portarla a essere scambiata nella lettura con una *b*).

M e V_1 sono bensì reciprocamente indipendenti. Che M non dipenda dalla stampa veneziana è provato da parecchi errori di V_1 difficilmente emendabili per congettura, alcuni dei quali neppure ravvisabili in quanto errori. Ad esempio nella facezia 146 (numerata 144 in MV_1V_2): *non ossando mutare li nomi* M *non essendo mutati li nomi* V_1V_2, ambedue le frasi di per sé accettabili nel testo (ma in Poggio: *cum non auderent nomina immutare*). Similmente nella facezia 153 (numerata 151 in MV_1V_2), V_1, seguito da V_2, legge *questo vase puza molto: mai non meterò il mio vino cossì gentile in questo vase – a quello che t'à mandato reportalo*. La frase ha perfettamente senso, ma è M a portare la lezione incorrotta: *questo vaso puza molto: mai non metterò il mio vino così gentile in questo. Vane a quello che t'ha mandato e reportalo* (*vas istud admodum foetet: numquam in hoc vinum meum infundam. Vade atque ad eum qui te misit istud reporta*). Decisive, ad ogni buon conto, sono le lacune. Ad esempio nella facezia 129 (numerata 127 in MV_1V_2): *diceme che io me dia al ocio* V_1V_2 contro *diceme che io voglia stare nel calore del lecto e che io me dia al ocio* M, ciò che in V_1 viene tralasciato si trova già in Poggio (*in calore lecti permanendum*). Nella facezia 141 (numerata 139 in MV_1V_2), M reca *poscia questionando uno fiorentino et un venitiano de questa cosa insieme e dicendo il venitiano «voi...»* (*Florentino Venetoque postmodum de hac re disceptantibus, cum Venetus diceret «nobis...»*); in V_1V_2 si legge: *poscia questionando uno fiorentino e uno venitiano «voi...»*.

---

12 Appartenuto a Renouard, Heber, Marchetti. Cfr. A.-A. RENOUARD: *Catalogue de la bibliothèque d'un amateur*. Paris 1819, t. III, p. 164. – *Catalogue of the Library of the Late Richard Heber, Esq., Part the Seventh, Removed from his House at Pimlico*. London 1835, n° 4874. – GIUSEPPE MARCHETTI: *La parte migliore de' miei libri*. Torino 1875, t. I, n° 428. – *Catalogue of the Rich Italian Library of the Late J. Marchetti Esq. of Turin*. London 1876, n° 87. – BERNARD QUARITCH: *Catalogue of Romances of Chivalry; Novels, Tales, Allegorical Romances*. N° 342. London 1882, n° 7748.

13 Appartenne a Martini che lo descrisse nel catalogo dei proprî incunaboli. Cfr. *A Catalogue of the Library of George Hibbert, Esq. of Portland Place*. London 1829, n° 6479. – *Catalogo della libreria di Giuseppe Martini compilato dal possessore. Parte prima: incunabuli*. Milano 1934, n° 85. Sbaglia Martini – insolitamente – nell'indicare un esemplare nella BSB, dove si conservano bensì due copie dell'edizione latina dovuta allo stesso Valdarfer H 13189 (BSB-Ink B-783). Egli ha bensì ragione di notare che l'edizione è «descritta due volte da Brunet e dal Passano come due differenti edizioni». Cfr. JACQUES-CHARLES BRUNET: *Manuel du libraire et de l'amateur de livres*. Paris 1843, t. III, p. 795 – GIAMBATTISTA PASSANO: *I novellieri italiani in prosa*. Milano 1864, pp. 350/1. – BRUNET e PASSANO citano prima V_2, asserendo esserne stato venduto un esemplare all'asta Hibbert per 4 sterline e 5 scellini – ciò che è falso: Hibbert possedeva solo M, venduto appunto a quel prezzo; citano poi M, di cui conoscono l'esemplare Hibbert (venduto, dicono, per 4 sterline e 4 scellini); citano nuovamente M come edizione differente, infine V_3. La falsa notizia sui prezzi della vendita Hibbert deriva probabilmente da BARTOLOMMEO GAMBA: *Delle novelle italiane in prosa – Bibliografia. Edizione seconda*. Firenze 1835, p. 72. La confusione che caratterizza le compilazioni di BRUNET e PASSANO si trasferisce in GIUSEPPE PITRÈ: *Bibliografia delle tradizioni popolari d'Italia*. Torino, Palermo 1914. Per chiarezza si può dunque porre:
V_1 = Pitrè 784;
V_2 = Pitrè 782;
V_3 = Pitrè 786;
M = Pitrè 783 = 785.

All'inverso, altri guasti, anch'essi dovuti a *sauts du même au même*, sono riscontrabili in M. Nella facezia 95 (numerata 93 in M, 94 in V_1V_2), V_1 legge *voleva martitare una sua figlia ad uno giovene del castello; al giovene parea fosse tropo fanciulla e di tenera etate* (*cupiebat ... desponsare uni ex vicinis iuvenem filiam. Quam ille conspicatus ut cum nimium teneram et adolescentiorem respueret*). Così M: *el quale volea maritare una sua figlia ad uno giovene parea fosse tropo fanciula e di tenera etate*. Altro caso nella facezia 128 (numerata 126 in MV_1V_2). Dove V_1V_2 leggono *Rispose: è uno cavallo e sì 'l tengo per andare a caciare. Poscia dixe: questo che tu tieni in mano come se domanda et a quale cosa l'usi tu? Rispose: egli è uno sparavero*, M reca *Rispose: egli è uno sparavero*. Chi vorrà ricostruire il testo della traduzione volgare potrà dunque dispensarsi dal ricorrere a V_2, ma avrà bisogno sia di M sia di V_1.

M si caratterizza, rispetto alle stampe veneziane, per qualche dialettismo fonetico (ad es. *giaramente* «chiaramente»). Soprattutto da segnalare è l'occorrenza, per due volte, nella facezia 135 (irregolarmente numerata 133 in MV_1V_2), della parola *scarmassa* (contro *carogna* di V_1V_2). La parola deve un suo particolare prestigio al fatto di essere stata registrata da Leonardo nel codice Trivulziano (p. 81 della paginazione più recente). È cosa da tempo accertato che i vocaboli confluiti nelle liste lessicali di Leonardo venivano da lui raccolti nella lettura.[14] Ora *scarmassa* è voce a tal punto rara (irreperibile, c'è da ritenere, in altri testi a stampa), da permettere d'identificare in M l'edizione delle *Facezie* posseduta da Leonardo. È a Milano, d'altronde, sul finire del nono decennio del secolo, ch'egli allestiva nel codice Trivulziano – operando sui libri che soleva leggere –[15] il suo primo spoglio lessicale; l'edizione di Valdarfer era uscita nella stessa città pochi anni prima.[16]

---

14 Cfr. ORNELLA OLIVIERI: Gli elenchi di voci volgari nei codici di Leonardo da Vinci. In: *Lingua nostra*. III (1941), pp. 29–32. – AUGUSTO MARINONI: Leonardo: «Libro di mia vocaboli». In: *Studi in onore di Alberto Chiari*. Brescia 1973, t. II, pp. 751–66.

15 Cfr. VECCE (vedi nota 8), p. 100: «I testi spogliati sono semplicemente quelli che si trovano sullo scrittoio di Leonardo in quegli anni, non sono frutto di una scelta meditata».

16 Lo stesso Valdarfer aveva dato fuori nel 1483 il *Novellino* di Masuccio (HC 10885), cui le compilazioni lessicali di Leonardo sono largamente debitrici: cfr. GIOVANNI PONTE: Una fonte lessicale vinciana: il *Novellino* di Masuccio Salernitano. In: *Esperienze letterarie*. I (1976), pp. 62–72. Spunti riguardo alla congenialità del *Novellino* ai gusti di Leonardo mi pare si possano trarre da FRANCESCO D'EPISCOPO: Il motto di Masuccio. In: *Quaderni di retorica e poetica*. II (1986), pp. 41–9.

ANETTE LÖFFLER

Neue Fragmente mit der Postilla des Nikolaus von Lyra aus dem Duisburger Stadtarchiv

DIE *POSTILLA SUPER TOTAM BIBLIAM* des Nikolaus von Lyra mit den Auslegungen des Guillelmus Britonis und den Zusätzen des Paulus Burgensis sowie den Korrekturen des Matthias Doering ist ein während des gesamten Mittelalters recht häufig anzutreffender Text. Trotz des großen Umfangs des Werkes existieren heute eine Vielzahl an Handschriften und Drucken. Auch als Inkunabel erfreute sich die *Postilla super totam bibliam* großer Beliebtheit. Insgesamt fünf Ausgaben gab es alleine bis 1500. Ferner existieren aber weitere Exemplare unter dem Titel *Biblia latina*, welche im Unterschied zur *Postilla super totam bibliam* nach dem eigentlichen Textende einen weiteren Druck *Contra perfidium Judaeorum* angehängt haben. Von dieser *Biblia latina* gibt es acht Druckausgaben mit sehr vielen heute überlieferten Exemplaren.[1]

Der älteste Druck der *Postilla super totam bibliam* wurde nicht nach 1472 in der Offizin von Johannes Mentelin in Straßburg hergestellt.[2] Nach den Angaben im ISTC sind hiervon heute 84 mehr oder weniger komplette Exemplare bekannt. Die nächstjüngere Ausgabe entstand zwischen 1474 und 1477 beim Drucker des Henricus Arminensis, ebenfalls in Straßburg.[3] Hier beherbergen 77 Bibliotheken oder vergleichbare Institutionen weltweit ein Exemplar oder zumindest Teile davon. Ein dritter Druck erschien 1481 bei Anton Koberger in Nürnberg;[4] hiervon sind 122 Exemplare erhalten. Zum vierten Mal wurde die *Postilla* nicht nach 1483 bei Ulrich Zell in Köln gedruckt.[5] In 75 Institutionen hat der ISTC Exemplare nachgewiesen. Der letzte Druck entstand in Basel 1494 in der Werkstatt von Johann Petri und Johann Froben.[6] Dieser Druck ist am seltensten, denn lediglich zwei Exemplare in der De Paul Library der University of St. Mary in Leavenworth (Kansas/USA) sowie in der Friedsam Memorial Library der St. Bonaventure University in St. Bonaventure (New York/USA) sind heute bekannt.

Während der Bearbeitung der mittelalterlichen und frühneuzeitlichen Makulatur-Sammlung des Stadtarchivs Duisburg fanden sich zwölf Blatt-Teile, welche inhaltlich prinzipiell als das oben genannte Werk der *Postilla super totam bibliam* des Nikolaus von Lyra identifiziert werden konnten. Schwieriger gestaltete sich eine genaue Zuordnung zu einer konkreten Ausgabe mit entsprechendem Drucker, Druckort und Offizin.

Wie bereits erwähnt gibt es fünf Inkunabel-Auflagen der Postilla. Nach Augenschein des Druckbildes kam primär die vierte Ausgabe aus der Kölner Offizin von Ulrich Zell, nicht nach 1483, in Frage. Da es sich bei den Duisburger Fragmenten um Teile der Apokalypse mit den Additiones handelte, schien eine Suche im ISTC zur Verifizierung der Werk-

[1] ISTC ib00612000, ib00613000, ib00614000, ib00615000, ib00616000, ib00617000, ib00618000 und ib00619000.
[2] ISTC in00133000.
[3] ISTC in00134000.
[4] ISTC in00135000.
[5] ISTC in00136000.
[6] ISTC in00137000.

statt relativ einfach zu sein, denn bei der Apokalypse gilt die Suche nach dem Ende des Textes.

Mehrheitlich war der voluminöse Druck in vier Bänden angelegt. Auf der Grundlage der Überlieferung dieses Druckes in deutschen Bibliotheken und Museen schieden die Bände mit einer Teilüberlieferung von Band 1 bis 3 zum Textvergleich von vornherein aus. Dies waren laut den Angaben im ISTC die Staatliche Bibliothek Amberg (Bd. 1), die Kunstbibliothek der Staatlichen Museen zu Berlin (Bd. 1), die Universitäts- und Landesbibliothek Bonn (Bde. 1 bis 3), die Universitäts- und Landesbibliothek Düsseldorf (Bd. 3, unvollständig), die Landesbibliothek Eutin (zwei Blätter), das Buchmuseum der Deutschen Bücherei Leipzig (Bd. 2, unvollständig), die Diözesanbibliothek Limburg (Bd. 2), das Gutenberg-Museum Mainz (ein Blatt), die Bayerische Staatsbibliothek München (ein Blatt von Bd. 2), die Alte Kapelle Regensburg (Bd. 2, unvollständig), die Württembergische Landesbibliothek Stuttgart (Bd. 2, unvollständig) und die Universitätsbibliothek Würzburg (Bd. 2, unvollständig).

Unvollständige Exemplare ohne Kenntnisse der Bandangaben sollten in der Universitätsbibliothek Greifswald,[7] der Stadtbibliothek Soest und der Ratsschulbibliothek Zwickau vorhanden sein. Teilüberlieferungen mit Band 4 gab es angeblich in der Bibliothek des Nikolaus-Hospitals Bernkastel-Kues (Bde. 3 und 4), der Universitäts- und Stadtbibliothek Köln (Bde. 3 und 4) und der Universitäts- und Landesbibliothek Münster (4 Bde.).

Laut ISTC waren komplette Ausgaben aller vier Bände schließlich in der Gymnasialbibliothek St. Michael Bad Münstereifel, der Staatsbibliothek Preußischer Kulturbesitz Berlin, der St. Albert-Bibliothek Bornheim-Walberberg, der Stadt- und Universitätsbibliothek Frankfurt, der Gaesdonck-Bibliothek Goch, der Staatsbibliothek Regensburg, der Stadtbibliothek Trier, der Stadtbibliothek Worms, der Diözesanbibliothek Köln sowie der Hessischen Landesbibliothek Wiesbaden zu erwarten.

In 15 Bibliotheken einschließlich der drei Institutionen ohne Angaben der Bände war der vierte Band demnach nicht vorhanden. Drei Bibliotheken besaßen ihn vielleicht, zehn Bibliotheken sicher. Sollte die Zuordnung der Fragmente zu dieser Werkstatt zutreffend sein, wären diese Stücke eine willkommene Bereicherung der insgesamt als überraschend selten heute noch vorhandenen Apokalypse zu werten.

Die Recherchen nach einer Bibliothek mit der Inkunabel des Nikolaus von Lyra, um einen Textabgleich vornehmen zu können, gestalteten sich jedoch überraschend, was das Vorhandensein dieser Inkunabel mit ihrem Band 4,2 anbelangt. Aus der Gruppe der Bibliotheken mit Teilüberlieferung ergab sich, dass die Württembergische Landesbibliothek Stuttgart sogar zwei Exemplare des Druckes besaß, beide jedoch unvollständig und teilweise ohne Band 4.[8] Ein Exemplar umfasst jedoch die Apokalypse, wenngleich nicht vollständig.

In der Bibliothek des Cusanus-Stifts in Bernkastel-Kues finden sich zwei Bände, wobei der letzte Band die Apokalypse umfasst. Allerdings scheinen die Cusaner Bände ehedem in mindestens drei Bänden gebunden worden zu sein, von denen heute mutmaßlich der mittlere fehlt.[9] Die

---

7 In der UB Greifswald sind lediglich Teile von Band 4 unter der Signatur BW 198 (B Wolgast) vorhanden laut freundlicher Mitteilung von Ivo Asmus, UB Greifswald, 14./15. 2. 2011. Siehe auch THOMAS WILHELMI: *Inkunabeln in Greifswalder Bibliotheken. Verzeichnis der Bestände der Universitätsbibliothek Greifswald, der Bibliothek des Geistlichen Ministeriums und des Landesarchivs Greifswald*. Wiesbaden 1997, Nr. 451, S. 246.

8 Freundliche Mitteilung von Dr. Eberhard Zwink, Württembergische LB Stuttgart, 23. 10. 2009 und 23. 11. 2009. Die Ausgaben besitzen die Signaturen Inc. fol. 10368-1 sowie
Inc. fol. 10368 (HB)-1 bis
Inc. fol. 10368 (HB)-3 und
Inc. fol. 10368 (HB, 2)-1. Die Stuttgarter Inkunabeln sind online beschrieben (www.inka.uni-tuebingen.de).

9 JAKOB MARX: *Verzeichnis der Handschriften-Sammlung des Hospitals zu Cues bei Bernkastel a. Mosel*. Trier 1905, Nr. 9 und 10. Für die Auskünfte bezüglich der Bände danke ich Frau Gabriele Neusius, Bernkastel-Kues.

Universitäts- und Stadtbibliothek in Köln besitzt den dritten und vierten Band vollständig.[10] In der Universitäts- und Landesbibliothek Münster hingegen ist der vierte Band nicht vollständig, die Apokalypse fehlt.[11] Die Stadtbibliothek in Soest besitzt die gesuchte Ausgabe der Postilla des Nikolaus von Lyra, wie sie im ISTC aufgeführt wird, gar nicht.[12] Vielmehr lagern in den Soester Beständen jeweils zwei Bibeln mit Kommentaren des Nikolaus von Cues sowie die Ausgabe der Postilla aus dem Jahr 1481.[13] In der Ratsschulbibliothek in Zwickau wird nur Band 1 aufbewahrt.[14]

Unter den Bibliotheken, welche nach ISTC die vollständige Ausgabe besitzen, gab es ebenfalls Abweichungen. Aus der Stadtbibliothek Worms waren leider keine Angaben zu erhalten. Alle fünf Bände besitzen lediglich die Staatsbibliothek zu Berlin,[15] die Stadt- und Universitätsbibliothek Frankfurt,[16] die BSB München, die Staatsbibliothek in Regensburg sowie die Hessische Landesbibliothek in Wiesbaden.[17] Gleiches gilt für die Bibliothek des Michael-Gymnasiums in Bad Münstereifel, das eine vollständige Ausgabe sein Eigen nennt.[18] Die Bibliothek St. Albertus Magnus in Bornheim-Walberberg wird heute in der Erzbischöflichen Diözesan- und Dombibliothek Köln aufbewahrt. Hier sind neben den Bänden 1 und 3 beide Teile von Band 4 vorhanden.[19] In der Stadtbibliothek Trier hingegen ist der Druck des Ulrich Zell gar nicht präsent.[20] Die Diözesanbibliothek in Köln besitzt den vierten Band, aber ohne Apokalypse. Die Klosterbibliothek des Collegium Augustinianum Gaesdonck in Goch ist derzeit wegen ihrer Katalogisierung ausgelagert, so dass nähere Angaben momentan noch nicht möglich sind.[21] Somit bleiben sieben Bibliotheken in Deutschland, die den gesuchten Text überhaupt aufweisen.

Ein Textabgleich mit der Inkunabel in der Stadt- und Universitätsbibliothek Frankfurt bestätigte die Vermutung, es handelte sich bei den Duisburger Fragmenten um Erzeugnisse aus der Werkstatt des Ulrich Zell. Die Fragmente umfassen den ursprünglichen Quinio am Textende, die Lagen J ii bis J iiii. Das äußere Doppelblatt J i sowie das innerste J v fehlen. Die einzelnen Blätter wurden horizontal zerschnitten, dabei gab es einen geringen Textverlust. Deshalb ist jedes Blatt mit zwei Fragmenten vertreten. Der Text setzt am Ende von Kapitel 21 ein und umfasst Kapitel 22 sowie die Additiones zur Apokalypse.

Auf Blatt J iii ist die Bleistiftsignatur *104* zu erkennen. Mit dieser Signatur wurden alle Fragmente versehen, die in den 1970er Jahren aus der Stadtrechnung von 1572/73 abgelöst worden waren. Neben den Inkunabelfragmenten des Nikolaus de Lyra waren dies weiterhin mehrere Blätter mit Schreibübungen (Katalognr. 69), ein Blatt aus einem Graduale (Katalognr. 24) und aus einer Missale-Handschrift (Katalognr. 11), ein Blatt aus einem Canon Missae (Katalognr. 10), ein kleines Stück aus einem Kollektar (Katalognr. 28) sowie ein kleiner Rest eines Briefes (Katalognr. 66).[22] Woher diese Inkunabel- und Handschriftenfragmente stammen, lässt sich nicht mehr feststellen. Selbst die Frage, ob diese aus der Stadtrechnung von 1572/73 abgelösten Fragmente als ehemals komplette Handschriften beziehungsweise Inkunabeln überhaupt ursprünglich in derselben Bibliothek aufbewahrt worden waren, kann nicht mehr beantwortet werden. Bis auf das Graduale-Fragment (Nr. 24), das in Frankreich ent-

[10] Freundliche Mitteilung von Irene Bischoff, UuStB Köln, 2. 10. 2009. Die Signatur lautet Ennen 49 und 50.
[11] Freundliche Mitteilung von Reinhard Feldmann, UuLB Münster, 5. 8. 2009.
[12] Freundliche Mitteilung von Dirk Elbert, Stadt Soest, 30. 9. und 11. 11. 2009.
[13] Die Inkunabel 8 entspricht dem Druck Anton Kobergers von 1481. Die beiden Bibeln mit den Soester Signaturen Inkunabel 47 und 69 sind im ISTC mit dem Sigle ib00613000 nachgewiesen.
[14] Diese Angaben beziehen sich auf HOLGER NICKEL: *Die Inkunabeln der Ratsschulbibliothek Zwickau. Entstehung, Geschichte der Sammlung und Bestand.* Diss. phil. HU Berlin 1976, S. 61, Nr. 350.
[15] Freundliche Mitteilung von Sandra Lubinski, SB Berlin/GW, 1. 10. 2009.
[16] Freundliche Mitteilung von Dr. Bernhard Tönnies, 9. 9. 2009. Siehe auch Inkunabelkatalog der Stadt- und Universitätsbibliothek Frankfurt und anderer öffentlicher Sammlungen in Frankfurt. Bearb. von KURT OHLY und VERA SACK. Frankfurt a. M. 1967 (*Kataloge der SUB Frankfurt.* 1), Nr. 2108, S. 388, mit der Signatur Inc. qu 662.
[17] Freundliche Mitteilung von Dr. Martin Mayer, Hessische LB Wiesbaden, 30. 9. 2009 sowie von Dr. Bernhard Lübbers, Staatl. B Regensburg, 30. 9. 2009.
[18] Vgl. HEINZ SIGEL: *Katalog der ehemaligen Jesuiten-Kollegbibliothek in Münstereifel.* Bad Münstereifel 1960, S. 16, Nr. 37.
[19] Freundliche Mitteilung von Dipl.-Theol. Harald Horst, Köln, 30. 9. 2009.
[20] Freundliche Mitteilung von Dr. Reiner Nolden, StB Trier, 1. 10. 2009.
[21] Freundliche Mitteilung von Schuldirektor H.-G. Steiffert, Bistum Münster, 30. 9. 2009. Frühestens für Frühsommer 2010 war die Rücklagerung der Bibliothek anberaumt.
[22] Die folgenden Nummern beziehen sich auf den Katalog der abgelösten und in-situ-Handschriften- und Druckfragmente im StArch. Duisburg. Er soll in der Reihe Duisburger Forschungen erscheinen.

standen ist, weisen die anderen eine Provenienz aus dem deutschen Sprachgebiet auf.

Der für die Stadt Duisburg arbeitende Buchbinder verwendete für die Stadtrechnungen recht umfangreiches Handschriften- und Druckmaterial. Abgelöste Makulatur ist in Duisburg weiterhin von den Stadtrechnungen der Jahre 1566/67,[23] 1574[24] sowie 1574/75[25] vorhanden.

Inzwischen ist im Duisburger Bestand noch ein weiteres Fragment aus dieser Inkunabel aufgetaucht. Hier handelt es sich um ein Einzelblatt aus dem zweiten Brief an die Korinther, mit dem Ende des achten und dem Beginn des neunten Kapitels.[26] Herausgelöst wurde das Blatt aus dem Erbbriefbuch aus der Zeit von 1572–76.[27] Damit dürfte kaum noch ein Zweifel daran bestehen, dass dem Buchbinder große Teile beziehungsweise der gesamte letzte Inkunabelband der *Postilla* vorgelegen haben dürfte, denn die Korinther-Briefe befinden sich im ersten Drittel des Bandes. Außerdem bedeutet dies aufgrund der Laufzeit des Erbbriefbuchs bis 1576, dass die Fragmente nicht vor diesem Zeitpunkt eingebunden worden sein konnten.

Bei dem Fund von 12 dieser 13 Fragmente handelt es sich um eine willkommene Bereicherung für den Apokalypse-Teil der *Postilla* des Nikolaus de Lyra. Alle 13 Fragmente zusammen erweitern unsere Kenntnisse von diesem fünften Teilband der *Postilla* beträchtlich.

---

[23] Katalognummern 1, 43 und 50.
[24] Katalognummer 51.
[25] Katalognummern 6, 13–5, 21, 30, 33, 39/40, 46, 48, 59/60, 67 und 69.
[26] Verglichen wiederum mit UuLB Frankfurt, Inc.qu 662, Druckbogen h^v.
[27] Die heutige Signatur des Bandes lautet Best. 10A/254.

HANS-WALTER STORK

»Hir hefft an dat Landrecht aver Ditmarschen.«
Neue Fragmente des gedruckten Dithmarscher Landrechts
(Lübeck: Steffen Arndes, 1487/88)

EIN VOLLSTÄNDIGES EXEMPLAR des 1487 von Steffen Arndes in Lübeck gedruckten Dithmarscher Landrechts[1] suchen die Landes- und Rechtshistoriker seit Jahrhunderten. Auch dieser Beitrag kann nicht mit der Fundmeldung eines vollständigen Exemplars aufwarten, aber wenigstens mit der Entdeckung weiterer acht Textseiten aus der seltenen Inkunabel [Abb. 1–4].

Die Inkunabelblätter befinden sich als vorderer und hinterer Vorsatz in einer im Jahr 2010 durch eine Edition vorgestellten Musikhandschrift der Staats- und Universitätsbibliothek Hamburg.[2] Die Handschrift ND VI 471 ist ein Antiphonar mit einem jeweils vollständigen Marien- und Annen-Offizium, das in den Jahren um 1470 für den Hamburger Dom entstand und nur in dieser einen Ausfertigung erhalten geblieben ist. Die Provenienz der Handschrift aus dem Hamburger Dom ist gesichert; eine Eintragung auf dem vorderen Vorsatzblatt [siehe Abb. 2 und 9] besagt: »Missale membranaceum, ad usum Ecclesiae Cathedral : (is) Hamburgens : (is) cum lit . (eris) initiali deaurata complectens Folia 19.« Wann diese Eintragung vorgenommen wurde, ist nicht mehr festzustellen; von der Schrift her wird sie aus dem 18. Jahrhundert stammen. Sie erlaubt aber, über die Provenienzzuweisung hinaus, die Handschrift in dem Versteigerungskatalog der Hamburger Dombibliothek vom 18. Oktober 1784 zu verifizieren. Dort ist sie als Nr. 6 in der Gruppe der »Codices membranaceos et manuscriptos« aufgeführt.[3] Nächster Besitzer der Musikhandschrift war die Gräflich Stolbergsche Bibliothek in Wernigerode; der genaue Zeitpunkt, wann das Manuskript in die Stolbergsche Sammlung kam, kann nicht bestimmt werden, möglicherweise direkt aus Anlass der Hamburger Auktion, möglicherweise erst später. Jedenfalls wird die Musikhandschrift unter jenen Büchern aufgelistet, die ab 1928 durch den Berliner Antiquar Martin Breslauer aus der Stolbergschen Bibliothek zum Verkauf angeboten wurden. Unter der Wernigeroder Bibliothekssignatur Za 68 wird angezeigt ein »Missale, 19 Blätter in Gross-Folio. Pergament, zum Gebrauch in der Hauptkirche in Hamburg«. Der Band erregte nun doch das Interesse der Hamburger Bibliothekare; im Verlauf des Jahres 1931 erwarb man ihn und akzessionierte ihn unter der Nummer [19]31. 1865.[4]

Bislang war es nur die Provenienzeintragung auf dem vorderen Inkunabelblatt, der Beachtung geschenkt wurde. Die eigentliche Bedeutung der Inkunabelblätter erschloss sich erst bei der Vorbereitung der Edition.

Frau Dr. Klara Erdei, UB Kiel, danke ich für die Publikationserlaubnis der Kieler Blätter.

1 Zum Dithmarscher Landrecht vgl. ULRICH-DIETER OPPITZ: Dithmarscher Landrecht. In: *Verfasserlexikon*. 2. Aufl. Bd. 11. Berlin 2002, Sp. 370–2.

2 *Das Hamburger Antiphonar* ND VI 471. *Ein wiederentdecktes Musikdenkmal des 15. Jahrhunderts aus dem Hamburger Dom. Einführung, Edition und Faksimile.* Bearbeitet von VIACHESLAV KARTSOVNIK (†). Hrsg. von JÜRGEN NEUBACHER. Wiesbaden 2010. Darin: HANS-WALTER STORK: Die Antiphonarhandschrift ND VI 471. Bemerkungen zu ihrer Geschichte und Kodikologie, S. 19–30, zu den Inkunabelblättern S. 23–6 (Text und Abbildungen).

3 Abb. der entsprechenden Seite des Versteigerungskataloges bei STORK (siehe Anm. 2), Abb. 1.

4 Die Akzessionsnummer ist noch heute auf dem ersten Blatt zu sehen. Im Akzessionsjournal ist die neu erworbene Handschrift kurz beschrieben und auch das erste handschriftliche Blatt vor dem eigentlichen Beginn des Marienhymnus verzeichnet; die Inkunabelblätter werden nicht erwähnt.

Der Buchbinder, dem wir den gediegenen Ledereinband über Holzdeckeln des Musikmanuskripts verdanken, klebte als Verbindung zwischen Buchblock und Deckel die beiden hier vorzustellenden Blätter aus der seltenen Lübecker Inkunabel ein.[5] Es handelt sich jeweils um ein Doppelblatt, das aufgefaltet (und damit um 45° zur Leserichtung gedreht) eingeklebt wurde; das für die Transkription wichtige Verhältnis von Vorder- und Rückseiten bzw. das der beiden Doppelseiten zueinander zeigen die jeweils zusammengestellten Vorder- und Rückseiten [Abb. 1–4].

Ursprünglich waren die Seiten fest auf die Holzdeckel aufgeklebt. Nachdem ihre Bedeutung feststand, entschloss man sich dazu, die Seiten abzulösen, um auch die Rückseiten lesen zu können. Wie die zuvor angefertigten Fotos belegen, waren die als Spiegel verwendeten, etwas zu kleinen Seiten gerissen, da das Holz der Deckel arbeitete, und an einigen Stellen lösten sich die Blätter bereits vom Holz.[6]

Zum Vorschein kamen insgesamt acht Seiten des Dithmarscher Landrecht-Drucks aus der Offizin des zunächst in Schleswig, dann in Lübeck tätigen Druckers Steffen Arndes (um 1450 Hamburg – 1519 Lübeck),[7] den dieser in den Jahren 1487/88 vorlegte. Von diesem Druck hat sich kein einziges vollständiges Exemplar erhalten; die der Frühdruckausgabe folgende Ausgabe des Dithmarscher Landrechts erschien im Jahr 1539 bei Johann Balhorn dem Älteren in Lübeck.[8] Die Editionen von Arndes und Balhorn führen die handschriftliche Überlieferung des Landrechts weiter, die in zwei zeitlich aufeinanderfolgenden Fassungen vorliegt. Die frühere – Codex I aus dem Kirchspielarchiv Büsum, jetzt im Dithmarscher Landesmuseum in Meldorf – ist 1447 datiert und weist Nachträge bis 1467 auf; die zweite – erhalten in mehreren Codices, von denen die Kieler Handschrift der Universitätsbibliothek Ms. 534 (394) die älteste ist – kodifiziert die Fassung von 1480 mit Zusätzen von 1483.[9]

Arndes legte also mit seinem bis auf die wenigen erhaltenen Blätter untergegangenen Druck die Fassung von 1480/83 vor, die auf der von 1447 fußte. Bis in die Jahre um 1840 kannte man aus dem Druck lediglich einige Textstellen, die der Hamburger Rechtsgelehrte Heinrich Giesebert (1604 – nach 1677), dem noch ein vollständiges Exemplar vorlag, in einem 1665 erschienenen Buch zitierte.[10] Giesebert nennt den Titel des Rechtsbuches: *Hir heff an dat Landrecht aver Ditmarschen / welcker upgenamen is mit Vulwort der Acht und vertig / und des gantzen Landes.*

Über diese Zitate Gieseberts waren die Meinungen geteilt. Johann Carl Henrich Dreyer bemerkt dazu in seinem Anhang »Von einigen seltenen gedruckten teutschen und nordischen Rechts- und Gesetz-Büchern« seiner 1783 vorgelegten *Beyträge zur Litteratur und Geschichte des Deutschen Rechts*:

> Die Landschaft Dithmarschen hatte [...] ihre alte Landes-Gewohnheiten [...] im Jahr 1447 in eine Sammlung gebracht. [...] Es soll aber davon ein, muthmaßlich im Jahr 1485 in folio geschehener Abdruck vorhanden seyn, der aber so selten ist, daß einige Gelehrte, die sich wegen der Kenntniß der Holsteinischen Litteratur vorzüglich ausgezeichnet, gezweifelt haben, ob er jemalen existiret, und ob nicht Henrich Giesebert, der dieses Abdruckes zuerst gedacht hat, der Nachwelt eine gute litterarische Legende aufgebürdet habe. Die Ehrlichkeit dieses alten Zupflegers, der zwar sonst in Hinsicht seiner höchstelenden Schmiererey

---

5 CONRAD BORCHLING / BRUNO CLAUSSEN: *Niederdeutsche Bibliographie. Gesamtverzeichnis der niederdeutschen Drucke bis zum Jahre 1800.* Neumünster 1931–36, Bd. 1: 1473–1600, Nr. 94. – KARL F. A. SCHELLER: *Bücherkunde der Sassisch-Niederdeutschen Sprache, hauptsächlich nach den Schriftdenkmälern der Herzoglichen Bibliothek zu Wolfenbüttel entworfen.* Braunschweig 1826, Nr. 416.

6 Die zwei Blätter wurden zunächst gelöst, dann neu verleimt, geglättet und auf neuen Fälzen wieder so an den ursprünglichen Stellen eingebunden, dass Vorder- und Rückseite lesbar bleiben. Der Restauratorin Frau Brigitte Hauswaldt sei für zahlreiche Hinweise zum Einband und den Fragmenten herzlich gedankt.

7 Zu Steffen Arndes vgl. zuletzt ALKEN BRUNS / DIETER LOHMEIER: *Die Lübecker Buchdrucker im 15. und 16. Jahrhundert. Buchdruck für den Ostseeraum.* Heide (Holstein) 1994, S. 69–71 (Literatur).

8 BORCHLING / CLAUSSEN (siehe Anm. 5), Nr. 1307. – Die Drucker Balhorn hatten keine glückliche Hand bei der Herausgabe von Gesetzestexten; der Ausdruck »verballhornen« kam – zu Recht oder Unrecht – in Folge eines schlecht redigierten Druckes des Lübecker Rechtes von 1586 auf, den Johann Balhorn der Jüngere vorlegte; vgl. HANS-BERND SPIES: »Verbessert durch Johann Balhorn«. Neues zu einer alten Redensart. In: *Zeitschrift des Vereins für lübeckische Geschichte und Altertumskunde.* 62 (1982), S. 285–92.

9 Auflistung der Handschriften – der erhaltenen wie der vermissten – bei OPPITZ (siehe Anm. 1).

10 HEINRICH GIESEBERT: *Periculum Secundum Harmoniae Practicae: Statutorum praecipuorum praesentium Magnae Germaniae & Antiqvorum Teutonum morum & ... aliarum Gentium Legum.* Hamburg: Pape, 1665, passim [benutztes Exemplar: SUB Hamburg, A/42937].

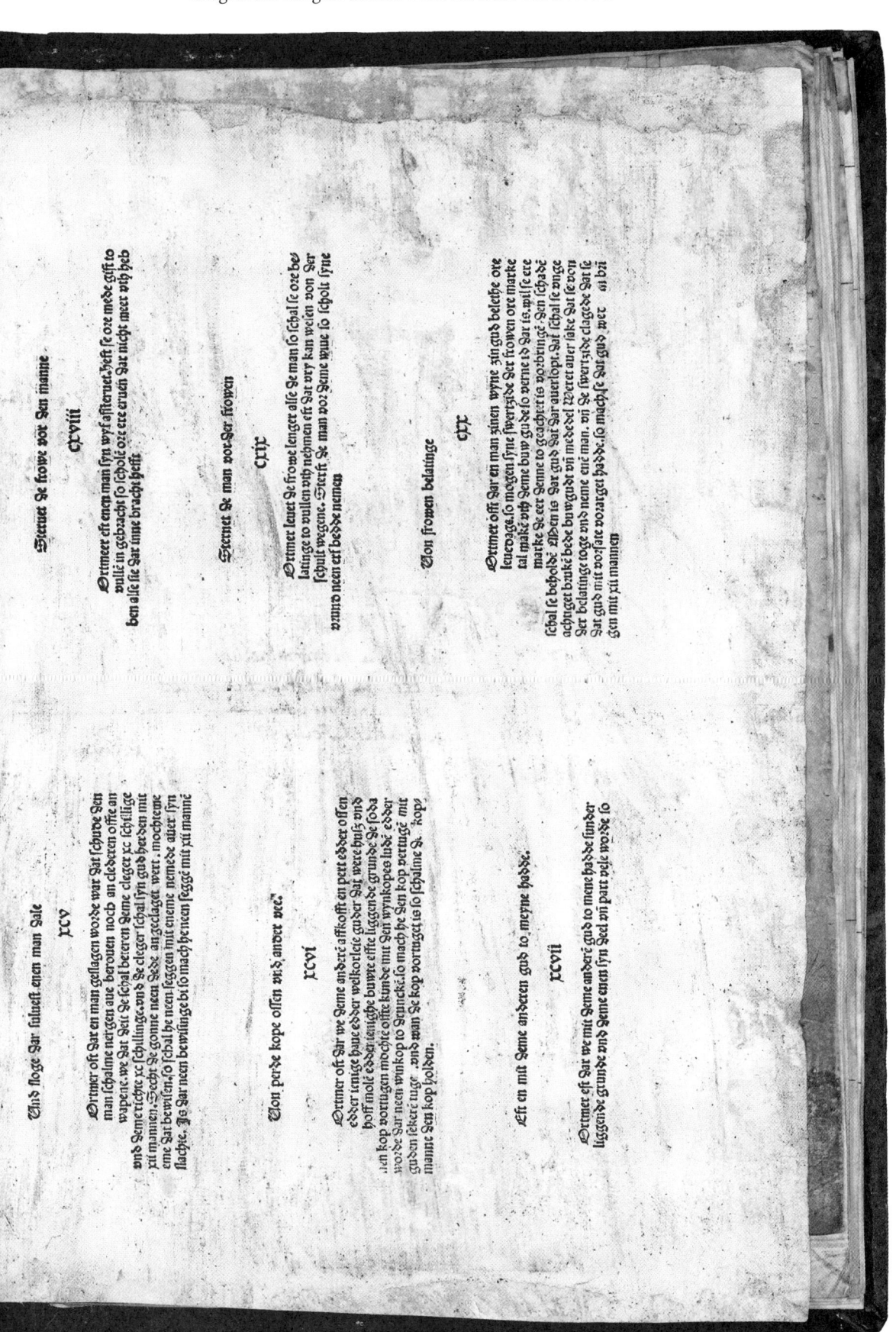

[Abb. 1–4] Hamburg, SuUB, Inkunabelblätter im Einband
der Musikhandschrift ND VI 471

Fol: 19.

Missale membranaceum
Dusum Ecclesiæ Cathedral: Hamburgens:
cum lit. initiali deaurata
complectens Folia 19.

ND VI, 471

cxv

Ortmer offt dar en man hadde enen fünbergē sone edder meer vnd de erigede na en wyf dar he ock enen sone me de hadde. storue de moder den vnd hadde se vryē acker so eruet se erē acker an erē sone Storue de sone hen so ar uet de sone den acker an den vader. wan de vader sterui be sen acker an syne sone Ofte de vader storue err de sone de me latere wue hadde bat, so sterui de sone den acker an de halue broder allyke wol so hyr vorschreuen steit

cxvi

Efft en man wil erigen de late syck nicht bedinge̅

Ortmer offt dar we erigede ene frowen edder iunckfrowē let he syck gelt aff bedingen in to zendende. Se zodane gelt bedinget vnde nympt de kerspel braken hebben xxx marck ie kert. dat richte an deme kerspel so man wanet de sodane gelt me lande dar richte.

cxvii

Neen bruth schal gaue vergen̅ in des brutmakers hus

Ortmer so schal neen frowe efte iunckfrowe gaue geuen dar se to des mannes huse gefamt wert by broke xxx lub. marken

cxxiiii

mach de ander dem is wede hort dar ene del mit deme anderen bescholde vnme so velc alle em en ander dar ōne geut wil dar bewillick is.

Sunte Oswaldus dach schalmen vyrē

xcviii

Ortmer so schal en ieweliek in vnsen lade sunte oswalds dach vyren by broke leistlich lub. marcken Und ock schal en iewelick in vnseme lande Sen eerliken erigedach in den nyen manen vaften vnd vyren beth tho mydbage vnd schal to syner horet ke ken in der bede missen wesen alle tact in allen to kamende maneten by broke iij lub.marck

Von acker kope

xcix

Ortmer dar we mē fromden synen acker vorkofte, so fin den wy de swertzyden neger kop also den vrōmeden. Se gōne de deme fromden den acker vorkoff vnde neme neger en wynich ac ker es an op dat de negesten nicht scholden neger kop wesen. konde se swertzyde deme vrōmeden koepmanne syne acker nicht vernogē mit gelde ofte anderen acker, so mach de swertzyde deme fromeden koep manne von deme salnen acker so vele af doen dat de neger kop to we sen vul also des clauert ackers belopen mach na gelde tale alle vier se ker man dorten bekant wesen. men de fromede kopman mach den ko repchūō to welker iszō he den acker afsneem wil

c

Ortmer offt dar we men fromden synen acker vorkofft, so fin...

Ortmer off de negeste sweertsyde beschulbet worde dat en de acker erst to kope haden were, so mach he to slan slist sorde vnd sweren dat de den acker so in al nicht kopē mochte, edder konde efte so na laten were allo de ander ene kost hadde, so mach he neger kop wesen. schal de gonne de den acker hest to slan sust sorde vnd mit den ... kopmanne vñ swere dat in sen vulgi dat oft kop so grot is sunder valsch vñ ... de ander weder kopē ...

Off der sweertsyden de acker worde erst to kope haden

De sweertsyde is neger kop alle des kopmās dochter

Ortmer ist en man syne acker efte verkopen wolde, so schal se sweertsyde neger kop wesen alle esyne egene dochter

Dere kost acker wise vñ quit lage banket hest

cij

Ortmer off dar en man hadde acker kost vñ he de acker hadde quit vnd wise siner bilpake vorst en iar edder teyne, so be ene behollen spricht dar na we vp so mach he dar by stan mit xii mannen

Ortmer est dar we siner dochter edder der soberen dochter acker mede lauede den schal se over rechte vort solgen laten vnd de he den ock siluū denken to siner lift vordinge, so schal se mede gist neine macht hebben

Est en man were vorumber ener iungkfrowe

cxiii

Ortmer oft dar en man siner dochter ofte suster efte ieniger inckfrow dat he vorumber auer were vn or acker mede geue vñ de acker or vn or maine na dele worde, so dolet or frumtneger kop wesen alle syne erste. ... syne frumtneger kop alse oz ... darso wesen allo hyr vorschreuen is est he oer mede geuen were

Est en man were vorumber ener iungkfrowe

cxiiij

Ortmer est en man hadde enen zone dat he nicht hadde als goedelet, vñ wisne zone ein wist vñ de zone stone den er he en afsodele, so mach de vader zene de sinen vsteren myt xij manně wes he sint sone besitt hadde, edder oz marke de schal allike wol hebbe allo veme se dar in gekome is mit erres mannes vnde willen

Est en man hadde vñ sunderge sone edder mer-mannen

über das neue Landrecht kein günstiges Vorurtheil vor sich hat, indessen doch als ein ehrlicher Mann allen Glauben verdienet, leistet aber für die Richtigkeit der Sache die Gewähr. Er beschreibet die Ausgabe; das Format; und die Aufschrift, und da auch Anton Vieth,[11] dem doch keine Urkunde seines Vaterlandes so leicht verborgen geblieben, ein zustimmendes Zeugniß abgegeben, so kann man wohl das Daseyn eines a.[nno] 1485 gedruckten Ditmarser Land-Rechts nicht weiter bezweifeln. Eben dieses Land-Recht ließ Wiehen Peters, ein in der Landes-Geschichte sehr bekannter Mann im Jahr 1539 unter der Rubrik: *Copia ut des Landesboken to Ditmarschen Recht lüdende und folgende von Artikul to Artikul nach sinen rechten Original gedruckt*[12] in 4. wieder auflegen.

Giesebert hatte einige Passagen der Landrechtsausgaben sehr kritisch kommentiert; darauf bezieht sich die Bemerkung Dreyers von der »höchstelenden Schmiererey«.

Die zwischen 1665 und 1783 bekannt gewordenen Erwähnungen des Dithmarscher Landrecht-Drucks beschränken sich auf bloße Nennungen der Inkunabelausgabe, so bei Johann Moller (1661–1725) in seiner *Isagoge ad historiam Ducatuum Slesvicensis & Holsatici* (Frankfurt/Hamburg 1691)[13] und bei dem schon von Dreyer herangezogenen Anton Vieth in dessen Geschichtswerk (Hamburg 1733), der, ausgehend von der ersten Kodifizierung im Jahre 1447 (wie sie in der Hs. I des Dithmarscher Museums in Morhof vorliegt) die Ergänzungen und Erweiterungen des Landrechts kurz nennt: »wie solche zum theil anführet die gedruckte Edition de Ao. 1485, so unter dem Titul heraus gekommen: Hier hefft an dat Land-Recht aver Dithmarschen, welcker upgenahmen is mit Vull Wort der der Acht und Veertig und des gantzen Landes.«[14]

Als im Jahre 1840 Johann Martin Lappenberg seine Geschichte der Hamburger Buchdruckerkunst[15] vorlegte, berichtete er von dem Fund zweier einseitig bedruckter Blätter durch »Professor Homeyer« im Einband eines Buches der Königlichen Bibliothek zu Berlin.[16] Obwohl Lappenberg keine näheren Angaben zu diesem Professor Homeyer macht, spricht viel dafür, dass es sich um Carl Gustav Homeyer (1795–1874) handelt, der damals an seiner Veröffentlichung *Die deutschen Rechtsbücher des Mittelalters und ihre Handschriften* arbeitete, die 1856 in Berlin erschien.[17]

Die Nachricht von den aufgefundenen originalen Inkunabelseiten wurde bereits 1842 von Andreas Ludwig Lacob Michelsen (1801–81) in dessen *Sammlung altdithmarscher Rechtsquellen* verwertet. Er sieht die Angaben von Giesebert aufs Schönste bestätigt und formuliert: »Das Reich der Hypothesen ist gestürzt« – die Annahme einer Inkunabelausgabe des Landrechts ist nicht länger hypothetisch, sondern beweisbar.[18]

Die Blätter, die Carl Gustav Homeyer 1840 auffand, wurden aus dem Berliner Band herausgelöst und der Königlichen Universitätsbibliothek Kiel zum Geschenk gemacht. Noch heute liegen den Inkunabelseiten ein Brief Johann Martin Lappenbergs und weitere diesbezügliche Korrespondenz bei. Erhalten sind [vgl. Abb. 5 und 6] die Reste eines vorder- und rückseitig bedruckten Blattes, das waagerecht zu den Druckzeilen in zwei annähernd gleichgroße Teile auseinandergetrennt ist; wie die Abbildung [Abb. 6] zeigt, hängen an dem unteren Teil der Vorderseite oben noch Reste eines beschriebenen Pergamentblattes an.

11 JOHAN CARL HENRICH DREYER: Von einigen seltenen gedruckten teutschen und nordischen Rechts- und Gesetz-Büchern. In: DERS.: *Beyträge zur Litteratur und Geschichte des Deutschen Rechts*. Lübeck 1783. Wortlaut der bei Dreyer gesetzten Anmerkung (Anm. 5): »Anton Vieth Beschreibung und Geschichte des Landes Dithmarschen, III. Th. c. 4, S. 157. Hrn. Christiani Geschichte der Herzogth. Schleswich und Holstein unter der Oldenburgischen Hoheit, I. Band S. 433. [...].«

12 Im Original nicht kursiv. Zum Druck »Dyth ys eyne Copia ⟨ut des Landesboken⟩« vgl. BORCHLING/CLAUSSEN (siehe Anm. 1 Nr. 1307 und VD 16 D 2089.

13 Bd. 3 des Sammelwerkes, S. 635: »An. 1485. autem luce publica, Typorum Beneficio, donatum.«

14 ANTON VIETH: Beschreibung und Geschichte des Landes Dithmarschen. Hamburg 1733, S. 157.

15 JOHANN MARTIN LAPPENBERG: *Zur Geschichte der Buchdruckerkunst in Hamburg am 24. Juni 1840*. Hamburg 1840, hier der »Anhang von einigen alten niedersächsischen Drucken«, S. 113–22, zum Dithmarscher Landrecht S. 115/6; mit Transkription der Artikel 187/8 der Vorderseite und 191, 194 und 196 der Rückseite.

16 »Herr Prof. Homeyer zu Berlin hat [...] kürzlich zwei Fragmente dieses Druckes auf einem Bücherdeckel entdeckt, welche er der Universitäts-Bibliothek zu Kiel bestimmt hat.«

17 Vgl. die bis heute gültige Neubearbeitung von CONRAD BORCHLING, KARL AUGUST ECKHARDT und JULIUS VON GIERKE, Weimar 1931/34.

18 Das Zitat stammt aus ANDREAS LUDWIG JACOB MICHELSEN: Sammlung altdithmarscher Rechtsquellen. Altona 1842, S. XIV; der Band auch als Internetquelle online bei google books verfügbar.

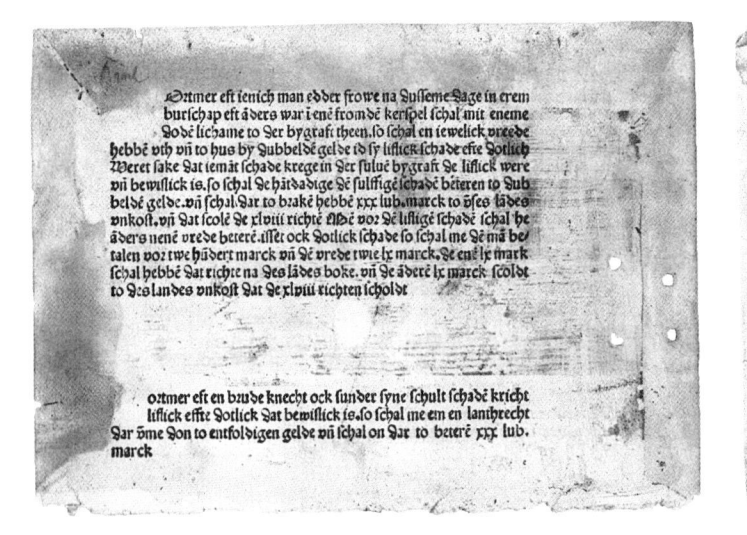

[Abb. 5a und 5b] Kiel, UB, Ink. 151 (1), Vorder- und Rückseite

[Abb. 6a und 6b] Kiel, UB, Ink. 151 (2), Vorder- und Rückseite

[Abb. 7] Kiel, UB, Ink. 151 (3), bedruckte Vorderseite. Das Inkunabelblatt aus Hamburg, St. Katharinen, aus dem untergegangenen Druck 4° 1151, in zwei Hälften geteilt. Obere und untere Hälfte nebeneinander. Rückseite leer bis auf die ehemalige Hamburger Signatur und den Kieler Bibliotheksstempel

Nachdem die Fragmente Jahre später nicht mehr auffindbar waren, entdeckte der schwedische Reichsbibliothekar Isak Collijn sie im Jahr 1915 erneut und publizierte sie.[19]

1919 fand der Bibliothekar der Hamburger Stadtbibliothek Willy Lüdtke in den Deckeln zweier Reformationsdrucke der Bibliothek von St. Katharinen in Hamburg[20] drei weitere textidentische Blätter aus dem Arndes-Druck und publizierte sie 1925; er edierte den gesamten Wortlaut dieses Fragments.[21] Der Kirchenvorstand von St. Katharinen entschloss sich, die identischen Blätter aufzuteilen: Das erste Exemplar der Druckseite behielt die Kirchenbibliothek selbst, das zweite erhielt die Kieler Universitätsbibliothek am 20. Juni 1920 als Geschenk, das dritte die Hamburger Stadtbibliothek zum selben Datum.[22] Nachdem die Bestände der Bibliothek von St. Katharinen im April 1923 von der Staats- und Universitätsbibliothek Hamburg – so bezeichnete sich die ehemalige Stadtbibliothek Hamburg ab dem Jahr 1919 – übernommen wurden, kam das bislang in der Bibliothek von St. Katharinen verwahrte Bruchstück ebenfalls in die Staatsbibliothek, die somit also über zwei der drei bekannten Exemplare dieser Druckseiten verfügte – aber nur bis zum Jahr 1943. Im Zweiten Weltkrieg wurde ein Teil dieser Sammlungen zerstört; seitdem ist in Hamburg nur noch ein Blatt erhalten.[23]

Nur diese drei Seiten des Dithmarscher Landrechts in Kiel und Hamburg kannte man durch die geschilderten Textblätter; die Rückseiten dieser Blätter waren unbedruckt. Jetzt erweitert sich der Bestand um bemerkenswerte vier Doppelseiten, die vorder- und rückseitig mit den Artikeln xcii bis cii sowie cxiii bis cxxiii bedruckt sind.

Aus der Verwendung von datierbaren Druckseiten für einen ansonsten undatierten Einband lassen sich Rückschlüsse ziehen. Da Steffen Arndes seinen Inkunabeldruck 1488 fertig gestellt hatte und auch er wie damals üblich überschüssige Druckseiten in Buchbindereien gab, wo sie weiterverwendet wurden, stützt dies die Annahme, dass die Antiphonarhandschrift direkt nach 1488 eingebunden wurde.

Die bislang gefundenen Einzelseiten bzw. Blätter aus dem Arndes-Druck des Dithmarscher Landrechts stammen, so wird man die Vergleiche der Seiten untereinander auswerten dürfen, aus drei verschiedenen Exemplaren, die zudem noch verschiedene Korrektur- bzw. Druckzustände aufweisen.

Das heutige Kieler Inkunabelblatt 151 (3), das aus dem Deckel des Katharinen-Druckes 4° 1151 herausgelöst wurde, stammt aus einem ersten Exemplar. Diese Druckseite weist, anders als die Seiten im Antiphonar und in Kiel Ink. 151 (1) und 151 (2), keine Durchnummerierung der Paragrafen auf; der Durchschuss zwischen den Textabschnitten entspricht aber schon genau dem in der durchnummerierten und deshalb wohl späteren Fassung. Bei diesem Textzeugen wird der Zustand als Probeabzug durch die leere Rückseite noch unterstrichen.

Die Kieler Inkunabelblätter 151 (1) und 151 (2) stammen aus einem zweiten Exemplar bzw. Abzug des Landrechts-Druckes; es sind jene Seiten, auf denen die von Arnim'sche Hausmarke aufgezeichnet wurde. Hier sind bereits beide Seiten bedruckt und Paragrafennummern einge-

19 UB Kiel, Signatur: Ink. 151; auch dieses Blatt wird im Zusammenhang mit den anderen hier transkribiert. – ISAK COLLIJN: Återfunna fragment af den äldsta tryckta upplagan af Dithmarscher Landrecht. In: *Nordisk tidskrift för bok- och biblioteksväsen*. 2 (1915), S. 105–10. – Der Kieler Bibliothekar Emil Steffenhagen publizierte eine Miszelle über die Hausmarke des Geschlechtes von Arnim, die handschriftlich auf eines der Fragmente gesetzt ist: S-n [Steffenhagen] unter »Notizen« in: *Literarisches Zentralblatt*. 66 (1915), Sp. 703–4.

20 Signaturen: Kath. 1151 und Kath. 1189 4°; die Bände wurden im Zweiten Weltkrieg zerstört. – Zur Bibliothek von St. Katharinen siehe allg. *Die Bau- und Kunstdenkmale der Freien und Hansestadt Hamburg Bd. 3. Innenstadt: Die Hauptkirchen St. Petri, St. Katharinen, St. Jakobi*. Bearbeitet von RENATA KLÉE GOBERT. Hamburg 1968, zu St. Katharinen S. 101–54. – UWE CZUBATYNSKI: Eine Quelle zur Geschichte der Kirchenbibliothek St. Katharinen in Hamburg. In: *Auskunft. Nordhausen*. 12 (1992), S. 328–30.

21 WILLY LÜDTKE: Neue Bruchstücke des gedruckten Dithmarscher Landrechtes. In: *Nordelbingen*. 4 (1925), S. 166–9.

22 Das Einzelblatt ist bei den Hamburger Inkunabeln aufgestellt; Signatur: AC IV, 112.

23 Es handelt sich um das aus dem Druck Kath. 1189 herausgelöste Exemplar.

fügt; und bei § cxcvi hat jemand kunstvoll den jeweils zu Beginn der Paragrafen fehlenden Initialbuchstaben V eingefügt. Der Druck war nicht zufriedenstellend ausgeführt; der Abstand zwischen den einzelnen Wörtern in der ersten Zeile ist zu gering; die zu kleinen Spatien sind durch senkrechte Striche markiert.

Die in der Hamburger Musikhandschrift neu aufgefundenen Abschnitte aus dem Landrecht weisen sowohl durchgezählte Paragrafen als auch gut spationierte Zeilen auf; sie stammen deshalb wohl aus einem dritten Exemplar und sind schon in Bögen montiert gewesen (Bogenzeichen d und d ii). Die beiden Doppelblätter ergeben ein Textkontinuum mit einer größeren Lücke (Paragrafen 92 bis 102 und 112 bis 123; dazwischen fehlt ein Doppelblatt mit dem Text der Paragrafen 103 bis 112 [Beginn]).

Warum die Ausgabe so selten geworden ist, können wir nicht mit Bestimmtheit sagen. Michelsen führt ja noch 1842 die Auffassung älterer Rechtshistoriker an, »dass nach der Eroberung Dithmarschen's die vorhandenen Exemplare des alten Rechts absichtlich auf die Seite geschafft seyen«.[24] Durch den Neufund weiterer acht Seiten des gedruckten Dithmarscher Landrechts in der Inkunabelausgabe des Steffen Arndes 1487 erweitert sich die Kenntnis von diesem seltenen Druck und seiner Texte.

Übersicht zu den erhaltenen Seiten und Blättern des Dithmarscher Landrechts

SuUB Hamburg, ND VI 471 [Abb. 1–4]
Blattgröße 20,5 – 21,5 × 28/9 cm, Schriftspiegel 19,8 × 12,6 cm
1. vorderer Vorsatz recto, links: Paragrafen 94 (Rest) bis 97
2. vorderer Vorsatz recto, rechts: Paragrafen 117 (Rest) bis 120
3. vorderer Vorsatz verso (= mit dem Besitzeintrag des Hamburger Doms), links: Paragrafen 120 (Rest) bis 123, rechts 93/4
4. vorderer Vorsatz verso (= mit dem Besitzeintrag des Hamburger Doms), rechts: Paragrafen 92 (Rest) bis 94
5. hinterer Vorsatz recto, links: Paragrafen 115–7
6. hinterer Vorsatz recto, rechts: Paragrafen 98/9
7. hinterer Vorsatz verso, links: Paragrafen 99 (Rest) bis 102
8. hinterer Vorsatz verso, rechts: Paragrafen 112 (Rest) bis 114

UB Kiel, Ink. 151 (1) und 151 (2) [Abb. 5 und 6]
Zwei Hälften. Vorder- und rückseitig bedruckt, Blattgröße (zusammengefügt, interpoliert) 28 × 16,5 cm, Schriftspiegel 19,8 × 12,6 cm
9. Vorderseite: obere Blatthälfte: Paragraf 190 (Rest), 191, untere Blatthälfte: Paragraf 194
10. Rückseite: obere Blatthälfte: Paragraf 187/88, untere Blatthälfte: Paragraf 196

SuUB Hamburg, AC IV 112 4° [Abb. 8] *und UB Kiel, Ink. 151 (3)* [Abb. 7]
Einseitig bedruckt, Blattgröße 20 × 29,5 cm, Schriftspiegel 19,8 × 12,6 cm
11. Artikel 227/8 der Edition von 1539

---

[24] MICHELSEN (siehe Anm. 17), S. XIV.

Ortmer efft ienich man edder frowe na dussem dage in eren
burschap efft anders war in ene fromden kerspel schal mit eneme
doden lichame to der bygraft theen so schal ein ewelick vrede
hebbe vth vn to hus by dubbelden gelde idt sy liflick schade efte dotlick
Weret sake dat iemant schade krege in der sulue bygraft de liflick were
vn bewißlick is so schal de hartdadige de sulftige schade beteren to dubbelden gelde vn schal dar to brake hebbe xxx lub. marck to dses landes
vnkost vn dat scolen de xlviii richten Und vor de lifligen schade schal he
anders nene vrede beteren Isset ock dotlick schade so schal me den man be-
talen vor twe hundert marck vn de vrede twie lx marck De ene lx marck
schal hebbe dat richte na des landes boke vn de andere lx marck scoldt
to des landes vnkost dat de xlviii richten scholdt

Ortmer efft en brude knecht ock sunder sine schult schade kricht
liflick effte dotlick dat bewißlick is so schal wem en lantrecht
dar vmme don to entfolgen gelde vn schal on dar to beteren xxx lub.
marck

Ortmer oft dar ienich man in vnsem lande were dede korne tho
hope hadde vnde wolde to borge don vnde etlige vnser lantlu-
de des kornes bedarf dede so syn wi endrechtligen ens worden datme
vor de tunne nicht mer schal geuen alse ene schillinck mer alse me se ko-
pen kan vor rede gelt

Ortmeer weret sake dat dar etlige weren in vnseme lande to dit-
merschen dede gelt wolden vp renthe don efte dar ock gilde offte
andere gudere dede werlike achte mechtich were dat dar nymant schal
meer to renthe gelde nemen als von xv marcken ene marck lub. men vp de
geistelige acht de don alse se dorren vn vor gode bekant mogen wesen

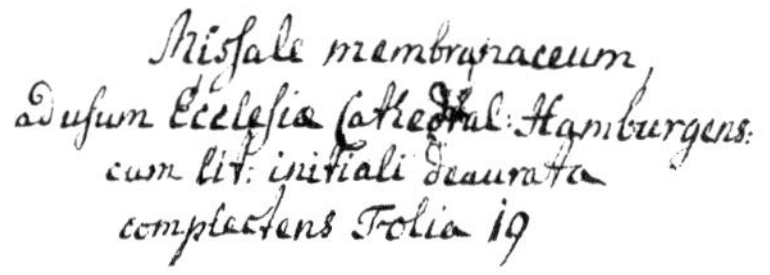

Missale membranaceum
usum Ecclesiæ Cathedral: Hamburgens.
cum lit: initiali deaurata
complectens Folia 19

[Abb. 9]

Transkription

Um die Transkription der erhaltenen Landrechts-Texte nicht zu überlasten, werden die Texte in der Abfolge der Paragrafen gebracht; die »Fundstelle« der einzelnen Textabschnitte erschließt sich aus der voranstehenden Übersicht der erhaltenen Seiten und Blätter.

SuUB Hamburg, ND VI 471
(Schluss) XCII

... des landes Eft hir bauen ienich man worde heret efte haue edder syn / gud toflagen worde effte wech genome(n) dat bewislick vere so schalme / eme syn gud weder don so hoge alse he dat herden dar mit xii manne(n). heft de cleger gude bewisinge, und secht he neen dede a(n)geclaget wert. / so mach he neen seggen mit eneme nemede auer sin slachte. heft de cle / ger nene bewisinge so mach he em entgan mit xii mannen. were id sa- / ke date m syn hus zo bauen recht worde af gebernet. und he dat bewi / sen mochte mit nogeaftige(n) tugen. unde secht he neen de so angeclaget worde so mach he neen seggen mit enem kercknemede. Heft de cleger / nene bewisinge so mach de gonne dede angeclaget wert neen seggen / mit twelf mannen.

[H]Efft dar en lanthsamelt gelecht worde XCIII

[V]Ortmeer efft dar en lantsamelt gelecht worden so schal en is-/lick dedeto deme lantsamelt kumpt vrede hebben dat sie vre-/de efte neen. offt dar en schade bauen iummende to dreue zi-/ner partye. de schade worde liflick offte dotlick. Den schaden schalme/beteren to dubbelden gelde. und den vrede ock to dubbelden gelde.

[H]Eft en man ene rulinge makede in deme samelde XCIIII

[V]Ortmer efft dar en lantsamelt gelecht worde unde dar we ene/rulinge makede an deme samelde dat bewislick were. de dat deit de schal deme lande beteren druttich marck.   [Lage:] d

neue Seite

(Schluss) XCIIII
Und floge dar suluest enen man dale. XCV

[V]Ortmer oft dar en man geslagen worde dat schude den/man schalme nergen aue berouen noch an clederen offte an/wapene. we dat deit de schal beteren deme cleger xc schilli(n)ge/und deme richte xc schillinge. und de cleger schal syn gud herden mit/xii mannen. Secht de gonne neen dede angeclaget wert. mochteme/eme dat bewisen. so schal he neen seggen mit eneme nemede auer syn/slachte. Is dar neen bewisinge bi so mach he neen segge(n) mit xii manne(n)

Von perde kope ossen und ander vee. XCVI

[V]Ortmer oft dar we deme andere(n) affkofft en pert edder ossen/edder einige haue edder welkorleie guder dat were husz und/hoff mole(n) edder ienighe buwte effte liggende grunde de soda/nen kop vortugen mochte offte kunde mit den wynkopes lude(n) edder/worde dar neen winkop to druncke(n). so mach he den kop vertuge(n) mit/guden sekere(n) tuge. und wan de kop vortuget is so schalme de kop-/manne den kop holden.

[H]Eft en mit deme anderen gut to meyne hadde. XCVII

[V]ortmer eft dar we mit deme ander$_3$(n) gud to meine hadde sunder/liggende grunde und deme enen syn deel un(d) part vele worde so//

neue Seite

(Schluss) xcvii

Mach de ander dem id mede hort date ne del mit deme anderen behol/de(n) umme so veele alse em en ander dar u(m)me geue(n) will dat bewislick is.

Sunte Oswaldus dach schalmen vyre(n) xcviii

[V]ortmer so schal en iewelick in unsen la(n)den sunte oswald(us) dach/vyren by broke sestich lub. marcken Und ock schal en iewe/lick in unseme lande den eersten vrigedach in den nyen ma-/nen vasten und vyren beth tho middage und schal to syner houet ker-/ken in der bede missen wesen alle iaer in allen to kamende(n) manten by/broke lx lub. marke(n)

Von acker kope xcix

[V]ortmer offt dar we enen fromden synen acker vorkofte. so fin/den wy de sweertzyden neger kop also den vromeden. De go(n)ne/de deme fromden den acker vorkoft unde neme daer en weynich ac-/kers an up dat de negesten nicht scholden neger kop wesen. konde de/swertzide deme vromeden koepmanne zyne(n) acker nicht vernoge(n) mit/gelde ofte anderen acker. so mach de swertzyde deme fromeden koep manne von deme suluen acker so vele af doen dar he neger kop to we-/sen will also des cleuere(n) ackers belopen mach na gelde tale alse vier se/ker man dorren bekannt wesen. men de fromede kopman mach den ko/re hebben to wel-/ker syden he den acker afneemen will.   [Lage:] d ii

neue Seite

[H]Offt der swertziden de acker worde

Erst to kope baden c

[V]ortmer oft de negeste sweertzyde beschukdet worde dat/em de acker eerst to kope baden were. so mach he to staen sulff dorde und sweren dat he den acker so na nicht kope(n) mochte edder konde efte so na laten were also de ander ene/kofft hadde. so mach he neger kop wesen. schal de gonne de den ac/ker koft heft to stan sulf dorde und mit deme kopmanne un(d) swere(n) dat/in den hilge(n) dat ore kop so grot is sunder valsch un(d) vul. dat schal em/de ander weder keren. und wilme em denne des nicht to loue(n) so schal/he syn gelt herden mit xii mannen. und in der teringhe der twelf man-/ne schal de ander em to hulpe kamen myt xxiiii schillingen und nicht/hoger Vortmer war en man eneme an dere(n) vrome de(r) synen acker ver/kofft. so schal de negeste swertsyde dem fromden kopman weder afdri(n)en in den eersten sos weken wen de acker verkoft is zo verne id em/anders to weten wert in iaren un(d) dagen

De swertsyde is neger kop alse des kopma(n)s dochter ci

[V]ortmer eft en man syne(n) acker verkoft efte verkoepen wolde. so/shal de swertzide neger kop wesen alse syne egene dochter

Dede koste(n) acker vrihe un(d) quit la(n)ge bruket hefft cii

[V]ortmeer oft dar en man hadde acker koft un(d) de de(n) acker hadde/quit und vrihe su(n)der bisprake voret en iar edder teyne. so trach / he ene beholden. spricht dar na we up so mach he daer by stan mit xii/mannen.

neue Seite

‹CXII›

[V]ortmeer efft dar we syner dochter edder fedderen dochter ac/ker mede lauede den schal se oer rechte vort folgen laten wol/de he den ock sulue(n) bruke(n) to syner liff vo dinghe. so schal de/medegift nene macht hebben

 Est en man were vormunder ener iungkfrowe(n) CXIII

[V]ortmeer oft dar en man zir er dochter ofte suster efte ieniger/ iunckfrowe(n) dar he vormunder auer were un(d) or acker mede/ geue un(d) de acker or un(d) ore(n) ma(n)ne na vele worde. so scholet ore/ frunt neger kop wesen alse syne Sterft he henne und heft se kynder. so/ synt syne frunt neger kop alse ore Oft or ock acker an storvvue so schal/ dat so wesen also hyr vorschreuen is eft he oer mede geuen were

 Eft en unafdelet zone wif neme un(d) storue hen CXIIII

[V]Ortmer eft en man hadde enen zone den he nicht hadde af-/gedelet. un(d) wu(n)ne deme zone ein wiff un(d) de zone storue hen er/he on afdelede. so mach de vader de(n)ne de suaren utheren myt xii manne(n) wes he syne(n) sone besunt hadde. su(n)der ore marke de schal se-/allike wol hebbe(n) also verne de dar in gekome(n) is mit erers mannes va-/ders willen

 Eft en man hadde ene(n) sunderge(n) sone edder meer CXV

[V]Ortmer offt dar en man hadde enen sunderge(n) sone edder/meer und he urigede na en wyf dar he ock enen zone me-/de hadde. storue de moder heen und hadde se vrye(n) acker/so eruet se ere(n) acker an ere(n) zone Storue de zone hen so ar/uet de sone den acker an den vader. wan de vader steruet so leuet he den acker an syne sons Oft de vader storue eer de sons de he mit de/me latere(n) wiue hadde hat. so steruet de sone den acker an de halue bro/der allyke wol so hyr vorschreuen steidt

 Efft en man will urigen de late syck nicht bededinge(n) CXVI

[V]Ortmer ooft dar we urigede ene frowen edder iunckfrowe(n)/let he syck gelt aff dedingen er in to zendende. do zodane gelt bedinget unde nympt de schal braken hebben xxx marck ie/ge(n) dat richte an deme ker-spel dar de man wandet de sodane gelt schat-/tet Deyt dat richte an deme kerspel id nicht. so schal dat richte in de-/me lande dat richten

 Keen bruth schal gaue vergene(n) in des brutmakers hus CXVII

[V]Ortmer so schal neen frowe efte iungkfrowe gaue geuen dar se/to des mannes husze gesant wert by broke xxx lub. marken//

neue Seite

---

 stervet de frowe vor den manne CXVIII

[V]ortmeer eft enen man syn wyf afstervet. heft so ore medegift to/vulle(n) in gebracht so schole(n) ore ere eruen dar nicht meer uth heb/ben alse sie dar inne bracht hefft

 sternet (!) de man vor der frowen CXIX

[V]Ortmer leuet de frowe lenger alse de man so schal se ore be-/latinge to vullen uth nehmen eft dat vry kann wesen von der/schult wegene. Sterft de man vor deme wiue so scholt syne/vrund neen erf bedde nehmen

 Von frowen belatinge CXX

[V]Ortmer offt dar en man zine wyne zin gud belethe ore/leuedage. so mogen syne swertzide der frowen ore marke/tal make(n) uth deme buw gude so uerne id dar is. wil se ere/marke de eer denne to geachtet is vorbringe(n) den schade(n)/schal se beholde(n) Men is dar gud dat dar auerlopt. dat schal se ungeachtiget bruke(n) bede buwgudt un(d) mededel

Weret auer sake dat se von/der belatingen toge und neme ene(n) man. un(d) de swertzide clagede dat se/dat gud mit vorsate vorarget hadde. so mach se dat gud wet an bri(n)/gen mit xii mannen

neue Seite

Eft me ener verstzoruen frowen cleder schal von sick don CXXI

[V]Ortmet oft ene frowe edder inngkfrowe storue un(d) dat mod/deren kunne spreke umme de wiffligen ware. so schalme se or/folgen laten so uerne se dat bewisen mogen dat de frowe ed-/der iungkfrowe or to baren se an dat verde von beden syden susteren/und bruderen uth to reken de also de hillige kerke leeth na to frige(n)de./ Vorder mer weret sake dat dat moddere(n) ku(n)ne so verne uth gestorve(n)/were so scholen de cleder weder in dar se uth gestoruet syn. Vorder/mer is dar buwgud dat schal steruen an dat negeste bloth.

En nalatene frowe schal ore cleder mit nyma(n)de dele(n) CXXII

[V]ortmer est dar ene frowe eren man vorlore so schal de frowe ne-/ne cleder delen van eren clederen mit oren dochtere(n)

Wat ene frowe in erem latesten vorgeuen mach CXXIII

[V]Ortmer so mach nene frowe mer vorgeuen dorch ere sele(n) sa/licheit an ereme latesten alse veftehalue marck zunder id we/re mit willen und vulborde erer eruen. unde dat geuene gut/schalme nehmen uth deme buwgude und nicht uth den clederen. so ver/ne dat dar buwgud is Des suluen glick oft en man ock wat vergeve(n)/will dat schal stan na dusser vorscreuen wyse.

UB Kiel, Ink. 151 (1), obere Blatthälfte

(Schluss) CXC

[V]ortmer so schal nymandt von den anderen nehmen my de ofe/gaue u(m)me nenerleye sake wille(n). eft dat we dede dat bewislick/were de schal beteren den xlviii xxx marck. Secht he neen so/schal he neen seggen mit eneme nemede auer syn slachte.

Efft en angesproken worde. CXCI

[V]Ortmer offt welck richtet enen man ansprecke u(m)me sak⟨...⟩/kerleye se were und hadde dar rechtt vor dan alse ehm hogest dar vor funden wer-de dar bauen schal en neen richter edder ny/mant schatten by broke des landes lx lub. marck

Von rechte to gevende

UB Kiel, Ink. 151 (1), untere Blatthälfte

gudt. CXCIIII

[V]Ortmer eft dar fromde koplude quemen so ieniger haue(n) an/unsen ⟨...⟩nde und em dat we vorbode dat he nicht schepen mo/ste. De dat deit unde bewislick were. De schal betereff en me richte xxx/marck. Secht he neen so schal he dar vor stan mit eneme nemede auer/syn slachte.

UB Kiel, Ink. 151 (2), obere Blatthälfte

CLXXXVII

[V]Ortmer eft dar wy volste medede an syn arbeid. welker dat ni=/cht en holt. De schal deme anderen dat halue loen geuen.

[Leerraum]
Eft en man synen volste schuldt geue CLXXXVIII

[V]ortmer weret sake dat da..ve zynen uolste schuldt geue um/me lenich gud date m entwent werde dat scal he don wand at/volste mit em an zyneme bro de is edder achte dage dar na al/se dat volste van em geit. Na deme dage schal de wert dar nene claghe/up geuen.

UB Kiel, Ink. 151 (2), untere Blatthälfte
CXCVI

[V (Initial eingemalt)]Ortmer oft dar en man enen borge(n) uth stettet uppe recht un(d)/bode allent dat recht were und syn borge worde dar baue(n) an/den kroch gebaden. und we en dar in buth und dwinghet de schal em dar weder uth losen un(d) die borge schal sunder schal wesen

Vortmer oft de borge wolde ock meer holden olse he laued hadde de/der alse recht were dat bewis⟨li⟩ck were. nympt he des schade(n) den schal/he beholden

SuUB Hamburg, AC IV 112 4° und UB Kiel, Ink. 151 (3)
einseitig bedruckt, ohne Paragrafennummern; Blattgröße 20,2 × 29,4 cm, Schriftspiegel 19,9 × 12,9 cm. Artikel 227/8 der Edition von 1539

[V]Ortmer eft ienich man edder frowe na dusse medage in erem/burschap eft a(n)ders war i(n) ene(m)e fromde(n) kerspel schal mit eneme/doden lichame to der by graft theen. so schal en iewelick vreede hebb(n) uth un(d) to hus by dubbelde(m) gelde id sy liflick schade efte dotlich./Weret sake dat ieman(t) schade krege in der sulue(n) bygraft de liflick were/un un(d) bewislick is. so schal de ha(n)tdadige de sulffige(n) schaden beteren to dub/belde(m) gelde. un(d) schal dar to brake(n) hebben xxx lub. marck to u(n)ses la(n)des/unkost. un(d) dat scole(n) de xlviii richte(n) Me(n) vor de(n) liftige(n) schade(n) schal he/a(n)ders nene(n) vrede betere(n). isset ock dotölick schade so schal me de(n) ma(n) be-/talen vor twe hu(d)dert marck un(d) de(n) vrede twie lx marck. de ene(n) lx mark/schal hebbe(n) dat richte na des landes boke. un(d) de andere(n) lx marck scoldt to des landes unkost dat de xlviii richten scholt.

[V]ortmer est en brude knecht ock sunder syne schult schade(n) kricht/liflick effte dotlick dat bewislick is. so schal me em en lanthrecht/dar umme don to entfoldigen gelde und schal on dar to beteren xxx lub./marck.

[V]ortmer oft dar ienich ma(n) in unseme la(n)de were dede korne tho/hope hadde unde wolde to borge don unde etlige unser lanthlu/de des kornes bedarf dede. so syn wi endrechtlige(n) en worden datme/vor de tunne(n) nicht mer schal geuen alse ene(n) schillinck mer alseme se ko/pen kann vor rede gelt.

[V]Ortmeer weret sake dat dar etlige weren in unseme la(n)de to dit⸗/mersche(n) dede gelt wolde(n) up renthe don efte dar ock gilde offte/andere gudere dede werlike(n) achte mechtich were(n) dat dar nyma(n)t schal/meer to renthe gelde neme(n) als von xv marcke(n) ene marck lub. me(n) up de/geistelige acht de don alse se dorre(n) un(d) vor gode bekannt mogen wesen

16. Jahrhundert

SIEGFRIED RISSE †

Zwei Auflagen von Michael Furters Psalterium im Jahr 1503

DER DRUCKER MICHAEL FURTER gab 1503 in Basel eine Neuauflage des lateinisch-deutschen *Psalterium cum apparatu vulgari*[1] heraus, das er schon 1502 aufgelegt hatte.[2] Die Auflage des Jahres 1503 fand offenbar eine so starke Nachfrage, dass in demselben Jahr noch eine zweite Auflage erfolgte. Beide Auflagen aus dem Jahr 1503 stimmen in der Titelseite, im Kolophon und der Seiteneinteilung so sehr überein, dass sie in neuerer Zeit nicht unterschieden wurden.[3] Im VD 16 zum Beispiel ist nur eine Ausgabe angegeben: ZV 1738. Bei genauerem Vergleich ist aber festzustellen, dass es zwei Auflagen gibt, deren Drucksätze sich durch zahlreiche Abweichungen unterscheiden. Allein sechs Seiten (r^v, r ij^r, r iij^v, r iiij^r, r v^v, r vj^r) der letzten Lage beider Auflagen stimmen genau überein. Auch die zwei letzten Seiten (r vij^v, r viij^r) beider Ausgaben stimmen bis auf wenige Zeichen, die geringfügig verschoben sind, überein.[4]

Hinweise früherer Autoren

Auf diese zweite Auflage im gleichen Jahr ist schon vor mehr als 200 Jahren hingewiesen worden. Im Jahr 1768 berichtete Christian Carl am Ende, dass er »in D. S. J. Baumgartens Nachrichten von merkwürdigen Büchern, im fünften Bande S. 16 bis 18« auf eine Version des Furter'schen Psalters von 1503 gestoßen sei, die nicht mit der Version des Exemplars übereinstimmte, das er in Händen hielt.[5] Auf diesen Artikel hin äußerte Johann Bartholomäus Riederer, der offenbar nicht wie Christian Carl am Ende die spätere, sondern die frühere Ausgabe vor sich hatte, die Vermutung: »Bey dem baselischen Psalter von 1503 merke ich nur an, daß es vermutlich zweyerley Ausgaben dieses Jares geben müsse.«[6] Diese Vermutung war für Christian Carl am Ende Anlass zur Nachprüfung. Ein Jahr später, also 1769, verteidigte er sich: »Ich konnte nicht vermuthen, daß Michael Furter einen solchen Psalter in einem Jahre zweymal gedruckt haben solte [...] Und doch hätte ich es vermuthen und annehmen sollen: denn es ist sicher und gewiß.«[7] Georg Wolfgang Panzer referierte in seinen Annalen diese Abhandlungen, hatte aber selber nur eine Ausgabe des Psalters aus dem Jahr 1503 gesehen.[8] Im 19. Jahrhundert hat Wilhelm Walther die Frage nach den zwei Ausgaben neu geprüft. Er fasste 1889 sein Ergebnis wie folgt zusammen: »Die Vermuthung, [...] daß es zwei verschiedene Ausgaben des Furter'schen lateinisch-deutschen Psalters vom Jahre 1503 geben dürfte, können wir zur Gewissheit erheben.«

Walther gab für die beiden Auflagen von 1503, von ihm als Nr. 6 und Nr. 7 gezählt, folgende Unterscheidungsmerkmale an:

---

1 *Psalterium cum apparatu vulgari firmiter appresso Lateinisch Psalter mit dem teutschen nutzbarlichen da bey getruckt.* Basel: Michael Furter, 1503.

2 Dieses Psalterium ist schon 1494 und 1499 von Erhart Ratdolt in Augsburg herausgegeben worden. – Einen Überblick über alle acht Auflagen dieses Psalteriums bietet SIEGFRIED RISSE: *Gedruckte deutsche Psalter vor 1524, dem Erscheinungsjahr von Martin Luthers deutschem Psalter.* Nordhausen 2010, S. 50–4 und 226–36.

3 Nur im OPAC der UB Basel, die beide Ausgaben aus dem Jahr 1503 besitzt (FB 95 und FNP VIII 41), fand ich bei der Titelvollanzeige für das Exemplar mit der Signatur FB 95 den Hinweis: »Anderer Druck als FNP VIII 41.«

4 Für den Vergleich der beiden Auflagen wurden folgende Exemplare benutzt: für die erste Auflage das Exemplar der Thüringischen UuLB Jena (4 Theol. XXI, 40[2]) und für die zweite Auflage das Exemplar der UB Heidelberg (Q 393-1 INC [1]).

5 CHRISTIAN CARL AM ENDE: VIIII. Eben desselben Beschreibung eines lateinisch-teutschen Psalters, so zu Basel im Jahr 1503, in Quart, gedruckt worden. In: JOHANN BARTHOLOMÄUS RIEDERER: *Nüzliche und angeneme Abhandlungen aus der Kirchen- Bücher- und Gelerten-Geschichte. Zweytes Stück.* Altdorf 1768, S. 140–54, hier S. 144/5.

6 JOHANN BARTHOLOMÄUS RIEDERER: *Nüzliche und angeneme Abhandlungen aus der Kirchen- Bücher- und Gelerten-Geschichte von verschiedenen Verfassern zusammen getragen, Gesammelt und mit eigenen Beiträgen herausgegeben.* Altdorf 1768/69, S. 163/4.

7 CHRISTIAN CARL AM ENDE: XXIIII. Beschreibung eines lateinisch-teutschen Psalters, Strasburg, 1506, in Quart. In: JOHANN BARTHOLOMÄUS RIEDERER: *Nüzliche und angeneme Abhandlungen aus der Kirchen- Bücher- und Gelerten-Geschichte. Viertes und letztes Stück.* Altdorf 1769, S. 379/80.

8 GEORG WOLFGANG PANZER: *Annalen der älteren deutschen Litteratur oder Anzeige und Beschreibung derjenigen Bücher welche von Erfindung der Buchdruckerkunst bis MDXX in deutscher Sprache gedruckt worden sind.* Nürnberg 1788, S. 259. (Nachdruck: Hildesheim 1961.)

> Auf dem Titelblatt liest No. 6: teutschen, N. 7 dagegen: teütschen, und die Worte »Lateinisch Psalter mit« sind in N. 6 weitläufiger gedruckt als in N. 7, sodaß sie dort 6,9 cm, hier nur 6,4 cm einnehmen. Da – wie wir wissen – einigen Exemplaren der Titel fehlt, fügen wir hinzu, daß die rotgedruckte Ueberschrift auf fol. 1. bei No. 6 liest: ritum cuz, bei N. 7: ritum : cū, und daß das 36. Blatt des eigentlichen Psalters in N. 6 irrthümlich mit xxxii, in N. 7 dagegen richtig mit xxxvi bezeichnet ist.[9]

Mit den von Walther genannten Unterscheidungsmerkmalen lassen sich aber nur die Exemplare der späteren Auflage (Walthers N. 7) bestimmen, die frühere Auflage und die im Folgenden beschriebenen Mischexemplare dagegen nicht.

Kurt Erich Schöndorf führte 1967 beide Ausgaben an mit dem Vermerk, dass von der früheren Ausgabe »nach Walther noch 8 Exemplare vorhanden« seien und von der späteren »nach Walther 1 Exemplar in Heidelberg«.[10]

Vergleich der beiden Ausgaben

Deutliche Übereinstimmungen in Buchaufbau, Seiteneinteilung und Druckbild sind festzustellen. Die zweite Auflage von 1503 entspricht weitgehend der ersten Auflage aus demselben Jahr. Die Folge verschieden großer Lagen ist die gleiche wie in der ersten Auflage. Die zweite Ausgabe stimmt im Seitenumbruch und in den Blattzahlen fast vollständig mit der ersten überein. Um die Gleichheit in den Blattzahlen zu erreichen, wurden sogar Unstimmigkeiten der ersten Ausgabe mit nur geringfügiger Änderung in die zweite Ausgabe übernommen. Bei der Seiteneinteilung sind die Unterschiede gering. Beide Auflagen wurden mit den gleichen Drucktypen gesetzt.

Ferner haben beide Auflagen die gleichen Lagen. In beiden Auflagen haben die Lagen mit den Signaturen i, k, p und q sechs Blätter, alle anderen Lagen dagegen acht Blätter: a⁸, ²a⁸ b–h⁸, i–k⁶, l–o⁸, p–q⁶, r⁸. Die erste Lage a enthält die Titelseite, einen Kalender und ein Register. Mit der zweiten Lage a beginnen der Psalter und auch die Nummerierung der Blätter von I bis CXX.

Bei Fehlern in der Blattzählung sind geringe Unterschiede feststellbar [siehe Tab. 1]. Beim Seitenumbruch konnten nur zwei geringfügige Abweichungen festgestellt werden: Erstens stehen die Wörter »vnd Dathan vnd abirō die« im Titulus des Psalms XLVIII in der früheren Auflage auf Seite XXXVIIIʳ, in der späteren auf der vorangehenden Seite XXXVIIᵛ. Zweitens beginnt in der früheren Ausgabe der lateinische Text auf Seite CVIᵛ mit dem Wort »Lunam«. In der späteren Ausgabe steht die Silbe »Lu« am Ende des lateinischen Textes der vorangehenden Seite CVIʳ.

Die Unterschiede in der Seitengestaltung sind zahlreicher. Die Gestaltung der Textblöcke (lateinischer Psalmtext, deutscher Psalmtext, deutsche Psalmtituli) weist in den beiden Auflagen geringfügige Unterschiede auf. Auch die Positionen der Überschriften, Blattzahlen und Signaturen sind in den beiden Auflagen geringfügig verschieden.

Bei den kleinen Initialen, die im deutschen Text zu Beginn eines Psalms stehen, zeigen sich hin und wieder Unterschiede darin, dass diese

9 WILHELM WALTHER: Die eine deutsche Übersetzung bietenden Psalterien des Mittelalters. In: *Centralblatt für Bibliothekswesen*. VI.1 (1889), S. 23–8, hier S. 25. – Vgl. DERS.: *Die deutsche Bibelübersetzung des Mittelalters*. 3 Teile. Braunschweig 1889–92, S. 611.

10 KURT ERICH SCHÖNDORF: Die Tradition der deutschen Psalmenübersetzung. Untersuchungen zur Verwandtschaft und Übersetzungstradition der Psalmenverdeutschung zwischen Notker und Luther. Köln, Graz 1967 (*Mitteldeutsche Forschungen*. 46), S. 87.

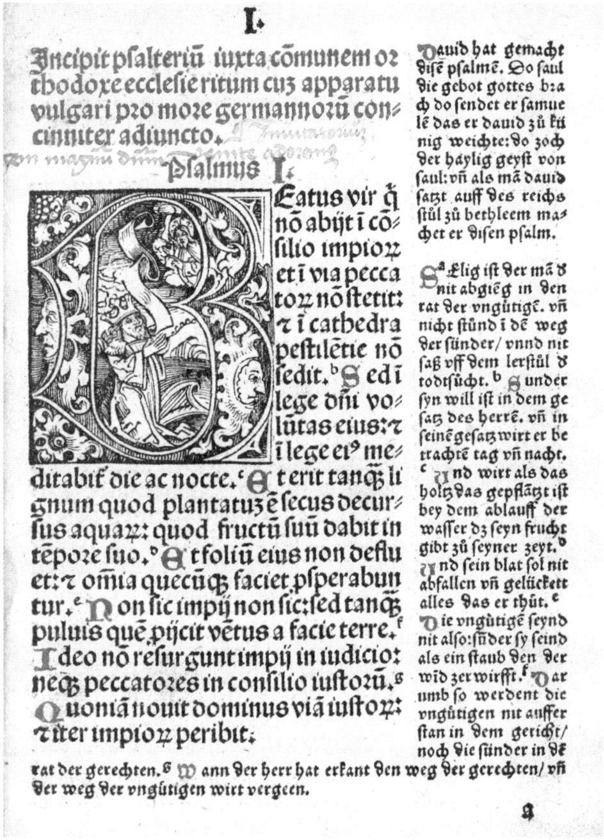

I.

Incipit psalteriū iuxta cōmunem or thodoxe ecclesie ritum cū3 apparatu vulgari pro more germannorū con- cinniter adiuncto.

Psalmus I.

Beatus vir q̄ nō abijt i cō- silio impiorꝫ et i via pecca- torꝫ nō stetit: ꝛ i cathedra pestilētie nō sedit. b Sed i lege dñi vo- lūtas eius: ꝛ i lege ei9 me- ditabit die ac nocte. c Et erit tanq̄ li- gnum quod plantatū ē secus decur- sus aquarꝫ: quod fructū suū dabit in tēpore suo. d Et foliū eius non deflu- et: ꝛ oīa quecūq̄ faciet psperabun- tur. e Non sic impij non sic: sed tanq̄ puluis quē pijcit vētus a facie terre. f Ideo nō resurgunt impij in iudicio: neq̄ peccatores in consilio iustorū. g Quoniā nouit dominus viā iustorꝫ: ꝛ iter impiorꝫ peribit.

Dauid hat gemacht dise psalmē. Do saul die gebot gottes brach do sendet er samuel das er dauid zū künig weichte: do zoch der haylig geyst von saul: vñ als mā dauid satzt auff des reichs stül zū bethleem machet er disen psalm.

a Selig ist der mā d nit abgieng in den rat der vngütigē. vñ nicht stünd i dē weg der sünder/ vnnd nit saß vff dem lerstül d todsücht. b Sunder syn will ist in dem gesatz des herrē. vñ in seinē gesatz wirt er betrachtē tag vñ nacht. c Und wirt als das holtz das gepflätzt ist bey dem ablauff der wasser dz seyn frucht gibt zū seyner zeyt. d Und sein blat sol nit abfallen vñ gelückett alles das er thüt. e Die vngütigē seynd nit also: sūder sy seind als ein staub den der wid zerwirfft. f Darumb so werdent die vngütigen nit auffer stan in dem gericht/ noch die sünder in dē rat der gerechten. g Wann der herr hat erkant den weg der gerechten/ vñ der weg der vngütigen wirt vergeen.

a

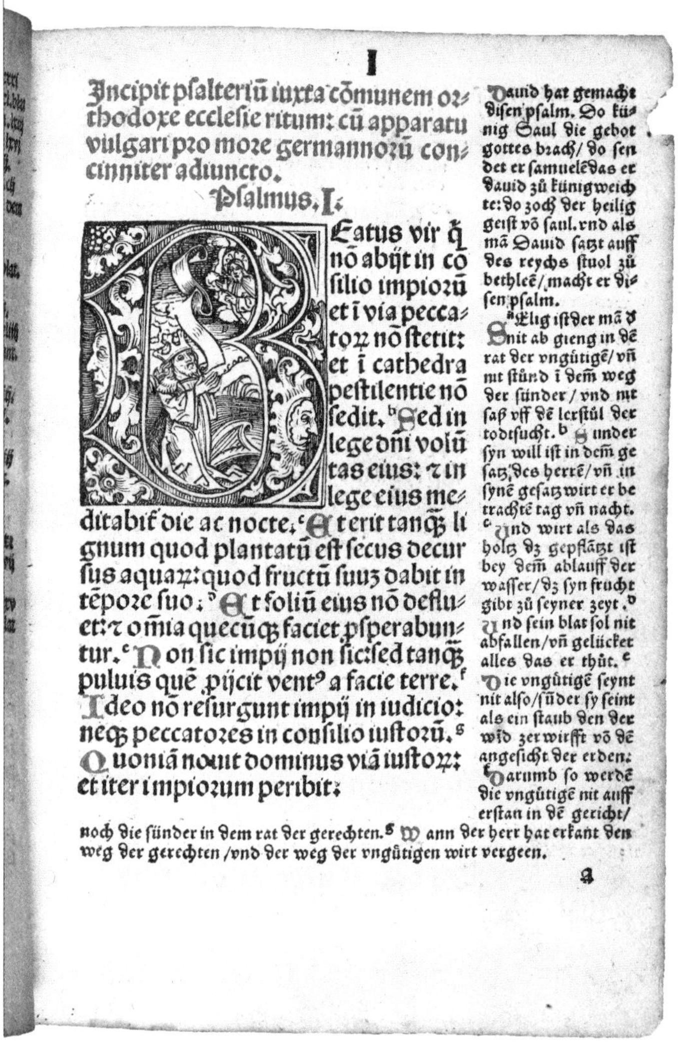

I

Incipit psalteriū iuxta cōmunem or thodoxe ecclesie ritum: cū apparatu vulgari pro more germannorū con- cinniter adiuncto.

Psalmus. I.

Beatus vir q̄ nō abijt in co silio impiorū et i via pecca- torꝫ nō stetit: et i cathedra pestilentie nō sedit. b Sed in lege dñi volū tas eius: ꝛ in lege eius me- ditabit die ac nocte. c Et erit tanq̄ li gnum quod plantatū est secus decur sus aquarꝫ: quod fructū suū dabit in tēpore suo. d Et foliū eius nō deflu- et: ꝛ oīa quecūq̄ faciet psperabun- tur. e Non sic impij non sic: sed tanq̄ puluis quē pijcit vent9 a facie terre. f Ideo nō resurgunt impij in iudicio: neq̄ peccatores in consilio iustorū. g Quoniā nouit dominus viā iustorꝫ: et iter impiorum peribit.

Dauid hat gemacht disen psalm. Do künig Saul die gebot gottes brach/ do sendet er samuelē das er Dauid zū künig weichte: do zoch der heilig geist vō saul. vnd als mā Dauid satzt auff des reychs stuol zū bethleē/ macht er disen psalm.

a Selig ist der mā d nit ab gieng in dē rat der vngütigē/ vñ nit stünd i dem weg der sünder/ vnd nit saß vff dē lerstül der todtsucht. b Sunder syn will ist in dem gesatz des herrē/ vñ in synē gesatz wirt er betrachtē tag vñ nacht. c Und wirt als das holtz dz gepflätzt ist bey dem ablauff der wasser/ dz syn frucht gibt zū seyner zeyt. d Und sein blat sol nit abfallen/ vñ gelücket alles das er thüt. e Die vngütigē seynt nit also/ sūder sy seint als ein staub den der wid zerwirfft vō dē angesicht der erden. f Darumb so werdē die vngütigē nit auff erstan in dē gericht/ noch die sünder in dem rat der gerechten. g Wann der herr hat erkant den weg der gerechten /vnd der weg der vngütigen wirt vergeen.

a

[Abb. 1a und 1b] Frühere Auflage, UB Marburg, Sign. XIXB B 261 t [1a], und spätere Auflage, UB Heidelberg, Sign. Q 393-1 INC :: [1] [1b]. Zahlreiche Unterschiede zwischen beiden Auflagen sind erkennbar. Die spätere Auflage weist in der Vorbemerkung zu Psalm 1 zusätzlich das Wort »künig« auf und im Vers e zusätzlich die Worte »von dem angesicht der erden«. Außerdem gibt es zwischen beiden Auflagen ca. 65 Unterschiede bei Buchstaben und Zeichen

Initialen in der einen Ausgabe fehlen oder zu tief stehen, in der anderen dagegen vorhanden sind beziehungsweise richtig stehen.

Unterschiede im Text

Die meisten Unterschiede zeigen sich im Text. Die einzelnen Seiten weisen durchschnittlich circa 60 Unterschiede auf, maximal 145. Im deutschen Text sind die Unterschiede im Durchschnitt gut dreimal häufiger als im lateinischen.

Im lateinischen Text unterscheiden sich die beiden Auflagen fast nur dadurch, dass Wörter abgekürzt oder nicht abgekürzt werden, verschiedene Arten von Abkürzungen gewählt und Satz- oder Trennungszeichen gesetzt oder ausgelassen werden. Vor allem durch die Abkürzungen entstehen oft auch Unterschiede im Zeilenumbruch.

Der lateinische Text der früheren Auflage enthielt nur wenige Fehler, so dass in der späteren Auflage nur wenig zu korrigieren war. Auch im lateinischen Text der späteren Auflage finden sich kaum Druckfehler. Als einziger bedeutender Fehler wurde festgestellt: S. XLIII^{v} Ps 55c: »A multitudine diei timebo« statt wie richtig in der ersten Auflage »Ab altitudine diei timebo«.

Die Unterschiede im deutschen Text bestehen nicht nur wie im lateinischen Text darin, dass Wörter abgekürzt oder nicht abgekürzt, verschiedene Arten von Abkürzungen gewählt und Satz- oder Trennungszeichen gesetzt oder ausgelassen werden. Variationen entstehen auch dadurch, dass verschiedene Drucktypen (besonders für d und h) benutzt und manche Wörter mit einfachem oder doppeltem Buchstaben gedruckt werden (»got/gott«, »her/herr«, »mit/mitt«, »nit/nitt«, »vnd/vnnd«). Ferner werden Vokale und Diphthonge unterschiedlich wiedergegeben (i/y, ai/ei/ey), ebenso Konsonanten (d/t, f/v, p/b, s/ß). Es kommen sowohl »min, din, sin« mit langem i vor als auch »mein, dein, sein« mit Diphthong. Auch die Flexionsformen können unterschiedlich sein (»werden/werdent«, »die übel ding/die übeln ding«, »ain strick/einen strick«, »vor sein augen/seinen augen«). Ein Trend von der früheren zur späteren Auflage ist bei diesen Unterschieden kaum auszumachen.

Eine Reihe von Druckfehlern der ersten Auflage wurde in der zweiten korrigiert, es schlichen sich aber auch neue Fehler in die zweite Auflage ein. Im Gegensatz zum lateinischen Text weist der deutsche auch zahlreiche Unterschiede im Wortlaut auf. In den meisten Fällen (circa fünfzig Mal) geht es um eine genauere Anpassung an den Text der Vulgata.

Zeitliche Einordnung der Auflagen

Walther spricht von der früheren beziehungsweise von der späteren Auflage, ohne für die zeitliche Einordnung Kriterien zu nennen. Für die von ihm aufgestellte Abfolge sprechen die Angleichungen an die Vulgata in der deutschen Übersetzung. Als spätere Auflage ist diejenige anzusehen, die genauer dem Text der Vulgata entspricht. Das trifft für die von Walther als später angesetzte Auflage zu.

Ein weiteres Kriterium für die zeitliche Abfolge der Auflagen ist, dass vereinzelt in der zweiten Auflage weniger gebräuchliche oder veraltete Begriffe ersetzt werden. Zum Beispiel wird »allwege« fast immer durch »allzeit« ersetzt.

Nachweis der Exemplare

Anhand der Tabelle im Anhang lassen sich die beiden Auflagen und die in zahlreichen Exemplaren vorhandene Mischform bestimmen.[11] Zusätzlich sollten die oben angeführten Unterscheidungsmerkmale von Walther berücksichtigt werden. Im Falle der nicht von mir geprüften Exemplare wurden die Notiz von Walther und die Tabelle den unten genannten Bibliotheken zugesandt mit der Bitte nachzuprüfen, welcher Auflage die jeweils vorhandenen Exemplare zuzuordnen sind oder ob eine Mischform vorliegt.

11 Der in dem OPAC einiger Bibliotheken angeführte Fingerprint (isal isis ieri ofde 3 1503R) bezieht sich auf die frühere Auflage. Er ist im vorliegenden Fall wenig hilfreich. Die Mischexemplare sind damit gar nicht zu unterscheiden, da sie den gleichen Fingerprint haben. Der Fingerprint der späteren Auflage unterscheidet sich nur durch einen Buchstaben, und zwar in der dritten Gruppe (neri statt ieri).

Frühere Auflage[12]

Basel, UB, fb 95
Berlin, SB, Bn 2924⟨a⟩ R
Bonn, UuLB, Ga 156/30
Dresden, SuUB, Biblia. 850
Eichstätt, UB, 04/1 B III 260
Freiburg i. B., UB, L 4065,fi
Göttingen, Niedersächsische
    SuUB, 8° H. E. Rit. I, 8904
Hamburg, SuUB,
    Inc App A/76
*Jena, Thüringer UuLB, 4
    Theol. XXIV, 40 (2)
London, BL, 3090.d.1
*Marburg, UB, XIXB B 261 t
*München, BSB, Res/4 B. lat. 11 k
Strasbourg, BN et U, R. 103. 578
Wolfenbüttel, HAB, H: 62.4° Helmst.
Wolfenbüttel, HAB, A: 77 Theol. (1)

Spätere Auflage

Aschaffenburg, StiftsB, G-715
Basel, UB, FNP VIII 41
Bern, UB, ZB AD 174
Greifswald, UB, 541/Inc. 32 4°
*Heidelberg, UB, Q 393-1 INC:: [1],
    http://digi.ub.uni-heidelberg.de
    [27. 12. 2010]
Kopenhagen, Kgl. B, 30, 95, S-30
*Mainz, Gutenberg M, Stb Ink 481
*Tübingen, UB, Ga XXXVI 14.4:1
Tübingen, UB, Ga XXXVI 14.4:2
Würzburg, UB, I. t. q. 338a

Mischexemplare

Folgende Exemplare sind zusammengesetzt aus Teilen der früheren und Teilen der späteren Auflage. Die Lagen a–h entsprechen der früheren Auflage. In den Lagen i und k gehören die Blätter i iij, i iiij und k iij, k iiij zur späteren Auflage, die anderen Blätter zur früheren. Die Lagen l–r entsprechen der späteren Auflage.

Augsburg, UB, 02/XIII. 10. 4. 102
Bamberg, SB, Bibl. q 72
Cambridge, UL, BSS. 228. B03
Cambridge, UL, BSS. 228. B03. 2
Cambridge, UL, Norton. d. 224. In diesem Exemplar ist das Blatt mit der Signatur a nachträglich eingefügt worden. Dieses Blatt entspricht der späteren Auflage.
*Frankfurt a. M., UB, 15/463 Nr. 2 (sehr schlecht erhalten)
Frauenburg, Kantonsbibliothek Thurgau/CH, X 628
Halle, ULB, Id 3674
London, BL, 3090. d. 2
Manchester, UL, R 213846
*München, BSB, Res/4 B. g. cath. 11 a
*München, BSB, Res/4 B. g. cath. 11 b
*München, BSB, Res/4 B. g. cath. 11. Die ersten beiden Blätter (Titelseite, Januar, Februar, März) dieses Exemplars sind eingeklebt. Sie unterscheiden sich von den übrigen Seiten durch festeres, glatteres Papier ohne Wurmlöcher. Anscheinend handelt es sich um Farbkopien, die bei der Restaurierung des Buches erstellt und eingefügt wurden. (Bleistift-Eintrag auf der Innenseite des rückwärtigen Einbandes: »v. S. 1979«.) Diese Blätter entsprechen der zweiten Auflage.
Regensburg, SB, Script. 906 a
Regensburg, SB, Script. 911 b
Stuttgart, Württembergische LB, Ba lat. 150301
Stuttgart, Württembergische LB, Ba lat. 150302
Würzburg, UB, I. t. q. 394 angeb.
Wien, UB, I-230165

Weitere Exemplare

*München, UB, W 4 Bibl. 983. Dieses Exemplar ist ein Sonderfall. Es besteht nicht nur aus Teilen der beiden Auflagen von 1503, sondern enthält auch einige Blätter der Auflage von 1502. Die Herkunft der Lagen ist folgende: a (Titel, Kalender, Register) entspricht der späteren Auflage von 1503; ²a (Anfang des Psalters) der früheren; b und c der späteren; d der früheren; e der späteren Auflage von 1503. f enthält vier Blätter der späteren Auflage von 1503 und vier Blätter (f iij bis f 6) der Auflage von 1502; g entspricht der früheren; h der späteren Auflage von 1503. i enthält zwei Blätter der späteren Auflage von 1503 und vier Blätter (i und i ij; i v und i 6) der Auflage von 1502. k–r entsprechen der späteren Auflage von 1503.
Ottobeuren, B der Abtei, F-1263. Dieses Exemplar ist anhand der von Walther genannten Merkmale als Mischexemplar zu erkennen. Eine nähere Untersuchung war leider nicht möglich.
Wernigerode. Walther führt ein Exemplar für Wernigerode an, das er der früheren Auflage zuordnet.[13] Die dortige Stolbergische B wurde in der ersten Hälfte des 20. Jahrhunderts aufgelöst. Wo das Exemplar von Furters Psalterium verblieben ist, konnte ich nicht feststellen.[14]
Nikolsburg / Mikulov. Von den als noch zu untersuchenden Exemplaren nennt Walther eines in Nikolsburg (heute: Mikulov, Tschechien). Auf Anfrage wurde mir mitgeteilt, dass dieser Psalter in der sogenannten "Library of Mikulov's Castle" nicht vorhanden sei.

Deutung der Ergebnisse

Wie lässt sich erklären, dass dieses Psalterium in demselben Jahr 1503 in zwei verschiedenen Auflagen gedruckt wurde und dass es so viele Mischexemplare gibt, die aus den gleichen Teilen der früheren und der späteren Auflage zusammengesetzt sind? Dieses lateinisch-deutsche Psalterium, das Michael Furter 1502 zum ersten Mal herausgab, war bereits 1494 und 1499 bei Erhart Ratdolt in Augsburg erschienen. Die wichtigste Änderung in Furters Ausgabe besteht darin, dass er die Psalmtituli vor die einzelnen Psalmen gesetzt hat und dass diese nicht mehr wie in den Ausgaben von Ratdolt im Register stehen. Furters Auflage von 1502 war offenbar so erfolgreich, dass er das Psalterium 1503 erneut herausgab. Als der Druck bis zu den Lagen mit den Signaturen i und k gelangt war (vermutlich wurde auf zwei Pressen gedruckt), muss etwas eingetreten sein, was dazu führte, dass der Druck nicht weiter in gleicher Auflagenhöhe fortgeführt wurde. War vielleicht ein Druckauftrag eingegangen, der sehr dringlich war und eine der Druckpressen beanspruchte? Und/oder wurde in einer kleineren Auflage weitergedruckt, um die Fertigstellung des Buches zu beschleunigen, weil ein Termin einzuhalten war? Dass die Lagen i und k nicht vollständig gedruckt wurden, könnte ein Hinweis darauf sein, dass man unter Zeitdruck stand.[15]

Als dann die erste Ausgabe von 1503 in einer geringeren Auflagenhöhe erschien, konnte damit der großen Nachfrage nach diesem Werk nicht entsprochen werden. Der erste Teil des Werkes bis zur Lage k war offenbar in einer größeren Anzahl noch vorhanden und konnte durch einen Neudruck der Lagen l bis r vervollständigt werden. Die Zahl der Mischexemplare reichte aber nicht aus, um die Nachfrage zu befriedigen. Es musste daher das ganze Buch neu gesetzt werden. Von der ersten Auflage stand der Widerdruck der beiden Bögen der letzten Lage für die zweite Auflage wohl noch zur Verfügung, da die entsprechenden Seiten in beiden Auflagen übereinstimmen.

Nimmt man an, dass der Schwund an Exemplaren bei den drei Formen prozentual ungefähr gleich groß war, kann man an der Anzahl der noch vorhandenen Exemplare das Größenverhältnis der früheren Auflage, der späteren Auflage und der gemischten Ausgabe ablesen. Von der früheren Auflage konnten für diese Untersuchung 15 noch vorhandene Exemplare nachgewiesen werden, von den Mischexemplaren 19 und von der späteren Auflage 10 Exemplare. Die Mischexemplare waren schließlich wohl der Grund, weshalb Furter die zweite Auflage 1503 nicht als solche kenntlich gemacht hat.

Verhältnis der beiden Auflagen

Die beiden Auflagen aus dem Jahr 1503 stimmen in der Seiteneinteilung nahezu vollständig überein. Das war für die Herstellung der Mischexemplare wichtig, aber auch für den Fall, dass zwei oder mehrere Setzer zugleich für das Buch arbeiteten. Eine völlige Übereinstimmung beider Auflagen wurde offensichtlich nicht angestrebt. Das hätte mehr Zeit in Anspruch genommen und die Auslieferung verzögert. Außerdem war man ja auch bestrebt, Fehler und Unvollkommenheiten auszumerzen.

Frühere / Spätere Auflage

32	XXXII	XXXII
33	XXXV	–
34	XXXII	–
35	–	XXXV
36	–	XXXVI
37	XXXVII	XXXVII
38	XXXVIII	XXXVIII
72	LXXII	[zwischen 72 und 79
73	LXIII	gleiche Fehler in der
74	LXIIII	Blattzählung]
75	LXXV	
76	LXXVI	
77	LXVII	LVXII [Vertauschung]
78	LXVIII	
79	LXXIX	
91	XCI	
92	CXII	[gleiche Vertauschung]
93	XCIII	

[Tab. 1] Fehler in der Blattzählung

12 Die mit * markierten Exemplare wurden von mir geprüft, die übrigen von den Bibliothekarinnen beziehungsweise Bibliothekaren der betreffenden Bibliotheken. Ihnen gilt mein Dank für ihre freundliche Hilfe. Besonders bedanken möchte ich mich bei Nicholas Smith von der University Library Cambridge und Karin Zimmermann von der Universitätsbibliothek Heidelberg für ihre ausführlichen Auskünfte und Hilfen.
13 WALTHER (siehe Anm. 9), S. 25.
14 Ein Teil der Bestände der Stolbergischen B befindet sich heute in der UuLB Halle. Die UuLB Halle besitzt ein Exemplar des Furter'schen Psalteriums. Auf Anfrage teilte man mir mit, dass es nicht das Exemplar aus Wernigerode sei.
15 Von Arbeit unter Zeitdruck heißt es in einem etwa 30 Jahre später erschienenen Psalter: »Dieweil die zeit verlauffen war/ vnnd die Meß vorhanden/ das man seer hat müssen eylen mit der arbeid/ mocht nit feylen (so man in der eyle nicht alles sehen kan) es feilen dann etlich errata dareinn/« (JOHANNES PEDIANUS: *Der rechte alte Psalter*. Gedruckt zů Cöln für S. Lupus. Jm jar M.D.XXXII.)

Dass die Abweichungen im deutschen Text wesentlich zahlreicher sind als im lateinischen, ist dadurch bedingt, dass der deutsche Text umfangreicher ist als der lateinische, aber auch dadurch, dass Orthografie, Zeichensetzung und Textfassung im Deutschen noch nicht so festgelegt waren wie im Lateinischen.

Eine Tendenz der zweiten Auflage lässt sich deutlich feststellen: An den zahlreichen Stellen, wo der Wortlaut geändert wurde, geschah dies meistens, um die Übersetzung genauer der Vulgata anzupassen.

Unterscheidungsmerkmale der beiden Auflagen

Seite, Stelle	frühere Auflage 1503	spätere Auflage 1503
xv^r Dt. unten Ps 21i (2)	Sy as-sen alle faißte d' erd v̇ anbettē in	Sy assen vnd anbetten in alle feißte der erd
xvii^r Dt. unten Ps 25e	die kirchen d' boßhait	die kirchen der b∻sen
xxv^v Dt. Ps 35 Titulus	so vil waren in sůchen zet∻tten	so vil waren die in sůchten zet∻ttē
xxix^r Dt. Ps 38bc	^b Ich hab gesetzet dle hůt minē mund : dē d' sund' stůnd wider mi ch: ^c Ich erstumpt v̇ bin gedemütiget ich schwig	^b Ich hab gesetzet die hůt meinē mūd / do d' sünd' stůnd wider mi ch ^c Ich erstumpt vnd bin gedemɸtiget v̇ schwig
xxxvii^v Dt. Ps 48 xxxviii^r Titulus	vnd dathan vnd abirō die [oben auf Seite xxxviii^r]	vnd Dathan vnd abyrō die [unten auf Seite xxxvii^v]
xliii^r Dt. Ende der letzten Zeile Ps 54 d(2)	aber herr ich wird hoffē in dich	aber ich wird hoffen ī dich herr.
liiii^r Dt. Ps 70 Titulus	Als Dauid die warnůg vō ionathas vernā : flo he er zů Samuel. do sendet im saul knecht nach in zefahen.	Als Dauid die warnůg vō ionathas vernā / flo he er zů samuel. do sendet i⊥ samuel knecht nach in zeuahē.
lxiii^r Lat.-Spalte	Psalmus lxxviii [am Ende der letzten Zeile von Ps 77]	Psalmus lxxviii [in einer eigenen Zeile vor dem Titulus des Ps 78]
lxvii^v Lat.-Spalte	Psalmus lxxxv. [am Ende der letzten Zeile von Ps 84]	Psalmus. lxxxv. [in einer eigenen Zeile vor dem Titulus des Ps 85]
lxviii^v Dt. Ps 86a	die thor	die portē
lxix^r Lat. 3. Zeile	o ɔspectu tuo oratio mea: oclina	in ɔspectu tuo orō mea: inclina
lxxv^v Dt. Ps 88y	»wirt i⊥ nit schadē zůsetzē.«	»wirt nit zůsetzē i⊥ zů schadē.«

LXIII (= 73ʳ) Dt. Ps 90o	Wa] er hat ī mich ge hoffet ich wird in be schirmen	Wā er hat ī mich ge=hoffet ich werd in erl-sē ich wird in bschir mē
LXIII (= 73ᵛ) Dt. Ps 91m	Der gerecht wirdt plϕen als d' zweyg	Der gerecht wirdt plϕen als der pal⊥
LXXVʳ Dt. Ps 93z	vnser gott wirt sy zerstrewen.	vnnser got wirt sy zerstreüwen.
LXXVᵛ Dt. unten Ps 95g	Bringen dem herren der gegent der haiden / bringent dem herren die glory synem namen.	Bringent dem herren ir gegent d' haidē bringent dē herren glory vnd eer brīgent dē herrē die glory seynē namen.
LXXVIᵛ Dt. oben Ps 96e	Die berg sind geflos sen als dα wachs vor dem antlütz des her=ren alle erd.	Die berg sind geflos sen als dα wachs vor dē antlütz des herrē vor dē antlütz de_ her ren alle erd.
77ʳ / Seitenzahl	LXVII	LVXII
77ᵛ Dt. unten Ps 98k	Erh= hent eüwern herren gott	Erh=ēt got euwern herren
LXVIIIʳ (= 78ʳ) Dt. Ps 99d	syne thor	seyne portē
LXXIXᵛ Lat. Ps 102a	BᵃEnedic aīa meo d]o:	BᵃEnedic aīa mea d]o:
LXXXVIIʳ Dt. 2. Zeile v. u. Ps 107v	die barmhertzigkaiten des hertzen.	die barmhertzigkaitē des her ren.
XCIXʳ Lat. 3. Zeile v. u.	Rectū iudiciū tuū	rectum iudicium tuū.
CVIᵛ Latein 1. Zeile	Lunā & stellas in ptātē noctis:	nā & stellas in potestatē noctis:
CXIIᵛ Latein 1. Zeile	Prope est d]s o⊥ibus inuocātibus	Prope ē d]s o⊥ibus inuocantibus
CXXIIᵛ Latein 1. Zeile	Quia r̄spexit hūilitatē ¶ ancille sue:	Quia respexit hūilita=¶ tē ācille sue:
CXXVIᵛ drittletzte Zeile	Sācte ianuari cum socijs tuis: ora,p.	Sctē ianuari cū socijs tuis: ora,p n.

FEDERICA FABBRI

Tridenti: per Mapheum de Fraçacinis,

M.cccccxj

*Note su un frammento
di lessico italiano-tedesco
del secolo decimosesto*

[…] compito della scienza non è soltanto quello di fondare nuovi edifici; sì bene quello di finire e di rifinire gli edifici già incominciati. […]. Repertori […], indici, cataloghi di edizioni, e studi bibliografici particolari, e repertori di tipi: tutto un lavoro immenso e minuzioso di preparazione già fatto. Da una parte resta ora da collaudare e da ripulire questo materiale ingente.   ROBERTO RIDOLFI

COM'È NOTO, QUESTE PAROLE DI ROBERTO RIDOLFI sono riportate nel saggio *Proposta di ricerche sulla stampa e sugli stampatori del Quattrocento* apparso nel 1949 sulla rivista *La Bibliofilia*;[1] si tratta di un grande classico degli studi bibliografici in cui lo studioso toscano sostiene fermamente la necessità di procedere ad una verifica di repertori e cataloghi di incunaboli per un controllo delle attribuzioni, in particolare delle edizioni *sine notis*, al fine di ripulire questi sussidi da eventuali attribuzioni errate e/o mancate segnalazioni, risolvere i casi incerti e fornire all'utente finale un'immagine il più attendibile possibile della produzione a stampa del XV secolo.

A sessant'anni di distanza non si può dire che l'opera di collaudo e ripulitura auspicata da Ridolfi sia stata completata, come cercherò di dimostrare in questo mio contributo in cui sono esposti i risultati di alcune ricerche condotte per il conseguimento della tesi di laurea in Bibliologia presso la Facoltà di Conservazione dei Beni Culturali dell'Università degli Studi di Bologna di cui è stato relatore il Professor Lorenzo Baldacchini e correlatrice la Dottoressa Bettina Wagner, responsabile del centro di catalogazione del manoscritto e consulente per il fondo incunaboli della Bayerische Staatsbibliothek di Monaco di Baviera e attuale *chair* della Rare Books and Manuscripts Section dell'International Federation of Library Associations and Institutions.

Le ricerche hanno avuto ad oggetto le edizioni dei lessici italianotedeschi stampate in Italia nel secolo decimoquinto e, come fine, la ricognizione di tutte le edizioni e di tutti gli esemplari superstiti nonché l'analisi bibliologica di questi ultimi. Le indagini condotte su repertori, cataloghi e in alcuni fondi archivistici, la verifica personale della quasi totalità degli esemplari sopravvissuti, la loro collazione e le informazioni recuperate dallo studio di opere monografiche, spogli di riviste e banche dati hanno portato alla scoperta di errori di attribuzione e datazione compiuti in fase di catalogazione, così come all'individuazione di esemplari fino ad oggi sconosciuti e di esemplari di cui è nota l'esistenza, ma dei quali si è persa ogni traccia. Ai lessici italiano-tedeschi stampati nel XV secolo si sono aggiunte un'edizione uscita dai torchi di Giovan Battista

[1] ROBERTO RIDOLFI: Proposta di ricerche sulla stampa e sugli stampatori del Quattrocento. In: *La Bibliofilia. Rivista di storia del libro e di bibliografia.* LI (1949), pp. 1–8, qui pp. 1/2.

Sessa nel dicembre 1500[2] ed una grammatica *sine notis*, ma stampata quasi certamente alla fine del Quattrocento, in cui il testo tedesco precede quello italiano. L'edizione di Sessa del 1500 è stata presa in considerazione in quanto costituisce la ristampa di una precedente realizzata dallo stesso tipografo due anni prima;[3] quanto alla grammatica tedesco-italiana, essa ha in comune con i lessici non solo lo stesso contesto di produzione (Venezia e la zona del Fondaco dei Tedeschi), ma anche gli stessi destinatari (coloro che, per lavoro o per studio, avevano necessità di intendere e farsi intendere nella lingua italiana e tedesca) e la stessa destinazione d'uso (l'autoapprendimento delle due lingue). La mia analisi parte proprio da questa grammatica di cui si fornisce di seguito la descrizione:

Vocabolario tedesco e italiano. [Venezia: Johann Hamman, XV sec. *exeunte*?]. 4°; [8] c.; a⁸, bianca c. a₁ᵛ. Car. got. (occhietto, 11:130G M88; c. a₂ʳ, ll. 1–3, 2:103G M20; testo, 12:73G M87). Stampa su 4 coll. (cc. a₂ʳ–a₅ᵛ) e su due coll. (cc. a₅ᵛ–a₈ᵛ); 26 e 44 ll. Iniziale silografica fitomorfa in cornice su fondo bianco a c. a₂ʳ. Impr.: gtst enen enir didi (C) 1499–1500 (Q). GW M51227; ISTC iv00315700; C 6303;[4] Claes 144;[5] Graesse VI 383.[6]

Attualmente ISTC segnala cinque esemplari dell'edizione, in Gran Bretagna (BL[7]), in Germania (UB Freiburg i. B.;[8] BSB;[9] StB Nürnberg[10]) e in Austria (Bischöfliche Gurker Mensal B Klagenfurt). Gli stessi esemplari sono segnalati anche in GW; quello della Bischöfliche Gurker Mensalbibliothek figura anche nell'*Österreichischer Inkunabelzensus*.[11] GW-M, la versione a schede cartacee manoscritte del *Gesamtkatalog der Wiegendrucke* in parte digitalizzate e visibili online,[12] omette l'incunabolo di Klagenfurt e segnala quello della collezione dei principi Dietrichstein di Mikulov (città meglio nota con il nome tedesco di Nikolsburg), non rilevato da ISTC e GW e di cui al momento non si trova traccia.

In questa sede non mi soffermerò tanto sull'edizione attribuita a Hamman, che sarà invece oggetto di un prossimo saggio, quanto sull'esemplare conservato a Klagenfurt di cui, secondo quanto si evince da ISTC e GW, si sarebbe conservato un solo frammento.

Nel catalogo dattiloscritto degli incunaboli della biblioteca di Klagenfurt compilato da Peter Hans Pascher all'inizio degli anni Ottanta del secolo scorso,[13] il frammento è così descritto:

Vocabulario Italiano-Tedesco. Venedig: Johann Hamman, [um 1490]. 8 Bl. 4 + 2 Sp. 44 Z. Typen: 2:103G, 11:130G, 12:73G. C 6303, Pr 5207. Sign. In XXV b 24 (Nachsatz).[14]

Il frammento sarebbe dunque contenuto nel volume con segnatura In XXV b 24. Tuttavia, già dalla descrizione di Pascher si nota qualcosa di strano: anzitutto l'incunabolo è descritto come *Vocabulario Italiano-Tedesco*; inoltre, né il luogo di stampa né lo stampatore sono posti tra parentesi quadre (a differenza della data), il ché lascia intendere che nel frammento sia stampato il *colophon* in cui Johann Hamman figura chiaramente quale stampatore dell'edizione in Venezia. Quanto alla descrizione, essa corrisponde effettivamente alla grammatica attribuita a Hamman; anche i riferimenti ai repertori bibliografici di Copinger e Proctor coincidono.

---

[2] GW M51150; ISTC iv00321600.

[3] GW M51147 e M51148; ISTC iv00321500.

[4] È indicato il 1490 come anno di stampa.

[5] FRANZ CLAES: *Bibliographisches Verzeichnis der deutschen Vokabulare und Wörterbücher, gedruckt bis 1600*. Hildesheim 1977.

[6] Graesse ritiene erroneamente che l'esemplare citato, venduto dalla libreria antiquaria berlinese J. A. Stargardt GmbH & Co., sia stato stampato a Bologna tra il 1478 e il 1480.

[7] IA.23409.

[8] Ink. E 308, accessibile online. Si veda l'indice dei siti a p. 374.

[9] 4 Inc. s. a. 1960 b (BSB-Ink V-285), accessibile online. Si veda l'indice dei siti a p. 374.

[10] Phil. 401. 4°.

[11] *Inkunabelzensus Österreich*, accessibile online. Si veda l'indice dei siti a p. 374.

[12] GW, consultato online.

[13] PETER HANS PASCHER: *Die Wiegendrucke der Bischöflichen Mensalbibliothek im Archiv der Diözese Gurk*. s. l. [post 1982], datt., n° 612. La stessa scheda è riportata in Ibid.: *Die Wiegendrucke in den öffentlichen und privaten Bibliotheken Kärntens. Catalogus incunabulorum in bibliothecis Carinthiae*. Klagenfurt 1997 (*Beiträge zur Kodikologie und zu den Historischen Hilfswissenschaften*. 12), n° 2080.

[14] Trad. it.: *appendice*.

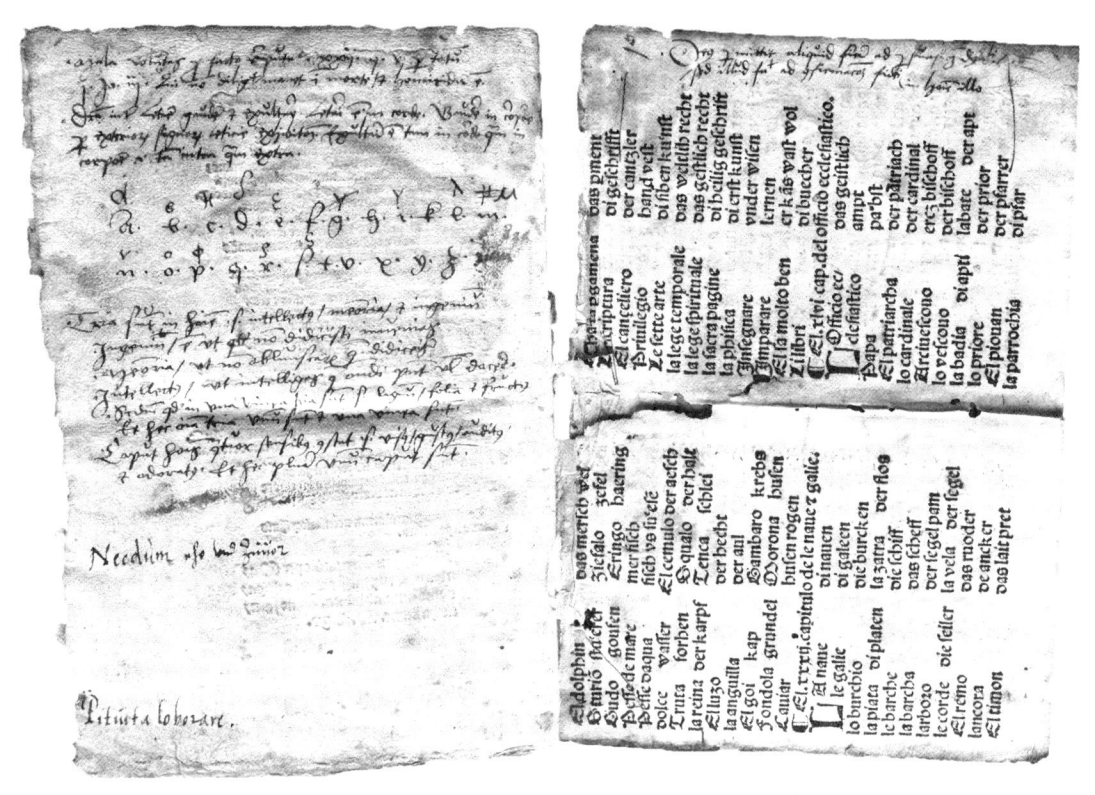

[Fig. 1a e 1b] HERMANNUS TORRENTINUS: *Elucidarius carminum & historiarum*.
Argentine: per Mathiam Hupfuff, 1515, c. L8ᵛ [1a]; recto del frammento di *lessico italiano-tedesco* usato come controguardia posteriore. Bischöfliche Gurker MensalB Klagenfurt, In xxv b 24 [1b]

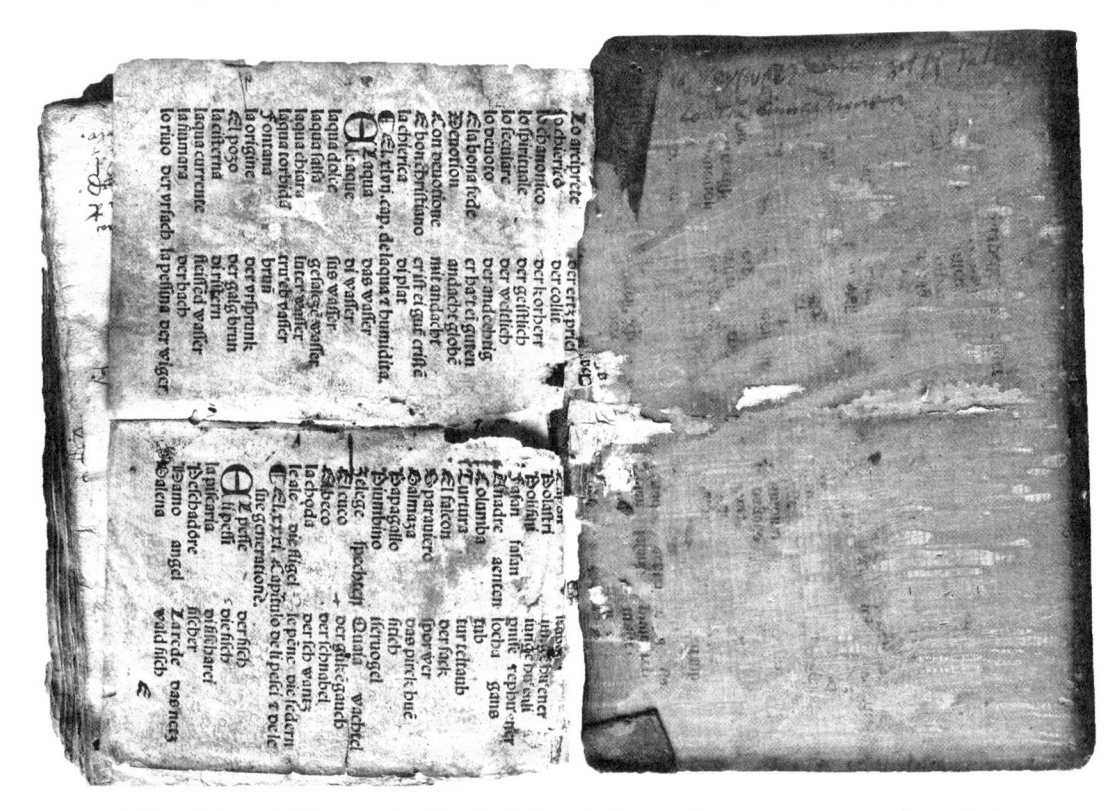

[Fig. 2] Verso del frammento di *lessico italiano-tedesco* usato come controguardia posteriore.
Bischöfliche Gurker MensalB Klagenfurt, In xxv b 24

A questo punto sono opportune alcune considerazioni: (1) l'unico lessico stampato da Johann Hamman è in realtà una grammatica in cui, come già detto, la versione tedesca precede quella italiana. Mentre in ISTC e GW il frammento di Klagenfurt è identificato come vocabolario tedesco-italiano, nel catalogo di Pascher esso figura come vocabolario *italiano-tedesco*; (2) la grammatica è priva di note tipografiche, tant'è che in ISTC e GW il nome dello stampatore, il luogo e la data di stampa sono riportati tra parentesi quadre; Pascher, invece, utilizza le parentesi quadre solo per la data cronica. Le ipotesi possibili sono due: o la dicitura *Vocabulario italiano-tedesco* riportata nel catalogo di Pascher è un errore, oppure il frammento conservato a Klagenfurt è effettivamente ciò che resta del lessico *sine notis* attribuito a Hamman il cui nome tuttavia avrebbe dovuto essere posto tra parentesi quadre dal catalogatore.

A risolvere ogni dubbio è l'esame diretto del frammento [fig. 1 e fig. 2] ed il confronto con gli altri esemplari segnalati da ISTC e GW [fig. 3 e fig. 4]. È evidente che la copia di Klagenfurt non può appartenere al *Vocabolario tedesco e italiano* attribuito a Hamman; un'indagine più accurata del frammento austriaco ha, infatti, evidenziato che si tratta di un caso di errata attribuzione alla produzione a stampa del Quattrocento di due carte appartenenti ad un'edizione del secolo successivo.

Il frammento di Klagenfurt è utilizzato come controguardia posteriore di un volume miscellaneo segnato In XXV b 24 contenente due esemplari di edizioni del Cinquecento:

ANTONIUS LIBER:[15] *Vocabularius gemma gemmarum noviter impressus multarum dictionum additione exornatus*, impressus in Lor,[16] per wilhelmu[m] schaffner, anno .M.D.xiiij. 4°; [152] c.; a^8 b–c^4 d^8 e–f^4 g^8 h–i^4 k^8 l–m^4 n^8 o–p^4 q^8 r–y^4 z^8 A–B^4 C^8 D^4 E^8, bianca c. E$_8$^{v}. VD 16 G 1101.

Legato con: HERMANNUS TORRENTINUS: *Elucidarius carminum & historiarum: vel vocabularius poeticus: continens fabulas: historias: provincias: urbes: insulas: fluvios & montes illustres: diligenter denuo revisus. Item vocabula et interpretationes Graecorum & Hebraicorum: una cum vocabulis communibus Sarracenorum in latinum translatis: et aliis in fine adiunctis*, Excussum Argentine[17]: per Mathiam Hupffuff, anno salutis humane .M.D.xv. 4°; [64] c.; A^8 B–C^4 D^8 E–F^4 G^8 H^4 I^8 K^4 L^8, bianca c. L$_8$v. VD 16 T 1603; PA VI 381.

Klagenfurt. Bischöfliche Gurker Mensalbibliothek. In XXV b 24. C. a$_1$: 14 × 19,7 cm. Mezza legatura a banda del XVI secolo di area tedesca in cuoio con decorazione a secco (doppia filettatura longitudinale centrale, successione di volute terminanti con rosette gotiche) su assi in legno di faggio. Sul piatto anteriore, traccia di tenone perduto ed etichetta con attuale segnatura di collocazione a inchiostro bruno (25 | B. 24). Sul piatto posteriore, traccia di contrograffa perduta. Tagli rustici. Dorso a due nervi doppi in cuoio a vista e tre scomparti; al centro, cartiglio con *titulus* e numero progressivo di catalogo a inchiostro bruno (Vocabulari[us] latino-germ. Anonym. 174).[18] Sul contropiatto anteriore, IOHANNES HEROLT: *Sermones discipuli de tempore*, frammento (Dominica quarta, Sermo IX, *De conscientia*: In hac d[omi]nica agit[ur] [de] q[ua]rto adue[n]tu qui erit | ad morte[m] cuiuslib[et] ho[min]is [...]), [Metz?: Kaspar Hoch-

---

15 Nome dell'autore da c. a$_1$^{v}.
16 Lahr (fonte: CERL *Thesaurus*, online. Si veda l'indice dei siti a p. 374).
17 Straßburg (fonte: CERL *Thesaurus*, online. Si veda l'indice dei siti a p. 374).
18 Il numero 174 è il progressivo del volume nel *Catalogus Librorum Bibliothecae Episcopalis Gurcensis* (Hs. XXX b 11) risalente al 1700 ca. (Sezione *Gram[m]atici, Anonijmi*). Sulla Bischöfliche Gurker Mensal B Klagenfurt si veda BERNHARD FABIAN: *Handbuch der historischen Buchbestände in Österreich*. Bearb. von WILMA BUCHINGER u. KONSTANZE MITTENDORFER. Hildesheim 1994–97. Vol. 1–4. Accessibile in linea. Si veda l'indice dei siti a p. 374.

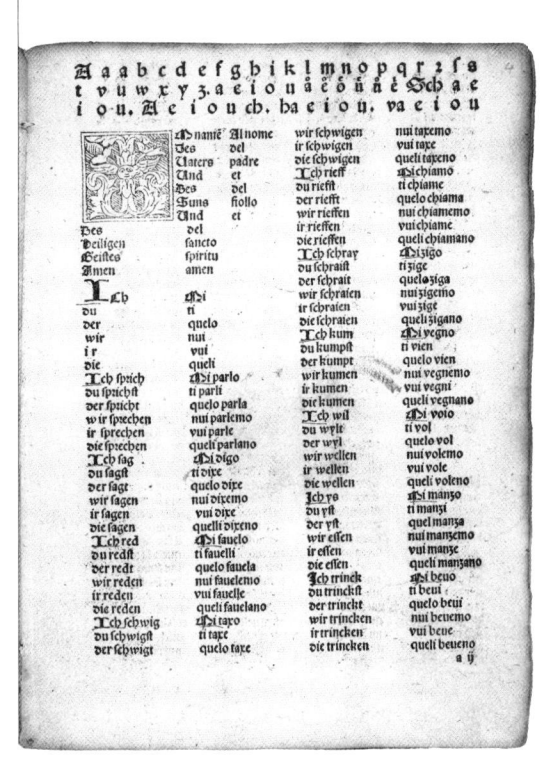

[Fig. 3] *Vocabolario Todescho e Italiano.* [Venezia: Johann Hamman, XV sec. exeunte?], c. a1ʳ. StB Nürnberg, Phil. 401.1°

[Fig. 4] *Vocabolario Todescho* [...], c. a2ʳ. StB Nürnberg, Phil. 401.4°

feder?, *post* 1500]; 2°; car. got., 3:65G M49; sul frammento, etichetta con attuale segnatura di collocazione (Philologi. | XXV. | B-24). Sul contropiatto posteriore, frammento di lessico italiano-tedesco del XVI secolo con nota manoscritta a inchiostro bruno di mano cinquecentesca. Esemplare in discreto stato conservativo: perdita del rivestimento in cuoio sul piatto anteriore e lacerazione dello stesso nella parte inferiore del piatto posteriore, perdita del rivestimento del dorso, vistosa lacuna sulla controguardia anteriore, bruniture e tracce di *foxing*, gore di liquido sulle carte del secondo esemplare, lacerazione della maculatura anteriore e posteriore (in quest'ultimo caso dovuta al distacco dal contropiatto), bruniture dovute ai residui del legno del contropiatto e fori di sfarfallamento di coleotteri anobidi sulla maculatura posteriore.

Da un confronto con gli esemplari segnalati da ISTC e GW appartenenti alla grammatica presumibilmente stampata da Johann Hamman emergono alcune importanti differenze, alcune delle quali già evidenziate: anzitutto, nella grammatica attribuita a Hamman il testo tedesco precede quello italiano, mentre nel frammento di Klagenfurt la traduzione tedesca segue quella italiana; inoltre, nell'edizione attribuita a Hamman il testo è stampato su quattro e due colonne, mentre sull'esemplare di Klagenfurt il testo è stampato solo su due; come dimostra il segno di piegatura al centro della carta, le quattro colonne visibili tanto al recto quanto al verso del frammento di Klagenfurt appartengono a due pagine distinte. Siamo dunque in presenza di una carta con quattro pagine stampate (due al recto e due al verso); la cosa interessante è che non si tratta di pagine contigue: infatti, al recto [fig. 1] sulla pagina di sinistra è riportato l'inizio del capitolo 32 (¶ El .xxxij. capitulo de le naue [et] galie), mentre sulla pagina di destra si trova l'inizio del capitolo 46 (¶ El .xlvi cap. del officio ecclesiastico); al verso [fig. 2], sulla pagina di sinistra è stampato il capitolo 47 (¶ El .xlvij. cap. de laqua [et] humidita), sulla pagina di destra l'inizio del capitolo 31 (¶ El .xxxi. Capitulo de li pesci [et] de le | sue generatione). Già questi elementi sarebbero sufficienti a dimostrare che il frammento di Klagenfurt non può appartenere all'edizione attribuita a Hamman, il cui testo peraltro non è suddiviso in capitoli; ma c'è di più: sulla pagina di destra stampata al verso della carta di Klagenfurt è visibile una segnatura (E) che ci conferma ulteriormente che non può trattarsi della grammatica di Hamman, composta da un solo fascicolo di appena otto carte, le prime quattro segnate con la lettera a.

La carta di Klagenfurt, un tempo incollata al contropiatto posteriore del volume miscellaneo e da questo distaccata con ogni probabilità in occasione della catalogazione ad opera di Peter Hans Pascher, appartiene dunque chiaramente ad un'altra edizione, ossia al *Libro utilissimo a chi si diletta di intendere tedesco* stampato a Trento da Maffeo Fracassini per Giovanni Pietro Pezzoni[19] il 18 settembre 1511 [figg. 5–7]. Si tratta della prima edizione trentina del Cinquecento e dell'unico lessico italiano-tedesco stampato da Maffeo Fracassini. In un breve saggio sulla tipografia di Collio apparso nel 1992,[20] Ennio Sandal fa riferimento per ben due volte ad una precedente edizione che sarebbe stata stampata dallo stesso Fracassini nel 1509 col titolo di *Piccolo libro da l'imparar todescho*.[21] Se l'edizione del 1509 fosse realmente uscita dai torchi di Fracassini, non è chiaro

---

19 Su Maffeo Fracassini, tipografo bresciano attivo a Collio Valtrompia e a Trento, e su Giovanni Pietro Pezzoni, editore e libraio bresciano e proprietario di una tipografia a Trento si veda FERNANDA ASCARELLI: La tipografia cinquecentina italiana. Firenze 1996 (*Contributi alla biblioteca bibliografica italica*. 1), pp. 86 e 221. – EAD.: La tipografia del '500 in Italia. Firenze 1989 (*Biblioteca di Bibliografia italiana*. 116), pp. 170, 175 e 301/2. – GIOVANNI BAMPI: Della stampa e degli stampatori nel Principato di Trento fino al 1564. In: *Archivio trentino*. II (1883), pp. 202–21, qui p. 210. – UGO BARONCELLI: Editori e stampatori a Brescia nel Cinquecento. In: *Studi di biblioteconomia e storia del libro in onore di Francesco Barberi*. Ed. GIORGIO DE GREGORI e MARIA VALENTI. Roma 1976, pp. 97–107, qui pp. 103/4. – GEDEON BORSA: *Clavis typographorum librariorumque Italiae 1465–1600*. Vol. 1/2. Aureliae Aquensis 1980, vol. I, p. 145 e vol. II, pp. 77, 349 e 384. – LAMBERTO DONATI: *Spigolature bresciane: omaggio offerto a Duilio Grazioli nel suo settantesimo compleanno (Brescia il 27 Maggio 1949)*. Milano 1949, pp. 15/6. – EDIT16 CNCT 462 e CNCT 687. – GIUSEPPE FUMAGALLI: *Lexicon typographicum Italiae: dictionnaire géographique d'Italie pour servir à l'histoire de l'imprimerie dans ce pays*. Florence 1966, pp. 92 e 431. – GERMANO JACOPO GUSSAGO: *Memorie storico-critiche della tipografia bresciana*. Brescia MDCCCXI, pp. 207–9. – MAURO HAUSBERGHER: La stampa a Trento. Il Quattrocento e il Cinquecento. In: Ibid.: Annali della tipografia Zanetti: Trento 1625–1683. Trento 1997 (*Annali della tipografia trentina*. 1), pp. 25–33, qui p. 27. – L'attività tipografica ed editoriale in Trentino nei secc. XV–XVII. Cronologia, notizie storiche e bibliografia. Ed. MAURO HAUSBERGHER e FABRIZIO LEONARDELLI. In: *Studi trentini di scienze storiche*. Sezione I, LXXV (1996), 4, pp. 431–44, qui p. 432. – FRITZ MILCKE: Il primo libro stampato a Collio di Val Trompia. In: *La Bibliofilia. Rivista di storia del libro e di bibliografia*. I (1899/1900), pp. 55–7. – GIORGIO MONTECCHI: *Fracassini, Maffeo und Gabriele*. In: LGB², vol. III, pp. 9/10. – FREDERICK JOHN NORTON: Italian printers: 1501–1520. An annotated list. London 1958 (*Cambridge Bibliographical Society*. 3), pp. 18/9. – GIUSEPPE NOVA: Stampatori, librai ed editori bresciani in Italia nel Cinquecento. Brescia 2000 (*Strumenti di lavoro. Fondazione civiltà bresciana*. 5), pp. 55–7 e 129/30. – CARLO PASERO: I libri di Collio in Valtrompia. In: *Brescia nelle industrie e nei commerci. Organo ufficiale della Camera di Commercio ed Industria di Brescia*. VII (1927), 5, pp. 119–21 (parzialmente riprodotto in VALENTINO VOLTA: Collio XVI secolo. Brescia 1980). – CARLO PASERO: *Francia Spagna Impero a Brescia: 1509–1516*. Brescia 1958, p. 133. – *Bibliotheca Tridentina: libri trentini del XV e del XVI secolo nelle collezioni della Biblioteca comunale. Dall'introduzione della stampa a Trento alla prima tipografia stabile della città*. Ed. ELENA RAVELLI e MAURO HAUSBERGHER. Trento 2000, p. 13. – I primordi della stampa a Brescia: 1472–1511. Atti del convegno internazionale (Brescia, 6–8 giugno 1984). Ed. ENNIO SANDAL. Padova 1986 (*Medioevo e Umanesimo*. 63), pp. 20, 21 e 23. – ENNIO SANDAL: *La tipografia di Collio V. T. (1502–1538)*. Collio 1992. – Ibid.: Fracassini, Maffeo, Iacopo e Gabriele. In: *Dizionario dei tipografi e degli editori italiani. Il Cinquecento*. Vol. I: A–F. Ed. MARCO MENATO, ENNIO SANDAL e GIUSEPPINA ZAPPELLA. Milano 1997 (*Grandi opere*. 9), pp. 447/8. – ENNIO SANDAL: *Maffeo, Gabriele e Giacomo Fracassini stampatori in Collio, 1502–1538*. Verona 2002. – Ibid.: Uomini, lettere e torchi a Brescia nel primo Cinquecento. In: *Aevum. Rassegna di scienze storiche linguistiche e filologiche*. LXXVII.3 (2003), pp. 557–91, qui p. 558. – VOLTA (vedi sopra), pp. 71–116.

20 SANDAL 1992 (vedi nota 19). A Collio Valtrompia Maffeo Fracassini introdusse nel 1502 la stampa a caratteri mobili.

21 SANDAL 1992 (vedi nota 19), p. 11: «la bellissima iniziale O su fondo nero che appare nella *Chronica* di Elia Capriolo [...] venne riutilizzata come Q nel *Piccolo libro da l'imparar todesch* (Trento 1509)»; più in basso, citando Aldo Chemelli: «Ma egli ignora due edizioni che riportano esplicitamente Trento come luogo di stampa: si tratta del *Piccolo libro da l'imparar todescho* (1509) e gli *Statuti* del 1528».

perché l'autore abbia inserito solo l'edizione del *Piccolo libro* del 1511 nell'indice cronologico posto in appendice alla stessa pubblicazione;[22] si tratta infatti di un errore, come confermatomi personalmente dal Professor Sandal, peraltro ripetuto nella voce sui tipografi Fracassini curata dallo stesso per il *Dizionario dei tipografi e degli editori italiani del Cinquecento* apparso nel 1997.[23] L'edizione del 1509 è dunque un fantasma bibliografico in quanto non esiste alcuna edizione del lessico italiano-tedesco stampata da Fracassini anteriore a quella del 1511.

EDIT 16[24] segnala due soli esemplari di questa edizione conservati alla Biblioteca Universitaria di Bologna[25] e alla Biblioteca Queriniana di Brescia.[26] Nella monografia di Ennio Sandal apparsa nel 2002 su Maffeo, Giacomo e Gabriele Fracassini[27] sono indicati due ulteriori esemplari conservati alla Biblioteca Comunale di Trento; anche nel Catalogo Bibliografico Trentino (CBT Trento) figurano due esemplari dell'edizione suddetta,[28] mentre su ESTeR[29] è segnalata la sola copia della Biblioteca Universitaria di Bologna identificata come Pontificia biblioteca per la presenza di un doppio timbro di possesso a c. A$_2^r$ dell'esemplare bolognese. Da una verifica nel catalogo degli incunaboli e delle cinquecentine conservate nel Fondo trentino della Biblioteca Comunale di Trento[30] non risulta tuttavia alcun esemplare del lessico stampato da Fracassini; infatti, come indicato in CBT Trento, le due copie della biblioteca sono solo riproduzioni dell'esemplare di Bologna.[31]

---

22 SANDAL 1992 (vedi nota 19), p. 14.

23 Ibid., pp. 447/8: «Tra i materiali portati da Brescia a Collio vi è una grande iniziale O silografica su fondo nero [...], trasformata in Q nel *Piccolo libro da l'imparar todesco* (1509). [...] Più diversificati i destinatari di altre tre operette dei F[racassini] e forse offerte a uno smercio più ampio: [...], il *Libro utilissimo a chi se dileta de intender todescho* (1511)».
Rigranzio sentitamente il Professor Ennio Sandal per la cortesia e l'utile informazione fornitami.

24 CNCE 60973.

25 A.V. Caps.LXXXVII/8.

26 Lechi.71.

27 SANDAL 2002 (vedi nota 19), p. 93, n° 8. Non è chiaro quali fossero i rapporti di parentela che legavano i tre Fracassini: fratelli o padre e figlio (Maffeo e Gabriele).

28 *Catalogo Bibliografico Trentino*. Versione online. Si veda l'indice dei siti a p. 374.
Doc. 1762891: primo esemplare, coll.: t-TT II b 146; secondo esemplare, coll.: t-TTF 1.

29 *Editori e stampatori di Trento e Rovereto*. Versione online. Si veda l'indice dei siti a p. 374. ID. 10290.

30 *Gli incunaboli della Biblioteca Comunale di Trento. Catalogo*. Ed. MAURO HAUSBERGHER e SILVANO GROFF. Trento 2006 (*Patrimonio storico e artistico del Trentino*. 29). – *Incunaboli e cinquecentine del Fondo trentino della Biblioteca comunale di Trento. Catalogo*. Ed. MAURO HAUSBERGHER e ELENA RAVELLI. Trento 2000 (*Patrimonio storico e artistico del Trentino*. 23).

31 Primo esemplare: fotoriproduzione originale alla Pontificia B di Bologna; secondo esemplare: microfilm, originale presso B Universitaria, Bologna. I due esemplari coincidono.

32 Cc. E$_3^r$ e E$_2^v$ riprodotte in VOLTA (vedi nota 19), pp. 92/3.

33 GIUSEPPINA ZAPPELLA: *Le marche dei tipografi e degli editori italiani del Cinquecento. Repertori di figure, simboli e soggetti e dei relativi motti*. Vol. 1/2. Milano 1986 (*Grandi opere*. 1), vol. I, XVId. Riprodotta in: DONATI (vedi nota 19), p. 15. – EDIT 16 CNCM 841. – ALDA ROSSEBASTIANO BART: Per le stampe trentine di Maffeo Fracassini. In: *Studi trentini di scienze storiche*. Sezione I, LV.1 (1976), pp. 43–5 fig. 1, parzialmente riprodotto in VOLTA (vedi nota 19), pp. 83/4. – ALDA ROSSEBASTIANO BART: Antichi vocabolari plurilingui d'uso popolare: la tradizione del «Solenissimo Vochabuolista». Alessandria 1984 (*Lessicografia e lessicologia*. 1), p. 75, tav. 16. – SANDAL 2002 (vedi nota 19), p. 44. – Sander, V, fig. 136. – VOLTA (vedi nota 19), p. 72. – ZAPPELLA (vedi sopra), vol. II, fig. 114.

34 SANDAL 2002 (vedi nota 19), p. 45: lettera Q su fondo nero con «scena bucolica ambientata in un paesaggio con alberi, un corso d'acqua e uccelli e un amorino alato che cavalca il dorso di un cervo»; p. 46: «La bella iniziale decorata passerà a Collio trasformata in una Q, segno dei rapporti e degli scambi esistenti tra Brescia e Collio». – L'iniziale è un riadattamento della lettera O utilizzata per la prima volta nella *Chronica de rebus Brixianorum* di Elia Capriolo (Brixiae: per Arundum de Arundis hortatu et auspicio Francisci Bragadini, [ca. 1505]), EDIT 16 CNCE 9279; ISTC ic00126000; GW VI col. 125a. – CARLO PASERO: *Le xilografie dei libri bresciani dal 1483 alla seconda metà del XVI secolo*. Brescia 1928, p. 172, n° LXXX. – ENNIO SANDAL: *La stampa a Brescia nel Cinquecento. Notizie storiche e annali tipografici (1501–1553)*. Baden-Baden 1999 (*Bibliotheca bibliographica aureliana*. CLXXIV), p. 52, n° 42. – C. A$_1^r$ riprodotta in SANDAL 2002 (vedi nota 19), p. 46. – Secondo CARLO PASERO si tratterebbe di un asinello cavalcato da un putto: PASERO 1927 (vedi nota 19), p. 120. – PASERO (vedi sopra), p. 173: «Un O (fondo nero, base cm. 4,8): un prato, una staccionata ed un asinello cavalcato da un putto con cornucopia». – Iniziale Q riprodotta in: ROSSEBASTIANO BART 1976 (vedi nota 33), fig. 2. – ROSSEBASTIANO BART 1984 (vedi nota 33), p. 74. – SANDAL 1992 (vedi nota 19), p. 10. – VOLTA (vedi nota 19), pp. 91 e 115.

35 Riprodotta in: ROSSEBASTIANO BART 1976 (vedi nota 33), fig. 3. – ROSSEBASTIANO BART 1984 (vedi nota 33), p. 75, tav. 15. – VOLTA (vedi nota 19), p. 114.

36 Larghezza della carta di difficile misurazione per lo stato conservativo della stessa.

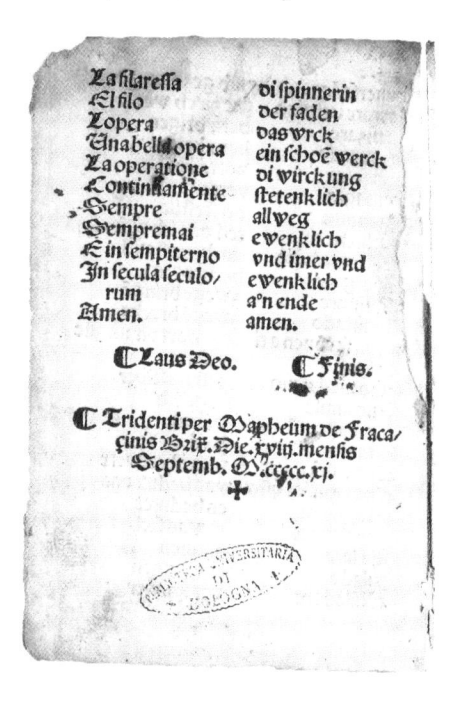

Gli unici due esemplari ad oggi conosciuti sono dunque quelli di Bologna e Brescia di cui si fornisce di seguito la descrizione analitica:

Libro utilissimo a chi si diletta di intendere tedesco [Vocabolario italiano-tedesco]. Tridenti: per Mapheum de Fracaçinis Brix., Die .xviij. mensis Septemb. M.ccccc.xj. 8°; [60] c.; A–G⁸ H⁴, bianca c. H₄ʳ.³²

Car. got. (99G). Stampa a piena pagina (cc. A₁ᵛ–A₆ᵛ) e su 2 coll. (cc. A₆ᵛ–H₃ᵛ); 25 ll. Occhietto a c. A₁ʳ; doppio frontespizio (cc. A₁ᵛ e H₄ᵛ): sul primo titolo in italiano; sul secondo titolo in tedesco [fig. 7]. Doppia marca editoriale riconducibile al libraio trentino Giovanni Pietro Pezzoni alle cc. A₁ʳ e H₄ᵛ: aquila ad ali spiegate con gli artigli sul globo; tra le zampe un nastro con le iniziali Z P (5,5 × 7,8 cm).³³ Iniziali semplici; iniziale silografica Q abitata a c. A₂ʳ (4,8 × 4,8 cm);³⁴ iniziale calligrafica P a c. A₈ᵛ (14 ll.).³⁵

Bologna. Biblioteca Universitaria. A. V. Caps. LXXXVII/8. C. A₁: 9,7 × 14,7 cm.³⁶ Esemplare mutilo delle cc. C₄ e C₅. Impr.: e.lo m.er dara ElOg (C) 1511 (R). Legatura coeva in pergamena floscia di vitello. Tagli rustici. Capitelli in seta rossa e blu. Anima del capitello superiore in pergamena a vista sul piatto anteriore. Al margine di testa del piatto anteriore, attuale segnatura di collocazione a inchiostro bruno (Aul. V. Caps. LXXXVII. Nº 8) e antica (?) segnatura di collocazione a inchiostro bruno depennata. Dorso liscio. Nervi in cuoio. Controguardie coeve; carte di guardia perdute. Sulla controguardia anteriore, attuale segnatura di collocazione a lapis di mano moderna e iniziali di possessore (?) a inchiostro bruno (V L). Timbro ellissoidale a inchiostro nero della Biblioteca Universitaria di Bologna al centro del piatto anteriore (non più leggibile) e alle cc. B₃ʳ, H₃ᵛ e H₄ᵛ. Doppio timbro ellissoidale a inchiostro nero e circolare a inchiostro verde della Pontificia Biblioteca Universitaria a c. A₁ʳ. Nota di possesso a inchiostro bruno di mano cinquecentesca a c. H₄ʳ (Jacomo Phi). Prove di penna e annotazioni manoscritte a inchiostro bruno di mano cinque-

[Fig. 5] *Libro utilissimo a chi si diletta di intendere tedesco* [Vocabolario italiano-tedesco]. Tridenti: per Mapheum de Fracaçinis, 1511, c. A1ʳ. B Civica Queriniana Brescia, Lechi. 71. Su concessione della B Civica Queriniana di Brescia. È vietata ogni ulteriore riproduzione o duplicazione con qualsiasi mezzo.

[Fig. 6] *Libro utilissimo* [...], colophon (c. H3ᵛ). B Universitaria di Bologna, A. V. Caps. LXXXVII/8. Tutti le immagini della B Universitaria Bologna riprodotte su concessione della B Universitaria di Bologna. È vietata ogni ulteriore riproduzione o duplicazione con qualsiasi mezzo

[Fig. 7] *Libro utilissimo* [...], frontespizio tedesco (c. H4v). B Universitaria di Bologna, A. V. Caps. LXXXVII/8

centesca alle cc. H_4^{r-v} parzialmente tagliate dalla rifilatura e dal risarcimento al margine superiore interno della carta. Disegni a inchiostro bruno a c. H_4^v, marche editoriali sulle cc. A_1^r e H_4^v parzialmente colorate. Esemplare in cattivo stato conservativo: allentamento del filo di cucitura, distacco di c. G_8, lacerazioni sulle controguardie e in corrispondenza della marca editoriale a c. A_1, vistose gore di liquido e bruniture, macchie di inchiostro, fori di sfarfallamento di coleotteri anobidi, pergamena di rivestimento dei piatti notevolmente macchiata. Esemplare descritto nel catalogo a schede cartacee delle cinquecentine della biblioteca (voce *Libro utile per intendere la lingua tedesca*).[37]

Brescia. Biblioteca Civica Queriniana. Lechi. 71. C. A_1: 10,3 × 16 cm. Esemplare mutilo del fascicolo *H*. Impr.: e.lo m.er dara ElOg (C) 1511 (Q). Errore in fase di rilegatura dei fascicoli *B* e *G*:[38] il fascicolo *B* è legato dopo il fascicolo *F*; il fascicolo *G* segue il fascicolo *A*.[39] Le cc. C_3 e C_6, coese, rilegate per errore alla fine del volume (dopo c. B_8). Mezza legatura moderna in marocchino marrone su piatti in cartone rivestiti in carta a colla spugnata con gocce e spruzzi in rosa (ultimo quarto del XIX secolo).[40] Tagli rustici. Dorso liscio con filetti impressi in oro (quattro visibili); al margine superiore, etichetta con attuale segnatura di collocazione a inchiostro bruno (Incunabuli | LECHI | 71) su tracce di precedenti etichette; al centro, *titulus* impresso in oro in lettere capitali (LIBRO | DELL IMPARAR | TODESCO); al margine inferiore, data topica impressa in oro in lettere capitali (COLLIBVS). 1 + 1 carte di guardia coeve ai piatti e coese alle controguardie. Sulla controguardia anteriore, antica collocazione del volume a inchiostro bruno (71) di mano ottocentesca (Luigi Lechi?), attuale ubicazione del volume a lapis di mano moderna (Biblioteca | Queriniana) ed etichetta identica a quella incollata sul dorso. Al recto della carta di guardia anteriore, riferimento repertoriale di mano moderna a lapis (V. Lechi, p. 111.8). Nota manoscritta di possesso (?) a inchiostro bruno sul globo visibile nella marca su c. A_1^r; provenienza dell'esemplare: Conte Luigi Lechi (1786–1867).[41] Esemplare in discreto stato conservativo: risarcimenti coevi alla legatura ai margini esterno ed inferiore e agli angoli interni di alcune carte, vistose gore di liquido, bruniture, fori di sfarfallamento di coleotteri anobidi.

Entrambi gli esemplari sono dunque scompleti; quello di Brescia, in particolare, è privo del *colophon*, il ché spiegherebbe la presenza di *Collibus* (Vallis Trompiae / Collio Valtrompia) quale luogo di stampa impresso sul dorso del volume al posto di *Tridenti* sulla base della descrizione fornita da Luigi Lechi, cui l'esemplare bresciano è appartenuto, nel catalogo cronologico delle edizioni della provincia di Brescia stampate tra XV e XVI secolo.[42]

Tornando all'esemplare di Klagenfurt, la carta impiegata come controguardia posteriore è un bifolio ove al recto sono stampate le carte E_1^v (pagina di sinistra) e E_8^r (pagina di destra), e al verso le carte E_8^v (pagina di sinistra) e E_1^r (pagina di destra) del lessico italiano-tedesco stampato da Fracassini. Il fascicolo *E*, di otto carte, è ottenuto da due fascicoli di quattro carte ciascuno, inseriti l'uno dentro l'altro, in cui la prima carta è legata inevitabilmente all'ottava. L'esemplare di Klagenfurt è il bifolio

---

37 Direzione generale per i Beni Librari e gli Istituti Culturali (ICCU). Cataloghi storici. Accessibile online. Si veda l'indice dei siti a p. 374.

38 Il legatore ha confuso le lettere B e G molto simili tra loro.

39 L'ordine delle carte è: A_1–A_8, G_1–G_8, C_1–C_2, C_4–C_5, C_7–C_8, D_1–D_8, E_1–E_8, F_1–F_8, B_1–B_8, C_3, C_6.

40 Simile a Civiche raccolte d'arte applicata e incisioni Milano. Raccolta Bertarelli: carte decorate. Milano 1989 (*Musei e gallerie di Milano*), p. 213, n° 1615.

41 Su Luigi Lechi si veda LUCIANO FAVERZANI: *sub voce*. In: Dizionario biografico degli italiani, vol. LXIV. Roma 2005, pp. 275–7. – ROSA ZILIOLI FADEN: Legato Luigi Lechi. In: I fondi delle biblioteche lombarde. Censimento descrittivo. Ed. FRANCO DELLA PERUTA. Vol. 1/2. Milano 1996-8 (*Fonti e strumenti*. 28), vol. II, p. 212.

42 LUIGI LECHI: *Della tipografia bresciana nel secolo decimoquinto: memorie*. Brescia 1854, p. 111, n° 8. Anche PASERO sostiene erroneamente che l'esemplare sia stato stampato a Collio: PASERO 1927 (vedi nota 19), p. 120: «Mercè la marca fu riconosciuta come appartenente ai Fracassini un curiosissimo *Libro dell'Imparar Todesco* senz'anno e mutilo (Queriniana di Brescia), breve vocabolarietto di valore filologico limitatissimo. Ma esso dimostra la necessità fortemente sentita nell'Italia settentrionale di strette relazioni col nord; e proprio a Collio venne stampato questo significativo documento».

più esterno del fascicolo E che contiene le carte 1 (recto e verso) e 8 (recto e verso): ecco dunque chiarita l'origine della piegatura al centro della carta [figg. 8–11].

Il bifolio misura 19,8 × 14 cm (c. E_1: 9,8 × 14 cm; c. E_8: 10 × 14 cm), le linee per pagina sono 25 stampate in carattere gotico (99 G): si tratta chiaramente dell'edizione di Fracassini. Tuttavia, confrontando il frammento di Klagenfurt con gli esemplari di Bologna e Brescia si notano alcune differenze inerenti la *mise en texte*, la *mise en page* e alcuni errori di composizione; qualche esempio dall'esemplare di Klagenfurt: l'uso della ç al posto della z (c. E_8^r, col. sin., l. 3, *el cançeliero*); l'uso di d con asta ascendente diritta al posto di quella di derivazione onciale con asta corta e coricata (c. E_1^v, col. sin., l. 1, *El dolphin*; c. E_8^r, l. 14, *del officio*; c. E_8^v, col. sin., l. 15, *laqua dolce*); l'applicazione della regola di Meyer a c. E_1^v, col. sin., l. 21 in presenza del tratto curvo di o che precede (*larboro*); la diversa ortografia di alcune parole (c. E_1^r, col. sin., l. 14, *El cuco*; c. E_8^r, col. sin., l. 1, *L[a] Chata* [sic!] *p[er]gamena*; c. E_8^v, col. sin., l. 2, *lo chierico*); il diverso uso delle maiuscole e minuscole (c. E_1^r, col. sin., l. 16, *la choda*; c. E_1^v, col. sin., l. 8, *la reina*; c. E_8^r, col. sin., l. 19, *lo cardinale*; c. E_8^v, col. des., l. 25, *la pessina*); l'uso di segni abbreviativi con significato proprio, come la linea retta al di sopra di una vocale in sostituzione delle lettere m e n (c. E_8^v, col. des., l. 23, *fleisse[n]d*); l'uso di segni abbreviativi con significato relativo, come la linea retta che taglia la gamba di p indicante *per* (c. E_1^r, col. des., l. 4, *p[er] nise*); l'uso di abbreviature per troncamento (esemplari di Bologna e Brescia, c. E_1^r, l. 18, *[de] li pesci*); la diversa impaginazione della segnatura a c. E_1^r (sotto la a di *das netz* – col. des., l. 24 – nell'esemplare di Klagenfurt, tra la s e la n della stessa parola negli esemplari di Bologna e Brescia); la diversa impaginazione delle parole *fasan, aenten* (c. E_1^r, col. sin., ll. 4/5), *sue generatione* (c. E_1^r, ll. 18/9), *der segel* (c. E_1^v, col. des., l. 22) e *der apt* (c. E_8^r, col. des., l. 22); errori di composizione (c. E_8^r, col. sin., l. 1, *Charta*; c. E_8^v, col. sin., l. 3, *la chanonico*).

Se la composizione degli esemplari di Bologna e Brescia risulta essere la medesima, il bifolio di Klagenfurt è chiaramente frutto di una diversa composizione del testo riga per riga da parte del tipografo. L'esemplare della Bischöfliche Gurker Mensalbibliothek, dunque, non solo è un frammento del lessico italiano-tedesco stampato da Maffeo Fracassini a Trento nel 1511 ma una variante di stampa del bifolio più esterno del fascicolo E contenente le carte $E_1^{r/v}$ e $E_8^{r/v}$.

Da ultimo, qualche breve riflessione sulle descrizioni del lessico di Fracassini fornite da alcuni repertori; in particolare, mi preme evidenziare alcune imprecisioni e lacune rilevate nella formulazione del formato, della consistenza e nell'indicazione delle copie esistenti a riprova di come il pensiero di Roberto Ridolfi riportato in apertura risulti ancora una volta calzante.

Nella monografia di Fernanda Ascarelli sulla tipografia italiana del Cinquecento si legge:[43] «Il 18 settembre del 1511 il Fracassini sottoscriveva a Trento un vocabolarietto italiano-tedesco (in 16°, di 58 carte): due gli esemplari noti, conservati nella Biblioteca Universitaria di Bologna e nella Civica Queriniana di Brescia (mancante però del *colophon*)».

43 ASCARELLI 1989 (vedi nota 19), p. 301.

Oui	ayer	Lapon	kapaun
Pullisini	lunge buenlin	Polastri	iunge hue̊ner
Chorno	horn	Polisini	iunge hue̊nli
		Fasan	fasan Pernise repbue̊ner

C El. xxx. cap. de li vselli τ de le sue generatione.

L vsello	der vogel	Anadre aenten	Locha gans
le vselle	die fogel	Columba	tub
le penne	die federn	Turtura	turteltaub
la piuma	die pflumfeder	El falcon	der fack
le ale	die flue̊gel	Sparauiero	sporuer
la granffa	die crempel	Galmaza	das pirckhue̊
la agla	der adler	Papagallo	sitich
Zigognia	storch	Piumbino	iseruogel
Struzo	strus	Zelege spechten	Quaia vachtel
Grifon	greyff	El chuco	der guke̊gauch
Coruo	rap	El beco	der schnabel
Tatula	tul	La choda	der schwantz
li corui die rappen		le ale die fligel	Le pe̊ne die federn
Cornachia	krae		
la gaza	aglaster		
Rusignolo	nachtigal		
Chalandra	kalander		
Faganelo	hantf vogel		
Gardelin stiglitz	lugarin zeisel		
li stornelli die starii	Tuordo trostel		
Merlo amsel	Alocho eul		
zueta kuczli	Notula fledermus		
zisilla schwalb	Pauon pfaw		
Pauonessa	pfuein		

C El. xxxi. capitulo d̊ li pesci τ de le sue generatione.

O L pesse	der fisch		
Li pessi	die fisch		
La piscaria	di fischarei		
Peschatore	fischer		
Hamo angel	La rede das netz		
Balena	vald fisch		

[Fig. 8] *Libro utilissimo* […], cc. D8v – E1r. B Universitaria di Bologna, A. V. Caps. LXXXVII/8

El dolphin	das mersch vel	La sentina	der sunck
Sturio stue̊rer	Ziefalo zefel	Al fondo	am boden
Budo goufen	Eringo haering	In fontego	im leger hus
Pesse de mare	mer fisch	in casa di todeschi	in teutschen hus
Pesse daqua dolce	fisch vs sue̊ese̊ wasser	C El. xxxiij. cap. del aiere τ de li venti.	
Truta forhen	El cemulo der aesch	L Aiara	der luft
La reina der karpf	Squalo der halt	El vento	der vind
El luzo	Tenca schlei	Fredo kalt	Relente kue̊l
La anguilla	der becht	Frescho frisch	Chaldo hels
El goi kap	der aul	Tepido	law
Fondola grundel	Gambaro krebs	la nuobola	di wolcken
Cauiar	Morona husen	La nebia	der nebel
	husen rogen	Trone	tonder
C El. xxxij. capitulo de le naue τ galie.		Tonizare	donren
L A naue	di nauen	Ventoso	vindig
Le galie	di galeen	El tra lampa	est pliczget
Lo burchio	die burcken	La saeta	der dōner schlag
La piata di platen	la zatra der flos	Lampezare	hemligezen
le barche	die schiff	larco vergene	der regē poge
la barcha	das scheff	El splendor del sole	der sunne̊ schi
larboro	der segelpam	Chiaro tempo	heiter veter
le corde die seiler	la vela der segel	Tristo tempo	bos zeit
El remo	das ruoder	Bruto tempo	heslich veter
lancora	de ancker	C El. xxxiiij. capitulo de le montagne τ valle τ pianure.	
El timon	das lait pret		

[Fig. 9] *Libro utilissimo* […], cc. E1v – E2r. B Universitaria di Bologna, A. V. Caps. LXXXVII/8

In EDIT 16[44] la notizia relativa all'edizione di Fracassini può essere recuperata solo digitando la trascrizione fedele del titolo così come riportato sull'occhietto del volume (*Questo sie vno libro vtilissimo, a chi se dileta de intendere todesco, dechiarando in lingua taliana* [fig. 5]); nella scheda è indicato che il libro è un 4° di 62 carte prive di cartulazione coeva alla stampa; gli esemplari segnalati sono quelli della Universitaria di Bologna e della Queriniana di Brescia. Anche in ESTeR[45] il formato indicato è in-4°, mentre diversa è la consistenza: 116 pagine, e dunque 58 carte, in accordo con Ascarelli. Quanto agli esemplari, è segnalato solo quello della Pontificia biblioteca di Bologna, oggi Biblioteca Universitaria.

Come in EDIT 16 anche in CBT Trento[46] l'edizione di Fracassini si recupera solo attraverso la trascrizione del titolo stampato a c. A$_1^r$ anche se con un errore (*si e vno* invece di *sie vno*). Come precisato in nota, la descrizione si basa sulla riproduzione in fotocopia dell'esemplare conservato alla Universitaria di Bologna che, stando a quanto indicato, è un 4° di [62] carte. Oltre alle note tipografiche (sia pure ripartite su due linee distinte: Tridenti: per Mapheum de Fracaçinis Brix.(IS), 1511; Trento: Fracassini, Maffeo die. xviij. mensis Septemb.) sono riportate la formula collazionale (π A–G^8 H^4) e l'impronta che coincide con quella indicata da EDIT 16 compreso l'errore di rilevamento del terzo gruppo su c. B$_2^r$ (*tnt invece di *dara*);[47] diverso invece è il segno di controllo per la data: R in EDIT16, Q in CBT Trento ad indicare che, in quest'ultimo caso, la data cronica è stata dedotta. Le due copie segnalate sono entrambe, come già detto e come confermatomi dal responsabile della Sezione Trentina della Biblioteca Mauro Hausbergher, riproduzioni dell'esemplare bolognese (completo): non si spiega dunque la presenza della lettera Q in corrispondenza della data nell'impronta.

Alla fine del XIX secolo Luigi Lechi descriveva così l'edizione di Fracassini inserendola tra quelle stampate a Collio tra il XV e il XVI secolo:[48] «*Questo sie uno libro utiliss. a chi se dilecta de intender Todesco, dechiarando in lingua Taliana*, in 16°. Da un nostro esemplare mancante in fine, ma impresso co'l solito carattere gotico dei Fracassini, e con la solita insegna [...] Ristampa di un dizionarietto già pubblicato a Venezia l'an. 1499».[49]

L'esemplare descritto da Lechi coincide con quello di cui parla Frederick John Norton[50] il quale ipotizza possa essere stato stampato non da Maffeo bensì da Gabriele Fracassini dato che l'esemplare preso in visione è privo delle carte finali: "[Date not known] *Questo sie uno libro utiliss. a chi se dilecta de intender Todesco, dechiarando in lingua Taliana*... 16°. (Lechi 8.[51] His copy was imperfect at the end. Contains the Z. P. device.)."

Nella monografia di Ennio Sandal su Maffeo, Giacomo e Gabriele Fracassini[52] l'edizione è descritta come un 4° di 62 carte prive di cartulazione, composta da sei quaternioni, un ternione e un binione: ð^4, A, B^8 C^6 D–G^8 H^4. Non è chiaro cosa indichi il segno ð dal momento che il fascicolo A è il primo del volume. E' improbabile che l'autore abbia voluto indicare le controguardie e le carte di guardia; si tratta dunque quasi certamente di un *lapsus*. Quanto agli esemplari, oltre a quelli di Bologna e Brescia, Sandal ne segnala due presso la Biblioteca Comunale di Trento che, come già detto, sono due riproduzioni dell'esemplare bolognese.

44 Vedi nota 24.
45 Vedi nota 29.
46 Vedi nota 28.
47 Caratteri rilevati sulla colonna di destra invece che sinistra.
48 LECHI (vedi nota 42).
49 Si tratta del *Libro utilissimo a chi si diletta di intendere tedesco* stampato a Venezia da Manfredo Bonelli di Monferrato il 5 luglio 1499 (GW M51143; ISTC il00201000). Dato confermato anche da Rossebastiano Bart: ROSSEBASTIANO BART 1984 (vedi nota 33), p. 74.
50 NORTON (vedi nota 19), p. 19.
51 LECHI (vedi nota 42).
52 SANDAL 2002 (vedi nota 19), p. 93, n° 8.

Rossebastiano Bart accenna all'esemplare mutilo del *colophon* della Queriniana di Brescia descritto da Lechi il quale «ne aveva individuato lo stampatore in uno dei Fracassini attraverso l'esame dei tipi» e lo aveva «datato topicamente Collio».[53] La descrizione fornita si basa sull'esemplare della Universitaria di Bologna che l'autrice afferma di aver consultato; non corrisponde invece il formato (in-16°), evidentemente desunto dalla descrizione di Lechi e ritenuto corretto: «Diverse illustrazioni ornano anche il volumetto oggetto del nostro studio, che è in 16°, di mm. 149 × 106, composto di 58 carte non numerate, segnate A–B^8, C^6, D–G^8, H^4, stampato in caratteri semigotici».[54]

Valentino Volta parla prima di un «vocabolarietto tedesco-italiano [sic!], senza data, [nel quale] compare la medesima iniziale veduta nel *Capreolus-Chronica* (Brescia, Aronte degli Aronti, senza anno)»[55] poi, citando Carlo Pasero, di un «curiosissimo *Libro dell'imparare Todescho* senz'anno e mutilo (Queriniana di Brescia)», di cui l'autore fornisce anche la descrizione:[56]

Senza data: LIBRO DELL'IMPARARE TODESCHO.[57] Senza copertina: questo libro sie uno libro utilissimo: a chi deleta da intendere todescho: dechiarando in lingua taliana. S. n. t. (Collio Fracassini). Lechi, 111, 8. Norton, 19. In 8°, 16 × 10 × 5 cm[58], cc. 56 non num., mutilo cart. got. iniziali ornate. Secondo Lechi si tratta della ristampa di un dizionarietto pubblicato a Venezia nel 1499.[59] Lechi 71.

Nella tabella [tab. 1] sono riportate schematicamente le principali differenze tra gli elementi delle descrizioni. L'unico ad indicare il formato corretto è Valentino Volta. Ascarelli, Norton e Rossebastiano Bart hanno ritenuto valido quello fornito da Luigi Lechi (in-16°). EDIT 16 ha ripreso con ogni probabilità quello indicato da Ennio Sandal, e così anche ESTeR e CBT Trento.

Quanto alla consistenza, nessuno indica il numero esatto di carte della copia ideale (60 non numerate). Ascarelli e Rossebastiano Bart riportano chiaramente la consistenza dell'esemplare di Bologna mutilo delle carte C_4 e C_5 e dunque composto di 58 carte prive di numerazione. Volta fornisce il numero di carte dell'esemplare bresciano, privo dell'intero fascicolo H (di quattro carte), e dunque composto di 56 carte prive di numerazione. Sandal (e EDIT 16 e CBT Trento che ne riprendono il dato) recupera l'informazione fornita da Rossebastiano Bart, includendo tuttavia nel computo anche un fascicolo iniziale ∂ di quattro carte di fatto inesistente (58 + 4). In ESTeR è riportato il numero delle pagine (116) corrispondenti a quelle dell'esemplare bolognese (58 cc.), l'unico segnalato dalla banca dati trentina. Lechi non fornisce alcun dato, ma nella descrizione della copia attualmente conservata alla Queriniana di Brescia afferma che essa è priva delle ultime carte («Da un nostro esemplare mancante in fine»).

La formula collazionale è riportata solo da Rossebastiano Bart, Sandal e da CBT Trento. Le prime due formule non descrivono tuttavia la copia ideale: Rossebastiano Bart basa la sua descrizione sulla copia della Biblioteca Universitaria mutilo delle carte C_4 e C_5 e dunque con il fascico-

---

53 ROSSEBASTIANO BART 1976 (vedi nota 33), p. 43.

54 ROSSEBASTIANO BART 1976 (vedi nota 33), p. 44; misurazione effettuata presumibilmente su c. A_1. – ROSSEBASTIANO BART 1984 (vedi nota 33), p. 74: «La descrizione del Lechi (s. n. t, [Collio, Fracassini]) e la citazione del Norton (Gabriele de Fracassini) si basano su un esemplare incompleto (56 cc.), attualmente conservato nella biblioteca di Brescia e mancante del *colophon*. L'altro esemplare, emerso durante le mie ricerche, conferma che lo stampatore fu uno dei Fracassini, ma precisamente Maffeo, mentre il luogo di stampa risulta Trento invece di Collio». – Va tuttavia precisato che l'attribuzione dell'edizione a uno dei Fracassini formulata dal Lechi fu fatta non solo sulla base dei caratteri ma anche della marca tipografica: LECHI (vedi nota 42), p. 111: «impresso co'l solito carattere gotico dei Fracassini, e con la solita insegna». Inoltre, la descrizione così come riportata da Rossebastiano Bart, (s. n. t, [Collio, Fracassini]) è tratta non dall'opera di LUIGI LECHI ma da quella di VALENTINO VOLTA (vedi nota 19), p. 81.

55 VOLTA (vedi nota 19), p. 74. Per l'edizione di Elia Capriolo, vedi nota 34.

56 VOLTA (vedi nota 19), pp. 75 e 81.

57 Titolo riportato sul dorso dell'esemplare bresciano usato da Volta per la descrizione.

58 Misurazione effettuata presumibilmente su c. A_1.

59 Vedi nota 49.

ximo come ti stesso	nechstē als dich selbs	Charta pgamena	das pment
Sāctificař el sabato	feyr die hailigē tag	La scriptura	di geschrifft
Honora el padre	er vater vnd	El canzeliero	der canczler
e la madre	mueter	Priuilegio	hand vest
Non occidere	tot niemant	Le sette arte	di siben kunst
Non furare	stil nicht	la lege temporale	das weltlih recht
Non mechare	brich kein ee nit	la lege spirituale	das geistlich recht
Non fare testi/	gib nit falschē	la sacra pagine	di heilig geschrift
monio falso	zu'gnus	la phisica	di erst kunst
Non desiderare	beger des ander	Insegnare	vnderwisen
le roba daltrui	guot nit	Imparare	lernen
Nō desiderare la	beger nit dines	El ia molto ben	er kās vast vol
mogliere daltrui	naechstē wib	Li libri	di buecher

C El. xlv. ca. de lo studio e de la schola. C El. xlvj. cap. del officio ecclesiastico.

Lo studio	di hoch	Officio ec	das geistlich
la vniuersita	schuol	clesiastico	ampt
Studiare	studieren	Papa	pabst
La schola di schuol	Doctore doctor	El patriarcha	der patriach
Scholaro	schuoler	Lo cardinale	der cardinal
El discipulo	der iunger	Arciuescouo	ercz bischoff
El scriuan	der schriber	Lo vescouo	der bischoff
El calamaro	das tintēfas	la badia di apti	labate der apt
El canzello da scriuere	der scrib zu'g	lo priore	der prior
Lindchiostro	di tint	El piouan	der pfarrer
La foia	ein blat	la parrochia	di pfar

[Fig. 10] *Libro utilissimo* [...], cc. E7v–E8r. B Universitaria di Bologna, A. V. Caps.LXXXVII/8

Lo arciprete	der erzt priester	El lago	der see
lo chiericho	der collit	Lo paludo	das mos oder pfutz
la chanonico	der korherr	lo reno der rin	la tana di tuonaw
lo spirituale	der geistlich	la marina das mer	lo fundo der grūd
lo seculare	der weltlich	Basso cioe laqua	saecht
lo deuoto	der andechtig	lumido	di fu'chti
El a bona fede	er ha't ei guten	la humidita	di fuchtikeit
Denotion	andacht globē	Bagniare neczē	Bagniato geneczet
Con deuotione	mit andacht	la rosata der taw	la bruina der riff
E bon christiano	er ist ei gut cristē	la pioza der regē	la tēpesta der hagel
la chierica	di plat	la neue der schne	Neuare schneien
		E gran neue	es ist ein grosser schne

C El. xlvij. ca. de laqua e humidita.

L aqua	das wasser	Giazo eiser	Giazare gefrieren
le aque	di wasser	Giazado	gefroren

C El. xlviij. cap. del fuocho e del caldo

laqua dolce	sus wasser	El fuocho	das fu'r
laqua salsa	gesalczē wasser	le brase	di glut
laqua chiara	luter wasser	lo carbon der kol	li carboni die koel
laqua torbida	tru'eb wasser	Abrusare	verbrennen
Fontana	brun	Brusa bren	El arde es bren
la origine	der vrsprunk	El chaldo	es ist warm
El pozo	der galg brun	Schaldare	wermen
la cisterna	di cistern	El e teuido	es ist law
laqua currente	fleissend wasser	Asmorzare	leschen
la humara	der bach	Asmorzato	erloeschet
lo riuo der vrfach La pessina der wiger			f

[Fig. 11] *Libro utilissimo* [...], cc. E8v–F1r. B Universitaria di Bologna, A. V. Caps.LXXXVII/8

lo C di sei carte invece che di otto; Sandal riporta nella sua scheda la stessa formula collazionale, integrandola tuttavia di un fascicolo iniziale di quattro carte, ma si tratta evidentemente di un errore.[60] Quanto a CBT Trento, la formula sarebbe corretta se non fosse per il π che precede il primo fascicolo che non può indicare né una carta iniziale bianca, né tantomeno la carta di guardia iniziale in quanto l'esemplare della Universitaria usato per la descrizione ne è privo. Rispetto agli altri cataloghi, quello trentino segnala anche le carte bianche: $π^r$ (ma non è chiara l'origine di questa carta), e H^4 (ma solo il recto della carta è bianco).

Ascarelli, EDIT 16 e Rossebastiano Bart segnalano due esemplari conservati alla Universitaria di Bologna e alla Queriniana di Brescia. ESTeR, Lechi, Norton e Volta indicano un solo esemplare (ESTeR quello della Pontificia Biblioteca di Bologna, oggi Biblioteca Universitaria; Volta quello della Queriniana di Brescia; Lechi e Norton non precisano la localizzazione della copia descritta, ma è evidente che si tratta di quella bresciana). Sandal segnala anche i due esemplari della Comunale di Trento, ma si tratta di riproduzioni della copia bolognese come indicato in CBT Trento.

Quanto alle note tipografiche, Ascarelli, EDIT 16, ESTeR, CBT Trento e Sandal riportano data topica e cronica nella forma completa. EDIT 16 e Sandal precisano anche il nome dell'editore; Ascarelli fa il nome di Fracassini ma non precisa quale dei tre. Nel Catalogo bibliografico trentino la data cronica è suddivisa su due linee. Rossebastiano Bart intesta la scheda al solo anno di stampa ma inserisce all'interno la trascrizione del *colophon*;[61] sull'editore afferma in nota: «La marca tipografica fa supporre che l'opera sia stata approntata per l'editore trentino Zoan Pezoni».[62] Lechi, che basa la propria descrizione sulla copia della Queriniana, precisa che l'esemplare è privo delle ultime carte e lo inserisce tra le edizioni stampate a Collio tra il XV e il XVI secolo da Fracassini («impresso co'l solito carattere gotico dei Fracassini, e con la solita insegna»). Norton, che descrive la stessa copia, omette la data topica e cronica ("Date not known"), ma indica il nome dell'editore ("contains the Z. P. device"). Anche Volta, che descrive lo stesso esemplare, indica che esso è senz'anno (s. n. t.) e mutilo ma fornisce tra parentesi tonde la data topica ed il nome del tipografo (Collio Fracassini).

Allo stesso modo, lascia spazio a qualche riflessione la descrizione dell'esemplare fornita dal catalogo online della Queriniana di Brescia:

Questo sie vno libro vtilissimo a chi se dileta de intendere todesco dechiarando in lingua italiana. – [Trento: Giovanni Pietro Pezzoni, 1511]. – [62] c.; 8° (16 cm). EDIT 16 (60973). – Marca (acronimo ZP). – Segn.: A–G^8. – Una iniziale xil. Altra edizione di: *Piccolo libro da imparar todescho*. Trento Pezzoni, Giovanni Pietro. Biblioteca Queriniana BQo Lechi. 71. Inv.: BQ000681141 (Leg. moderna in carta decorata, dorso in pelle. – Mancano 6 carte finali (cfr. Lechi, Della tipografia bresciana, p. 111 n. 8). – Le c. C^3 (e la successiva, probabilmente C^7 o C^8) sono rilegate, per errore, dopo c. G^8.

---

60 L'asterisco in corrispondenza della copia bresciana fa pensare che la descrizione si basi su questa. Se tuttavia ciò fosse vero e la formula collazionale si riferisse all'esemplare della Queriniana, priva del fascicolo *H* ma completa di tutte le carte del fascicolo *C*, sarebbe stato più corretto indicare come completo il fascicolo *C* ed omettere il fascicolo *H*.
61 ROSSEBASTIANO BART 1984 (vedi nota 33), p. 73. La stessa trascrizione anche in ROSSEBASTIANO BART 1976 (vedi nota 33), p. 43.
62 ROSSEBASTIANO BART 1984 (vedi nota 33), p. 74.

Notiamo che la scheda è suddivisa in due parti; nella prima sono riportati i dati dell'edizione: titolo, note tipografiche, consistenza, formato e dimensione del volume; nella seconda, quelli dell'esemplare della Queriniana: collocazione, inventario, legatura, note sulle carte mancanti e sull'ordine delle carte nell'esemplare. Senza soffermarsi sulle problematiche e la correttezza della scelta del titolo per l'identificazione dell'edizione così come riportato sull'occhietto (problema peraltro riscontrabile anche in EDIT 16, ESTeR e CBT Trento), non si può fare meno di notare che la trascrizione non è del tutto fedele (*italiana* invece di *taliana*). Le note tipografiche sono poste tra parentesi quadre in quanto nell'esemplare bresciano mancano le ultime carte tra cui il *colophon*. Inoltre, la formulazione di consistenza riportata nell'area di descrizione dell'edizione, [62] c., non è pienamente corretta in quanto il lessico stampato da Fracassini si compone di [60] carte. Il dato potrebbe riferirsi all'esemplare bresciano con l'inclusione nel computo delle carte anche di quelle di guardia, due appunto; in questo caso, allora, andrebbe inserito nella sezione sottostante della scheda tra le note d'esemplare. Tuttavia, anche con questa ipotesi, i conti non tornerebbero perché nella copia della Queriniana manca l'intero fascicolo *H*, sicché l'esemplare risulta composto di [56] carte. Quanto all'informazione sull'altezza del libro (16 cm), essa non è tradizionalmente ritenuta un dato identificativo dell'edizione quanto piuttosto dell'esemplare; pertanto andrebbe inserita più correttamente nella sezione inferiore della scheda. Allo stesso modo, la formula collazionale A–G^8 è quella della copia bresciana; pertanto sarebbe più corretto inserirla tra le note d'esemplare. Dalla descrizione emerge inoltre che quella del 1511 sarebbe una riedizione del *Piccolo libro da imparar todesco*; l'informazione è ricavata con ogni probabilità dalla voce di Ennio Sandal nel *Dizionario dei tipografi e degli editori italiani*[63] che riprende un saggio dello stesso autore pubblicato nel 1992[64] in cui si accenna ad una presunta edizione del 1509, il *Piccolo libro* appunto. Tuttavia, come accennato in precedenza, si tratta di un errore in quanto l'unico lessico stampato da Fracassini è quello del 1511. Da ultimo, le carte mancanti non sono sei bensì quattro (fascicolo *H*) e le carte C_3 e C_6 (e non C_7 o C_8) sono legate dopo c. B_8 (e non G_8).

63 SANDAL 1997 (vedi nota 19).
64 SANDAL 1992 (vedi nota 19).

[Tab. 1]

	Consistenza	Formula collazionale	Totale esemplari	Localizzazione	Note tipografiche
Ascarelli	16° [58] c.	Tace	2	Universitaria Bologna Queriniana Brescia	Il 18 settembre del 1511 il Fracassini sottoscriveva a Trento un vocabolarietto italiano-tedesco; esemplare bresciano mancante del *colophon*
EDIT 16	4° [62] c.	Tace	2	Universitaria Bologna Queriniana Brescia	[Trento: Giovanni Pietro Pezzoni] (Tridenti: per Mapheum de Fraçaçinis Brix., die xviij mensis Septemb. 1511)
ESTeR	4° 116 p. = 58 c.	Tace	1	Pontificia Biblioteca Bologna	Tridenti per Mapheum de Fraçaçinis Brix., 1511 die. xviij. mensis septemb
CBT Trento	4° [62] c.	π A–G⁸ H⁴ Bianche π^r, H⁴	2 (riproduzioni dell'esemplare della U di Bologna)	Comunale Trento	Tridenti: per Mapheum de Fraçaçinis Brix., 1511 Trento: Fracassini, Maffeo, die. xviij. mensis Septemb.
Lechi	16° Tace, ma esemplare privo delle ultime carte	Tace	Non indicato, ma 1	Tace, ma Queriniana Brescia	Esemplare privo delle ultime carte, ma impresso col solito carattere gotico dei Fracassini, e con la solita insegna (Collio, tra XV e XVI secolo)
Norton	16° Tace	Tace	Non indicato, ma 1	Tace, ma Queriniana Brescia	[Date not known]; contains the Z. P. device
Sandal	4° [62] c.	∂⁴, A, B⁸ C⁶ D–G⁸ H⁴	4	Universitaria Bologna Queriniana Brescia* Comunale Trento (2)	Trento, Maffeo Fracassini [per Giovan Pietro Pezzoni], 18 settembre 1511
Volta	8° 56 c.	Tace	1	Queriniana Brescia	Senz'anno e mutilo (Queriniana Brescia): S. n. t. (Collio Fracassini)
Rossebastiano Bart	16° [58] c.	A–B⁸, C⁶, D–G⁸ H⁴	2	Universitaria Bologna Queriniana Brescia	Trento, 1511 Mapheus de Fraçaçinis; esemplare bresciano mutilo del *colophon*

GISELA MÖNCKE

Ein wieder aufgefundener Erfurter Lutherdruck von 1523 mit einem Bildnis des Reformators

LUTHERS WOHL ANFANG JULI 1523 im Druck erschienene Schrift *Wider die Verkehrer und Fälscher kaiserlichs Mandat* richtete sich gegen eine nach seiner Auffassung irrige Auslegung des Religionsartikels aus dem Abschied des zweiten Nürnberger Reichstags.[1] Den beiden Wittenberger Erstdrucken von Cranach und Döring folgten noch im selben Jahr sechs Nachdrucke.[2] Davon konnten fünf Drucke, die unfirmiert außerhalb Wittenbergs erschienen, aufgrund ihres typografischen Befundes Pressen in Erfurt (Johann Loersfeld, Matthes Maler, Wolfgang Stürmer), Augsburg (Philipp Ulhart) und Straßburg (Reinhard Beck, Erben) zugewiesen werden.

Straßburg als Druckort vermutete Gustav Kawerau auch für eine ebenfalls unfirmierte Ausgabe, die er mit einer knappen Beschreibung des Titelholzschnittes nach einem Exemplar der Königlichen Bibliothek Berlin in der Weimarer Ausgabe nachwies.[3] Dieses Exemplar gehört heute zu den Kriegsverlusten, und da sich kein weiteres feststellen ließ, beließ man es zunächst bei der Zuschreibung an eine Straßburger Offizin.[4] Erst die Einsicht in die nachgelassene Materialsammlung, die Johannes Luther für eine intensivere Beschreibung der Lutherdrucke zusammengetragen hatte, führte zu berechtigten Zweifeln, denn die von ihm notierten Maße des Holzschnittes stimmen nicht überein mit dem Schnitt, der in einem Straßburger Druck von 1520 überliefert ist.[5] So blieb in der zweiten, von Helmut Claus besorgten Auflage der *Lutherbibliographie* Druckort und Drucker unbestimmt.[6]

Mit einem Exemplar, das vor kurzem in den Auktionshandel kam[7] und von der Bayerischen Staatsbibliothek München erworben wurde, kann diese bibliografische Lücke nun geschlossen werden:

(W)ydder die verkerer vnd felscher | keyßerlichs mandats. |
Martinus Luther. M.D.XXiij | [Holzschnitt]
[Erfurt: Michel Buchfürer 1523] 4°. [4] Bl. a⁴.
VD 16 L 7509. – München BSB: Res/H.ref. 755 f.

Die W-Initiale begegnet in Buchfürers Nachdruck einer Zwinglischrift.[8] Die Auszeichnungstype, eine mittelgroße Missale, verwendete er in beinahe allen seinen Drucken, die Texttype nur bis 1523. Letztere bezeichnet von Hase ungenau als »Schwabacher«.[9] Sie gehört zu jenen lateinischen rundgotischen Texttypen, die Johnson als "germanised" charakterisiert.[10] Buchfürer hatte sie wahrscheinlich aus Leipzig von Valentin Schumann bezogen, in dessen Drucken sie uns seit 1518 bis 1520 als "germanised" begegnet.[11] Seine Ausgabe ist also ein weiterer in Erfurt hergestellter

1 MARTIN LUTHER: *Werke*. Kritische Gesamtausgabe. Bd. 12. Weimar 1891, S. 58–67. – Vgl. dazu MARTIN BRECHT: *Martin Luther*. Bd. 2. Stuttgart 1986, S. 111–6. – ARMIN KOHLE: *Reichstag und Reformation*. Gütersloh 2007, S. 124–32.
2 JOSEPH BENZING/HELMUT CLAUS: Lutherbibliographie. Bd. 2. Aktualisierte Neuaufl. Baden-Baden 1994 (*Bibliotheca bibliographica Aureliana*. 143), Nr. 1647–54.
3 LUTHER (siehe Anm. 1), S. 61/2 G.
4 MARIA-CONSUELO OLDENBOURG: *Die Buchholzschnitte des Hans Baldung-Grien*. Baden-Baden, Straßburg 1962, Nr. 543, L 158. – BENZING/CLAUS (siehe Anm. 2), Nr. 1653.
5 HELMUT CLAUS/MICHAEL A. PEGG: *Ergänzungen zur Bibliographie der zeitgenössischen Lutherdrucke*. Gotha 1982, S. 93.
6 BENZING/CLAUS (siehe Anm. 2), Nr. 1653.
7 Antiquariat PETER KIEFER, Pforzheim. *Katalog*. 71 (2010), Nr. 342.
8 VD16 Z 815, hier auf Bl. B1b.
9 MARTIN VON HASE: Johann Michael genannt Michel Buchfürer alias Michel Kremer. Straßburg 1928 (*Studien zur deutschen Kunstgeschichte*. 260), S. 27, T 2. Dort zusammen mit der Auszeichnungstype auf Abb. 17 und 18.
10 ALFRED FORBES JOHNSON: Notes on some German Types used in the Reformation Period. In: *Festschrift für Josef Benzing zum 60. Geburtstag*. Hrsg. von ELISABETH GECK. Wiesbaden 1964, S. 226–52, hier S. 228/9 (Bastarda 80).
11 Gegen VON HASE (siehe Anm. 9), der S. 92, Anm. 58 meint, Buchfürers Type sei »auf kleineren Kegel gegossen«, messe ich doch auch in dessen Erfurter Drucken 20 Zeilen mit 79 mm. Das entspricht genau der Schumannschen Type. Nach 1523 wurde sie anscheinend in keiner anderen Offizin weiter verwendet.

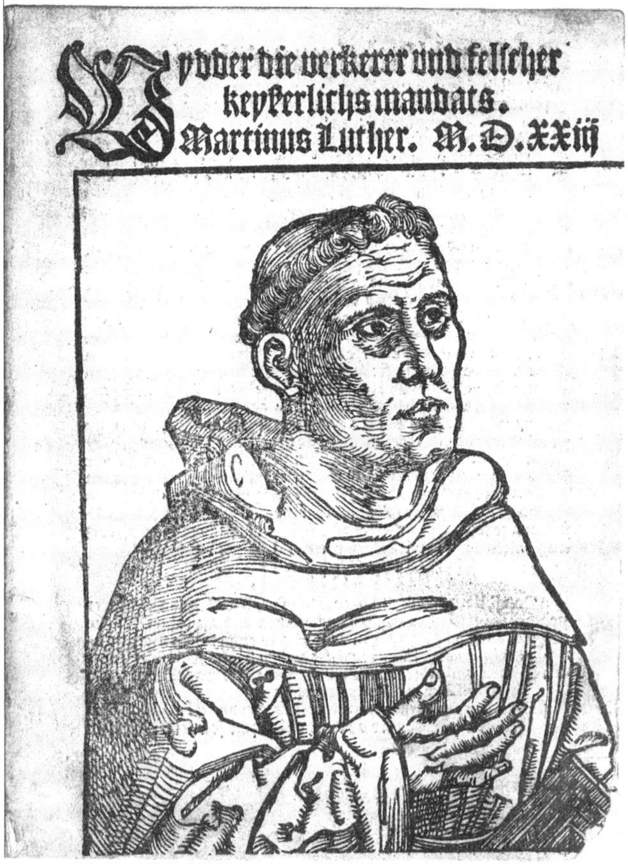

Widder die verkerer und felscher keyserlichs mandats. Martinus Luther. M.D.XXiij

[Abb. 1] BSB, Titelseite

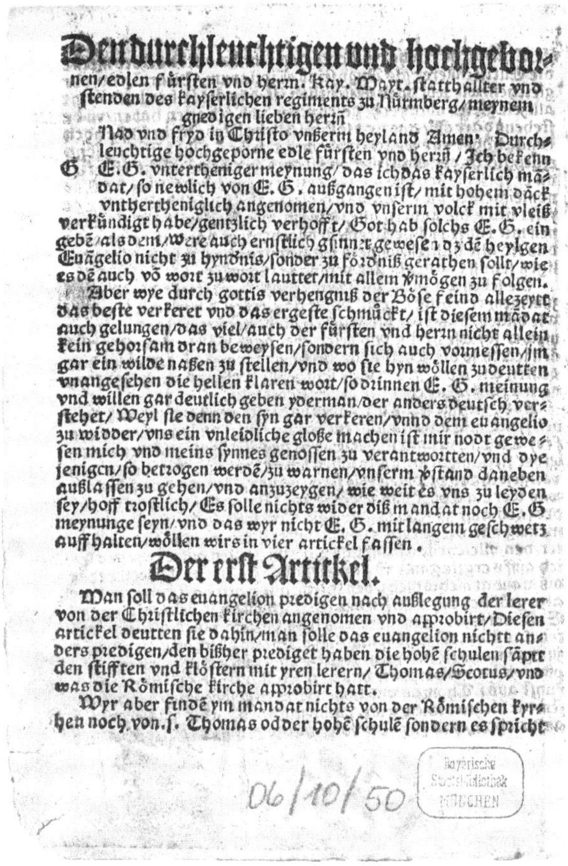

Den durchleuchtigen und hochgebornen/edlen fürsten vnd herrn. Kay. Mayt. statthallter vnd stenden des kayserlichen regiments zu Nürmberg/meynem gnedigen lieben herrn

Gnad vnd fryd in Christo vnßerm heyland Amen. Durchleuchtige hochgeporne edle fürsten vnd herrn / Ich bekenn E. G. vnterteniger meynung/ das ich das kayserlich mandat/ so newlich von E. G. außgangen ist/ mit hohem danck vntherthenigclich angenomen/vnd vnsern volck mit vleiß verkündigt habe/gentzlich verhofft/ Got hab solchs E. G. eingebē/als dem/were auch ernstlich gsinnet geweßen dz dē heylgen Euāgelio nicht zu hyndnis/sonder zu fördniß gerathen sollt/wie es dē auch vō wort zu wort lauttet/mit allem vermögen zu folgen.

Aber wye durch gottis verhengniß der Böse feind allezeyt das beste verkeret vnd das ergeste schmückt/ ist diesem mandat auch gelungen/das viel/auch der fürsten vnd herrn nicht allein kein gehorsam dran beweysen/sondern sich auch vormessen/im gar ein wilde naßen zu stellen/vnd wo sie hyn wöllen zu deutten vnangesehen die hellen klaren wort/so drinnen E. G. meinung vnd willen gar deutlich geben yderman/der anders deutsch verstehet/ Weyl sie denn den syn gar verkeren/vnnd dem euangelio zu widder/vns ein vnleidliche gloße machen ist mir nodt gewesen mich vnd meins synnes genossen zu verantwortten/vnd dye jenigen/so betrogen werdē/zu warnen/vnserm verstand daneben außlassen zu gehen/vnd anzuzeygen/ wie weit es vns zu leyden sey/hoff trostlich/ Es solle nichts wider diß mandat noch E. G meynunge seyn/vnd das wyr nicht E. G. mit langem geschwetz auffhalten/wöllen wirs in vier artickel fassen.

Der erst Artickel.

Man soll das euangelion predigen nach außlegung der lerer von der Christlichen kirchen angenomen vnd approbirt/ Diesen artickel deutten sie dahin/man solle das euangelion nichtt anders predigen/den bißher prediget haben die hohē schulen sampt den stifften vnd klöstern mit yren lerern/ Thomas/Scotus/vnd was die Römische kirche approbirt hatt.

Wyr aber findē ym mandat nichts von der Römischen kyrchen noch von .s. Thomas odder hohē schulē sondern es spricht

06/10/50
Bayerische Staatsbibliothek MÜNCHEN

[Abb. 2] BSB, Textanfang (A1b)

12 BERND MOELLER: Erwägungen zur Bedeutung Erfurts als Kommunikationszentrum der frühen Reformation. In: Erfurt. Geschichte und Gegenwart. Hrsg. von ULMAN WEISS. Weimar 1995 (*Schriften des Vereins für die Geschichte und Altertumskunde von Erfurt.* 2), S. 275–82.

13 Aus Buchfürers Produktion kannte man bisher nur die Abbildung Luthers als ganzer Figur neben Teufel und Emser auf dem Titelholzschnitt der Flugschrift *Ein schöner Dialogus von Martin Luther und der geschickten Botschaft aus der Hölle* (VD 16 A 1523). Vgl. dazu VON HASE (siehe Anm. 9), S. 54 mit Anm. 100 und Abb. 4.

14 Luther als Mönch vor einer Nische. *Lucas Cranach. Gemälde, Zeichnungen, Druckgraphik*. Hrsg. von DIETER KOEPPLIN u. TILMAN FRANK. Ausstellungskatalog Kunstmuseum Basel. Bd. 1. Basel u. a. 1974, Nr. 36 mit Abb. 35. – *Köpfe der Lutherzeit.* Hrsg. von WERNER HOFFMANN. Ausstellungskatalog Kunsthalle Hamburg. München 1983, Nr. 41 mit Abb.

15 ROBERT W. SCHRIBNER: *For the Sake of simple Folk. Popular Propaganda for the German Reformation.* Cambridge, London 1981, hier insbesondere das zweite Kapitel (Images of Luther 1519–1525), S. 14–36. – MARTIN WARNKE: *Cranachs Luther. Entwürfe für ein Image.*

Nachdruck dieser Lutherschrift, derer sich hier auch Loersfeld, Maler und Stürmer annahmen. Der Fund unterstreicht einmal mehr die immense Bedeutung, die dem Erfurter Buchdruck bei der überregionalen Verbreitung reformatorischer Schriften insbesondere in den Jahren zwischen 1521 und 1525 zukam.[12] Interesse verdient er aber auch wegen seines Titelschmucks, eines bisher unbekannten Holzschnittportraits des Reformators.[13]

Das Brustbild zeigt Luther als Mönch, den Blick (vom Bild aus) nach halbrechts gewendet. Die rechte Hand ist nach Art eines Lehrers oder Predigers leicht angehoben, die linke Hand hält ein Buch. Leider ist der Abdruck nicht vollständig erhalten, denn das Titelblatt ist sehr knapp beschnitten. Dem Holzschnitt, der nach den Angaben Johannes Luthers 153 mm hoch und 131 mm breit sein müsste, fehlen auf der rechten und unteren Seite die Begrenzungslinien. Außerdem ist rechts unten eine kleine Ecke abgerissen. Die Darstellung gehört zu jenen Lutherbildnissen, die in Anlehnung an einen von Lukas Cranach d. Ä. geschaffenen Kupferstich[14] als Holzschnitte im Buchdruck verwendet wurden.[15] Die größte Verbreitung erfuhr eine Nachbildung, die seit 1520 in Straßburger Drucken begegnet, Hans-Baldung Grien zugeschrieben wird und als Vorlage auch für Lutherportraits in Basler, Augsburger und Wiener Drucken diente.[16] Dagegen ist das Erfurter Bild nach einem anderen Holzschnitt kopiert, der seinerseits direkt auf den Kupferstich Cranachs zurückgeht, nur dessen Nischenhintergrund und die unter dem Portrait angebrachte Inschrift weglässt. Auch diese freie Kopie (145 × 125 mm) ist bisher nur in einem einzigen Druck überliefert, nämlich auf der Titelseite der ins Jahr 1520 zu datierenden, von Melchior Ramminger in Augsburg gedruckten Erstausgabe der Flugschrift *On Applas von Rom kann man wol selig werden*.[17] Frank Muller weist die Zeichnung dem Künstler Heinrich Vogtherr d. Ä. zu, der während seiner Augsburger Jahre eng mit Ramminger zusammenarbeitete.[18] Wer die Kopie für Buchfürers Druck angefertigt hat, bleibt vorerst ungewiss.[19] Sie steht, leicht vergrößert, jedenfalls ihrem Vorbild, das ja erst die Umsetzung vom Tiefdruck zum Hochdruck leisten musste, nicht nach, ist qualitativ sogar besser gelungen.

Buchfürers Druck ist nicht zuletzt seines bisher unbeschriebenen Autorenportraits wegen eine wertvolle Ergänzung der *Lutherbibliographie*. Es ist zu hoffen, dass sich künftig auch von anderen Lutherdrucken, die dort nach ehemals unikalem Berliner Besitz noch immer ohne Druckerzuweisung und ohne aktuellen Nachweis verzeichnet sind,[20] Exemplare auffinden. Die Neuerwerbung ergänzt darüber hinaus die Bibliografie Erfurter Drucke der ersten Hälfte des 16. Jahrhunderts, an der Martin von Hase seit seiner Dissertation von 1928, die Michel Buchfürer galt, gearbeitet hat. Seine Bibliografie erschien in dritter, erweiterter Auflage 1968.[21] Es gibt mittlerweile zwei Supplemente mit insgesamt mehr als 280 zusätzlichen Drucken dieses Zeitraums.[22] Der neue Fund macht einmal mehr deutlich, dass auch damit die Überlieferung Erfurter Drucke keineswegs vollständig verzeichnet war. Nachzutragen ist ein Wiener Besitznachweis für den bei von Hase unter der Nummer 1027 nur ungenau verzeichneten Stürmer-Druck von 1550 (VD 16 C 5863).

Hinzu kommen neben Buchfürers Lutherausgabe weitere sieben mir erst in jüngster Zeit bekannt gewordene Erfurter Drucke:

Frankfurt a. M. 1984 (*Fischer-Taschenbücher*. 3904). – ILONKA VAN GÜLPEN: *Der deutsche Humanismus und die frühe Reformationspropaganda 1520–1526. Das Lutherportrait im Dienst der Bildpublizistik*. Hildesheim 2002 (*Studien zur Kunstgeschichte*. 144).
16 Zuerst auf der Titelrückseite der Lutherschrift *De captivitate ecclesiae* in einem Nachdruck von Johann Schott von 1520. OLDENBOURG (siehe Anm. 4), Nr. 343, L 152 (mit Abb. 176). – VAN GÜLPEN (siehe Anm. 15), S. 136/7 mit Abb. 9–14.
17 ADOLF HAGELSTANGE: Die Wandlungen eines Lutherbildes in der Buchillustration des XVI. Jahrhunderts. In: *Zeitschrift für Bücherfreunde*. 11 (1907/08), S. 98–107, hier S. 106 und Abb. 5. – JOHANNES FICKER: Älteste Bildnisse Luthers. In: *Zeitschrift des Vereins für Kirchengeschichte der Provinz Sachsen*. 17 (1920), S. 1–50, hier S. 16 Anm. 4. – VAN GÜLPEN (siehe Anm.15), S. 140 mit Abb. 15. – VD 16 O 526 (digitalisiert nach einem Exemplar der UuLB Halle).

18 FRANK MULLER: *Heinrich Vogtherr l'Ancien (1490–1556). Un artiste entre Renaissance & Réforme*. Wiesbaden 1997 (*Wolfenbütteler Forschungen*. 72), Nr. 63. – DERS.: Heinrich Vogtherr d. Ä. In: *Jahrbuch des Historischen Vereins Dillingen an der Donau*. 92 (1990), S. 173–224, hier Abb. S. 225. – Auf die Nähe zu Cranach oder seiner Werkstatt könnte auch das C auf der zurückgeschlagenen Kapuze hindeuten, wenn es denn nicht nur eine auf allen anderen Nachschnitten fehlende Falte darstellt.
19 Die für Buchfürer tätigen Illustratoren behandelt ausführlich VON HASE (siehe Anm. 9), S. 46–64. Als Ergänzung dazu sei vermerkt, dass MULLER (siehe Anm. 18), hier S. 98 Nr. 18, auch die Darstellung Marias auf der Mondsichel auf Buchfürers frühem Einblattdruck Heinrich Vogtherr zuschreibt und auf circa 1513 datiert.
20 Das gilt beispielsweise für eine Ausgabe vom *Papsteesel und Mönchskalb*, die bisher nur vage einer süddeutschen Presse zugeschrieben werden kann.

BENZING / CLAUS (siehe Anm. 2), Nr. 1555.
21 MARTIN VON HASE: Bibliographie der Erfurter Drucke von 1501–1550. In: *Börsenblatt für den deutschen Buchhandel. Frankfurter Ausgabe*. 99 (1966), S. 2586–2794. 2. Aufl. In: *AGB* 8 (1967), Sp. 655–1096. 3. erweiterte Aufl. Nieuwkoop 1968.
22 HELMUT CLAUS: Erfurter Drucke der ersten Hälfte des 16. Jahrhunderts. In memoriam Dr. phil. Martin von Hase. In: *Erfurt 742–1992. Stadtgeschichte, Universitätsgeschichte*. Hrsg. von ULMAN WEISS. Weimar 1992, S. 295–314. – GISELA MÖNCKE: Weitere Ergänzungen zur Bibliographie Erfurter Drucke der ersten Hälfte des 16. Jahrhunderts. In: *Buchwesen in Spätmittelalter und Früher Neuzeit. Festschrift für Helmut Claus zum 75. Geburtstag*. Hrsg. von ULMAN WEISS. Epfendorf 2008, S. 73–107.

Stürmer

HESSUS, HELIUS EOBANUS: *DE PVGNA STVDENTVM EROHORDIENSIVM ... Carmen*. [Holzschnitt] – (Erfurt: Wolfgang Stürmer, 1507.) 4°. [4] Bl. – Wien NB 16 E 397 mit Abbildung des Titels und des Impressums); VD 16 ZV 27231. – Wien ÖNB.

ERASMUS, DESIDERIUS: *Ausslegung vber das heylig Götlich gepet des vater vnsers* ... [Titeleinfassung = v. Hase, Bibliographie, Stürmer 14.] [Erfurt: Wolfgang Stürmer], 1526. 8°. – VD 16 ZV 27232. – Arnstadt, KirchenB.

Etliche tröstliche Gebet, Psalmen vnd Geistliche Lieder ... [Erfurt: Wolfgang und/oder Gervasius Stürmer], 1547. 8°. [24] Bl. – Wien NB 16 E 848; VD 16 E 4085. – Wien ÖNB.

Sachse

Gemeyne stimmen von der Müntz ... [Holzschnitt] – [Erfurt] (Melchior Sachse d. Ä., 1530.) 8°. [14] Bl. – Wien NB 16 G 256a; VD 16 ZV 27252. – Wien ÖNB.

JOHANN FRIEDRICH, KURFÜRST VON SACHSEN UND PHILIPP, LANDGRAF VON HESSEN: *Wahrhafftiger Bericht v[[ñ]] Summari Ausführung* ... [Wappenholzschnitte] – [Erfurt: Melchior Sachse], 1546. 4°. [34] Bl. A–E⁴ A–C⁴ D². Variante zu von Hase 960b (= VD 16 ZV 27077) mit abweichender Bogenkollation und teilweise unterschiedlichem Satz. – VD 16 S 1076 – München BSB; Wolfenbüttel HAB.

HELPHRICHIUS, BONIFACIUS: *DECLAMATIO IN LAVDEM POETICAE CARMINE ELEGIACO conscripta* ... (Erfurt: Melchior Sachse), 1548. 8°. [16] Bl. – VD 16 ZV 23265. Michelstadt, Nicolaus-Matz-B; Zwickau, RatsschulB.

von Dolgen

(FINGIUS NOLANUS:) *PASQVILLVS*. [Erfurt: Merten von Dolgen, 1545.] 8°. [4] Bl. – VD 16 P 835. – München BSB.

H. GEORGE FLETCHER

A Manuscript Aldine Catalogue from the
Mid-Sixteenth Century

THE APPEARANCE of a contemporary manuscript catalogue of the Aldine Press – one, moreover, that had hitherto escaped the attention of the many workers in a field often deemed overly tilled – is a cause for interest and (dare one of the gleaners say?) pleasure. Moreover, I say this even though, as will emerge, the manuscript derives from a printed text.

Yale manuscript 59, in the Beinecke Rare Book and Manuscript Library, a listing of approximately 150 publications of the Aldine Press, is the only hand-written, sixteenth-century Aldine catalogue currently known to me that has remained unedited and largely unnoticed. It was presented to Yale by Thomas E. Marston in 1935. Its published record, apart from brief listings, is restricted for all practical purposes to its summary description in Barbara Shailor's *Catalogue* of Yale manuscripts.[1]

The manuscript
Ledger folio in format, 32,3 × 10,2 cm, it consists of two sheets of paper folded vertically into one gathering of four leaves or eight pages, neither foliated nor paginated. It is written in a single column by one hand, perhaps at different times to judge from the different shades of ink and slight changes in ductus, in brown (i.e., scribal, or water-based) ink. The script is a somewhat unpolished, spiky chancery hand or italic. A small arabic 3 at the foot of leaf 2^r, arabic 5 at the foot of 3^r, and arabic 7 at the foot of 4^r suggest collation guides; they appear to be similar to a majuscule B at the foot of 4^v, all of which I attribute to the binder, Bretherton. The manuscript is preceded by 4 stubs and followed by 12 stubs in its workaday binding of half-leather with cloth-covered boards. Its mid-nineteenth-century English binding obscures some few letters or numerals within the sewing folds, as well as the watermark(s).[2]

The leaves began as folio half-sheets of approximately 33 × 21 cm overall; this fits within the tolerances for the standard sheet termed the *Reçute* in the paper statute enacted by the Commune of Bologna in 1389, a full sheet of which measured 31,5 × 45 cm. This size sheet enjoyed long use, and was employed by early generations of printers to produce so-called Chancery folios for much of the fifteenth and sixteenth centuries.[3]

There has been some very minor attrition through wear at the extremities and marginal discoloration, but the paper is still virtually original size; there is no sign of trimming, and the bottom edge of the final leaf (leaf 4), for example, still retains a strong irregularity in the deckle, which caused the scribe to write around the resultant curve in the paper. The

*With an Appendix on the
Fourth Aldine Press Catalogue of
[March 1527]*

1 BARBARA A. SHAILOR: *Catalogue of Medieval and Renaissance Manuscripts in the Beinecke Rare Book and Manuscript Library, Yale University*. Vol. I. Binghamton 1984, pp. 83/4 nº 59 is speculatively assigned to Italy, 1534; the listing is not repeated in vol. III (1993), which is devoted to the Marston manuscripts, but not the general manuscripts at Yale previously described. It is listed in SEYMOUR DE RICCI: *Census of Medieval and Renaissance Manuscripts in the United States and Canada*. 3 vols. New York 1935–40, vol. II, p. 2252 (nº 59), and in PAUL OSKAR KRISTELLER: *Iter Italicum*. London 1990, vol. V, p. 276 nº 59. – See also note 5.
2 I am grateful to Dr. Robert G. Babcock, at the time the Edwin G. Beinecke Curator, for bringing the manuscript to my attention, and to the late Frank Turner, former Director of the Beinecke L, and Yale U for permitting its publication.
3 PAUL NEEDHAM: Aldus Manutius's Paper Stocks. In: *Princeton University Library Chronicle*. 55.2 (1994), pp. 287–307, here pp. 287–90. The original measuring stone, incised with the actual proportions of the paper sizes and preserved in Bologna's Museo civico medievale, is illustrated in CONOR FAHY: La carta nelle edizioni aldine del 1527 e del 1528. In: *La Bibliofilía*. 103.3 (2001), pp. 263–89, here p. 270, tav. I.

watermark, described in Shailor as an unidentified coat of arms, is concealed by the vertical folding of the sheets. The manuscript was in England by 1850, when it was bound by George Bretherton, who had plied the bookbinder's trade in Gloucester from no later than 1840.[4] Acquired by Sir Thomas Phillipps (1792–1872) around 1860, it was Phillipps ms 15644. The manuscript appears to have remained in steady, recorded ownership for the past century and a half. It was lot 13 in the 1899 Phillipps sale, when it sold for a shilling, and lot 26 in the Hodgkin sale (Sotheby, 12 May 1914), when it was knocked down to Tregaskis for £4 10s. It was sold by C. A. Stonehill in 1934 to Thomas E. Marston, who presented it to Yale in 1935. Its known provenance, which is limited to the past century and a half, is therefore Phillipps ▷ Hodgkin ▷ Tregaskis ▷ Stonehill ▷ Marston ▷ Yale.[5]

Gesner's Pandectae

The direct source, the apograph, of the scribe's manuscript is Conrad Gesner (in German sources commonly Konrad Gessner; 1516–65), *Pandectarum sive partitionum universalium Conradi Gesneri Tigurini, medici & philosophiae professoris, libri xxi* (Zurich: Christoph Froschauer, 1548/49). This, the second volume of his *Bibliotheca universalis* (the first volume, of 1545, is the author bibliography), is the subject index, dedicated to contemporary printers – Paulus Manutius is the dedicatee of Book XI –, with lists of their publications.[6] The catalogue of Aldine publications is printed in italic, in two columns.

It merits repeating that the *Pandectae* volume is quite distinct from Gesner's *Bibliotheca universalis, sive catalogus omnium scriptorum locupletissimus ...* (Zurich: Froschauer, 1545), with which it is often, and erroneously, conflated. A recent search on WorldCat suggests that seven copies of the *Pandectae* can be located in institutions, but even this record is misleading, because it includes a microfilm copy in the tally, and the book remains very rare. Thanks to information provided by T. Kimball Brooker and Roland Folter, I know of five copies, all but one in private hands, in the United States; it is likely that one or more of the four untraced copies that have appeared at auction in Europe and the United States since 1976 may be among these copies.

An external fact thus enables us to establish a terminal date before which the manuscript cannot have been written. The compilation cannot date from before 1548, since the author cites Conrad Gesner's *Pandectarum ... libri xxi* in the opening lines, as a kind of subtitle to the heading, and bases the manuscript upon Gesner. The manuscript has the physical appearance of a private production, rather than, for example, a bookseller's list. Its creation falls chronologically late in the span between Renouard's fourth Aldine Press catalogue, hitherto variously dated [c. 1526] and [1534], and his fifth, of 1563.[7] One copy of that fourth catalogue is known to survive, and I am comfortable dating it to the spring of 1527. It is treated at some length in the Appendix at the end of this Introduction.

Renouard reported in 1834 that the sole copy of the fourth catalogue of which he was aware was part of the Aldine collection of Count Etienne

---

4 The front pastedown is stamped Bretherton, | ligavit | 1850. CHARLES RAMSDEN: *Bookbinders of the United Kingdom (outside London), 1780–1840.* London 1954, p. 42; cf. p. 17 (misspelled Brotherton), under Gloucester. Bretherton worked almost exclusively for Phillipps.

5 Its history prior to 1850 is a dead end, in the present state of my knowledge. See ALAN N. L. MUNBY: *Phillipps Studies. Nº 4: The Formation of the Phillipps Library between 1841 and 1872.* Cambridge 1956, Appendix A: The Sources from which Phillipps obtained mss. 10818–23837 (pp. 172–211): 15597-659 »*Miscellanea ex Bibl. variis*« (p. 195). Phillipps himself recorded it in his immense and diffuse printed *Catalogus* (THOMAS PHILIPPS: *Catalogus librorum manuscriptorum in bibliotheca D. Thomae Phillipps, Bart.* Middle Hill 1837–71.) laconically: "15644 Catalogue of Books printed by Aldus. *thin fol. ch. s. xviii. half red cf.*" (p. 298). By no stretch of the imagination could this be an eighteenth-century manuscript. It falls within the numbers headed as MUNBY records them, and its location before and after various contemporary entries giving specific sources in 1860 indicates that it came into Phillipps's possession during or around that year, although Bretherton may have bound it for him a decade earlier. I am indebted to Paul Naiditch, formerly of UCLA, for some of the provenance history subsequent to Phillipps.

6 CONRAD GESNER [in German sources commonly KONRAD GESSNER; 1516–65]: *Pandectarum sive partitionum universalium Conradi Gesneri Tigurini, medici & philosophiae professoris, libri xxi.* 2 vols. Zurich: Christoph Froschauer, 1548/49. This is quite distinct from his *Bibliotheca universalis, sive catalogus omnium scriptorum locupletissimus ...* (Zurich: Froschauer, 1545), with which it is often, and erroneously, conflated. Various revised and abridged editions of the *Bibliotheca universalis*, but not of the *Pandectae*, appeared as early as 1551, 1555, 1574, and 1583. Cf. STC, p. 357 and GRAHAM POLLARD / ALBERT EHRMAN: *The distribution of books by catalogue from the invention of printing to AD 1800.* Cambridge 1965, pp. 47–50. POLLARD / EHRMAN is in the course of revision by Giles Mandelbrote (Lambeth Palace L). Cf. also *Printing and the Mind of Man.* Ed. JOHN CARTER and PERCY H. MUIR. 2nd, rev. ed. Munich 1983, nº 204, and BERNARD H. BRESLAUER / ROLAND FOLTER: *Bibliography: Its history and development.* New York 1984, nº 14. The contents of the entire work are extensively summarized and analyzed in ALFREDO SERRAI: *Storia della Bibliografia.* 11 vols. Rome 1988–2001, vol. II pp. 209–614; the Aldine Press catalogue component of Book XI, esp. pp. 326/7.

Méjan (1766–1846). Méjan's copy of the fourth Aldine Press catalogue of [March 1527] has rested in obscurity these many years, but it survives uniquely in Berlin, assigned to or after the year 1526.[8] It consists of one gathering of six leaves, the first five of which contain printed entries.

Renouard owned a copy of the printed 1563 Aldine catalogue, which was bought at his 1854 sale by Edwin Tross. It may have been sold soon thereafter; at least it was not in the group Tross sold to the British Museum (Library) in 1876, and its current status remains as unknown as it was to Pollard and Ehrman.[9]

Internal evidence suggests strongly that the Yale manuscript either was written not long after 1548 or was based upon no later sources. In other words, I have not been able to identify with any assurance the citation in the manuscript of an Aldine edition published later than 1548. Scribal practice would place the manuscript in the sixteenth century.

Our manuscript does not derive from Renouard's 1563 catalogue, which was set in type, consisted of six leaves, and bore the Aldine device. Gesner himself reports (fol. 21r, col. 2) his source as being a three-leaf folio catalogue, which equates with Aldus's published list of 24 November 1513, the third and final list of his lifetime. Since Gesner's various catalogues reflect knowledge on his part that cannot be equated with surviving lists of books, the sources of his additional knowledge remain unknown in many instances, but are assumed to be the cumulative result of years of note-taking.

Our manuscript's literal dependence, in whole or in part, upon the [March 1527] fourth Aldine catalogue remains unclear to me, but I can find no compelling evidence that it was a direct source. The fourth catalogue repeats its predecessors when it opens with the heading *Aldus studiosis s[alutem].*, although Aldus had been dead for a full dozen years, and when it continues with a paragraph of advertising for the works that follow. Also like its predecessors, it repeats seriatim and verbatim in chronological order of original publication the contents listings of the earlier catalogues, though the entries are expanded and updated to reflect the most recent re-edition or reprint of particular works, and new works are added. Unlike its 1513 predecessor, it does contain an entry for the *Hypnerotomachia* (fol. A4v, col. 1, final entry), described as *Poliphili Hypnerotomachia, ubi humana omnia non nisi somnium esse ostendit, atq[ue] obiter plurima scitu sanè quàm digna commemorat, forma folij.*

Even this descriptive listing is not a clear source for the Yale manuscript's terse entry »Poliphili Hypnerotomachia. in fol.« Gesner uses the same brief wording for his entry.

But the extensive listing in the [1527] catalogue raises an interesting question. The wording is directly linked to what would emerge as the now-vernacular title of the second edition, of 1545,[10] which reads in part «[...] dov'egli mostra, che tutte le cose humane non sono altro che sogno». This phrase is accurately rendered in Latin as »ubi humana omnia non nisi somnium esse ostendit«. By no means, however, could the fourth Aldine Press printed catalogue be as late as the mid-1540s, so what is the connection? Does the Latin follow or precede the Italian version, and

7 ANTOINE-AUGUSTIN RENOUARD: *Annales de l'imprimerie des Alde*. 3rd ed. Paris 1834, pp. 264.3 and 339/40. RENOUARD (p. 339) gives a very brief, summary description of the printed catalogue (see also note 8), which he dated [c. 1526]. POLLARD/EHRMAN (see note 6), pp. 60/1, assign the date [1534], because the Aetius was completed in September 1534. *The Aldine Press: Catalogue of the Ahmanson-Murphy Collection*. Ed. NICOLAS BARKER, SUE A. KAPLAN and PAUL NAIDITCH. Berkeley 2001, nº 240 ("[after 1526]"). On all this, see the Appendix.

8 RENOUARD (see note 7), p. 339. For the later fate of this unique copy, see the Appendix, esp. note 21 and its related text.

9 POLLARD/EHRMAN (see note 6), pp. 67/8. Christian Coppens (see also note 15) has located seven copies of the 1563 catalogue; an additional recorded copy was not on the shelf.

10 RENOUARD (see note 7), 1545.14; *The Aldine Press* (see note 7), nº 335; *Aldine Press Books at the Harry Ransom Humanities Research Center, The University of Texas at Austin: a Descriptive Catalogue*. Ed. CRAIG KALLENDORF and MARIA X. WELLS. Austin 1998, nº 302 (p. 275). From here on, abbreviated as HRHRC.

does this wording derive from an oral tradition within the printing house, which one would presume to have been vernacular?

The fourth Aldine catalogue might be the source for the format designation that concludes each entry in the manuscript, because it is the first printed list of Aldine publications to have this feature. The richness of each of the fourth catalogue's individual entries, however, renders the manuscript's listings absolutely jejune by comparison. If Gesner saw a copy of the fourth catalogue, in other words, he drew no inspiration from its great detail.

The scribe

The scribe I believe to be from the historically Germanic lands, the »Länder deutscher Zunge« or the »deutscher Sprachbereich«: who but a German-speaker and -writer would automatically surmount many a *u* with a diacritical mark – a wavy macron (the U-Bogen), written at various angles as space permitted or required – to differentiate it from *n* or even *e* in German cursive? Whereas the unfortunate corollary is that the scribe's usage here equates with the customary Latin suspension for *-um*, easily creating false readings for the unwary, this problem would not have arisen for the writer, and would not have confused another German-speaker. Moreover, certain variants in his entries, such as Aphtonius for Aphthonius and chose for cose, reflect German pronunciation.

Apart from the Aldines, the writer once, following Gesner, refers to a book published in Basel, which may suggest a Swiss or Alsatian or at least upper-Rhenish connection. One should not stress this unduly, however, since the trade in books was highly efficient and very widespread, and the focal point of publishing had migrated from Venice to such locales as Basel, Lyon, and Paris, with Antwerp coming to the fore, by the second third of the sixteenth century. The devotion to Aldus's books is all the more notable, on this score alone; some of Aldus's editions had been superseded in the intervening years. Considering the linguistic clues and given the dependence upon Gesner, one could reasonably postulate a geographical origin in German-speaking Switzerland or along a Rhenish trade-route.

Generally, the writer has been reasonably careful in his writing and in his Latinity. His text, while apparently hastily written in many spots, is the product of thought and planning. There are relatively few abbreviations, contractions, or suspensions. The hand has an idiomatic ductus, indicating that the writer was compiling for his own uses, rather than with an eye to consumption by others. While presenting occasional difficulties, though, the whole is generally legible after a bit of practice in reading it, and growing familiarity with the manuscript and occasional consultation of the books themselves clarify many a potential crux, along with direct comparison with Gesner's published text. It is a deliberately Italianate hand, which is to say that the scribe is using a humanistic script to record works in the classical languages. I can detect no intrusions of a vernacular hand, beyond the overall ductus with its tendency toward the spiky style that suggests a writer accustomed to using a gothic cursive for vernacular vocabulary.

[**Fig. 1**; fol. 1ʳ] Yale Manuscript 59, Beinecke Rare Book and Manuscript L, Yale U

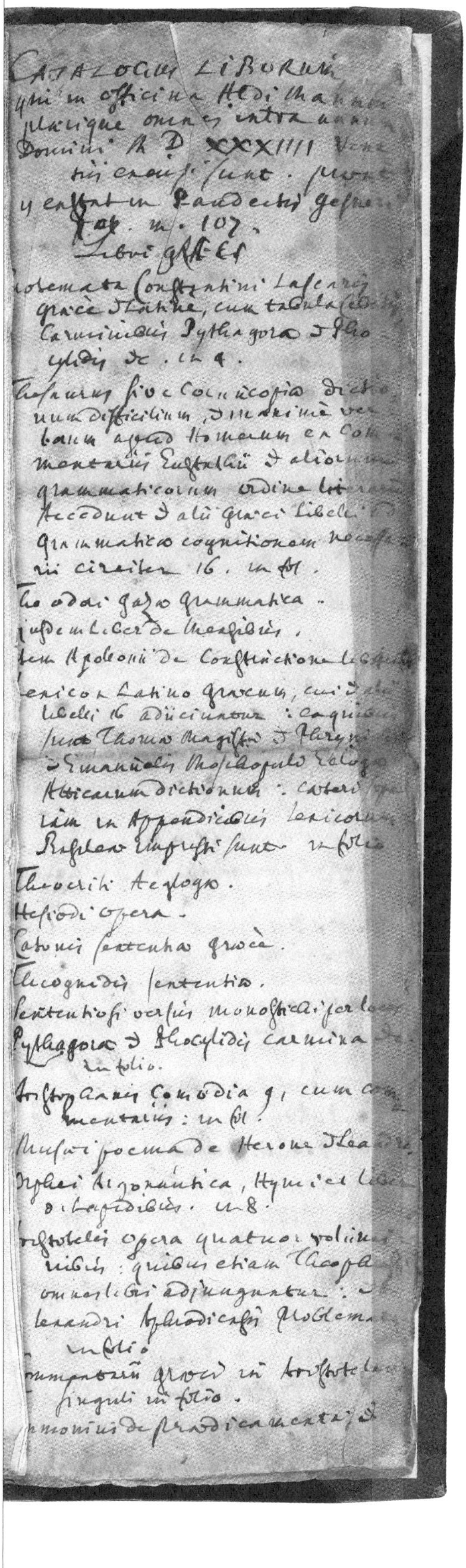

Catalogus Librorum
qui in officina Aldi Manutii
plerique omnes intra annos
Domini M.D.XXXIIII Vene-
tiis excusi sunt. sumpt-
9 extat in Pandectis Gesneri
pag. m. 107.
Libri graeci

Progemmata Constantini Lascaris
graece & latine, cum tabula etc.
Carminibus Pythagorae & Phocylidis &c. in 4.

Thesaurus sive Cornucopia dictionum difficilium, & maxime verborum apud Homerum ex commentariis Eustathii & aliorum
grammaticorum ordine literarum
Accedunt & alii graeci libelli
grammaticae cognitionem necessarii circiter 16. in fol.

Theodori Gazae grammatica.
ejusdem liber de Mensibus.
Item Apollonii de Constructione &c.

Lexicon latino graecum, cui & alii
libelli 16 adjiciuntur : Ecloga
item Thomae Magistri & Harpo-
& Emanuelis Moschopuli Ecloga
Atticarum dictionum. Caetera optima in Appendiculis lexicorum
Aldina impressa sunt in folio.

Theocriti Aeglogae.
Hesiodi opera.
Catonis sententiae graecae.
Theognidis sententiae.
Sententiosi versus monostichi per locos
Pythagorae & Phocylidis carmina &c.
in folio.

Aristophanis Comoedia 9, cum commentariis : in fol.

Musaei poema de Herone & Leandro.
Orphei Argonautica, Hymni et liber
o Lapidibus. in 8.

Aristotelis opera quatuor voluminibus
nibus ; quibus etiam Theophra-
omnes libri adjunguntur.
Alexandri Aphrodisaei Problemata
in folio.

Commentarii graeci in Aristotelem
singuli in folio.
Ammonius de Praedicamentis &c.

in libram de enutiatione : cum
Magentio in eundem
Alexander Aphrodis. in priora analiticorum
Joan. grammaticus & Eustratius in
Posteriora.
Alexander Aphrodisiensis in Topica
Idem in Elenchos.
Simplicius in 8 libros physicorum
Idem in libros de Coelo.
Joan. grammaticus in libros de gene-
ratione & interitu : cum Alexandro
Aphrodisiensi in Meteora.
Themistius in libros de Anima. &
Alexander Aphrodis. in eosdem, cum
eiusdem libro de fato.
Simplicius in libros de anima, una cum
Michaele Ephesio in parva natu-
ralia.
Eustratius in Ethica.
    Alii libri graeci
Psalterium graecum. 4.
Officium in honorem B. Virginis cum
psalmis poenitentialibus a Latino
in graecum . in 16.
Quaestionum mille & septuaginta trium
volumen, quorum auctores sunt
40. in 4.
Gregorii Nazianzeni diversa poema-
ta : cum Latina translatione,
inserto Evangelio Joannis . in 4.
Nonni paraphrasis in Evangelium
Joannis . in 4.
Dioscoridis de materia medica et
venenis libri, cum indice. Accedunt
carmina de virtutibus quarundam
plantarum, in antiquis exempla-
ribus reperta.
Nicandri Theriaca & Alexipharma-
ca cum commentariis.
De Ponderibus & Mensuris . in 4.
Julii Pollucis Vocabularium. in fol.
Stephanus de Urbibus. in fol.
Thucydidis libri . 8 . in fol.
Herodoti lib. 9. in fol.
Luciani omnia. Icones eiusdem fratris
eiusdem Heroica
Icones Junioris Philostrati 22.
Quarrationes Callistrati in Statuas
Philostrati vitae Sophistarum 58 in
       folio.

Philostrati de vita Apollonii libri
    graeci, & Latini Alemanno Rhi-
    naccio interprete.
Eusebius contra Hieroclem graece et
    Latine Zenobio Accialo interpre-
    te, in folio.
Sophoclis Tragoediae 7. in 8
Euripidis Tragoediae 22. in 4.
Epigrammatum graecorum libri 7.
Homeri omnia : cum vita eius ex
    Plutarcho, Herodoto & Dione. in 8.
Q. Calabri poetae Paralipomena Ho-
    meri, libris 14 . in 8.
Demosthenis orationes . in folio .
Ulpiani Commentarii in 28 Demos-
    thenis orationes
Harpocration de Dictionibus Rheto-
    rum ordine literarum . in folio
Plutarchi Moralia . in folio .
Phornuti de natura Deorum
    cum Palaephato de fabulosa histo-
    ria.
Vita et fabulae Aesopi graece & Latine
Gabriae fabulae graece & Latine
Heraclidis Pontici de allegoriis
    apud Homerum
Orus de hieroglyphicis
Proverbia per ordinem Alphabeti
Libri ex Rhetorum de arte Rheto-
    rica . in fol.
In Aphtonii progymnasmata commen-
    tarii; item in Hermogenis omnia
Theodori Gazae grammatica
Georgii Lecapeni de constructione
    verborum
Manuel Moscopuli de constructione
    nominum et verborum
Idem de Accentibus . in 8.
Grammatica Chrysolorae, cum libro
    1. Theodori Gazae, & sententiis Pin-
    dari, Phocylidis, Catone, & Theocriti
    Idylliis . in 8.
Pindarus, Callimachus, Dionysius
    situ Orbis, Lycophron. in 8.
Isocratis, Alcidamantis, Gorgiae & Lysiae
    studiis orationes quaedam
Harpocration de Dictionibus Isocrati-
    corum
Platonis opera . in fol.
Suidas . in fol.
Athenaei Symposiaca . in fol.

[left column — Fol. 2v]

Lexici Graecorum ... in fol.
Caesaris Commentarii Graece ... in fol.
Strabo ... in fol.
Sacrae Scripturae veteris novique ... omnia in fol.
Artemidori cum Synesio de interpretatione somniorum ... ms.
Plutarchi illustrium virorum graecae latinaeque nominis vitae 49 ... in fol.
Oppiani de piscibus libri 5, una cum Laurentii Lippii tralatione
Eiusdem de venatione libri 4 ... in 8.
Aeschylii tragoediae 6 ... in 8.
Aldi Manutii Romani grammaticae institutiones graecae ... in 4.
Gregorii Nazianzeni orationes 16 ... in
Apollonii Rhodii Argonautica cum commentariis ... in 8.
Commentarii in Homeri Iliadem et Porphyrii duo opuscula ... ms.
Herodiani historiarum libri 8, cum interpretatione latina Angeli Politiani ... in fol.
Xenophontis omnia ... in fol.
Galeni omnia in quinque voll. in fol.
Hippocratis omnia ... in fol.
Didymi scholia in Odysseam Homeri ...
Paulus Aegineta ... in fol.
Aëtii medici libri primi 8 ... in fol.
Xenophontis paralipomena
Commentarii in Thucydidem
Herodianus
Plethonis historia ... in fol.
Greg. Nazianzeni orationes 9 et Hyssenii quaedam ... ms.

LIBRI LATINI

Angeli Politiani Opera ... in fol.
Julii Firmici et M. Manilii Astronomica
Arati Phaenomena, Germanico interprete, cum commentariis et imaginibus
In eadem fragmentum interpretationis Ciceronianae et Rufi Festi breviarium paraphrasis
Eadem graece cum comment. Theonis
Procli Sphaera graece et Thomae Linacro interprete ... in fol.
Nicolai Perotti Cornucopiae &c.
Varronis libri de lingua latina et analogia

[right column — Fol. 3r]

Pompeii Festus et Nonius Marcellus
Grammaticae institutiones Aldi Manutii
Bessionis Cardinalis libri 4 in calumniatorem Platonis
Eiusdem liber in quo ex 12 libris Platonis de legibus quamplurima recitantur et a Georg. Trapezuntio male versa ostenduntur
Eiusdem tractatus an natura et ars consulto agant ... in fol.
Aristoteles de Animalibus
Theophrastus de Plantis
Problemata Aristotelis et Alexandri Aphrodisiei Theodoro Gaza interprete ... in fol.
Iamblichus de mysteriis
Proclus in Alcibiadem. Idem de sacrificio et magia
Porphyrius de divinis atque demonibus
Synesius de Somniis. Psellus de daemonibus
Expositio Pisciani et Marsilii in Theophrastum de sensu et phantasia et intellectu
Alcinous de doctrina Platonis
Speusippus de Platonis definitionibus
Pythagorae Carmina aurea et Symbola
Xenocrates de morte
Mercurii Trismegisti Pimander. Eiusdem Asclepius
Marsilii Ficini de triplici vita lib. 2
Eiusdem libri de Voluptate, de Sole et Lumine, de Magis: Quod necessaria sit animi tranquillitas ... in fol.
Desiderii proverbia ... in fol.
Polyphili Hypnerotomachia ... in fol.
Lud. Coelii Antiquarum lectionum libri 16 ... in fol.
M. T. Ciceronis omnia. Formis diversis
C. Crispi Sallustii historiae et orationes eis adiungi solitae ... ms.
M. F. Quintilianus ... in 4.
Cato, Varro, Columella, Palladius de re rustica
Georgii Alexandrini enarrationes piscarium dictionum in eiusdem libris ... in 4.
Virgilius ... in 8.
Diversorum veterum poetarum priapeum lusus
Marionis catalecta, copa, Rosa, Culex, Dirae, Moretum et alia quae falso Virgilii creduntur

Argumenta in Virgilii libros, & alia
    diversorum coniectura. m8.
P. Ovidii omnia cum annotationibus
Terentius. m8.
T. Livii Decades 3.
L. Flori libri 4.
Polybii historiarum libri 5. Nico-
    lao Perotto interprete. m8.
Eiusdem Livii omnia accurata de-
    nuo impressa. in fol.
C. Plinii secundi epistolae
Eiusdem Panegyricus, & liber de vi-
    ris illustribus
Suetonius Tranquillus & clarii
    grammaticis & Rhetoribus.
Iulii Obsequentis prodigiorum liber
Catullus, Tibullus, Propertius. m8.
Lucanus. m8.
Valerius Maximus. m8.
C. Iulii Caesaris & A. Hirtii aut Oppii
    Commentarii de bello diversi, cum
    picturis quibusdam. & locorum ac
    populorum nominibus. m8.
L. Coelii Lactantii Opera cum Ter-
    tulliani Apologetico. m8.
A. Gellii Noctes Atticae. m8.
T. Lucretius. m8.
Nerva, Traiani & Hadriani Caesa-
    rum vitae ex Dione G. Merula
    interprete. Item Aelius Spartia-
    nus, Iul. Capitolinus, Lampridius,
    Fl. Vopiscus, Trebellius Pollio, Vulca-
    tius Gallicanus, omnes à Ioanne
    Baptista Egnatio castigati.
Heliogabali ad meretrices oratio.
Ioan. Bapt. Egnatii de Caesaribus libri
Eiusdem in Spartiani Lampridii vi-
    tas & reliquorum annotationes
Aristidis Smyrnaei oratio de laudibus
    urbis Romae, Scipione Carteromā-
    cho interprete
Conflagratio Vesuvii montis ex Dio-
    ne, Georg. Merula interprete. m8.
Pomponius Mela. Iulius Solinus.
Itinerarium Antonini Augusti. Vi-
    bius Sequester.
P. Victorius de regionibus urbis
    Romae
Dionysius Afer de situ orbis, Pris-
    ciano interprete. m8
Senecae tragoediae. m8
Martialis. m8.
Dec. Ausonius. m8.

Iulii Iocumata. m8.
Ioviani Pontani opera soluta oratio-
    ne m4.
Eiusdem Poemata duobus voluminibus
Posteriori accedunt (Calpurnii Aeglogae)
Aurelii Nemesiani Aeglogae
Strozii poetae ferrarienses pater & filius
Euripidis Hecuba & Iphigenia Eras-
    mo interprete Gr. m8.
Luciani opuscula quaedam Des. E-
    rasmo & Thoma Moro interpretibus. m8.
Des. Erasmi Moria. m8.
Eiusdem Querela Pacis, & alia opuscula
    diversa. m8.
Christophori Longolii perduellionis rei
    defensiones duae. m8.
L. Apuleii Opera. m8.
Q. Curtius. m8.
Plauti Comoediae. m4.
Prudentii libri 5. De affectu. m8.
Asconii Paediani expositio in ora-
    tiones aliquot Ciceronis: cum
    Victorini commentariis in libros
    De Inventione, & Georg. Trapezun-
    tii in orationem pro Q. Ligario. m8.
Petrus Alcyonius de exilio. m4.
Iustinus de exteris historiis, cum
    Aemylio Probo de exteris Im-
    peratoribus. m8.
Claudiani Opera. m8.
Valerii Flacci Argonautica, cum
    Ioan. Bapt. Pii carmine in quarto
    Argonauticorum Apollonii: & Orphei
    Argonauticis innominato inter-
    prete. m8.
Silius Italicus De bello Punico. m8.
Georg. Trapezuntii Rhetoricorum
    libri 5. his accedunt Consulti
    Chirii Fortuniani libri 3.
Aquila Romani de figuris senten-
    tiarum & elocutionis lib. 1.
P. Rutilii Lupi earundem figurata à
    Georgio lib. 1.
Aristotelis Rhetoricon ad Theode-
    cten Georg. Trapezuntio interprete. lib. 6.
Eiusdem Rhetorica ad Alexandrum,
    F. Philelpho interprete
Ἐγχειρίδιον Rhetoricum Hermogenis,
    Hilarione monacho Veronensi
    interprete.
Prisciani praeexercitamenta ex Her-
    mogene. A. Phesciæ prog... aquatu fr. Maria

Cetraeo interprete. in fol.
Macrobius. in 8. Prisciani[us]. in[...]
Sannazarius de partu virginis, de nu[...]
 impressis d auctoris. in 8.
Recognitio veteris testamenti. [...]
Quinq libri quintæ decadis T. Livi[i...]
Corn. Celsus cum Q. Sereno. in 4.
Corn. Tacitus. in 4.
Gratianus de venatione. Ovidius, de P[isc...]
Marc. Aur. Olympius Nemesianus de
 venatione. in 8.
Laur. Vallæ Elegantiæ. in 4.

ITALICI LIBRI

Dantes. in 8. Petrarcha. in 8. Be[...]
di quædam. in 8. Ph. Jo. Bocatius. [...]
Il Cortegiano, del Conte Baldisser Ca[sti]
 glione. in fol. & in 8.
Anthropologia Galeatii Capellæ. in 8

Nota. Hæc omnia ex Aldi [...]
officina publicum acceperunt. Filius
autem Pauli in Manutiis quæ na[...]
 enudi curaverit, certum fam no[...]
habeo, præter pauca hæc.

Ambrosii Calepini Dictionarium. in fol.
Appendix dictionorum in idem. in fol.
Annotata propria, castigationes & obs
 ervationes in M. Tullii Ciceronis libros,
 præcipuæ Philosophicos
Commentarii delle cose de Turch[...]
 Paulo Giovio & Andrea Gambini, [...]
 gli fatti & la vita di Scanderbey.
 in 8. A[nn]o. 1541.
De itineribus ex urbe Veneta in Po[...]
 siam Tanam & Constantinopolim,
 liber Italicus. in 8.
Lexicon Italicum difficiliorum præ
sertim & rariorum dictionum, qui
bus Bocatius & alii utuntur,
 in fol.
M. Antonii Flaminii ff bene memi[...]
 explanatio in Psalmos

Supplex, sic, se habeo sup[ra]
 scriptis Catalogis.

Phillipps MS
 15644

All the scribe's numerals are arabic, again reflecting Gesner. This is a progressive feature, but the writer occasionally employs an archaic practice that goes beyond Gesner's. Straightforward written Latin, including numerals, consists exclusively of letters. As medieval and Renaissance Latin developed, its writers created a feature to enable readers to grasp instantly that the writer was employing numerals, even though everything was written in minuscules. On a given occasion, the author wanted the reader, upon seeing, for example, *ii* or *ij*, to envisage and say (for one commonly read aloud) *duo* or "two" rather than *ii* or "they." The method of distinguishing the numerals was to precede and follow the letters with a period or full-stop. Our writer has occasionally flanked his arabic numerals with periods. This is, of course, a needless embellishment for arabic numerals, which cannot be misread as letters. Gesner's text regularly follows a numeral with punctuation, but it is the scribe who sometimes expands the practice to flanking the numerals with a period or full-stop.

To remove a possible question, the scribe is not Gesner himself: the manuscript is not written in his hand. His manuscripts are in the Zentralbibliothek Zürich, and examples of his handwriting may be viewed on the Internet. While I have been thus far unable to locate instances of the handwriting of Christoph Froschauer the elder (1521–64), I do not consider this in any sense a setting-copy manuscript prepared by someone in the printing house for use by Froschauer's compositors. With its opening citation of the specific page in Gesner on which Gesner's printed catalogue opens, all this is idle, because the manuscript clearly postdates the publication of Gesner's *Pandectae*. So I conclude that it is a private production for personal use.

Contents and analysis

The writer begins his text with the introductory comment that all the books that follow were published in Aldus's own shop up to the year 1534, and cites Gesner's *Pandectae* as his authority and source. So, and as I have previously said, the manuscript cannot date from before the 1548 date of publication. Another way of putting this is that the writer, for the most part, repeats Gesner's wording, while adding the occasional comment, and adjusting some entries, for both good and ill.

The catalogue is assembled in a sequence that effectively follows the consecutive publishing order of the titles, which Aldus established in the three catalogues issued in his lifetime, in 1498, 1503, and 1513,[11] and was observed by the Torresani in compiling the fourth Aldine catalogue of [March 1527]. We have Gesner's citation as his own source of what, in the present state of our knowledge, can seem from its physical description to be only the November 1513 Aldine Press catalogue. The sequence in the manuscript is: title and introductory passages (fol. 1r); Libri Graeci (fol. 1r–v); Alii libri Graeci (fols. 1v–2v); Libri Latini (fols. 2v–4v); Libri Italici (fol. 4v); first concluding passage, and introductory passage to final section (fol. 4v); publications by Paulus Manutius (fol. 4v); conclusion (fol. 4v).

Each entry tends to be more than a bald citation, especially in the case of the composite volumes. The writer gives the authors and a contextual

---

11 RENOUARD (see note 7), pp. 329–38; see now the excellent facsimiles of the catalogues in Aldo Manuzio editore: dediche, prefazioni, note ai testi. Ed. CARLO DIONISOTTI. 2 vols. Milan 1975 (*Documenti sulle arti del libro*. 11), tavv. IX (I 22/3), X–XIII (I 78/9), and XIV–XVIII (I 126/7), respectively. The extant and essentially unique copies (but see below in this note) of all three catalogues – 1 Oct. 1498, 22 June 1503, 24 Nov. 1513 – are part of Paris, BnF, Mss, grec 3064. The three catalogues are reproduced less satisfactorily in *Aldo Manuzio tipografo, 1494–1515*. Ed. LUCIANA BIGLIAZZI, ANGELA DILLON BUSSI, GIANCARLO SAVINI, and PIERO SCAPECCHI. Florence 1994, entries 30, 76, and 118, respectively. The descriptive entry 118 cites a surviving second copy of the 1513 catalogue as being preserved at the B Comunale V. Joppi in Udine, and it was exhibited in Florence at the B Medicea Laurenziana from June to July 1994. In the notes to my critical edition of the manuscript text, I cite the third catalogue as Aldus's 1513 Catalogue.

listing of the contents, often clearly drawn from an analysis of the books themselves. An indication of format – folio, quarto, octavo – normally concludes each entry. The writer expects them to be read as »in folio« (in fol.), »in quarto« (in 4°), and »in octavo« (in 8°); there is also a single »in sextodecimo« (in 16°), for the Greek Hours of the Virgin (in fact, 32°).

In studying the roughly 150 individual and composite publications, one encounters no great surprises in the relative proportions of Greek authors (101) versus Latin authors (109) or in the individual entries, and the paucity of Italian authors (6), almost all of whom, moreover, are cited in Latin, suggests Gesner's or his cataloguer's limited familiarity with the Italian vernacular.[12] Both literary and patristic texts are to be found, with a sprinkling of grammatical aids and dictionaries, and a healthy proportion of then-modern writers, either as authors or as editors and commentators. The *Hypnerotomachia Poliphili* is there; while it is in Gesner, it is not in Aldus's 1513 catalogue, and this could derive from the [1527] catalogue, or be a citation to the 1545 reprint edition, despite the new vernacular title of that edition, as mentioned above. Many of these books have subsequently become great rarities: the incunabula in general, and the various works of Erasmus, for example. The assemblage is reasonably complete. Obvious gaps are few, such as additional volumes of multi-volume works apparently present only in part, the *Organon* volume of Aristotle, and Horace. There are many more works cited than in Aldus's 1513 catalogue, but one also searches in vain for a number of works that had been listed in November 1513.

The cataloguer's, which is to say Gesner's, interest in the books I take to be primarily scholarly and textual: he knows them well enough to compile his entries from a variety of sources, including actual contents, as opposed to merely parroting the contents listings given in the books or in the 1513 Aldine catalogue. A basic premiss behind the whole enterprise is a clear note of admiration for the work of Aldus himself, and the books obviously represent for the cataloguer important artifactual links with the great scholar-printer.

The frequent occurrence of the books in sequences that come very close to or concur with chronologies of their original appearance is noteworthy; a quick glance down the textual notes will show what I mean. This reflects the deliberate bibliophilic motivations of Gesner, who made use of the best sources he could find. The occurrence of this trend in the 1540s is a real eye-opener. Gesner, it seems to me, reflects a degree of analytical bibliography rather in advance of its time. He also has rearranged certain works, rather than follow the 1513 catalogue slavishly. Because Gesner extended his listings well beyond the November 1513 published catalogue and the death of Aldus on 6 February 1515, and again employed considerable detail, he has been at pains to locate and report from authoritative sources.

Midway down the final page, leaf 4ᵛ, a pair of comments treats two elements in the history of the Press. First comes the writer's conclusion of all his preceding listings, with the observation reiterated from Gesner that all the books come from the shop of "Aldus the father." Then follows

12 The author tallies are taken from SERRAI (see note 6), vol. II p. 327.

the notation, highlighted by the scribe, that he possesses only a very few of son Paulus's publications, a mere seven of which he subsequently lists summarily.¹³

It is a bit odd that Gesner did not have knowledge of, or access to records of, a much more extensive collection of Paulus's publications. His dedicatory letter to Paulus, opening Book XI, speaks glowingly and in detail of Paulus's scholarly and editorial attainments and achievements. This suggests that he would have had greater access to a range of Aldine Press books that had appeared during the Sons of Aldus period in the 1540s, but the catalogue does not reflect this beyond the most exiguous extent.

Editorial procedures

My goal has been to present a reasonably consistent and accurate diplomatic transcript of the manuscript, occasionally modified for clarity or specificity. I have sought to emend only potentially substantive problems in presenting this edited text, and these interpolations are clearly indicated, both in the text and in the pertinent notes. Relatively minor differences of orthography – *exilio* for *exsilio*, for example – have been allowed occasionally to stand. Simple expansions of contractions or suspensions are given within square brackets [ ]; editorial interpolations, within angle brackets ⟨ ⟩. I have selectively expanded the names of Byzantine and Renaissance translators, editors, and commentators, but not those of the classical writers. Where I have also regularized median and terminal punctuation in accord with what I believe to be the writer's intentions, I have indicated these changes as well.

Each edition is identified, as feasible, by citation to the long-standard Aldine bibliography, the *Annales des Alde*, by Antoine-Augustin Renouard. Following his intentions and structure, I have cited Renouard annalistically in most instances: that is, by year and item number, rather than by page. (An example: RENOUARD 1517.8 means that the writer is listing a copy of the octavo reprint edition of MUSAEUS: *De Herone et Leandro* of 1517, described by Renouard under nº 8 of his listings for the year 1517, rather than the incunabular Aldine quarto editions.) Although this is not entirely satisfactory from a rigidly scholarly viewpoint — Renouard occasionally and erroneously assigned Venetian Style chronology to many January and February dates that can be proved to be New Style, thereby creating misleading annual sequences and assignments — it offers the general benefit of providing a year at quick glance. I cite Renouard by page and item for the undated books, which of course do not lend themselves to annalistic assignment; the attributed date is also given. Whenever it seems helpful in clarifying the specific edition or extended contents of a work I believe to be at issue, I have added a citation to the respective location in the printed catalogues of the very extensive holdings of the Ahmanson-Murphy Collection, at the University of California, Los Angeles, and the Harry Ransom Humanities Research Center, at the University of Texas, Austin. On some occasions I cite Annaclara Cataldi Palau's monumental study of Gian Francesco Torresani, responsible for the Aldine Press in the years following Aldus's death.

---

13 Some discussion of Paulus's career and motivations based upon more recent discoveries and investigations or revisited evidence, a topic to which I have contributed, has appeared latterly. Cf. T. KIMBALL BROOKER: Paolo Manutio's Use of Fore-edge Titles for Presentation Copies (1540–1541). In: *The Book Collector*. 46 (1997). Part I (Spring), pp. 27–68 and Part II (Summer), pp. 193–209, here pp. 29/30 and passim. Cf. also MARTIN LOWRY: Aristotle's *Poetics* and the Rise of Vernacular Literary Theory. In: *Viator*. 25 (1994), 411–25, passim and MARTIN LOWRY: Facing the Responsibility of Paulus Manutius. Los Angeles 1995 (*University Research Library Occasional Paper*. 8), passim. Cf. H. GEORGE FLETCHER: *In Praise of Aldus Manutius: a Quincentenary Exhibition*. New York, Los Angeles 1995, esp. pp. 8/9, 16/7, 65–77 and H. GEORGE FLETCHER: Paulus Manutius in Aedibus Populi Romani. In: Aldus Manutius and Renaissance Culture: Studies in Memory of Franklin D. Murphy. Ed. DAVID S. ZEIDBERG. Florence 1998 (*Villa I Tatti*. 15), pp. 287–321, passim.

As often as possible, I have narrowed the citation to a single edition. My decisions have been based on a combination of such factors as Gesner's initial date of 1534 and publication date of 1548, his exclusion of Paulus's publications until the final section of his catalogue, the format designations (though not without the occasional problem), and the precise contents and wording of each actual edition that is a potential candidate. The cataloguer's individual compilations and vocabulary regularly narrow the choice dramatically. I cite more than one edition, sometimes with and sometimes without further comment, when I cannot delimit the candidates more precisely. When it is either not apparent from such basic facts as limited choices or specific wording, however, my underlying assumption is that an edition close to the 1548 publication date of the *Pandectae* is the likely candidate among a group of options.

Conclusions

Our objective knowledge of certain details surrounding the publication of the many titles that emerged from the Aldine Press in the periods 1514–29, 1533–36, and from 1539 up to the date of Gesner's *Pandectae*, 1548–49, is hampered by a certain want of published catalogues from these periods. The re-emergence of the [1527] fourth catalogue is a major advance, but there are still extensive lacunae. In the absence of this kind of knowledge, we are thwarted in seeking to draw conclusions from all the entries in Gesner, and we still have serious gaps in our ability to determine the source or sources of his entries about editions published after November 1513.

The only other recorded catalogue of this period that might have had some pertinence turns out to be at best peripheral. The Parisian bookseller Nicolas le Riche, who advertised his books as bearing the device of twin, or crossed, anchors, ran a shop at the sign of Aldus in the rue des Prêtres next to the Collège de Cambrai from 1540 to 1548. Renouard reports having seen two issues of his seventh catalogue, «non pas d'Alde, mais di Cose d'Aldo». This catalogue, which is undated, lists books published in the years 1547 and 1548, both Greek and Latin Aldines and Italian vernacular works. No extant copy is currently recorded.[14]

Aldine catalogues from this long span of years have not surfaced during the course of the investigation that Christian Coppens, of Katholieke Universiteit Leuven, has been conducting for many years.[15]

Given the paucity of firm evidence, we are bound to find the Aldine catalogue in Gesner's *Pandectae* all the more valuable, and its relative obscurity and demonstrable inaccessibility have produced a lacuna in our knowledge of the advance of bibliographical inquiry in the middle years of the sixteenth century. Indeed, my old friend Dr. Brooker posited the ingenious suggestion[16] that Gesner had access to the fourth Aldine Press catalogue of [1527] and in fact based his own list upon it, although that does not now seem to have been the case.

How to explain the creation of the Yale manuscript compounds our present want of known surviving sources. Has Gesner's *Pandectae* been essentially difficult to consult from its origins, and was it too expensive for those needing it? Gesner was placed on the *Index librorum prohibitorum* by

14 Nicolaus Dives (Nicolas le Riche, or Le Riche, or Leriche) is probably described accurately as a seller of books imported from Italy. According to RENOUARD (see note 7), pp. 344/5, he published two issues of an 8º *Index librorum tam Graeca & Latina, quam uulgari Italorum lingua, ex officina Aldi, & aliunde ex Italia aduectorum*. These were »Libri per Nicolaum Divitem excusi ad insigne geminae anchorae uia sacerdotum, & iuxta collegium Cameracense ad insigne Aldi uaenales.« POLLARD/EHRMAN (see note 6), pp. 56 and 59 (Table III).
15 I am grateful to Dr. Coppens for generous access to his research (CHRISTIAN COPPENS: *Census of Printers' and Booksellers' Catalogues before 1600.* [Unpublished work in progress.]), including his presentation at the conference on "Book Catalogues, Tomorrow and Beyond," held in New York at The Grolier Club on 22 January 2008, and subsequent personal correspondence.
16 Personal correspondence, February to March 2008 and February to March 2009.

the Council of Trent, because he wrote approvingly of heretical authors, and he himself was Zwinglian.¹⁷ Indeed, the censors used his *Bibliotheca universalis* as a convenient guide to heretical authors, beginning with the Milanese and Venetian Indices of 1554, and Gesner himself was designated in the first class of condemned authors, which meant that all that author's works were prohibited. Even before this, however, the University of Louvain condemned Gesner's work as early as 1550. So his proscribed works were defaced, destroyed, or discarded in certain instances, especially in Catholic countries and locales, reducing the numbers of what was probably a relatively small print run to begin with. On the other hand, surviving copies may yet lie unrecognized in libraries of eastern Europe still awaiting modernization, and not readily locatable in libraries around the world that have not updated their holdings records.

The scribe seems to me to have been someone in the middle decades of the sixteenth century who was eager to have a private record of the publications of the Aldine Press, had access to, but did not own, a copy of Gesner, and made a personal copy of the catalogue in Book XI. Was it an easily carried shopping list, to accompany its creator on a voyage of bibliophilic exploration and acquisition? Did its creation imply that it was simply all its writer could afford? This would conform to the regular pattern, long in use following the introduction of printing from movable type in the West, of the survival of the manuscript copy, made from the printed edition, often for personal reasons of interests and means, alongside texts already available in printed form.¹⁸

The simple fact of the survival of this manuscript catalogue is, of course, a positive thing, providing an extant artifact in an otherwise sparsely inhabited landscape. Whether judged a valuable resource or dismissed as a mere curiosity, it offers a surviving witness only marginally rarer than the first edition of Gesner's *Pandectae* itself. It testifies to a personal interest in Aldine publications during a period from which we have almost no surviving witnesses, and it adds another element to our repertory of records of the continuing pertinence of the Aldine Press in the decades well after the death of its eponymous founder and guiding spirit.¹⁹

---

17 ALBERTO MORENI: La *Bibliotheca Universalis* di Konrad Gesner e gli Indici dei libri proibiti. In: *La Bibliofilía*. 88.2 (1986), pp. 131–50, here pp. 137 (»quorum libri et scripta omnia prohibentur«), 138 (»totius bibliothecae atque pandectarum C. Gesneri«), 139, 142, and passim.

18 On this interesting topic, see CURT F. BÜHLER: *The Fifteenth-century Book: the Scribes, the Printers, the Decorators. The 1959 Rosenbach Lectures in Bibliography*. Philadelphia 1960, sect. I (*Scribes*) passim, esp. pp. 15/6, 32/3, 35–7. "Readers [...] continued to use manuscripts and incunabula indifferently; quotation and reference to texts unpublished [...] imply the continued use of the hand-written book into the late Quattrocento"; "the routine, prosaic copy of a classic can only be accounted for on the basis that, as the fifteenth century was dying, it still was more economical to write out your own manuscript than to buy a printed version, even a second-hand one" (p. 33). While BÜHLER treats mostly the transitional century, his commentary extends well into later periods. One might also consult SANDRA HINDMAN/JAMES DOUGLAS FARQUHAR: *Pen to Press: Illustrated Manuscripts and Printed Books in the First Century of Printing*. Baltimore 1977, so long as one takes into account W. H. BOND's review in *Speculum*. 2 (1979), pp. 386–8.

19 A personal note to conclude this Introduction. I first saw this manuscript in the autumn of 1988, and began this investigation tentatively not long afterward, but was forced by circumstances to put it aside for very long intervals. A major circumstance was my frustration with elements of the manuscript caused by my thwarted attempts to find a copy of Gesner's *Pandectae* that I might consult. While the intervening years also brought the benefit of additional information that I discovered, or that colleagues supplied, it was Paul Naiditch, formerly of UCLA, who pointed out to me, in his customarily thoughtful and generous way, that my real problem was the rarity of the Gesner. It is indeed a surprisingly inaccessible work, perhaps at least four or five times scarcer than Gesner's *Bibliotheca universalis*, and it was a long time before I discovered that the only copies I might consult were those owned by the late Bernard H. Breslauer and Roland Folter. Dr. Folter was so generous as to provide me with a photocopy of the requisite pages of Book XI taken from his copy, which advanced my editorial work very substantially; moreover, he has saved me from numerous errors of commission and omission. The Breslauer copy, it is pleasing to note, is now in The Morgan L & M, where it had been a perennial desideratum. An invitation from Richard Ovenden of the Bodleian L and Ian Mclean of All Souls College to present a paper on an Aldine topic at the 29 Feb. to 1 March 2008 Oxford conference "The Sixteenth-century Book: European Perspectives" provided the impetus to my completing this study. T. Kimball Brooker's close reading of the final draft sagely challenged some of my conclusions and enabled me to avoid certain errors, while offering a number of most thoughtful hypotheses. Conor Fahy's review of *Im Zeichen von Anker und Delphin* (see note 21) in *La Bibliofilía* (CONOR FAHY: Review of *Im Zeichen von Anker und Delphin*. In: *La Bibliofilía*. 110.1 [2008], pp. 93/4.), which I chanced upon as a posthumous benefaction, enabled me to push aside a major stumbling-block.

I regret that Conor did not live to see this present study, which he would have critiqued admirably; its inadequacies notwithstanding, it is dedicated to his memory.

ALDVS STVDIOSIS. S.

LIBRORVM Et græcorum, et latinorum nomina, quotquot in hunc usq; diem excudendos curauimus, sacre uos uoluimus. Vbi etiam quædam de libris singulis, tanquam eorum argumenta dicuntur, ut inde quid singulo quoq; libro eractatur, facile cognoscatis. Quod ideo factum est, q̄, cum undiq; ad nos scribatur, qui nam libri cura nostra excussi sint, sic satisfaciamus, cum aliter, propter summas occupationes nostras, non liceat.

LIBRI GRAECI.

Erotemata Constantini Lascaris tribus libris, in quibus hæc habentur, uidelicet. De quatuor grammatices, et octo orationis partibus. De formatione uerborum per tempora, et modos omneis. De accentibus, et punctis, et locis tonorum. De præpositionum constructione. De figuris. De anomalis uerbis. De aspiratione, et exilitate uocalium, et diphthongorum, hæc primo libro. De constructione uerborum, libro secundo. De nomine, et uerbo abunde admodum, libro tertio. De pronominibus secundum diuersas linguas, et quemadmodū eis poëtæ utantur. Quæ omnia habent latinam trālationem propter græcarum literarum rudes, ita tamen, ut et amoueri, et additi tinum queat pro cuiusq; arbitrio. In medio latinæ trālationis habetur Cebetis Thebani tabula, et oratio quædā ad Virginem tam græce, quàm latine, ne charta, quæ superat, periret. Inest et nostrum Opusculum de literis, et diphthongis græcis, ut possint, qui præceptore carent, uel per seipsos discere principia literarum græcarum. Item quæ admodum literæ, et diphthongi græcæ ad nos ueniant. Abbreuiationes etiam græcæ. Oratio dominica, et duplex salutatio ad B. Virginem. Symbolum Apostolorum. Euangelium diui Ioannis. Carmina aurea Pythagoræ. Phocylidis documenta. Omnia habent latinam interpretationem. Inest etiam perbreuis ad hebraicam liguam introductio. Nec non de Dialectis, et græce, et latine, ubi multa digna lectu dicuntur, forma paulo echiridij maiore.

Canonismata, quæ thesaurus, et Cornucopiæ appellatur dictionum difficilium, et maxime uerborum, quæ apud Homerum ex commentarijs Eustathij, et aliorum gramaticorum per ordinem literarum. Aelij Dionysij de indeclinabilibus uerbis. Declinationes uerborum sum, et eo, utilissimæ. De ijs, quæ sedere significant. Quot sint quæ ire significant. Ex scriptis Herodiani excerpta de magno uerbo sciu dignissima, et rara inuentu. Ex scriptis eiusdem de ductionibus uerborum difficulter declinatorum. Chœrobosca ad eos, qui in omnibus uerbis regulas quærunt, et similitudines. Eiusdem in quibus ob malesonantiam atrahatur r. litera. De anomalis, et inæqualibus uerbis secundum ordinem alphabeti. Herodiani de inclinatis, et encliticis, et coenecliticis distinauculis. Ex scriptis Chœrobosca de ijs, quæ inclinantur, encliticisq;. Sine authore deijs, quæ inclinatur. Ex scriptis Ioãnis Grãmatici de idiomatis. Eustathius de idiomatis, quæ apud Homerum. Item de idiomatis, ex ijs, quæ à Corintho decerpta. De fœmininis noibus, quæ desinūt in o magnum, forma folij.

Grãmatica doctissima, et (pace aliorum dixerim) omnium utilissima Theodori Gazæ uiri ingenio, et doctrina uel cum antiquissimis cōferēdi. Eiusdē de mēsibus pulcherrimū opus. Itē quatuor libri Apollonij de constructione, forma folij.

Dictionarium græcum cum interpretatione latina, omnium, quæ hactenus impressa sunt, copiosissimum. Collectio dictionum, quæ differunt significatu, per ordinem literarum. Dictiones latinæ græce redditæ. Ammonius de similibus, et differentibus dictionibus. Vetus instructio, et denominationes præfectorum militum. Orbicius de nominibus ordinum militarium. Significata τῶ ἥ κοσμοῖς. Io. Grammatici quædam de proprietatibus linguarum. Eustathij quædam de proprietatibus linguarū apud Homerum. Corinthus de proprietatibus linguarum. Verborum anomalorum declinationes secundum ordinem literarum. Herodiani quædam de encliticis. Io. Grammatici Charcis quædam de encliticis. Chœrobosca quædam de encliticis. Thomæ Magistri eclogæ atticorum nominum, et uerborum. Phrynichi eclogæ atticorum nominum, et uerborum. Emanuelis Moschopuli eclogæ atticarum dictionum, nunc primū impressæ, forma folij.

Theocriti eclogæ triginta. Hesiodi theogonia. Eiusdem scutum Herculis. Eiusdem georgicorū libri duo. Maximi Planudæ ex latino libro, qui Cato dicitur, Sententiæ parœneticæ distichi. Caput De inuidia. Theognidis Megarensis Siculi sententiæ elegæcæ. Sententiæ putiles monostichi per capita ex uarijs poëtis. Aurea Carmina Pythagoræ. Phocylidæ poëma admonitorium utilissimum. Carmina Sibyllæ erythrææ de Christo IESV. Differentia uocum, forma folij.

Aristophanis cum antiquis commentarijs Comediæ nouem. Plutus. Nebulæ. Ranæ. Equites. Acharnes. Vespæ. Aues. Pax. Concionatrices fœminæ, forma folij.

Musei opusculum de Herone et Leandro, una cum Orphei argonautica, et hymnis, et de lapidibus, forma enchiridij.

Logica Aristotelis, quod organum græce dicitur, ubi habētur hæc. Porphyrij introductionis, siue uniuersalium liber unus. Prædicamentorum Aristotelis liber unus. Perihermenias liber unus, siue sectiones sex. Priorum resolutoriorum libri duo. Posteriorum resolutoriorum libri duo. Topicorū libri octo. Elenchorū libri duo, forma folij.

Primum uolumen in Philosophia.

Vita Aristotelis per Laërtium, et Philopoũ, et uita Theophrasti. Aristotelis phisicorum libri octo. De cœlo libri quatuor. De generatione, et corruptione libri duo. Meteorologicorum libri quatuor. De mundo ad Alexandrum liber unus. Philonis iudæi de mundo liber unus. Thephrasti de igne liber unus. De uentis liber unus. De lapidibus liber unus. De signis aquarum, et uentorum incerti authoris, forma folij.

Secundum uolumen.

De historia animaliū libri octo. De partibus animalium libri quatuor. De gressu animalium liber unus. De anima libri tres. De sensu liber unus. De memoria liber unus. De somno, et uigilia liber unus. De somnijs liber unus. De diuinatione p̃ somniorum liber unus. De motu animalium liber unus. De generatione animaliū libri quinq;. De longitudine, et breuitate uitæ liber unus. De iuuentute, et senectute, et respiratione, et uita, et morte libri tres. De spiritu liber unus. De coloribus liber unus. Physiognomicorum liber unus. De mirabili bus auditionibus liber unus. De Xenophanis, Zenonis, & Gorgiæ opinionibus liber unus. De indiuisibilibus lineis liber unus. Theophrasti de piscibus liber unus. De uertigine oculorū liber unus. De laboribus liber unus. De odoribus liber unus. De sudoribus liber unus, forma folij.

Tertium Volumen.

Theophrasti de historia plantarum libri decem. Eiusdem de causis plantarum libri sex. Aristotelis problematum sectiones duodequadraginta. Alexandri Aphrodiensis problematum libri duo. Aristotelis mechanicorum liber unus. Eiusdē metaphysicorum libri quatuordecim. Theophrasti metaphysicorum liber unus, forma folij.

Quartum volumen.

Aristotelis magnorum moralium ad Nicomachum patrem libri duo. Ethicorum ad Eudemum discipulū libri octo. Ethicorum ad Nicomachum filium libri decem. Oeconomicorum libri duo. Politicorum libri octo, forma folij.

Psalterium græcum, forma paulo enchiridij maiore.

Officium in honorem Beatissimæ uirginis cum Psalmis pœnitentialibus è latino in græcum, per quam parua forma.

Epistolarum mille, & septuaginta trium volumen, quarum authores sunt quadraginta, uidelicet. Basilius. Libanius. Chion. Aeschines. Isocrates. Phalaris. Pythagoras. Mithridates. Brutus. Apollonius. Iulianus. Synesius. Demosthenes. Plato. Aristoteles. Philippus, & Alexāder Macedonū reges. Hippocrates. Artaxerxes rex. Pætus. Istanes. Democritus. Darius. Heraclitus. Diogenes. Crates. Anacharsis. Euripides. Theano. Myia. Melissa. Alciphron. Philostratus. Theophilactus. Aelianus. Aeneas. Proxpias. Lysis. Amasis. Musonius. Epistolarum typi, & characteres, forma paulo enchiridij maiore.

Gregorij Nazanzeni opusculum, ubi philosophatur, atq; enarrat, quæ in tota uita expertus est, heroicis. 610. Eiusdem uirginitatis carmen, heroicis. 711. Eiusdem documenta uirginibus, heroicis. 684. Eiusdem luctus de suæ ipsius animæ passionibus, elegis. 350. Eiusdem commiserationum de ipsius animæ affectibus, heroicis. 170. De uitæ stultitia, & perfidia, & communi omniū fine, heroicis. 69. Lamentatio suorum laborum, & ad Christum oratio de solutione suæ uitæ, heroicis. 31. Ad se ipsum per interrogationem, & responsionem, heroicis. 31. Insomnium de Anastasiæ ecclesia, quā struxit in Cōstātinopoli, elegis. 104. De uitæ differentijs, & contra falsos sacerdotes, elegis. 108. Ad episcopos, heroicis. 227. Ad sacerdotes Constantinopolis, & ipsam urbem, elegis. 26. De humana natura, elegis. 132. De extrinseca hominum, uita, elegis. 164. De uitæ itineribus, heroicis. 40. Diuersarum uitarum beationes, elegis. 66. Iuramenta, uel promissiones per iusiurandum, elegis. 30. Contra carnem, elegis. 50. Contra diabolum, heroicis. 10. Conuersuatio ergo Deum admonitio, heroicis. 16. Expulsio diaboli, & Christi inuocatio, elegis. 24. Luctus, elegis. 8. Ad animum suum, elegis. 6. De fatali humana natura, elegis. 12. Aliud epigramma, elegis. 12. De desyderio erga Deū, elegis. 24. Lamentabile pro sua anima, heroicis. 36. Luctus, elegis. 8. Supplicatorium, heroicis. 24. Funebris, & compendium suæ uitæ, elegis. 2. Pœnitentiarium, et hortatorium, elegis. 12. Contra diabolum, elegis. 4. De le=

gitimus libris diuinitus inspiratæ scripturæ, tum heroicis, tum elegis, tum iambicis. 39. Verbera Aegypti, elegis. 12. Mosis dialogus, heroicis. 10. De duodecim Patriarchis, heroicis. 5. De duodecim Apostolis, heroicis. 5. De Christi genealogia, heroicis. 102. Christi miracula secundum Matthæum, elegis. 38. Eiusdem parobolæ, & ænigmata, elegis. 18. Eiusdem miracula secundum Ioannem, heroicis. 11. Eiusdem miracula secundum Lucam, legis. 20. Eiusdem parabolæ, iambicis. 22. Christi miracula secundum Marcum, heroicis. 17. Parabolæ quatuor euangelistarum, heroicis. 106. Ad monachos in cōmuni uitæ, heroicis. 15. Ad græcos de monachis hortatorium, elegis. 368. Ad Iulianum, elegis. 30. A'Nicobulo ad patrem, heroicis. 207. Nicælij ad filium, heroicis. 283. Ad Vitalianum à filijs, heroicis. 352. In nobilem male moratum, elegis. 40. Itineraria, heroicis. 33. In silentium in ieiunijs, elegis. 10. Hymni ad Christum post silentium in pascha, elegis. 52. Admonitorium, heroicis. 111. Ad se ipsum post reditum ex Constantinopoli, elegis. 53. Ad se ipsum, heroicis. 117. In carpentem, solitariam uitam degentem, elegis. 50. In mortuum, elegis. 118. Ad Nemesium, heroicis. 333. Sententiæ disticha, elegis. 124. Contra mulieres ornatas, elegis. 334. In magnum Basilium duodecim epitaphia, elegis. 52. Sententiosa disticha iambicis. 115. Sententiosa tetrasticha, iambicis. 132. Quæ omnia habent latinam tralationem, quæ & addi, & amoueri potest pro legentis arbitrio. In medio quaternionum tralationis totius operis habetur historia euangelij secundum Ioannem græcè, & latinè, forma paulo enchiridij maiore.

Nonni poetæ Panopolitani Paraphrasis totius historiæ Euangelicæ secundum Ioannem carmine heroico excellenti. Incipit enim sic.

ἄχρονος ἦν ἀκίχητος, ἐν ἀῤῥήτῳ λόγος ἀρχῇ,
ἰσοφυὴς γενετῆρος ὁμήλικος, ὁμὸς ἀμήτωρ.
καὶ λόγος αὐτοφύτοιο θεοῦ φῶς ἐκφάος φῶς.

Sunt autem carminum tria milia, et supra, forma paulo enchiridij maiore.

Pedacij Dioscoridis de materia medica, libri sex. Eiusdem de uenenatis animalibus libri duo, quibus canis rabidi signa, & curatio eorum continetur, quibus uenenata animalia morsum defixerint. Index omnium plantarum, animalium, metallorum, quorum utilitatem author Dioscorides præsenti in libro docet. Carmina de uirtute, siue facultate quorundam plantarum in antiquis reperta exemplaribus, Nicandri præterea Theriaca. Eiusdem Alexipharmaca. Interpretatio etiam innominati authoris in Theriaca. Commētarij diuersorum authorū in Alexipharmaca. Expositio poderum, ac mensurarum signorum, et characterum, forma paulo enchiridij maiore.

Iulij pollucis uocabularium, quod indicat multa de eodem dici, & quo nam modo singula appellentur, nititur enim non tam multitudine, q̃ pulchri delectu. Totum uero opus diuiditur in decem libros, nec per ordinem literarum uocabula denotantur, sed sunt præposita capita rerum omnium summatim ante singulos libros ab ipso authore. Sed ego, ut facilius inueniri oīa queant, quæ libris singulis ante id ipsum uolumen pertractantur, copiosius'q;, & dilucidius, & latinè, & græcè imprimenda curaui, numeris arithmeticis annotatis, quibus ad columnulam, in qua id est, quod quæritur, studiosus lector remittitur. quādoquide singulas quasq; libri totius columnulas ijsdem numeris signandas curaui,uis forma folij.

Stephanus de urbibus opus perq́ utile, maximéq́; necessariu ijs, qui humanitati incumbunt. nam & urbes multas, quae apud historicos & poëtas leguntur καρὰ ϛοιχεῖον docet, et quo nam modo gentilia ab urbibus nomina deducantur, ostendit. Adde, q́ huiusmodi nominum orthographiam, in qua plurimum errare solent graecarum literarum rudes, ex Stephano operaepretium est discere, forma folij.

Thucydides de bello inter Peloponenses, & Athenienses libri octo, quibus haec praemittuntur. Aphthonij Sophistae laudatio in Thucydidem ex ipsius in rhetoricis exercitamentis. Vita Thucydidis. Item aliter Marcellini de uita Thucydidis, & ipsius orationis forma ex tota conscriptione extracta fio. Item aliter de Thucydide ex Suda. Dionysius Alicarnaseus de Idiomatis apud Thucydide, forma folij.

Herodoti libri noue, quibus musarum Clius. Euterpes. Thaliae. Melpomenes. Therpsichores. Eratus. Polymniae. Vraniae. Caliopes indita ab eo nomina. Vbi notandum primum librum abundare à caeteris, quibus cum contulimus exemplar nostrum, multis chartis, quae et in eo desunt, qui à Laurentio Valla translatus habetur, quod conferendo licet cognoscere, forma folij.

Luciani opuscula. 171. quibus propter rerum uarietatem, & copiam, & dicendi elegantiam, & facilitatem, perbreui proficere quis graecis literis potest. Insunt & Icones quinq́ & sexaginta Philostrati, idest imagines, & species rerum quarundam, quae in tabellis, in porticu quadam Neapoli erant depictae, quas Philostratus hospitis sui filio enarrat, cum is admodum puer discendi cupidus rogasset Philostratum, ut sibi eas depictas imagines declararet. Item eiusdem heroica, est enim dialogus in quo uinitor quidam cum Phoenice hospite suo multa commemorat, et inter caetera ideas, & species heroum, qui apud Troiam pugnauerunt, ut ipse à Protesilao didicerat, breuiter docet, describit autem heroas unum & uiginti. Adduntur praeterea Icones Iunioris Philostrati duodeuiginti. Item enarrationes Calistrati in statuas quatuordecim. Necnon Philostrati uitae sophistarum. 58. duobus libris. Index etiam duplex, alter ante Luciani dialogos, eorum, quae in eo uolumine tractantur, alter post opuscula Philostrati eorum omnium, quae habentur inibi, forma folij.

Philostrati de uita Apollonii Tyanei libri octo, in quibus mirabilia de eo uiro narrantur. Iidem libri latini Alemano Rinuccino Florentino interprete. Eusebius contra Hieroclem, q́ Tyaneum Christo humani generis redemptori conferre conatus fuerit. Idem latinus interprete Zenobio Acciaiolo Florentino ordinis praedicatorum, forma folii.

Ammonius in praedicamenta Aristotelis. Idem in librum περὶ ἑρμηνείας .i. de interpretatione. Margentinus in eundem, forma folii.

Ioannes Grammaticus in posteriora resolutoria Aristotelis, forma folii.

Sophoclis tragoediae septem, quarum nomina Aiax flagellifer. Electra. Oedipus tyrannus. Antigone. Oedipus Coloneus. Trachiniae. Philoctetes, forma enchiridii.

Euripidis tragoediae duodeuiginti, quarum nomina Hecuba. Orestes. Phoenissae. Medea. Hippolytus. Alcestis. Andromache. Supplices. Iphigenia in Aulide. Iphigenia in Tauris. Rhesus. Troades. Bacchae. Cyclops. Heraclidae. Helena. Ion. Hercules furens, forma enchiridii.

Epigrammata graeca, à diuersis composita antiquis q́; ac doctis authoribus, quae diuiditur in libros septe. habet autem unusquisq́; liber in fronte indicem eorum, quae inibi tractantur per capita secundum ordinem alphabeti, forma enchiridii.

Homeri libri 48. & uita eius ex Plutarcho, Herodoto, & Dione, forma enchiridii.

Quintus Calaber de derelictis ab Homero, quatuordecim libris, forma enchiridii.

Orationes Demosthenis. Olynthiacae tres. Philippicae quatuor. De coordinatione, seu instructione 1. De classib. reip. 1. De pace 1. De Halonesso 1. De rebus Cherronesi 1. Ad Philippi epistolam 1. Epistola Philippi. De Rhodiorum libertate 1. Pro Megalopolitanis 1. Pro pactionibus cum Alexandro 1. De Corona, uel pro Ctesiphonte 1. De uiolata legatione 1. De immunitate ad Leptinem 1. Contra Midiam 1. Contra Androtionem 1. Contra Aristocratem 1. Contra Timocratem 1. Contra Aristogitonem 2. Contra Aphobum 2. Ad Aphobum falsi testimonii 1. Contra Onetorem 2. Translatio ad Zenothemum 1. Translatio aduersus Apaturium 1. Ad Phormionem pro pecunia mutuo data 1. Translatio pro Phormione 1. Translatio ad Pantaenetum 1. Translatio ad Nausimachum, et Xenopiten 1. Ad Boeotum de nomine 1. Ad Boeotum pro dote materna 1. Ad Spudiam pro dote 1. Ad Phaenippum de permutando censu 1. Ad Macartatum de Hagnithaereditate 1. Aduersus Leocharen de haereditate 1. Contra Stephanum falsi testimonii 2. Contra Eueygum, et Mnesibuli falsi testimonii 1. Contra Olympiodorum nocumenti 1. Ad Timotheum pro debito 1. Ad Polyclẽ De tpe, quo praefuit classi 1. De praefectura classis Stephani 1. Ad Calippum 1. Ad Nicostratum de descriptione mancipiorum Arethusij 1. Contra Cononum contumeliosorum uerborum 1. Ad Calliclem de praedio 1. Contra Dionysodorum nocumenti 1. Prouocatio ad Eubuliden 1. Acusatio contra Theocrinum 1. Contra Neaeram 1. Funebris 1. Amatoria 1. Prooemia concionatoria 1. forma folij.

Vlpiani Commentaria in duodeuiginti Demosthenis orationes scilicet in Olynthiacas treis. In Philippicas quatuor. Ad Philippi epistolam. Contra Androtionem. Contra Midiem. De Corona. De uiolata legatione. Contra Aristocratem. Contra Timocratem. Ad Leptinem. De Coordinatione, seu instructione. De classibus reip. Pro Megalopolitanis. Pro libertate Rhodiorum. Pro pactionibus cum Alexandro. Harpocration de dictionibus rhetorum per ordinem literarum, forma folij.

Moralia Plutarchi, uidelicet. De liberis educandis. Quomodo oportet nouitium audire poëmata. De audiendo. Quonam modo queat quis assentatorem ab amico discernere. Quonam modo quis sentiat se uirtute proficere. Quo modo quis iuuari possit ab inimicis.

De multiplici amicitia. De fortuna. De uirtute, et uitio. Consolatoria ad Apollonium. Salubria praecepta. Nuptialia praecepta. Septem sapientum conuiuium. De Superstitione. Dicteria Regum, ac Imperatorum. Dicteria lacunica. Mulierum uirtutes. Vtrum aqua, an ignis utilior. Res, acrius Romanorum capitibus 113. Res, & ritus graecorum Cap. 61. De placitis philosophorum libri quinque. De comparatione Graecorum, & Romanorum Cap. 84. Compendium Commentarii, in quo stoicos inopinatiora, quàm poëtas asseruisse tradit. De unius, & populi, & paucorum dominatu. Belluas ratione uti. Quod ne uiuere quidem datur suauiter secundum Epicurum. An recte dictum sit, lateat, te uixisse.

A ij

An satis sit nitiui ad infelicitatem. De charitate erga sobolem. De Iside, & Osiride. De Iis, qui à Deo sero puniuntur. Quod doctrina acquiri potest uirtus. Quod sé ipse quis laudet sic, ut nulla contrahat inuidiam. De non irascendo. De curiositate. De tranquillitate animi. De nimia uerecundia. De amore fraterno. De loquacitate. De studio erga diuitias. Vtrum animi, an corporis morbi peiores. De fortuna Romanorum. De fortuna, & uirtute Alexandri libri duo. De esu carnium libri duo. Quod maxime oportet philosophum cum principibus degere. Ad principem indoctum. De morali uirtute. An seniori uersandum sit in rep. De capessenda rep. praecepta. Quod non oportet mutuari. Quaestiones Platonis. De animi potestatibus. De primo frigido. Vtrum Athenienses ob res bellicas, an ob doctrinam gloriosiores. De exilio. De inuidia, & odio. Consolatoria ad suam uxorem. De fato. De musica. Compendium coparationis Aristophanis, & Euandri. Vitae decem oratorum. Antiphontis. Andocidae. Lisiae. Isocratis. Isaei. Aeschinis. Lycurgi. Demosthenis. Hyperidis. Dynarchi. De oppugnantibus inter se stoicorum dictis. Otho. Vita animalia prudentiora, terrena, an aquatilia. Galba. De animae generatione in Timaeo. Compendium de eo, de animae generatione in Timaeo. Amatoriae narrationes. Causae naturales. Coniuiorum libri nouem. De facie apparente in circulo lunae. Quod non dat nunc oracula carminibus pythia. Ad Colotem. De communibus conceptibus aduersus stoicos. De daemonio Socratis. De malignitate Herodoti, forma folij.

P hornutus de natura deorum cum Palaephato de fabulosa historia cum uita, & fabulis. Aesopi graece, & latine cum Gabriae fabulis uersu iambico, graece & latine, cum Heraclide pontico de allegorijs apud Homerum cum Orode hieroglyphis, cum prouerbijs per ordinem alphabeti, forma folij.

L iber duodecim rhetorum de arte rhetorica uidelicet. Aphthonij progymnasmata. Hermogenis ars rhetorica. Aristotelis Rhetoricorum ad Theodecten libri tres. Eiusdem Rhetoricae ad Alexandrum. Eiusdem ars poetica. Sopatri quaestiones de componendis declamationibus in causis praecipue iudicialibus. Cyri differentiae statuum. Dionysij Alicarnasei ars rhetorica. Demetrij Phalerei de interpretatione. Alexandri de figuris sensus, & dictionis. Annotationes innominati de figuris rhetoricis. Menacri diuisio causarum. Aristidis de ciuili oratione. Eiusdem de simplici oratione. Apsini praecepta de arte rhetorica, forma folij.

I n Aphthonij progymnasmata commentarij innominati authoris. Syriani. Sopatri. Marcellini in status Hermogenis commentarij. Innominati in reliqua Hermogenis commentarij, forma folij.

G rammatica Chrysolorae cum libro quarto Theodori de constructione cum sententijs monostichis per ordinem alphabeti ex uarijs poetis una cum Catone, & Erotematibus Guarini, forma enchiridij.

P indarus cum Callimacho, Dionysio de situ orbis. Lycophrone, forma enchiridij.

I socratis orationes, & Alcidamantis contra dicendi magistros, & Gorgiae de laudibus Helenae, & Aristidis de laudibus Atheniensium, & de laudibus urbis Romae, forma folij.

A eschinis orationes cum Lysiae orationibus. Alcidamantis. Antisthenis. Demadis. Andocidis. Isei. Dinarchi. Antiphontis. Lycurgi. Gorgiae. Lesbonactis. Herodis. Aeschinis uita. Lysiae uita, forma folij.

P latonis opera per nouem quaternitates secundum Trasillum, ut Laërtius scribit. Prima quaternitas. Euthyphron, uel de sancto. Socratis defensio. Criton, uel de agendo. Phaedon, uel de anima. Secunda. Cratylus, uel de rectitudine nominum. Theaetetus, uel de scientia. Sophista, uel de Ente. Ciuilis, uel de regno. Tertia. Parmenides, uel de Ideis. Philebus, uel de uoluptate. Coniuium, uel de amore. Phaedrus, uel de pulchro. Quarta. Alcibiades I. uel de natura hominis. Alcibiades II. uel de noto. Hipparchus, uel quaestiosus. Amatores, uel de philosophia. Quinta. Theages, uel de sapientia. Charmides, uel de temperantia. Laches, uel de fortitudine. Lysis, uel de amicitia. Sexta. Euthydemus, uel litigiosus. Protagoras, uel sapientiae professores. Gorgias, uel de Rhetorica. Menon, uel de uirtute. Septima. Hippias maior, uel de honesto. Hippias minor, uel de mendacio. Ion, uel de Iliade. Menexenus, uel epitaphius. Octaua. Clitophon, uel exhortatorius. De rep. ut unus liber, uel de Iusto. Timaeus, uel de natura. Critias, uel Atlanticus. Nona. Minos, uel de lege. Leges ut unus liber, uel de legum latione. Appendix legum, uel philosophus. Epistolae. Suntque hi omnes octo, et legitimi Platonis Dialogi numero sex & quinquaginta, diuiso libro de rep. in X. Dialogos de legibus autem abs. corollario, in duodecim. Nothi uero, ad dubij, sex, qui sequuntur. Axiocus, uel de morte. De uirtute, si doceri potest. Demodochus, uel de consultando. Sisyphus, uel de consulendo. Eryxias, uel Erasistratus, uel de diuitijs. Definitiones. Adduntur his Platonis libris, Timaeus Locrus de natura, scriptus lingua dorica, forma folij.

S uidas denuo impressus, forma folij.
A lexander Aphrodiseus in Topica Aristotelis, forma folij.
A thenaei Symposia, forma folij.
H esychij dictionarium, forma folij.
P ausaniae Commentarij Graeciam describentes, forma folij.
S trabo de situ orbis, forma folij.
S acrae scripturae ueteris, nouaeq́s omnia, forma folij.
A rtemidorus cum Synesio de interpretatione somniorum, forma enchiridij.
P lutarchi illustrium uirorum graeci, ac latini nominis uitae nouem & quadraginta, forma folij.
O ppiani de piscibus libri quinque una cum Laurentij Lippij translatione, Eiusdem de uenatione libri iiii. forma enchiridij.
A eschyli tragoediae VI, forma enchiridij.
A ldi Manutii Grammaticae institutionis graecae, forma quadrati.
G regorii Nazazeni theologi orationes 16, forma enchiridij.
A lexandri Aphrodisensis in sophisticos Aristotelis Elenchos commentaria, forma folij.
A lexandri Aphrodisensis in Priora analitica commentarii, forma folij.
A pollonij Rodij Argonautica cum commentarijs, forma enchiridij.
I nterpraetationes & antiquae, & perquam utiles in Homeri Iliada, necnon quaedam Porphirii in Odyssea, forma enchiridij.
H erodiani historiarum libri VIII. cum interpretatione latina Angeli Politiani, forma enchiridij.
X enophontis uolumen, in quo haec insunt, ex Laertio uita Xenophontis. Xenophontis Cyri pediae libri VIII. Cyri anabaseos, & ascensus in Persidem libri VII. De rebus Graecorum lib. 7. In Agesilaum. Apomnemoneumaton i. de dictis Socratis lib. IIII. Oeconomica. Hieron. Lacedaemoniorum resp. Atheniensium resp. De Vestigalibus. Symposium. De

disciplina equestri. De equis. De uenatione, forma folij.

GALENI, quæcunq; extant in quinq; uoluminibus, in quorum primo hæc insunt.

Hortatio ad artes discendas. De optima doctrina. Optimū medicum, eundem esse philosophum. De sectarū narietate ad introducendos. De optima secta. De constitutione medicinæ. De elementis libri duo. De cōplexionibus libri tres. De potentiis naturalibus libri tres. Anatomici libri nouem. De uenarum, & arteriarum dissectione. De neruorum dissectione. De odoratus instrumento. De uuluæ dissectione. De foetuum formatione. An sanguis, natura in arteriis contineatur. De spmate libri duo. De optima corporis constitutione. De bona habitudine. De inæquali dyscrasia. De Hippocratis, & Platonis dogmatibus, libri octo sine primo. De substantia facultatum naturalium. Animi mores temperaturā corporis sequi. De uitiis, & passionibus animæ. De curatione. De usu partium corporis humani, libri decem, & septem. De musculorum motu libri, duo. forma folij.

IN SECVNDO HAEC.

De temperatura medicaminū simpliciū, libri .11. De compositoe medicaminū per singulas corporis partes lib. 10. De compositione medicaminum per genera, libri .7. De Antidotis libri .2. De Theriaca ad Pisonem. De Theriaca ad Pamphilianum. De habendis facile remediis, liber sine principio. De purgantium medicaminū ui. Quos nā oportet purgare, & qualibus medicamentis purgatibus, & quando, liber. De Ptisana, liber. forma folij.

IN TERTIO HAEC.

De pulsibus, ad eos qui introducuntur liber. 1. De differentia pulsuū, libri .4. De pulsuum dignotione, libri .4. De causis pulsuum libri .4. De prænotione ex pulsibus, libri .4. De usu pulsuum liber .1. De usu spirationis liber. 1. De causis spirationis liber. 1. De difficultate spirationis libri .3. De differentia morborū liber. 1. De causis morborum liber. 1. De differentia symptomatum liber. 1. De causis symptomatum libri .3. De locis affectis libri. 6. De differentia febrium libri .2. De plenitudine liber. 1. De tumoribus præter naturam liber. 1. De atra bile liber. 1. De tremore, & palpitatione, et conuulsione, & rigore liber .1. De tabe liber. 1. De temporibus morborum liber .1. De teporibus morbi totius, liber .1. Quomodo cōarguendi sint, qui fingunt se ægrotare. De iudiciis libri. 3. De diebus iudicialibus libri. 3. De prænotione liber. 1. De dignotione ex insomniis liber. 1. Aduersus eos, qui de formis siue circuitibus scripserūt, liber .1. De formis liber. 1. Ars medica liber. 1. forma folij.

IN QVARTO HAEC.

De uenæ sectione aduersus Erasistratum liber. 1. De uenæ sectione aduersus sequaces Erasistrati Romæ agentes, liber. 1. De curatione per uenæ sectione liber. 1. De hirudinibus reuulsione, cucurbitula, & concasione cutis, siue scarificatione liber. 1. Consilium puero morbo comitiali laboranti scriptum. De captionibus, quæ in dictione cōsistunt liber. 1. Curandi ratio libri. 14. De curatione ad Glauconem libri. 2. De tuenda ualetudine libri. 6. Ad Thrasybulum utrum medicinæ an gymnasticæ sit tueri ualetudinem liber. 1. De ea, quæ parua pila sit exercitatione liber. 1. De facultate alimentorum libri. 3. De boni & mali succi cibis liber. 1. De libris suis liber. 1. De ordine librorum suorum liber. 1.

Libri Galeno adscripti.

Introductio, uel medicus, liber. 1. Definitiones medicæ liber. 1. Qd qualitates sine corpore sint, liber. 1. An animal sit, quod in corpore continetur liber. 1. De urini liber. 1. Dignotio passionum, quæ in renibus sunt, ac eorum curatio liber. 1. De philosophi narratione liber. 1. De facile parabilibus medicamentis ad Solonem liber. 1. De facile parabilibus medicamentis liber alius. De mensuris, & ponderibus liber. 1. De atra bile ex libris Galeni, Ruphi, & Aetij Sicamij excerpta. De medicamentis quæ inter se commutantur liber. 1. De decubitu prænotiones, ex mathematica scientia liber. 1. forma folij.

IN QVINTO HAEC.

Commentariorum Galeni in librum Hippocratis de natura hominis libri. 2. Commentarij in librū Hippocratis de ratione uictus salubris. Commentariorū in Hippocratem de ratione uictus acutorum libri. 4. Commētariorum in prænotiones Hippocratis libri. 3. Cōmentariorum in prædictiones Hippocratis, libri. 3. Commentariorum in aphorismos Hippocratis libri. 7. Galenus aduersus Lycum, qd nihil delinquitur ab Hippocrate, in aphorismo illo, cui principium est τὰ αὐξανόμενα πλεῖστον ἔχει θερμόν. Galenus aduersus ea, quæ contra Hippocratis aphorismos, scripta sunt à Iuliano. Commentariorū in primū librū Hippocratis, de morbis passim grassantibus libri. 3. Commentariorum in tertium Hippocratis eiusdem argumenti librū, libri. 3. Commentariorum in sextum eiusdē argumenti librū, libri. 6. Commentariorum in librum Hippocratis de fracturis libri. 3. Commentariorum in librum Hippocratis de articulis, libri 3. Commentariorū in librū Hippocratis de medici uulnerarij munere, libri. 3. Galeni expositio de linguis Hippocratis, forma folij.

OPERA HIPPOCRATIS.

Iusiurandum Hippocratis. De arte. De prisca medicina. De medico. De probitate. Hippocratis præcepta. Lex Hippocratis. De natura hominis. De ratione uictus salubris, Polybi discapuli Hippocratis. De semine Polybi. De natura foetus. De carne. De septimestri partu. De octomestri partu. De superfoetatione. De extractione foetus. De dentitione. De dissectione. De corde. De glandibus. De natura ossium. De locis in homine. De aëre, aqua, locis. De uictus ratione. De insomniis. De alimento, quē esse Hippocratis negat Galenus. De usu humidorū. De humoribus. De flatibus. De sacro morbo, docti cuiusdā. De morbis. De affectibus, Polybi. De internarū partiū affectibus. De morbis uirginū. De natura muliebri. De morbis mulierū. De sterilibus. Supposititia quædā calci primi de morbis mulierū, adscripta. De morbis passim grassantibus. De ra=

tione uictus acutoru̅. De iuditijs. De diebus iuditialibus.
Hippocratis definitæ sententiæ. Hippocratis prænotio=
nes. Hippocratis prædictiones. Cuacæ præcognitiones.
De fracturis. De articulis. Hippocratis de medici mu=
nere. Hippocratis de curandis luxatis. De ulceribus.
De fistulis. De hæmorrhoidibus. De uisu. Hippo=
cratis epistolæ. Decretum Atheniensium. Epibomios.
Oratio Thesali Hippocratis filij legati ad Athenienses, for
ma folij.

S implicij Commentarij in octo libros Phisicæ auscultationis
Aristotelis.

E iusdē in quatuor de cœlo. Eiusdē item in tres de anima,
quos et si adhuc nō ædidimus, tamē quia iam proxime ædē
tur, huic indici inseruimus. sunt enim commentarij illi in
physica, penè perfecti, forma folij.

A etij etiam medici præstantissimi opera, iampridem à no=
bis incæpta, breui in lucem euuttemus. forma folij.

L ibros græcos, qui sequuntur, & si ab alijs impressi sunt,
tamen, quia in biblio polio nostro habentur uenales, adno=
tauimus. sunt uero hi.

E tymologicum magnum.

S implicius in prædicamenta Aristotelis.

A mmonius in prædicabilia Porphyrij.

*Libros etiam illos impres-
si alibis qui quoniam
huic Catalogo non
dum sunt additi,
hic adscripsi.*

*Alexandri aphrodisien. Comentarij
in libru̅ de sensu et sensibili.*

*Michaelis Ephesy in omā quæ
uocant parua Naturalia.*

*Joan. gramaticus in lib. de gene-
ratione et interitu.*

*Alex. aphrodisien. in quatuor libros
Meteorum.*

*Pauli æginete libri medicinæ
artis. vij.*

*Sophoclis septem tragœdiæ cum
Scholijs antiquiss.*

LIBRI LATINI

Opera Politiani·i·epistolæ eius, & eorum ad quos scripsit, qui sunt Ioannes Picus Mirandula·Hermolaus Barbarus·Pōponius Lætus·Baptista Guarinus·Philippus Beroaldus·Nicolaus Leonicænus·Hieronimus Donatus·Callimachus·Ludouicus Odaxius·Marcus Antonius Sabellicus·Lucius Phosphorus episcopus Signinus·Iacobus Antiquarius·Cæsar Carmentus·Bartholomæus Scala·Antonius Codrus Vrceus·Franciscus Pucinus·Augustinus Mapheus·Ioannes Franciscus Benedictus·Marsilius Ficinus·Macarius Mutius eques·Tydeus Acciarinus·Baccius Vgulinus·Aldus Manutius Romanus·Matthæus Vero·Cano regularis·Innocētius Papa VIII·Iacobus Cardinalis Papiēsis·Frācis cus Picol·Cardinalis Senēsis·Paulus Cortesius·Ioānes rex Portugalliæ. Laurentius Medices· Ludouicus Maria Dux Mediolani· Georgius Merula· Bartholomæus Chalcus· Petrus Crinitus·Michael Aciarius Vtianēsis·Scipio Carteromachus Pistoriensis. Sequntur postea nonnulla Hermolai Barbari lectu dignissima, & inter cætera erudita epistola de serculis, ac oratio ad Federicum Imperatorē, & ad Maximilianū Romanorum Regem·Deinde opuscula Angeli Politiani hæc, uidelicet, Præfatio in Carmidem Platonis e græco in latinum. Miscellaneorum uolumen eruditiss. Herodiani historia de imperio post Marcum e græco in latinum, libris octo. Enchiridion Epicteti Stoici e græco in latinum. Plutarchi amatoriæ narrationes e græco in latinum. Lamia. De ira ad Laurentium Medicem. Præfatio in Homerum. In Quintilianum. In Syluas Statij. In Suetonium. Oratio pro oratoribus Senensium, ad Alexandrum VI·Pont·Max. Pro Florentinis, ad Alphonsum Siciliæ regem. Pro eisdem ad eundem. Pro prætore Florentino ad Dominos Florentinos. Athanasij opusculum in Psalmos, e græco in latinum. Dialectica. Prælectio de dialectica. In Persium. Siluæ. Nutricia. Rusticus·Manto. Ambra carmine heroico. Epicedion in Albieram. Liber epigrammatum latinorum. Liber epigrammatum græcorum, forma folij.

Iulij firmici Astronomicorum libri octo integri, et emendati·allatum enim fuit exemplar ex Scythia. Marci Malij astronomicorum libri quinq; heroico carmine. Arati Phænomena Cæsare Germanico interprete cū commentarijs, & imaginibus. Arati eiusdem Phenomenon fragmentum M·T·Cicerone interprete. Arati eiusdem Phænomena Rufo Festo Auienio Paraphraste. Arati Phænomena græce. Theonis comentaria in Aratum, græce. Procli Sphæra græca·Eadem latina Thoma Linacro Britanno interprete, forma folij.

Nicolai Perotti Sypontini Cornucopiæ, seu commentaria in primū librū Martialis, ubi plurima emendata sunt· Græcum etiam, quod ita inuersum habebatur, ut ne legi quidē posset, in eo libro emendatum est. Index ad inuenienda uocabula nouo, & pulchro ordine. Eiusdem Sipontini libellus in epistolam Plinij in librum de naturali historia· Cornelij Vitellij in cum ipsum Sypontini libellum annotationes. Varronis libri de lingua Latina, & Analogia· Sextus Pompeius Festus. Nonius Marcellus, in quo multa addita, non ante impressa, forma folij.

Gramaticæ institutioēs nostræ latinæ, libris quatuor. In primo libro habētur præcipua hæc. De Gramaticæ partibus. De nomine. De generibus nominū. De inflexione nomi-nu. De casuū terminatione. De Heteroclitis. De Pronoie. In Secundo, hæc. De uerbo. De Inchoatiuis, et religs deriuatiuorum uerborum speciebus. De inflexione uerborum. De præteritis, & supinis. De Aduerbio, et cæteris orationis partibus. In Tertio, hæc. De constructione uerborum. Aduerbiorum localium. Participiorum. Nominum. De duodecim figuris dictionis, et octo constructionis. In Quarto, hæc. De quantitate syllabarum. De pedibus metrorum græcis, et latinis cum exemplis, quantitatem syllabarū signis longo, et breui indicantibus, usq ad hexasyllabos. De uersu Hexametro. Pentametro. Iambico senario. Hendecasyllabo Saphico. Trochaio. ubi & græca habentur exempla. De Accentibus. De distinctionibus, quadrati forma.

Bessarionis Cardinalis Niceni, libri quatuor in calumniatorem Platonis, ubi multa præclara, utiliaq traduntur. Eiusdem liber, in quo ex duodecim libris Platonis de legibus q plurima recitantur, quæ etiam in latinū traducit, tum passim ostendit, q perperam tralata eadem fuerunt à Georgio Trapezuntio. Quod ijs, qui græce discunt existimamus adiumento fore non mediocri. Additur præterea eiusdem tractatus, ut natura, & ars consulto agant. Nam cum Gemisto Constantinopolitanus, qui alio nomine Pletho appellatur, Platonis doctrinæ perq studiosus, & Theodorus Gaza thessalonicensis peripateticæ sectæ defensor, acriter super ea quæstione contenderent, ac Bessario Cardinalis rogatus, ut sententiam suā diceret, ex scriptis Platonis breui libello respondisset, contradixissetq ei libello Georgius Trapezuntius, hoc tractatu Nicenus respondet, forma folij.

Aristoteles de animalibus. Theophrastus de Plantis. Problemata Aristotelis, & Alexandri Aphrodisei, Theodoro Gaza interprete. Quæ, ut emendata exirent ex ædibus nostris, conulimus cum exemplaribus græcis, & latinis archetypis. Addidimus etiam duos indices secundum ordinem literarum, alterum græcum, latinum alterum, ut animalium, & plantarum nomina, de quibus Aristoteles, & Theophrastus meminerunt, queat quis & græce, & latine q facillime discere, forma folij.

Iamblicus de mysterijs Aegyptiorum, Chaldæorum, Assyriorum. Proclus in Platonicum. Alabiadem de anima, atq dæmone. Proclus de sacrificio, & magia. Porphyrius de diuinis, atq dæmonibus. Synesius Platonicus de somnijs. Psellus de dæmonibus. Expositio Prisciani, & Marsilij in Theophrastum de sensu, phantasia, & intellectu. Alcinoi Platonici philosophi liber de doctrina Platonis. Speusippi Platonis discipuli liber de Platonis definitionibus. Pythagoræ philosophi aurea uerba. Symbola Pythagoræ philosophi. Xenocratis philosophi Platonici liber de morte. Mercurij Trismegisti Pimander. Eiusdē Asclepius. Marsilij Ficini de triplici uita libri.II. Eiusdē liber de uoluptate. Eiusdē de sole, et lumine lib.II. Apologia eiusdem in librum suum de lumine. Eiusdem libellus de magis. Quod necessaria sit securitas, & tranquillitas animi præclarissimarum sententiarum huius operis breuis annotatio, forma folij.

Prouerbiorum Erasmi Rhoterodami Adagiorum Chiliades quatuor, Centuriæq totidem. Quibus etiam quinta additur imperfecta, forma folij.

Poliphili Hypnerotomachia, ubi humana omnia non nisi somnium esse ostendit, atq obiter plurima scitu sane q dignum commemorat, forma folij.

Lodouicī Cælij Rhodiginī antiquarum lectionum libri XVI, forma folij.

Rhetricorum ad C. Herēnium libri 4. M.T. Ciceronis de inuentione libri 2. Eiusdem de oratore ad Quintum fratrem lib.3. Eiusdem de claris oratoribus, qui dicitur Brutus, lib.I. Eiusdē orator ad Brutum lib.I. Eiusdem Topica ad Trebatium lib.I. Eiusdē oratoriæ partitiones lib.I. Eiusdem de optimo genere oratorum præfatio quædam, quadrati forma.

M. F. Quintilianus, quadrati forma.

M. Catonis lib.I. M. Terentij Varronis lib.3. L. Iunij Moderati Columellæ lib.12. Eiusdem de arboribus liber separatus ab alijs, quare autem id factum fuerit: ostenditur in epistola ad lectorem. Palladij lib.14. De duobus dierum generibus, simulq de umbris, & horis, quæ apud Palladium, in alia epistola ad lectorem. Georgij Alexandrini enarrationes priscarum dictionum, quæ in his libris Catonis, Varronis, Columellæ, quadrati forma.

Ioannis Iouiani Pontani opera omnia soluta oratione composita, tribus digesta partibus, in quarum prima hæc continentur. De Obedientia lib.5. De Fortitudine lib.2. De Principe. Liber de Liberalitate. Liber de Beneficēta. Liber de Magnificentia. Liber de Splendore. Liber de Contiuentia. De Prudentia lib.5. De Magnanimitate lib.2. De Fortuna lib.3. Liber de Immanitate. In Altera. De Aspiratione libri 2. Charon Dialogus. Antonius Dialogus. Actius Dialogus. Aegidius Dialogus. Asinus Dialogus. De Sermone libri 6. Belli, quod Ferdinādus Senior Neap. Rex cum Ioanne Andegauiensum duce gessit lib. In Tertia. Centū Sententiæ Ptolemæi cum expositionibus. De rebus cœlestibus lib. 14. Liber de Luna imperfectus, forma quadrati.

Virgilius. Diuersorū ueterū poëtarū in Priapū lusus.P.V. M. Cataletca. Copa. Rose. Culex. Diræ. Moretum. Ciris. Aetna. Elegia in Mecœnatis obitum, et alia nonnulla, quæ falso Virgilij creduntur. Argumenta in Virgilij libros, & alia diuersorum complura, forma enchiridij.

Q. Horatij Flacci poëmata omnia. Centimetrum Marij Sergij. Annotationes Aldi Ma. Ro. in Horatiū. Ratio mensuum, quibus odæ eiusdem poëtæ tenentur, eodem Aldo authore. Nicolai Perotti libellus eiusdem argumenti, forma enchiridij.

Omnia opera Ouidij tribus uoluminibus partita, in quorum primo hæc continentur. P. Ouidij Nasonis uita per Aldū ex ipsius libris excerpta. Heroidum epistolæ. Amorum libri.3. De arte amandi libri.3. De remedio amoris libri.1. De medicamine faciei. Nux. Somnium. Pulex & philomela. In Altero. Cla. Ptolemæi inerrantiū Stellarum significationes per Nicolaū Leonicum è græco traslatæ. XII Romanorum menses in ueteribus monumentis Romæ reperti. Sex priorum mensum digestio, ex sex Ouidij Fastorum libris excerpta. P. Ouidij Nasonis Fastorum lib.6. Tristium lib.5. De ponto lib.4. In Ibin. Ad Liuiam. In Tertio. Annotationes in omnia Ouidij opera. Index fabularum, & cæterorum, quæ insunt hoc libro secundum ordinem alphabeti. Ouidij Metamorphoseon libri.15, forma enchiridij.

Terentius, forma enchiridij.

M.T.C. Officiorum lib.3. Cato maior, siue de senectute. Lælius, siue de amicitia. Somniū Scipionis ex VI. de Rep. excerptum. Παράδοξα. Θεοδώρου περὶ τρόπων ἑρμηνείας. Ὅπερος Ἐπιτάφιος, forma enchiridij.

M.T.C. Epistolæ familiares accuratius recognitæ, Index etiã ad inueniendũ, quota nam charta habeantur singulæ quæ q epistolæ, forma enchiridii.

M.T.C. Epistolarum ad Atticum, ad Brutum, ad Quintum fratrem, libri 20. Latina interpretatio eorum, quæ in iis ipsis epistolis græce scripta sunt, ubi multa & mutata, & addita sunt. Admonemus igitur lectorem, ut inde sibi librum corrigat suum, forma enchiridii.

M.T.C. Orationes LVII, tribus digestæ voluminibus, in quorũ primo hæ continentur. Pro P. Quintio. Pro Sex. Roscio Amerino. Pro Q. Roscio Comœdo. Diuinatio in C. Verrem. In C. Verrem liber 1. In C. Verrē lib. 3. In C. Verrem lib. 4. In C. Verrem lib. 5. In C. Verrem lib. 6. In C. Verrem lib. 7. Pro M. Fonteio. Pro A. Cæcinna. In altero. Pro Lege Manilia. Pro A. Cluentio. De Lege Agraria contra P. Seruilium Rullũ in senatu. De Lege Agraria ad populum contra P. Seruilium Rullum. De Lege Agraria ad populum contra Rullum. Pro C. Rabirio Perduellionis reo ad populum. IN L. Catilinam in senatu. In L. Catilinam ad populum. In L. Catilinam ad populum. In L. Catilinam in senatu. Pro L. Murena. Pro L. Flacco. Pro P. Sylla. Pro Archia poëta. Ad Equites romanos antequam iret in exilium. Ad Quirites post redditum. Post reditum in senatu. Pro domo sua ad Pontifices. De Aruspicum responsis in senatu. Pro Cn. Plancio. In tertio. Pro P. Sestio. In Vatinium. Pro M. Cœlio. Pro L. Cornelio Balbo. De Prouinciis consularibus. In L. Pisonem. Pro T. Annio Milone. Pro C. Rabirio Posthumo. Pro M. Marcello. Pro Q. Ligario. Pro Rege Deiotaro. In M. Antonium Philippica prima. In M. Antonium Philippica 2. In M. Ant. Philip. 3. In M. Ant. Philip. 4. In M. Ant. Philip. 5. In M. Ant. Philip. 6. In M. Ant. Philip. 7. In M. Ant. Philip. 8. In M. Ant. Philip. 9. In M. Ant. Philip. 10. In M. Ant. Philip. 11. In M. Ant. Philip. 12. In M. Ant. Philip. 13. In M. Ant. Philip. 14. Epistola ad Octauium. Crispi Sallustij in Ciceronem oratio. M. Tullij Ciceronis in Sallustium responsio, forma enchiridij.

C. Crispi Sallustij de coniuratione Catilinæ. Eiusdem de bello Iugurthino. Orationes quædam ex libris historiarũ C. Crispi Sallustij. Eiusdem oratio contra M. T. Ciceronem. M. T. Ciceronis oratio contra C. Crispum Sallustiũ. Eiusdē orationes quatuor contra Luciũ Catilinam. Porcij Latronis declamatio contra Luciũ Catilinā, forma enchiridij.

T. Liuij Patauini Historici Decades tres, una cum indice ad singula queq; facillime inueniēda maxime necessario. Eiusdem Decadum XIIII Epitomæ. Lucij Flori libri 4. Polybii historiarum libri V. à Nicolao Perotto in Latinũ conuersi sermonem. Quæ omnia nunc accuratius q̃ unquã antea, & recognita, & omnibus elustrata sunt erroribus, forma enchiridij.

Eiusdem Liuij omnia accuratissime denuo impressimus, forma folij.

C. Plinij Secundi Nouocomensis epistolarum lib. X, in quibus multæ habentur epistolæ non ante impressæ, tum Græca correcta, & suis locis restituta, atq; reiectis adulterinis, uera reposita. Item fragmentatæ epistolæ, integræ factæ. In medio etiam epistolæ libri Octaui de Clitumno fonte, non solũ uertici calx additus, et calci uertex, sed. X quoq; epistolæ interpositæ, ac ex Nono libro Octauus factus, & ex Octauo Nonus, Idq; beneficio exẽplaris correctissimi, et miræ, ac potius uenerãdæ uetustatis. Eiusdẽ Panegyricus Traiano Imp. dictus. Eiusdem de uiris illustribus in Re militari, & in administranda Rep. Suetonij Tranquilli de claris Grammaticis, & Rhetoribus. Iulii obsequentis prodigiorum liber. Epistolæ Decimi libri ad Traianum probantur esse Plinii in sequenti epistola. Ibi etiam liber de uiris illustribus, non Tranquilli, sed Plinii esse ostenditur, forma enchiridii.

Catullus. Tibullus. Propertius, forma enchiridii.

Lucanus, forma enchiridii.

Valerius Maximus, cui exempla quatuor & uiginti nuper inuenta, sunt addita, forma enchiridii.

Commentariorũ de bello Gallico lib. 8. De bello ciuili pompeiano lib. 4. De bello Alexandrino lib. 1. De bello Afri cano lib. 1. De bello Hispaniensi lib. 1. Pictura totius Galliæ, & Hispaniæ secundum C. Cæsaris Comentarios. Nomina locorum, urbiumq;, & populorum Galliæ, et Hispaniæ, ut olim dicebantur latine, et nunc dicãntur, secundum ordinem alphabeti. Pictura pontis in Rheno. Item Auarici. Alexiæ. Vxelloduni. Massiliæ, forma enchiridij.

Suetonii Tranquilli XII Cæsares. Sexti Aurelii Victoris à D. Cæsare Augusto usq; ad Theodosium excerpta. Eutropii de gestis Romanorũ lib. 10. Pauli Diaconi lib. 8. ad Eutropii historiam additi, forma enchiridij.

L. Cœlii Lactantii Firmiani diuinarum institutionum lib. 7. De ira Dei lib. 1. De opificio Dei lib. 1. Epitome in libros suos liber acephalos. Phœnix. Carmen de Dominica Resurrectione, forma enchiridii.

Auli Gellii noctium atticarum libri undeuiginti, forma enchiridii.

Lucretius, forma enchiridii.

Iuuenalis & Persius, forma enchiridii.

Nerua & Traiani, atq; Adriani Cæsarum uitæ ex Dione, Georgo Merula interprete.

Aelius Spartianus.
Iulius Capitolinus.   Ab Ioanne Baptista
Lampridius.   Egnatio Veneto dili-
Flauius Vopiscus.   gentissime castigati.
Trebellius Pollio.
Vulcatius Gallicanus.

Heliogabali principis ad meretrices elegantissima oratio. Eiusdem Io. Baptistæ Egnatii de Cæsaribus libri tres à dictatore Cæsare ad Constantinum Palæologum, hinc à Carolo magno ad Maximilianum Cæsarem. Eiusdem in Spartiani, Lãpridiiq; uitas, & reliquorum annotationes. Aristidis Smyrnæi oratio de laudibus urbis Romæ, à Scipione Carteromacho in latinum uersa. In extrema operis parte addita Conflagratio Vesuui montis ex Dione, Georgo Merula interprete, forma enchiridii.

Pomponius Mela. Iulius Solinus. Itinerarium Antonini Augusti. Vibius Sequester. P. Victor de regionibus urbis Romæ. Dionysius Afer de situ orbis, Prisciano interprete, forma enchiridii.

Senecæ tragœdiæ, forma enchiridii.

Martialis, forma enchiridii.

Ausonius, forma enchiridii.

Statii Syluarum lib. 5. Achilleidos libri 2. Thebaidos libri. 2. Orthographia & flexus dictionum græcarum omnium apud Statium cum accentibus, et generibus ex uariis utriusq; linguæ authoribus, forma enchiridii.

Pontani Vrania siue de Stellis lib. 5. Meteororum lib. 1. De hortis hesperidum lib. 2. Lepidina siue pastorales pompæ. 7. Itē Meliseus. Mæon. Acon. Hendecasyllaborũ lib. 2.

Tumulorum lib. 1. Neniæ 12. Epigrammata 12, forma enchiridij.

Ioannis Ioviani Pontani amorum libri 2. De amore coniugali 3. Tumulorum 2, qui in superiore aliorum poëmaton editione desyderabantur. Lyrici 1. Eridanorum 2. Eclogæ duæ Coryle, et Quinquennius superioribus quatuor additæ. Calpurnij Siculi Eclogæ 7. Aurelij Nemesiani Eclogæ 4. Explicatio locorum omnium abstrusorum Pontani, authore Petro Summontio viro doctissimo. Index rerum, quæ in his Pontani lusibus contineantur, forma enchiridij.

Strozii poetæ Ferarienses, pater, et filius, forma enchiridij.

Hecuba, & Iphigenia in Aulide Euripidis tragœdiæ in latinum tralatæ, Erasmo Rhoterodamo interprete. Eiusdē Ode de laudibus Britaniæ, Regisq; Henrici Septimi, ac regiorum liberorum eius. Eiusdem Ode de senectutis incōmodis, forma enchiridij.

Luciani opuscula Erasmo Rhoterodamo interprete. Toxaris, siue de amicitia. Alexander, qui et Pseudomantis. Gallus, siue somnium. Timon, seu Misanthropus. Tyrannicida, seu pro tyrannicida. Declamatio Erasmi contra Tyrannicidam. De ijs, qui mercede conducti degunt, & quædam eiusdem alia. Eiusdem Luciani Thoma Moro interprete. Cynicus. Menippus, seu Necromancia. Philopseudes, seu incredulus. Tyrannicida. Declamatio Mori de eodem, forma enchiridij.

Erasmi Rhoterodami opusculū, cui titulus est Moria, idest Stultitia, quæ pro concione loquitur, forma enchiridij.

Pacis Quærela Erasmi. De regno administrando. Institutio principis Christiani. Panegyricus ad Philippum, & carmen. Item ex Plutarcho. De discrimine adulatoris, & amici. De utilitate capienda ex inimicis. De doctrina principum. Principi cum philosopho semper esse disputandū. Item Declamatio sup mortuo puero, forma enchiridij.

Christophori Longolij ciuis Romani perduellionis rei deffensiones duæ, forma enchiridij.

Dantes, forma enchiridij.

Petrarcha, forma enchiridij.

Archadia Sannazari, forma enchiridij.

Asulani Petri Bembi, forma enchiridij.

Centum facetissimæ narrationes Ioannis Boccacij, quas vulgari sermone eleganti uocabulo il Decamerone uocauit, quibus adiunctæ sunt de nouo tres aliæ non minus facetæ, forma quadrati.

Hore Beatæ uirginis per quàm parua forma.

Luceij Metamorphoseos, siue lusus Asini libri 11. Floridorum libri 4. De Deo Socratis liber 1. De philosophia liber 1. Asclepius Trismegisti dialogus codē Apuleio interprete. Eiusdē Apuleij liber de dogmatis Platonicis. Eiusdem liber De mundo, quem magna ex parte ex libro Aristotelis eiusdem argumenti in latinum traduxit. hic sanè liber mutilatus ante nostram impressionem circumferebatur. eum nos fidem antiquissimi codicis secuti, restituimus. Apologiæ duæ. Isagogicus liber Platonicæ philosophiæ græcè impressus, forma enchiridij.

Quintus Curtius de rebus Alexandri Regis Macedonum, forma enchiridij.

Ex Plauti comœdijs uiginti, quarum carmina magna ex parte in mensum suum restituta sunt. Adduntur singularum Commœdiarum argumenta. Item Index uerborū, quibus paulo abstrusioribus Plautus utitur. Authoris uita. tralatio etiam dictionum græcarum, forma quadrati.

Guillielmi Budæi Parisiensis Secretarii Regij, libri 5. De Asse, & partibus eius, post duas Parisienses impressiones ab eodem ipso Budæo castigati, forma quadrati.

Asconii Pædiani expositio in quatuor orationes M. Tulij. C. contra C. Verrem, & in orationem pro Cornelio. In orationem contra C. Antonium, & L. Catilinam. In orationem pro M. Scauro. In orationem contra L. Pisonem. In orationem pro Milone. atq; harum rerum omnium Index. adduntur præterea Victorini commentarii in libros M. Tulii de inuentione, & Georgii Trapezuntii in orationem pro Q. Ligario, forma enchiridii.

Petri Alcyonii medices legatus de exilio, forma quadrati.

L. Annei Senecæ naturalium quæstionum lib. 7. Matthæi Fortunati in eosdem libros annotationes. Index præterea rerum notatu dignarum, forma quadrati.

Iustinus de externis historijs, cui adiunximus Aemilium Probum de externis Imperatoribus, forma enchiridij.

Cl. Claudiani opera q̃ diligentissime castigata, quæ hæc sunt. In Rufinum libri 2. De bello Gildonico liber 1. In Eutropium libri 2. De laudibus Stiliconis libri 3. De Bello Getico liber 1. De nuptiis Mariæ, & Honorij lib. 1. De eiusdem tertio, quarto, & sexto consulatu, lib. 1. De Cōsulatu Probini, et Olibri fratrum, liber 1. De Manlij Theodori consulatu liber 1. De Raptu Proserpinæ libri 3. Complures lusus elegantissimi, quorū primus est de Herculis laude, secundus de Sirenis, qui duo nunc primum à nobis è uetustissimo codice in medium afferuntur, forma enchiridij.

C. Valerii Flacci Setini Balbi Argonautica, cui adiungitur Io. Baptistæ Pii carmen ex quarto Argonauticon Apollonii, & Orphei Argonautica, innominato interprete, forma enchiridii.

Silii Italici de bello Punico secundo libri 17. diligentissimè castigati, forma enchiridii.

M. T. Ciceronis Philosophiæ duo uolumina, in quorum primo hæc continentur, Academicarum quæstionum æditionis primæ liber secundus. Aeditionis secundæ liber primus. De finibus bonorū, & malorum libri 5. Tusculanarum quæstionum libri 5. Secundo uolumine hæc insunt. M. T. C. de natura deorum libri 3. De diuinatione libri 2. De fato libri 1. Scipionis somnium, quod è sex de republica libris superest. De legibus libri 3. De uniuersitate liber 1. Quinti Ciceronis de petitione consulatus ad Marcum fratrem liber 1. forma enchiridii.

Georgii Trapezuntii rhetoricorum libri 5. His adduūtur Consulti Chirii Fortunatiani libri 3. Aquilæ Romani de figuris sententiarum, & elocutionis liber 1. P. Rutilii Lupi earundem figurarum è Gorgia liber 1. Aristotelis præterea rhetoricorum Ad Theodecten Georgio Trapezūtio interprete libri 3. Eiusdem rhetorices Ad Alexandrū, à Francisco Philelpho in latinū uersæ, liber 1. Itē paraphrasis rhetoricæ Hermogenis, ex Hilarionis mōachi Veronensis traductione. Priscianus etiam de rhetoricæ præexercitamentis ex Hermogne, denum Aphthonii Declamatoris rhetoricæ, progymnasmata. Io. Maria Cataneo tralatore, forma folii.

Iosephi Calvinj Sapientissimj paraphrasis Graeca Cantici Canticorum 1589
Eiusdem Paraphrasis in lib. de fronte menseal Galeni. 18 Epistolae de Varijs Argum: De
Cautione a Veneno ad Clemen: VII. Epistolae Ciceronis ad Varios missae.

AL   DVS.

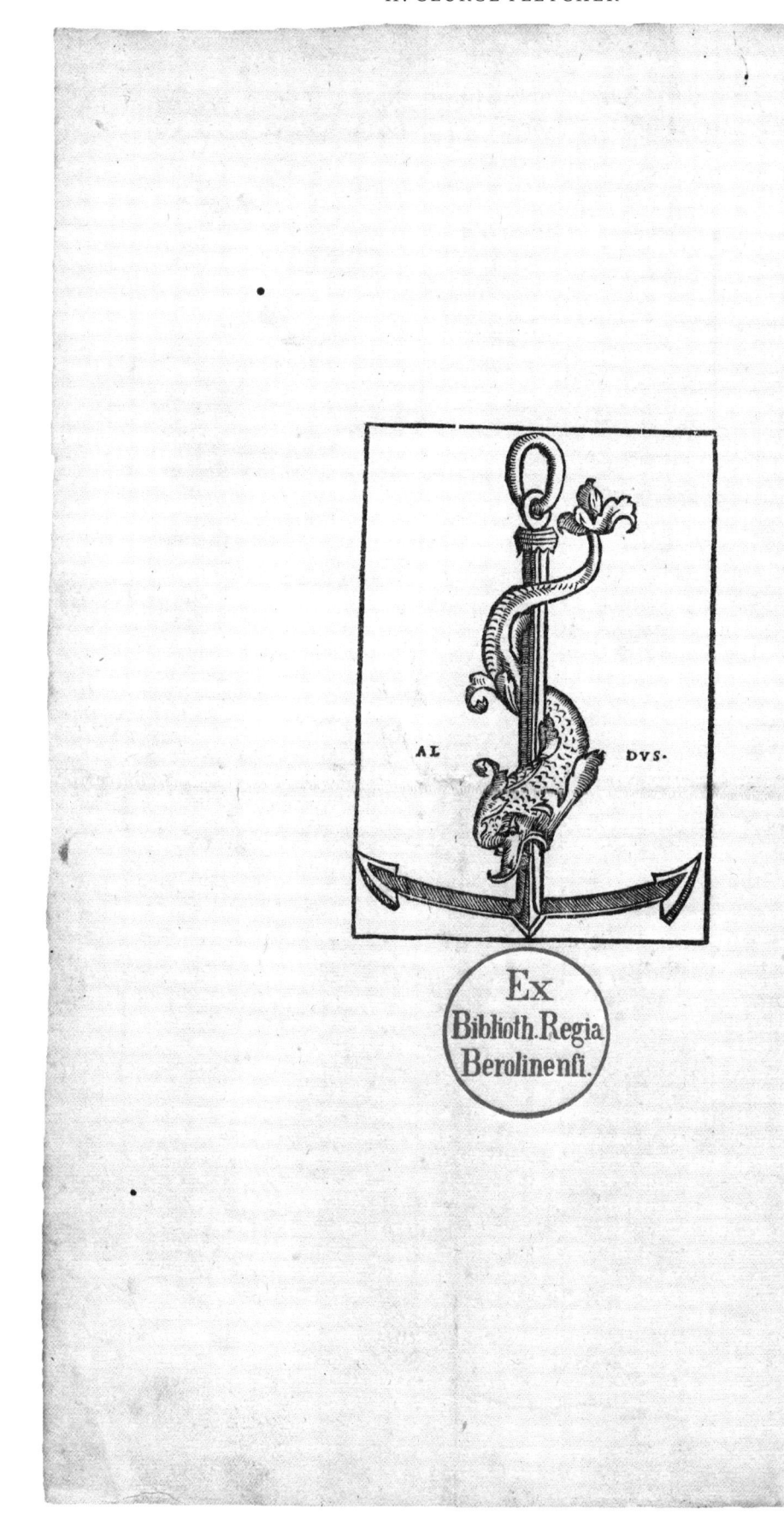

Ex
Biblioth. Regia
Berolinensi.

The Fourth Aldine Press Catalogue of [March 1527]

The publishing list that Renouard designated the fourth Aldine Press catalogue has been variously dated [c. 1526] and [1534], and, with a sole exception, scholars have not had access to a copy since Renouard's 1834 report.[20] One copy of that fourth catalogue survives, however, and it is the same unique copy Renouard reported. I am comfortable dating it to the spring of 1527, and specifically to March of that year.

Renouard reported in 1834 that the sole copy of the fourth catalogue of which he was aware was part of the extensive Aldine collection of Count Etienne Méjan (1766–1846). The Méjan collection, acquired en bloc in 1847 by King Friedrich Wilhelm IV of Prussia and donated by him to the Königliche Bibliothek, the Bibliotheca Regia Berolinensis, survives essentially intact in the Staatsbibliothek zu Berlin – Preussischer Kulturbesitz, Abteilung Historische Drucke, which houses 843 Aldine editions in 1150 volumes from the Méjan collection. Additional Méjan volumes, their numbers variously reported, are recorded at the Biblioteka Jagiellońska in Kraków. Relatively few Méjan books remain unaccounted for after the destruction and upheavals of World War II, during which the collection was widely dispersed. The recently published, exhaustive catalogue of the 1448 volumes in the collection, comprising the Méjan and other Aldines in Berlin and the volumes in Kraków, records Méjan's copy of the fourth Aldine Press catalogue of [1527] as present in Berlin, described as a folio but classed as a quarto, and assigned to or after the year 1526.[21]

Thanks to the courtesy of colleagues in the Abteilung Historische Drucke at the Staatsbibliothek zu Berlin – Preussischer Kulturbesitz, I

---

20 RENOUARD (see note 7), pp. 264.23 and 339/40; RENOUARD, p. 339, gave a summary description of the printed catalogue (see also note 21). POLLARD/ EHRMAN (see note 6), pp. 60/1, assign the date [1534], because the Aetius was completed in September 1534; it was announced in this catalogue as being in preparation, and they judged it a complement to the 1525/26 Galen then published. From this same comparison, RENOUARD drew his date of [c. 1526]. The text of the preface of the Aetius, »Medicinae studiosis«, in which the details of the decade's delays are recorded, is given in the text below, from RENOUARD (see note 7), 1534.7. ANNACLARA CATALDI PALAU: *Gian Francesco d'Asola e la tipografia Aldina: la vita, le edizioni, la biblioteca dell'Asolano*. Genoa 1998, nº 137 (pp. 660/1); *The Aldine Press* (see note 7), nº 195. RENOUARD reported that the catalogue carried the folio device flanked by AL|DVS thus divided, which has now turned out to be the device Fletcher f 6 in its damaged state (= March 1527).

The sole exception to its scholarly unavailability is a study by the late Fredric J. Mosher (1914-99), in which he made a substantial number of valuable observations, based upon a photocopy obtained c. 1976, when he was on sabbatical at the BL from the University of California, Berkeley. (FREDRIC J. MOSHER: The Fourth Catalogue of the Aldine Press. In: *La Bibliofilía*. 80.3 [1978], pp. 229–35.) He dated the catalogue, which he engagingly termed Aldus IV, to the autumn of 1526, and he believed that it was a partial source of what he termed Aldus G (for Gesner, *Pandectae*). The further research promised in that article never materialized, and the preliminary study itself has slipped into obscurity; I am indebted to Dr. Folter for bringing the 1978 article to my attention.

21 RENOUARD (see note 7), p. 339, commented that he knew of only one copy, in Germany, which he believed to be at the court of the King of Bavaria, in the Méjan collection. This is reasonably accurate, because Méjan moved to Bavaria in 1816, in the suite of Eugène de Beauharnais, dying in Munich thirty years later. But it was Friedrich Wilhelm IV of Prussia who purchased the Méjan collection, for 64 000 Prussian Talers, by outbidding the British Museum and Ludwig I of Bavaria, among several others, including Payne and Lord Spencer. See *Im Zeichen von Anker und Delphin: die Aldinen-Sammlung der Staatsbibliothek zu Berlin – Preussischer Kulturbesitz*. Ed. KARLA FAUST, VERONIKA MANTEI, ET AL. Leipzig 2005, passim, and therein KARLA FAUST: Zur Geschichte der Sammlung, pp. 10–7. See also FAHY'S (see note 19) review of the Berlin catalogue. The additional recorded Méjan volumes are at the Biblioteka Jagiellońska in Kraków, brought there after 1945 from former German remote-storage repositories in areas ceded to Poland. They are reported variously: 171 (*Im Zeichen von Anker und Delphin*, p. 17), 180 (ibid., p. 54), and 154 by my count from the catalogue itself (ibid., pp. 57–227). This would leave relatively few of the 193 Méjan books not now in Berlin (either 22 or 13 or 39, respectively) unaccounted for. One notes that the Kraków volumes include quite strong holdings of the Lyonnaise counterfeits and the Paris: Turrisan editions. Dr. Folter reports that many other Méjan copies, duplicating other Königliche Bibliothek holdings, were sold at auction in Berlin by Th. Muller on 28 July 1851. – The copy of the fourth Aldine Press catalogue is *Im Zeichen von Anker und Delphin*, nº 408 (p. 110), and it is shelved under the SSB-PK classmark 4º Ald. Ren. 339.

obtained a complete facsimile of this unique copy of the fourth catalogue of books in print issued by the Aldine Press, as photocopies from microfiche, and subsequently as digital captures. This is a preliminary note to record its characteristics. The catalogue's complete illustration within this present study is a most valuable bibliographical resource.

Initial physical description

The catalogue, printed on paper in black ink, was probably originally Chancery folio in format (approximately 31 × 22 cm folded), here trimmed to 27 × 18,4 cm by sight, which is perhaps 10% less than actual size, to judge from the device. At present, I know nothing about the paper stock's chainlines and watermarks. The Staatsbibliothek zu Berlin has catalogued it as a folio but given it a classmark as a quarto – one assumes, from its trimmed proportions – but the type area is too deep and wide for the standard Aldine quarto format (roughly 21,5 × 15 cm folded). It consists of one gathering of six leaves (A6, signed A *i* – A *iij*), typographically foliated correctly 1–3 in arabic in the upper-right-hand corner of the first three rectos, respectively, and erroneously foliated typographically »4« on the fifth recto; folios A4^r and A6^r remain unfoliated. It is printed in two columns in italic, the initials in small-cap roman, the type area of each column measuring 25,4 × 7,5 cm, including the small-cap initials set off in the respective left-hand margins, imposed on an overall type area of 25,4 × 15,5 cm. These measurements are made from the photocopies, and are thus only tentative, although they are reasonably close, being the result of comparison with actual italic two-column typography in Aldine folios of the period; however, the device measures only 9,9 × 6,9 cm on the photocopy, vs. 10,7 × 7,6 cm in reality, and thus my rough calculation of about a 10% reduction. The Berlin cataloging entry describes the book as incorrectly bound, but this is not the case; only the erroneous typographical foliation »4« of A5^r is at fault, the textual continuity of the listings being sequentially and chronologically correct.

Folio A6^r is blank, although there are three lines of entries in contemporary manuscript at the top of the leaf, described later. Folio A6^v carries only a folio-size device on A6^v. This is the device Fletcher f6 (10,7 × 7,6 cm; within a heavy single-rule border, and there are prominent scales and shading on the figure of the dolphin), found in works dated between October 1520 and March 1527.[22] On folio A6^v it is found in its final state, with small breaks in the top border, and it is reproduced in this damaged condition as Ahmanson-Murphy device A8.[23] It is to be found in this damaged condition solely within the fourth edition of Perottus, in the final part dated March 1527, on which basis I assigned this state of the device to that month and year.[24]

Dating

While, given the final state of the device, I am comfortable assigning the catalogue to March 1527, there is considerably more to help us determine the actual date of completion of printing. Beyond the evidence of the device, the printed catalogue may also be dated from internal evidence

---

22 It is reproduced actual size in intact condition in H. GEORGE FLETCHER: *New Aldine Studies: Documentary Essays on the Life and Work of Aldus Manutius*. San Francisco 1988, p. 57, and also in intact condition but in much-reduced size in CATALDI PALAU (see note 20), p. 716.

23 *The Aldine Press* (see note 7), p. 558, actual size; in addition to the breaks in the top rule, notable workups of type shoulders are apparent in the AL|DVS inserted within the woodblock.

24 FLETCHER (see note 22), pp. 55–8.

to the period after January 1526/27 and before May 1527. The internal evidence is as follows.

The entries follow the general pattern of the three previous catalogues, all published in Aldus's lifetime, which regularly repeated the sequence of entries and expanded upon earlier wording, suggesting that each new list of publications in print was set from a revised copy of its predecessor. The works in Greek come first, followed by those in Latin, and they are cited in the chronological sequence of their original publication. That is to say, the works are listed in the order in which they first appeared, but more recent editions replace their predecessors, as may be determined by the detailed contents of each edition in its respective listing.

The *Dictionarium graecum cum interpretatione latina*, an example that enables us to establish its specific date, is the first entry of the second column of the first leaf (fol. A1^r, col. 2, li. 1–18). Its citation ends *Emanuelis Moschopuli eglogae atticarum dictionum, nunc primu[m] impressae, forma folij*. This is the edition dated December 1524.[25]

The Perottus, a significant example, is here (fol. A4^r, col. 2, li. 48–57) in the fourth edition, of 1526/27, as the contents listings indicate, ending in *Nonius Marcellus, in quo multa addita, non ante impressa, forma folij*. ("Nonius Marcellus, to which much has been added, not previously printed, in folio format."). Its parts are dated May 1526, September 1526, and March 1527, this last part being the location of the damaged version of device Fletcher f6, as stated just above.[26]

As mentioned briefly in my main study of the Yale manuscript catalogue (see note 7), there has been some discussion about the presence of the Aetius at the end of the Greek listings. (This is the final entry for works in Greek published by the Aldine Press, followed only by listings of three other Greek works available for sale at, but not published by, the Aldine Press. See below.) The listing of the Aetius has been interpreted to indicate that the fourth catalogue dates to or near 1534, when the edition was actually published. The entry reads: »Aetii etiam medici praestantissimi opera, iampridem à nobis incoepta, breui in lucem emittemus, forma folij.« This translates as: "Also the works of the most renowned physician Aetius, already begun by us, which we shall release shortly, in folio format."

This is anything but convincing evidence for a date closer to 1534. The setting manuscript or manuscripts might have been prepared, and even initial proof composition of the Aetius might have begun, but this is not in the least likely, and the real evidence is against it. The fourth catalogue was intended, like its predecessors, to have a reasonably long life, and it would have made sense to Gian Francesco Torresani, his father, Andrea, and their colleagues to list what they expected to be the next major Greek folio. But their expectations were dashed. This publication was greatly delayed, and languished during the interim period 1529–33, following the death of Andrea Torresani (20/21 October 1528), while the Manutio and Torresani branches of the Aldine family were feuding over proprietary rights, and the Press was closed from some point in 1529 until the late winter of 1533. The Aetius might have been about to begin composition,

25 RENOUARD (see note 7), 1524.3; CATALDI PALAU (see note 20), nº 94 (pp. 638/9).
26 RENOUARD (see note 7), 1527.1; FLETCHER (see note 22), p. 55; CATALDI PALAU (see note 20), nº 104 (pp. 644/5). See note 23.

but in fact it was held in abeyance until after the Press reopened in or before March 1533, now with Paulus Manutius a youthful partner, and only then was it put into production.

The most conclusive evidence is to be found in Gian Francesco Torresani's preface »Medicinae studiosis« in the September 1534 Aetius itself, in which he writes about the delays of the intervening years, and that the edition has just then been completed. Renouard reprints the text, and Cataldi Palau has a short excerpt.[27] The opening text of the preface reads as follows: »ETsi iampridem, cum Galenum ederemus, Aëtii quoque nos opera in usum uestrum emissuros polliciti sumus: factum est tamen primum fato nescio quo officinae nostrae, quae superioribus temporibus diutius omnino, quàm oportuit, otiosa fuit: deinde uero uetustarum exemplarium inopia, ut & uestram expectationem fefellerimus, & nos in hunc usque diem authoris tam excellentis editionem differe coacti simus.« This translates as: "Even though, when we were publishing Galen a long time ago [April 1525 – May 1526], we also had promised to issue the works of Aetius for your use, the event nevertheless turned out otherwise. First, in past times, through ill fortune, silence settled upon our publishing house for far longer than it should have. Then, there was a complete lack of ancient manuscripts. So that caused us to fail your expectations, and to have to put off an edition of such an excellent author right up to the present day." The lack of adequate manuscripts was never resolved, because the Aldine Aetius comprises only the first eight books, which is merely half the work.

Another complication worth noting is that the events of the intervening years, when Paulus was fighting with his Torresani uncles over the ownership of his late father's proprietary typefaces, especially the italic, can be detected in an ancillary aspect of the 1534 Aetius. The volume contains the first appearance of the publishing privilege granted on 27 January 1525 by Pope Clement VII (Giulio di Giuliano de' Medici, 1478–1534; card. 1513; r. 1523–34), who died on 25 September 1534, and thus within the very month of the completion of printing. The papal privilege, addressed *Dilectis filiis Andreae de Torresanis de Asula, & haeredibus quondam Aldi Manutii R[omani]. in ciuitate Venetiarum commorantibus*, stresses that the late Aldus was the creator and discoverer of the typefaces now being used by the dual-family firm of Andrea's sons and Aldus's heirs.

All of this notwithstanding, the conclusive listing for me in determining the date of the fourth catalogue is the entry immediately preceding the Aetius. This entry concerns the edition of Simplicius: »Simplicij Commentarij in octo libros Phisicae auscultationis Aristotelis. Eiusde[m] in quatuor ⟨libros⟩ de caelo. Eiusde[m] in tres ⟨libros⟩ de ani[m]a, quos etsi adhuc no[n] aedidimus, tame[n] quia iam proxime aede[n]tur, huic indici inseruimus. sunt enim commentarij illi in physica, penè perfecti, forma folij.« This entry translates into English as follows: "Simplicius's Commentaries in eight books on Aristotle's Physics of audiology. The same author's four books on the heavens. The same author's three books on the soul, which, even though we have not yet published them, nevertheless, because they will be published next, we have listed them

27 RENOUARD (see note 7), 1534.1 (p. 112 cols. 1–2); CATALDI PALAU (see note 20), nº 137 (pp. 660/1). See also note 7.

28 RENOUARD (see note 7), 1526.2–3 and 1527.5; CATALDI PALAU (see note 20), nº 108 (pp. 646/7).

29 RENOUARD (see note 7), 1527.5; CATALDI PALAU (see note 20), nº 108 (pp. 646/7); *The Aldine Press* (see note 7), 246; HRHRC (see note 10), nº 223. This is a component of the Simplicius.

30 RENOUARD (see note 7), 1527.5; CATALDI PALAU (see note 20), nº 108 (pp. 646/7). This is another component of the Simplicius.

31 RENOUARD (see note 7), 1527.7; CATALDI PALAU (see note 20), nº 112 (pp. 648/9); *The Aldine Press* (see note 7), nº 248; HRHRC (see note 10), nº 225. This is a component of the Philoponus.

32 RENOUARD (see note 7), 1527.7; *The Aldine Press* (see note 7), nº 248; CATALDI PALAU (see note 20), nº 112 (pp. 648/9). This is another component of the Philoponus. The title page reads »eis ta Meteōrologika« and »in Meteorologica« in Greek and Latin, respectively; in the manuscript entry this word is written in Greek, in a defective genitive plural, Meteorōn [sic!].

33 RENOUARD (see note 7), 1528.5; CATALDI PALAU (see note 20), nº 117 (pp. 650/1).

in this index. These are, in fact, commentaries on the Physics, nearly finished, in folio format."

The Simplicius composite folio contains a variety of dates at the conclusion of its constituent parts, reflecting the completion of printing. The Aristotle commentary is dated October 1526; his four books on the heavens, January 1526/27 (apparently an Old Style or Venetian Style date); the three books on the soul, June 1527.[28]

We have further evidence of a terminus post quem non for printing the fourth catalogue in the contemporary manuscript entries that follow the Greek listings and the Latin listings, respectively, and which I have transcribed diplomatically.

The blank bottom half of the first column of folio A3ᵛ, at the end of the printed Greek entries, is filled out in manuscript with the following heading and list: Libros etiam Illos Impres|sit aldus⟨.⟩ quj[a] quonia[m] | huic Catalogo non|dum sunt additj | hic adscripsj || Alexandrj aphrodiesien[sis] Com⟨m⟩entarij in libru[m] de sensu et sensibilj [June 1527][29] || Michaelis Ephesij In om[ni]a qu[a]e vocant parua Naturalia [June 1527][30] || Joann[es] gram[m]aticus In lib[rum] de gene|ratione Et Interitu [September 1527][31] || Alex[andri]. Aphrodisien[sis] In quatuor libros || Meteōrōn [Gk.]. [September 1527][32] || Paulj Aegineti librj medicin[a]e artis vij. [August 1528][33] || Sophoclis septem tragoedi[a]e Cum Scholijs antiquiss[imis]. [1518?][34]

The foot of column two of folio A5ᵛ, following the printed Latin entries, carries this briefer heading and list: Impressi sunt et Illj ⟨libri⟩ Latinj | Nuper || Priscianus [May 1527][35] || Cornelius Celsus Cum Sereno [March 1528][36] || recognitio Veteris testamentj. [the Steuchus, of 1529][37]

Both manuscript additions are written in the same hand, which is probably Gian Francesco Torresani's.[38] This copy was therefore available for annotation – likely in the printing establishment itself – over the course of at least two years after it came off the press. This would bring us into the era of the death of Andrea Torresani, followed not long thereafter by the closing of the Press for some four years.

The three lines of manuscript at the top of folio A6ʳ, in a different hand, concern a "1539" medical work that is extraneous to this catalogue of the Aldine Press. They read as follows:

Prosper Calani[us] Sarzinensis paraphrasin scripsit sup[er] libru[m] de In[a]eq[ua]le Intemp[er]ie 1539 ⟨.⟩ | Promisit Paraphrasin in lib[rum] de fami|lia atra bileni ⟨.⟩ 18 Co[n]silia de Varijs syris ⟨.⟩ De | Cautione a Venenatis ad Clemen[tem] .VII. ⟨.⟩ Epistolas Curationu[m] ad Varios missas ⟨.⟩ |[39]

Summary description of arrangement and contents
The catalogue begins, like its predecessors of 22 June 1503 and 24 November 1513, with the heading ALDVS STVDIOSIS. S[ALVTEM]., followed by the verbatim reprint of a paragraph of general comments, advertising the value and importance of the works that follow: »LIBRORVM Et graecorum, et latinorum nomina, quot quot in hunc usq[ue] diem excudendos curauimus, scire uos uoluimus. Vbi etiam quaedam de libris singulis, tanquam eorum argumenta dicuntur, ut inde quid singulo quoq[ue] libro

34 This manuscript entry raises a complication because the Sophocles entry is already among the printed citations (fol. A2ʳ col. 1). The sole Aldine edition of Sophocles, dated August 1502 (RENOUARD [see note 7], 1502.6; *The Aldine Press* [see note 7], nº 60; HRHRC [see note 10], nº 53), never contained the commentaries, the scholia, even though the title page lists the plays »cum commentariis«. The respective entries in the 1503 and 1513 printed catalogues, the latter copied from the former, give the title and the names of the seven individual plays; there is no notice of the scholia. This same formula is repeated in the [1527] catalogue (fol. A2ʳ col. 1), which reprints the previous listings. So is this a citation to the Rome: Medici Greek College Press, 1518 edition (the editio princeps) of the scholia, edited by Janus Lascaris?

35 RENOUARD (see note 7), 1527.2; CATALDI PALAU (see note 20), nº 105 (p. 645).

36 RENOUARD (see note 7), 1528.1; CATALDI PALAU (see note 20), nº 113 (p. 649).

37 RENOUARD (see note 7), 1529.1; CATALDI PALAU (see note 20), nº 119 (pp. 651/2).

38 For examples of Gian Francesco Torresani's autograph, see his ex libris reproduced in CATALDI PALAU (see note 20), tav. 41 (p. 764) »A me Jo. Francesco Asulano« and tav. 75 (p. 798) »A me Jo. Fr« (the balance cropped with the excision of part of the leaf).

39 Prospero Calani (also Calani Centurione; b. 1480), was an Italian cleric and physician from Sarzana, in Liguria. The scribe must be citing, if idiosyncratically, *Prosperi Calanii Sarzinensis medici excellentissimi Paraphrasis in librum Galeni de inaequali intemperie. Huic alia quaedam, eodem autore, Medicinae candidatis haud uulgariter profutura, subjecimus: quae pagella proximè sequens declarabit*. Lyon: Sebastian Gryphius, 1538. This collective volume, an 8º of 287 pages printed in roman, includes several of the works listed here, with variant versions of their titles. No other contemporary published work in Latin by Calani seems to be recorded, in particular one dated 1539. BAUDRIER, vol. VIII p. 120; THOMAS STC, p. 89; SYBILLE VON GÜLTLINGEN: *Bibliographie des livres imprimés à Lyon au seizième siècle*. Baden-Baden 1992–2006 (*Bibliotheca Bibliographica Aureliana*), nº 432 (V 80), as Calanio. I am indebted to Dr. Fred Schreiber for his counsel on this matter.

tractatur, facile cognoscatis. Quod ideo factum est, q[ui]a, cum undiq[ue] ad nos scribatur, qui nam libri cura nostra excussi sint, sic satisfaciamus, cum aliter, propter summas occupationes nostras, non liceat.« This translates as: "We wish you to know the titles of all the Greek and Latin books that we have been at pains to publish up to the present day. Thereby, you will easily determine the details of individual books, what their arguments entail, and what a specific book treats. We do this because from wherever one may write to us, we are determined to give satisfaction in the books we have carefully published, since to do otherwise, given our extensive and serious efforts, would not be acceptable."

Under the heading LIBRI GRAECI., the various works in Greek are described in extenso, beginning with *Erotemata Constantini Lascaris tribus libris ...*, from column one of folio A1^r through the middle of column one of folio A3^v. The Greek editions end with *Aetij ... opera* for works published by the Aldine Press. The following short paragraph and three entries for non-Aldine Greek publications available in the bookshop for sale conclude the Greek component of the list: »Libros graecos, qui sequ⟨u⟩ntur, & si ab alijs impressi sunt, tamen, quia in bibliopolio nostro habentur uenales, adnotauimus. sunt vero hi. || Etymologicum magnum. || Simplicius in praedicamenta Aristotelis. || Ammonius in praedicabilia Porphyrij.«

This is also a verbatim reprint of the comparable material in the 1503 and 1513 catalogues, except that the works offered diminish in number with each of the three successive lists. In 1503, five works are offered; in 1513, four, here, in [1527], three.

The lower half of folio A3^v column one and the entirety of column two are blank. Seventeen lines of contemporary manuscript entries, given in detail above, fill out most of column one, reporting books published since the printing of the catalogue was completed.

Under the heading LIBRI LATINI., the works in Latin start with the second column of folio A4^r (column one being entirely blank), beginning with *Opera Politiani*, and continuing almost to the end of column two of folio A5^v. The final entry for Aldine Press publications is *Georgii Trapezuntii rhetoricorum libri.5*. The small remaining unprinted space at the foot of this column is taken up with five lines in contemporary manuscript, listing three books that appeared after the completion of printing, as reported above.

Each entry in the fourth catalogue ends with a format statement, and the different formats are now intermingled, as opposed to the segregation by format maintained in the November 1513 catalogue and apparent in the June 1503 catalogue. This format statement is a novel feature of the fourth Aldine catalogue. An evolutionary development may be perceived from catalogue to catalogue.

In the first catalogue, of 1 October 1498, which is printed in roman type in a broad-measure single column, only Greek works are listed, but individual prices are printed at the conclusion of each entry.

In 1503, printed in roman type in a narrow-measure single column, an indication of format appears for the first time, but only for the octavos, and they are grouped at the end of the Greek and Latin titles, respectively. The Greek octavos, at the top of folio 2ʳ, have no distinctive heading, whereas the Latin octavos are listed chronologically beneath the heading »Libelli portatiles in formam enchiridii.« (The accusative *formam* is used in each instance.) They constitute the penultimate paragraph on folio 2ᵛ. The prices, entered in manuscript and attributed to Aldus, appear in the margins.

In 1513, printed in italic in double columns, the octavos again constitute the only size to be described by format. Five Greek works, without a separate heading, are grouped in column one of folio 2ʳ, each with its individual format notation, but these five octavos are described within the overall listings of works in Greek. The Latin octavos enjoy a separate entry, in column two of folio 3ʳ, beneath the heading »Libelli forma enchiridij.« No prices are indicated, either in type or in manuscript.

The [1527] catalogue is modeled most closely upon the 1513 list, although it is now nearly twice its size, and the individual entries are in general more detailed in their contents, and in some instances expanded exponentially. The titles are listed in chronological sequence of initial publication, without regard to format, and I judge this to be one reason for the format designation that ends each overall entry. No prices are given. In addition to its listings of the new works published since 1513, the fourth catalogue is longer in part because many suspensions and contractions in the third catalogue have now been spelled out.

The occasional updating is to be found. For example, when in 1513 Aldus listed his own Latin grammar, probably the April 1508 edition, he inserted a brief phrase to the effect that he is currently pressing on with his Greek grammar (»nam graecas ⟨scil. institutiones⟩ adhuc premimus«). This phrase is not to be found in the comparable entry in the fourth catalogue, in which Aldus's posthumous Greek grammar of November 1515 is among the works appearing for the first time and enjoys its own listing.[40] The other side of the coin is reflected in the Plutarch listing. The entry in 1513 begins M*oralia Plutarchi*; in setting [1527], however, the compositor misread M*oralia*, and the entry now begins M*ordia Plutarchi*.[41]

The format terminology employed in [1527] is *forma folii* (or *folij*), *forma paulo enchiridij maiore*, *forma quadrati* (or *quadrati forma*), and *forma enchiridii* (or *enchiridij*). There is a single entry *per quàm parua forma* for the diminutive (32°) Greek Hours of the Virgin (fol. A5ᵛ, col. 1, li. 45) – here, for the June 1521 edition.[42] The extensive composite works are clearly delineated by the format citation occurring only at the very end, even when sub-sections of contents descriptions are very lengthy and require multiple paragraphs.

A new format, or certainly one new to me, emerges in this list, the *forma paulo enchiridii maiore*, or "somewhat larger than octavo format," as I understand the phrase, which I find puzzling at best. This format is assigned only to six works within the Greek listings, namely: Psalterium Graecum [undated; c. 1498];[43] Lascaris [probably the October 1512 ed.];[44] Epistolae Graecae, vol. II [15 Calends May (= 17 April) 1499];[45] Gregorius Nazianzenus [*Poetae Christiani veteres*, vol. III (June 1504)];[46] Nonnus Panopolitanus [undated, but 1504?];[47] Dioscorides [June 1518].[48]

40 Aldus's April 1508 Latin Grammar: 1513 catalogue fol. 3ʳ col. 1; [1527] catalogue fol. A4ʳ col. 2, still listed in Aldus's personal style as »Gra[m]maticae institutio[n]es nostrae latinae«. RENOUARD (see note 7), 1508.1; *The Aldine Press* (see note 7), n° 97. – Aldus's November 1515 Greek Grammar (edited by Marcus Musurus and dedicated to Jean Grolier): [1527] catalogue fol. A2ᵛ col. 2. RENOUARD (see note 7), 1515.10; CATALDI PALAU (see note 20), n° 10 (p. 600).

41 Plutarch, *Moralia*: 1513 catalogue fol. 2ʳ col. 2. Plutarch, *Mordia*: [1527] catalogue fol. A2ʳ col. 2.

42 See the critical edition of the manuscript catalogue, note 72.

43 RENOUARD (see note 7), p. 260.8; *The Aldine Press* (see note 7), p. 29; HRHRC (see note 10), n° 8; *Aldo Manuzio tipografo* (see note 11), n° 29; *Aldo Manuzio e l'ambiente veneziano, 1494–1515*. Ed. SUZY MARCON and MARINO ZORZI. Venice 1994, n° 26.

44 RENOUARD (see note 7), 1512.1; *The Aldine Press* (see note 7), n° 105; HRHRC (see note 10), n° 95; *Aldo Manuzio tipografo* (see note 11), n° 107; *Aldo Manuzio e l'ambiente veneziano* (see note 43), n° 124.

45 RENOUARD (see note 7), 1499.1; *The Aldine Press* (see note 7), n° 30; HRHRC (see note 10), n° 24; *Aldo Manuzio tipografo* (see note 11), n° 31; *Aldo Manuzio e l'ambiente veneziano* (see note 43), n° 30.

46 RENOUARD (see note 7), 1504.4; *The Aldine Press* (see note 7), n° 84; HRHRC (see note 10), n° 76; *Aldo Manuzio tipografo* (see note 11), n° 86; *Aldo Manuzio e l'ambiente veneziano* (see note 43), n° 96.

47 RENOUARD (see note 7), p. 261.12; *The Aldine Press* (see note 7), p. 46; HRHRC (see note 10), n° 46; *Aldo Manuzio tipografo* (see note 11), n° 53; *Aldo Manuzio e l'ambiente veneziano* (see note 43), n° 52. Judging from the treble signature guides, I believe this large fragment to have been intended for inclusion in the third volume of the *Poetae Christiani veteres*.

48 RENOUARD (see note 7), 1518.2; CATALDI PALAU (see note 20), n° 38 (p. 612); *The Aldine Press* (see note 7), n° 167; HRHRC (see note 10), n° 151.

All these works are uniformly described as quartos in various modern catalogues, with an average leaf height of 20 to 21 cm when measurements are recorded.[49] Actual trim sizes of surviving copies of these six works (listed in the notes) conform to the overall appearance of Aldine quartos. While this novel terminology might suggest that the books are in the elongated format that the trimmed *Reçute* sheet can furnish, surviving copies reflect the standard quadratic appearance of the Aldine quarto. In general, I find nothing to distinguish them in bound and trimmed appearance from the many quartos described in [1527] as being in *forma quadrati*. The only thing I could suggest is that the unbound and untrimmed copies in stock and available for sale did not appear to be quite as square as those in *forma quadrati*, so this new term was created for the six books; however, this is purely speculative and doubtless of very little merit. The precise intent or meaning of *forma paulo enchiridii maiore* remains a riddle to me: while I might risk positing a reference to large-paper copies, I would do so most tentatively.

49 These six works are described as quartos, without leaf measurements, in *Aldo Manuzio tipografo* (see note 11), HRHRC (see note 10), CATALDI PALAU (see note 20), and *Im Zeichen von Anker und Delphin* (see note 21). The following measurements of the bound and trimmed leaves are reported in *The Aldine Press* (see note 7) and *Aldo Manuzio e l'ambiente veneziano* (see note 43), the latter for the first five works because of the 1515 terminal date of coverage. – Psalterium Graecum: *The Aldine Press*, nº 29 is 19,8 × 12,9 cm. *Aldo Manuzio e l'ambiente veneziano*, nº 26 is 20 × 14,8 cm (in a restored contemporary binding). – Lascaris: *The Aldine Press*, nº 105 is 21,5 × 15,7 cm (in a Rome c. 1515–27 binding); nº 105A is 19,2 × 14 cm. *Aldo Manuzio e l'ambiente veneziano*, nº 124 is 20,8 × 14,4 cm. (My own copy measures 21,3 × 16,1 cm.) – Epistolae Graecae: *The Aldine Press*, nº 30 is 20,9 × 14,2; nº 30A is 21,3 × 15,7; nº 30B is 20,9 × 15,3 cm. *Aldo Manuzio e l'ambiente veneziano*, nº 30 is 21,2 × 15,6 cm. – Gregorius Nazianzenus: *The Aldine Press*, nº 84 is 19,8 × 14,8 cm. *Aldo Manuzio e l'ambiente veneziano*,

Catalogue

CATALOGUS LIB⟨R⟩ORUM, qui in officina Aldi Manutii plaerique omnes intra annum Domini M.D.XXXIIII Venetiis excusi sunt, prout is exstat in Pandectis Gesneri fol[io]. in[eunte]. 107.[50]

Libri GRAECI

Erotemata Constantini Lascaris Graecè & Latine, cum tabula Cebetis, Carminibus Pythagorae & Phocylidis &c. in 4.[51]

Thesaurus sive Cornucopiae dictionum difficilium, & maximè verborum apud Homerum ex Commentariis Eustathii & aliorum grammaticorum ordine literarum. Accedunt & alii graeci libelli ad grammaticae cognitionem necessarii circiter 16. in fol.[52]

Theodori Gazae Grammatica. Ejusdem liber de Mensibus. Item Apollonii de Constructione lib[ri]. 4⟨.⟩ in fol.[53]

Lexicon Latino Graecum, cui & alii libelli 16 adiiciuntur: ex quibus sunt Thomae Magistri & Phrynichi & Emanuelis Moschopuli Eclogae Atticarum dictionum: caeteri saepe iam in Appendicibus Lexicorum Basileae impressi sunt. in folio.[54]

Theocriti Aeglogae. Hesiodi opera. Catonis sententiae Graecè. Theognidis sententiae. Sententiosi versus monostichi per locos. Pythagorae & Phocylidis carmina &c. in folio.[55]

Aristophanis comoedia⟨e⟩ 9, cum commentariis: in fol.[56]

Musaei poema de Herone & Leandro. Orphei Argonautica, Hymni et liber de Lapidibus. in 8.[57]

Aristotelis opera quatuor voluminibus: quibus etiam Theophrasti omnes libri adjunguntur: & Alexandri Aphrodi⟨si⟩ensis Problemata. in folio⟨.⟩[58]

Commentarii Graeci in Aristotelem, singuli in folio.⟨:⟩[59]

---

nº 96 is 21,4 × 15,4 cm. – Nonnus: *The Aldine Press*, nº 46 is 19,8 × 15 cm. *Aldo Manuzio e l'ambiente veneziano*, nº 52 is 20,2 × 14,6 cm. – Dioscorides: *The Aldine Press*, nº 167 is 20 × 13,1 cm.

50 The scribe states that the books have been published up to the year 1534 because he is copying Gesner's opening sentences of the catalogue in Book XI. Gesner's dedicatory letter to Paulus Manutius fills folio 107ʳ, the catalogue itself beginning on fol. 107ᵛ and ending on fol. 109ʳ. In fact, Gesner's catalogue contains numerous examples from the 1533–36 period of the Press's brief and troubled reflorescence, and additional publications from the Sons of Aldus period in the 1540s are included, up to the 1548 publication date of the *Pandectarum ... libri xxi*. – Gesner lists many of his sources for compiling his bibliographies, including on fol. 21ʳ: »Aldi Manutii in fol. chartis 3«. This refers to the published list of 24 November 1513, which consists of three leaves (facs. in *Aldo Manuzio editore* [see note 11], vol. I, pp. 126/7). Gesner follows the basic outline of this third published Aldine Press catalogue (cited in the notes below as Aldus's 1513 Catalogue), compiling entries from its contents, though with great condensation, extensive overall rearrangement, and with many additions from the years between 1513 and 1548. – Librorum is spelled correctly in Gesner.

51 RENOUARD (see note 7), 1495.1 and 1512.1.

52 Ibid., 1496.1.

53 Ibid., 1495.2.

54 Ibid., 1524.3; HRHRC (see note 10), nº 209 (p. 216). The allusion may be to Walder's reprint edition of JOHANNES CRASTONUS: *Dictionarium*, published at Basel in 1541, Ex officina Valderiana, but there is more than one possibility. HIERONYMUS CURIO: *Lexicon Graecolatinum ...* (Basel: Johann Walder, 1541); CONRAD GESNER: *Lexicon Graeco-Latinum* (Basel: Hieronymus Curio, 1545).

55 RENOUARD (see note 7), 1495.3.

56 Ibid., 1498.3. Gesner reads »comoediae« correctly, reflecting the listing in Aldus's 1513 Catalogue (fol. 1ʳ). The spelling in the [1527] catalogue is »comediae« (fol. A1ʳ).

57 RENOUARD (see note 7), 1517.8.

58 Ibid., 1497.1–3 and 1498.1. Note that the scribe omits the first volume of the Aristotle, the 1495 *Organon*, reflecting its absence in Gesner. The volume is present in Aldus's 1513 Catalogue, however, as *Logica Aristotelis*, followed by an entry per volume for each of the four subsequent volumes »in philosophia« (fol. 1ʳ). This pattern is repeated in the [1527] catalogue (fol. A1ʳ⁻ᵛ). Aldus himself mirrored the views of his contemporaries when he segregated his monumental edition of Aristotle into one and four volumes, respectively: the *Organon* (1495), comprising the six treatises on logic, followed by the additional four volumes (1497/98) comprising the balance of the Aristotelian corpus along with allied works by Theocritus and others. Gesner's text reads Theophrasti libri omnes, which the scribe has reversed, and Aphrodisiensis is correctly spelled.

59 I.e., this is the heading for the eleven works that immediately follow, each in a separate folio volume; I have added terminal punctuation to indicate this.

Ammonius de praedicamenta: & [f. 1ᵛ] in librum de enunciatione: cum Magentio in eundem.[60]

Alexander Aphrodis[iensis]. in primum priorum.[61]

Joan[nes]. Grammaticus & Eustratius in Posteriora.[62]

Alexander Aphrodisiensis in Topica.[63]

Idem in Elenchos.[64]

Simplicius in 8 libros physicorum.[65]

Idem in libros de Coelo.[66]

Joan[nes]. Grammaticus in libros de Generatione & interitu: cum Alexandro Aphrodisiensi in Meteora.[67]

Themistius in libros de Anima. Alexander Aphrodis[iensis]. in eosdem, cum ejusdem libro de fato.[68]

Simplicius in libros de anima, una cum Michaele Ephesio in parva naturalia[69]

Eustrathius in Ethica.[70]

Alii libri Graeci

Psalterium graecum. ⟨in⟩ 4.[71]

Officium in honorem D. Virginis cum psalmis poenitentialibus à Latino in graecum. in 16.[72]

Epistolarum mille & septuaginta trium volumen, quorum authores sunt 40. in 4.[73]

Gregorii Nazianzeni diversa poemata: cum Latina translatione, inserto Evangelio Joannis. in 4.[74]

Nonni paraphrasis in Evangelium Joannis. in 4.[75]

Dioscoridis de materia medica et venenis libri, cum indice. Accedent carmina de viribus quarundam plantarum, in antiquis exemplaribus reperta. Nicandri Theriaca & Alexipharmaca cum Commentariis. De Ponderibus, & Mensuris. in 4.[76]

---

60 RENOUARD (see note 7), 1503.4; note the spelling Magentio, not quite Gesner's correction to Magentino, against the misspelled title-page reading Margentini or Aldus's 1513 Catalogue entry Margentinus (fol. 2ʳ), which is repeated in the [1527] catalogue (fol. A2ʳ).

61 RENOUARD (see note 7), 1520.3.
62 Ibid., 1534.9.
63 Ibid., 1513.5.
64 Ibid., 1520.4.
65 Ibid., 1526.2.
66 Ibid., 1526.3.
67 Ibid., 1527.7.
68 Ibid., 1534.3.
69 Ibid., 1527.5.
70 Ibid., 1536.6.

71 [Undated; c. 1498]: RENOUARD (see note 7), p. 260.8.

72 I believe this to be the 32° June 1521 reprint edition: RENOUARD (see note 7), 1521.10; *Aldo Manuzio tipografo* (see note 11), n° 92; CATALDI PALAU (see note 20), n° 70 (pp. 626/7). *Aldo Manuzio tipografo*, n° 92 also mentions a 1534 reprint edition, in Latin, but this seems to be a ghost. The 1521 edition is thus closest to the date of the catalogue, having already replaced the 1505 reprint edition (RENOUARD [see note 7], 1505.3). It seems most unlikely that the citation is to the original December 1497 edition (RENOUARD, 1497.13). There is no indication of the *Brevissima introductio ad litteras Graecas*, which is known to be extant in only three copies (Cf. MARTIN DAVIES: *Aldus Manutius: Printer and Publisher of Renaissance Venice*. London 1995, p. 28); considering the detail of the entries, one would judge this to be conclusive as to its absence, and also a help in excluding the 1497 edition from consideration. It is also worth noting that, while the Greek Hours of the Virgin is recorded in Aldus's 1513 Catalogue (fol. 1ʳ), the *Brevissima introductio* is not.

73 RENOUARD (see note 7), 1499.1 (i.e., the *Epistolae diversorum philosophorum*).

74 Ibid., 1504.4 (i.e., *Poetae Christiani veteres* III).

75 [1501]: RENOUARD (see note 7), p. 261.12; cf. 1504.4.

76 This entry is a puzzle, since it combines discrete elements of the two Aldine editions, the fol. 1499 and the 4° 1518. The first two sentences (»Dioscorides [...] cum indice. Accedunt carmina [...] reperta.«) manifestly derive from RENOUARD (see note 7), 1518.2 (see the verso of the title page); however, this 4° edition does not contain Nicander. RENOUARD, 1499.4, while comprising the catalogue's contents, is differently structured and is entirely in Greek apart from Aldus's preface and the colophons; it thus does not provide the basic vocabulary for this entry. Moreover, the large size of its type page, which includes both text and commentary set in different fonts, cannot feasibly be trimmed down to 4° format. It is as though the cataloguer picked up the vocabulary of part of the 1518 edition to describe the 1499 edition, and assigned the 1518 edition's format as well. The entry in Aldus's 1513 Catalogue (fol. 1ᵛ), for the 1499 edition, does not help to clarify this. The much more extensive entry in the [1527] catalogue (fol. A1ᵛ) is clearly for the 4° edition of 1518, and is discussed at some length in the Appendix.

Julii Pollucis vocabularium. in fol.⁷⁷
Stephanus de Urbibus. in fol.⁷⁸
Thucydidis libri .8. in fol.⁷⁹
Herodoti lib[ri]. 9. in fol.⁸⁰
Luciani omnia. Icones Philostrati 66. Ejusdem Heroica⟨.⟩ Icones junioris Philostrati 22. Enarrationes Callistrati in Statuas 14.
Philostrati vitae Sophistarum 58. in folio.⁸¹

[f. 2ʳ]

Philostrati de vita Apollonii libri 8 Graeci, & Latini⟨,⟩ Alemanno Rhinuccio interprete.
Eusebius contra Hierodem Graece et Latine⟨,⟩ Zenobio Accialo interprete, in folio.⁸²
Sophoclis Tragoediae .7. in 8.⁸³
Euripidis Tragoediae .⟨18⟩. in 8.⁸⁴
Epigrammatum graecorum libri .7. in 8.⁸⁵
Homeri omnia: cum vita ejus ex Plutarcho, Herodoto & Dione. in 8.⁸⁶
Q. ⟨Smyrnaei⟩ Calabri poetae Paralipomena Homeri, libris 14. in 8.⁸⁷
Demosthenis orationes. in folio.⁸⁸
Vlpiani Commentarii in ⟨13⟩ Demosthenis orationes⟨.⟩
Harpocration de Dictionibus Rhetorum ordine literarum. in folio⟨.⟩⁸⁹
Plutarchi Moralia. in folio.⁹⁰
Phornutus de natura Deorum cum Palaephato de fabulosa historia. Vita et fabulae Aesopi Graecè & Latinè⟨.⟩ Gabriae fabulae Graecè & Latinè. Hieraclides Ponticus de allegoriis apud Homerum⟨.⟩ Orus de hieroglyphicis. Proverbia per ordinem Alphabeti. in fol.⁹¹
Liber 12 Rhetorum de arte Rhetorica. in fol.⁹²

77 RENOUARD (see note 7), 1502.1.
78 Ibid., 1502.15.
79 Ibid., 1502.4.
80 Ibid., 1502.8.
81 This is more likely to be a citation to the 1503 edition: RENOUARD (see note 7), 1503.3. The second digit of the 66 is hidden by the manuscript's sewing; Gesner reads 66; Aldus's 1513 Catalogue (fol. 2ʳ) reads 65 (i.e., »quinq[ue] & sexaginta«), for the 1503 edition. The [1527] catalogue carries a much-expanded entry, for the 1522 edition (RENOUARD, 1522.4), and now specifies, using arabic numerals, that it contains 171 minor works (fol. A2ʳ).
82 RENOUARD (see note 7), 1501.2 (i.e., 1501–1502–1504); the title-page readings are Rinuccino and Acciolo. Gesner reads Rhinuccino. Aldus's 1513 Catalogue reads Accialo corrected in manuscript to Acciolo (fol. 2ʳ); however, the spelling is still Accialo in the [1527] catalogue (fol. A2ʳ), so the correction was not noted.
83 RENOUARD (see note 7), 1502.6.
84 Ibid., 1503.10; for my ⟨18⟩, the scribe has written a very haphazard arabic 22, reflecting Gesner. Gesner, however, has copied Aldus's 1513 Catalogue entry »duodeviginti« (fol. 2ʳ), which itself is a correction. The [1527] catalogue entry, while still reading »duodeuiginti«, provides an itemized list of all eighteen plays (fol. A2ʳ). Whereas the title page reads »heptakaideka« [Gk.] | »septendecim«, the volume itself, as is well known, comprises eighteen tragedies, including the »Hercules furens« not listed among the contents. Gesner is thus responsible for introducing yet another error, by his seeming to have read duodeviginti (i.e., the Roman fashion of stating eighteen as two from twenty) as duoetviginti, and I wonder if he subconsciously translated it into German as zweiundzwanzig in making his entry. See note 89.
85 RENOUARD (see note 7), 1503.9 and 1521.17 (i.e., *Anthologia Graeca*).
86 Ibid., 1504.6, 1517.3 and 1524.1.
87 [c. 1505]: RENOUARD (see note 7), p. 261.14.
88 Ibid., 1504.7 (i.e., 1504; [1520–1527]).
89 Ibid., 1503.6 and 1527.4. My ⟨13⟩ replaces the scribe's arabic 18, following Gesner, which raises an interesting point. Aldus's 1513 Catalogue reads (fol. 2ʳ) »duodeviginti« (see note 84), which is repeated in the [1527] catalogue (fol. A2ʳ), and Gesner has followed this accurately. The title page reads »dekatreis« [Gk.] | »tredecim« for both editions and the 1513 Catalogue reads »duodeviginti«; however, my attempts to tally the slightly ambiguous listings in Aldus's 1513 Catalogue produce a total of twenty, plus Harpocration. A comparable attempt with the [1527] catalogue again produced a total of twenty, plus Harpocration.
90 RENOUARD (see note 7), 1509.1.
91 Ibid., 1505.6. For the scribe's Hieraclides, perhaps influenced by the »hieroglyphicis« on the following line, Gesner reads Heraclides, reflecting the title-page reading, and the entry in Aldus's 1513 Catalogue reads »cum Heraclide« (fol. 2ᵛ), which is repeated in the [1527] catalogue (fol. A2ᵛ).
92 RENOUARD (see note 7), 1508.4 (i.e., *Rhetores Graeci* I).

In Aphtonii progymnasmata Commentarii: item in Hermogenis omnia. in fol.[93]

Theodori Gazae grammatica. Georgius Lecapenus de constructione verborum⟨.⟩ Emanuel Moscopulus de constructione nominum et verborum⟨.⟩ Idem de Accentibus. in 8.[94]

Grammatica Chrysolorae, cum libro 4. Theodori Gazae, & sententiis monost⟨i⟩chis, Catone, & Erotematibus Guarini. in 8.[95]

Pindarus. Callimachus. Dionysius de situ Orbis. Lycophron. in 8.[96]

Isocrates. Alcidamantis, Gorgiae & Aristidis orationes quaedam. Harpocration de Dictionibus Isocratis. in fol.[97]

⟨Aeschinis & aliorum 12. rhetorum orationes. In fol.⟩ [98]

Platonis opera. in fol.[99]

Suidas. in fol.[100]

Athenaei Symposiaca. in fol.[101]

[f. 2ᵛ]

Hesychii dictionarium. in fol.[102]

Pausaniae Commentarii Graeciam describentes. in fol.[103]

Strabo. in fol.[104]

Sacrae Scripturae veteris novaeque omnia. in fol.[105]

Artemidorus cum Synesio de interpretatione Somniorum. in 8.[106]

Plutarchi illustrium virorum Graece ac Latine nominis vitae 49. in fol.[107]

Oppiani de piscibus libri 5. una cum Laurentii Lippii tralatione⟨.⟩ Ejusdem de venatione libri 4. in 8.[108]

Aeschilii tragoediae 6. in 8.[109]

Aldi Manutii Rom[ani]. grammaticae institutiones graecae. in 4.[110]

Gregorii Nazianzeni orationes .16. in 8.[111]

Apollonii Rhodii Argonautica cum Commentariis. in 8.[112]

Commentarii in Homeri Iliadem: & Porphyrii duo opuscula. in 8.[113]

Herodiani historiarum libri 8. cum interpretatione Latina Angeli Politiani. in 8.[114]

Xenophontis omnia. in fol.[115]

Galeni omnia in quinq[ue] vol[uminibus]. in fol.[116]

Hippocratis omnia. in fol.[117]

---

[93] Ibid., 1508.4 (i.e., *Rhetores Graeci* II, of May 1509). The scribe's Aphtonii reflects the unvoiced *h* of a German-speaker's *th*. Gesner reads Aphthonii; the title page, Aphthonius. See also note 175. Aldus's 1513 Catalogue reads Aphthonij consistently in three listings (fols. 1ᵛ & 2ᵛ), as does the [1527] catalogue (fol. A2ᵛ).

[94] Ibid., 1525.2.

[95] Ibid., 1517.6. The scribe's reading is monostochis, whereas Gesner reads monostichis, reflecting the title page. The [1527] catalogue follows the title-page reading (fol. A2ᵛ).

[96] Ibid., 1513.9.

[97] Ibid., 1534.4.

[98] Text from Gesner, the scribe having failed to make this entry. Gesner's tally is based upon Aldus's 1513 Catalogue listing (fol. 2ᵛ). Ibid., 1513.2 (i.e., *Oratores Graeci* I); see *The Aldine Press* (see note 7), nº 112 (p. 106), HRHRC (see note 10), nº 99 (pp. 124/5) for detailed contents.

[99] RENOUARD (see note 7), 1513.4.

[100] Ibid., 1514.11.

[101] Ibid., 1514.4.

[102] Ibid., 1514.3.

[103] Ibid., 1516.3.

[104] Ibid., 1516.7.

[105] Ibid., 1518.8 (i.e., the complete Bible in Greek).

[106] Ibid., 1518.4.

[107] Ibid., 1519.9.

[108] Ibid., 1517.9.

[109] Ibid., 1518.9; the reduplicative genitive form of Aeschylus may be simple inadvertence; Gesner reads correctly Aeschyli.

[110] Ibid., 1515.10.

[111] Ibid., 1516.1.

[112] Ibid., 1521.5.

[113] Ibid., 1521.6 (i.e., Didymus). This entry has been made apparently from the book rather than after the contents listing on the title page: the title announces the commentary on the *Odyssey* as well, but it is not present, and would not appear until 1528 (see the text at note 118).

[114] Ibid., 1524.2. Gesner has the suspended forms Ang. Politian.

[115] Ibid., 1525.1.

[116] Ibid., 1525.3. What I have expanded as vol[uminibus] is written voll., indicating the plural; the word is spelled out (»uoluminibus«) in Gesner.

[117] Ibid., 1526.1.

[118] Ibid., 1528.4; cf. note 113.

Didymi scholia in Odysseam Homeri. in 8.[118]
Paulus Aegineta. in fol.[119]
Aetii medici libri primi 8. in fol.[120]
Xenophontis paralipomena. Commentarii in Thucydidem⟨.⟩ Herodianus. Plethonis historia. in fol.[121]
Greg[orii]. Nazianzeni orationes 9 & Greg[orii]. Nysseni quaedam. in 8.[122]

LIBRI LATINI

Angeli Politiani Opera. in fol.[123]
Julii Firmici & M. Manilii Astronomica⟨.⟩ Arati Phaenomena, Germanico interprete, cum commentariis & imaginibus. In eadem Fragmentum interpretationis Ciceronianae: & Rufi Festi Avieni Paraphrasis⟨.⟩ Eadem Graece cum comment[ariis]. Theonis⟨.⟩ Procli sphaera Graecè, & Latinè Thoma Linacro interprete. in fol.[124]
Nicolai Perotti Cornucopiae &c. Varronis libri de lingua latina & analogia.

[f. 3ʳ]

S. Pompeius Festus. Nonius Marcellus. in fol.[125]
Grammaticae Institutiones Aldi. in 4.[126]
Bessarionis Cardinalis libri 4 in calumniatorem Platonis. Ejusdem liber in quo ex 12 libris Platonis de legibus quam plurima recitantur, & à Georg[io]. Trapezuntio male versa esse ostenduntur. Ejusdem tractatus an natura & ars consulto agant. in fol.[127]
Aristoteles de Animalibus. Theophrastus de Plantis. Problemata Aristotelis & Alexandri Aphrodisaei⟨,⟩ Theod⟨oro⟩. Gaza interprete. in fol.[128]
Jamblichus de mysteriis⟨.⟩ Proclus in Alcibiadem. Idem de sacrificio & Magia. Porphyrius de divinis atq[ue] daemonibus.
Synesius de Somniis. Psellus de daemonibus.
Expositio Prisciani & Marsilii in Theophrastum de sensu⟨,⟩ phantasia & intellectu. Alcionius de doctrina Platonis. Speusippus de Platonis definitionibus. Pythagorae Carmina aurea & symbola. Xenocrates de morte. Mercurii Trismegisti Pomander. Ejusdem Asclepius. Marsilii Ficini de triplici vita lib[ri]. 2. Ejusdem libri, de Voluptate, de Sole & lumine, de magis: Quod necessaria sit animi tranquillitas. in fol.[129]

119 Ibid., 1528.5.
120 Ibid., 1534.7. Gesner reads Aëtij. The [1527] catalogue uses the form Aetius (fol. A3ᵛ), i.e., without diaeresis, whereas the work itself uses Aëtius.
121 Ibid., 1503.7. Gesner reads Paraleipomena, accurately reflecting the title page's »Paraleipomena« [Gk.], with a ligatured epsilon-iota typesort. Aldus's 1513 Catalogue has Paralipomena, in Latin (fol. 2ʳ), whereas the word does not appear in the entry in the [1527] catalogue (fols. A2ᵛ–A3ʳ), which now opens *Xenophontis* Volumen.
122 Ibid., 1536.5.
123 Ibid., 1498.4.
124 Ibid., 1499.3.
125 Ibid., 1513.6 and 1517.10.
126 Ibid., 1508.1, 1514.10 and 1523.7. The first Aldine edition (Ibid., 1501.9), titled *Rudimenta grammatices Latinae linguae*, is unlikely to be a candidate.
127 Ibid., 1503.5.
128 Ibid., 1504.2 and 1513.11. The scribe seems to have written a ligatured *ae*, although I am not absolutely certain of this. Gesner reads Aphrodisiei. Aldus's 1513 Catalogue reads aphrodisiei, with lower-case *a*; in the [1527] catalogue, this has become Aphrodisiei (fol. A4ᵛ).
129 Ibid., 1516.8. For the scribe's Alcionius, Gesner reads Alcinous; the title page, Alcinoi. Was the scribe thinking of PETRUS ALCYONIUS: *De exsilio* (Ibid., 1522.6)? See note 170 and text. For Pomander, read Poimander (i.e. Poimandres); Gesner reads Poemander, with the ligature; the title-page reading is Pimander.

Des[iderii]. Erasmi proverbia. in fol.[130]

Poliphili Hypnerotomachia. in fol.[131]

Lud[ovici]. Coelii ⟨Rhodigini⟩ Antiquarum lectionum libri 16. in fol.[132]

M. T. Ciceronis omnia. Formis diversis.[133]

C. Crispi Sallustii historiae & orationes eis adjungi solitae. in 8.[134]

M. F. Quintilianus. in 4.[135]

Cato, Varro, Columella, Palladius. de re rustica. Georgii Alexandrini enarrationes priscarum dictionum in ejusdem libris. in 4.[136]

Virgilius. in 8.[137]

Diversarum veterum poetarum in Priapum lusus. Maronis Catalecta, Copa, Rosae, Culex, Dirae, Moretum & alia quae falso Virgilii creduntur.

[f. 3ᵛ]

Argumenta in Virgilii libros, & alia diversorum complura. in 8.[138]

P. Ovidii omnia, cum annotationib[us]. ⟨in⟩ 8⟨.⟩[139]

Terentius. in 8.[140] T. Livii Decades .3. L. Flori libri 4. Polybii historiarum libri 5. Nicolao Perotto interprete. in 8.[141]

Ejusdem Livii omnia accurate denuo impressa. in fol.[142]

C. Plinii secundi epistolae⟨.⟩ Ejusdem Panegyricus, & liber de viris illustribus⟨.⟩ Suetonius Tranquillus ⟨de⟩ claris grammaticis & Rhetoribus. Iulii Obsequentis prodigiorum liber. ⟨in⟩ 8.[143]

Catullus, Tibullus, Propertius. in 8.[144]

Lucanus. in 8.[145]

Valerius Maximus. in 8.[146]

C. Julii Caesaris & A. Hirtii aut Opii Commentarii de bellis diversis: cum picturis quibusdam: & locorum ac populorum nominibus. in 8.[147]

L. Coelii Lactantii Opera cum Tertulliani Apologetico. in 8.[148]

130 Ibid., 1508.2 and 1520.2 (i.e., the *Adagia*). Aldus's 1513 Catalogue entry reads *Prouerbia Erasmi* (fol. 3ʳ), which is changed to the genitive plural and expanded in the [1527] catalogue (fol. A4ᵛ).

131 Ibid., 1499.5 and 1545.14. See the text of the Introduction, at note 10.

132 Ibid., 1516.11. Gesner reads Caelij, with the ligature, which is the reading in the [1527] catalogue (fol. A4ᵛ).

133 The candidates are far more extensive than their formats; only Gesner's and the scribe's terminal date of 1534 and the exclusion until folio 4ᵛ of Paulus Manutius's publications (see the text at notes 191 and 192) keep our choices to manageable proportions, though the entry is too generic to warrant attempts at specifying editions. The formats, at any rate, can be only 4⁰ and 8⁰, and very few of the former; the folio Ciceros date from much later in the Press's existence.

134 RENOUARD (see note 7), 1509.3 and 1521.16.

135 Ibid., 1514.5 and 1521.14.

136 Ibid., 1514.2; 1533.9. Gesner has a comma after Palladius, but the scribe differs. For the scribe's erroneous ejusdem, Gesner reads eisdem (as »ejsdem«); the title page of the 1514 edition reads »his«, whereas the title page of the 1533 edition changes the relevant wording. The listing in the [1527] catalogue (fol. A4ᵛ), while very extensive and somewhat diffuse, offers the grammatically correct reading »in his libris«; at this time, it would of necessity have referred to the 1514 edition.

137 Ibid., 1514.8, 1527.3, 1541.7, and 1545.11. The first edition, 1501.3, is spelled Vergilius on the title page; the 1514, 1527, and 1541 editions, Virgilius. Gesner's presumptive source, Aldus's 1513 Catalogue, reads Vergilius (fol. 3ʳ), whereas Gesner reads Virgilius. The [1527] catalogue again reads Virgilius (fol. A4ᵛ), and the details of the entry seem to refer to the June 1527 edition (Ibid., 1527.3).

138 Ibid., 1517.12. It is interesting to find the Priapeia and Appendix Vergiliana volume immediately following the Virgil itself; however, since Gesner and thus the scribe consistently and clearly record two separate octavos, we should not suspect that this volume and the immediately preceding one are in fact the very rare composite Aldine Virgil of 1505 (Ibid., 1505.7).

139 Ibid., 1515.3 and 1516.9–10, 1533.8 (i.e., 3 vols.).

140 Ibid., 1517.5 and 1521.9.

141 Ibid., 1521.1.

142 Ibid., 1520.6.

143 Ibid., 1508.3 and 1518.1. For my interpolated ⟨de⟩ the manuscript reads &, whereas Gesner reads de. The correctly printed preposition, however, lies immediately beneath an ampersand in the line above, so the scribe's eye wandered as he copied Gesner. The title page reads »de«; the entry for the 1508 edition in Aldus's 1513 Catalogue reads *Epistolae Plinij* in its entirety. The [1527] catalogue, on the other hand, contains a very extensive entry for this work, far exceeding, and differing in content and wording from, what Gesner and the scribe list, and it would thereby seem not to be a source for this entry.

144 Ibid., 1502.16 and 1515.1.

145 Ibid., 1502.3 and 1515.6.

146 Ibid., 1502.10 and 1514.9.

A. Gelli⟨i⟩ Noctes Atticae. in 8.[149]

T. Lucretius. in 8.[150]

Nervae, Trajani & Adriani Caesarum vitae ex Dione, G[eorgio]. Merula interprete. Item Aelius Spartianus, Jul. Capitolinus, Lampridius, Fl. Vopiscus, Trebellius Pollio, Vulcatius Gallicanus, omnes à Joanne Baptista Egnatio castigati. Heliogabali ad meretrices oratio. Joan[nis]. Bapt[istae]. Egnatii de Caesaribus libri 3. Ejusdem in Spartiani Lampridiiq[ue] vitas & reliquorum annotationes. Aristidis Smyrnaei oratio de laudibus urbis Romae, Scipione Carteromacho interprete⟨.⟩ Conflagratio Vesuvii montis ex Dione, Georg[io]. Merula interprete. in 8.[151]

Pomponius Mela. Julius Solinus. Itinerarium Antonini Augusti. Vibius Sequester.

P[ublius]. Victorius de regionibus urbis Romae.

Dionysius Afer de situ orbis, Prisciano interprete. in 8.[152]

Senecae tragoediae. in 8⟨.⟩[153]

Martialis. in 8.[154]

Dec. Ausonius. in 8.[155]

[f. 4ʳ]

Statii Poemata. in 8.[156]

Io[annis]. Ioviani Pontani opera soluta oratione. in 4.[157]

Ejusdem Poemata duobus volum[inibus]. in 8. Posteriori accedunt, Calpurni Aeglogae .7. Aurelii Nemesiani Aeglogae 4⟨.⟩[158]

Strozii poetae Ferrarienses pater & filius. in 8⟨.⟩[159]

Euripidis Hecuba et Iphigenia⟨,⟩ Des[iderio]. Erasmo interprete &c. in 8.[160]

Luciani opuscula quaedam⟨,⟩ Des[iderio]. Erasmo & Tho[ma]. Moro interpretibus &c. in 8.[161]

147 Ibid., 1513.1 and 1519.11.
148 Ibid., 1515.2.
149 Ibid., 1515.9. The author's name can be read as either Gelli or Gelii, because of overwriting, and I have taken it as the former; Gesner reads Gellii, as does the title page.
150 Ibid., 1515.11.
151 Ibid., 1519.8. For the scribe's G. Merula, Gesner reads Ge. Merula. For the scribe's Vesuvii, Gesner reads Veseui, following the title page. The lengthy entry in the [1527] catalogue, with a typographically striking inset shoulder note citing Egnatio's skillful editing, spells out Georgio and uses the form Veseui (fol. A5ʳ). CATALDI PALAU (see note 20), nº 48 (p. 616).
152 RENOUARD (see note 7), 1518.6. Gesner reads P. Victor, after the title page, which is the form employed in the [1527] catalogue (fol. A5ʳ). The scribe may have been thinking of Petrus Victorius (Pier Vettori). CATALDI PALAU (see note 20), nº 41 (p. 613).
153 RENOUARD (see note 7), 1517.4. One should probably not make too much of the correct spelling of the author's name, versus the title page's famous misspelling Scenecae, which is repeated in the [1527] catalogue (fol. A5ʳ). The correction, which is in Gesner, is an obvious one on the face of it.
154 Ibid., 1501.7 and 1517.11.
155 Ibid., 1517.7.
156 Ibid., 1502.7 and 1519.12.
157 Ibid., 1519.3. Since Gesner is absolutely consistent in citing multiple-volume works, and only this first volume of Pontanus's prose works in 4º is thus titled, I assume that only the first volume is cited, rather than all three, thereby excluding the concluding two 4º volumes of the following year (Ibid., 1519.6–7). Gesner reads Iouiniani and Calpurnij. The [1527] catalogue states explicitly that the prose works are in three volumes (tribus digesta partibus), the contents of which are then listed in detail (fol. A4ᵛ), so it appears not to have provided a source for Gesner.
158 Ibid., 1513.7 and 1518.10. This entry immediately supports my comments in note 157 about multiple volumes. For once, the format (8º) is indicated at the beginning of the entry.

CATALDI PALAU (see note 20), nº 35 (pp. 610/1). There is a composite entry in the [1527] catalogue (fol. A5ᵛ).
159 RENOUARD (see note 7), 1513.10. The interesting qualifier that these are the Ferrarese Strozzi derives from Aldus's 1513 Catalogue entry »ferrarienses« (fol. 3ʳ), repeated with the variant spelling »Ferarienses« in the [1527] catalogue (fol. A5ᵛ), and thus via Gesner to the scribe.
160 Ibid., 1507.1.
161 Ibid., 1516.2.

Des[iderii]. Erasmi Moria. in 8.[162]

Ejusdem Quaerela Pacis, & alia opuscula diversa. in 8.[163]

Christophori Longolii perduellionis rei defensiones duae. in 8.[164]

L. Apuleii Opera. in 8.[165]

Q. Curtius. in 8.[166]

Plauti Comoediae. in 4.[167]

Guil[lielmi]. Budaei libri 5. de asse. in 4⟨.⟩[168]

Asconii Paediani expositio in orationes aliquot Ciceronis: cum Victorini commentariis in libros de Inventione, & Georg[ii]. Trapezuntii in orationem pro Q. Ligario. in 8.[169]

Petrus Alcyonius de exilio. in 4.[170]

Iustinus de externis historiis, cum Aemylio Probo de externis Imperatoribus. in 8.[171]

C. Claudiani Opera. in 8.[172]

C. Valerii Flacci Argonautica, cum Joha[nnis]. Bapt[istae]. Pii carmine ex quarto Argonauticorum Apollonii: & Orphe⟨i⟩ Argonauticis innominato interprete. in 8.[173]

Silius Italicus de bello Punico. in 8.[174]

Georg[ii]. Trapezuntii Rhetoricorum libri 5. His accedunt, Consulti Chirii Fortun⟨at⟩iani libri 3. Aquilae Romani de figuris sententiarum & elocutionis lib[er] .1. P. Rutilii Lupi earundem figurarum e ⟨Gorgia⟩ lib[er] 1. Aristotelis Rhetoricorum ad Theodecten⟨,⟩ Georg[io] Trapezuntio interprete, lib[er] .1. Eiusdem Rhetorica ad Alexandrum, Fr[ancisco]. Philelpho interprete. Paraphrasis Rhetoricae Hermogenis, Hilarione Monacho Ve-

162 Ibid., 1515.7.
163 Ibid., 1518.5.
164 [undated; but 1521]: RENOUARD (see note 7), p. 263 nº 22 (erroneously attributing the date to 1518). On the date, determined from the dolphin and anchor device employed (Fletcher 7), see FLETCHER (see note 22), p. 50; cf. THE ALDINE PRESS (see note 7), device A7 (p. 557); CATALDI PALAU (see note 20), nº 59 (p. 621).
165 RENOUARD (see note 7), 1521.8.
166 Ibid., 1520.1.
167 Ibid., 1522.2.
168 Ibid., 1522.3. Gesner reads Gulielmi; the title-page reading is Guillielmi, as is the entry in the [1527] catalogue (fol. A5ᵛ).
169 Ibid., 1522.8.
170 Ibid., 1522.6. The writer's *exilio*, which is Gesner's reading, is a defective if common variant of the *exsilio* of the title page. The [1527] catalogue entry reads *exilio* (fol. A5ᵛ). See note 129.
171 Ibid., 1522.9.
172 Ibid., 1523.1.
173 Ibid., 1523.3.
174 Ibid., 1523.6.
175 Ibid., 1523.2. Gesner reads Fortunatiani, as does the title page, as well as the [1527] catalogue (fol. A5ᵛ). For my interpolated ⟨Gorgia⟩, the manuscript reads Georgio, perhaps a dittography caused by the neighboring listing of

George of Trebizond, whereas Gesner's text correctly reads Gorgia. Once again (see note 93), the scribe's Aphtonii indicates the unvoiced h of a German-speaker's th; Gesner reads Aphthonii, in agreement with the title page.
176 Ibid., 1528.2.
177 Ibid., 1527.2.
178 A contemporary Aldine edition of Sannazaro, *De partu Virginis* and other works, literally described as *denuo impressus et auctus* on its title page or within the volume, does not exist. Four successive editions, the second, third, and fourth each reprinted (»denuo impressus«) with expanded contents (»auctus«) from its predecessor, appeared in the years 1527 (RENOUARD [see note 7], 1527.6; 1ˢᵗ Aldine ed.), 1528 (Ibid., 1528.6), 1533 (Ibid., 1533.11), and 1535 (Ibid., 1535.3). From its titling, however, RENOUARD 1535.3, Sannazaro's *Opera omnia Latine scripta, nuper edita*, which includes his *De partu Virginis*, and also lists his *Elegiarum libri tres … nuper emissi*, is the likeliest candidate. For its detailed contents, see esp. HRHRC (see note 10), nº 255 (pp. 249/50), then The Aldine Press (see note 7), nº 279 (p. 198); CATALDI PALAU (see note 20), nº 142 (p. 663), while still detailed, is less extensive. The next Aldine edition appears 35 years later (RENOUARD 1570.20), and is described in detail in HRHRC (see note 10), nº 478

(pp. 359/60). No edition of JACOPO SANNAZARO: *De partu Virginis* appears in the [1527] catalogue, either in print or added in manuscript; only his September 1514 *Arcadia* (RENOUARD 1514.7) is cited there (fol. A5ᵛ), as *Archadia Sannazari*.
179 RENOUARD (see note 7), 1529.1 (i.e., [Steuchus]).
180 Ibid., 1533.4. The scribe has introduced T[iti].; Gesner does not indicate the praenomen, either in whole or by initial; the title page reads Titi.
181 Ibid., 1528.1.
182 Ibid., 1534.8.
183 Ibid., 1534.10. For my interpolated ⟨Gratius⟩ (i.e., Grattius), the manuscript reading is Gratianus; Gesner reads Gratius.
184 Ibid., 1536.3.
185 Ibid., 1502.5 and 1515.8.
186 Ibid., 1501.5, 1514.6, 1521.12, 1533.5 and 1546.19.
187 Only ibid., 1515.5, the 8º edition of PIETRO BEMBO: *Gli Asolani*' seems to fit the description.
188 I.e., GIOVANNI BOCCACCIO: *Il Decamerone*; however, the sole feasible Aldine edition (Ibid., 1522.5) is 4º in format. Gesner reads Boccatius.
189 Fol.: Ibid., 1528.3 and 1545.4. 8º: Ibid., 1533.2 and 1547.1.
190 Ibid., 1533.10.
191 This is by and large true, so long as one construes the writer's meaning as

ronensi interprete. Prisciani praeexercitamenta ex Hermogene. Aphtonii progymnasmata⟨,⟩ Io[anne]. Maria [f. 4ᵛ] Catanaeo interprete. in fol.[175]
Macrobius. in 8.[176] Priscianus. in 4.[177]
Sannazarius de partu virginis, denuo impressus & auctus. in 8.[178]
Recognitio veteris Testamenti. in 4.[179]
Quinq[ue]. libri quintae Decadis T. Livii. in 8.[180]
Corn. Celsus cum Q. Sereno. in 4.[181]
Corn. Tacitus. in 4.[182]
⟨Gratius⟩ de Venatione. Ovidius de Piscibus. Marc. Aur. Olympius Nemesianus de Venatione. in 8.[183]
Laur[entii]. Vallae Elegantiae. in 4.[184]

ITALICI LIBRI

Dantes. in 8.[185] Petrarcha. in 8.[186] Bembi quaedam. in 8.[187] M[agister]. Jo[annes]. Bocatius. in 8.[188] Il Cortegiano, del Conte Baldissar Castiglione. in folio & in 8.[189]
Anthropologia Galeatii Capellae. in 8.[190]
Nota. Haec omnia ex Aldi patris officina publicum acceperunt.[191] Filius autem Paulus Manutius quaenam excudi curaverit, certum jam non habeo, praeter pauca haec.[192]
Ambrosii Calepini Dictionarium. in fol.[193]
Appendix Additionum in idem. in fol.[194]
Annotata propria, castigationes & observationes in M. Tullii Ciceronis libros praecipue Philosophicos.[195]

restricted to books issuing from the first two sequential locations of the Press, at Sant' Agostino and San Paternian, until Aldus's death in February 1515, past the death of Andrea Torresani in October 1528 to the closing of the Press in 1529; then the second phase of publishing, 1533–36, under the varying imprints up to and including the 1533–36 imprint In aedibus haeredum Aldi et Andreae Asulani soceri (i.e., In the House of the Heirs of Aldus and of Andrea of Asola, His Father-in-Law). While this would honor the cut-off date of 1534, the point is minor and basically irrelevant, since neither Gesner nor the scribe pays strict attention to this terminal date.

192 The opening »Nota« is the scribe's addition to Gesner's text, which begins simply with Haec. This could mean that he is struck by the absence of many of Paulus's publications and editions, or that he is drawing attention to this want. It is curious that Gesner makes this comment within his catalogue, after having prefaced Book XI with a long dedicatory letter (fol. 107ʳ), dated 13 Feb. 1548, to Paulus Manutius, filled with detailed compliments about Paulus's editorial achievements. On the other hand, this is an understandable comment if one concludes that Gesner has followed the 3-leaf published catalogue of November 1513 as the basis of his own listings, deriving his later editions, for which he had no such authoritative guide, from other sources.

193 RENOUARD (see note 7), 1542.3 (1ˢᵗ Aldine ed.) and 1548.1. Editions later than the *Pandectae* are ibid., 1552.2, 1558.7, 1559.5, 1563.8, and 1564.8. See also note 194.

194 The separate listing indicates that this part of Calepino's dictionary was bound separately or even unbound, but at least was distinct from the 1542 edition of the dictionary itself. See ALBERT LABARRE: Bibliographie du Dictionarium d'Ambrogio Calepino. Baden-Baden 1975 (*Bibliotheca Bibliographica Aureliana*. 26), n° 97 (p. 53). RENOUARD's (see note 7) entry for the 1542 edition (1542.3) describes the second part, the 26-leaf additions (*Additiones*), with its own title page, dated 1543. *The Aldine Press* (see note 7), n° 308 (p. 210): "without the separate section containing the additions (with title page dated 1543) issued with the 1542 edition of the Dictionary." The wording »appendix additionum« suggests that precisely this is being described. There is another, if remote, possibility. The first edition of Paulus's own *Additamenta* to the dictionary appeared in 1558, more than doubling the size of the composite publication (1558.7); if the entry were for this, which I believe it is not, it would provide a misleading terminus ante quem non for our manuscript catalogue.

195 The choices are not quite endless, since the cataloguer (Gesner) wrote this in the late 1540s. Then again, Paulus commented Cicero's philosophical works the least of any Ciceronian category, so RENOUARD (see note 7), 1546.11 and 1546.12, which are 8vos, are virtually the sole firm citations one can make. *The Aldine Press* (see note 7), nos. 354/5 (p. 230), HRHRC (see note 10), nos. 313/4 (pp. 282/3).

Commentarii delle chose de Turchi, de Paulo Giovio & Andrea Gambini, con gli fatti & la vita di Scanderbeg. in 8. A[nno]. 1541.[196]

De itineribus ex urbe Veneta in Persiam, Tanam & Constantinopolim, liber Italicus in 8.[197]

Lexicon Italicum difficiliorum praesertim & rariorum dictionum, quibus Bocatius & alii utuntur. in fol.[198]

M. Antonii Flaminii (si bene memini) explanatio in Psalmos.[199]

Huc usque sic se habet supra scriptus Catalogus./.[200]

---

196 RENOUARD (see note 7), 1541.11. The scribe's aspirated »chose« would represent a hard *c* for a German-speaker. Gesner reads delle cose, following the title page. Note the correct spelling of Scanderbeg, versus the title page's erroneous Scanderberg. Gesner's entry carries the correct form of the name, and »anno« is spelled out in full, with lower-case a.

197 RENOUARD (see note 7), 1543.8 and 1545.18 (i.e., *Viaggi fatti da Venezia ...* by GIOSOFAT BARBARO, AMBROGIO CONTARINI, LUIGI DI GIOVANNI, ET AL.). 1543 ed.: *The Aldine Press* (see note 7), nº 317; HRHRC (see note 10), nº 292. 1545 ed.: *The Aldine Press*, nº 338; HRHRC, nos. 305 & 305a.

198 RENOUARD (see note 7), 1543.2. FRANCESCO ALUNNO: *Le Ricchezze della lingua volgare ...* was reprinted more specifically as *Le Ricchezze della lingua volgare . . . sopra il Boccaccio* (RENOUARD, 1551.7), but this latter edition was published some three years after the *Pandectae*. 1543 ed.: *The Aldine Press* (see note 7), nº 312 (p. 212); 1551 ed.: *The Aldine Press*, nº 404 (p. 250). Gesner reads Boccatius.

199 RENOUARD (see note 7), 1545.1; a later edition (1564.2) is unlikely to be at issue. The aside appears within slashes, which I have replicated as parentheses; in Gesner, the phrase is set off by commas. The implication of the phrase is that Gesner wrote this entry from memory, which is another curious matter; whatever the nature of his comment, he remembered correctly.

200 I.e., Gesner's printed catalogue, which concludes about a third of the way down folio 109 recto, followed by a contents listing of the sections of Book XI.

ANDRÁS NÉMETH

Willibald Pirckheimer and his Greek codices from Buda

New data on the manuscripts used for the first editions of several Greek Patristic works

AMONG HIS VARIOUS HONORABLE ACTIVITIES, Willibald Pirckheimer (1470–1530), a distinguished humanist scholar from Nuremberg, is known as the editor and translator of a number of Greek authors who became accessible through his Latin and German translations for a large readership during the first decades of the sixteenth century.[1] His portrait made by Albrecht Dürer in 1524 expresses their close friendship and the artist's gratitude to his patron [see fig. 1]. His extensive correspondence reflects an exceptional network which connected him with almost all prominent humanist scholars of his age from Austria, Bavaria, Switzerland, Silesia, and the Netherlands.[2] Relying on his broad horizon of education and knowledge, Pirckheimer possessed a good sense for collecting books and artefacts. After studying law in Italy (Padua and Pavia), he became one of the few collectors in the German-speaking countries who attempted to acquire a copy from each printed Greek edition produced in the printing shop of the famous Venetian printer, Aldus Manutius.[3] The ex libris that Pirckheimer pasted onto his printed volumes – which was designed by his friend Albrecht Dürer – expressed both his devotion and philological sensitivity through its use of the proverb »Initium sapientiae timor Domini« ("The fear of the Lord is the source of wisdom"; Prov. 1:7), featured in Hebrew, Greek and Latin above the coats of arms of Pirckheimer and his wife, Crescentia.[4]

Historians studying the provenance of the Arundel collection in the British Library maintain the view that Pirckheimer managed to acquire a substantial part of the famous humanist library of the Hungarian King, Matthias Corvinus, called the Corvina library.[5] The enigmatic story about

This study is the part of the "Corvina Graeca" project (K 75693), supported by the Hungarian Scientific Research Fund, OTKA.

1 On Willibald Pirckheimer with detailed bibliography, see WILLEHAD PAUL ECKERT / CHRISTOPH VON IMHOF: *Willibald Pirckheimer Dürers Freund im Spiegel seines Lebens seiner Werke und seiner Umwelt*. Cologne 1971. – Cf. also NIKLAS HOLZBERG: *Willibald Pirckheimer: Griechischer Humanismus in Deutschland*. Munich 1981.

2 Pirckheimer's correspondence was published in seven volumes. *Willibald Pirckheimers Briefwechsel*. Ed. EMIL REICKE, ARNOLD REIMANN, HELGA SCHEIBLE and DIETER WUTTKE. Munich 1940– 2009 (henceforth, REICKE = vol. 2, SCHEIBLE / WUTTKE = vol. 3, SCHEIBLE 2004 = vol. 6, SCHEIBLE 2009 = vol. 7).

3 Cf. JULIUS SCHÜCK: *Aldus Manutius und seine Zeitgenossen in Italien und Deutschland*. Berlin 1862, p. 57.

4 Cf. LES GRONBERG: The Cover. In: *The Journal of Library History*. 19 (1984), pp. 426–30, here pp. 426/7.

5 In 1739 William Maitland described the origin of volumes that were donated to the Royal Society by Henry Arundel. "This collection originally was (kept at the City of *Buda*) Part of the Royal Library, belonging to the Kings of *Hungary*; which, upon the Demise of *Matthias Corvinus*, the last king of the *Hungarian* Race, was dispos'd of; about Two Thirds whereof being bought by the Emperor, they are now in the Imperial Library at Vienna; and this Part coming to *Bilibaldus Perkeymberus* of *Nuremberg*, it was bought of him by the Earl of *Arundel*, on his Return from his Embassy to the Imperial Court." WILLIAM MAITLAND: *The history of London: from its foundation by the Romans, to the present time*. London 1739, p. 656. On his description, see LINDA LEVY PECK: Uncovering the Arundel Library at the Royal Society: Changing Meanings of Science and the Fate of the Norfolk Donation. In: *Notes and Records of the Royal Society of London*. 52 (1998), pp. 3–24, here pp. 6–8, notes 17, 22, and 23.

[Fig. 1] The engraving of Willibald Pirckheimer by Albrecht Dürer 1524 (18,2 × 11,4 cm)

Pirckheimer's acquisitions from the Corvina library seems to have originated in the seventeenth century,[6] thereafter developing into a widespread view through a series of inexplicit references.[7] Despite the common view disseminated in various handbooks, there is not a single manuscript in the Arundel collection that wears traces of an origin from the royal library of Buda.[8]

When Pirckheimer died, he did not leave a male heir. Thus, Pirckheimer's possessions went to the hands of his sister, Caritas Pirckheimer, and his daughters. First, it was his daughter, Barbara, married to Hans Straub, who acquired Pirckheimer's goods. When she died without children in 1560, Pirckheimer's possessions passed on to the hands of Willibald Imhoff, his grandson from his daughter Felicitas' side.[9] After Willibald Imhoff's death in 1580, some items of the art collection were transported to the imperial court of Prague. However, the entire book collection remained in Nuremberg. From among this rich collection, 14 printed volumes (11 incunabula and three sixteenth-century prints) were sold to a Dutch antiquarian, Matthaeus van Overbeck, in 1634.[10] It was Thomas Howard, Earl of Arundel (1585–1646), who purchased the majority of Pirckheimer's books in 1636 in Nuremberg.[11] His grandson, Henry Howard, Duke of Norfolk (1628–84) enriched the collection he had inherited from his grandfather. After returning from his European tour, Henry Howard finally donated his entire book collection to the Royal Society in 1667.[12] On the one hand, the Royal Society sold the manuscripts in Western languages in 1830–32 and the Eastern manuscripts in 1835 to the British Library, the British Library created the so-called Arundel collection from these acquisitions. Some of Pirckheimer's manuscripts, however, must

6 William Perry, the first "Library Keeper" of the Royal Society, the compiler of the 1681 catalogue (see note 12), mentioned the Corvina Library as a major source of the Arundel collection. JOHN WARD: *The Lives of the Professors of Gresham College*. London 1740, pp. 232/3. This myth may have originated from Henry Howard himself who visited Hungary where he met Peter Lambeck who showed great interest in the Corvina volumes and had much knowledge on this subject due to his activities in the HofB in Vienna. On their meeting, see NOÉMI VISKOLCZ: Peter Lambeck budai utazása a corvinákért 1666-ban. In: *Magyar Könyvszemle* [Hungarian Book Review]. 125 (2009), pp. 149–188, here pp. 159–61.

7 CHARLES ISAAC ELTON, MARY AUGUSTA ELTON: *The Great Book Collectors*. London 1893, p. 86 (reprint: Fairford 2009, pp. 44/5). The information about the origin of the "Arundel collection" from King Matthias library relies on the description of the Gresham College Library William Oldys (1697–1761) compiled in the first half of the eighteenth century. *A literary antiquary. Memoir of William Oldys. Together with his diary, choice notes from his Adversaria, and an account of the London libraries*. London 1862, pp. 79–80. The same notion appears in WILLIAM HENRY BLACK: *Catalogue of the Arundel manuscripts in the library of the College of Arms*. [not published] London 1829, p. ix; *Catalogue of Manuscripts of the British Museum*. New Series. Vol. I. Part I. *The Arundel Manuscripts*. London 1840, p. v. Following these references, book historians often emphasized the Corvina library in the context of Pirckheimer and the "Arundel collection".

8 It is possible that volumes of Hungarian origin will be identified within the Arundel collection. However, the volumes themselves do not provide physical evidence: none of the volumes is bound in Corvina binding or is furnished with the coat of arms of Matthias Corvinus. The only basis of such a provenance can be Pirckheimer's correspondence or his editions and translations. Such volumes may occur among mss Arundel 516–49. Cf. DAVID PAISEY: Searching for Pirckheimer's books in the remains of the Arundel Library at the Royal Society. In: Enea Silvio Piccolomini nördlich der Alpen: Akten des interdisziplinären Symposions vom 18. bis 19. Nov. 2005 an der Ludwig-Maximilians-Universität München. Ed. FRANZ FUCHS. Wiesbaden 2007 (*Pirckheimer Jahrbuch für Renaissance und Humanismusforschung*. 22), pp. 159–218 (on Pirckheimer's activity as a collector and his library, see pp. 161–75). He inherited a Greek manuscript from his father, Johann Pirckheimer, who had acquired it from Johann Tröster, a city councillor in Nuremberg (Arundel 526). Cf. PAUL LEHMANN: Dr. Johann Tröster ein humanistisch gesinnter Wohltäter bayerischer Büchersammlungen. In: *Historisches Jahrbuch*. 60 (1940), pp. 646–63, here pp. 662/3. In Nuremberg, W. Pirckheimer also acquired two other Greek manuscripts from Johannes Löffelholz (Arundel 517, 525). Cf. THOMAS SMITH PATTIE / SCOT MCKENDRICK: *Summary Catalogue of Greek manuscripts in the British Library*. London 1999, pp. 4/5 and 8/9.

9 Cf. PATTIE / MCKENDRICK (see note 8), pp. 1–25 and PAISEY (see note 8), p. 163.

10 Cf. ERWIN ROSENTHAL: Dürers Buchmalereien für Pirckheimers Bibliothek. Berlin 1928 (*Jahrbuch der Preuszischen Kunstsammlungen*. 49), pp. 2/3. Cf. also EMIL OFFENBACHER: La Bibliothèque de Wilibald Pirckheimer. In: *La Bibliofilia*. 40 (1938), pp. 241–63.

have left the collection rather early and drifted though different channels of owners. On the other hand, Pirckheimer's printed books remained at the Royal Society that sold some of these volumes to Bernard Quaritch, antiquarian in London, in 1873; the majority of the rest was sold at Sotheby's in London in 1925.[13]

Despite the lack of manuscripts and printed volumes of Buda origin in the Arundel collection, it has become obvious that Pirckheimer was well informed regarding the Greek holdings of the royal library at Buda. Scholars studying the Corvina library used to mention Pirckheimer in the context of four Greek codices: Firstly, it was through the secretary Jacobus Banissius in 1514 that Emperor Maximilian I (1459–1519) sent his request to Pirckheimer, asking him to translate the Greek *World Chronicle* by Johannes Monachus (Zonaras), which was transported by Johannes Cuspinianus from Buda in 1513, into Latin.[14] First, Pirckheimer refused the imperial request, being busy with his other duties.[15] Later on, Cuspinianus ceased to deliver the valuable Zonaras manuscript.[16] Secondly, the other volume Pirckheimer was well informed about was a valuable humanist copy of the *Geography* by Ptolemy, frequently referred to by humanist scholars visiting the Buda court since the end of the fifteenth century.[17] The German humanist Ulrich von Hutten provided valuable data on the variant readings of the Buda *Geography* manuscript in 1518 to Pirckheimer who was preparing a Ptolemy edition that time.[18]

This study strives to explore the other two manuscripts with an origin from Buda, which are known to scholars studying the Corvina library as two of the "lost" Corvinas.[19] Their significance appears in the fact that these two manuscripts proved influential in the early Reformation by

---

11 On Hans Heronymus Imhoff's 1636 sale to Thomas Howard, see ROSENTHAL (see note 10), pp. 51/2.

12 On the volumes donated by Henry Howard, see [WILLIAM PERRY]: *Bibliotheca Norfolciana, sive, Catalogus libb. manuscriptorum & impressorum in omni arte & lingua quos illustriss princeps Henricus Dux Norfolciae, &c.; Regiae societati Londinensi pro scientia naturali promovenda donavit*. London 1681.

13 On the volumes returned to Germany, cf. ROSENTHAL (see note 10), p. 4. On the considerable part which remained in possession of the Royal Society, London (Carlton House Terrace), cf. PAISEY (see note 8), pp. 160 and 185–218.

14 The Zonaras manuscript is now in Vienna, ÖNB, hist. gr. 16. See Emperor Maximilian's letter to W. Pirckheimer through his secretary Jacobus Banissius (Gmuden, 20.08.1514) in REICKE (see note 2), n° 328, pp. 454–6.

15 See the letter by Beatus Rhenanus to W. Pirckheimer after July 1515 in REICKE (see note 2), n° 364, pp. 560–2.

16 In a letter (dated 16.05.1515), W. Pirckheimer asked J. Cuspinianus to send him the Zonaras codex. *Johann Cuspinians Briefwechsel*. Ed. HANS ANKWICZ-KLEEHOVEN. Munich 1933, n° 31, pp. 67/8. In a letter (dated 18.10.1518), J. Cuspinianus excused himself for not sending the manuscript. REICKE (see note 2), n° 372, pp. 577/8.

17 ÖNB, hist. gr. 1. See its description in JULIUS HERMANN: *Beschreibendes Verzeichnis der illuminierten Handschriften in Österreich*. VI. *Die Handschriften und Inkunabeln der italienischen Renaissance*. 3. *Mittelitalien: Toskana, Umbrien, Rom*. Leipzig 1932, n° 11, pp. 19–21, table IV. – Cf. also *Katalog der griechischen Handschriften*. Ed. HERBERT HUNGER. Vienna 1961–94, vol. 1, p. 1 and ERNST GAMILLSCHEG / BRIGITTE MERSICH: *Matthias Corvinus und die Bildung der Renaissance*. Vienna 1994, Cat. n° 29, pp. 69/70. Conrad Celtis ordered a copy for himself. This direct copy, made in 1482 in Buda, is now in Oxford, Bodleian L, Arch. Selden B 45. On f. 1ʳ, the scribe wrote: »ὁ Ἰοάννης Ἀθεσινος δοῦλος ποιητὴς Κονραδα Κέλτις Γερμανου γεγραφα ἐν ἔτει αυπβ', In Buda inferioris Pannoniae«. At the end of the copied text (f. 176ᵛ, lower margin), the scribe repeated the colophon of the Vienna Ptolemy (ÖNB, hist. gr. 1, f. 98ᵛ). Cf. HENRY OCTAVIUS COXE: *Bodleian Library, Quarto Catalogues*, I. *Greek manuscripts*. Oxford 1853, p. 603. On the humanists' correspondence regarding this copy of Ptolemy' *Geography*, see CSABA CSAPODI: *The Corvinian Library: History and Stock*. Budapest 1973, n° 554.

18 Pirckheimer's edition of the Latin translation of Ptolemy's *Geography* came to light in Strasbourg in 1525 (VD16 P 5211). Ulrich von Hutten mentioned in his letter (Augsburg, 25.10.1518) that Sigmund von Herberstein, an envoy from Vienna to Moscow, visited Buda and consulted a Greek Ptolemy manuscript, which can be identified as the Vienna Ptolemy. SCHEIBLE / WUTTKE (see note 2), n° 561, pp. 400–25 (especially p. 420, ll. 714–6).

19 Cf. CSAPODI (see note 17), n° 306: the codex with more than 50 works by Gregory of Nazianzus; n° 107: the codex with the epistles by Gregory of Nazianzus and Basil the Great, both as lost Corvinas. PECK (see note 5), p. 17 and VISKOLCZ (see note 6), p. 161.

providing material for first printed editions of several Patristic works (both in original Greek and Latin translation). Thus, it seems equally helpful for a deeper understanding of the role the Greek Church Fathers played in the formation of King Matthias' library and for the identification of these manuscripts to analyze the various contexts which correlate these two codices with Pirckheimer. As a main contribution of this study, solid arguments will be provided, for the first time, that one of the two "lost" Corvinas can in fact be identified as Vienna, ÖNB, suppl. gr. 177. Concerning the other codex, relying on Przychocki's and Crimi's results (see below), I will provide additional arguments that it can be identified as ms Oxford, Corpus Christi College (henceforth, CCC), 284. This identification, although first suggested almost one hundred years ago, has remained unknown to the scholars of the Corvina library. In order to go beyond the single references mentioning that each of the two manuscripts derived from Buda royal library, I collected the entire series of references mentioning either of the two "lost" Corvinas. The data thus amassed have been cross-checked with the candidate manuscripts themselves and the various editions and Latin translations of the early sixteenth century. This new method resulted in the successful identification of both manuscripts.

A new authentic Corvina: the archetype of Pirckheimer's translation of the homilies by Gregory of Nazianzus

One of the documents mentioning the origin from Buda was Pirckheimer's letter (15 May, 1529) to Georg Spalatin (1484–1545),[20] a Lutheran theologian. In this letter, Pirckheimer referred to a Greek manuscript obtained from the booty of Hungary.

> And I am sending you the homily by Gregory of Nazianzus "On the bishop's duty" [or. 2] as well, in order to show you how I can heal gout. In addition, a Greek codex by the same Gregory came to my hands, from the booty of Hungary, which contains more than fifty works by this very holy and learned man. If God permits, I will translate more of these works into Latin although I am almost always sick.[21]

The codex mentioned here was registered on the list of the lost Corvina volumes; neither the scholars studying the Corvina library,[22] nor those

---

20 Cf. IRMGARD HÖSS: *Georg Spalatin, 1484–1545: ein Leben in der Zeit des Humanismus und der Reformation.* 2nd, revised and enlarged ed. Weimar 1989.

21 SCHEIBLE 2009 (see note 2), nº 1227, pp. 210–2 (Pirckheimer's letter to Georg Spalatin: Nuremberg, 15. 05. 1529; ll. 34–40): »Interim mitto orationem Nazianzeni De officio episcopi [oration 2, VD 16 G 3073: Nuremberg, 1529], ut videas, quemadmodum podagram meam consoler. Nactus praetera sum codicem graecum eiusdem Gregorii ex Ungariae spoliis ultra quinquaginta opuscula eiusdem sanctissimi et doctissimi viri continentem. Ex quibus, si deus voluerit, pleraque latine eloqui incipiam, licet assidue fere aegrotem.«

22 Cf. CSAPODI (see note 17), nos. 306 and 307 as lost Corvinas.

23 Cf. HOLZBERG (see note 1), pp. 352/3 and 358/9 (!) notes 405/6.

24 Cf. JULIUS KÖSTLIN: Johann Heß, der Breslauer Reformator. In: *Zeitschrift des Vereins für Geschichte und Alterthum Schlesiens.* 6 (1864), pp. 97–131 and 181–265. – ADOLF HENSCHEL: *Dr. Johannes Heß der Breslauer Reformator.* Halle 1901. – GEORG KRETSCHMAR: Johann Heß. In: ADB, vol. 9, pp. 7/8.

25 SCHEIBLE 2009 (see note 2), nº 1219, pp. 190–2 (Johannes Heß's letter to W. Pirckheimer: Wrocław, 04. 04. 1529) »S⟨alutem⟩. Indicem thesauri verius quam libri ideo ad te opt⟨imum⟩ patronum misi, ut mecum gauderes graciasque ageres deo nostro, quod haec dona ex media Grecia nobis largitus est et Nazianzenum vetustiss⟨imum⟩ servavit utcunque et nostris oculis, licet non omni ex parte integrum (desunt enim aliquae membranae). [...] Magnum hoc volumen vel hodie mecum est (est enim vel precipium ornamentum ornatissimae meae bibliothecae). [...] Sunt qui iurarent viso volumine vel ipsa etate autoris librum scriptum«.

26 Cf. SCHEIBLE 2009 (see note 2), nº 1324, pp. 419/20 (Johannes Heß's letter to Pirckheimer: Wrocław, 13. 10. 1530; ll. 4–11) »Tacui itaque ad aliquot menses, ut nihil litterarum ad tuam mag.⟨am⟩ darem. Nunc autem nacta oportunitate rupto silencio cogor esse sollicitus pro meo Nazianzeno, quem indies expecto non solum grece sed et latine loquentem.

constructing Pirckheimer's biography[23] have hitherto managed to identify the manuscript.

Another letter by Pirckheimer reveals that it was Johannes Heß (1490–1547),[24] a humanist theologian in Wrocław, who sent Pirckheimer the substantial Gregory codex between 4 April and 15 May, 1529, in order to help him complete the translations of some homilies by Gergory of Nazianzus he published during the previous years. The edition comprising Pirckheimer's new translations based on Heß's manuscript only came out in print in 1531 after Pirckheimer's death.

> I am sending to you, my great patron, a register, which seems to be an inventory of treasures rather than a register of the contents of a book. I hope that you share my pleasures and express gratitude to God for giving these gifts from the middle of Greece into our hands and for rescuing this ancient Gregory of Nazianzus volume as if it were only for our eyes. The volume is not intact (it has lost some parchment leaves) […] This huge volume is with me today (an exceptional gem of my magnificent library) […] When observing the volume, some people insist that the book was copied in the times of its author [i.e. Gregory of Nazianzus].[25]

After receiving the codex, Pirckheimer seems to have kept it with him in Nuremberg at least until mid-October 1530.[26] However, it must have been returned to Heß as Philipp Melanchthon (1497–1560) mentioned in his letter to Heß that Joachim Camerarius was using Heß's volume in 1543.[27]

About the codex sent to Pirckheimer, Heß mentioned that he obtained the outstanding manuscript from the middle of Greece (»ex media Grecia«). This statement seems to parallel another expression in which Pirckheimer described the provenance of the other manuscript credited with an origin from Buda (»qui e miseranda Graecia«),[28] as well as the phrasing Johannes Alexander Brassicanus used in the impressive description of his astonishing encounter with the royal library at Buda court (»ex media Graecia«).[29] Based on the similarity of these phrases and their contexts, the phrase »ex media Graecia« does not seem to report on the direct provenance of the manuscripts in concern. It rather seems to have emphasized that these codices were not brand new Italian copies but old ones manufactured in the Greek-speaking world, i.e., in the Byzantine

Hanc enim spem meam nuper auxit epistola Uldarici Zasii doctissimi viri ad tuam mag.⟨am⟩ scripta, in qua gracias agit pro translacione Nazianzeni«.

27 On Johannes Heß's library, see PAUL LEHMANN: Aus der Bibliothek des Reformators Johannes Hessius. In: *Aus der Welt des Buches: Festgabe zum 70. Geburtstag von Georg Leyh*. Leipzig 1950, pp. 100–24 (on the lost codex comprising the works by Gregory of Nazianzus, see p. 105). »Tuus codex Nazianzeni est penes Camerarium, ut opinor. Nam Basileae habent similem, et ut audio, locupletiorem. Perspexi totum, et quamquam monumentum est dignum bibliothecis, propter controversiam de trinitate, tamen praeter eam causam, non multa continent διδασκαλικά«.

Philippi Melanchthonis opera quae supersunt omnia: epistolae, praeformationes, consilia. Ed. CAROLUS GOTTLIEB BRETSCHNEIDER. Halle 1838. Reprint New York 1963 (*Corpus Reformatorum*. 5), n° 2655, coll. 56/7.

28 In the preface to the translation of St Nilus' sentences, Pirckheimer mentioned the provenance of the Greek codex he used. As will be demonstrated below, this manuscript seems to have passed through Buda, yet Pirckheimer emphasizes an origin from Greece. REICKE (see note 2), n° 377, pp. 596–8 (Pirckheimer's letter to Clara Pirckheimer: Nuremberg, 29. 12. 1515): »codicem pervetustum, qui e miseranda Graecia elapsus captivitatis iugum evaserat«.

29 »Tantum erat hic antiquorum, graecorum simul & hebraicorum voluminum, quae Matthias ille rex capta iam Constantinopoli, eversisque multis amplissimis Graeciae urbibus, ex media Graecia inaestimandis sumptibus coemerat, ac tanquam mancipia ex barbarorum catastis atque compedibus receperat«. This sentence is cited from the preface to the edition of Salvianus by Alexander Brassicanus (Basle 1530: VD 16 S 1511, f. a₃ʳ).

[Fig. 2] Upper cover of the ms ÖNB suppl. gr. 177 (37 × 24 cm, »G. NAZIANZENUS GRECE AN MDXXVIII«), prepared by Jannes Heß's binder in Wrocław; the coat of arms of Johannes Heß features in the center (in a medallion a lion standing on his hind legs with an inscription »ARMA HESSICA ANNO 1525«)

Empire. At the same time, the expressions reflect the topos of rescuing the Greek manuscripts conquered by the Barbarians from slavery.[30] Thus, Heß's statement on the "Greek origin" of the Gregory of Nazianzus manuscript does not necessarily negate Pirckheimer's implicit statement that the same manuscript passed through Hungary. Keeping this interpretation in mind, I have read through Pirckheimer's extensive correspondence, which convinced me to identify the codex as a manuscript in Vienna (ÖNB, suppl. gr. 177). In addition to Pirckheimer's letters, the Viennese manuscript itself provided evidence verifying that the codex was in fact in the royal library at Buda in the 1480s. The method of identification which has confirmed Pirckheimer's information may also help complete the scarce evidence which so far has proved insufficient to define the nature of the relationship of some other manuscripts with the Buda royal library.

The method of identification

First of all, the fact that Johannes Heß was the possessor of the manuscript ÖNB suppl. gr. 177 supports the identification. As mentioned above, it was the same humanist who sent the codex to Pirckheimer. The centers of the upper and lower covers of the Viennese Gregory hold Johannes Heß's coat of arms [see fig. 2]. At the top of the upper cover, the date of binding (1528) appears with the inscription »G. NAZIANZENUS GRECE AN MDXXVIII«. It seems that the Viennese Gregory was bound in its present binding two years after the disastrous battle of Mohács and one year before Johannes Heß delivered the manuscript to Pirckheimer in the "restored form".

In addition, Pirckheimer's biographer Holzberg already noticed that a list among Pirckheimer's documents (BL Arundel 175, ff. 37r–38r),[31] which comprises the contents of a Gregory of Nazianzus manuscript, provides a clue for the identification of the "lost" Greek Gregory manuscript Pirckheimer frequently alluded to in his correspondence. Holzberg thought that this list was the one Heß sent to Pirckheimer together with his letter (April 4, 1529). Holzberg could not find an extant manuscript based on the register of its contents.[32] However, if we carefully compare this list with the contents of all the extant codices[33] containing the homilies by Gregory of Nazianzus it will turn out that only a tenth-century codex, now in Vienna (ÖNB, suppl. gr. 177), embraces Gregory's

---

30 This is why I cannot accept the views of basic handbooks, based on Brassicanus' statement, which say that King Matthias acquired Greek manuscripts from Greece. If such acquisitions took place, Brassicanus could not have known about them.

31 HOLZBERG (see note 1), p. 356–8. London, BL Arundel 175, ff. 37r–38r (see its description in PAUL OSKAR KRISTELLER: *Iter Italicum*. Vol. 4. Leiden etc. 1989, p. 128). SCHEIBLE 2009 (see note 1), nº 1219, pp. 190–2 (Johannes Heß' letter to Pirckheimer: Wrocław, 04.04.1529): »Indicem thesauri verius quam libri ideo ad te opt⟨imum⟩ patronum misi«.

32 HOLZBERG (see note 1), p. 91 did not find any notes by Pirckheimer in ms London, BL Arundel 549 (245 folia), which contains the homilies by Gregory of Nazianzus. This volume is only half as large as the volume with more than 50 works by Gregory. At the same time, the sequence of these works is different from that of the list preserved in Pirckheimer bequest. For these two reasons, ms Arundel 549 cannot be the manuscript Pirckheimer used.

33 I. R. H. T. Pinakes. Available online. See index of websites on p. 374.

34 See the descriptions of the manuscript in HERBERT HUNGER / CHRISTIAN HANNICK: Katalog der griechischen Handschriften der österreichischen Nationalbibliothek. Vol. 4. Supplementum Graecum. Vienna 1994 (*Museion: Veröffentlichungen der Handschriftensammlung*. NF 1,4), nº 177, pp. 304–10. – MARIA LUISA AGATI: *La minuscula «bouletée»*. Vatican City 1992, vol. 1, pp. 147/8, plate: vol. 2, p. 100. – EDUARD GOLLOB: Verzeichnis der griechischen Handschriften in Österreich außerhalb Wiens mit 11 Tafeln. Vienna 1903 (*Sitzungsberichte. Akademie der Wissenschaften in Wien, Philolosophisch-Historische Klasse*. 146.7), pp. 81–6. – *Bibliothek Fürst Dietrichstein Schloss Nikolsburg*,

more than fifty works in the same sequence as summarized in the register mentioned above.³⁴ In addition to the content being identical with the register, the list itself appears a faithful rendering of the tenth-century Greek majuscule text in ÖNB suppl. gr. 177, ff. 2/3, almost a facsimile copy. The paper used for the register possesses a watermark originating from the paper-mill of Wrocław.³⁵ These aspects also verify Holzberg's view that the exemplar behind the register, namely ms ÖNB, suppl. gr. 177, was used by Pirckheimer for his Latin translations from Gregory of Nazianzus. It is these works that were published in Froben's printing shop in Basle in 1531, under the supervision of Pirckheimer's son-in-law, Hans Straub.³⁶

The first table [table 1] summarizes how Pirckheimer's translation (Basle 1531) depended on ms ÖNB, suppl. gr. 177. The sequence of the homilies in the first third of the 1531 edition does not follow that of the Viennese codex; some clusters still demonstrate the direct interdependence between the two (e.g., *or.* 8, 6, 23). The fact that in each case the homilies are partially organized in a different sequence might be explained by the following hypothesis: the codex used by Pirckheimer was returned to Heß before Straub started to organize Pirckheimer's translations which he must have put together in an order different from that of the codex he was working from (Straub may have neglected the register sent by Heß).³⁷ In two thirds of the 1531 edition, however, the translated homilies are arranged in a sequence (pp. 163–304) identical with that of the Viennese codex (ff. 179ʳ–497ᵛ); only those homilies were omitted which had already been published (1521, 1528, and 1529)³⁸ or which had been accessible in the translation by Petrus Mosellanus. The content of the Viennese codex sheds light on the surprising phenomena that a poem, numbered as Homily xxix, and four letters (*ep.* 101, 102, 202, and 243) were inserted among the translated homilies in a sequence identical with that of the Viennese Gregory.

In addition, Straub appended the homilies of Gregory, published in 1521 and 1528 in Pirckheimer's translation, subsequent to the new corpus of translations (pp. 1–126).³⁹ Moreover, Straub inserted Pirckheimer's translation of the *Life of Gregory of Nazianzus* by Gregorius Presbyter which also seems to have been based on the text of ÖNB suppl. gr. 177 (ff. 512ʳ–530ʳ = pp. 1–23).⁴⁰ Apart from the partially different sequence of the homilies, all previously unpublished works of ms ÖNB, suppl. gr. 177

Versteigerung am 21. und 22. November 1933, Luzern. Ed. H. GILHOFER & H. RANSCH-BURG AG. Luzern 1933, nº 407, p. 82. On the position of the codex in the manuscript transmission, see *Gregorii Presbyteri Vita Sancti Gregorii Theologii.* Ed. XAVIER LEQUEUX. Turnhout 2001 (Corpus Christianorum. Series Graeca. 41), pp. 84/5. – VÉRONIQUE SOMERS: *Histoire des collections complètes des Discours de Grégoire de Nazianianze.* Louvain-la-Neuve 1997, pp. 77, 129, 368–74 (it is marked as siglum x7).

35 The watermark is the head of St John the Baptist, the patron saint of Wrocław featuring in a shield round in base (4,2 × 3,5 cm). I owe Jenő Pelbárt, the president of the Hungarian Paper and Watermark Association, a debt of gratitude for the identification from his database (cf. similar types MVA 4355/6, both from archival material dated to 1536). On the paper-mill in Wrocław, see GEORG EINEDER: *The Ancient Paper-Mills of the Former Austro-Hungarian Empire and their watermarks.* Hilversum 1960. Vol. VIII. pp. 145, 147.

36 VD 16 G 3082.

37 The foliation of ÖNB suppl. gr. 177 appears in parentheses: VD 16 G 3082, pp. 1–23 (ff. 512ʳ–530ʳ), pp. 23–5 (ff. 39ᵛ–41ᵛ), pp. 25–30 (ff. 82ᵛ–87ᵛ), pp. 30–3 (ff. 80ʳ–82ᵛ), pp. 30–3 (ff. 80ʳ–82ᵛ), pp. 33–5 (ff. 88ʳ–90ᵛ), pp. 36–43 (ff. 123ᵛ–130ᵛ), pp. 43–56 (ff. 41ᵛ–53ʳ), pp. 56–94 (ff. 138ʳ–179ʳ), pp. 94–119 (ff. 53ᵛ–79ᵛ), pp. 119–26 (ff. 356ʳ–363ʳ), pp. 126–57 (ff. 91ʳ–123ʳ), pp. 157–62 (ff. 131ʳ–136ᵛ), pp. 163–304 (ff. 179ʳ–500ʳ).

38 1521 (VD 16 G 3038): *or.*38–41, 44, 45; 1528 (VD 16 G 3081): *or.*4/5; 1529 (VD 16 G 3073): *or.*2. On these editions, cf. HOLZBERG (see note 1), pp. 287–98, 343–51 and 352–62.

39 Gregory of Nazianzus, *or* 27–41.

40 SCHEIBLE 2009 (see note 2), nº 1288: Pirckheimer's letter (29.04.1530). Pirckhemer sent his translation of *the*

Work	Suppl. gr. 177 (ff.)	Suppl. gr. 177 (no.)	PG (coll.)	Basle 1531(pp.)	Basle 1531(no.)
or. 1	5ʳ – 6ʳ (fr.)	(Α')	35, 396–401	—	—
or. 2	6ᵛ – 39ʳ	(Β')	35, 408–514	(1529: VD16 G 3073)	—
or. 3	39ᵛ – 41ᵛ	(Γ')	35, 517–25	23–25	(I)
or. 7	41ᵛ – 53ʳ	(Δ')	35, 756–88	43–56	(VII)
or. 8	53ᵛ – 62ᵛ	(Ε')	35, 789–817	94–103	(IX)
or. 6	63ʳ – 73ᵛ	(ΣΤ')	35, 721–52	103–113	(X)
or. 23	74ʳ – 79ᵛ	(Ζ')	35, 1152–68	13–119	(XI)
or. 9	80ʳ – 82ᵛ	(Η')	35, 820–5	30–33	(IV)
or. 10	82ᵛ – 84ʳ	(Θ')	35, 828–32	25–27	(II)
or. 11	84ᵛ – 87ᵛ	(Ι')	35, 832–41	27–30	(III)
or. 12	88ʳ – 90ᵛ	(ΙΑ')	35, 844–9	33–35	(V)
or. 16	91ʳ – 101ᵛ	(ΙΒ')	35, 933–64	126–136	(XIII)
or. 18	102ʳ – 123ʳ	(ΙΓ')	35, 985–1044	136–157	(XIV)
or. 19	123ᵛ – 130ᵛ	(ΙΔ')	35, 1044–64	36–43	(VI)
or. 17	131ʳ – 136ᵛ	(ΙΕ')	35, 964–81	157–162	(XV)
or. 43	138ʳ – 179ʳ	(ΙΣΤ')	36, 943–605	56–94	(VIII)
or. 14	179ʳ – 198ʳ	(ΙΖ')	35, 857–909	163–181	(XVI)
or. 20	198ᵛ – 203ᵛ	(ΙΗ')	35, 1065–80	181–186	(XVII)
or. 27	204ʳ – 208ᵛ	(ΙΘ')	36, 12–25		—
or. 28	209ʳ – 226ʳ	(Κ')	36, 25–72		—
or. 29	226ʳ – 237ʳ	(ΚΑ')	36, 73–104	(P. Mosellanus)	—
or. 30	237ᵛ – 248ᵛ	(ΚΒ')	36, 104–33		—
or. 31	248ᵛ – 263ᵛ	(ΚΓ')	36, 133–72		—
or. 38	264ʳ – 271ʳ	(ΚΔ')	36, 312–33		—
or. 39	271ʳ – 280ʳ	(ΚΕ')	36, 336–60		—
or. 40	280ʳ – 302ʳ	(ΚΣΤ')	36, 360–425	(1521: VD16 G 3038)	—
or. 45	302ʳ – 315ᵛ	(ΚΖ')	36, 624–64		—
or. 44	315ᵛ – 319ʳ	(ΚΗ')	36, 608–21		—
or. 41	320ʳ – 327ᵛ	(ΚΘ')	36, 428–52		—
or. 21	327ᵛ – 342ʳ	(Λ')	35, 1081–128	186–201	(XVIII)
or. 24	342ʳ – 349ᵛ	(ΛΑ')	35, 1169–93	201–210	(XIX)
or. 15	349ᵛ – 356ʳ	(ΛΒ')	35, 912–33	210–217	(XX)
or. 22	356ʳ – 363ʳ	(ΛΓ')	35, 1132–52	119–126	(XII)
or. 32	363ʳ – 376ʳ	(ΛΔ')	36, 173–212	217–231	(XXI)
or. 25	376ʳ – 385ᵛ	(ΛΕ')	35, 1197–225	231–240	(XXII)
or. 34	385ᵛ – 390ᵛ	(ΛΣΤ')	36, 241–56	240–245	(XXIII)
or. 33	390ᵛ – 397ᵛ	(ΛΖ')	36, 213–37	245–252	(XXIV)
or. 36	398ʳ – 401ᵛ (fr.)	(ΛΗ')	36, 265–380	253–258	(XXV)
or. 26	405 – 412ʳ	(ΛΘ')	35, 1228–52	258–267	(XXVI)
or. 42	412ʳ – 423ᵛ	(Μ')	36, 457–92	267–280	(XXVII)
ep. 101	424ʳ – 429ʳ	(ΜΑ')	37, 176–93	280–285	
ep. 102	429ʳ – 431ᵛ	(ΜΒ')	37, 193–201	286–288	
ep. 202	431ᵛ – 433ʳ	(ΜΓ')	37, 329–33	288–289	
or. 4	433ʳ – 470ᵛ	(ΜΔ')	35, 532–64	(1528: VD16 G 3081)	—
or. 5	471ʳ – 486ʳ	(ΜΕ')	35, 664–720		—
or. 13	486ᵛ – 487ᵛ	(ΜΣΤ')	35, 852–6	290–291	(XXVIII)
carm.I/2.3	487ᵛ – 489ʳ	(ΜΖ')	37, 632–40	291–293	(XXIX)
carm.I/1.32	489ʳ⁻ᵛ	(ΜΗ')	37, 511–4	—	
or. 37	489ᵛ – 497ᵛ	(—)	36, 281–308	293–302	(XXX)
ep.243	497ᵛ – 500ʳ	(ΜΘ')	46, 1101–8	302–304	
CPG 3060	500ʳ – 501ʳ	(Ν')	36, 665–9	—	—
A	501ʳ–511ʳ	(—)	10, 988–1017	—	—
B	512ʳ–530ʳ	(—)	35, 244–304	1–23	

feature in the 1531 Basle edition except for the texts on ff. 489ʳ⁻ᵛ, 500ʳ–511ʳ. It is only Homily 1 that was omitted in a way which requires explanation because it was not accessible in earlier translations. It is the physical state of the Viennese codex, a phenomenon also hinted at by Heß in the passage quoted above, that provides an answer. The fact that the first two folios (ff. 5/6), carrying Homily 1, are mutilated clarifies why Pirckheimer could not translate this homily into Latin. The other codex with a purported Hungarian origin was in the possession of Pirckheimer.

Oxford, Corpus Christi College (CCC), ms 284

In the Hagenau printing shop of Johannes Setzer,[41] Vincent Opsopoeus published the first Greek edition of the letters by Cappadocian fathers, Basil the Great and Gregory of Nazianzus in 1528. As a preface to the edition, a letter was inserted which Opsopoeus wrote to Pirckheimer in April 1528. In this letter, Opsopoeus described the direct provenance of the exemplar he used for the edition and clearly stated that it was a two-hundred-year-old codex, originating from the royal library of Buda.

> To Thou, most glorious lord, Bilibald Pirckheimer, patrician in Nuremberg, Vincent Opsopoeus [is sending his] greetings. Recently Georg Leutius transferred from your library, most glorious Pirckheimer, to me to study the codex comprising the letters by Basil and Gregory. I was excited to see it as much for the characters of the letters as for the old age of the volume, – because it was copied, as far as I can judge, at least two hundred years ago or even earlier, and was kept in the library of the Hungarian king –, and when I had become avidly engaged in reading the volume, I started to copy a few letters [...][42]

Based on Opsopoeus' statement on the Hungarian provenance of the exemplar used for the edition, Csaba Csapodi registered the volume among the lost Corvinas in his 1973 repertory under the names of »Basilius Magnus« and »Gregorius Nazianzenus«.[43] As far as the identification is concerned, there has not yet been any progress in the scholarly literature on the Corvina library.[44]

However, scholars studying the textual tradition of the two Church Fathers already suggested in the 1910s that the codex mentioned in Opsopoeus' letter can be identified as the fourteenth-century manuscript kept

[Table 1] Ms ÖNB suppl. gr. 177 and Pirckheimer's Latin translation of the homilies by Gregory of Nazianzus in the edition by Hans Straub (Basle 1531, VD 16 G 3082)

A Gregorius Thaumaturgus: *Metaphrasis in Ecclesiasticen*
B Gregorius Presbyter: *Vita Gregorii theologi*
CPG Maurice Geerard: *Clavis Patrum Graecorum*

Life of Gregory to G. Spalatin. HOLZBERG (see note 1), pp. 355–62 and cf. SCHEIBLE 2009 (see note 2), nº 1176.

41 KARL STEIFF: Johannes Setzer (Secerius), der gelehrte Buchdrucker in Hangenau. In: *Zentralblatt für Bibliothekswesen*. 9 (1892), pp. 297–317.

42 The letter by Vintentius Opsopoeus to W. Pirckheimer is attached as a preface to this edition: *Basilii Magni et Gregorii Nazianzeni, Theologorum, Epistolae Graecae, nunquam antea editae*. Hagenau: Johann Setzer, 1528. (VD 16 B 688). See the critical edition of the letter, in SCHEIBLE 2009 (see note 2), nº 1159, pp. 36–43. The cited passage is as follows: »Clarissimo viro domino Bilibalde Pyrckheimero, Patritie Norimbergensi, Vintentius Opspopoeus Sal⟨utem⟩. Cum nuper inspiciendum mihi obtulisset ex bibliotheca tua, Bilibalde clariss⟨ime⟩, Georgius Leutius codicem epistolarum Basilii et Gregorii, quem cum ob litterarum characteras, tum ob vetustatem vehementer videre cupiebam – est enim, ut mihi coniecturam facienti scribi est, ante ducentos aut amplius annos descriptus inque regis Ungariae bibliothecam repositus – in eo ergo cum avidissime versarer, coepi epistolas quoque aliquot excutere, [...]«.

43 CSAPODI (see note 17), nos. 107 and 307. On a possible identification of ms Munich, BSB cod. gr. 497, see HENRY SIMONSFELD: Einige kunst- und literaturgeschichtliche Funde. In: *Sitzungsberichte der philosophisch-philologischen und der historischen Classe der k. b. Akademie der Wissenschaften zu München*. (1902), pp. 521–68, here p. 550. WEINBERGER refused SIMONSFELD's suggestion based on the fact that cod. gr. 497 was purchased by the city council of Augsburg in 1545 from Antonius Eparchus in Venice. WILHELM WEINBERGER: Beiträge zur Handschriftenkunde. I. Die Bibliotheca Corvina. Wien 1908 (*Sitzungsberichte der Kaiserliche Akademie der Wissenschaften in Wien Philosophisch-Historische Klasse*. 159,6), p. 41.

44 ISTVÁN MONOK: La Bibliotheca Corviniana et les imprimés. In: *Mathias Corvin, les bibliothèques princières et la genèse de l'État moderne*. Ed. JEAN-FRANÇOIS MAILLARD, ISTVÁN MONOK and DONATELLA NEBBIAI. Budapest 2009, pp. 161–75, here p. 170.

in Oxford, CCC, ms 284.⁴⁵ A number of arguments such as the sequence of the letters, the age of the manuscript as well as the variant readings lead to the conclusion that among the extant manuscripts of letters of Basil and Gregory it is only ms 284 in Oxford, CCC that corresponds to Opsopoeus' description.⁴⁶

The first edition of the Epistles by Basil and Gregory

The 59 epistles by Basil the Great and the 80 epistles by Gregory of Nazianzus are mixed in a unique way in ms 284 CCC, Oxford. The table [table 2] shows the sequence of the epistles in ms 284 CCC, Oxford (columns 5/6) with references to its foliation (column 1), to the Greek numbers labelling the epistles in the manuscript (column 2), the page numbers in Opsopoeus' edition (Hagenau, 1528) (column 3 referred to with quire signatures), and the pagination of the edition by Erasmus of Rotterdam (Basle 1532: column 4).⁴⁷ Column 6 gives the number of the letters according to the modern editions. The sequence of the epistles in ms Oxford, CCC, 284 almost exactly follows the order found in the editions by Opsopoeus and Erasmus. There are only minor differences. On the one hand, Opsopoeus mistakenly omitted Epistle 8 by Basil. In addition, preceding Epistle 61 by Gregory, he jumped exactly ten leaves (ff. 276ʳ–286ʳ) with sixteen epistles on them; subsequent to Gregory, Epistle 61, Opsopoeus also failed to copy the last seven epistles in the codex (ff. 287ᵛ–292ᵛ). At the end of his edition, Opsopoeus published Basil, Epistle 8 that seems to have been omitted before (ff. Y₄ʳ–Z₇ᵛ) when compared to ms 284 CCC, Ox-

---

45 See its more detailed description – with a focus on the decoration – in IRMGARD HUTTER: Corpus der byzantinischen Miniaturenhandschriften. Vol. 5.1. Oxford College Libraries. Stuttgart 1997 (*Denkmäler der Buchkunst.* 13), n° 9, pp. 20–2.

46 Cf. GUSTAV PRZYCHOCKI: De Gregorii Nazienzeni epistularum codicibus Britannicis, qui Londinii, Oxoniae, Cantabrigiae asservantur. In: *Rozprawy Akademii Umiejętności Wydział Filologiczny.* 3.5 (1913), pp. 230–46, here p. 240. – STIG Y. RUDBERG: Études sur la tradition manuscrite de Saint Basil. Uppsala 1953, pp. 48–52. – GALLAY concluded that a manuscript close to ms Oxford, CCC 284 was the basis of the edition. PAUL GALLAY: *Les manuscrits des lettres de Saint Grégoire de Nazianze.* Paris 1957, pp. 50/1 and 105–9 (especially p. 106). – See also PAUL JONATHAN FEDWICK: *Bibliotheca Basiliana Universalis: A Study of the Manuscript Tradition, Translations and Editions of the Works of Basil of Caesarea.* Vol. 1: The letters. Turnhout 1993, pp. 34/35 (siglum Eb5) and 203–7.

47 Table 2 is based on the summary by CARMELO CRIMI: »Editiones principes« dell'Epistolario di Basilio di Cesarea. In: »Editiones principes« delle opere dei padri greci e latini. Ed. MARIAROSA CORTESI. Florence 2006 (*Millennio medievale. Atti di convegni.* 19), pp. 313–54,

here pp. 350–4 and is supplied with references to the foliation of the Oxford manuscript (CCC 284) and the editions by Opsopoeus and Erasmus, respectively.

48 Opsopoeus mentioned that Pirckheimer was willing to lend his Greek manuscript containing the letters of Basil the Great and Gregory of Nazianzus to Opsopoeus when he asked him through Andreas Rüttel. SCHEIBLE 2009 (see note 2), n° 1159: »Itaque ego hoc tuo iam liberali responso sum non mediocriter erectus et exhilaratus tuaeque cohortationi non illibenter obsequutus«. Opsopoeus cleary said that he copied the sections which were not edited by Aldus Manutius. Although both Opsopoeus' request and Pirckheimer's reply were lost, it is clear that Opsopoeus worked from his copy where he combined Aldus' edition with the letters found in Pirckheimer's manuscript.

49 By the 1528 edition, Opsopoeus wanted to complete the previous edition by Manutius (Venice 1499; ll. 29–39): »Eas vel hoc nomine diligentius transscripsi, partim quod antea nunquam editas compererim, partim quod sperarem studiosis et candidis lectoribus me non vulgariter gratificaturum, si nostra opera tanti ac tam rari thesauri potirentur. Promiserat quidem Aldus ille optime de literis meritus in epistolio ad Codrum Urceum, quod secundo libro Graecarum

Epistolarum praefixum est, eas aliquando se editurum. Verum quid eius voluntatem ab edendo retraxerit, parum compertum habeo. Paucas saltem Basilii ad Libanium sophistam et alios nonnullos in secundo volumine edidit, quas nos in hoc libello consulto praetermisimus«. SCHEIBLE 2009 (see note 2), n° 1159. On the 1499 edition by Aldus, cf. FEDWICK (see note 46), 199–201. On ff. α₁ʳ–β₇ᵛ, there are 44 letters by Basil the Great. The location of the letters in the Aldina edition: n° 151: ff. 9ᵛ–10ʳ, n° 20: f. 11ʳ⁻ᵛ, n° 14: ff. 15ʳ–16ʳ, n° 2: 16ʳ–20ʳ, n° 19: 20ᵛ. The other thirty-nine letters were inserted by Erasmus of Rotterdam.

50 Cf. CRIMI (see note 47), pp. 325–7. In note 45, CRIMI provided instances when Opsopoeus followed Aldus' edition. However, the variant readings of the Oxford codex as well as the editions by Opsopoeus and Erasmus demonstrate that the latter two were primarily based on the Oxford codex (CCC 284). The differences can be explained as editorial corrections or conjectures. CRIMI, pp. 336–43.

ms 284	gr. no	Hagenau 1528	Basle 1532	author	Epistle Aldina 1499
86ʳ – 101ʳ	(α' – ια')	B1ʳ–C7ʳ	504–14	Basil	2, 7, 19, 47, 34, 27, 30, 138, 268, 239, 271
101ʳ – 113ᵛ	(ιβ')	–	–	Basil	8
113ᵛ – 116ᵛ	(α' – ζ')	C7ʳ–D2ʳ	515–8	Gregory	53, 54, 114, 91, 186, 172, 120
117ʳ – 118ᵛ	(ιγ')	D2ʳ–D3ᵛ	518/9	Basil	14
118ᵛ – 130ᵛ	(η' – κ')	D3ᵛ–E6ʳ	519–28	Gregory	60, 1, 2, 4, 5, 6, 46, 8, 19, 16, 41, 43, 58
130ᵛ – 132ʳ	(ιδ')	E6ʳ–E7ᵛ	528/9	Basil	71
132ʳ – 137ᵛ	(κα' – κζ')	E8ʳ–F4ᵛ	529–33	Gregory	59, 48, 49, 50, 45, 47, 40
137ᵛ – 243ʳ	(ιστ' – νγ')	F4ᵛ–S4ᵛ	533–608	Basil	9, 277, 38, 58, 60, 59, 61, 66, 80, 67, 82, 69, 25, 24, 197, 57, 68, 120, 129, 140, 90, 28, 207, 210, 261, 246, 29, 97, 92, 243, 139, 251, 226, 263, 204, 53, 203, 125, 223, 189
–		S4ᵛ–S5ᵛ	608	Basil	151
243ʳ – 256ᵛ	(νδ' – νθ')	S5ᵛ–V1ᵛ	609–18	Basil	244, 20, 32, 250, 51, 115
256ᵛ – 275ᵛ	(κη' – νστ')	V1ᵛ–Y3ʳ	618–33	Gregory	79, 80, 30, 92, 81, 72, 73, 76, 182, 11, 195, 196, 141, 154, 130, 90, 193, 194, 25, 26, 138, 153, 20, 7, 29, 93, 135, 190, 191
275ᵛ – 286ʳ	(νζ' – οβ')	–	634–42	Gregory	178, 32, 87, 34, 33, 35, 36, 31, 224, 147, 148, 173, 132, 94, 112, 113
286ʳ – 287ᵛ	(ογ')	Y3ʳ–Y4ʳ	–	Gregory	61
287ᵛ–292ᵛ	(οδ' – π')	–	643–6	Gregory	64, 44, 65, 131, 125, 140, 199
–	–	–	647	Gregory	61
–	–	Y4ʳ–Z7ᵛ	648–56	Basil	8
–	–	–	656–74	Basil	(Aldina 1499, ff. 1ʳ–15ʳ, f. 20ᵛ) 335–356, 112, 1, 293, 135, 16, 4, 211, 12, 13, 3, 116, 10, 330, 332, 333, 86, 334

[Table 2] Ms Oxford, CCC 284 and the first two editions of the epistles of Gregory of Nazianzus and Basil the Great by Opsopoeus (Hagenau 1528) and Erasmus (Basle 1532)

ford. From the edition by Aldus Manutius (Venice 1499), Opsopoeus inserted only one epistle by Basil (nº 151), which is surprising because Opsopoeus intended his new edition to complement the earlier one by Aldus.[48] However, Opsopoeus did not omit the four epistles (nos. 2, 19, 14, and 20) that Aldus Manutius published in 1499,[49] and collated them with ms 284 CCC, Oxford.[50] Compared to the latter, the single peculiarity in Opsopoeus' edition is the fact that he inserted Epistle 151 by Basil in his own copy from Aldus Manutius' edition although it is absent in the Oxford manuscript that seems to have been the exemplar he used. This oddity might be explained by the addressee (»Eustathios archiiatros«) of Epistle 151, identical with that of Epistle 189 after which it was inserted. Thus, the act of inserting an item from Manutius' edition can be regarded as an editorial attempt to complete the deficiency of the other exemplar. As a further explanation, it is worth observing that Epistles 151, 244, and 20 feature in an identical sequence in both the Aldina and Opsopoeus' edition; thus, the editor might have used the printed edition when he was transcribing this part of Pirckheimer's manuscript (ff. 9ᵛ–11ᵛ).

On the other hand, it is well known that Erasmus asked Pirckheimer for the manuscript that Opsopoeus employed when preparing a more complete edition of the two Church Fathers (Basil and Gregory).[51] After comparing Opsopoeus' edition with Pirckheimer's manuscript, Erasmus complained about the inaccuracy of Opsopoeus' Hagenau edition.[52] Erasmus pointed out that Opsopoeus omitted almost one third of the epistles featured in Pirckheimer's manuscript. In order to correct these shortcomings, Erasmus promised that he would include the absent epistles in his new edition. Erasmus' edition that was published in Basle in 1532 demonstrates that he kept his word. His edition contains the 23 epistles that Opsopoeus omitted, in a sequence identical with that of ms 284 CCC, Oxford.[53] The only difference is that Epistle 61 by Gregory and Epistle 8 by Basil are arranged according to Opsopoeus' edition. Subsequent to the epistles that appear in the Oxford manuscript, Erasmus inserted the correspondence between Basil and Libanius (39 epistles) from the 1499 edition by Aldus Manutius (ff. 1r–15r, 20v), which Opsopoeus did not want to include due to its being available in an alternative edition.

In addition to the letters of the two Church Fathers, some other texts copied in ms 284 CCC, Oxford also demonstrate its possession by Pirckheimer. Quite recently, relying on former arguments, Carmelo Crimi demonstrated with even stronger evidence that Opsopoeus referred to ms 284 CCC, Oxford. Among his arguments, Crimi emphasized that the sequence of the letters of the two Church Fathers in ms 284 is basically identical with that of the *editio princeps* by Opsopoeus and share a great number of distinctive readings with it. In addition, Crimi used a passage in Pirckheimer's early biography by Konrad Rittershausen as a further argument. This passage provides a selection of Pirckheimer's translations: sentences by St Nilus of Ancyra († c. 430), extracts from St John Damascene (c. 676–749), and a treatise by St Maximus the Confessor (c. 580–662).[54] Relying on Holzberg's view, Crimi believed that Rittershausen's list of these translations implies that all of them are based on a single manuscript because all these works can be found in ms 284 CCC, Oxford.

Nevertheless, the statement by Rittershausen can be understood in a different way as well. I do not think that Pirckheimer's biographer had

---

51 Cf. SCHEIBLE 2009 (note 2), nº 1174 (28. 05. 1528); nº 1190, pp. 125/6 (25. 08. 1528): »Existimo tibi redditas litteras, quibus rogabam, ut codicem calamo descriptum epistolarum Basilii et Nazianzeni ad me mitteres. Vehementer enim hoc cupio nec levibus de causis et fiet absque de tuo detrimento. Sed expecto his nundinis scripta tua« (cf. nº 1176).

52 Cf. SCHEIBLE 2009 (note 2), nº 1242, pp. 241/2 (also edited in *Opus epistolarum Des. Erasmi Roterodami*, ed. PERCY STAFFORD ALLEN. Oxford 1934, nº 2214, vol. 8, pp. 276/7). Erasmus sent his edition of the letters to W. Pirckheimer through Hieronymus Froben (Freiburg i. Br., 07. 09. 1529) with a letter: »De codice graeco ignoscat tua humanitas mihi, quod non praesto fidem. Sub nundinas coepimus conferre. Quo sumus ingressi altius opus, hoc plus offendimus portentorum. Interdum toti versus omissi sunt, multa mutata studio, ut videtur. Quin et epistolae multae omissae. Postremo plusquam tertia pars voluminis abest. Collatio peracta est; sed coepimus, quod nobis deest, describere. De codice ne sis sollicitus; erit domino suo incolumis. Fortasse curabimus excudendum exemplar nostrum«. SCHEIBLE 2009 (see note 2), nº 1254, pp. 266–9 (Johannes Baptista Egnatius' letter to Pirckheimer: Venice, 13. 11. 1529). The letter mentions a codex comprising Gregory of Nazianzus from which Pirckheimer made the sections copied for him, which were missing in his manuscript. This copy was sent to Pirckheimer from Venice through a merchant, Jakob Wesler.

53 Basle, VD 16 B 338 and VD G 3040. Erasmus' edition of the letters of the two Cappadocian Fathers was appended to Froben's edition of Basil's homilies (*En amice lector ...*, Basle 1532, pp. 504–674). See also the digitalized copy. See index of websites on p. 374. On this edition, see FEDWICK (see note 46), pp. 208–17.

54 »Sibi comparavit ex graecis [auctoribus] Epistolas sanctorum Patrum atque episcoporum, Basilii Magni, et Gregorii Nazianzeni, quibuscum etiam Nili capita gnostica: Item Iohannis Damasceni quaedam, et Maximi Confessoris: Quae omnia ante aliquot centenos

any information regarding the exemplars Pirckheimer used for his translations. This sentence seems to have been compiled exclusively based on the editions which were easily accessible for the biographer. Thus, Rittershausen's statement about Pirckheimer's translations cannot be used as a proof of the hypothesis that all derive from a single manuscript. So far, this supposition has not been examined through comparison of the manuscript with the editions. For the identification of the exemplars used by Pirckheimer, the letters and St Nilus' sentences seem to provide solid grounds by the sequence of the short literary pieces because they are arranged in an identical and distinctive way in both cases (see below). At the same time, the distortion generated by the translation makes this task rather difficult in longer texts such as the treatise by St Maximus. The extracts from St John Damascene, however, seem to originate from a manuscript other than ms 284 CCC, Oxford.

The first Latin translation of St Nilus' sentences

Pirckheimer translated the sentences by St Nilus both in Latin and German in December 1515.[55] A clear sign of their popularity was that Pirckheimer found five different publishers who printed his Latin translation in the subsequent year (1516). An edition, dedicated to Georg Spalatin, was published in Johann Rhau-Grunenberg's printing shop in Wittenberg.[56] In addition, Pirckheimer's Latin translation of St Nilus's sentences was published in the printing shop of Friedrich Peypus in Nuremberg (VD 16 N 1759–1760) and in an edition by Matthias Schürer in Strasbourg (VD 16 N 1761). Moreover, it was also published by Lotter Melchior in Leipzig (VD 16 N 1758) and in Cologne (VD 16 N 1757). In addition to St Nilus' sentences, three editions (those by Peypus, Schürer, and Melchior) contain Pirckheimer's Latin translation of a set of short extracts from the homilies by St John Damascene (VD 16 J 525–9). Later, Pirckheimer translated both texts into German as well,[57] and his Latin translation came out in a number of subsequent editions.[58] As a preface to the translation, all editions are preceded by a letter Pirckheimer wrote to his sister. This letter narrated the acquisition of the exemplar used for the editions in the same phrases as cited here:

annos in ipsa Graecia scripta sunt, nec unquam viderant lucem, quam ab ipso fuissent edita«. KONRAD RITTERSHAUSEN / GOLDAST MELCHIOR, V.: *Illvstris Bilibaldi Pirckheimeri... Opera Politica, Historica, Philologica Et Epistolica.* Frankfurt 1610, p. 14. Cited by: HOLZBERG (see note 1), pp. 90, 223 and 226–30. – CRIMI (see note 47), p. 343, note 105. – HOLZBERG, p. 227, did not manage to identify the manuscript used for the edition.

55 On this translation (MAURICE GEERARD: *Clavis Patrum Graecorum.* Vols. I–IV. Turnhout 1974–83, n° 6583) and its significance, see PAOLO BETTIOLO: Le Sententiae di Nilo: patristica ed umanesimo nel XVI secolo. In: *Cristianesimo nella Storia, Ricerche Storiche Esegetiche Teologiche Bologna.* 1 (1980), pp. 155–84, here pp. 165–8.

56 VD 16 N 1762: the dedication is dated 11.03.1516. On this edition, see CRIMI (see note 47), p. 344, note 106.

57 Cf. HOLZBERG (see note 1), pp. 232–6. London, Arundel 503, ff. 1ʳ–17ʳ (sentences by St Nilus), ff. 17ᵛ–20ʳ (excerpts from St John Damascene), described by KRISTELLER (see note 31), p. 131. Pirckheimer's German translation of St John Damascene has not yet been edited in print. The German translation of the sentences by St Nilus was published in Nuremberg in 1536 (VD 16 ZV 25849).

58 Cf. HOLZBERG (see note 1), p. 232. Pirckheimer sent the small volume to many of his friends. REICKE (see note 2), n° 377, pp. 596–8 and SCHEIBLE / WUTTKE (see note 2), n° 380, pp. 2/3. Both translations were published in a number of later editions: Leipzig 1517: VD 16 ZV 11740; Basle 1517: VD 16 ZV 11741 (without St John Damascene); Basle 1518: VD 16 ZV 11742; Strasbourg 1519: VD 16 ZV 11743; Cologne 1520: VD 16 ZV 11739; Augsburg 1540: VD 16 N 1763; Augsburg 1542: VD 16 N 1764; Ingolstadt 1556: VD 16 N 1765; and Ingolstadt 1568: VD 16 N 1766.

ms Oxford CCC 284	/ 1516 Nuremberg	VD 16 N 1759	/ PG 79 / work
66ᵛ–70ʳ, l. 21	A₂ʳ l. 1–A₄ʳ l. 18	1251–7	(cap. 25–96)
70ʳ l. 21–71ʳ l. 14	A₄ʳ l. 19–A₄ᵛ l. 17	1241–3	(sen. 19–33)
71ʳ l. 15–73ᵛ l. 6	A₄ᵛ l. 18–A₆ʳ l. 3	1243–7	(sen. 35–72)
73ᵛ l. 7–74ʳ l. 23	A₆ʳ l. 4–A₆ᵛ l. 1	1257–60	(cap. 97–109a)
74ʳ l. 19–23	A₆ᵛ l. 1–5	—	
74ʳ l. 23–74ᵛ l. 21	A₆ᵛ l. 6–21	1260	(cap. 110–117)
74ᵛ l. 22–24	A₆ᵛ l. 22–23	—	
75ʳ Z. 1–19	A₆ᵛ l. 24–B₁ʳ l. 5	1260	(cap. 118–123)
75ʳ l. 19–75ᵛ l. 7	B₁ʳ l. 6–15	1261/2	(cap. 127–128, 130–132, 136)
75ᵛ l. 7–11	B₁ʳ l. 16–18	1262	(cap. 139a)
75ᵛ l. 11–24	B₁ʳ l. 19–32	1240	(sen. 1–6)
76ʳ l. 1–4	—		
76ʳ l. 4–19	B₁ᵛ l. 1–11	1241	(sen. 8–12)
76ʳ l. 19–76ᵛ l. 10	B₁ᵛ l. 12–22	1261	(cap. 125–126, 129–130, 134)
76ᵛ l. 11–12	B₁ᵛ l. 22–23	?	
76ᵛ l. 12–19	—	1261	(cap. 137–138)
76ᵛ l. 19–77ʳ l. 9	B₁ᵛ l. 24–B₂ʳ l. 3	1241	(sen. 13–18)
77ʳ l. 10–24	B₂ʳ l. 4–12		(sen. 73–77a)
= 76ᵛ l. 15–19	B₂ʳ l. 13–15	1261	(cap. 138)
77ᵛ l. 1–78ᵛ l. 2	B₂ʳ l. 16–B₂ᵛ l. 21	1248	(sen. 78–97)
78ᵛ l. 3–5	—	—	—
77ᵛ–78ᵛ l. 5–14	B₂ᵛ l. 22–29	—	—

[table 3] St Nilus' sentences in ms Oxford, CCC 284 and in the editions of Pirckheimer's Latin translation

> Jacobus Banissius, the councilor and secretary of his imperial majesty, dean of Trident, sent us a rather old codex which escaped the yoke of slavery by being rescued from a miserable Greece through our common friend, the imperial historian and prominent mathematician Johannes Stabius. I was skimming over it and reading bits and pieces when I suddenly arrived at the wise sentences by Father Nilus, saint bishop and Christ's confessor.[59]

The sentences by St Nilus (ff. 66ᵛ–78ᵛ) were copied down behind an extract from St John Damascene (ff. 56ʳ–66ᵛ) in ms 284 CCC, Oxford. I compared the Greek text with the Latin translation of the sentences by St Nilus, which has decisively confirmed the hypothesis that Pirckheimer used ms 284 CCC. Except for three sentences among the more than two hundred, Pirckheimer's translation faithfully follows the sequence of the sentences as transmitted in ms 284 CCC, Oxford [see table 3].[60] All of the three cases can be regarded as Pirckheimer's slips of attention; he recognized one of them, as his correction manifests.[61] However, the extracts from the homilies of St John Damascene derive from a selection different from the one in ms 284 CCC, Oxford.[62] Thus, in this particular case the exemplar used by Pirckheimer must have been a manuscript other than ms 284 CCC, Oxford.

In the preface mentioned above – the letter to Clara Pirckheimer – Pirckheimer did not mention the extracts from St John Damascene.

Among the manuscripts that can be traced as a part of Pirckheimer's bequest, the identical selection of extracts from St John Damascene appears in a single manuscript: London, BL, Arundel 528, ff. 107ᵛ–110ᵛ. This composite manuscript moved together with Arundel 527 and seems to have been transferred from Johannes Gremper's († 1519) possession (cf. f. 193: »Jo. Gremperij Memor Sis«) to Pirckheimer.⁶³ The various parts of the composite manuscript were put together by a certain Makarios, Bishop of Halicz (now Ukraine).⁶⁴ As far as the date of Pirckheimer's edition allows a precision, he translated it at the very end of the year 1515. The ms Arundel 527/8 could easily have been acquired in Hungary, perhaps in Buda by Gremper who visited the Hungarian royal court in 1513 and 1514 and acquired a number of volumes from the royal library.⁶⁵ It seems in 1515 through Jacobus Banissius (Jakov Baničević, † 1532), the secretary of Emperor Maximilian I and Johannes Stabius who devised the iconographic

---

59 REICKE (see note 2), nº 377, pp. 596–8 (W. Pirckheimer's letter to Clara Pirckheimernek, Nuremberg, 29. 12. 1515): »Jacobus Banissius, Caesareae maiestatis a consiliis et secretis, decanus Tridentinus, codicem pervetustum, qui e miseranda Graecia elapsus captivitatis iugum evaserat, per communem amicum Joannem Stabium, imperialem historiographum et mathematicum insignem, ad me misisset egoque levi transcursu illum delibassem, sorte quadam in beatissimi patris Nili, episcopi et martiris Christi, sententiosa incidi dicta«. This phrase also features in the preface to the edition by Johann Rhau-Grunenberg, which was dedicated to Georg Spalatin: VD 16 N 1762, f. A iiʳ, cf. CRIMI (see note 47), p. 344, note 107.

60 See also the table in HOLZBERG (see note 1), p. 228, who was not familiar with the Oxford manuscript.

61 Pirckheimer omitted three sentences: Oxford, CCC, ms 284, f. 76ʳ, ll. 1–4; 76ᵛ, ll. 16–9 (the latter one is inserted on p. B₂ʳ ll. 13–5); f. 78ᵛ, ll. 3–5. There is no evidence for such sentences that Pirckheimer translated and do not feature in the Oxford codex.

62 Subsequent to the Nilus sentences, there is a short section excerpted from St John Damascene: *Patrologiae Cursus Completus, Series Graeca*. 95 (1864), 83B–86C: (*Octo sunt Passiones* ...), GEERARD (see note 55), nos. 8110 and 3975. MIGNE published this redaction from Pirckheimer's translation without the Greek original. The CCC, ms 284 contains a redaction GEERARD nº 8111 (*Patrologiae Cursus Completus, Series Graeca*. 95 [1864], pp. 85–96.) different from Pirckheimer's translation, which refutes the hypothesis that RITTERSHAUSEN (see note 54) referred to a single manuscript.

63 PATTIE/MCKENDRICK (see note 8), pp. 9–12. RALPH CLEMINSON: *A Union Catalogue of Cyrillic Manuscripts in British and Irish Collections*. London 1988, nº 94/5, pp. 144–6. Cf. also HANS ANKWICZ-KLEEHOVEN: Magister Johannes Gremper aus Rheinfelden, ein Wiener Humanist und Bibliophile des XVI. Jahrhunderts. In: *Zentralblatt für Bibliothekswesen*. 30 (1913), pp. 197–216, here pp. 212/3. The extracts from St John Damascene on ff. 107ᵛ–110ᵛ are verbatim identical with the edition in *Patrologiae Cursus Completus, Series Graeca*. 95 (1864), 83B–86C: (*Octo sunt Passiones* ...), GEERARD (see note 55), nos. 8110. Within Part ff. 63–110, the heading of the exact Pirckheimer translated (ff. 107ᵛ–110ᵛ) does not tell the name of its author, the title of f. 85ᵛ yet gives the name of St John Damascene, who could easily be understood as the author of all the subsequent writings: f. 85ᵛ: »τοῦ ἁγίου Ἰωάννου τοῦ Δαμασκηνοῦ περὶ ἀρετῶν καὶ κακιῶν ψυχϊκῶν καὶ σωματικῶν« (GEERARD (see note 55), nº 8111); f. 97ʳ: »περὶ τῶν ψυχϊκῶν δυναμεων« (Michael Psellos: De anima, extract); f. 107ᵛ: »Περὶ τῶν ὀκτὼ πονηρίας πνευματος« from which Pirckheimer translated the extracts with the Latin heading »ex sanctissim⟨i⟩ patris Ioannis Damasceni sermonibus«. Compared to the latter redaction, Pirckheimer's translation is a condensed paraphrase. The closing summary added after the final section of the Greek text discussing the fight against arrogance seems Pirckheimer's own composition.

64 Arundel 528 was bound from at least five parts. Part 1: ff. 1–8; Part 2: ff. 9–62 (quire signatures: α'–ζ'); Part 3: ff. 63–110 (quire signatures: α'–στ', some are not well visible); Part 4: ff. 111–82 (quire signatures: α'–θ', some are not well visible); Part 5: 183–94. See Makarios' notes »ΜΑΚΑΡΙΟΥ ...« in Slavonic on f. 110ᵛ; »Τοῦ ταπεινοῦ ἐπισκόπου Γαλίτζης μακαρίου« in Greek on f. 60ᵛ; »ὁ γαλίτζης μακάριος« a *monokondylion* (a signature written in a single continuous line) on f. 162ʳ and f. 181ᵛ; »μακάριος« on f. 182ᵛ. Cf. PANAYOTIS G. NIKOLOPULOS: Αἱ εἰς τὸν Ἰωάννην Χρυσόστομον ἐσφαλμένως ἀποδιδόμεναι ἐπιστολαί. Athens 1973, p. 279. Makarios, a monk of Serbian origin in the monastery of St Cyprian in Constantinople, was appointed as a bishop of Halicz by Pope Callistus III (1455–8) in 1458. ANTONI PROCHASKA: Miscellanea Archiwalne: Nieznane dokumenta do unji Florenczkiej w Polsce. In: *Ateneum wilneskie*. 1 (1923), pp. 58–74, here pp. 64/5, 68/9. GEORG HOFMANN: Papst Kalixt III und die Frage der Kircheneinheit im Osten. In: *Miscellanea Giovanni Mercati*. Vol. 3. Letteratura e storia bizantina. Vatican City 1946, pp. 209–37, here pp. 227–9. – *Repertorium der griechischen Kopisten, 800–1600*. Vol. I. Handschriften aus Bibliotheken Grossbritanniens Ed. ERNST GAMILLSCHEG, DIETER HARLFINGER and HERBERT HUNGER. Vienna 1981 (*Veröffentlichungen der Kommission für Byzantinistik*. 3), nº 244. *Prosopographisches Lexikon des Palaiologenzeit*. Wien 1976–96, vol. 7, nº 16192.

65 Vienna, ÖNB Cod. Lat. 138 (Marcellinus comes Illyricus, Gennadius Massiliensis, Isidorus Hispalensis, Ildefonsus Toletanus), 218 (*In perversionem problematum Aristotelis*), 977 (*Dialogus S. Iohannis Chrysostomi et [Pseudo-] Sancti Basilii* ...) and Budapest, OSZK, Cod. Lat. 417 (Philostratus), CSAPODI (see note 17), nos. 418, 669, 170, 478, and 503. In addition to these volumes, Gremper's interest in theology is also manifested by his annotations in Bessarion's three theological works in Latin, later rebound in a Corvina binding in Buda (today Budapest, OSZK, Cod. Lat. 438) and, presumably in Vienna, copied the entire manuscript comprising the Latin translation of two works by Basil the Great (*De divinitate filii et spiritus sancti* and *Adversus Eunomium*) from a Corvina manuscript today kept in Budapest (OSZK, Cod. Lat. 415). His apograph is kept in HAB Wolfenbüttel (4. 7. Aug. 4º). ANKWICZ-KLEEHOVEN (see note 63), pp. 213–5.

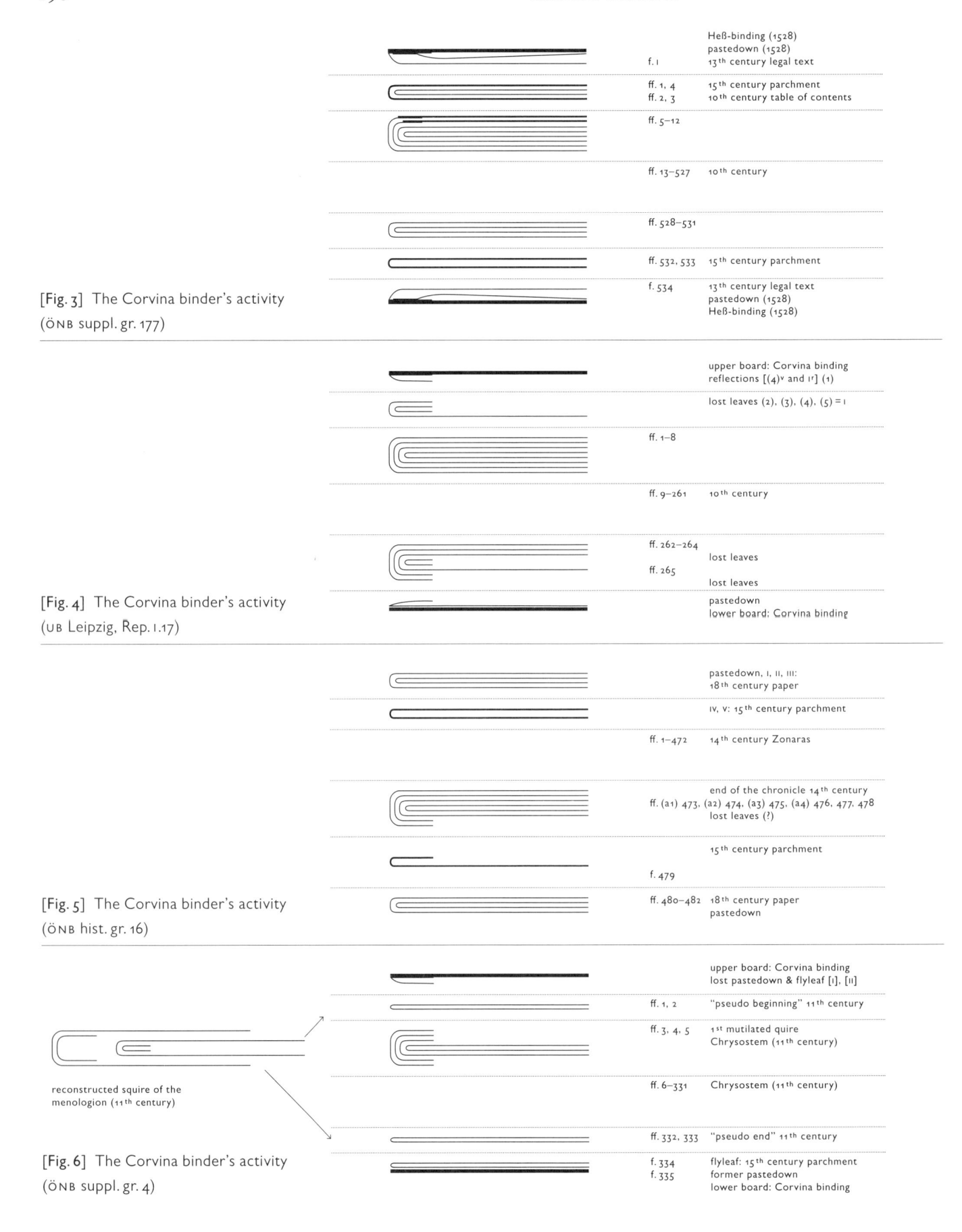

[Fig. 3] The Corvina binder's activity
(ÖNB suppl. gr. 177)

f. 1		Heß-binding (1528) pastedown (1528) 13th century legal text
ff. 1, 4 ff. 2, 3		15th century parchment 10th century table of contents
ff. 5–12		
ff. 13–527		10th century
ff. 528–531		
ff. 532, 533		15th century parchment
f. 534		13th century legal text pastedown (1528) Heß-binding (1528)

[Fig. 4] The Corvina binder's activity
(UB Leipzig, Rep. I.17)

	upper board: Corvina binding reflections [(4)v and 1r] (1)
	lost leaves (2), (3), (4), (5) = 1
ff. 1–8	
ff. 9–261	10th century
ff. 262–264	lost leaves
ff. 265	lost leaves
	pastedown lower board: Corvina binding

[Fig. 5] The Corvina binder's activity
(ÖNB hist. gr. 16)

	pastedown, I, II, III: 18th century paper
	IV, V: 15th century parchment
ff. 1–472	14th century Zonaras
ff. (a1) 473, (a2) 474, (a3) 475, (a4) 476, 477, 478	end of the chronicle 14th century lost leaves (?)
f. 479	15th century parchment
ff. 480–482	18th century paper pastedown

[Fig. 6] The Corvina binder's activity
(ÖNB suppl. gr. 4)

reconstructed squire of the menologion (11th century)

	upper board: Corvina binding lost pastedown & flyleaf [I], [II]
ff. 1, 2	"pseudo beginning" 11th century
ff. 3, 4, 5	1st mutilated quire Chrysostem (11th century)
ff. 6–331	Chrysostem (11th century)
ff. 332, 333	"pseudo end" 11th century
f. 334 f. 335	flyleaf: 15th century parchment former pastedown lower board: Corvina binding

program of Maximilian's "Triumphal Arch" (*Ehrenpforte*) with Pirckheimer's assistance that the exemplar was transferred to him. This is known from a letter (January 1516) in which Pirckheimer expresses his gratitude for more than one volume and states that he had translated more works by referring to the name of Banissius as it stands in the preface to the edition of the sentences by St Nilus, which was expanded with the excerpts from St John Damascene.[66] The use of the plural (»libellos quosdam graecos«) also supports the identification of Arundel 527/8 as Pirckheimer's exemplar because it consisted of several short manuscripts at the beginning of the sixteenth century.

Liber Asceticus by St Maximus the Confessor
In addition to the epistles of the two Cappadocian Fathers, and the sentences by St Nilus, Pirckheimer translated two other works from ms 284 CCC, Oxford. One of them is the *Liber Asceticus* by St Maximus the Confessor, which was published in 1530.[67] This work does not feature in any manuscripts of the Arundel collection in the British Library, a reservoir of Pirckheimer's bequest, and copies preceding the year 1530 are considerably scarce, almost not attested in the West. Thereafter, ms 284 CCC, Oxford seems an acceptable candidate to be regarded as the exemplar Pirckheimer used (ff. 293ᵛ–324ʳ). Regrettably, there is not a preface preceding the edition which can inform us about the provenance of exemplar.

The two codices and the Corvina library
The other work is *De officio episcopi* (or. 2) by Gregory of Nazianzus, a homily which Pirckheimer already decided to translate in 1528 when he published his translations of two other homilies by Gregory.[68] Pirckheimer's translation of Homily 2 came out in print at the beginning of 1529.[69] It is in the context of this 1529 edition of Homily 2 that Heß expressed his debt of gratitude to Pirckheimer for sending a copy. In addition, it was the same letter to which Heß appended the index of contents of ÖNB suppl. gr. 177. Because of this chronology and Pirckheimer's turn of phrase (»praeterea«), he must have used a manuscript other than the one sent by Heß; thus it could be easily ms 284 CCC, Oxford. The title of the trans-

66 Cf. SCHEIBLE/WUTTKE (see note 2), nº 379, pp. 1/2: Pirckheimer's letter to Jacobus Banissius (Nuremberg, January 1516): »Interim vero, cum Stabius noster libellos quosdam graecos a dominatione tua attulisset, quaedam ex illis convertimus ac in publicum non sine nominis tui, ut decet, praeconio edidimus«. Pirckheimer sent his friend twenty copies of his translation of Nilus' sentences. On the occasions when Bannisius, the imperial secretary, disposed of the acquired manuscripts according to Maximilian's wish, see a manuscript sent by Gremper through Georg von Slatkonia, Bishop of Vienna (1456–1522) to Bannisius in ANKWICZ-KLEEHOVEN (see note 63), p. 203 and Maximilian's request from Johannes Cuspinianus (1443–1529) to transfer the Zonaras manuscript from Buda to Bannisius who would forward it to Pirckheimer for translation in *Johann Cuspinians Briefwechsel* (see note 16), nº 18, pp. 39–41 (Weißenburg, 05. 02. 1513). On Pirckheimer's cooperation with Stabius, see HOLZBERG (see note 1), pp. 176/7. – JOHN MONFASANI: A tale of two books: Bessarion's *In Calumniatorem Platonis* and George of Trebizond's *Comparatio Philosophorum Platonis et Aristotelis*. In: *Renaissance Studies*. 22 (2007), pp. 1–13, here pp. 12/3. – ANDRÁS NÉMETH: I. Miksa Willibald Pirckheimernek küldött ajándékkönyvei: Újabb budai eredetű görög kódexek? In: *Művészettörténeti Értesítő* [Bulletin of History of Arts]. 59 (2011), pp. 275–291.

67 Cf. GEERARD (see note 55), nº 7692. – VD 16 1664. – HOLZBERG (see note 1), pp. 351/2.

68 Cf. SCHEIBLE 2009 (see note 2), nº 1176, p. 97: »et si deus annuerit, bervi alia quoque theologi huius – ita enim a Graecis apellatur – scripta in publicum exire videbis, precipue vero orationem elegantissimam de munere episcopali, quam me tunc in manibus habere vidisti«, see full citation in note 52. See the edition as VD 16 G 3081.

69 VD 16 G 3073: HOLZBERG (see note 1), pp. 348–51.

[Fig. 7] Upper cover of the *alla greca* gilded leather binding of ms UB Leipzig, Rep. I. 17 (34,5 × 23,3 × 9 cm) prepared in Buda in the late 1480s; at the bottom of the upper cover features the title »⟨DE⟩ REGALIBUS INSTITUTIONIBUS«; the coat of arms of King Matthias Corvinus appears in the centre

lated homily is a verbatim translation of the title in the Oxford manuscript. Otherwise, the distortion of the Latin translation cannot provide decisive evidence for the identification of the archetype of these two texts.

It is also in connection with the homily *On the bishop's office* (or. 2) that Pirckheimer mentioned the Hungarian provenance of the Gregory codex in a letter to his friend, Georg Spalatin, in 1529 as a seemingly unfitted and redundant piece of information. The note that the substantial Gregory codex was acquired as booty from Hungary appears rather suddenly and without an adequate context. Pirckheimer seems to have more reasons to refer to the substantial unique codex he received from Heß. The homily (*On the bishop's office*) of which Pirckheimer was sending a Latin translation to Georg Spalatin featured in both codices: in Heß's manuscript it was the work subsequent to the truncated Homily 1 (ff. 6^v–39^v, incomplete at the beginning); in the other manuscript, which seems to have been ms 284 CCC, Oxford, on ff. 5^r–56^v. The additional note that Heß's codex originated from Hungary can be best explained through the origin shared by the exemplar Pirckheimer used for the 1529 edition – as we have already learned from Opsopoeus in connection with other texts edited from the same manuscript. On the one hand, Opsopoeus is likely to have learned from Pirckheimer that the codex comprising the epistles of the two Cappadocian Fathers was once housed in the royal library in Buda. On the other hand, Pirckheimer seems to have come to know about the provenance of the old volume comprising more than 50 works by Gregory of Nazianzus from Heß who also mentioned his Gregory codex in the context of the homily *On the bishop's office*. Regrettably, neither of the two sources survives.

The value of an origin from the Hungarian royal library in Buda, which immediately increased after its pillage by the Turks in 1526, can be viewed as an additional explanation. This change of appreciation might explain the differences between the preface to St Nilus' sentences, where the Greek origin was emphasized, and Pirckheimer's letter to Spalatin. In the latter, the Nuremberg scholar found the Hungarian provenance worth mentioning in the case of Heß's codex; Heß had previously emphasized the Greek origin of his manuscript in a letter to Pirckheimer (as cited above). A similar difference can be observed concerning the provenance of Munich, BSB, cod. gr. 157 in Vincent Opsopoeus' Polybius edition (Hagenau 1530: VD 16 P 4082) where he does not mention the provenance of the manuscript, and his Heliodorus edition (Basle 1534: VD 16 H 1673) where he describes the adventures how a soldier obtained the manuscript from King Matthias' library. Philological studies have demonstrated that both editions rely on Munich, BSB, cod. gr. 157.[70]

The personage of Georg Spalatin might provide a further supportive argument. Pirckheimer dedicated an edition of Nilus' sentences to Spalatin (Wittenberg 1516: VD 16 N 1762). This translation is also based on the same codex from which the homiliy *On the bishop's office* seems to have been made. This dedication may have given Pirckheimer an opportunity to share his knowledge of the origin of this codex with Spalatin although

70 Cf. KERSTIN HAJDU: Codices Graeci Monacenses 110–180. Wiesbaden 2003 (*Catalogus codicum manu scriptorum Bibliothecae Regiae Monacensis*. 2,3), pp. 255–9 with literature.

such a letter does not survive. However, Opsopoeus' 1528 Basle edition certainly revealed the provenance of its archetype to Spalatin if he knew that the homiliy *On the bishop's office* and the epistles of the two Greek fathers were in the same manuscript. All these aspects together may explain why Pirckheimer mentioned the direct Hungarian provenance of Heß's Gregory codex, being of secondary importance for theological discussions he focused on, in his letter to Georg Spalatin. These connections between the two codices seem to corroborate Opsopoeus' statement that scholars used to distrust.

It is true that in the Oxford manuscript there is not any evidence left for its history before the turn of the eighteenth century when Christopher Wase donated it to Corpus Christi College in 1704.[71] Wase enrolled in the college in 1677 and became a scholar in 1690. His father, also named as Christopher Wase (1625?–90) was a famous classical scholar and is credited with English translations of several works such as Sophocles' *Electra* and Phaedrus' *Fables*. He was the *architypographus* of Oxford University Press for some time and also bequeathed manuscripts to Corpus Christi College. Wase may have acquired the volume in England because Thomas Howard, as shown above, purchased Pirckheimer's manuscripts and brought them to England in 1636. Shortly after Henry Howard donated his books to the Royal Society, Oxford University initiated negotiations with the earl to consent with the exchange of some manuscripts donated to the Royal Society.[72] Thus, it could easily have been in the 1670s or 1680s, when negotiations took place with Oxford University, that the elder Wase obtained this manuscript with an origin from Pirckheimer's library.

The scholars who described ms 284 CCC, Oxford (Irmgard Hutter and Nigel Wilson)[73] rejected Opsopoeus' report on its provenance from the Hungarian royal library, which might have come from Pirckheimer, for two major reasons. Firstly, because the coat of arms of Matthias Corvinus is absent from the manuscript, and secondly because there are not any marks left in the margins that were introduced in Hagenau in Setzer's printing shop when Opsopoeus edited the epistles of Basil and Gregory. The characteristics of the other Greek manuscripts that were certainly available at Buda for a couple of decades refute the first objection, as none of them is furnished with the coat of arms of the king on the title pages. In addition, Opsopoeus stated in the preface to his edition that it was based on his own selection which he transcribed from Pirckheimer's manuscript.[74] Opsopoeus did so in his other editions as well. For example, the *editio princeps* of Heliodorus was based on manuscript Munich, cod. gr. 157, ff. 124ʳ–167ᵛ. Instead of the precious parchment manuscript itself, however, there was a copy in Ospopoeus' hands (Leiden, UL, BPG. 61a) which was directly used for the edition (Basle 1534: DV 16 H 1673); this copy is supplied with the editorial marks introduced in the printing shop.[75] The same procedure can be observed in Erasmus' edition (Basle 1532) who also worked from an apograph because he handled the old Greek codex, lent from Pirckheimer, with care and avoided writing in the manuscript.[76] Thus, neither of the two editions was based directly on

71 I owe a debt of gratitude to Dr. Julian Reid, archivist of Corpus Christi College for assisting me. It was Christopher Wase († 1711) who donated the volume to Corpus Christi College (see f. 1ʳ: »ex dono Christophori Wase«). THOMAS FOWLER: *The History of Corpus Christi College with Lists of Its Members*. Oxford 1893, pp. 401/2. On the 1704 donation, see ms Oxford, CCC, D/2/2: *Donations to the library C. C. C. Oxon. from 1695*: »a. 1704: Vol. mss. in pergam. continens quoddam Gregorii, Damasceni, Nili, Basilii«. Although the entry speaks about a parchment manuscript, it cannot be anything else but cod. 284.

72 Cf. PAISEY (see note 8), pp. 173/4.

73 Cf. HUTTER (see note 45), nº 9, pp. 20–2. – CRIMI (see note 47), p. 347. I owe a debt of gratitude to Prof. Nigel Wilson for providing me with his notes on the provenance of ms 284 CCC, Oxford.

74 Cf. SCHEIBLE 2009 (see note 2), nº 1159 (ll. 15–23): »Sed enim cum animadverterem huius tam rari codicis pretium nulla tua invidia premi, cum alias tuae instructissimae bibliothecae utriusque linguae auctores studiosis a te flagitantibus candidiss⟨ime⟩ et libentiss⟨ime⟩ utendos dare soleas, sed potius librarii penuria hactenus in obscuro delituisse, cepi te per Andream Rutellium familiarem tuum interpellare […] me describendi laborem et taedium libenti animo suscipere et devorare velle«. Ll. 29–33: »Eas vel hoc nomine diligentius transscripsi, partim quod antea nunquam editas [compared to the edition (1499) by Aldus Manutius] compererim, partim quod sperarem studiosis et candidis lectoribus me non vulgariter gratificaturum, si nostra opera tanti ac tam rari thesauri potirentur«. He omitted the epistles edited by Aldus Manutius (Venice 1499; ll. 37–9): »Paucas saltem Basilii ad Libanium Sophistam et alios in secundo volumine edidit, quas nos in hoc libello consulto praetermisimus«.

75 Cf. KAREL ADRIAAN DE MEYER: *Codices bibliothecae publicae Graeci*. Leiden 1965 (*Codices manuscripti / Bibliotheca Universitatis Leidensis*. 8), pp. 90/1. On the collation of both manuscripts with Opsopoeus' edition, see the literature in HAJDU (see note 70), p. 258.

76 Cf. SCHEIBLE 2009 (see note 2), nº 1242, pp. 241/2: »De codice ne sis sollicitus; erit domino suo incolumis«, see full citation in note 52.

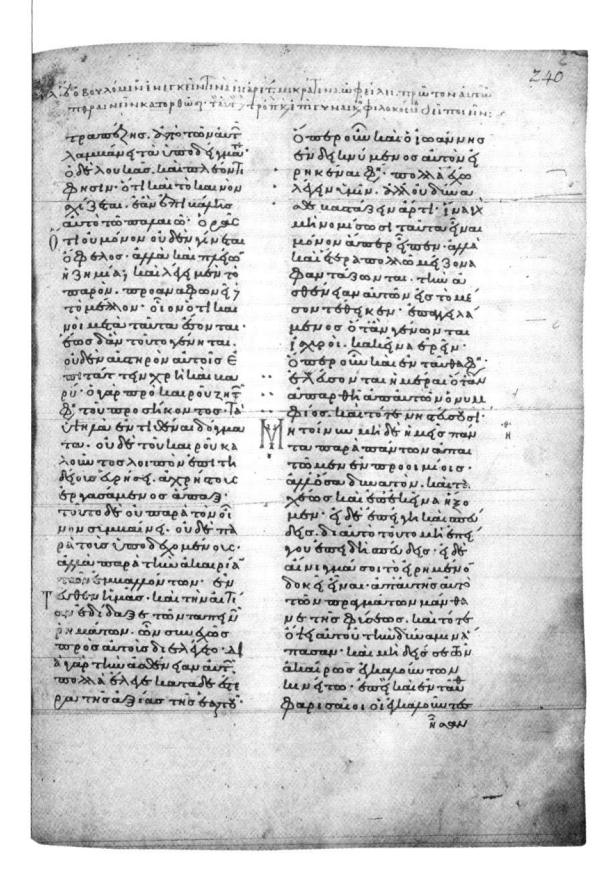

[Fig. 8] UB Leipzig, Rep. I. 17, f. 83ʳ
(33 × 23 cm, quire number: 13)

[Fig. 9] Vienna, ÖNB suppl. gr. 4, f. 240ʳ
(34 × 25 cm, quire number: 32)

Pirckheimer's codex: Opsopoeus worked from his apograph and Erasmus from his notes, which have not been identified so far. There is no reason to distrust the information deriving from Pirckheimer and Opsopoeus.[77] The quire signatures in ms ÖNB suppl. gr. 177 demonstrate that his knowledge of the origin of the Gregory codex was correct.

Pirckheimer's reliability

As far as Pirckheimer's reliability is concerned, the careful study of ms ÖNB suppl. gr. 177 demonstrates with material evidence that the huge codex he received from Heß in fact originates from the Corvina library:

(a) In the upper right corner of the first leaf of each quire, there are Arabic quire numbers in ÖNB suppl. gr. 177, ff. 5ʳ–173ʳ, which are identical in function (all facilitate the job of a binder) with the other codices with Corvina bindings and similar to them with regard to their ductus [see tab. 4].[78] The other three manuscripts are UB Leipzig, Rep. I. 17,[79] Vienna, ÖNB hist. gr. 16,[80] and suppl. gr. 4 [see fig. 3–6, 8–10].[81] In addition, in the outer corner of the lower margin there are quire signatures which could be ascribed to Johannes Heß's binder: ff. 5ʳ–173ʳ: lower case Gothic letters from b–z; ff. 151ʳ–352ʳ: also lower case Gothic letters from a–z; finally ff. 360ʳ–528ʳ: upper case Gothic letters from A–Y [see fig. 11].

(b) The hand identical with that of the quire numerals numbered the first four leaves of each quire in the entire codex (ÖNB suppl. gr 177), occasionally jumping several numbers between subsequent leaves. This demonstrates that an assistant of the binder numbered the folia in order to facilitate the job of reassembling the double leaves in the correct order when rebinding the vast volume. The double-leaf numbers demonstrate that the Gregory of Nazianzus codex was disbound between the mid-fifteenth-century and 1528 with the purpose of rebinding. The fact that the double-leaf numbers in the identical function appear in the truncated initial and final quires in other Corvina codices leads to the conclusion that the Gregory of Nazianzus codex arrived at the Buda court in a loose binding.[82] Because the process of rebinding lasted relatively short time, cod. suppl. gr. 177 seems to have received an *alla greca* type of gilded leather Corvina binding, similar to those of ms UB Leipzig, Rep. I. 17 [see fig. 7] and ms ÖNB suppl. gr. 4 (35,5 × 25,5 × 9,5 cm). In 1528, however, Heß's binder deprived the manuscript of all evidence necessary to answer this question. The execution of the 1528 re-binding, prepared with a different binding technique, necessitated the dis-binding the Corvina volume, stitching the double leaves into quires and sewing together the quires again. This procedure explains the new system of quire signatures copied by Heß's binder in the lower margin's outer corner [see fig. 3 and fig. 11].

(c) The state of preservation must have been also damaged because several truncated leaves of ms ÖNB suppl. gr. 177 were completed with fine Italian parchment [see fig. 3].[83] In addition to the humanist quire numbers, the insertion of the fifteenth-century fine parchment leaves might also be ascribed to the binding workshop at Buda. Similarly to ff. 532/3, ff. 1 and 4 could have functioned as flyleaves before the codex was rebound for Heß. It could have been Heß's binder who transferred the double leaf of ff. 1 and 4 in order to protect ff. 2/3 that comprise the table of contents of the volume. Three other manuscripts demonstrate that the Corvina binder

---

77 As shown above (see notes 14–8), Pirckheimer was well informed on other manuscripts of the royal library in Buda and also in the news from Hungary such as, e.g., on the Hungarians' preparations against the Turks. SCHEIBLE 2004 (see note 2), nº 1028 (Vienna, 26. 04. 1526), pp. 138–42.

78 On these four manuscripts (ÖNB hist. gr. 16, suppl. gr. 4, 177 and UB Leipzig, Rep. I. 17), see ANDRÁS NÉMETH: The Mynas codex and the Bibliotheca Corviniana. In: *Matthias Corvinus und seine Zeit. Europa am Übergang vom Mittelalter zur Neuzeit zwischen Wien und Konstantinopel.* Ed. CH. GASTGEBER et alii. Vienna 2011 (forthcoming), pp. 158–63. See numerals copied by the assistant of the Corvina binder and those of Heß's binder in parentheses: (in the humanist complement of the truncated leaf) 1 (b); f. 13ʳ: 2 (c); f. 21ʳ: 3 (d); f. 29ʳ: 4 (e); f. 37ʳ: 5 (f); f. 45ʳ: 6 (g); f. 53ʳ: 7 (h); f. 61ʳ: 8 (i); f. 69ʳ: 9 (k); f. 77ʳ: 10 (l); f. 85ʳ: 11 (m); f. 93ʳ: 12 (n); f. 101ʳ: 13 (o); f. 109ʳ: 14 (p); f. 117ʳ: 15 (q); f. 125ʳ: 16 (r); f. 133ʳ: 17 (s); f. 141ʳ: 18 (t? washed); f. 149ʳ: 1⟨9⟩ (trimmed) (v); f. 157ʳ: 20 (x); f. 165ʳ: 2⟨1⟩ (y); f. 173ʳ: ⟨22⟩ (z).

79 UB Leipzig, Rep. I. 17: f. 1ʳ: 2; f. 9ʳ: 3; f. 17ʳ: 4; f. 25ʳ: 5; f. 33ʳ: 6; f. 41ʳ: 7; f. 43ʳ: 8; f. 51ʳ: 9; f. 59ʳ: 10; f. 67ʳ: 11; f. 75ʳ: 12; f. 83ʳ: 13; f. 91ʳ: 14; f. 99ʳ: 15; f. 107ʳ: 16; f. 115ʳ: 17; f. 123ʳ: 18; f. 131ʳ: 19; f. 139ʳ: 20; f. 147ʳ: 21 (trimmed upper part); f. 155ʳ: not visible; f. 163ʳ: 23 (trimmed upper part); f. 171ʳ: leaf lost after the binding was made; f. 179ʳ: not visible; f. 187ʳ: not visible, f. 195ʳ: not visible; f. 203ʳ: leaf lost after binding; f. 211ʳ: ⟨2⟩9 (trimmed upper part); f. 222ʳ: 31 (trimmed upper part); f. 230ʳ: 32; f. 238ʳ: 33; f. 246ʳ: 3⟨4⟩; f. 254ʳ: not visible; f. 262ʳ: not visible.

80 ÖNB hist. gr. 16: f. 17ʳ: 3; f. 25ʳ: 4; f. 33ʳ: 5; f. 41ʳ: 6; f. 49ʳ: 7; f. 57ʳ: 8; f. 65ʳ: 9; f. 73ʳ: 10; f. 81ʳ: 11; f. 89ʳ: 12; f. 97ʳ: 13; f. 105ʳ: 14; f. 114ʳ: not visible; f. 121ʳ: 16; f. 129ʳ: 17; f. 137ʳ: not visible; f. 145ʳ: 19; f. 153ʳ: 20; f. 161ʳ: not visible; f. 169ʳ: ⟨2⟩2; f. 177ʳ: ⟨2⟩3; f. 185ʳ: not visible; f. 193ʳ: 25; f. 201ʳ: 2⟨6⟩; f. 209ʳ: ⟨2⟩7; f. 217ʳ: not visible; f. 225ʳ: 29; f. 233ʳ: 30; f. 241ʳ: 31; f. 249ʳ: 32; f. 257ʳ: 33; f. 265ʳ: 34; f. 273ʳ: 35; f. 281ʳ: 36; f. 289ʳ: 37; f. 297ʳ: not visible; f. 305ʳ: 39; f. 313ʳ: 4⟨0⟩; f. 321ʳ: not visible; f. 329ʳ: not visible; f. 337ʳ: 43; f. 345ʳ: not visible; f. 353ʳ: 45; f. 361ʳ, f. 369ʳ and f. 377ʳ: not visible; f. 385ʳ: ⟨4⟩9; f. 393ʳ: not visible; f. 401ʳ: 5⟨1⟩; f. 409ʳ: 5⟨2⟩; f. 417ʳ: ⟨5⟩3; f. 425ʳ: 54; f. 433ʳ: 55; f. 441ʳ: 56; f. 449ʳ: 57; f. 457ʳ: 58; f. 465ʳ: 59.

81 ÖNB suppl. gr. 4: f. 1ʳ: 1; f. 3ʳ: 2; f. 6ʳ: 3; f. 14ʳ: 4; f. 22ʳ: 5; f. 30ʳ: 6; f. 39ʳ: 7; f. 48ʳ: 8; f. 56ʳ: 9; f. 64ʳ: 10; f. 72ʳ: 11; f. 80ʳ: 12; f. 88ʳ: 13; f. 96ʳ: 14; f. 104ʳ: 15; f. 112ʳ: 16; f. 120ʳ: 17; f. 128ʳ: 18; f. 136ʳ: 19 crossed out by the hand foliating the volume; f. 144ʳ: 20; f. 152ʳ: 21; f. 160ʳ: 22; f. 168ʳ: 23; f. 176ʳ: 24; f. 184ʳ: 25; f. 192ʳ: 26; f. 200ʳ: 27; f. 208ʳ: 28; f. 216ʳ: 29; f. 224ʳ: 30; f. 232ʳ: 31; f. 240ʳ: 32; f. 248ʳ: 33; f. 256ʳ: 34; f. 264ʳ: 35; f. 272ʳ: 36; f. 280ʳ: 37; f. 288ʳ: 38; f. 296ʳ: 39; f. 304ʳ: 40; f. 312ʳ: 41; f. 320ʳ: 42; f. 328ʳ: 43; f. 330ʳ: 44.

82 See numerals in similar hand and function in mss Vienna, ÖNB hist. gr. 16, f. 473ʳ: a1; f. 474ʳ: a2; f. 475: a3; f. 476ʳ: a4 and ÖNB, suppl. gr. 4, f. 328ʳ: 1 and f. 329ʳ: 2.

83 See a similar attempt in ms UB Leipzig, Rep. I. 17, f. 91 where the lower margin (3,8 cm) was completed in Buda as the gilded edges of the fine Italian parchment, used for the completion, demonstrates.

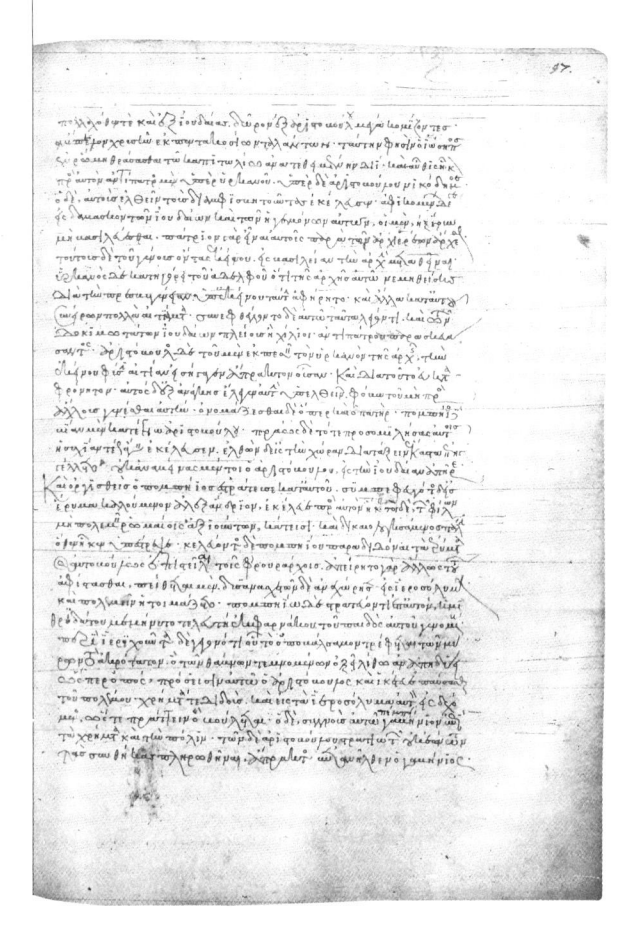

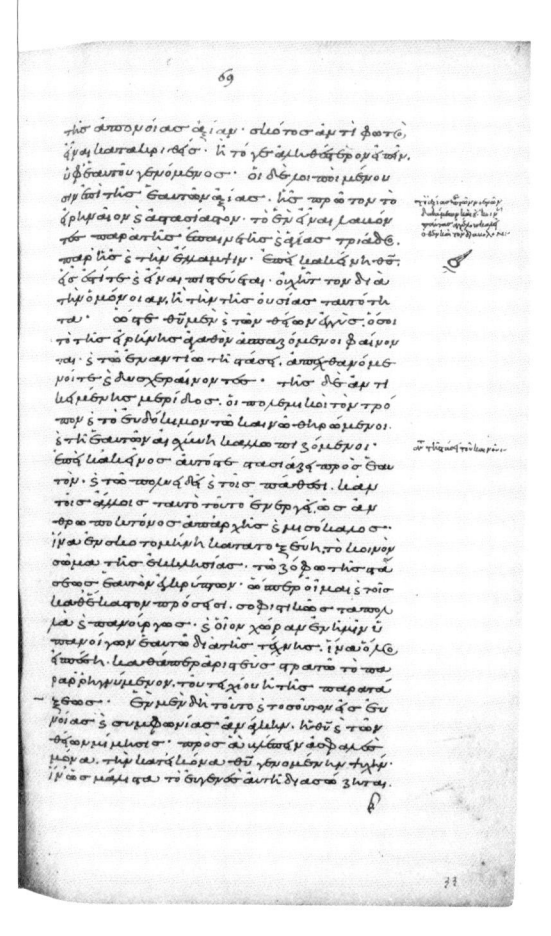

[Fig. 10] Vienna, ÖNB hist. gr. 16, f. 97ʳ (31,5 × 23,5 cm, quire number: 12)

[Fig. 11] Vienna, ÖNB suppl. gr. 177, f. 69ʳ (34 × 23 cm, quire number copied in Buda: 9, double-leaf number copied in Burda: 33, Heß's quire signature: k)

84 The insertion of the central double leaf (ff. 402–4: nº 404 appears on f. 403ᵛ) could easily have taken place in Buda.

85 The ÖNB purchased the Gregory of Nazianzus codex together with the other Greek manuscripts of the Dietrichstein library. Cf. *Bibliothek Fürst Dietrichstein …* (note 34), nº 407, p. 82.

used to insert a double leaf of fine Italian parchment in the front and in the back of the aged Greek codices that were rebound in Buda in the 1480s [see figs. 3–6]. As remarkable evidence of how the old Greek volumes were approached as objects, the heavily truncated leaves (ff. 5/6) were complemented in the fifteenth century because the quire number 1 on f. 5ʳ was copied in the newly complemented part and belongs to the Corvina binder's quire system.[84] The flyleaves (ff. 1 and 534) carrying legal texts from the thirteenth century might have been inserted only by Heß's binder.

The several hundreds of Arabic numerals copied in mss ÖNB hist. gr. 16, suppl. gr. 4, 177, and ms UB Leipzig, Rep. I. 17 seem to have been copied in Buda in order to assist the Corvina binder's work. Supplied with additional data, thus, the similarities in the ductus of these numerals, especially that of nº 3 [see tab. 4], may help identify other old Greek manuscripts that were rebound in Buda. The codex of Gregory of Nazianzus left Buda only after 1526, reached Johannes Heß in Wrocław, was transported to Pirckheimer in 1529, returned to Heß in 1530, and arrived at Nikolsburg (the Dietrichstein collection, today Mikulov in Czech Republic) afterwards. It did not turn up in Vienna before 1936 so that the numerals could not have been copied there in the early sixteenth century.[85] Thus, the information Pirckheimer first shared with Georg Spalatin regarding the provenance of the Gregory codex from the Hungarian booty has been confirmed with some material evidence for its presence in Buda.

Willibald Pirckheimer and his Greek codices from Buda

[Table 4] Numerals written to assist the Corvina binder (Buda 1480s)

A = UB Leipzig, Rep. I. 17
f. 67ʳ (1), f. 1ʳ (2), f. 75ʳ (12), f. 9ʳ (3), f. 83ʳ (13), f. 17ʳ (4), f. 91ʳ (14), f. 25 (5); f. 99ʳ (15), f. 33ʳ (6), f. 107ʳ (16), f. 41ʳ (7), f. 115ʳ (17), f. 43ʳ (8). f. 123ʳ (18), f. 51ʳ (9), f. 131ʳ (19), f. 59ʳ (10), f. 139ʳ (20)

B = Vienna, ÖNB, suppl. gr. 4
f. 72ʳ (11), f. 3ʳ (2), f. 80ʳ (12), f. 6ʳ (3), f. 88ʳ (13), f. 14ʳ (4), f. 96ʳ (14), f. 22ʳ (5), f. 104ʳ (15), f. 30ʳ (6), f. 112ʳ (16), f. 120ʳ (17), f. 48ʳ (8), f. 128ʳ (18), f. 56ʳ (9), f. 136ʳ (19), f. 64ʳ (10), f. 144ʳ (20)

C = Vienna, ÖNB, hist. gr. 16
f. 473ʳ (α1), f. 89ʳ (12), f. 474ʳ (α2), f. 97ʳ (13), f. 475ʳ (3), f. 265ʳ (34), f. 25ʳ (4), f. 465ʳ (59), f. 41ʳ (6), f. 49ʳ (7), f. 57ʳ (8), f. 457ʳ (58), f. 465ʳ (59), f. 73ʳ (10)

D = Vienna, ÖNB, suppl. gr. 177
f. 85ʳ (11), f. 93ʳ (12), f. 426ʳ (234), f. 467ʳ (259), f. 482ʳ (267), f. 238ʳ (123), f. 21ʳ (3), f. 125ʳ (63), f. 426ʳ (234), f. 101ʳ (49), f. 426 (234), f. 37ʳ (5), f. 53ʳ (25), f. 467ʳ (259), f. 125ʳ (63), f. 61ʳ (8), f. 101ʳ (49), f. 467ʳ (259), f. 77ʳ (10)

Conclusion

The horizon of this study does not allow me to locate these two manuscripts within the Corvina library. Their acquisition coincides with the increasing interest in the Greek Fathers, which received a major impetus in the Council of Florence in 1438/9 when the theological debates with the eastern Churches highlighted the significance of the old Greek codices of the Fathers, especially the Cappadocian Fathers.[86] This interest continued after the council. In this context, such a complete selection of the homilies by Gregory of Nazianzus, especially in an early manuscript as recognized and emphasized by Heß's theologian friends in Wrocław (see the citation above), must have been of a great value and appreciation. Both codices mainly contained writings that were not accessible in Latin. At the same time, the homilies and epistles by Basil and Gregory were considered to be valuable both for their rhetorical and theological merits, which then became accessible in Greek and Latin. This process was fostered by the increasing interest of early sixteenth-century audiences, which was a period of expanding activity of printing shops in the territory of the early Reformation. Opsopoeus described the Arrianism, a heresy in the times of the Cappadocian Fathers – Basil the Great and Gregory of Nazianzus –, as comparable with the heresy of his own age exemplified in the teachings of Thomas Müntzer, Oecolampadius and Martin Luther.[87] It was also in these years that J. A. Brassicanus primarily saw the works of the Greek Fathers as being worth editing from his own manuscripts, which would bring him fame and fortune.[88]

The humanist scholars who were active in Matthias' court discovered the value of the Greek manuscripts at a rather early point in time. Like the Medicis, the Hungarian king collected paper manuscripts, fragments of codices in the form of unbound gatherings,[89] primarily for the value of the texts and not for their beauty.[90] Most of these works have not been translated into Latin, or were accessible in alternative Latin translations competing for acknowledgment, for which the Greek original must have served as a decisive basis. Ms ÖNB suppl. gr. 177 elucidates how much respect the Greek codices received as objects: in the procedure of rebinding, the damaged leaves were treated with care and the truncated leaves were complemented. Interestingly enough, only considerably old large folio size parchment manuscripts received *alla greca* type gilded leather Corvina binding.[91] Thus, it is the dis-binding and re-binding of the aged volumes, which left quire signatures in the manuscripts, that may provide an opportunity to expand the scarce knowledge provided in the correspondence of humanist scholars.

---

86 Cf. PAUL HETHERINGTON: Vecchi, e non antichi: Differing Responses to Byzantine Culture in Fifteenth-century Tuscany. In: *Rinascimento*. 32 (1992), pp. 203–11.

87 Cf. SCHEIBLE 2009 (see note 2), nº 1159 (ll. 55–60): »Vixerunt enim eo tempore in Caesarea Cappadotiae quidem Basilius, Constantinopoli autem Gregorius, quo vehementissime viguit arriana haeresis «. Ll. 75–80: »Neque enim minore multorum ruina et offendiculo iam furiunt haeretici munzerani et omnium maxime oecolampadiani, qui olim insaniebant Arriani«.

88 See the passage in the *editio princeps* of Salvianus by J. Alexander Brassicanus, Basle 1530 (VD 16 S 1511), ff. Biiv–Biiiv. On the manuscripts Brassicanus saw in the royal library in 1525 he said: »Vidimus grandem librum apostolicorum canonum, opus incomparabile; vidimus Theodoretum Cyrensem in Psalterium integrum. Vidimus Chrysostomi, Athanasii, Cyrilli, Nazianzeni, Basilii Magni, Gregorii Nysseni, Theophanis, Dorothei infinita opera. Vidimus Marcum monachum, cognomento Anachoritam«. Subsequent to this list, Brassicanus enumerated some of his manuscripts he planned to publish in print, among which appear Philo's eleventh-century manuscript (Vienna, ÖNB, suppl. gr. 50), a number of works by Gregory of Nazianzus and Basil the Great, 14 homilies by Severianus of Gabbala, and the commentary on Genesis by Gregory of Nyssa.

89 Cf. NÉMETH (see note 78), pp. 158–63.

90 Cf. ENNEA S. PICCOLOMINI III.: Inventario della libreria medicea privata compilato nel 1495. In: *Archivio storico italiano*. 20 (1875), pp. 51–94. See *capsae* nos. 1, 3/4 and 8/9. In the Medici collection, the Greek manuscripts were mainly paper codices, while the Latin ones parchment codices. The inventory registered separate cases which contained the unbound paper and parchment gatherings (p. 79). King Matthias' collection must have shown a similar picture.

91 Cf. MARIANNE ROZSONDAI: Sulle legature in cuoio dorato per Mattia Corvino. In: *Nel Segno del Corvo: libri e miniature della biblioteca di Mattia Corvino re d'ungaria (1443–1490)*. Modena 2002, pp. 249–59, here p. 259, nos. 16, 46. Available online. See index of websites on p. 374.

HERMANN BAUMEISTER

Universalis Cosmographiae descriptio

Der Editionsplan Gauthier Luds aus Saint-Dié mit dem Humanisten Matthias Ringmann und dem Kartografen Martin Waldseemüller

DIE STADT SAINT-DIÉ (lat. Deodatus) liegt in einer Talmulde am Ufer der Meurthe, am Westrand der Vogesen, etwa 80 km südwestlich von Straßburg, der Hochburg des elsässischen Humanismus und neben Basel eine der bedeutendsten Metropolen der Buchdruckkunst. Saint-Dié, ein aus einem ehemaligen Benediktinerkloster hervorgegangener Ort im Herzogtum Lothringen mit etwa zweitausend Einwohnern, war Sitz eines Stiftskapitels. Nur zehn Kilometer entfernt lagen die ergiebigen Silberminen von La Croix. Das Herzogtum gehörte dem Heiligen Römischen Reich Deutscher Nation an; es wurde seit 1473 von Herzog René II., Titularkönig von Jerusalem, regiert. In der Schlacht von Nancy besiegte René II. am 5. Januar 1477 mit Hilfe der Eidgenossen Herzog Karl den Kühnen von Burgund, der dort den Tod fand. Nach seinem Sieg belohnte Herzog René seine Getreuen mit gut dotierten Ämtern, so auch Angehörige der Familie Lud (Ludwig), die aus dem elsässischen, also deutschsprachigen Pfaffenhofen stammte. Gauthier (auch Vaudrin, Walter) Lud (1448–1527)[1] war zunächst Sekretär des Herzogs und wurde 1490 zum Kanoniker im Kapitel seiner Heimatstadt ernannt. Im Dienst der Kirche errichtete er am nördlichen Stadtrand auf seine Kosten ein Haus für Pestkranke, verbunden mit einer Rochuskapelle. 1504 ernannte ihn der Herzog als Nachfolger seines Bruders Johannes Lud zum Generaldirektor des Bergwerkes von Ste. Croix-aux-Mines, eines Unternehmens, das zeitweilig bis zu zweitausend Bergleute beschäftigte. Als Förderer der Künste stiftete er zwei kostbar illuminierte Seiten eines Graduales, also eines liturgischen Buches für den Chorgesang.

1490 gründete Gauthier Lud mit Hilfe des Herzogs das *Gymnasium Vosagense*, eine Vereinigung gelehrter Humanisten, die sich neben philologischen Studien vor allem der Kosmografie, also der Erd- und Himmelskunde, widmete. Mitglieder dieser Gruppe waren Jean Basin, Magister der Philosophie und der Schönen Künste, Pfarrer von Wisembach, Hofnotar und Kanonikus am Stift von Saint-Dié, ein hervorragender Latinist († 1524), weiterhin Pierre de Blarru (1437–1508), Magister der Philosophie und Verfasser eines 5044 lateinische Verse umfassenden *Liber Nanceidos*, eines Lobgedichts auf René II. als dem Sieger über Karl den Kühnen – Blarru war angeblich ein Kommilitone des Vagantendichters François Villon –, schließlich Jean Pelérin, genannt Viator (um 1435–1527), aus Anjou, ebenfalls Kanonikus in Saint-Dié, später in Toul, Kirchendiplomat im Dienste des Hauses Anjou und des Herzogs von Lothringen. Dieser betrieb astronomische und geografische Studien, schrieb eine Abhandlung *De Artificali*

1 Vgl. ALBERT RONSIN: L'Imprimerie humaniste à Saint-Dié au XVIe siècle. In: *Refugium animae bibliotheca. Festschrift für Albert Kolb*. Wiesbaden 1969, S. 382–425. – DERS.: *La fortune d'un nom: America*. Grenoble 1991. – J. FRANK: Walther Lud. In: ADB 19, S. 361–5. – HEINRICH CHARLES: *Der deutsche Ursprung des Namens Amerika*. New York 1922.

Perspectiva und zeichnete Karten nach Ptolemäus. Gauthier Lud selbst befasste sich mit Astronomie, mit der Bewegung der Fixsterne und Planeten.

In diesem *Gymnasium Vosagense* entstand der ehrgeizige Plan einer *Universalis Cosmographiae descriptio*, einer Beschreibung des gesamten Kosmos und der Erde nach der Überlieferung des Ptolemäus und nach dem neuesten Stand der Entdeckungen. Im April 1507 veröffentlichte Gauthier Lud bei Johann Grüninger in Straßburg seine Schrift *Speculi orbis declaratio*,[2] eine Erklärung eines *Astrolabiums*, eines astronomischen Instruments zur Bestimmung von Länge und Breite der Gestirne. In der Widmung dieses Weltspiegels an René, König von Jerusalem und Sizilien, Herzog von Lothringen, kündigte Gauthier Lud an:

> Wir können nicht nur ausführlich und genau die Topographie Europas darstellen, sondern auch die unbekannten Landstriche [ignota terra], die durch den portugiesischen König schon früher, vor der Erfindung dieses Weltspiegels entdeckt worden waren, oberflächlich [propere] anzeigen. Eine genaue und exakte Beschreibung dieser Küsten ist aus dem Ptolemäus zu ersehen, den wir bald, mit Gottes Hilfe und auf unsere Kosten, vollkommen revidiert und großartig erweitert mit Martin Ilacomylus [Waldseemüller], den in dieser Materie erfahrensten Fachmann, herausgeben werden. Die Beschreibung dieser Region, die dir, erlauchtester König René, aus Portugal zugesandt wurde, wurde auf meine Bitte aus der französischen Sprache von dem ausgezeichneten Dichter Jean Basin aus Sandaucourt in elegantes Latein übersetzt. Es sind auch bei den Buchhändlern einige Epigramme von unserem Philesius Vogesigena [Matthias Ringmann] in der Schrift von Vespucci in Umlauf, die der Venezianer Architekt Giovanni Giocondo aus Verona ins Latein übersetzte.[3]

Der Astronom und Geograf Claudius Ptolemäus aus Alexandria (um 100–170 n. Chr.)[4] hatte bewiesen, dass die Erde eine Kugel ist, auf der Land- und Wassermassen untermischt sind. In seiner *Geographia* gibt er in acht Büchern eine Anleitung zur Anfertigung von Karten. Grundlage seines Systems sind die Koordinaten von Breiten- und Längengraden. Der Null-Meridian läuft über die *Insulae fortunatae*, die Kanarischen Inseln, der von der heutigen Einteilung von Greenwich um +18° abweicht. Das Werk enthält eine Tabelle von rund achttausend Orts-, Fluss- und Gebirgsnamen mit ihren Breiten- und Längengraden. Im Westen verschollen, wurde sein Werk aus griechischen und arabischen Quellen Anfang des XV. Jahrhunderts aus Byzanz nach dem Westen Europas tradiert. Hier übersetzte 1406 Jacobo d'Angelo da Scarperia die griechische Ausgabe der *Geographia* des Ptolemäus ins Lateinische. Zahlreiche Druckausgaben erschienen seit den siebziger Jahren des XV. Jahrhunderts [siehe Tab. 1].

Die Ausgaben des Ptolemäus enthielten in der Regel 27 alte Grundkarten. Die frühen italienischen Ausgaben wurden von Kupferplatten gedruckt. Sie sind im Ergebnis flach und wenig ausgefeilt. Bei der Ulmer Ausgabe von 1482 wurde zum ersten Mal die Holzschnitttechnik angewandt. Der gezeichnete Entwurf wurde von einem Reißer auf einen Holzstock übertragen. Von einem Formschneider wurden die Linien und Texte mit dem Schneidemesser aus dem Holzblock erhaben herausgearbeitet und eingeschwärzt. Mit Hilfe der Presse wurde die Karte mit ihrem Text in einem Arbeitsgang gedruckt.

---

[2] GUALTERUS LUDD: *Speculi Orbis succinctiss sed neque poenitenda neque inelegans Declaratio et Canon*. Straßburg Grüninger 1507. VD 16 L 3128.

[3] M. D'AVEZAC: *Martin Hylacomylus Waltzemüller, ses ouvrages et collaborateurs*. Paris 1867, S. 65.

[4] *Die Karte als Kunstwerk*. Hrsg. BSB. Unterschneidheim 1979, S.15/6. – Die Ulmer Geographia des Ptolemäus von 1482. Hrsg. von KARL-HEINZ MEINE. Weißenhorn 1982 (*Veröffentlichungen der Stadtbibliothek Ulm.* 2), S. 16/7.

1475	in Vicenza bei Hermann Liechtenstein, ohne Karten
1477	in Bologna bei Domenico de Lapi mit 27 Kupferstichkarten von Manfredi und Avogario
1478	in Rom bei Arnold Bucking mit 27 Kupferstichkarten von Conrad Sweynheym
1482	in Florenz bei Nicolo Tedescho mit 31 Kupferstichkarten von Francesco Berlingheri
1482	in Ulm bei Lienhart Holl mit 32 Holzschnittkarten von Nicolaus Germanus
1486	in Ulm bei Johannes Reger mit 32 Holzschnittkarten von Nicolaus Germanus
1490	in Rom bei Petrus de Turre mit 27 Holzschnittkarten von Nicolaus Germanus
1507 + 1508	in Rom bei Bernardus Venetus de Vitalibus mit 33 Kupferstichkarten von Marco Beneventanus und 1 Weltkarte von Ruysch
1511	in Venedig bei Giacomo Penzio mit 28 Holzschnittkarten von Bernardus Sylvanus Ebolensis

[Tab. 1] Druckausgaben der ptolemäischen *Geographia* seit den 70er Jahren des xv. Jahrhunderts

Die Entdeckungen der Portugiesen und Spanier im 15. Jahrhundert machten eine laufende Überarbeitung dieser Karten notwendig, die durch Korrektur der Küstenlinien auf den alten Karten oder durch Hinzufügen neuer Karten (*Tabulae novae*) angezeigt wurden. Die Portugiesen hatten, beginnend in den dreißiger Jahren des 15. Jahrhunderts, schrittweise die westafrikanische Küste erforscht. Bartolomeo Diaz erreichte 1482 die Südspitze Afrikas mit dem Kap der Guten Hoffnung. Den Seeweg nach Indien erschloss Vasco da Gama (um 1469–1524), der am 22. Mai 1498 nach Calicut in Indien gelangte. Der portugiesische Admiral Pedro Alvares de Cabral (ca. 1469–1520/26) segelte 1500 über Brasilien, das er als *Terra de Vera Cruz* für Portugal in Besitz nahm, nach Indien. 1501/02 erkundete der Florentiner Amerigo Vespucci (1452–1512) in portugiesischem Dienst die brasilianische Küste zwischen Pernambuco und dem Rio de la Plata. Auf der Suche nach einem Seeweg nach Westindien entdeckte 1492 Christoph Kolumbus (1451–1506) im Auftrag der spanischen Könige die Bahama-Insel Guanahani, Kuba und Hispaniola, d.h. Haiti. Auf seiner dritten Reise erreichte er am 30. Mai 1498 das südamerikanische Festland nahe der Orinoko-Mündung. 1499/1500 erkundete Alonso de Ojeda (um 1466–1501) die Nordküste Südamerikas von Guayana bis Venezuela. Giovanni Caboto (John Cabot; um 1450–99) landete 1497/98 auf der Suche nach einem nördlichen Seeweg nach Indien in Nordamerika. Dies war der Stand der Entdeckungen, als Gauthier Lud eine überarbeitete Neuausgabe der *Geographia* des Ptolemäus mit vollständig neuen Karten der Entdeckungen und mit Verbesserung aller durch Übersetzung aus dem Griechischen eingeschlichenen Irrtümer und Korrektur aller Druckfehler plante.

Der Humanist Matthias Ringmann und der Kartograf Martin Waldseemüller
In seiner Ankündigung nannte Gauthier Lud auch gleich die beiden Mitarbeiter, die er für sein Projekt gewonnen hatte: den Kartografen Martinus Ilacomylus (griech. ὕλη = Wald; λάκος = See; μύλη = Mühle), also Martin Waldseemüller, und den Humanisten Matthias Ringmann (um 1482–1511), der sich Philesius Vogesigena nannte. Martin Waltzemüller (ca. 1473–1520),[5] der sich später Waldseemüller schrieb, wurde wahrscheinlich in Wolfenweiler bei Freiburg im Breisgau geboren, nicht wie

5 Vgl. D'AVEZAC (siehe Anm. 3). – HERMANN MAYER: Der Freiburger Geograph Martin Waldseemüller und die neu entdeckten Weltkarten desselben. In: *Schau-ins-Land*. 31 (1904), S. 16–34. – HANS WOLFF: Martin Waldseemüller. Bedeutendster Kosmograph in einer Epoche forschenden Umbruchs. In: *America. Das frühe Bild der Neuen Welt*. Hrsg. von HANS WOLFF. München 1992 (*Ausstellungskataloge / Bayerische Staatsbibliothek*. 58), S. 111–26.

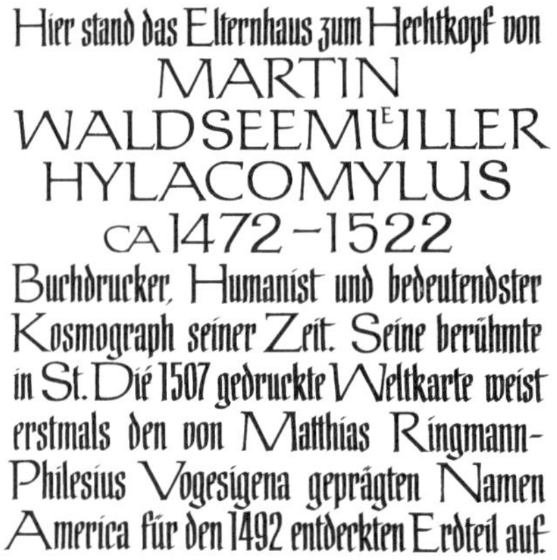

> Hier stand das Elternhaus zum Hechtkopf von
> **MARTIN WALDSEEMÜLLER HYLACOMYLUS CA 1472–1522**
> Buchdrucker, Humanist und bedeutendster Kosmograph seiner Zeit. Seine berühmte in St. Dié 1507 gedruckte Weltkarte weist erstmals den von Matthias Ringmann-Philesius Vogesigena geprägten Namen America für den 1492 entdeckten Erdteil auf.

[Abb. 1] Gedenktafel an den Kartografen Martin Waldseemüller an der Stelle seines Freiburger Elternhauses *Zum Hechtkopf* in der Löwenstraße 9–11

noch oft behauptet in Radolfszell.[6] Sein Vater Konrad Waltzemüller betrieb in Freiburg seit 1480 im Haus *Zum Hechtkopf* in der Löwenstraße 9–11 eine Metzgerei mit Viehhandel. Dort erinnert heute eine Gedenktafel [Abb. 1] an »Martin Waldseemüller Hylacolymus (ca. 1472–1522),[7] Buchdrucker, Humanist und bedeutendster Kosmograph seiner Zeit«. Konrad Waltzemüller galt als *Judenküng* und kam als Führer einer Bürgeropposition gegen den Rat der Stadt 1491 unter ungeklärten Umständen ums Leben. Als *Martinus Walzemüller de Friburgo Const. Dioc.* schrieb sich Martin Waldseemüller am 7. Dezember 1490 an der Universität seiner Heimatstadt ein. Sein Mentor war der gelehrte Gregor Reisch (ca. 1470–1525), seit 1489 Lehrer der *Artes Liberales*, später Prior des Freiburger Kartäuserklosters. Bei Reisch wurde Waldseemüller in die Mathematik, Geometrie und Astronomie eingeführt. Er dachte zunächst an eine geistliche Laufbahn und ließ sich als Subdiakon ausweihen, wie aus einer späteren Bewerbung als Kleriker der Diözese Konstanz um ein Kanonikat in Saint-Dié hervorgeht.[8] Bei seinem Onkel Jakob Waltzemüller in Basel erlernte er die Kunst des Buchdrucks. Um das Jahr 1504 wurde er mit dem Kanonikus Gauthier Lud aus Saint-Dié bekannt, der ihn für sein geplantes Projekt einer zeitgemäßen Ptolemäusausgabe anheuerte.

Ebenso nahm Gauthier Lud auch den Humanisten Matthias Ringmann[9] unter Vertrag, den er in seiner oben genannten Einleitung als »unseren Philesius« vorstellte. Geboren 1482 im elsässischen Eichhoffen, besuchte er wahrscheinlich das nahe gelegene humanistische Gymnasium in Schlettstadt und studierte in Heidelberg bei dem Humanisten Jakob Wimpfeling, dem Autor der *Germania*, der ersten deutschen Nationalgeschichte. Zu seinen Lehrern in Heidelberg gehörte auch Gregor Reisch. In Paris hörte er Vorlesungen bei dem italienischen Humanisten Publius Faustus Adrelinus und vertiefte seine mathematischen, astronomischen und geografischen Kenntnisse bei Faber Stapulensis, d. i. Jacques Levèvre d'Estables. Dort erwarb er auch bei einem Byzantiner Kenntnisse des Griechischen. In Straßburg kam er über seinen Lehrer Wimpfeling mit dem dortigen Humanistenkreis in Verbindung und stand auch in Kontakt mit Konrad Peutinger in Nürnberg und Heinrich Bebel in Tübingen. Nach einem Versuch als Schulleiter in Colmar und Straßburg arbeitete er als Korrektor in den Straßburger Druckereien von Johann Prüss, Johann Grüninger und Johann Knobloch und übersetzte *Julius der erst Römische Keiser von seinen kriegen*, eine Zusammenstellung von Caesars *Bellum Gallicum* und *Bellum Civile* und Plutarchs Caesaren-Vita. Als gelehrter Humanist fügte Matthias Ringmann in den von ihm herausgegebenen Werken als Einleitung lateinische Verse mit Inhaltsangabe und Lobgedichten über die Autoren bei.

1505 edierte Ringmann bei Matthias Hüpfuff in Straßburg unter dem Titel *De ora antarctica*[10] den Bericht Amerigo Vespuccis an Lorenzo di Pierfrancesco de' Medici über dessen dritte Entdeckungsreise vom 14. Mai 1501, die er mit einer Flotte von drei Schiffen von Lissabon über Cabo Verde (Dakar) unternommen hatte. Am 17. August 1501 landete er in Brasilien auf 5° Süd und segelte der brasilianischen Küste bis 32° Süd entlang; er kehrte über Sierra Leone und die Azoren am 7. September 1502

---

6 FRANZ GÖTZ: Wurde der Kartograph Martin Waldseemüller in Radolfszell geboren? In: *Hegau, Zeitschrift für Geschichte, Volkskunde und Naturgeschichte des Gebietes zwischen Rhein, Donau und Bodensee*. 17 (1964), S. 51–62.

7 Todesjahr 1519/20. RONSIN: L'Imprimerie (siehe Anm. 1), S. 410.

8 LUCIEN GALLOIS: Waldseemüller Chanoine de Saint-Dié. In: *Bulletin trimestrial de la Sociéte de l'Est.* NS. 21 (1900), S. 221–9, hier S. 222.

9 FRANZ JOSEF WORSTBROCK: Matthias Ringmann (Philesius Vogesigena). In: *Die deutsche Literatur des Mittelalters*. Verfasserlexikon. Bd. 11, Sp. 1310–26. – RICHARD NEWALD: *Elsässische Charakterköpfe aus dem Zeitalter des Humanismus*. Colmar o. J. [1944], S. 187–206.

10 *De ora antarctica per regem Portugallie pridem inventa*. Straßburg: Mathias Hüpfuff, 1505. VD 16 V 937.

zurück. In dieser Schrift beschrieb Vespucci die neuen Regionen, »die man als Neue Welt (Mundus Novus) bezeichnen könnte« und wie er »in den südlichen Breiten einen Kontinent fand, der mit Vögeln und Tieren dichter besiedelt ist, als unser Europa oder Asien und Afrika«.[11] Damit wandte sich Vespucci gegen die vorherrschende Meinung, dass Kolumbus auf seinen Entdeckungsfahrten Westindien bzw. die westindischen Inseln entdeckt hatte. Vespucci war damit zwar nicht der Entdecker des neuen Kontinents; er stellte aber fest, dass das neu entdeckte Land ein eigener Erdteil war. Wie Ringmann an seinen Freund Jakob Braun am 1. August 1505 schrieb, hatte er die Schrift Vespuccis durch Zufall zu Gesicht bekommen, sie voller Eifer durchgelesen und sie Stück für Stück mit dem Ptolemäus verglichen, dessen Karten er im Augenblick mit großer Sorgfalt studierte.[12] Ringmann fügte dieser Schrift ein eigenes Gedicht über diese neu entdeckte Welt bei. Gauthier Lud konnte also keinen fachkundigeren *Castigator*, also Korrektor, und mehr noch – Übersetzer, Lektor und Herausgeber – für seine geplante Ptolemäusedition gewinnen.

Die Kosmografie Matthias Ringmanns
Mit Unterstützung des Herzogs von Lothringen und der Hilfe von Pierre Jacobi, einem Priester und Drucker aus St. Nicolas de Port, richtete Gauthier Lud Anfang 1507 für sein Ptolemäusprojekt in seinem Haus in Saint-Dié eine *Officina Libraria*, eine Druckerwerkstatt, ein. Er besorgte sich einen Satz Antiqua-Schriften, wie sie besonders für lateinische wissenschaftliche Werke gebraucht wurden. Als Leiter der Druckerei setzte er seinen Neffen Nicolas Lud ein. Als erstes Werk aus seiner Presse erschien am 25. April 1507 eine *Cosmographiae Introductio*,[13] eine Einführung in die Kosmografie [Abb. 2]. Sie beschäftigt sich mit geometrischen und astronomischen Grundsätzen der Sphäre, der Trigonometrie der Kugeloberfläche, mit den Koordinatensystemen, den Breiten- und Längengraden, Achsen, Polen, Himmelskreisen, Parallelen, den Klimazonen und den Windrichtungen. Im neunten Kapitel werden die Einteilung der Erde, die Kontinente und die Grenzen der Meere, Inseln und die Entfernung der verschiedenen Orte beschrieben. Als Vorlage diente die Syntaxis Mathematica des Ptolemäus, bekannt in ihrer arabischen Bearbeitung als *Amalgest*, und ihrer lateinischen Version *Sphaera terrae* des Johannes de Sacrobosco (1230), der wichtigste mittelalterliche Text für das Studium der Astronomie und Kosmografie. Ringmanns Lehrer Faber Stapulensis hatte die Sphaera terrae 1499 neu herausgegeben.

Beigelegt wurde eine von Basin de Sandoucourt aus dem Französischen angefertigte lateinische Übersetzung der *Quattuor Americi Vesputii Navigationes*, der Philesius Vogesigena eine Widmung an den Leser beifügte. Amerigo Vespucci hatte diesen Bericht dem Gondolfiere (Stadthauptmann) Piero Soderini (1450–1513) übermittelt. Herzog René II. hatte neben Kartenmaterial aus Portugal eine französische Fassung der Briefe besorgt. Vespucci war nach humanistischen Studien bei seinem Onkel und nach mathematischem und astronomischem Unterricht bei Paolo del Pozzo di Toscanelli in das Bankhaus des Lorenzo di Pierfrancesco de'

COSMOGRAPHIAE
INTRODVCTIO
CVM QVIBVS
DAM GEOME
TRIAE
AC
ASTRONO
MIAE PRINCIPIIS AD
EAM REM NECESSARIIS

Insuper quattuor Americi
Vespucij nauigationes.

Vniuersalis Cosmographiæ descriptio tam in solido q̄ plano/ eis etiam insertis quæ Ptholomæo ignota a nuperis reperta sunt.

DISTHYCON

Cum deus astra regat/& terræ climata Cæsar
Nec tellus/nec eis sydera maius habent.

[Abb. 2] *Cosmographiae Introductio, eine Einführung in die Kosmographie mit den dafür notwendigen geometrischen und astronomischen Grundsätzen, zusammen mit den vier Seereisen des Amerigo Vespucci. 2. Aufl. Saint-Dié: Gauthier Lud, 1507.*
UB Freiburg T 2047, aa

11 *De ora antarctica* (siehe Anm. 10), f. 2ᵛ.
12 D'AVEZAC (siehe Anm. 3), S. 91/2.
13 *Cosmographiae introductio cum quibusdam geometriae ac astronomiae principiis ad eam rem necessariis.* Saint-Dié: Gaulthier Lud, 25. 4. 1507. Schlettstadt Humanisten Bibliothek. Faksimile: Die Cosmographiae introductio des Martin Waldseemüller (Ilacomylus) im Faksimiledruck. Hrsg. von FRANZ VON WIESER. Straßburg 1907 (*Drucke und Holzschnitte des XV. und XVI. Jahrhunderts in getreuer Nachbildung.* 12). Transskription und deutsche Übersetzung. In: MARTIN LEHMANN: *Die Cosmographiae Introductio Matthias Ringmanns und die Weltkarte Martin Waldseemüllers aus dem Jahre 1507.* München 2010, S 261–327.

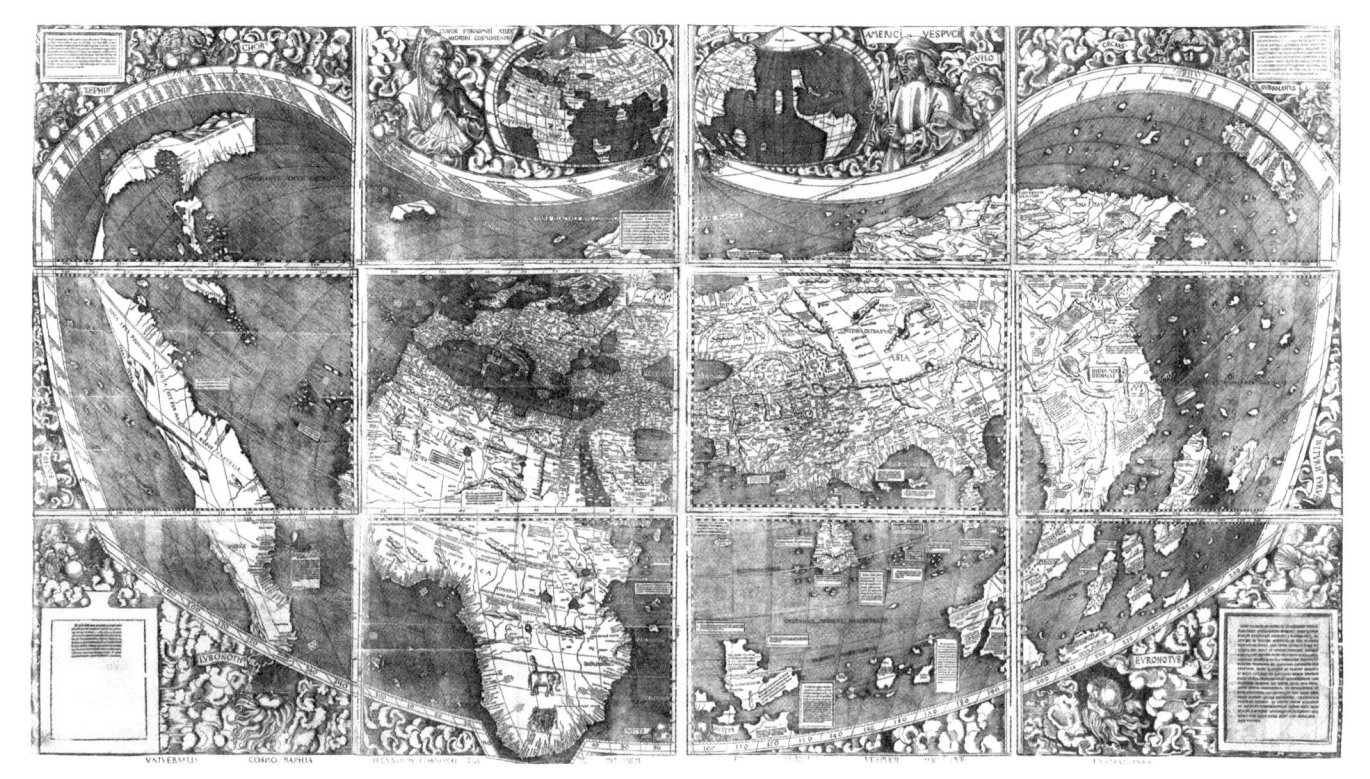

[Abb. 3] MARTIN WALDSEEMÜLLER: *Universalis Cosmographia secundum Ptolemei Traditionem.* Weltkarte im Format 232 × 129 cm, gedruckt auf 12 Holzstöcken 59 × 43 cm. Am linken Bildrand eine Insel mit dem Eindruck *America,* der erste Nachweis des Namens *America* auf einer Karte. Im Norden dieser Insel heißt es: »Diese Provinz wurde auf Befehl des Königs von Kastilien entdeckt«. Saint-Dié: Gauthier Lud, 1507. Washington DC, L of Congress

Medici eingetreten.[14] Im Dienst des Bankhauses half er 1491 in Sevilla bei der Ausrüstung der Flotte des Kolumbus. Vom 10. Mai 1497 bis 15. Oktober 1498 nahm er an einer Entdeckungsfahrt in die Karibik teil, die unter Diáz de Solis in die Karibik und entlang der Küste von Costa Rica, Mexiko und Florida führte.[15] Eine zweite Reise unter Alonso de Hojeda vom 18. Mai 1499 bis 22. April 1500 führte ihn an die südamerikanische Küste von Guayana und Venezuela. Im Auftrag des Königs von Portugal unternahm er die oben beschriebene dritte Reise mit Gonçalo Coelho an die brasilianische Küste von 5° bis 32° Süd. In einer vierten Reise, diesmal unter eigenem Kommando, ebenfalls im Dienste Portugals, erreichte er die Küste Südamerikas bis 18° Süd bei Baia de Todos os Santos, also Bahia. Die moderne Forschung bezweifelt die Echtheit der ersten und vierten Reise Vespuccis; über den Stand dieses äußerst schwierigen Diskurses sei deshalb eigens auf den Artikel über Vespucci in Dieter Henzes *Enzyklopädie der Entdecker und Erforscher der Erde* hingewiesen.[16]

Die Erstausgabe der *Cosmographia* und der *Quattuor Navigationes* vom 25. April 1507 (VII. Kal. Maij 1507) ist heute nur noch in wenigen Exemplaren nachweisbar: In der Humanistenbibliothek in Schlettstadt, in der Bayrischen Staatsbibliothek in München, in der British Library in London und in der Bibliothèque Nationale von Paris.

14 URS BITTERLI: Die Entdeckung Amerikas. Von Kolumbus bis Alexander von Humboldt. München 1999 (*Beck'sche Reihe.* 1322), S.113–6.
15 *Amerigo Vespucci. El nuevo mundo. Cartas relativas a sus viajes y descubrimientos.* Hrsg. von ROBERTO LEVILLIER. Buenos Aires 1951, S.17–9.
16 DIETER HENZE: *Enzyklopädie der Entdecker und Erforscher der Erde.* Graz 1978–2004, Bd. 5, S. 396–406.

[Abb. 4] MARTIN WALDSEEMÜLLER: *Universalis Cosmographia*. Kartusche vom oberen rechten Bildrand der Weltkarte. Amerigo Vespucci mit Zirkel und der Halbkugel mit dem Mundus novus. Südamerika mit dem Südlichen Nordamerika, links daneben die Insel Zipangu, d. i. Japan, und der asiatische Kontinent mit Indien. Im Gegensatz zur Hauptkarte fehlt hier der Hinweis auf *America* [siehe Abb. 3]

Die Weltkarte Universalis Cosmographia und die Globensegmentkarte Martin Waldseemüllers

Zusammen mit der *Cosmographia* erschien eine Weltkarte *Universalis Cosmographia secundum Ptolomaei traditionem et Americi Vespucii aliorumque Lustrationes*, nach der Tradition des Ptolemäus mit den Entdeckungen von Vespucci und anderen [Abb. 3]. Die monumentale Wandkarte im Format 129 × 232 cm wurde von zwölf holzgeschnittenen Druckstöcken im Format 59 × 43 cm gedruckt. Sie zeigt in einer Kartusche am oberen Bildrand Claudius Ptolemäus mit einem Quadranten und einer Halbkugel mit der alten Welt; rechts daneben erscheint Amerigo Vespucci mit einem Kompass und einer Halbkugel mit dem *Mundus Novus* [Abb. 4]. Am linken Bildrand ist der neu entdeckte vierte Erdteil »als eine Insel, die von Meer umgeben ist«, eingezeichnet, wie es in der *Cosmographia* beschrieben ist.[17] In einem Rahmentext bei den Westindischen Inseln wird festgestellt, dass »diese Inseln durch den Genueser Columbus als Admiral im Auftrag des Königs von Kastilien entdeckt wurden«. Neu ist die besondere Projektionsform der Weltkarte: Waldseemüller projizierte den Globus in einem herzförmigen Netz. Die Karte wurde als Holzschnitt hergestellt. Neben den als Holzschnitt herausgeschnittenen Namen der Erdteile, Länder, Berge und Flüsse wurden in einem neuen Verfahren erklärende

17 *Cosmographia* (siehe Anm. 13), Fol. 14ᵛ.

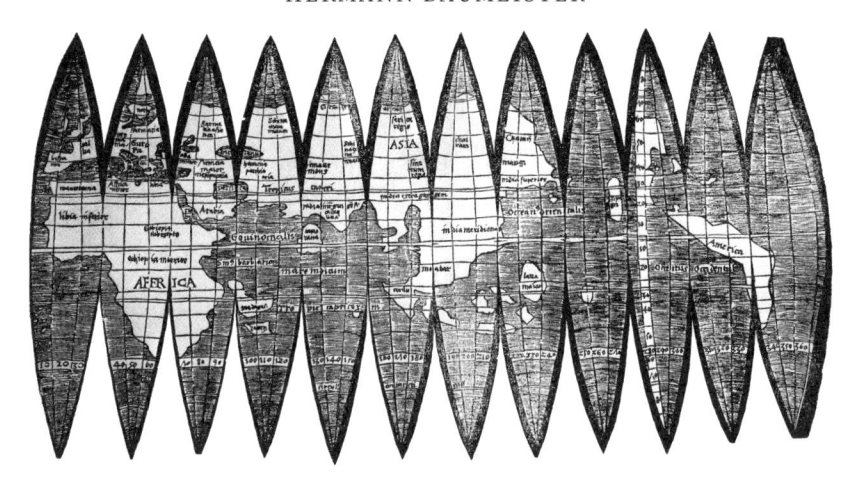

[Abb. 5] MARTIN WALDSEEMÜLLER: Globussegmentkarte (Korpus ca. 36 x 18 cm. Zum Anfertigen eines Erdglobus von ca. 11 cm Durchmesser). Rechts ist der neue Kontinent als eine Insel im Ozean sichtbar, mit dem Eindruck *America*. Saint-Dié: Gauthier Lud, 1507. StB Offenburg

Texte in Metalllettern in den Holzstock eingesetzt. Die Weltkarte wurde 1903 von dem Jesuiten Joseph Fischer in der Bibliothek des Fürsten von Waldburg-Wolfegg entdeckt und zusammen mit Franz von Wieser in einer Faksimileausgabe herausgegeben. Die Übereinstimmung des Titels, die gedruckten Legenden mit dem Text und den Wappen der Länder bei *Cosmographia* und Weltkarte und schließlich die Tatsache, dass die Karte in mehreren Blättern gedruckt wurde, beweisen nach Fischer die Identität der beiden Dokumente.[18] Die Karte, wahrscheinlich ein späterer Abdruck von 1516,[19] ist heute im Besitz der Library of Congress in Washington. Sie wurde von Bundeskanzlerin Angela Merkel am 30. April 2007 anlässlich der 500-Jahrfeier des Namens Amerika in Washington symbolisch übergeben; die Deutsche Bundespost gab aus diesem Anlass eine Sonderbriefmarke dieser Weltkarte heraus. Ein Faksimiledruck ist im Kartensaal der BSB in München ausgestellt.

Als *Universalis Cosmographiae descriptio in solido* erschien 1507 eine Globussegmentkarte, mit der der Benutzer eine Holzkugel bekleben und so einen Globus anfertigen konnte [Abb. 5]. Der älteste erhaltene Erdglobus ist der sogenannte Erdapfel (Durchmesser 51 cm) des Nürnberger Kaufmanns und Astronomen Martin Beheim (1457–1507). Er wurde 1492 von Georg Glockendon d. Ä. (tätig 1483–1514) in Nürnberg nach der Weltkarte des Henricus Martellus Germanus (Heinrich Hammer; tätig 1480–96) handgezeichnet und enthält noch das Weltbild, an dem sich Christoph Kolumbus bei seinen Entdeckungsreisen orientierte: Die Ostküste Afrikas wird durch ein Meer von der Westküste Asiens getrennt. Auf dem Erdapfel von Martin Beheim lassen sich die wichtigsten Länder, Städte und Flüsse der Erde feststellen. Der erste gedruckte kleine Globus Waldseemüllers (Durchmesser 11 cm) diente hingegen der Veranschaulichung der in der *Cosmographia* vorgebrachten wichtigsten Grundstrukturen der Erdkugel, mit den Kontinenten Europa, Afrika und Asien und Süd-Amerika als einer Insel, mit den Meeren *Oceanus occidentalis* (Atlantik),

18 *Die älteste Karte mit dem Namen Amerika aus dem Jahr 1507 und die Carta marina aus dem Jahr 1516 des M. Waldseemüller (Ilacomilus)*. Hrsg. von JOSEPH FISCHER u. FRANZ VON WEISER. Innsbruck 1903, S. 9/10.
19 ELIZABETH HARRIS: The Waldseemüller World Map: a Typographic Appraisal. In: *Imago Mundi*. 37 (1985), S. 30–53, hier S. 50.

Oceanus orientalis (Pazifik) und *mare indicum* (Indischer Ocean). Außerdem sind 360 Längengrade und je 90 Breitengrade Nord und Süd in Zehnerstufen eingezeichnet. Der Äquator wird als *Aequinoctalis*, der *Tropicus Cancri* und *Cabricorni*, die Wendekreise des Krebses und des Steinbocks auf 23° Nord beziehungsweise 23° Süd eingezeichnet. Ein Originalglobus ist nicht erhalten; eine Nachbildung steht im Deutschen Museum in München neben einer Replik des Erdapfels von Beheim. Lange Zeit war nur eine der oben erwähnten Globussegmentkarten aus dem früheren Besitz des Ritters von Hauslab in der James Ford Bell Library der University of Minnesota, Mineapolis bekannt. Im Jahre 1990 konnte die Bayerische Staatsbibliothek in München eine Karte erwerben, 1993 wurde ein weiteres Exemplar bei Restaurierungsarbeiten in der Historischen Bibliothek der Stadt Offenburg entdeckt. Eine vierte Karte fand ein Privatmann auf Grund eines Artikels in der Frankfurter Allgemeinen Zeitung.[20] Sie erzielte angeblich bei einer Auktion bei Christie's in London am 9. Juni 2005 einen Rekordpreis von € 812 000.[21]

Die *Cosmographiae Introductio*, die Weltkarte *Universalis cosmographia* und die Globensegmentkarte sind zusammen als Medienpaket[22] anonym erschienen. Als Druckerzeichen erscheint in der *Cosmographia* ein Doppelkreuz in einem Kreis, d. i. ein Globus, mit den Buchstaben SD, GL, NL und MI, für St. Dié, Gauthier Lud, Nicolas Lud und Martin Ilacomylus [Abb. 6]. In ihnen wird zum ersten Mal der Name *America* nach seinem vorgeblichen Entdecker Amerigo Vespucci benannt. In der *Cosmographia* heißt es:

> Jetzt aber nachdem diese Teile (Europa, Afrika, Asien) weithin erforscht sind und ein anderer, vierter Teil, wie aus dem Folgenden zu ersehen ist, durch Amerigo Vespucci entdeckt wurde, sehe ich nicht ein, welches Recht es verbietet, das Land des Americus nach seinem Entdecker, dem genialen Mann Ameri ge (griech. Land des Americus) zu benennen, beziehungsweise America, wie auch Europa und Asien nach Frauen benannt worden sind. Seine Lage und die Gebräuche seiner Völker sind aus den zweimal zwei Reisen des Americus, die unten folgen, leicht zu ersehen. [Abb. 7]

In der großen Wandkarte *Universalis Cosmographia secundum Ptolomaei traditionem* wird der neue Erdteil als *America* bezeichnet, ebenso in der Globussegmentkarte. In der Kartusche der Wandkarte mit Amerigo Vespucci wird in der Halbkugel die Neue Welt noch als *Terra incognita* benannt.

Aus Druckersignet und Widmung der zweiten Ausgabe der *Cosmographia* vom 28. August 1509 schloss Alexander von Humboldt, dass Martin Waldseemüller der Urheber aller drei Druckwerke war; auch Franz von Wieser folgte dieser These.[23] Waldseemüller galt deshalb lange Zeit als Namensgeber Amerikas. Eine kritische Untersuchung der Erstausgabe der *Cosmographiae introductio* vom 25. April (VII. Kal Maij) 1507 durch Franz Laubenberger[24] zeigte jedoch, dass Philesius Vogesigena, also Ringmann, dem Kaiser Maximilian I. »hinc tibi devota generale«, also das Gesamtwerk widmete. In einer zweiten Widmung dediziert Martinus Ilacomylus »totius orbis typum tam in solido quam plano«, also den Erdglobus (in

[Abb. 6] Druckersignet der Offizin von Gaulthier Lud in Saint-Dié. Globus mit Kreuz. SD für Saint-Dié; GL für Gaulthier Lud; NL für Nicolaus Lud; MI für Martin Ilacolymus (Waldseemüller). Aus: *Cosmographiae* [siehe Abb. 2]

20 FRANZ GEORG KALTWASSER: Taufschein in ausgesprochen drolliger Form. Wie Amerika zu seiner Bezeichnung kam. In: *Frankfurter Allgemeine Zeitung* vom 15. 2. 2003, S. 38.
21 UTE OBHOF: Der Erdglobus, der Amerika benannte. Die Überlieferung der Globensegmente von Martin Waldseemüller aus dem Jahre 1507. In: *Neue Welt und altes Wissen. Wie Amerika zu seinem Namen kam*. Hrsg. von SUSANNE ASCHE u. WOLFGANG M. GALL. Offenburg 2006, S. 46.
22 Ebd.
23 VON WIESER (siehe Anm. 13), S. 2.
24 FRANZ LAUBENBERGER: Ringmann oder Waldseemüller. In: *Erdkunde*. 13 (1959), S.163–79.

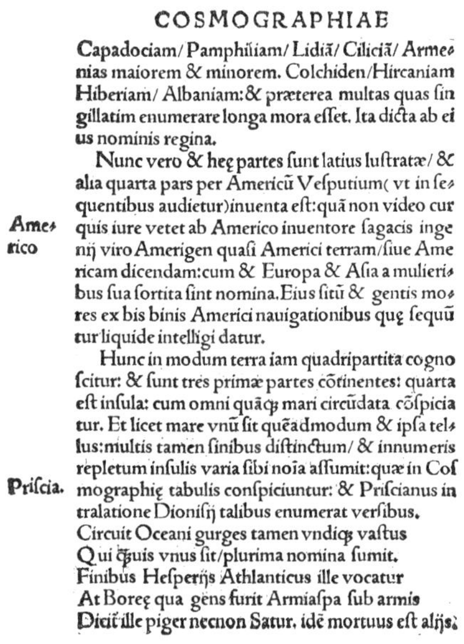

COSMOGRAPHIAE
Capadociam/ Pamphiliam/ Lidiã/ Ciliciã/ Armeniasmaiorem & minorem. Colchiden/Hircaniam Hiberiam/ Albaniam:& præterea multas quas sin gillatim enumerare longa mora esset. Ita dicta ab ei us nominis regina.
 Nunc vero & hęę partes sunt latius lustratæ/ & alia quarta pars per Americũ Vesputium(vt in sequentibus audietur)inuenta est:quã non video cur quis iure vetet ab Americo inuentore sagacis inge Ame- nij viro Amerigen quasi Americi terram/siue Ame rico ricam dicendam:cum & Europa & Asia a mulieribus sua sortita sint nomina.Eius situ & gentis mores ex bis binis Americi nauigationibus quę sequu tur liquide intelligi datur.
 Hunc in modum terra iam quadripartita cogno scitur: & sunt tres primæ partes cõtinentes: quarta est insula: cum omni quãq; mari circũdata cõspicia tur. Et licet mare vnũ sit quęadmodum & ipsa tel- lus:multis tamen finibus distinctum/ & innumeris repletum insulis varia sibi noĩa assumit:quę in Cos Priscia. mographię tabulis conspiciuntur: & Priscianus in tralatione Dionisij talibus enumerat versibus.
Circuit Oceani gurges tamen vndiq; vastus
Qui q̃uis vnus sit/plurima nomina sumit.
Finibus Hesperijs Athlanticus ille vocatur
At Boreę qua gens furit Armiaspa sub armis
Dicit ille piger necnon Satur. idẽ mortuus est alijs;

[Abb. 7] Taufurkunde Americas. Aus dem neunten Kapitel der *Cosmographiae* [siehe Abb. 2]

25 *Cosmographia* (siehe Anm. 13), f. 1ᵛ, 2ʳ.
26 RONSIN: L'Imprimerie (siehe Anm.1), S. 398 mit Karte; Anm. 30.
27 HENRY NEWTON STEVENS: The first delineation of the New World and the first use of the name America on a printed map, an analytical comparison of three maps for each of which priority of representation has been claimed [...] with an argument tending to demonstrate that the earliest in each case is the one discovered in 1893 and now preserved in the John Carter Brown Library in Providence. London 1928.
28 *Die Amerbachkorrespondenz. Band I. Die Briefe aus der Zeit Johann Amerbachs 1481–1513.* Hrsg. von ALFRED HARTMANN. Basel 1942, S. 312, Nr. 333.

solido) und die Weltkarte (in plano).[25] Matthias Ringmann ist demnach der Autor des Textes, während Waldseemüller die Weltkarte und den Erdglobus zeichnete. Das entspricht auch den Rollen der beiden Mitarbeiter Gauthier Luds. Matthias Ringmann war als *Castigator* für den Text verantwortlich, Martin Waldseemüller, der sich selbst als Drucker bezeichnete, entwarf die Karten. Nach dem Tod von Matthias Ringmann (1511) fehlt auf den Karten Waldseemüllers der Eindruck *America*, ein Indiz, dass Ringmann und nicht Waldseemüller der Urheber des Namens Amerikas war.

Die Quelle für die Arbeiten Ringmanns und Waldseemüllers war neben den oben aufgeführten Berichten Vespuccis eine Karte aus dem Besitz Herzog Renés II., die dieser sich auf diplomatischem Weg aus Portugal besorgt hatte. Die Könige von Portugal und Spanien ließen die sogenannten Portalankarten, d. h. die Navigationsunterlagen der Fahrten von Hafen zu Hafen, nach ihrer Rückkehr durch Kartografen systematisch auswerten. Zuständig dafür war ein *Pilota Mayor*, der Chef aller Steuerleute, ein Amt, das Amerigo Vespucci in der Casa de Contratacíon in Sevilla für die katholischen Könige von 1508–11 ausübte. Das dortige Kartenmaterial unterlag aus Konkurrenzgründen strengster Geheimhaltung; Kopieren und Weitergabe galt als Kapitalverbrechen. Die portugiesische Karte Renés entsprach der Weltkarte des Genuesen Nicola di Caverio (Canerio) von 1504/5, die die portugiesischen Entdeckungen der afrikanischen Küste auf dem Seeweg nach Indien und der östlichen Küste Südamerikas durch Cabral enthielt. Sie wurde 1544 bei einem Brand in Saint-Dié vernichtet. Ungeklärt ist, woher Waldseemüller seine Informationen über die westlichen Küstenlinien Südamerikas bezog, die erst 1525/26 von Guevara entdeckt wurden.

Neben der oben genannten Weltkarte *Universalis Cosmographia* erschien um 1507 eine Seekarte *Orbis typus universalis iuxta Hydrographorum Traditionem*. Diese Karte im Format 59 × 43 cm zeigt die Kontinente Europa, Asien und Afrika als Block, umgeben im Westen vom *Oceanus occidentalis*, im Süden vom *Mar Indicum*. Im Westen sind am Rand zwischen 30–5° die Inseln Hispaniola und Isabella eingezeichnet. Zwischen 15° Nord und 40° Süd befindet sich ein Festlandstreifen mit der Bezeichnung *America*. Titel, Namen der Kontinente und Ozeane sind in Holz geschnitten, circa 100 Orts-, Gebirgs- und Flussnamen sind von Lettern gedruckt. Diese Seekarte ohne Angabe von Ort, Datum und Drucker befindet sich heute in der John Carter Brown Library in Providence, Long Island.[26] Henry Newton Stevens beschrieb 1928 »drei Karten mit und ohne Eindruck America im Vergleich, mit dem Beweis, dass die 1893 entdeckte und in der John Carter Brown aufbewahrte Karte die älteste Karte mit dem ersten Gebrauch des Namens America ist«[27] und datierte sie auf 1506/07. Diese Karte war eine Musterkarte für die geplante Ptolemäusausgabe. In einem Brief vom 5. April 1507 an Johann Amerbach schrieb Waldseemüller: »Ich glaube, dass es dir nicht verborgen geblieben ist, dass wir in der Stadt Saint-Dié eine revidierte und mit einigen neuen Karten versehene Ptolemäusausgabe drucken werden [impressuros]«.[28] Aus dem Brief geht hervor, dass die große Weltkarte bereits fertiggestellt, der Erdglobus noch binnen Monatsfrist gedruckt werden sollte. Die Karte *Orbis typus universalis* ist demnach erst nach dem 25. April 1507 erschienen und nicht, wie Stevens vermutete, das Blatt mit der ersten Erwähnung Amerikas.

Weitere Arbeiten der Officin Gauthier Luds, Ringmanns und Waldseemüllers
Im gleichen Jahr 1507 erschien in der Druckerwerkstatt Gauthier Luds aus der Feder des Jean Basin, der auch die *Quattuor Navigationes* aus dem Französischen ins Lateinische übersetzt hatte, eine Stilkunde *Novus et elegansque conficiendas epistolas ac alias de arte dicendi modus*.[29] Das Buch enthielt Ratschläge für die Gestaltung von Briefen mit Hinweisen zur Fehlervermeidung, zum Satzaufbau und zur rhetorischen Ausschmückung. Laut Einleitung des Verfassers war das Büchlein sowohl für Anfänger wie auch für Fortgeschrittene bestimmt. Die Arbeit enthält einen Druckvermerk aus der Stadt Saint-Dié, ist aber mit den gleichen Lettern wie die *Cosmographia* gedruckt.

Die Verbindung Matthias Ringmanns und Martin Waldseemüllers zu ihrem Lehrer Gregor Reisch war nicht abgerissen. In der vierten Auflage der Margarita Philosophica, seines umfassenden Lehrbuchs der *Artes Liberales*, die 1508 bei ihrem Freiburger Kommilitonen, dem Straßburger Drucker Johann Schott erschien, schrieb Matthias Ringmann ein einleitendes lateinisches Distichon. Diese Ausgabe enthält auch einen Brief von Martin Waldseemüller an seinen Freund Matthias Ringmann, der zu dieser Zeit öffentliche Vorlesungen über die Kosmografie des Universums in Basel hielt:

> In dieser Zeit des Karnevals habe ich mich gewohnheitsgemäß zur Erholung nach Deutschland begeben und Frankreich, besser gesagt die Vogesenstadt Saint-Dié, verlassen. Dort haben wir erst neulich, nicht ohne meine große Anstrengung und Arbeit, eine Kosmografie sowohl als Karte als auch als Globus entworfen [composimus], gezeichnet [depinximus] und gedruckt [impressimus], nicht ohne weltweiten Lob und Ruhm zu ernten, den sich jetzt viele Andere fälschlicherweise zuschreiben. Während sich die Anderen vergnügten, habe ich verschiedenen Autoren zusammengetragen, die sich mit der Scenografie, einer Sektion der Architektur, und mit der positiven Perspektive befassen.[30]

So leitete Waldseemüller eine Abhandlung über *Architecturae et Perspectivae Rudimenta* ein. Er befasst sich mit der Scenografie, also mit der Messung von Linien, von Oberflächen und Festkörpern und mit den entsprechenden Messinstrumenten. Aus diesem Brief geht eindeutig hervor, dass neben der Cosmographia auch die Karte und der Globus bei Gauthier Lud in Saint-Dié entstanden sind.

Die Arbeiten an der Ptolemäusausgabe zogen sich länger hin als erwartet. Da die lateinischen Vorlagen nicht übereinstimmten, hatte Waldseemüller am Ostermontag 1507 in dem oben erwähnten Brief den Basler Drucker Amerbach um die Besorgung eines griechischen Originals aus dem dortigen Dominikanerkloster gebeten.[31] Diese Handschrift war nicht befriedigend. Deshalb unternahm Matthias Ringmann im Sommer 1508 eigens eine Reise nach Ferrara zu dem italienischen Humanisten Lilio Gregorio Giraldi (1479–1552), der ihn in die griechischen Ziffern einwies, und nach Novi zu Giovanni Francesco Pico della Mirandola (1463–94),

29 *Johannis Basini Sendacurtensi novus elegansque conficiendae epistulae ac alias de arte dicendi modus duos in principales de hoc in se complectens libros.* Saint-Dié 1507. BnF, 30064035. – RONSIN: L'Imprimerie (siehe Anm.1), S. 411, Anm.51.
30 GREGOR REISCH: *Margarita Philosophica*. Straßburg: Johann Schott, 1508, fol. 149ʳ.
31 *Die Amerbachkorrespondenz* (siehe Anm. 28), S. 312, Nr.333.

einem Neffen des großen Humanisten, der ihm eine griechische Handschrift mit dem Text des Ptolemäus aushändigte.

Im Juni 1509 erschien bei Gauthier Lud eine Grammatica figurata, eine lateinische Bildergrammatik.[32] In der Widmung an Hugo de Hazard, den Bischof von Toul, schreibt Gauthier Lud, dass er »unserem Philesius«, den er in seiner literarischen Anstalt als Korrektor beschäftige, und der in Tag- und Nachtarbeit Werke aus dem Griechischen (d. h. den Ptolemäus) übersetze, zur Entspannung aufgetragen habe, die Grundzüge der Grammatik in Bildern darzustellen. Wie in einem Kartenspiel werden die Elemente der Grammatik des Donat in acht Holzschnitten dargestellt: Nomen: Kurat; Pronomen: Vikar; Verb: König; Adverb: Königin; Partizip: Mönch; Konjunktion: Mundschenk, Präposition: Mesner; Interjektion: Narr. Aus dem Impressum vom 1. Juni 1509[33] geht hervor, dass Gauthier Lud und Philesius die Grammatica figurata in Saint-Dié gedruckt haben. Ein Holzschnitt zeigt einen Engel, in der Rechten ein Schild mit drei Wappen und einer Rose, dem Emblem von Lud, in der Linken ein Insignium mit drei Eicheln von Eichhoffen, dem Geburtsort Ringmanns. Gauthier Lud war so optimistisch, in der Grammatica figurata in der Widmung an den Bischof anzukündigen: »Du wirst demnächst mit Gottes Hilfe noch bedeutendere Werke aus meiner Werkstatt sehen. Unter Ihnen wird Dir, wenn ich mich nicht irre, besonders die Geographia des Claudius Ptolemäus gefallen, aus dem griechischen Original auf das Sorgfältigste ediert und mit vielfältigen Beigaben geschmückt«.[34] Aus der Widmung geht hervor, dass die Ptolemäusausgabe kurz vor ihrer Vollendung stand.

Am 1. März 1511 entwarf Martin Waldseemüller eine Carta Itineraria Europae in vier Holzschnitten im Format 106 × 140 cm aus den für die Ptolemäusausgabe bereits gezeichneten Einzelkarten von Spanien, Frankreich, Großbritannien, Deutschland, Italien, Griechenland, Böhmen und Ungarn und verzierte sie mit den entsprechenden Länderwappen. Matthias Ringmann schrieb dazu eine Gebrauchsanweisung (Instructio manducationem prestans in cartam itinerariam Martini Hilacomini) mit einer Beschreibung »der wichtigsten Gegenden der Christenheit, ihren Dörfern und Städten, Bergen und Flüssen, ebenso wie alles gelegen ist unter Berücksichtigung der festgestellten Entfernungen, ohne die Wappen ihrer Könige und Prinzen zu vergessen«.[35] Diese Karte ist nur in einem späteren Abzug von 1520 im Ferdinandeum in Innsbruck erhalten.

Das Scheitern des Projektes von Gauthier Lud

Zur Katastrophe kam es im Jahr 1511: Nachdem schon im Dezember 1508 der Mentor des Gymnasiums Vosagense René II. verstorben war, verschied Matthias Ringmann am 1. August 1511 im Alter von 29 Jahren an einer Lungenschwindsucht. Sein Freund Beat Bild, Beatus Rhenanus (1485–1547), widmete ihm im heute abgerissenen Kreuzgang der Kirche St. Johann in Schlettstadt eine Gedenktafel: »Dem Matthias Ringmann, Philesius der Vogeser, Verbreiter der Schönen Literatur im Elsass, hochgelehrt im Lateinischen, des Griechischen nicht unkundig, nicht ohne schweren Schaden für die Literatur von einem frühen Tode dahingerafft«.[36] Kurz zuvor hatte er den Druck eines Nachrufs auf René II. aus der

---

32 *Grammatica figurata. Octo partes orationis secundum Donati editionem et regulam Remigii ita imaginibus expressae.* Saint-Dié 1509. Faksimile. Grammatica figurata des Matthias Ringmann (Philesius Vogesigena) in Faksimiledruck. Hrsg. von FRANZ VON WIESER. Straßburg 1905 (*Drucke und Holzschnitte des XV. und XVI. Jahrhunderts in getreuer Nachbildung.* 11). – RONSIN: L'Imprimerie (siehe Anm. 1), S. 413–7.
33 *Grammatica figurata* (siehe Anm. 32), f. 32ʳ.
34 D'AVEZAC (siehe Anm. 3), S. 132/3.
35 Ebd., S. 137.
36 Ebd., S. 140.

Feder von Jean Loy besorgt, das letzte Werk der Offizin Gauthier Luds in Saint-Dié. Gauthier Lud selbst geriet in finanzielle Schwierigkeiten. Als Generaldirektor der Minen musste er mit zwei Kompagnons die Schürfrechte bestimmter Minen an den Herzog Anton zurückgeben: Ein Bürger der Stadt Breisach hatte sie wegen eines nicht erfüllten Vertrags zur Lieferung von Mineralien verklagt. Das Gericht in Ensisheim hatte Lud und seine Kollegen daraufhin zu einer Strafe von 9000 Gulden verurteilt. Als sie die Zahlung verweigerten, wandte sich der Kläger an den Herzog, der um des lieben Friedens willen die Schuld übernahm, dafür aber die Konzessionen einbehielt.[37] Gauthier und Nicolas Lud gaben wohl im Herbst 1511 ihre Druckerei auf. Ihr wichtigster Mitarbeiter, der Korrektor Ringmann, war verstorben und ihre finanziellen Mittel waren erschöpft. Die Suche nach einem einwandfreien Urtext mit einer eigens dafür unternommenen Reise Ringmanns nach Italien und die sorgfältige Übersetzung aus dem Griechischen hatten ihren Editionsplan unvorhergesehen verzögert; die Druckkosten waren nicht mehr weiter finanzierbar. Das Projekt der schon weit fortgeschrittenen Ptolemäusausgabe schien damit vereitelt.

Die glückliche Vollendung des Projekts: Der Straßburger Ptolemäus von 1513

Zwei Jahre später, am 12. März 1513, erschien bei Johann Schott in Straßburg die bereits erwähnte, repräsentative Ptolemäusausgabe in Groß Quart (33 × 48 cm) mit 181 Blatt[38] [Abb. 8]. Das Werk umfasst zwei Teile: Die acht Bücher der Geographia mit der Einführung des Ptolemäus und der Beschreibung der Regionen und Orte der Erde mit ihren lateinischen und griechischen Namen, mit der Angabe von Breiten- und Längengraden und einem alphabetischen Ortsverzeichnis. Zudem enthielt die Ausgabe 27 Karten in der Kegelprojektion des Nicolaus Germanus: eine Weltkarte, zehn Karten von Europa, vier von Afrika und zwölf von Asien. Dieser Teil war von Matthias Ringmann nach dem griechischen Urtext bearbeitet worden. Ein zweiter Teil In Claudii Ptolemei Supplementum umfasst 20 Tabulae modernae von Martin Waldseemüller: Die Weltkarte Orbis typus Universalis [Abb. 9], wie wir sie bereits in der Ausgabe von 1507 kennen, jedoch ohne den Eindruck America und eine Tabula Terre Nove [Abb. 11] mit den neuen Entdeckungen [Abb. 10]. Waldseemüller hielt nach dem Tod Ringmanns die Bezeichnung America nicht mehr aufrecht, ein Indiz, dass Ringmann und nicht Waldseemüller der Schöpfer des Namens America war. Neben neun Europa-, zwei Afrika- und drei Asienkarten sind vier Charte Chorographiae, das heißt Regionalkarten in größerem Maßstab, und zwar von der Schweiz, vom Oberrhein von Basel bis Mainz[39] [Abb. 10], von Kreta und von Lothringen beigegeben. Letztere ist zum ersten Mal in einem Dreifarbendruck ausgeführt. Ein Anhang De locis ac mirabilis mundi über die Namen, Orte, Sitten und Gebräuche der Völker beschließt das Werk. Dieser geht von den bislang bekannten drei Kontinenten aus und basiert auf der Übersetzung von Jacobo d'Angelo da Scarperia.

Die Lettern dieser Ptolemäusausgabe entsprechen der Antiquaschrift der Cosmologiae Introductio von 1507 aus Saint-Dié. Johannes Schott

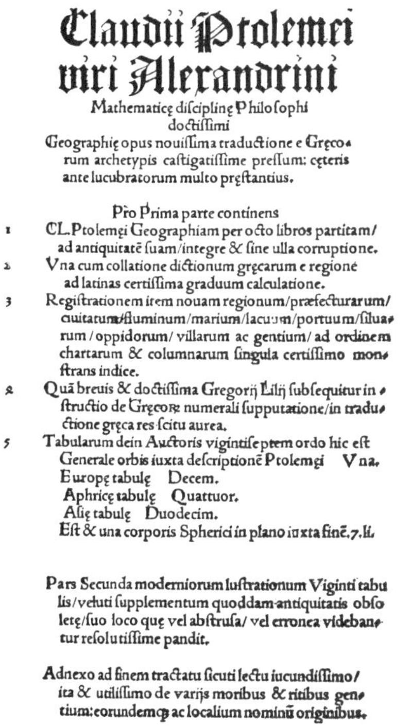

Claudii Ptolemei viri Alexandrini

Mathematicę disciplinę Philosophi doctissimi

Geographię opus nouissima traductione e Grecorum archetypis castigatissime pressum: cęteris ante lucubratorum multo prę̨stantius.

Pro Prima parte continens

1 CL. Ptolemęi Geographiam per octo libros partitam/ ad antiquitatē suam/integre & sine ulla corruptione.

2 Vna cum collatione dictionum gręcarum e regionē ad latinas certissima graduum calculatione.

3 Registrationem item nouam regionum/præfecturarum/ ciuitatum/fluminum/marium/lacuum/portuum/siluarum/oppidorum/ villarum ac gentium/ ad ordinem chartarum & columnarum singula certissimo monstrans indice.

4 Quā breuis & doctissima Gregorij Lilij subsequitur instructio de Grecorū numerali supputatione/in traductione gręca res scitu aurea.

5 Tabularum dein Auctoris vigintiseptem ordo hic est
Generale orbis iuxta descriptionē Ptolemęi Vna.
Europę tabulę Decem.
Aphricę tabulę Quattuor.
Asię tabulę Duodecim.
Est & una corporis Spherici in plano iuxta finē.7.li.

Pars Secunda moderniorum lustrationum Viginti tabulis/veluti supplementum quoddam antiquitatis obsoletę/suo loco quę vel abstrusa/ vel erronea videbantur resolutissime pandit.

Adnexo ad finem tractatu sicuti lectu iucundissimo/ ita & utilissimo de varijs moribus & ritibus gentium: eorundemq; ac localium nominū originibus.

[Abb. 8] CLAUDIUS PTOLEMÄUS: *Geographia*. Titelblatt mit Inhaltsverzeichnis. Im zweiten Teil sind zwanzig Karten Martin Waldseemüllers mit den modernen Entdeckungen und Korrekturen der alten Karten verzeichnet. Straßburg: Johann Schott, 12. März 1513. UB Freiburg D 3107, b.

37 RONSIN: *La fortune* (siehe Anm. 1), S. 58.

38 CLAUDIUS PTOLEMÄUS: *Geographia*. Straßburg: Johann Schott, 1513. VD 16 P 5210.

39 Vgl. RUTHHARDT OEHME: Martin Waldseemüller und der Straßburger Ptolemäus von 1513. In: *Beiträge zur Spachwissenschaft und Volkskunde. Festschrift für Ernst Ochs zum 60. Geburtstag.* Hrsg. von KARL-FRIEDRICH MÜLLER. Lahr 1951, S. 155–66. – DERS.: *Der deutsche Südwesten im Bild alter Karten*. Konstanz 1961, S. 11; Karte 3.

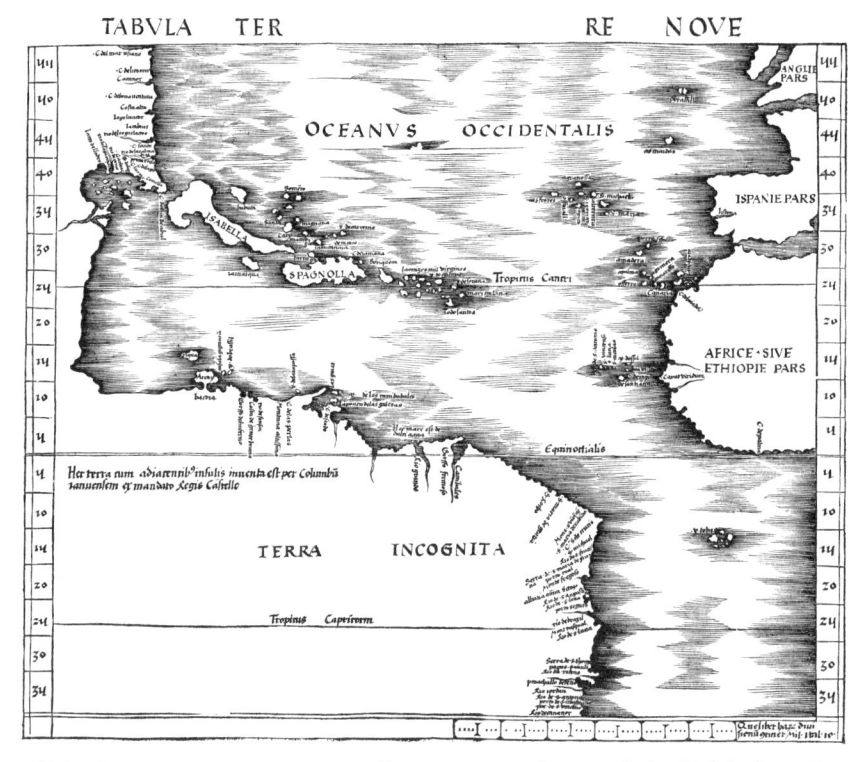

[Abb. 9] MARTIN WALDSEEMÜLLER: *Terra incognita*. Der nördliche Teil Südamerikas mit den Karibischen Inseln mit dem Vermerk: Dieses Land mit den anliegenden Inseln wurde von dem Genueser Kolumbus auf Befehl des Königs von Kastilien entdeckt. Auch hier ohne Namensnennung *America*. Aus: PTOLEMÄUS [siehe Abb. 8]

hatte also die Schriften der Druckerei Gauthier Luds übernommen und das Werk fertiggestellt. In ihrer Widmung an Kaiser Maximilian vom 15. März 1513[40] bezeichnen sich Jakob Äschler und Georg Übelin, Anwälte am bischöflichen Gericht in Straßburg, als Herausgeber des Werkes. Sie hätten das Werk in sechsjähriger Arbeit nicht ohne Mühen fertiggestellt. In einem angeblich von Giovanni Francesco Pico della Mirandola, dem Neffen des berühmten Humanisten, an Äschler und Genossen gerichteten Brief aus Novi vom 28. August 1508,[41] bedankt sich dieser, dass Philesius den Weg nach Italien nicht gescheut habe, um von ihm eine griechische Originalausgabe des Ptolemäus für das Gymnasium Vosagense in Empfang zu nehmen. Ebenso wird auch der Brief Lilio Gregorio Giraldis aus Ferrara vom 21. August 1508 abgedruckt, mit dem dieser die Einweisung Ringmanns in das griechische Zahlensystem bestätigt. In einem Hinweis an den Leser erfahren wir, dass »Philesius, dessen treue und gelehrte Hand das ganze Werk, das du vor dir siehst, übersetzte und noch in einer zweiten Revision alles Gedruckte überprüfte«.[42] Schließlich werden wir noch informiert, dass das Werk nach »einer Carta marina eines Admirals des portugiesischen Königs Ferdinand und nach anderen Vorlagen durch Vermittlung Herzog Renés in sechsjähriger Arbeit in den Schluchten der Vogesen erarbeitet und durch uns vollendet wurde«.[43] Daraus geht hervor, dass die wirklichen Urheber dieser Ptolemäusausgabe von 1513 Gauthier Lud, Matthias Ringmann und Martin Waldseemüller waren. Denn zu Beginn der sechsjährigen Arbeiten, also 1506, war

40 PTOLEMÄUS (siehe Anm. 38), f. 2r.
41 Ebd., f. 3v.
42 Ebd., f. 72v.
43 Ebd., f. 113v.

Gauthier Lud der Herausgeber der Edition, der sie, wie aus der Widmung der *Grammatica figurata* hervorgeht, 1509 schon fast fertiggestellt hatte. Äschler und Übelin ignorierten die Herausgeberschaft Luds, ebenso auch die Arbeit Waldseemüllers, während Ringmanns Bearbeitung des lateinischen Textes nach dem griechischen Original aus den oben zitierten Briefen ersichtlich ist. Die Mitarbeit Waldseemüllers wird später durch den in Colmar geborenen Metzer Arzt und Mathematiker Lorenz Fries (Laurentius Frisius, 1483–1531) in einem verkleinerten Nachdruck 1522 bei Johann Grüninger bestätigt, dass »diese Karten von Neuem [e novo] von Martinus Ilacomylus entworfen wurden, der sanft entschlafen ist«.[44] Die oben erwähnte Notiz der Kartenübergabe durch Herzog René ist irreführend: Portugiesischer König war zu dieser Zeit Manuel I. und nicht der katholische König Ferdinand von Kastilien. Mit dem Admiral war wahrscheinlich Christoph Kolumbus gemeint, da Vespucci nie diesen Titel trug. Wie die Transaktion von Lud zu den beiden Kirchenjuristen vor sich ging und wann sie vollzogen wurde, ist nicht nachprüfbar. Denkbar ist eine Mitarbeit von Waldseemüller, der sich von 1511 bis 1513 in Straßburg aufhielt.

Äschler und Übelin ließen sich von Kaiser Maximilian I. ein Druckprivileg auf vier Jahre ausstellen, für das im Übrigen Jakob Äschler als »Kaiserlicher Majestät verordneter Zensor und Rechtfertiger neu gedruckter Bücher«[45] selbst zuständig war. Damit war das Werk in diesem Zeitraum vor unberechtigten Nachdrucken geschützt. Die damaligen Druckprivilegien waren Vorläufer des Verlagsrechtes im Sinne einer Berechtigung zur ausschließlichen Vervielfältigung eines Werkes; ein Urheberrecht der Autoren war noch unbekannt, ebenso ein Autorenhonorar. Ihre Namen wurden nicht genannt; sie wurden als Castigator und als Drucker bezahlt und ihre Ansprüche galten damit als abgegolten. Der Autor konnte Exemplare mit einer Widmung an einen hochgestellten Gönner drucken lassen, um von ihm ein Honorar oder einen Ehrensold zu erhalten, und vom Verkauf von Freiexemplaren zusätzliche Einkünfte erzielen. Neben Ringmann bestritten auch andere Humanisten wie Johann Adolph Muling oder Beatus Rhenanus auf diese Weise ihren Lebensunterhalt. Ein Meister des Dedikationswesens war zu dieser Zeit Erasmus von Rotterdam (1466–1536), der es zu einem beachtlichen Vermögen brachte, wie sein Testament beweist.

Martin Waldseemüller als Kanonikus in Saint Dié und seine Carta Marina von 1516

Mit einer Order vom 23. März 1513 genehmigte Herzog Anton von Lothringen das Gesuch Martin Waldseemüllers, »Kleriker der Diözese Konstanz, Drucker, wohnhaft in Straßburg«, um eine Pfründe als Kanoniker an der Stiftskirche in Saint-Dié.[46] Dort vollendete er 1516 eine Carta Marina navigatoria Portugallen Navigationes in zwölf Holzstöcken von 59 × 43 cm, also insgesamt 232 × 129 cm. Diese Seekarte ist umrahmt von vier Winden, deren künstlerische Darstellung Josef Fischer der Dürerschule zuordnet.[47] Nordamerika wird zwischen 44° Nord und 38° Süd als Terra de Cuba, Asie partis, Südamerika zwischen 16° Nord und 38° Süd als

44 D'AVEZAC (siehe Anm. 3), S. 165.
45 KARL SCHOTTENLOHER: Druckprivilegien des 16. Jahrhunderts. In: GJ 1933, S. 89–110, hier S. 89.
46 GALLOIS (siehe Anm. 8), S. 222.
47 *Die älteste Karte* (siehe Anm. 18), S. 19.

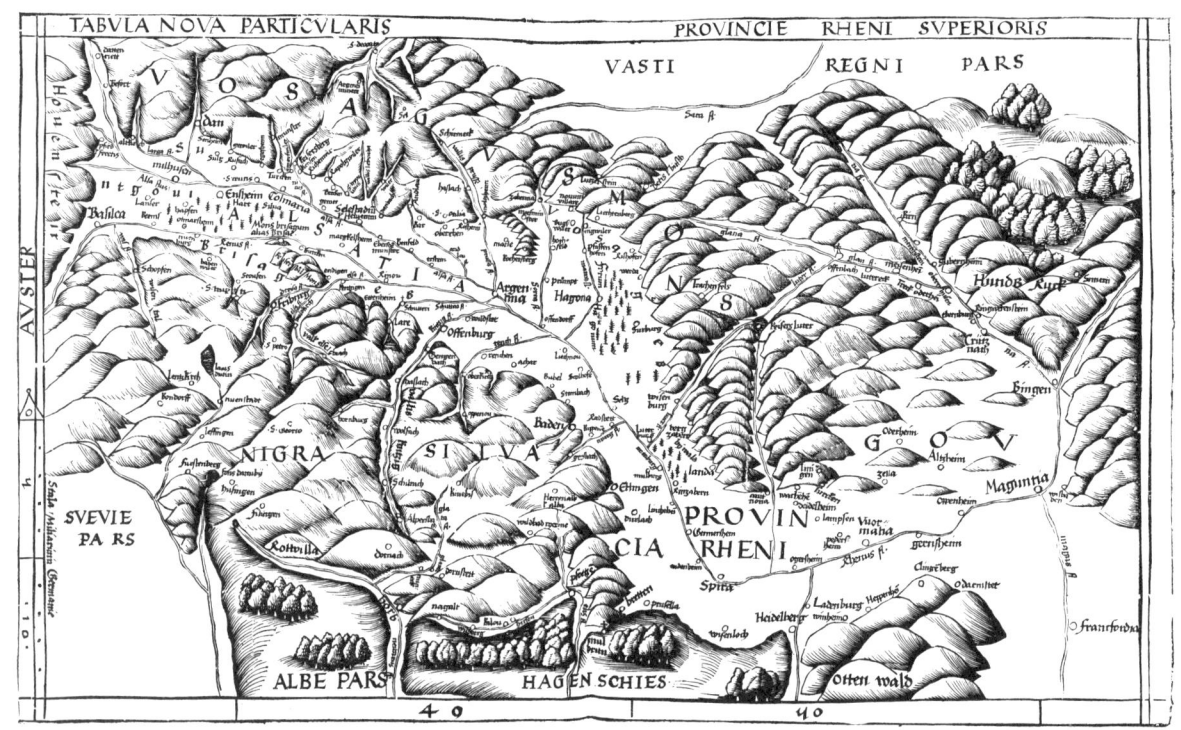

[Abb. 10] MARTIN WALDSEEMÜLLER: *Oberrheinkarte*. Der Reichtum an topografischen Angaben und genauen Standortbestimmungen um Freiburg und Saint-Dié lassen vermuten, dass Waldseemüller selbst in seiner Heimat die Berechnungen vorgenommen hat. Aus: PTOLEMÄUS [siehe **Abb. 8**]

Terra Nova bezeichnet. Brasilien wird bei 20° Süd als Brisilia sive Terra Papagalli aufgeführt. Die Karte ist von Waldseemüller signiert. Die einzige Ausführung dieser Karte befindet sich jetzt in der Library of Congress. Eine Kopie hängt im Kartensaal der Bayerischen Staatsbibliothek in München. Waldseemüller arbeitete noch an einer illustrierten Ausgabe einer Chronica mundi,[48] als er Ende 1519 oder Anfang 1520 starb. Am 17. März 1520 zahlte der Vikar Didier de Charmes jedenfalls 18 Livres für das Haus aus dem Besitz des verstorbenen Kanonikers an den Schatzmeister des Stifts in Sant-Dié.[49] Die Lettern der Cosmographia aus dem Bestand der Druckerei Luds tauchten 1513 in der Straßburger Ptolemäusausgabe und 1520 in einer antilutherischen Streitschrift von Nikolaus Gerbel und Thomas Murner auf: *Defensio christianorum de cruce*,[50] die bei Johann Schott in Straßburg mit dem oben erwähnten Druckersignet GL NL MI erschien. Dieser Name MI ist mit einem Kreuz bezeichnet, ein Zeichen, dass Martin Waldseemüller zu diesem Zeitpunkt bereits verstorben war. Gauthier Lud selbst starb 1527 als Kanoniker in Saint-Dié. In seinem Testament wird seine Tätigkeit als Drucker und Verleger mit keinem Wort erwähnt.

Die Wirkung Luds, Ringmanns und Waldseemüllers

Die von Gauthier Lud projizierten Editionen einer *Universalis Cosmographiae descriptio* sind bedeutende Wegmarken des Buchdrucks im frühen 16. Jahrhundert. Gauthier Lud war ohne Zweifel ein bedeutender Drucker

48 LEO BAGROW / RALEIGH ASHLIN SKELTON: *Meister der Kartographie*. 5. Aufl. Berlin 1985, S. 158.
49 RONSIN: L'Imprimerie (siehe Anm. 1), S. 410.
50 VD 16 G 2277.

und Verleger, auch wenn er sein Programm nicht selbst zu Ende führen konnte. In seiner eigenen Werkstatt in Saint-Dié erschien neben drei Arbeiten aus dem Kreis des Gymnasiums Vosagense nur die *Cosmographiae introductio* mit der Weltkarte und dem Erdglobus. Mit dieser großen Weltkarte schuf Waldseemüller eine der ersten gedruckten Karten der modernen Welt mit den Entdeckungen der Portugiesen und Spanier; Matthias Ringmann gab in der Cosmographia der Neuen Welt den Namen America. Mit dem Druck der Quattro Navigationes des Amerigo Vespucci veröffentlichte Lud eine der frühesten Dokumente der Entdeckungen und der Völkerkunde. Sensationell ist der erste gedruckte Erdglobus, mit dem Waldseemüller die Theorie des Ptolemäus von der Erde als einer Weltkugel plastisch darstellte. Gauthier Luds großer Wurf aber war die später von den Kirchenjuristen Äschler und Übelin finanzierte, 1513 bei Johann Schott in Straßburg gedruckte Geographia des Ptolemäus. Dieser erste moderne Weltatlas war ein Höhepunkt humanistischer Gelehrsamkeit am Oberrhein und ein Meisterwerk der Buchdruckkunst des frühen XVI. Jahrhunderts. Er enthielt einen nach dem griechischen Original philologisch sorgfältig edierten lateinischen Text von Ringmann, war in seiner Kartografie von Waldseemüller nach den neuesten geografischen Erkenntnissen über die Neue Welt erarbeitet worden und wurde in einer hervorragenden typografischen und künstlerischen Gestaltung dargeboten. Lud und seine Mitarbeiter revolutionierten mit der Darstellung des Mundus novus das Weltbild des Ptolemäus. Nach dem heutigen Verständnis signalisierten sie damit auch den Beginn des Zeitalters der Globalisierung der Welt, wenn man unter diesem schillernden Begriff eine Bildung weltumspannender Netze versteht. Die Karten Waldseemüllers waren epochemachend für die folgenden Generationen – für Johann Schöner (1477–1547), für Lorenz Fries, für Peter Bienewitz (Apian, 1495–1552), für Sebastian Münster (1488–1552), für die berühmten Kartografen Gerhard Mercator (1512–94) und Abraham Ortelius (1527–98). Sie alle stützten sich auf das Kartenwerk Martin Waldseemüllers, den man wohl mit Recht als den Vater der modernen Kartografie bezeichnen kann.

ANNELIESE SCHMITT

Alexius Bresnicer – Humanist, Dramatiker, Theologe und Reformator. Eine Bibliothek gibt Auskunft über ein Leben

ÜBER DEN AUS COTTBUS STAMMENDEN, vielseitig gebildeten Alexius Bresnicer, der den Reformatoren der zweiten und dritten Generation zuzurechnen ist und eine beachtliche Bibliothek hinterlassen hat, lässt sich in der einschlägigen neueren Literatur nur wenig in Erfahrung bringen. Die Schreibweise seines Namens variiert zwischen Alexis, meist Alexius Bresnicer (latinisiert Bresnicerus), Bresnitzer, Bresnizer, Bresnitius, Bresnitz und Brisnicerus. Bis zum Ende seiner Tätigkeit als Büchersammler kennzeichnete er jedes Buch durch ein in den vorderen Buchspiegel mit der Hand eingetragenes Exlibris, das in der Regel wie folgt lautet: *Liber (Libri) Alexii Breniceri Cotbusiani*. Dieses Exlibris variiert nur in der Schreibweise einzelner Buchstaben. Für sein handschriftliches Exlibris in den Büchern und in seinen eigenen Schriften verwendete er stets die latinisierte Form seines Namens. Diese durchgehende Kennzeichnung sowie die Nutzungsspuren von seiner Hand zeugen von einer engen Beziehung zu seinen Büchern und von ihrer Bedeutung für seine Person und seine Tätigkeit. Sein Lebenslauf lässt sich zwar nicht lückenlos rekonstruieren, doch berichten die Bücher, die sich in seinem Besitz befanden, über wichtige Lebensabschnitte und sein kulturelles Umfeld.

Ältere Nachschlagewerke geben sein Geburtsjahr meist mit 1504/05 an, denen sich Autoren aus jüngster Zeit angeschlossen haben.[1] Andere Wissenschaftler geben sich zurückhaltender und beschränken sich auf gesicherte Fakten. So formuliert Wilhelm Scherer in der ADB nur: »Alexius Bresnicer aus Cottbus, Superintendent aus Altenburg, deutscher Dramatiker«, und charakterisiert kurz dessen *Comoedia*.[2] In der DBE heißt es im Index: »Bresnizer, Alexius, evang. Theologe, Dramatiker, *1503/04, †1581«; in Band 2: »[...] *Cottbus. B. war Pastor in Neukirchen bei Crimmitzschau, seit 1545 Pastor zu Altenburg und von 1553 an Superintendent. 1562 wurde er des Amtes enthoben, 1568 wieder eingesetzt, 1573 wegen Verteidigung des Flacianismus abermals abgesetzt. Er schrieb geistliche Dramen [...]«.[3] Karl Goedeke schreibt über Bresnicer etwas ausführlicher:

»[...] aus Cotbus [...] *vor 1540, †nach 1573, 1546 Pfarrer zu Neukirch bei Crimmitzschau, dann als 3. Superintendent nach Altenburg berufen. 1558 beim Colloquium der Jenaer Theologen in Weimar gegenwärtig, wurde, als er Victorin Strigels Meinung nicht anerkennen konnte, am 10. Juli 1562 bis Michaelis suspendiert und dann am 20. Oktober mit 27 anderen Predigern des Landes verwiesen. Er ging nach Oettingen, von wo er, nach der Einnahme Gothas am 13. April 1567 und der Befestigung der kirchlichen Zustände, ehrenvoll zurückgerufen und am

---

[1] Im Text werden die folgenden Abkürzungen verwendet: IA = *Index Aureliensis. Catalogus librorum sedecimo saeculo impressorum*. T. 1–15. Baden-Baden 1962–2005. Moreau = BRIGITTE MOREAU: Inventaire chronologique des éditions Parisiennes du XVIᵉ siècle. P. 1–4. 1501–30. Paris 1972–92. (*Histoire général de Paris*).
UWE CZUBATYNSKI: Brandenburg. Domstiftsarchiv – Kirchenbibliothek St. Katharinen. In: *Handbuch der historischen Buchbestände in Deutschland*. Hrsg. von BERNHARD FABIAN. Bd. 16: Mecklenburg-Vorpommern. Brandenburg. Hrsg. von FRIEDHILDE KRAUSE. Hildesheim, Zürich 1996, S. 292. – STEPHAN FITOS: Zensur als Mißerfolg. Die Verbreitung indizierter deutscher Druckschriften in der zweiten Hälfte des 16. Jahrhunderts. Frankfurt a. M. u. a. 2000, Tabelle.
[2] ADB, Bd. 3, S. 317.
[3] *Deutsche Biographische Enzyklopädie* (DBE). Hrsg. von WALTHER KILLY. Bd. 2. München u. a. 1995, S. 120/1. – Vgl. auch MARGA HEYNE: Alexius Bresnicer. In: *Brandenburgische Jahrbücher*. 13 (1939), S. 79.

28. Juni 1568 wieder in seine Altenburger Superintendantur eingesetzt wurde. In Folge der flacianischen Streitigkeiten über die Erbsünde geriet er mit seinen Collegen in heftigen Streit und wurde auf Befehl des Consistoriums zu Jena, 17. Februar 1573 abermals abgesetzt. Weiteres nicht bekannt.«

Anschließend beschreibt Goedeke Bresnicers Komödie.[4] Erwähnt wird Bresnicer unter anderem im *Deutschen Theater-Lexikon* von Wilhelm Kosch als Verfasser von Dramen, zitiert wird nur die *Comoedia* von 1553, ohne Angabe weiterer Lebensdaten. Er hat also offensichtlich nur das eine Drama verfasst.[5] Andere Nachschlagewerke bieten keine neuen Fakten. Es sei erwähnt, dass das unzureichende Wissen über Alexius Bresnicer zum Beispiel im *Deutschen Biographischen Index* dazu geführt hat, zwei Personen hinter diesem Namen zu vermuten: einen Dramatiker und einen Theologen.[6] Die durchgehend als persönliches Eigentum ausgewiesene Bibliothek bietet jedoch keinen Anlass, den Dramatiker vom Theologen zu trennen.

Die Berücksichtigung des gesamten Wirkungs- und Kulturkreises, zu dem außer die Mark Brandenburg am Ende des Weges, die Niederlausitz, das heutige Sachsen, Sachsen-Anhalt und Thüringen sowie Schwaben und Österreich gehören, dürfte hilfreich werden bei der Suche nach dem Weg, den die Bibliothek Bresnicers genommen hat, bis sie von Joachim Garcaeus in Brandenburg an der Havel übernommen wurde und nach dessen Tod 1633 in der Bibliothek von St. Katharinen ihren Platz fand. Hier ist sie als Depositum seit 1951 in der Bibliothek des Domarchivs im Domstift Brandenburg öffentlich zugänglich.

Über Bresnicers familiäre Herkunft und soziale Situation ist bisher nichts bekannt. Ältere Quellen verweisen vor allem auf Verwandte und Vertreter aus Wissenschaft und Kultur; Auskunft über die Familie Bresnicers geben sie nicht. Die ersten sicheren Daten lassen sich den Universitätsmatrikeln entnehmen. Er studierte 1535 in Leipzig[7] und ab 1539 in Wittenberg[8] Theologie und erlangte hier den Magister. Ungewöhnlich erscheint, dass er sein Studium erst als bereits 30-Jähriger aufgenommen haben soll. Erfahrungsgemäß begannen im 16. Jahrhundert die Studenten in der Regel ihr Studium im Alter zwischen 15 und 18 Jahren, wenn nicht sogar noch etwas früher. Von diesem Erfahrungswert ausgehend scheint es wahrscheinlich, dass Bresnicer erst zwischen 1517 und 1520 geboren wurde. Es ist aber auch vorstellbar, dass er vor seinem Studium eine der berühmten Lateinschulen oder Gymnasien besuchte, die es zu jener Zeit selbst in kleineren Orten gegeben hat. Cottbus oder Freiberg (Sachsen) kämen zum Beispiel dafür in Frage.[9]

Für sein Studium wählte er anfangs die traditionsreiche Universität Leipzig, die aber bereits in jenen Jahren durch ihre Vorbehalte gegen jegliche Neuerungen den Anschluss an die Entwicklung der Zeit und damit sehr an Bedeutung verloren hatte. Der vier Jahre später erfolgte Wechsel an die Universität Wittenberg darf als eine bewusste Entscheidung gewertet werden, war doch diese Universität auf dem Weg zum Höhepunkt ihrer Entwicklung, von Studenten aus ganz Europa geschätzt und durch beste Fachwissenschaftler jener Zeit geprägt.[10] Hier geriet Bresnicer unter den Einfluss der antischolastischen Richtung und des

4 KARL GOEDEKE: *Grundriß zur Geschichte der deutschen Dichtung.* Bd. 2: Das Reformationszeitalter. 2. Aufl. Dresden 1886, S. 362.

5 WILHELM KOSCH: *Deutsches Theater-Lexikon.* Bd. 1. Klagenfurt, Wien 1953, S. 209.

6 *Deutscher Biographischer Index* (DBI). München 1998, S. 432. Der Dichter Bresnicer stirbt 1553 und der Prediger 1581.

7 Die Matrikel der Universität Leipzig. Bearb. von GEORG ERLER. Bd. I: Die Immatrikulationen von 1409–1559. Leipzig 1895 (*Codex Diplomaticus Saxoniae.* 16–8), S. 617, P 31. 1535: Theologische Fakultät, Sommersemester, unter dem Rektorat von Heinrich Gottschalek von Bodenwerder. »Alexius Bressnitzer de Cotwiß« findet sich in der Gruppe der Poloni, er hatte 6 gr. zu zahlen. Im Register ist sein Name unter »Kottbus« zu finden.

8 CARL EDUARD FOERSTEMANN: *Album Academiae Vitebergensis.* Vol. 1. Leipzig 1841. Neudruck Aalen 1976, S. 175b, 17. – Zitierweise des Namens im Index »Bresmitius, Kottbus: Alexius.«

9 Mein Dank gilt Frau Dr. Doris Teichmann, der Spezialistin für sorbische Kirchengeschichte, für zahlreiche Hinweise zur Geschichte bekannter Familien aus der Lausitz und auf besondere Quellen.

10 Vgl. u. a. HEINZ SCHEIBLE: Die philosophische Fakultät der Universität Wittenberg bis zur Vertreibung der Philippisten. In: *Archiv für Reformationsgeschichte.* 98 (2007), S. 7–44. – RALF THOMAS: Die Neuordnung der Schulen und der Universität Leipzig. In: *Das Jahrhundert der Reformation in Sachsen. Festgabe zum 450jährigen Bestehen der Evangelisch-Lutherischen Landeskirche Sachsens.* Hrsg. von HELMAR JUNGHANS. Berlin 1989, S. 113–31. – *Theologische Realenzyklopädie* (TRE). Hrsg. von GERHARD KRAUSE u. GERHARD MÜLLER. Bde. 1–36. Berlin, New York 1977–2004, Bd. 20, S. 721–9. Zum Thema allgemein vgl. BERNARD VOGLER: Rekrutierung, Ausbildung und soziale Verflechtung: Karrieremuster evangelischer Geistlichkeit. In: *Archiv für Reformationsgeschichte.* 85 (1994), S. 225–33.

Humanismus, Strömungen, die durch Luthers Bemühungen der Universität ihr modernes Profil gaben. Im Mittelpunkt standen Geschichts- und Sprachstudien, Griechisch, Hebräisch, Latein. Hier – und nicht in Leipzig – lernte er die reformatorische Botschaft Luthers kennen.

Die Laufbahn, die Bresnicer nach seinem Studium einschlug, lässt sich gut verfolgen. Für das Jahr 1541 ist eine Tätigkeit als Diakon und Schulmeister in Neukirchen bei Crimmitschau (Krymmitsch) nachzuweisen. Es war erwünscht, vor der Ernennung zum Pfarrer einige Jahre Dienst als Lehrer getan zu haben. Am 25. Mai 1541 erhielt er durch Johannes Bugenhagen seine Berufung zum Priesteramt: »Allexius Bresnitz vonn Cotbus, Schulmeister zu Krymmitzsch, Beruffenn doselbsthin zum Priesteramt«.[11] Bereits 1545 wechselte er als zweiter Stadtgeistlicher nach Altenburg. Seine berufliche Kompetenz muss er bewiesen und die in ihn gesetzten Erwartungen erfüllt haben, denn seit 1553 fungierte er als Superintendent Altenburgs, womit ihm unter anderem die Aufgabe zufiel, Pfarrer ins Amt zu berufen. Diese Stationen seiner beruflichen Laufbahn entsprechen dem seinerzeit üblichen Werdegang. Eine solche Berufung als Superintendenten erfolgte durch den Landesherrn; zudem befähigte ihn sein Magistertitel, das Amt eines Superintendenten zu übernehmen. Bresnicers Wirken als Superintendent fällt dabei in die Zeit der Entstehung der sächsisch-thüringischen Landeskirche.

Mit dieser verantwortungsvollen Tätigkeit war Bresnicer gefordert, sich innerhalb der reformatorischen Entwicklung zu positionieren und zu bekennen. Zur Feststellung seiner Position werden uns seine Biografie und seine überlieferte Bibliothek Belege liefern. Sie hilft auch, die tragische Wende in seinem Leben zu erklären: 1562 wurde er als Anhänger des Flacius Illyricus von Herzog Johann Friedrich entlassen und ausgewiesen. In der Sprache der Zeit und in den Protestdrucken ist von »Enturlaubung« die Rede, und er hielt sich nun, wie viele andere Gesinnungsgenossen, die dieses Schicksal ereilte, einige Jahre im schwäbischen Öttingen auf. 1568 wurde er als Superintendent nach Altenburg zurückgeholt, doch 1573 nochmals des Amtes enthoben und ausgewiesen. Diesmal ging er – wie viele andere Exulanten auch – nach Österreich, wo er als Pfarrer – ab 1574 in Schönbichl und Horn, ab 1578 in Feldsberg (Veldsberg) – tätig war. Dass seine Tätigkeit hier geschätzt wurde, wird durch Lucas Bacmeister (Backmeister) aus Rostock belegt, der im Jahre 1580 nach Österreich reiste mit dem Auftrag, dort Visitationen durchzuführen. Aus seinem Bericht erfahren wir, dass er Alexius Bresnicer in seine Kommission berief.[12] In Feldsberg verstarb Alexius Bresnicer im Jahr 1581. Diese Lebensdaten erklären, dass die letzten in seiner Bibliothek befindlichen Drucke aus den 1570er Jahren datieren. Später erschienene Bücher mit dem handschriftlichen Exlibris Bresnicers haben sich nicht gefunden.[13]

Schriftsteller und Dramatiker

Da die Reformatoren – vor allem die streitbaren – sehr produktiv und die Bedingungen für schnelles Publizieren günstig waren, liegt es nahe, Alexius Bresnicer auch als Autor zu betrachten und durch seine eigenen Schriften mehr über ihn zu erfahren. Die Zahl der Schriften, die sich mit

---

11 Vgl. GEORG BUCHWALD: *Wittenberger Ordiniertenbuch*. Bd. 1: 1537–1560. Leipzig 1894, S. 19 Nr. 302.
12 WALTHER BACMEISTER: Die Reise des D. Lucas Bacmeister nach Österreich im Jahre 1580. In: *Mecklenburgische Jahrbücher*. 102 (1938), S. 1–30.
13 Ob sich im Bestand der B der Katharinenkirche noch Bücher ohne sein Exlibris, wohl aber mit Notizen von seiner Hand finden lassen, ist vorerst nicht absehbar. Das lässt sich mit Sicherheit erst nach Abschluss der Katalogisierungsarbeit sagen.

dem Namen Bresnicers verbinden, ist überschaubar. Der früheste Druck ist eine Übersetzung bzw. Bearbeitung der Schrift *De mortalitate* des Caecilius Cyprianus, Bischof von Karthago, der 258 den Märtyrertod starb.[14] Gedruckt wurde diese 40 Blätter umfassende Schrift von Georg Hantzsch »um 1552« in Leipzig: *Ein sehr nuetzliches, troestliches vnnd geistliches regiment wieder die Pestilentz vnd sonst allerley gifftig vnd toedliche kranckheiten ... Zusamen gebracht vnnd gepredigt durch den heiligen Bischoff vnd Merterer S. Cyprianum. Vordeutzscht durch Alexium Bresnicerum prediger zu Aldenburg* (VD 16 C 6553; IA 149.090 – Ex. BSB). Bresnicers Übersetzung dieses Textes ist nicht die einzige; vor ihr erschienen verschiedene Bearbeitungen, unter anderem von Martin Luther (1519) und von Nikolaus Selnecker (1566). Wie sich Christen in Notzeiten und im Sterben verhalten sollen, gehörte, wie die Totentanzliteratur, zu den immer wieder behandelten Themen jener Zeit: Zwischen 1522 und 1600 erschienen über hundert Auflagen von verschiedenen Autoren zu diesem Thema, gedacht für Kranke und ihre Angehörigen, die in Zeiten des Hungers und von Seuchen des Trostes bedurften.

In Dresden erschien im Jahre 1552 *Von dem christlichen Pilgrim* (IA 124-856, mit Nachweis eines Exemplars in Kopenhagen).[15] In die Literaturgeschichte ist Bresnicer eingegangen mit seinem Drama *Lienhart Hirsing. Comoedia von dem geystlichen kampff, christlicher Ritterschafft, das ist, wie die Christen aus warheit der schrifft, sich legen müssen, wider die Heel, Todt, Teuffel, Sünde, Gesetz etc troestlich zu lesen, allen blöden gewissen, vorfasset vnd reymweis gestellet durch Alexium Bresnicerum Cotbusianum*. Bresnicer widmete sein Drama auf Blatt 2a »Der Edlen Gestrengen vnd Tugentsamen Frawen | Elisabet Pfluegin zum Steyn | meiner gebietenden Frawen«. Seine Zueignung umfasst 5 Blätter. Der Name Lienhard Hirsing kommt im Text nicht vor; der Begriff »Comoedia« wird in jener Zeit noch allgemein für das Drama verwendet. Der in Freiberg 1553 bei Wolfgang Meyerpeck erschienene Druck umfasst 56 Blatt (IA 124-857 – Das Ex. Berlin SBB-PK befindet sich in Krakau, Ex. vorhanden: Göttingen SuUB). Hans Rupprich hat dieses Stück in seinem Kapitel über das Drama der Reformationsepoche unter dem Thema »Die Moralitäten und allegorischen Humanistendramen« aufgenommen[16] und ordnet es in die Tradition der Jedermann-Dramen ein. In der ADB bewertet Wilhelm Scherer das Drama wie folgt: »trockene theologische Wortkämpfe des Ritters Christianus gegen seine Feinde Welt, Fleisch, Satan, Gesetz, Tod; er siegt durch den Glauben und die Schrift«.[17] Ebenso kritisch urteilt Wolfgang Michael über dieses Stück. Er bezeichnet das Thema als christlich, aber nicht als biblisch: »Der Christ ist hier als Ritter gesehen, nicht im mittelalterlichen Sinne, sondern im Sinne von Erasmus.« Er nennt das Stück »spießerisch pastorenhaft« und bezeichnet Bresnicers Stil und Sprache als »pedantisch«.[18]

Zu den Hauptanliegen der Reformationsdramen gehörte, ein dem Evangelium angemessenes Leben der Bürger zu fördern und auf die ethischen Konsequenzen zu verweisen. Schulmeister und Pastoren beherrschten im 16. Jahrhundert die Bühnen. Diese Entwicklung des protestantischen Schuldramas – inzwischen bevorzugt in deutscher Sprache

14 TRE (siehe Anm. 19), Bd. 8, S. 246–54.
15 Diese Schrift wird unter Bresnicers Namen angeführt. Das Exemplar in Kopenhagen konnte noch nicht überprüft werden.
16 HANS RUPPRICH: Die deutsche Literatur vom späten Mittelalter bis zum Barock. 2. Teil: Das Zeitalter der Reformation 1520–1570. München 1973 (*Geschichte der deutschen Literatur von den Anfängen bis zur Gegenwart*. 4,2), S. 331.
17 ADB, Bd. 3, S. 317.
18 WOLFGANG F. MICHAEL: *Das deutsche Drama der Reformationszeit*. Bern, Frankfurt a. M. 1984, S. 100. Im Gegensatz dazu hebt er das Lazarus-Drama des J. Criginger als eines der besten und wirksamsten Stücke hervor.

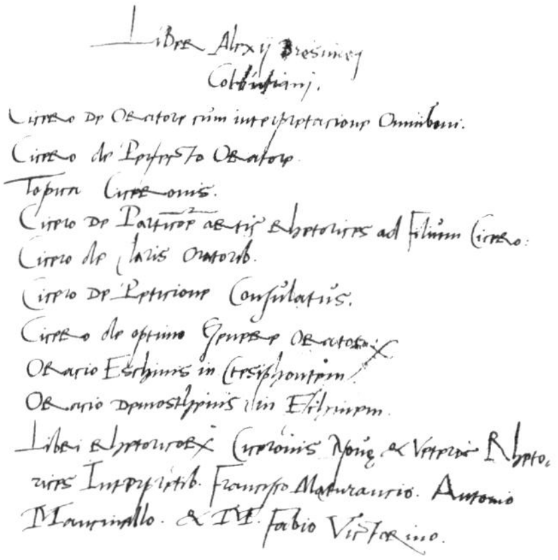

[Abb. 1] Handschriftliches Exlibris und Inhaltsverzeichnis von Alexius Bresnicer. Der Band enthält mehrere Schriften von Cicero (2° K 188)

19 Vgl. dazu bei JOHANN CHRISTOPH GOTTSCHED: *Nöthiger Vorrath zur Geschichte der deutschen Dramatischen Dichtkunst*. Leipzig 1757. Reprint: Hildesheim 1970, T. 2, S. 212. Er lobt dieses »starke Schauspiel« und den Appell an die Jugend durch Pfendtner und Bresnicer in den Vorreden.

20 Vgl. RUPPRICH (siehe Anm. 16), S. 383. – Zur Geschichte des Stoffes u. a. SIEGFRIED BRÄUER: Die Reformation und die Dichtung. In: *Das Jahrhundert der Reformation* (siehe Anm. 10), S. 179–93, besonders S. 187–9. Das Lazarus-Thema spielte in der gesamten Literatur des 16. Jahrhunderts eine große Rolle. Das gleichnamige Drama von Georg Rollenhagen aus dem Jahre 1590 wurde dessen letztes und bestes Stück.

verfasst – war seit den 1530er Jahren von Sachsen und den angrenzenden Gebieten und hier besonders von Zwickau und Freiberg ausgegangen. Dazu leistete Bresnicer einen Beitrag, auch wenn sein Drama nicht zu den herausragenden Leistungen gehört und weitere von ihm nicht bekannt sind.

Johannes Criginger (auch: Krüginger, 1521–71) ist ein in der Literatur viel zitierter Repräsentant des Schul- und Reformationsdramas. Als Schulmeister in Crimmitschau wurde er mit Bresnicer bekannt. Sein Drama *Vom armen Lazaro ...*, das er 1543 verfasste, erschien im gleichen Jahr in Zwickau: COMOEDIA *Von dem Reichen Mann vnd Armen Lazaro / Luce am 16. [Lukasevangelium, Kap. 16] beschrieben vnd Reimweis gestelt durch Johannem Kruegingerum Vallensem* (nicht im VD 16 – Ex. Berlin SBB-PK: Yp8611R). Eine zweite Ausgabe muss als verschollen gelten, die dritte, 1555 bei Matthias Stöckel in Dresden herausgekommen, ist eine erweiterte Fassung und enthält bereits Regieanweisungen. Für beide Ausgaben schrieben Wolfgang Pfendtner und Alexius Bresnicer je ein Vorwort; die Vorworte sind der ersten Ausgabe als Nachwort beigegeben. Bresnicers gereimte Vorrede in *Die Historia vom Reichen man vnd armen Lazaro aus dem Sechtzehenden Capittel Luce jnn ein Action verfasset sehr troestlich vnd nuetzlich zu lesen. Mit Zweien schoenen Vorreden D. Wolffgangi Pfentnerj Superintendenten auffm Annaberg vnd Alexij Bresniceri Cotbusiani Superintendenten zu Aldenburgk* (VD 16 C 5877 – Ex. Berlin SBB-PK: Yp8616R), die gleichlautend mit dem Anhang der ersten Ausgabe ist, umfasst drei Seiten (Blätter B3ʳ–B4ʳ). Die 66 Reimpaare beginnen mit der Beschreibung des schlechten Zustandes dieser Welt; Bresnicer erwähnt die eifrigen Bücherschreiber und erklärt den Sinn des christlichen Spiels mit seinen Figuren, das hauptsächlich für die Jugend gedacht ist: »Was jhm zu thun vnd lassen ist / Christlicher sach zu aller frist / So das kein entschuldigung bleibt / Den Gottlosen zu dieser zeit«. Darauf folgen Werbung und Aufruf zum Kauf: »Kauff dir den Lazarum in zeit / Dadurch du lernst fliehen das leidt / Welchs kommen wirdt vbr all person / Die weder glaub noch libe han / Drumb der Reich man leid grosse pein / Da kan keine erloesung sein«. Bresnicer lobt Crigingers Dichtung und endet mit den Versen »Er wirdt der jugent dienen mehr / Allein dem lieben Gott zu ehr / Damit die junge Welt allzeit / Gereitzt werd zur Gottseligkeit.« Darunter lässt er in größerer Type seinen Namen setzen – wie immer formuliert – in lateinischer Form und mit seiner Herkunft. Diese Vorrede kommt dem Prolog gleich, wie er im Reformationsdrama üblich wurde und Inhalt und Figuren zu erklären hatte.[19]

Bresnicer kannte Criginger aus seiner Zeit als Pfarrer in Crimmitschau und war vielleicht durch ihn bereits in den 1540er Jahren angeregt worden, selbst Dramen zu verfassen. Der aus Joachimsthal stammende Criginger, der dort die berühmte Lateinschule besucht hatte und sicher an Komödienaufführungen beteiligt war, hatte mit seinen Dramen, die große Simultanbühnen verlangten, viel Erfolg. Eine theatertechnische Neuerung war, dass – wie in der oben erwähnten dritten Ausgabe – für die Spieler bereits Regieanmerkungen beigegeben wurden.[20] Bräuer vertritt außerdem die Meinung, dass Criginger in den Jahren der Teuerung und des Wuchers sogar mit seiner Thematik aktueller war als seine berühmten Zeitgenossen Paul Rebhun oder Hans Ackermann.

Criginger war von ähnlichen persönlichen Schwierigkeiten betroffen, doch hatte er mehr Glück als Bresnicer, denn er wurde nicht seines Amtes enthoben. Vom Annaberger Superintendenten Philip Wagner wurde er beim Kurfürst August der Verbindung zu Matthias Flacius Illyricus angeklagt. Nach dem Verhör in Dresden, wo er sich auf die unveränderte Augsburgische Konfession von 1530 berief und belegen konnte, Flacius Illyricus persönlich nicht zu kennen, wohl aber seine Schriften gelesen zu haben – um sich über die Lehrmeinungen zu unterrichten –, wurde er jedoch freigesprochen. Einer ähnlichen Maßregelung unterlag Wolfgang Pfendtner (1510?–56), doch behielt auch er im Gegensatz zu Bresnicer seine Superintendentur in Annaberg, da die Pfarrer seiner Ephorie Ende Oktober 1549 ihre Bedenken zum »Auszug« nach Dresden erklärten.[21]

Wie bereits erwähnt war Criginger als Autor von Dramen relativ erfolgreich. Seine *Tragoedia von Herode vnd Joanne dem Tauffer, inn Deudsche Reymen verfasset* aus dem Jahre 1545 (Ex. Berlin SBB-PK: Yp 8628R) widmete er seinem Drucker, »den ersamen und fürsichtigen« Wolfgang Meyerpeck in Zwickau. Dies war eine sehr schöne Geste, da zu bedenken ist, in welche Gefahr sich auch die Drucker jener Autoren begaben, die in den Auseinandersetzungen von ihren Landesherren vertrieben wurden.

Weder von Bresnicers eigener Übersetzung noch von den genannten Dramen befindet sich ein Exemplar in seiner Bibliothek, die vermutlich nicht vollständig überliefert ist. Als Dramatiker wählte er die deutsche Sprache, doch keine seiner zahlreichen Annotationen in den von ihm benutzten Büchern schrieb er deutsch: Er annotierte konsequent lateinisch, wie es in jener Zeit üblich war.

Als Autor begegnet uns Bresnicer erst deutlich später, im Jahre 1579, wieder. Tätig als Pfarrer in Horn verfasste er die auch als Druck veröffentlichte Predigt für die verstorbene Helene von Starhemberg: *Leichpredigt Vber die Leich der … Frawen Helene, Frawen von Starhemberg, geborne Zaecklin Frayn, … Deß … Herrn Rudigers, Herrn von Starhembergs vnd zu Schoenbuehl Roem: Key: Mayt: etc Raths Ehegemahels. Gethan zu Horn in Sanct Stephans Kirchen den 21, Martij … Anno M.D. LXXIX. Durch* ALESIVM BRESNICERUM COTBVSIANUM … (o. O. u. Dr., VD 16 B 8013).

Im gleichen Jahr erschien im österreichischen Wildberg bei Horn in der Protestantischen Druckerei ein zehn Blatt umfassender Druck mit verschiedenen Beiträgen in lateinischer Sprache: VOTA HORNENSIA PRONVPTIIS GENEROSI DOMINI D. VITI ALBERTI BARONIS A. BVECHEIM, DOMINI HORNAE *et* Wildbergae: Austriae inclytae Dapiferi haereditarij, et sacrae Caesareae Maiestatis Consiliarij … SPONSI. ET … VIRGINIS … HELENAE, LIBERAE BARONISSAE A ROGENDORFF ET MOLLENBVRGO … *D. Johannes Guilielmi liberi Baronis à Rogendorff et Mollenburgo, Primarij Austriae Inferioris Aulae Magistri et Sacrae Caesareae Maiestatis consiliarij, Landmarschalli filiae* SPONSAE, CELEBRATIS HORNAE AVSTRIAE ANNO DOMINI M.D.LXXIX (VD 16 V 2783). Bresnicer ist einer der zehn genannten Autoren – alle wie er Emigranten.

21 GÜNTHER WARTENBERG: Die Entstehung der sächsischen Landeskirche von 1539 bis 1559. In: *Das Jahrhundert der Reformation* (siehe Anm. 10), S. 67–90, hier S. 86.

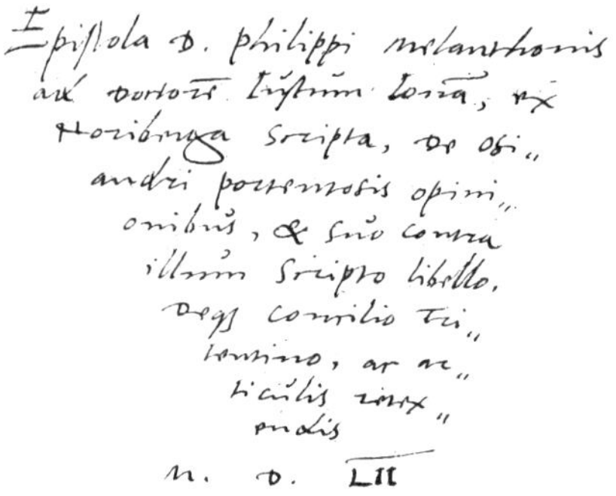

[Abb. 2] Titelblatt zur Abschrift eines Melanchton-Textes durch Alexius Bresnicer (4° K 765 (2))

22 Wegen seines Umfangs kann der Katalog nicht gedruckt werden. Den im Text zitierten Ausgaben werden Signatur und ein bibliografischer Nachweis, in Klammern gesetzt, beigegeben. Die B des Domstiftsarchivs in Brandenburg verfügt über eine CD mit dem vollständigen Katalog nebst Registern. Anfragen sind zu richten an: Domstift Brandenburg. Archiv und Bibliothek. Burghof 9, 14776 Brandenburg/Havel.

Der schreibende Alexius Bresnicer hatte in jüngeren Jahren literarische Ambitionen; die beiden letztgenannten Schriften sind seinem Pfarramt geschuldet. Der Druck von Leichenpredigten war seinerzeit weit verbreitet. Theologisch-reformatorische und programmatische Schriften hat er offensichtlich nicht verfasst. Das ist sicher einer der Gründe, weshalb er in der neueren Literatur zur Reformationszeit keine Erwähnung findet und wir ihm deshalb nur in der regionalgeschichtlichen Literatur des 19. Jahrhunderts begegnen. In die zahlreichen Auseinandersetzungen und Kämpfe der Reformationszeit mischte er sich mit eigenen Schriften nicht ein, wie es viele seiner Zeitgenossen und Freunde taten. Beim derzeitigen Forschungsstand lässt sich nicht sagen, ob er anonym an bestimmten Projekten beteiligt war. Sicher ist, dass er als Pfarrer konsequent seinen Standpunkt vertrat. So wurde er nicht wegen eigener Schriften oder Lehrmeinungen des Landes verwiesen, sondern wegen seiner Predigten und seiner in der Öffentlichkeit vertretenen Auffassungen.

Eine Privatbliothek gibt Auskunft[22]

Einen sichereren Zugang zu Bresnicers Wirken innerhalb der ausgebrochenen Kontroversen gibt uns seine überlieferte Bibliothek. Die große Zahl reformationsgeschichtlicher Texte ermöglicht ein Urteil über seine Entwicklung, sein kulturelles Umfeld, sein Denken und sein Handeln. Selbst die Herstellungsorte einzelner Bucheinbände erlauben Rückschlüsse auf Bresnicers Lebensstationen und weitreichenden Beziehungen.

Eine Besonderheit sei an dieser Stelle hervorgehoben: die auf uns gekommene Bibliothek hat zwei Besitzer. Beide haben sie ihren Besitz durch ein handschriftliches Exlibris gekennzeichnet, doch liegen dazwischen einige Jahrzehnte. Bresnicer ist Besitzer und Benutzer seiner Bücher bis um 1570; nach 1600 gilt dies auch für Joachim Garcaeus, der ebenfalls sein Eigentum durch seine handschriftliche Eintragung auf den Titelblättern, links unten, kenntlich macht: *Ex libris Garcaei*. Auch er hinterlässt seine Spuren in vielen dieser Bücher.

Auf Grundlage der überlieferten Titel lässt sich feststellen, dass Bresnicer von keinem in seiner Bibliothek vertretenen Autor das gesamte Werk besaß – wie dies zum Beispiel bei Verehrern des Erasmus oder Luthers der Fall ist. Von der Anzahl der Bücher einzelner Autoren lässt sich nicht auf eindeutige Vorlieben schließen, denn Bresnicer hat in diesem Sinne nicht »gesammelt«. Immerhin liegt Flacius Illyricus mit 27 Drucken vor Luther, von dem 20 Schriften nachzuweisen sind. Es folgen Johann Brenz und Johannes Wigand mit je 16 Titeln, Nikolaus von Amsdorf, Jakob Andreae und Philipp Melanchthon mit jeweils 15 Titeln – darunter jedoch keine Ausgabe der *Loci communes* –, Erasmus Rotterodamus und Nikolaus Gallus mit jeweils 13 Titeln, Georg Major und Joachim Westphal mit je acht, Geiler von Kaisersberg mit sieben, Augustinus von Alveldt, Johannes Bugenhagen, Tilemann Heshusius und Erasmus Sarcerius mit je fünf Ausgaben. Viele andere meist sehr bekannte Autoren, darunter Freund und Feind, sind jeweils durch weniger Drucke vertreten.

Bresnicer besaß 490 Druckschriften. 52 davon sind als Einzelbände, meist im historischen Einband, überliefert, darunter dreimal jeweils in zwei, je einmal in vier und acht Bänden gebunden. 438 Texte sind in Sammelbänden zusammengefasst, und zwar in 88 Bänden. Insgesamt sind 140 Buchbindereinheiten auf uns gekommen; es handelt sich also um keine sehr große Sammlung. Weder nach Umfang noch nach Inhalt gehört diese Bibliothek zu den bedeutenden Büchersammlungen, verglichen mit den aus den Zentren des Humanismus und der Reformation erhaltenen Bibliotheken. Für Mitteldeutschland jedoch – Altenburg liegt im heutigen Thüringen – und für ihren späteren Standort in Brandenburg an der Havel ist sie, neben weiteren Bibliotheken aus namhafter Provenienz in der Sammlung des Joachim Garcaeus, eine aussagekräftige Dokumentation der Zeitgeschichte. Czubatynski urteilt über sie: »Die Bibliothek dokumentiert in erster Linie die Entwicklung der evangelischen Theologie durch das gesamte 16. Jahrhundert hindurch«.[23] Bresnicers Sammlung setzt besondere Akzente. Sie zeichnet den Weg über die humanistisch-theologischen Studien – die Grundlagen für das Studium der *Artes liberales* zeichnen sich deutlich ab – zum Pfarrer und Superintendenten bis hin zu seinen besonderen und folgenreichen Aktivitäten als Anhänger des Matthaeus Flacius Illyricus nach.

Sein Exlibris notiert Bresnicer fast immer im oberen Drittel des vorderen Spiegels. Wortlaut und Schreibduktus haben sich im Verlauf der Jahre nicht verändert; in den späteren Bänden ist die Schrift nicht mehr ganz so groß und schwungvoll, was mit dem kleineren Format der Bücher zusammenhängen dürfte.

Der Buchbestand weist eine deutliche Zweiteilung auf: ein Teil umfasst die Drucke des 15. und des ersten Drittels des 16. Jahrhunderts und enthält vor allem die für das Theologiestudium notwendigen Texte; der andere, spätere Teil vereint jene Schriften, die die verschiedenen Strömungen des Reformationszeitalters prägten und umfasst die Themen, mit denen sich ein Pfarrer und Superintendent auseinanderzusetzen hatte. Die Sammlung schließt mit Drucken aus dem Jahre 1570 ab. Der früheste Druck – Anselmus von Canterbury – stammt aus dem Jahre 1491, die letzten Drucke aus dem Jahre 1570 mit Titeln wie »Antworten«, »Berichte«, »Bekenntnisse« und Schriften von Martin Luther, Johannes Wigand und Georg Major sowie eine Schrift von Nikolaus Selnecker: *Christliche und notwendige Verantwortung auf der Flaccianer Lästerung* (4° K 675 (15); VD 16 S 5498). Dieser zweite Teil der Bibliothek belegt Bresnicers Wirken als Theologe innerhalb der Richtung des Flacianismus und gewinnt dadurch einen speziellen Charakter. Die älteren Bücher bezeugen durch die zahlreichen Nutzungsspuren die besonderen und ursprünglichen Interessen und die intensive Arbeit des Besitzers. Bezogen auf die Entwicklung Bresnicers belegen sie, dass ihn in seinen jungen Jahren die humanistischen Studien sehr interessiert haben und er – noch in den früheren 1550er Jahren als Schriftsteller und als Übersetzer – über seine zukünftige Tätigkeit vielleicht andere Vorstellungen hatte, als sie sein späterer Lebensweg dokumentiert.

Da ihn seine Bücher durch sein Leben begleitet haben, sollen sie nach

[23] CZUBATYNSKI (siehe Anm. 1), S. 292.

[Abb. 3] Einband von Caspar Krafft, d. Ä., Wittenberg. Mittelplatte mit Monogramm des Alexius Bresnicer und Jahreszahl (2° K 13)

24 Da es sich um bekannte Autoren und Werke handelt, werden Hinweise auf Fachliteratur nur in Ausnahmefällen gegeben.
25 Sie findet sich nicht im VD 16. Ein Exemplar nach dem Microfiche BSB besitzt Berlin SBB-PK.
26 Zur Überlieferung der Briefe vgl. den Artikel von MICHAEL WEISSENBERGER: Libanios. In: *Der neue Pauly* (DNP). *Enzyklopädie der Antike*. Hrsg. von HUBERT CANCIK u. HELMUTH SCHNEIDER. Bd. 7. Stuttgart, Weimar 1999, Sp. 129–32, Briefe Sp. 131.

bestimmten Zeitabschnitten betrachtet werden. Zuerst finden die bis zu den Jahren 1539 erschienen Ausgaben Beachtung – jene Bücher also, die vor seinen Leipziger und Wittenberger Studienjahren und vor seiner Berufung und Tätigkeit als Schulmeister und Pfarrer erschienen sind. Für das moderne, humanistische Lehrprogramm der Wittenberger Universität war die Universität Tübingen mit ihrem berühmten Gelehrten Heinrich Bebel Vorbild. Von diesem Autor besaß Bresnicer drei Texte, und alle sind sie voller Notizen und Lesehilfen (4° K 78 (1); VD 16 B 1176 sowie 4° K 63 (2) und (3); VD 16 B 1174 und B 1207). Sicher waren es diese Qualitäten, die ihn veranlassten, seinen Magistertitel in Wittenberg zu erwerben und ihn zugleich zum Verfechter der Reformation werden ließen. Auf Melanchthons hervorgehobene Position und Qualität als Lehrer sei nur hingewiesen. Melanchthon durfte in Wittenberg lesen, was er wollte, und er las auch über Cicero, den Bresnicer sehr schätzte.

Der ältere Teil der Bibliothek Bresnicers umfasst 16 Inkunabeln und etwa 150 Drucke aus der Frühdruckzeit, die, bezogen auf Bresnicers Studienzeit, bis 1539 eingeordnet wurden. Nachfolgend werden einige typische Titel zitiert, um seine Interessen beurteilen zu können. In vielen dieser Bücher finden sich seine lateinischen und griechischen Notizen und Lesehilfen – oft eine handschriftliche Blattzählung, Kapitelmarkierung, Unterstreichung und Wiederholung von Begriffen sowie persönliche Randbemerkungen – teils sehr intensiv, teils vereinzelt oder auch nur in speziellen Kapiteln. In einigen Exemplaren wurde jeder Freiraum beschrieben. In durchschossenen Ausgaben ließ er zusätzlich leere Lagen einbinden, die weiteren Notizen dienten. Die Bibliothek enthält viele solcher »Handexemplare«. In einigen Texten der Kirchenväter notierte er mehrfach die Lehrmeinung Melanchthons. Manchmal ist es nur eine einzelne Unterstreichung, die Korrektur eines Druckfehlers oder einer fehlerhaft gedruckten Lagenbezeichnung, die seinen aufmerksamen Umgang mit dem Buch beweisen, wie zum Beispiel in einem Band, der Schriften von Laurentius Valla enthält (2° K 583). Die nachfolgenden Beispiele wurden der Übersichtlichkeit halber nach chronologischen und sachlichen Gesichtspunkten gruppiert.[24] Folgende Ausgaben von frühchristlichen Autoren und Kirchenvätern sind unter anderem vorhanden: ANSELMUS DE CANTERBURY: *Opera* (Nürnberg: Hochfeder, 1491; 2° K 24 (1); GW 2031); EUSEBIUS VON CAESAREA: *Autores historiae ecclesiasticae* (Hrsg. von BEATUS RHENANUS. Basel: Froben, 1544; 2° K 897; VD 16 E 4277); GREGORIUS I.: *Opera* (Paris: Rembolt, 1518; 2° K 403; Moreau II, S. 479 Nr. 1835); SOPHRONIUS EUSEBIUS HIERONYMUS: *Opera* (Bde. 1–9 u. Index. Hrsg. von ERASMUS. Basel: Amerbach, Froben, Rechburger, 1516–20; 2° K 473–480; VD 16 H 3882).

Dubletten gibt es in Bresnicers Sammlung nur wenige. Davon erweist sich allerdings eine als ein interessantes Dokument. Unter der Signatur 4° K 589 verbirgt sich eine lateinische Libanius-Ausgabe[25] aus dem Jahre 1504, gedruckt in Krakau: *Libanii greci declamatoris beati Iohannis Chrysostomi praeceptoris epistolae: cum adiectis Iohannis Sommerfeldt argumentis et emendatione et castigatione clarissimis.*[26] Die Humanisten sammelten zwar die Handschriften des Libanius, veranstalteten aber keine Ausgabe. Der

Übersetzer aus dem Griechischen war Francesco Zambeccari in der zweiten Hälfte des 15. Jahrhunderts. Eine der überlieferten Handschriften gelangte nach Krakau, wo sie Johannes Sommerfeld (Johannes Rhagius oder Aesticampanus) als Vorlage für eine Ausgabe verwendete.[27] Der Halbledereinband gehört zur Gruppe der vom Leipziger Buchführer K 107 eingebundenen Bände.[28] Auf dem Vorderdeckel wurde oben, im typischen Schreibduktus von Bresnicer, »PFLugius« notiert; im Spiegel des Vorderdeckels ist »LiBeR Huguldi Pflugii« eingetragen. Diese Eintragung wurde durchgestrichen, und darunter trug Bresnicer seinen bekannten Besitzvermerk ein. Von anderer Hand finden sich unter dem Titel einige handschriftliche Zeilen, darunter ein griechisches Wort und der Name Johannes Speiser. Stammt dieser Band etwa aus der berühmten Bibliothek des Meißner Bischofs Julius Pflug, dem Bresnicer, der zu dieser Diozese gehörte, begegnet ist? Leider lässt sich hierüber vorerst keine Klärung erreichen.[29]

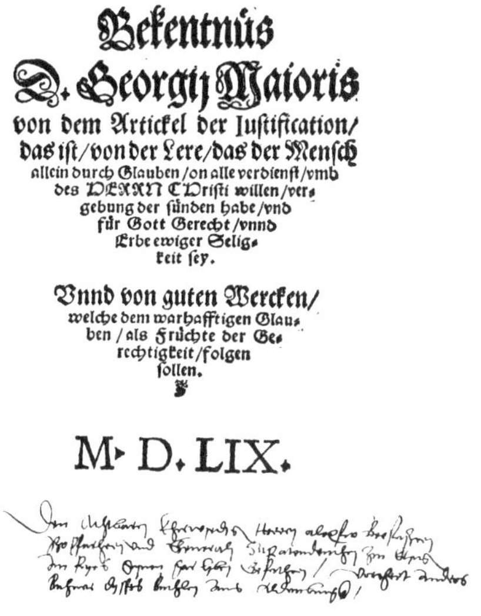
Bekentnüs D. Georgij Maioris von dem Artickel der Iustification/ das ist/ von der Lere/ das der Mensch allein durch Glauben/ on alle verdienst/ vmb des HERRN CHristi willen/ vergebung der sünden habe/ vnd für Gott Gerecht/ vnnd Erbe ewiger Seligkeit sey.
Vnnd von guten Wercken/ welche dem warhafftigen Glauben/ als Früchte der Gerechtigkeit/ folgen sollen.
M. D. LIX.

[Abb. 4] Widmung von Andreas Behmer aus Altenburg (4° K 675)

Die Gruppe antiker Philosophen und Literaten ist ebenfalls gut vertreten, dazu gehören AESOPUS: *Fabulae* (Reggio: Bertochus, 1497; 4° K 86 (3); GW 314); HOMER: *Ilias* (Leipzig: Lotter, 1512; 2° K 584; VD 16 H 4661); MUSAEUS: *Hero und Leander* (Venedig: Aldus Manutius, [um 1495/97]; 4° K 86 (4); H 11653); mehrere Texte von Aristoteles, zum Beispiel: *De Moribus alias Ethicorum a Johane Argyropylo ...* (Leipzig: [Landsberger], 1504; 2° K 36 (1); VD 16 A 3414); ZENOBIOS GRAMMATIKOS: *Epitome proverbiorum Tarrhaei et Didymi* (Florenz: für Giunta, 1497; 4° K 86 (1); H 16283); M. TULLIUS CICERO: *De oratore etc.* ([Nürnberg]: Koberger, 1497; 2° K 188 (1); GW 6753) [Abb. 1]. Von Cicero besaß Bresnicer noch zwei weitere Ausgaben aus dem frühen 16. Jahrhundert, darunter einen durchschossenen Druck mit einer zusätzlich eingebundenen Lage; alle Seiten sind voll beschrieben.

Werke von Autoren des frühen und späteren Mittelalters dienten dem Studium und finden sich also auch in Bresnicers Sammlung, zum Beispiel BOETHIUS: *De consolatione philosophiae* (Mit Kommentar des Pseudo-Thomas de Aquino. Nürnberg: Koberger, 1495; 4° K 116 (1); GW 4559); ANTONINUS FLORENTINUS: *Confessionale* (Straßburg: Flach, 1499; 4° K 25 (1); GW 2137); BIRGITTA: *Revelationes etc.* (Nürnberg: Koberger, 1500; 2° K 115 – GW 4392);[30] HENRICUS DE HASSIA: *Secreta sacerdotum* (Leipzig: Lotter, 1506; 4° K 25 (3) – VD 16 H 2137).

Aus der Literatur der Renaissancezeit sei die Ausgabe von GIOVANNI BOCCACCIO: *Genealogiae deorum* (Venedig: Locatellus für Scotus, 1494/95; 2° K 570 (2) – GW 4478) genannt. Werke von Humanisten, Philosophen und Philologen des 15. und 16. Jahrhunderts standen Bresnicer in größerer Auswahl zur Verfügung, wie zum Beispiel PHILIPPUS BEROALDUS: *Commentationes ... In Suetonium Tranquillum* (Paris: Hornken und Hittorp, 1512; 2° K 96; Moreau III S. 113 Nr. 247); ANTONIUS MANCINELLUS: *De componendis versibus opusculum ...* ([Leipzig: Thanner], 1504; 4° K 680 (3); VD 16 M 508); MARSILIUS FICINUS: *Epistolae* ([Nürnberg]: Koberger, 1497; 4° K 682; GW 9874); MARCUS ANTONIUS SABELLICUS: *Opera* (Venedig: de Lisone, 1502; 2° K 910 (1); Adams S 10); LAURENTIUS VALLA: *De lingua latina ...* (Paris: Poncet u. a., 1510; 2° K 583 (2); Moreau I, S. 389 Nr. 212).

27 Vgl. auch RICHARD FÖRSTER: *Francesco Zambeccari und die Briefe des Libanios. Ein Beitrag zur Kritik des Libanios und zur Geschichte der Philologie.* Stuttgart 1878.

28 Vgl. Kapitel weiter unten.

29 Zur B Pflugs siehe HOLGER KUNDE u. a.: Schatzhaus der Überlieferung – Stiftsbibliothek und Stiftsarchiv Zeitz. Petersberg 2005 (*Kleine Schriften der vereinigten Domstifter zu Merseburg und Naumburg und des Kollegiatsstifts Zeitz*. 1). – WALTER KALINER: Julius Pflug als Bibliophile. In: Pflugiana. Studien über Julius Pflug (1499–1564). Ein internationales Symposium. Hrsg. von ELMAR NEUSS u. J. V. POLLET. Münster 1990 (*Reformationsgeschichtliche Studien und Texte*. 129), S. 23–42.

30 Es ist der einzige Kettenband in Bresnicers Bibliothek; seine Herkunft ist noch ungeklärt.

Zwischen dieser und der nächsten Gruppe sei eines der erfolgreichsten Bücher jener Zeit erwähnt: DIONYSIUS CARTUSIANUS: *Specula omnis status vitae humanae* (Nürnberg: Wagner, 1495; 4° K 265 (1); GW 8419). Mit dem Einfluss der *Devotio moderna* aus dem Norden verbindet sich auch die Wirkung des Erasmus Roterodamus. Es ist eines der wenigen Exemplare, das eine weitere Provenienz aufweist: »Georgij Korichß sum compostum Anno ... 1512«. Er war der Vorbesitzer dieses Exemplars, das außer Bresnicers Notizen noch weitere Eintragungen von anderer Hand enthält.

Der praktizierende Theologe benötigte viele Texte, und Spuren von Bresnicers Arbeit zeigen unter anderem folgende Ausgaben: GUILLELMUS PARISIENSIS: *Postilla super Epistolas et Evangelia de tempore et de sanctis et pro defunctis* (Leipzig: Lotter, 1510; 4° K 409; VD 16 E 4378); *Psalterium latinum* (Nürnberg: Koberger, 1497; 4° K 265 (2); H 4013); *Viaticum Misnense* (Leipzig: Lotter, 1502; 4° K 1117; VD 16 B 8176).[31]

Seinen Textstudien diente eine gute Auswahl an Lexika, Grammatiken, Sprachlehren, wie zum Beispiel AUGUSTINUS: *Ars grammatica* (Straßburg: Grüninger, 1508; 4° K 63 (1); VD 16 A 4273); JOHANNES CRASTONUS: *Lexicon Graecolatinum* (Venedig: Manutius, 1497; 2° K 679; GW 7814); THEODORUS GAZA: *Grammaticae institutionis libri duo* (Basel: Froben, 1521; 4° K 357; VD 16 T 802); ALDUS MANUTIUS: *Rudimenta Grammatices latinae linguae etc.* (Leipzig: Lotter, 1510; 4° K 680 (1); VD 16 M 777); JOHANNES SULPITIUS: *Grammatica posterior edicio Sulpiciana* (Leipzig: Stöckel, 1511; 4° K 680 (2); VD 16 S 10149). Auch in diesen Nachschlagewerken finden sich viele Annotationen. Juristische Literatur ist nur mit einem Titel vertreten: IUSTINIAN: *Institutiones Imperiales novissime correcte* (Paris: Petit, 1508; 4° K 531; Moreau I, S. 272 Nr. 53).

Den größten Teil der Bibliothek bilden Schriften seiner Zeitgenossen – berühmter und einflussreicher Gelehrter. 1538 ist das Todesjahr von Erasmus; es fällt in die Zeit, als Bresnicer sein Studium begann. Welche Bedeutung Erasmus für ihn hatte, belegen verschiedene Ausgaben. Nur in defektem Zustand sind die *Annotationes Novi Testamenti* (Basel: Froben, 1516; 2° K 221 (2); VD 16 B 4146) erhalten. Am Schluss des Matthaeus-Evangeliums legte Bresnicer ein handschriftliches Register an, das Namen und Begriffe enthält. Weiterhin benutzte er die 1524 in Basel erschienene Schrift *De libero Arbitrio Diatribe, sive Collatio ...* (8° K 288 (1); VD 16 E 3147). Diese ist mit einer Schrift Luthers zusammengebunden.

Der früheste Lutherdruck in Bresnicers Bibliothek, *Sermo de duplici iustitia castigatus ...* (4° K 603 (6); VD 16 L 5998) erschien 1519 in Wittenberg. Mehrere Texte, die er intensiv benutzte, stammen aus den 1520er Jahren: *Epistola ad Leonem decimum summum pontificem. Tractatus de libertate christiana* (Wittenberg: Grunenberg, 1520; 4° K 603 (9); VD 16 L 4630); *De bonis operibus* (Leipzig: Lotter, 1521; 4° K 603 (2); VD 16 L 7150) und *De servo arbitrio Mar. Lutheri ad Erasmum Roterodamum* (Wittenberg: Lufft, 1525; 8° K 288 (2); VD 16 L 6660); bei Letzterem handelt es sich um die Schrift, die mit der oben genannten Erasmus-Ausgabe zusammengebunden ist.

Luther pflegte seine reformatorische Botschaft auch durch persönliche Verbindungen zu vermitteln. Er führte unter anderem Briefwechsel mit

---

[31] Dieses Breviarium erhielt Bresnicer von Alexius Crohner, Dr. der Philosophie und Canonicus in Altenburg.

Johannes Sylvius Egranus (d. i. Wildenauer aus Eger), der wie Luther humanistisch orientiert war. Egranus, seit 1517 Prediger in der Zwickauer Marienkirche, musste sich gegen die Angriffe des Leipziger Theologieprofessors Hieronymus Dungersheim zur Wehr setzen. Schriften beider Autoren sind in Bresnicers Sammlung vertreten: JOHANN SYLVIUS EGRANUS: *Contra Calumniatores suos Apologia* ... ([Nürnberg: Peypus], 1518; 4° K 301 (2); VD 16 W 3073) und HIERONYMUS DUNGERSHEIM: *Confutatio: apologetici cuiusdam sacre scripture falso inscripti* ... (Leipzig: Stöckel, 1514; 4° K 301 (5); VD 16 D 2947). Ein ausgewiesener Lutherfeind war zum Beispiel Johann Cochlaeus, der die *Articuli. CCCCC. Martini Lutheri. Ex sermonibus* ... (Köln: Quentell, 1525) herausgegeben hat (4° K 607; VD 16 L 6657). Im vorderen Spiegel ist eine Sentenz gegen Verleumder und Schmarotzer eingetragen. Von den verfügbaren Schriften des Lutherfreundes Johannes Bugenhagen hingegen zeigt seine *Interpretatio in libri Psalmorum* (Basel: [Petri], 1524; 2° K 143 (1); VD 16 B 3138) Spuren von Bresnicers Arbeit und Wertschätzung.

Die Bibliothek Bresnicers weist nur wenige zwischen 1530 und 1539 erschienene Drucke auf. Es wird aber deutlich, dass die reformatorischen Schriften während seiner Studienzeit eine prägende Rolle spielten. Zwar finden sich in der Zeit nur relativ wenige Spuren seiner Arbeit mit relevanten Texten, aber daraus lassen sich keine überzeugenden Schlüsse ziehen, was auch für die Tatsache gilt, dass sich in der Bibliothek Bresnicers keine Luther-Bibel findet. Intensive Nutzerspuren seiner Arbeit enthalten hingegen Bücher von JOHANNES AGRICOLA: *De duplici legis discrimine sententia, ad Wendelinum Fahrum et quosdam alios in Comitatu Mansfeldensi* (Wittenberg: Rhau, 1539; 8° K 408 (6); VD 16 A 971) und von JOHANNES BRENZ: *In acta apostolica Homiliae centum viginti duae* (Hagenau: Brubacher, 1536; 2° K 126 (1); VD 16 B 7682). In diesem Exemplar und in einer weiteren Brenz-Ausgabe – den Luther sehr schätzte – vermerkte Bresnicer: »sibi suisque comparavit«.

Handschriften

Die Sammlung enthält auch einige Handschriften, die noch genauer zu untersuchen sind, da es sich wahrscheinlich um Nachschriften handelt. Der Sammelband 4° K 952 vereint vier gedruckte und handschriftliche Texte mit Psalmen und *Sermones*. Die Drucke, beide aus Wittenberg, sind durchschossen. Die Psalmen bearbeitete Thomas Wolf (Wolphius), der zusammen mit Spalatin Schüler Mutians in Erfurt war und dessen Psalmen-Auslegungen mehrfach gedruckt worden sind. Der Verfasser der Scholien ist J. Bugenhagen. Der Band, dem die ersten Lagen fehlen, ist auf ungewöhnliche Art zusammengebunden: Die drei Texte sind in den vorderen handschriftlichen Text zwischengeordnet.

Ein zwanzig Texte umfassender Sammelband (4° K 765) enthält sieben Handschriften meist geringen Umfangs: *Collatio sententiae D. Martini Lutheri ..., de Iustificatione cum blasphemia et fanatica sententia Andreae Osiandri* 1551 (4 Bl.); *Epistola D. Philippi Melanchthonis ad Doctorem Iustum Ionam ...* M.D.LII. (4 Bl.); *Tres epistolae Ioannis Brentii de duobus scriptis in causa Osiandrica* (um 1553, 17 Bl.); *Victorini Strigelij pharmacon contra furores Andreae Osiandri* (um 1550, 25 Bl.); *Epicedion Draconis Regiomontani, organimendacis, ac homicidae diaboli, qui, laus Deo, praeter omnium opinionem XVII Octobris huius praeter extinctus est* (6 Bl.); *Bericht Herrn Johanßen Stolizen [Stoll] Hoffpredigers zu Weimar, an den Churfürsten zu Sachsen Herzog Johan fridrichen von Osianders Irthumb in preussen die Rechtfertigung belangent. Sampt S. C. f. G. Antworth. 1551* (11 Bl.); *Nobilitate generis virtute et pietate praestanti domino Vulfgango a Ketering iurisconsulto et consiliario Illustrißimi Prußiae principis suo Domino et amico Charißimo ... Maij 1551. Tui Studiosis.; ... I. Stol* [Stoll] (15 Bl.). Diese thematisch zusammengehörenden Schriften betreffen die Auseinandersetzungen mit Andreas Osiander in den 1550er Jahren. Der erste und zweite handschriftliche Text wurde von Alexius Bresnicer persönlich geschrieben [Abb. 2].

Aus Bresnicers Studienzeit hat sich ferner ein Handschriftenkonvolut erhalten, das einen Eindruck vermittelt, wie er arbeitete und seine Notizen anlegte, denn es handelt sich um seine eigenen »Studien« (4° K 421). Sie sind – leider inzwischen stark defekt – in braunes Leder gebunden, und mit großer Sicherheit hat er sie sich in Wittenberg einbinden lassen. Die acht lateinischen und griechischen Texte müssen ihm wichtig gewesen sein, denn auf dem Schmutzblatt verzeichnete er, sehr sorgfältig und mit schönen Majuskeln, ihren Inhalt. Seine Themen seien hier in knapper Übersetzung angegeben: *Kurzgefaßte Darstellung über die Behörden und Priesterschaften der Römer ...; Anweisung zur kunstvollen Beredsamkeit; Einführung in die griechischen Buchstaben; Griechische Redewendungen, die in den lateinischen Sprachgebrauch übertragen wurden; Regelwerk zur Zeichensetzung; Kurzgefaßte Anweisung zur Abfassung von Gedichten; Kleines Werk des I. B. P [Johannes Bugenhagen Pommeranus], welche Schriftsteller zu lesen sind, um gutes Latein mit feinem Geschmack zu verbinden; Kurzgefaßte Überlieferung, was zur Abfassung von Briefen und Reden am meisten hilft; Zeichensetzungslehre.*

Seine eigenen Texte versah er mit Randnotizen. Für die Überschriften benutzte er eine breitere Feder; Kopftitel setzte er in die Mitte und das Thema notierte er in der rechten oberen Ecke der Seite. Mit roter Tinte zog er doppelte Rahmenlinien. Am Schluss von S. 28, wo er das griechische Alphabet, Diphthonge, Präpositionen und Silben behandelte, schrieb er das griechische »Telos«, wie es bei den Humanisten – auch in vielen Drucken – üblich war.

Der Theologe: Superintendent und Flacianer

Seit den 1540er Jahren ist Bresnicer als Lehrer, Pfarrer und Superintendent tätig und wird in der Residenzstadt Altenburg sesshaft.[32] Es ist die Zeit des späten Luthers, des Nachrückens der zweiten Generation der Reformatoren, des Beginns und des Höhepunkts der Kontroverstheologie bis hin zur sogenannten »Spätreformation«.[33] In diesen Jahrzehnten wächst Bresnicers Bibliothek beachtlich an; bis 1570 haben mehr als 300 weitere Titel seine Sammlung bereichert. Theologie und seine Tätigkeit als Pfarrer sind es fortan, die den thematischen Schwerpunkt seiner Büchersammlung – mit ausschließlich aktuellem Zeitbezug – bestimmen. In die 1550er Jahre fallen auch seine schriftstellerischen Versuche, die er dann

32 Das StArch. in Altenburg verwahrt drei Dokumente, die sich auf Bresnicers Tätigkeit beziehen.

33 Vgl. u. a. HEINZ SCHILLING: Reformation – Umbruch oder Gipfelpunkt eines Temps des Réformes? In: Ausgewählte Abhandlungen zur europäischen Reformations- und Konfessionsgeschichte. Hrsg. von HEINZ SCHILLING. Berlin 2002 (*Historische Forschungen*. 75), S. 11–31. – DERS.: Die »zweite Reformation« als Kategorie der Geschichtswissenschaft. In: Ausgewählte Abhandlungen (siehe oben), S. 433–82. – PETER F. BARTON: Matthäus Flacius Illyricus. In: Die Reformationszeit. 2 Bde. Hrsg. von MARTIN GRESCHAT. Stuttgart 1981 (*Gestalten der Kirchengeschichte*. 6), Bd. 2, S. 277–93.

offensichtlich nicht fortgesetzt hat. Wie bereits erwähnt sind seine eigenen Werke in der nach Brandenburg gelangten Bibliothek nicht überliefert.

Die inhaltlichen Schwerpunkte seiner Bibliothek in den Jahren zwischen 1540 und 1570 spiegeln wichtige Entwicklungsphasen der Reformation und unterschiedliche Lehrmeinungen wider.[34] Die Bücher in diesem Teil der Bibliothek – der umfangreicher ist als der »historisch« und bildungsgeschichtlich orientierte ältere Bestand – sind aktuelle Texte, die ohne Zeitverzug erworben oder ihm als Schenkung übereignet wurden. Die aktuellen Streitschriften führen durch die Auseinandersetzungen mit Freund und Feind. Der Buchdruck expandiert in jenen Jahren, und über Bücher zu verfügen bedeutet, dass jederzeit mittels der Lektüre und der Möglichkeit des synoptischen Lesens eine fachlich-intellektuelle Stellungnahme möglich war und der Einzelne sich seine eigene Meinung bilden und in Marginalien und Exzerpten seine persönliche Position beziehen konnte. Dass für diese Notizen die lateinische Sprache auch in deutschsprachigen Texten verwendet wurde, beweist nur die Gewohnheit, das gebräuchliche Medium für die individuelle Erschließung des Inhalts zu nutzen.

Bresnicer stand aufgrund seiner beruflichen Stellung in der Pflicht, sich zu einer theologischen Richtung zu bekennen, und er entschied sich für den Magdeburger, später Jenaer Kreis um Flacius Illyricus.[35] Schriftlich hat er nicht Stellung bezogen, im Gegensatz zu vielen jener Autoren, deren Bücher in seiner Bibliothek standen. Auch Predigten von Bresnicer sind nicht überliefert. Dass auch die Schriften der Gegner – wie beispielsweise Victorinus Strigel – zum Bestand gehören, bedeutet, dass er sich intensiv und differenziert mit den aktuellen Fragen befasst haben muss und viele Werke zur Hand haben wollte, auf die sich die laufenden Auseinandersetzungen bezogen: von den *Adiaphora* bis zum Osiander-Streit. Wie bereits erwähnt handelt es sich niemals um das Gesamtwerk eines Autors; stattdessen sind immer nur wenige Grundschriften vorhanden, was auch für viele Hauptwerke gilt, zum Beispiel von Flacius Illyricus oder Johannes Wigand.

In dieser Zeit bildeten sich neue Druckerzentren heraus, die sich neben den traditionellen wie Köln, Mainz, Hamburg, Rostock, Heidelberg, Dillingen, Königsberg, Dresden, Frankfurt/Oder oder Kopenhagen etablieren konnten. Regional wichtiger wurden vor allem Magdeburg (41 Drucke), Jena (26 Drucke), Eisleben (13 Drucke) – Zentren, in denen die Anhänger des Flacius auf Zeit sesshaft wurden und wo vorrangig ihre Schriften im Druck erschienen. Aus den bisher bevorzugten Werkstätten wie in Erfurt (nur drei Drucke), Leipzig (17 Drucke) und vor allem Wittenberg (25 Drucke) gingen weniger Drucke hervor. Je nach Ausbreitung der Reformation sind auch Tübingen (22 Drucke), Ingolstadt (sieben Drucke), Frankfurt am Main (20 Drucke), Regensburg (10 Drucke) vertreten. Bedeutung behielten die traditionsreichen Zentren Straßburg und Basel. Wichtig war, wie und wo sich die Reformation ausbreitete, wie weit sich – gefördert durch namhafte Reformatoren – der Wirkungsbereich im Süden ausdehnte. Nicht zuletzt waren es die Exulanten, die auf Zeit oder für den Rest ihres Lebens in der Fremde blieben und dort publizierten. Auch in Österreich wurde eine protestantische Druckerei gegründet.

34 Vgl. den allgemeinen Überblick in HARM KLUETING: *Das konfessionelle Zeitalter. Europa zwischen Mittelalter und Moderne. Kirchengeschichte und Allgemeine Geschichte.* Darmstadt 2007, besonders S. 182–261: Das reformatorische Europa.

35 Zu den verschiedenen Stationen im Leben der Flacius Illyricus vgl. u. a. TRE (siehe Anm. 19), Bd. 11, S. 206–14, besonders S. 207–9. Zur Geschichte der Kirchenspaltung allgemein vgl. u. a. PAUL TSCHACKERT: *Die Entstehung der lutherischen und reformierten Kirchenlehre samt ihren innerprotestantischen Gegensätzen.* Göttingen 1979 (Neudruck der Erstauflage von 1910). – *Geschichte des Christentums.* Hrsg. von MARC VENARD. Deutsche Fassung von HERIBERT SMOLINSKY. 8 Bde. Freiburg, Basel, Wien 1992, hier Bd. 8: Die Zeit der Konfessionen 1530–1620/30.

Betrachten wir nochmal bereits genannte Autoren, die in Bresnicers Sammlung besonders zahlreich vertreten sind. Flacius kommt – statistisch gesehen – vor Luther. Das spricht deutlich dafür, dass er die Lehrmeinung des Ersteren anerkannte und selbst vertrat. Viele der grundlegenden Schriften des Flacius fehlen allerdings in Bresnicers Buchbestand; bei den meisten Drucken handelt es sich um Kleinschriften nur geringen Umfangs. Eine Ausnahme ist die 344 Seiten umfassende Schrift *De sectis, dissensionibus, contradictionibus et contusionibus doctrinae, religionis, scriptorum et doctorum pontificiorum Liber ...*, 1565 in Basel erschienen (4° K 523; VD 16 F 1496). Das Exemplar weist Notationen und Unterstreichungen – im Vorwort mit roter, im Text mit schwarzer Tinte – auf, allerdings nicht das ganze Buch hindurch. Bresnicer hat also mit diesem Text gearbeitet. Seine Lesespuren sind ab Mitte des Textes auch in der 1563 in Frankfurt am Main erschienenen Ausgabe *Pia et necessaria Admonitio de decretis et canonibus Concilii Tridentini ...* (4° K 1105 (1); VD 16 F 1468) zu finden; diese Schrift verfasste Flacius zusammen mit Nikolaus Gallus.

Ob Bresnicer die oben erwähnten Lutherdrucke aus den Jahren 1520 und 1525 als Student oder später als Pfarrer benutzt hat, lässt sich nicht feststellen. Tatsache ist, dass nur ein weiterer Lutherdruck Eintragungen von seiner Hand enthält, und zwar die 1553 in Jena erschienene Ausgabe *Der Prophet Joel durch Doct. Mart. L. in Latinischer sprach vnd ausgelegt Vnd newlich verdeutscht etc. Mit einer Vorrede von Nikolaus von Amsdorf* (4° K 918 (7); VD 16 B 3865). Dieser umfangreiche Band macht Bresnicers Bücherstudien besonders deutlich.

Schriften des Johann Brenz, der bereits für den Studenten Bresnicer wichtig geworden war, benutzte dieser auch weiterhin, wie die Anmerkungen in zwei seiner späteren Texte bezeugen. Die Schrift *In acta apostolica Homiliae centum viginti duae* (1536 in Hagenau publiziert; 2° K 126 (1); VD 16 B 7682), hat Bresnicer mit zahlreichen lateinischen und hebräischen Marginalien versehen. Vereinzelte Notizen enthält auch eines der umfangreichsten Werke von Brenz: *In evangelii secundum Lucam duodecim priora capita Homiliae ...* (1541 in Frankfurt am Main gedruckt; 2° K 129; VD 16 B 7731) – einer der beiden Bände, in die er den Vermerk »Alexius Bresnicerus sibi suisquem comparavit« eingetragen hat. In die leere Wappenkartusche der Titelbordüre setzte er sein Monogramm, zeichnete zwei gekreuzte Knochen und schrieb darunter die Worte »Memento mori«. Dagegen finden sich in nur einer in Wittenberg von Hans Lufft 1561 veröffentlichten Schrift des *Praeceptor Germaniae* Unterstreichungen, und zwar in den *Sententiae sanctorum patrum de coena Domini ...* (8° K 449 (4); VD 16 M 4223). Von Tilemann Heshusius' Werken zeigt der 1560 in Jena erschienene Druck *De praesentia corporis Christi in coena Domini* (8° K 651 (2), VD 16 H 3102) Bresnicers Arbeitsspuren. Diese und zahlreiche nicht erwähnte Autoren haben in den Kontroversen und Richtungskämpfen jener Jahrzehnte eine wichtige Rolle gespielt.

Dem Wortführer der Altenburger Religionsgespräche, Johannes Wigand, stand Bresnicer sicherlich nahe, wie dessen Widmungen beweisen. Nutzungsspuren Bresnicers finden sich jedoch in seinen Büchern nicht. Ohne Spuren blieben auch die Schriften von Nikolaus von Amsdorf,

Augustin von Alveldt, Nikolaus Gallus, Georg Major oder Joachim Westphal. Sie alle gehörten zum Kreis um Flacius Illyricus, mit vielen wird Bresnicer Kontakt gehabt haben. Wie bereits Luther seine reformatorische Botschaft durch persönliche Verbindungen weitergetragen hat, werden auch die Flacianer Kontakte gepflegt haben. Dass sich nicht in allen Büchern Bresnicers Spuren seines Umgangs mit ihnen finden lassen, hängt sicherlich auch damit zusammen, dass die Nachhaltigkeit eines Textes geringer und die Zeitereignisse schnelllebiger und innerhalb kurzer Zeit neue Stellungnahmen erforderlich wurden.[36]

Bucheinbände als Wegweiser

Stationen aus Bresnicers Leben sowie persönliche und berufsbedingte Kontakte vermitteln auch einige Bucheinbände. Soweit sie sich bestimmen lassen, führen uns die Einbände der vor 1539 erschienenen Bücher zu 17 verschiedenen Buchbinderwerkstätten. Unter den individuell gearbeiteten und mit Blindstempeln verzierten Ledereinbänden – meist aus Schweinsleder – gibt es in der früheren Zeit nur wenige Sammelbände, was mit Format und Umfang zusammenhängt. Einzelne Einbände kommen aus Werkstätten in Braunschweig, Görlitz, Wittenberg und Zwickau. Ein brauner Halbleder-Einband stammt aus dem Sächsischen Erzgebirge und fällt durch sein besonderes Stempelmaterial auf: ein springender Hase in rhombischen Feldern. Der Einband wurde für die 1494 erschienene Ausgabe des Alphonsus de Spina gearbeitet und ist mit einer beschrifteten Schließe versehen.[37] Ein weiterer Band mit diesem Stempel befindet sich in der Kirchenbibliothek St. Annen in Annaberg-Buchholz und gehörte einst dem dortigen Franziskanerkloster. Der Buchbinder ist also in dieser Gegend anzusiedeln, die Bresnicer aus den Anfangszeiten seines Wirkens gut gekannt hat. Einige Einbände schmückte der Buchbinder mit datierten Rollen, doch lassen sich Ort und Werkstatt nicht im Einzelnen ausmachen, wohl aber in Mittel- und Süddeutschland vermuten. Es sind vor allem datierte Rollen mit biblischen Motiven. Eine größere Anzahl von Büchern wurde in Erfurt, Magdeburg, Frankfurt/Oder, vor allem aber in Leipzig, unter anderem bei Valentin Bormann, gebunden. In Leipzig erhielten 23 Bücher einheitlich gestaltete Einbände, was auf einen Auftraggeber hinweist, der sie in Serie preiswert hat binden lassen. Es sind Buchführer-Einbände der Werkstatt K 107, auf Holzdeckel gearbeitet und mit zeittypischen Schließen in Lilienform versehen.[38]

Nur wenige Bände aus der ersten Hälfte des 16. Jahrhunderts erhielten einen flexiblen Einband mit Bändern. Die einheitlich wirkende Musterung wurde mit nur vier oder zwei Blindstempeln hergestellt. Es handelt sich um stabile, solide gearbeitete Gebrauchsbände, oft als preiswerte Halblederbände gearbeitet.[39] Ob Bresnicer während seines Aufenthalts in Leipzig diese Bücher bereits besaß und hat einbinden lassen oder sie später gebunden von einem Vorbesitzer übernommen hat, muss offen bleiben. Der Buchbinder K 107 war seit dem letzten Drittel des 15. Jahrhunderts bis in die 1530er Jahre aktiv, also vor Bresnicers Studienzeit. Die Bücher mit diesen schlichten Einbänden erschienen zwischen 1497 und 1518 vorwiegend in Basel und Straßburg. Inhaltlich gehören sie zur

[36] Auch die in seiner B vorhandenen Schriften einiger Landesfürsten hat er annotiert.

[37] Signatur 4° K 317; siehe Abb. bei ANNELIESE SCHMITT u. NINON SUCKOW: *Mein Name ist Hase*. In: *Einbandforschungen* (AEB). 8 (2001), S. 20/1.

[38] GERHARD LOH: *Die Leipziger Buchbinder im 15. Jahrhundert. Zugleich ein methodischer Beitrag zur Nutzung historischer Bucheinbände für die Erforschung der örtlichen Buchgewerbe- und Handwerkergeschichte.* Diss. Berlin 1990, S. 76–8, Werkstatt 16, Tafel 21 und 22.

[39] Abb. und ausführliche Beschreibung bei ANNELIESE SCHMITT: *Ein Großauftrag für K 107*. In: *Einbandforschung* (AEB). 23 (2008), S. 57–60, mit Verzeichnis der Buchtitel.

gefragten Literatur, die für humanistisch-theologische Studien benötigt wurde. Als Joachim Garcaeus diese Bände übernahm, müssen einige Schließen defekt gewesen sein, denn er ließ neue anbringen; ihre ursprüngliche Form ist darunter nur noch als Abdruck erkennbar.

Bresnicers Bibliothek dokumentiert auch den Wandel der Einbandgestaltung, der sich nach dem ersten Drittel des 16. Jahrhunderts vollzog. Von den nach 1539 erschienenen Schriften haben nur noch drei einen individuell gestalteten Ledereinband: einer ist in Stuttgart, zwei sind in Wittenberg gearbeitet worden. Die übrigen Bände wurden wegen ihres geringen Umfangs in sinnvoller thematischer Zusammenstellung als Konvolut gebunden und erhielten einen flexiblen Einband aus makulierten Handschriften, wozu auch eine hebräische Handschrift gehörte. Mehrere Bände sind in neutrales Pergament eingebunden, das teilweise eingefärbt wurde; darunter befinden sich einige Copert-Einbände mit Schließen. Dieser Teil der Bibliothek erhielt so ein einheitliches Aussehen und entsprach dem praktischen und sparsamen Einsatz vorhandener Materialien – in diesem Fall durch Recycling von Handschriften, die entsorgt und durch Buchbinder weiter genutzt werden konnten.

Der geschätzte und gefragte Kollokutor
In der Geschichte der Religionen haben Religionsgespräche eine lange Tradition und eine vielseitige formale und inhaltliche Gestaltung. Die Religionsgespräche der Reformationszeit sind nach dem Augsburger Religionsfrieden (1555), der eine Duldung verschiedener Glaubensrichtungen festschreibt, dadurch geprägt, dass sie sich mit den Differenzen innerhalb der verschiedenen Gruppierungen befassen. Den akzentsetzenden Auftakt bildet das 1557 geführte Wormser Religionsgespräch, das in der Organisation und Berufung der Teilnehmer typisch für diese Zeit wurde. Als notwendig erwiesen sich nunmehr auch innerprotestantische Religionsgespräche – Lutheraner mit Lutheranern –, die vor allem die nach dem Leipziger Interim ausgebrochenen Streitigkeiten innerhalb des lutherischen Lagers beilegen sollten. Diese Aufgabe hatte die nach Altenburg einberufene Diskussionsrunde.[40] Hier trafen sich – jeweils mit der gleichen Anzahl von Vertretern – eine ernestinische und eine albertinische Theologenkommission mit ihren Räten und Notaren.

Als Superintendent in Altenburg und als Sympathisant der Flacianer gehörte Bresnicer zu den Teilnehmern des Altenburger Religionsgespräches, das vom Herbst 1568 bis zum Frühjahr 1569 dauerte. In seiner Bibliothek befindet sich ein Exemplar des Erstdruckes des Protokollbandes in deutscher Sprache, der 1569 in Jena erschien: *Colloquium zu Altenburg in Meißen: Vom Artikel der Rechtfertigung vor Gott etc., zwischen dem Kurfürst und den Fürsten von Sachsen und Theologen gehalten, Oktober 1568 – März 1569* (2° K 13; VD 16 K 945). Beigedruckt wurden auf Veranlassung der Flacianer zwei Artikel über ihre wichtigsten Themen: »Vom freien Willen« und »Von den Mitteldingen«, mit denen neue Debatten ausgelöst wurden. 1570 erschienen vom *Colloquium* noch drei weitere Auflagen in lateinischer und deutscher Sprache.

Auf Blatt 8a des Protokollbandes werden die an diesem Gespräch teil-

---

[40] Vgl. TRE (siehe Anm. 19), Bd. 28, S. 631–80, bes. S. 667–80.

nehmenden Personen aufgelistet. Zuerst sind die Churfürstlich-Sächsischen politischen Räte und Theologen benannt,[41] dann folgen die Fürstlich-Sächsischen politischen Räte und Theologen, deren Namen alle in ihrer latinisierten Form zitiert werden. Die Fürstlich-Sächsischen Räte sind Eberhard von der Thanne, Dr. iur. Petrus Prem und Heinrich von Erffa. Der Wortführer der Fürstlich-Sächsischen »Fraktion« ist D. Johannes Wigandus. Die weiteren Teilnehmer sind in der gedruckten Reihenfolge D. Johannes Fridericus Coelestinus, M. Christophorus Irinaeus, M. Bartholomaeus Rosinus, M. Alexius Bresnicer, Timotheus Kirchnerus und als Notar Martinus Burggravius. Inoffiziell haben zeitweilig M. Martinus Wolfius und M. Jacobus Weber teilgenommen.

Das Altenburger Kolloquium blieb ohne Ergebnis, da die Auffassungen gegenüber den Theologen, die aus dem universitären Zentrum in Jena – dem Wirkungsfeld von Flacius Illyricus, der persönlich aber nicht teilnahm – kamen, zu gegensätzlich waren: »In ihren Auseinandersetzungen standen nicht mehr nur die Adiaphora zur Debatte, sondern gleich mehrere Aspekte der Rechtfertigungslehre: die Rolle der guten Werke im Blick auf die Seligkeit (majoristischer Streit), der Beitrag des freien Willens zur Bekehrung (synergistischer Streit) und die Funktion des Gesetzes (antinomistischer Streit)«.[42] Den zum 20. Oktober 1568 nach Altenburg in Meißen von Kurfürst August und Herzog Johann Wilhelm – letzterer war zeitweilig auch persönlich anwesend – berufenen Teilnehmern wurde die Aufgabe zuteil, in diesen Fragen einen Ausgleich zu finden. Beide Seiten wurden durch je drei politische Räte vertreten und hatten einen Notarius dabei. Die Gutachten zu den genannten Themen, die den Teilnehmern als Diskussionsgrundlage dienten, wurden von den Jenaer Theologen erstellt, doch kam es nur über das erste Thema zu Diskussionen. Da sich herausstellte, dass die lehrmäßige Differenzierung in Sachsens Luthertum bereits tief verankert war und Gnesiolutheraner (die Flacianer) und Philippisten keine Annäherung finden konnten, sondern es zu weiterer Spaltung kam, wurde das Kolloquium am 9. März 1569 durch die Abreise der kurfürstlichen Vertreter abgebrochen.

Neue Auseinandersetzungen ergaben sich, weil jede der beiden Seiten eigene Protokolle publizierte. Dazu kamen weitere Publikationen, die wiederum den Charakter von Streitschriften erlangten. Die Bemühungen um die Einheit der Kirchen der Wittenberger Reformation waren gescheitert, und die Eingriffe der Landesfürsten zu dieser Zeit wurden immer härter.[43] In der Zukunft wurde es für die Pfarrer entscheidend, in welchem Maße sie sich den Vorstellungen ihres Landesfürsten anpassten.

»Meinem guten Freund und Bruder« – Die Widmungsexemplare

Natürlich befindet sich unter den Bresnicer gehörenden Büchern der umfangreiche Protokollband über das Altenburger Religionsgespräch (2° K 13; VD 16 K 1945). Dieses Exemplar wurde ihm von Johannes Wigand, dem Wortführer der Theologen,[44] gewidmet: »Collocutorj D. M. Alexio Bresnicero Wigantus«. Als Teilnehmer stand ihm ein »Pflichtexemplar« zu, das durch seinen besonderen Einband auffällt. Er wurde aus Schweinsleder von Caspar Krafft d. Ä. in Wittenberg gestaltet und mit dem Mono-

[41] Auf der kurfürstlichen Seite waren vertreten die politischen Räte Hans von Bernstein, Johann von Zeschaw und Dr. iur. Laurentius Lindeman, die Theologen D. Paulus Eberus, D. Henricus Salmuth, D. Andreas Freyhub, D. Petrus, M. Caspar Cruciger jun., M. Christianus Schütz und als Notarius M. Heinricus Moller. Zeitweilig nahm D. Paulus Crellius teil.

[42] TRE (siehe Anm. 19), Bd. 28, S. 667/8.

[43] Vgl. u. a. ERNST KOCH: Ausbau, Gefährdung und Festigung der lutherischen Landeskirche von 1553 bis 1601. In: *Das Jahrhundert der Reformation* (siehe Anm. 10), S. 195–223, bes. S. 202.

[44] Flacius Illyricus nahm am Altenburger Religionsgespräch nicht teil.

gramm von Alexius Bresnicer sowie mit der Angabe des Jahres versehen, in dem das Kolloquium stattfand [Abb. 3]. Von einer guten persönlichen Beziehung zu Wigand zeugt eine weitere Widmung. Seine Schrift *De clave ligante in ecclesia Christi ...* (1561 bei Peter Brubach in Frankfurt am Main erschienen; 8° K 1180 (3); VD W 2737), übereignete er Bresnicer mit den Worten »Reverendo viro D. Mgrm Alexio Superint. Aldenburgensis fidelissimo suo fratrj Joh. Wigandus dd.« Wigands *Erinnerung von der neuen Buße D. Georg. Majors Repetition: Widerholung und endliche Erklärung der Bekenntnis*, wohl um 1568 in Eisleben erschienen (4° K 675 (4); VD 2558), ist ein Geschenk Cyriacus Spangenbergs: »Reverendo viro et docto [...] Alexio Bresnicero: fratri et amico suo Cyr. Spangenberg«. Spangenberg, der auch mit einer eigenen Schrift in Bresnicers Sammlung vertreten ist, gehört zu jenen, die sich für eine Rückberufung Bresnicers aus Öttingen eingesetzt hatten.

Ein weiterer Teilnehmer am Altenburger Religionsgespräch, Christoph Irinaeus, der ebenfalls mit eigenen Schriften in Bresnicers Bibliothek vertreten ist, widmete ihm ein Büchlein von Dietrich Schernberg: *Apotheosis Johannis VIII ... Ein schön Spiel von Frau Jutten*, 1565 in Eisleben bei Andreas Petri erschienen (8° K 535 (2); Ex. Berlin SBB-PK: Yp 7161 R, z. Zt. Krakau) mit den Worten »Reverendo viro D. Alexio Bresnicero superintendentii [...] fratri [...] donum dedit Christoph Irinej«. Die Tatsache, dass er ihm dieses Legenden-Spiel von Frau Jutten zueignete, lässt vermuten, dass er um die Interessen Bresnicers an dramatischer Literatur und dessen eigenen Beitrag wusste. Natürlich diente dieses Spiel, dessen erste Fassung um 1490 entstanden war und in dieser frühen Phase bereits eine Einzelperson in den Mittelpunkt der Handlung stellte, der Polemik gegen die katholische Kirche.[45] Immer wieder formulierten die Flacianer ihren Protest. Irinaeus nahm Stellung zu den Ausweisungen evangelischer Priester: *Rezept für die Verfolger. I. Wie große Sünde es sei, christliche Prediger zu verfolgen. II. Wie Gott die verfolger straft ...* (Eisleben, um 1566 erschienen; 8° K 535 (1); VD 16 I 1295). Auf das Titelblatt schrieb er die Widmung »D. M. Alexio Bresnicero«, leider ohne seinen Namen zu nennen. Der Flacianer Christoph Irinaeus, zuerst als Schulmeister und Diakon in Bernburg und Aschersleben tätig, wurde 1562 als Pfarrer nach Eisleben berufen und später wieder vertrieben; doch auch in Österreich ließ er von seiner kritischen Haltung nicht ab.

Teilnehmer am Altenburger Religionsgespräch war auch Johann Friedrich Coelestinus, von dem ein eigenes Werk in Bresnicers Bibliothek vorhanden ist. Er schenkte ihm den in Regensburg gedruckten Traktat von Wolfgang Waldner mit der Widmung »Domino Alexio d. d. I. F. Colestius [...]«. Der Titel lautet *Defensio: Das ist Entschuldigung und Ableinung der heidnischen und unchristlichen Verleumdung und Lästerung des übernatürlichen Sternsehers Christian Heiden* (4° K 204 (3); VD 16 W 874).

Der Jenenser Prediger Christoph Hoffmann übereignete Bresnicer zwei Bücher. Der Titel der 1546 erschienenen kleinen Schrift Martin Bucers lautet: *Ein wahrhaftiger Bericht vom Colloquio von Regensburg dies Jahrs angefangen und von dem Abzug der Auditoren und Colloquenten die von Fürsten und Ständen der Augsburgischen Konfession dahin verordnet*

---

45 Vgl. RUPPRICH (siehe Anm. 16), S. 328: Die Neuausgabe besorgte der Prediger und Magister Hieronymus Tilesius aus Hirschberg, Superintendent in Mühlhausen. Er fügte historische Zeugnisse bei und gab zum Schluss Christoph Irenaeus zu einer Konfessionspolemik das Wort; Abdruck des Textes u. a. bei GOTTSCHED (siehe Anm. 19), S. 84–138. – HANSJÜRGEN LINKE: Schernberg, Dieter. In: *Verfasserlexikon*. Hrsg. von FRANZ JOSEF WORSTBROCK u. a. Berlin, New York 1992, Bd. 8, Sp. 647–51.

waren (4° K 610 (8 = 3); VD 16 B 8946). Für ein weiteres Buchgeschenk mit Widmung wählte er eine Schrift Philipp Melanchthons: *Causae quare et amplexae sint et retinendam ducant doctrinam, quam profitentur, Ecclesiae, quae confessionem Augustae exhibitam in synodo Tridentina*, erschienen in Wittenberg 1556 bei Joseph Klug (4° K 610 (15 = 10); VD 16 M 2650). Seine beiden Widmungen sind kurz und nüchtern und lauten in beiden Büchern »D. Alexio suo Christophorus Hoffmann d. d.«.

Viele weitere Freunde, Bekannte und Mitstreiter schenkten Bresnicer ihre eigenen oder Schriften anderer Autoren und versahen sie mit Widmungen, die als Ausdruck einer besonderen Wertschätzung gelten dürfen. Dazu gehörten auch Personen aus Altenburg und Umgebung, die nicht unbedingt als Anhänger des Flacius namhaft gemacht werden können, aber offensichtlich Sympathisanten waren. Zwei Texte von Georg Maior (Meier) weisen auf den Titelblättern eine gleichlautende Widmung auf: »Dem achtbarn Ehrwirdigen Herrn Alexio Bresnizern Itzo Pfarhern vnd Ehrwird. Superintendenthen zu [...] Am Ryes seynem gar liben geferthen verehret Andres Behmer dysses Buchlin aus Aldenburg« [Abb. 4]. Es handelt sich um typische Programmschriften: *Bekenntnis von dem Artikel der Justifikation, das ist von der Lehre, daß der Mensch allein durch den Glauben ... Vergebung der Sünden habe* (Wittenberg 1558; 4° K 675 (2); VD 16 M 2005) und *Repetitio ... Artikel der Justifikation ...* (Dresden 1567; 4° K 657 (3); VD 16 M 2160). Major, der in Wittenberg studiert hatte und dort auch 1574 verstarb, war ein geschätzter Prediger und Schriftsteller, der viele verantwortungsvolle Ämter bekleidete. Mit seinen Auffassungen geriet er in die adiaphoristischen Streitigkeiten und somit auch zu gegensätzlichen Positionen gegenüber den Flacianern. Georg Melhorn, Bürgermeister von Altenburg, der später seines Amtes enthoben wurde, widmete Bresnicer die 1559 bei Kirchner in Magdeburg herausgekommene Schrift *De adiaphoristicis corruptelis ...* (4° K 1193a (5); VD 16 W 2702) mit den Worten »Clarissimo viro D. Alexio Bresnicero superintendenti Altenburgensi d.d. Georgius Melhorn«.

Melchior Runzler aus Mittweida dürfte zu den Bekannten bereits aus jüngeren Jahren gehören. Ihm verdankt Bresnicer zwei interessante Schriften, die jede für sich die Vielfalt reformatorischer Strömungen repräsentiert. Der Autor von *Widerruf, daß die Münch und Pfaffen im Herzogtum Bayern wider das Zeugnis ihres Gewissens ... Bäpstisch sein und bleiben wollen* (4° K 204 (4); VD 16 A 2719) – 1569 in Tübingen erschienen – ist Jakob Andreae, den Bresnicer persönlich in seinem Öttinger Exil kennengelernt hatte. Die Widmung lautet: »Reverendo et doctissimo viro Domini M. Alexio Bresnicero [...] Melchior Runzler Mituuediensis«. Der Verfasser der zweiten Schrift ist Lucas Osiander, der sich durch seine Bauernpostille und das erste evangelische Choralbuch einen Namen machte. Er ist der Sohn des berühmten Andreas Osiander d. Ä., der wiederum den Osiander-Streit ausgelöst hatte: *Ablehnung der Lügen, Verkehrungen und Lästerungen mit denen Bruder Nass ... die christliche Lehre der Augsburgischen Confession ... antastet* (4° K 204 (6); VD 16 O 1161). Osiander ließ diese Schrift 1569 in Tübingen drucken und reagierte damit auf die Polemiken des Johannes Nas, eines Anhängers der römischen Kirche.

Die Widmung lautet »Pro viro pietate et doctrina excellenti Domino M. Alexio Bresnicero superintendenti Ecclesiae Altenburgensis fratri suo in Christo [...] Melchior Runzler Mitvedensis«.

Auch Nikolaus Gallus, ein konsequenter Mitstreiter des Flacius Illyricus und Verfasser vieler Schriften, fühlte sich Bresnicer verbunden. Als Superintendent in Regensburg bemühte sich Gallus, den Vertriebenen zu einer neuen Existenzgrundlage zu verhelfen. Nach seinem Studium in Wittenberg hatte ihn Melanchthon nach Süddeutschland geschickt. Dort vertrieben, ging er für einige Zeit nach Magdeburg, wo er Anhänger der Flacianer wurde. Er durfte später nach Regensburg zurückkehren, wo er wegen seiner vorbildlichen Haltung sehr geschätzt war. Seine Schrift, *Gegenbericht auf D. Pfeffingers und der Adiaphoristen gesuchte Glossen über ihr Leipziger Interim ...*, die 1550 in Magdeburg erschienen war (4° K 664 (2); VD 16 G 276), übereignete er Bresnicer mit sehr persönlichen Worten: »Dem würdigen Herrn Alexio Bresnicero predigern zu Aldenburg meinen gutten freund und Bruder«. Es erübrigt sich beinahe darauf hinzuweisen, dass Bresnicer auch Schriften von Johann Pfeffinger, dem Leipziger Superintendenten, besaß; darunter befand sich eine in Leipzig 1553 erschienene Leichenpredigt für Kurfürst Moritz von Sachsen (4° K 918 (2); VD 16 P 2331).

Die Aktualität der Bücher Bresnicers aus der zweiten Hälfte des 16. Jahrhunderts machen die historischen Zeitabläufe nachvollziehbar. Dass er zu den Flacianern gehörte, belegt nicht nur seine zweimalige Absetzung und Ausweisung aus Altenburg, sondern der große Anteil von Schriften der Gnesiolutheraner,[46] unter denen Matthaeus Flacius Illyricus die streitbarste und zugleich profilierteste Persönlichkeit war. Seine lange kritisch eingeschätzte und unterschätzte Bedeutung wird heute anders bewertet: ohne ihn hätte sich Luthers Lehre nicht durchsetzen können. Flacius selbst widmete Bresnicer zwei Bücher, beide von bedeutenden Autoren und Weggefährten aus den Jahren der großen Auseinandersetzungen. Die eine hat den berühmten, aktiven und großes Vertrauen genießenden Nikolaus von Amsdorf zum Verfasser: *Das die Propositio »gute Werke sind zu Seligkeit schädlich« eine rechte wahre propositio sey, durch die heiligen Paul und Luther gelehrt und gepredigt* ([Magdeburg]: [Kirchner], 1559; 4° K 722 (14); VD 16 A 2335). Flacius notierte auf dem Titelblatt: »Eruditiss: & pietiss: viro D. M. Alexio superintendenti Aldenburgensis suo [...] et fratro illyricus«. Der andere Text stammt aus der Feder von Nikolaus Gallus: *Responsio de libro professorum Wittenbergensium data ecclesiae, ...* (4° K 1193a (4); VD 16 G 289); sie erschien 1559 in Regensburg bei Heinrich Geißler. Flacius variiert seine Widmung geringfügig: »Pro viro domino Alexio Bresnicero superintendenti Aldeburgensi suo fratri Illyricus«.

Auch Schriften anderen Inhalts wurden Bresnicer gewidmet. Der *Hymnus Christi qui lux est et dies etc*, übersetzt nach der deutschen Fassung des Erasmus Alberus, wurde zusammen mit anderen Hymnen von dem in Mansfeld wirkenden Christoph Singel herausgegeben (4° K 1105 (2a)).[47] Dieser Text umfasst nur vier Blätter, auf der ersten bedruckten Seite (Blatt 2a) unten schrieb der Autor seine Widmung »Accipe Singelius ... fratri D. Alexio Bresnicero Singilius d. d. 1562«.

46 Vgl. TRE (siehe Anm. 19), Bd. 13, S. 512–9; hier auch zum Begriff Adiaphora.

47 Ob diese vier Blätter einzeln gedruckt wurden oder zu einer größeren Ausgabe gehörten, wäre noch zu klären. Ein Anhaltspunkt ist, dass Singel seine Widmung datiert hat. Sowohl er als auch Erasmus Alberus sind durch ihre Kirchenlieder bekannt.

Einige andere der Bresnicer gewidmeten Schriften sind nur fragmentarisch erhalten, meist bedingt durch das Einbinden und Beschneiden des Buchblocks durch den Buchbinder. Sie bringen verschiedene Aspekte der Beziehungen und Interessen zum Ausdruck und zeugen von der Wertschätzung seiner Person. Viele gehören zu den führenden Kräften der Reformation und sind bekannt durch Wort und Schrift, sind praktizierende Pfarrer, in gehobenen Positionen und Ämtern, vereinzelt aus dem Schulwesen oder Kulturbereich. Bresnicer muss einen großen Bekanntheitsgrad besessen haben, obwohl er selbst als Autor nicht hervorgetreten ist.

Zweimalige »Enturlaubung« und Vertreibung

Im Jahre 1562 wurde Alexius Bresnicer das erste Mal abgesetzt und ausgewiesen. Über diese Entscheidung schreibt Rudolf Herrmann: »Er scheint aber bei einem Teil der Bürgerschaft sehr beliebt gewesen zu sein, denn es kam zu Unruhen in der Stadt, die zur Absetzung des Bürgermeisters Melhorn führten«.[48] Wie andere Betroffene auch ging Bresnicer nach Öttingen. Dort wirkte er als Pfarrer, bis er im Jahre 1568 wieder in sein Amt als Superintendent in Altenburg zurückberufen wurde. Das wurde durch das Ende der Willkürherrschaft Johann Friedrichs möglich, durch dessen Aktionen gegen die Flacianer zum Beispiel die theologische Fakultät in Jena aufgelöst worden war und auch Flacius Illyricus ins Exil gehen musste.[49] Vier Jahre verbrachte Bresnicer im Schwäbischen. Wenn sein Geburtsjahr wirklich 1504 gewesen wäre, wäre er bei seiner ersten Entlassung und Ausweisung 58 Jahre alt gewesen; wenn er um 1520 geboren wurde, wäre er circa 42 Jahre alt gewesen, als ihn dieses harte Schicksal ereilte. Vertrieben wegen seiner Gesinnung – das bedeutete Armut und Not. Im Exil nutzte Bresnicer jedoch die Möglichkeit, darüber zu sprechen, denn auch in Öttingen hatte er sich zu verantworten und zu rechtfertigen. Zeugnisse und Belege aus dieser Zeit hat T. F. Karrer[50] zusammengestellt, die es uns erlauben, Bresnicers Verhältnisse zu beurteilen.

Die Probleme begannen in Altenburg, als der Herzog die wichtigsten Theologen, zu denen auch Bresnicer gehörte, 1560 nach Weimar einlud. Bei der Diskussion der kursierenden theologischen Lehrmeinungen zwischen Flacius Illyricus und Victorin Strigel war Bresnicer einer der Schiedsmänner. Diese Diskussionen blieben ohne Ergebnis. Maßnahmen gegen Bresnicer und andere Pfarrer erfolgten aber erst, als im Jahre 1562 die Deklaration des Victorin Strigel (Declaratio Victorini) zu unterschreiben war und Bresnicer, der sich nicht vom Flacianismus distanzierte, seine Unterschrift verweigerte. Karrer stellt viele Belege aus den Öttinger Protokollen zusammen, darunter Anträge und Aussagen von namhaften Adligen und Theologen, die sich für Bresnicer aussprachen. Von diesem selbst stammt eine am 6. Juni 1564 verfasste schriftliche Rechtfertigung; veranlasst war sie durch eine Aussprache mit Dr. Jakobus Andreae, der aus Tübingen nach Öttingen gekommen war und mit dem sich Bresnicer auf Anweisung getroffen hatte; persönlich waren sich die beiden bisher noch nicht begegnet. Der einflussreiche Andreae war wegen seines mäßigenden Einwirkens gefragt.

48 RUDOLF HERRMANN: *Thüringische Kirchengeschichte*. Weimar 1947. Nachdruck: Jena 2000, Bd. II, S. 156.
49 Johann Stössel wirkte als Superintendent in Jena und wurde nach der Vertreibung der Flacianer an die Theologische Fakultät der Universität berufen. Nachdem Selnecker die Universität wieder verlassen hatte, verblieb er dort als einziger Theologe. Vgl. u. a. HERRMANN (siehe Anm. 48), S. 153/4.
50 T. F. KARRER: Geschichte der lutherischen Kirche des Fürstenthums Oettingen. Der Oettingischen Reformationsgeschichte zweites Kapitel. Ludwig XVI. Der Beständige 1557–1569. In: *Zeitschrift für die gesamte lutherische Theologie und Kirche*. 17 (1855), S. 656–725, Beilagen betr. Bresnicer S. 692–710.

Die nachfolgenden Auszüge vermitteln einen Eindruck von der Art der Anschuldigungen gegen Bresnicer, von seiner Rede- und Schreibgewandtheit, seiner Verteidigung und Argumentation und von seinem sozialen Empfinden.

> Gnediger herr, Je mehr ich den zustand der lieben, heiligen, Christlichen Kirchen, der jämmerlich durch anstifftung des Sathans angefochten wird, bedencke, Je mehr ich Gottes wunderbarliche Regierung sampt krefftiger erhaltung derselben befinde, und das auf göttliche weise, welche nicht in den starcken, klugen, reichen, verstendigen leuten dieser welt, sondern allzeit in den Schwachen mechtig ist, also das alle frommen Christen neben mir bekennen müssen, das die ewige göttliche Majestet in ihrem solchen hochmut sitzen lest alles, das etwas in der kirchen vor andern sein will und zeucht in seinem geliebten son Christo herfür die armen Aschenbrüdeln, das kehricht und Schabet, dadurch er in der welt verklärett, geliebet, gelobet und geehret wird, derwegen wir wol mit dem h. Apostolo Paulo fragen mügen: wo sein die klugen? wo sein die Schrifftgelerten? etc. wo seind die Eifferigen herren, die alle Corrupten mit ihren Confutationibus und wappen aus der Kirchen Christi ausmustern wolten? wo ist die bestendige Stadt die sich für allen andern ruhmte: wir sein bestendig blieben! Das Römische Reich hat uns jahr und tag umb gottes worts willen beklaget! wir haben gottes wort erhalten! wo bleibt der fromme alte herr Niclas Bischoff, der hiebevor über der warheit allein geeiffert hatt, itzt aber seinen eiffer fast wendet, die verfolger des reinen Ministerii zu rechtfertigen, nur unter dem verwahr und namen, das die verfolger noch das Ev. lassen predigen und der Sacrament (Gott geb lang) reichen, gleich als hette der gute alte herr von Luther seligen gedechtnis nie gehört, das Deutschland das h. Ev. unter dem schein des Ev. verlieren wurde? Welche Universitet schreibet itzo in specie wider das verfluchte Reich des Antichrists, so es doch bei uns kribel und wiebelt von Scribenten, die das Babstumb per force erhalten wellen, die die wahre kirche mit öffentlichem schänden und lestern angreiffen, und mit gewalt aufs blut lauren? Aber also muss es gehen, wenn gott die undankbare weltt straffen und sein heuflein wunderbarlicher weise mitten im grim und toben des Sathans erhalten wil. Gott erbarme sich unser. Amen.[51]

> ¶ Ich vermelde kürtzlich dem hern Cantzler ursachen, warumb ich D. Jakobs [d. i. Dr. Jakob Andreae aus Tübingen] muss müssig gehen, bitte unterthenig, mein mit D. Jak. gemeinschaft zu verschonen, alhie werde ich nu balde verdächtig, weil es Strigels Declaration betrifft, als lehrte ich von freiem willen nicht recht, wirt derwegen von mir begehrt erstlich Strigels Declaration, zum andern meine Ursachen, die mich bewegeten derselben nicht zu unterschreiben, zum dritten eine kurtz und runde bekentnis meiner lere vom freien willen schriftlich zu stellen. Solches alles thue ich schleunig mit repetirter Bitt, das ich D. Jakobs möchte müssig gehen […] hierauf argumentiren sie, ich würde eine böse sache haben, weil ich das licht scheuete und mit D. Jacoben, der es heftig begerte, auch mit meiner übergeben Confession vom freien willen gar wol zufrieden were, ich würde auch vieleicht ein Sächsischer, das ist, halsstarriger kopf sein, welches sie sich zu mir doch nicht versehen, und wie wol ich den guten herren hiebevor genugsam bericht von dem thüringischen Rath gethan hatte, also das sie nicht allein mit mir zufrieden waren, sondern auch zusagten, bei mir in solchen gueten sachen wider D. Jakoben, wenn er kommen solte, zu stehen […].[52]

---

[51] Ebd., S. 695/6.
[52] Ebd., S. 698/9.

¶ Darnach protestirte ich, das alles, was ich vorgenommen hätte, wider D. J. und noch furnehmen würde, nicht aus einem privat hass oder neid geschehe, weil mir auch seine person bis anher unbekant gewesen, were derhalben zwischen mir und ihm kein personale sondern jede certamen, den ich hette, vornehmlich nicht meine person, sondern der betrübten kirchen Christi, die er mit seiner Transaction hefftig betrübet hätte, zu thun. Letztlich zeigte ich die ursachen an, worumb ich mich billich seiner eussere, denn erstlich wäre mirs nit gelegen, das ich mein eigen exilium, wenn ich ihm die hand böthe oder mit ihm communicirte, solte billichen, ich wäre aber umb Strigels Declaration willen, deren ich mit gutem gewissen nit hett können unterschreiben, meines amptes entsetzet und des landes verjagt, welche Declaration er nit allein hätte gebilliget, sondern auch helffen machen, wie ich nun mit Strigeln nicht könte communiciren, also könte ich warlich mit ihm ohne versönung nicht gemeinschafft haben und mein Exilium also probiren. Zum andern könte ich viel weniger mit dieser meiner gemeinschafft, die ich mit ihm als mit einem Transactor Strigelianae Declarationis solte haben, frommer gelehrter redlicher männer Exilia, die mit ihren armen weibern und kindern noch im elend wären, approbiren und loben. Zum dritten, wolte ich auch darmit die falsche lehr Strigels vom freien willen, die er noch auff den heutigen tag vor recht hielte, nicht billichen. Zum vierden, könnte ich mit dieser meiner that die Tyrannei des fürsten in diesem handel vorgenommen nicht loben. Zum fünften, wolte ich hiermit die Synergisten und muttwilligen unterschreiber der falschen lehr Strigels in ihrem Irrthumb nicht confirmirt haben. Zum sechsten, solte ich auch die schwachen, die es mit der kirchen Christi gerne gut sehen, und doch noch nicht gewis gegründet sein, nicht stützig oder zweiffelhaftig machen. […].[53]

Nachdem Andreae sein Verhalten rechtfertigt und beteuert, dass er nicht beabsichtigt habe, dass Bresnicer und andere ins Exil getrieben wurden und ihm das leid täte, setzt Bresnicer seine Erklärung fort und erinnert ihn, dass er ja habe »Mediator« sein wollen, und als solcher nicht hätte beide Ohren nur Strigel leihen dürfen, sondern auch Flacius Illyricus und Johann Wigandus; außerdem argumentiert er gegen Strigels Haltung mit Zitaten aus der Bibel. Gegen die »entsetzung« und Vertreibung wurde nicht protestiert, um dem Landesfürsten zu gefallen.

Auf die Frage des Jakob Andreae, wie das Unrecht gut zu machen sei, antwortet Bresnicer:

Darauf ich antworte, er als ein verständiger solte selbs darauf dencken und man könte dem hertzögen schreiben und ihm den ergangenen schaden zu gemüt führen, desgleichen den Stössel [d. i. Johann Stössel, nach der Vertreibung der Jenenser Flacianer Superintendent und Theologe an der Universität in Jena] seiner freien visitation erinnern, ihn und andere zur buss vermahnen, das doch die armen Exules, die noch im Elend sitzen, mit gott, ehren und guten gewissen möchten recovirt werden. Darauf D. J. [Dr. Jakob Andreae] sich alles fleisses und freundlickeit nach seinem höhesten vermügen erbothen.[54]

Am Ende bedankt sich Bresnicer bei allen Beteiligten, dass ihm Gehör geschenkt wurde und er ausführlich über sich und seine Leidensgenossen sprechen durfte: »Hiermit E. G. mich auch in Unterthenickeit befehlende, Datum in Ottingen 6. Junii Anno domini 1564. E. G. ganz williger gehorsamer und untertheniger diener Alexius Bresnicerus«.[55]

[53] Ebd., S. 700.
[54] Ebd., S. 703.
[55] Ebd., S. 705.

Seine Rückberufung im Jahre 1568 als Superintendent in Altenburg verdankt er dem Fürsten Johann Wilhelm, der sich nach der Übernahme des ernestinischen Landesteils seines verstorbenen Bruders entschieden für die Flacianer einsetzte, wenn er auch später über das Gezänk und die Uneinigkeit enttäuscht war. So kam auch Wigand als Professor nach Jena zurück, Irinaeus wurde nach Eisleben berufen.

In zeitgenössischen Aussagen heißt es, dass Bresnicer Jakobus Andreae in Öttingen erst nicht getraut, sich später aber recht gut mit ihm verstanden habe. Dafür spricht, dass in seiner Bibliothek dessen Schriften – insgesamt 16 – einen gewichtigen Platz einnahmen. Diese Drucke sind zwischen 1560 und 1569 in Tübingen erschienen, und es liegt die Annahme nahe, dass er sie dort – im Exil – vom Autor erhalten oder erworben hat. Leider lassen die flexiblen, in Handschriftenmakulatur eingebundenen Texte keine regionale Eingrenzung zu.

Die zweite Amtsenthebung erfolgte am 17. Februar 1573, und diesmal sollte er nicht wieder in seine Heimat und an die Stätte seines Wirkens zurückkehren. Bevor er nach Österreich emigrierte, lebte er ein halbes Jahr in seiner Heimatstadt Cottbus. Diese Möglichkeit war ihm vom Hauptmann von Pannwitz zugesagt worden. Bresnicer konnte sich auf ein Dokument beziehen, das ihm von Wulff von Schönberg, Herr zu Glauchau, ausgestellt wurde und in dem auf das Bresnicer geschehene Unrecht verwiesen wird. Darüber berichtete der damalige Superintendent von Cottbus, Dr. Teckler, in einem Brief an die Ehefrau des Brandenburgischen Kurfürsten. Zumindest lässt sich daraus schließen, dass Bresnicer überregionale Kontakte gepflegt hat und ein bekannter Mann war.

Aus dem bereits zitierten Bericht des Rostocker Superintendenten Lukas Bacmeister, der von David Chytraeus[56] den Auftrag bekommen hatte, in Österreich Visitationen in Horn, Feldsberg und weiteren Orten durchzuführen, lässt sich entnehmen, dass ihm die Zusammenarbeit mit Bresnicer keine Schwierigkeiten bereitete. Wenig befriedigend muss das Resultat gewesen sein, da er in seinem Bericht von der »Schläfrigkeit in Sachen Religion«[57] spricht. Inwieweit Bresnicer sich selbst als strenger Flacianer zeigte, lässt sich nicht beurteilen, denn nicht über ihn hat sich Backmeister beklagt, wohl aber nennt er Friedrich Stock als seinen hartnäckigen und unbelehrbaren Gegner. Dieser bezeichnete Bacmeisters *Deklaration Norma doctrinae* als Werk des Teufels, und viele Pfarrer versagten die Unterschrift. Da er Bresnicer in seinem Bericht, in dem er mehrfach auf die geringe Bildung und den Fanatismus einiger Pfarrer hinweist, nicht noch einmal erwähnt, ist anzunehmen, dass er mit ihm, obwohl gleichfalls Flacianer, zusammenarbeiten konnte. Bresnicer war zuerst in Schönpühl, dann bis 1578 in Horn und danach, berufen durch Hartmann von Liechtenstein, in Feldsberg tätig.[58]

Während seiner Feldsberger Tätigkeit wird Bresnicer als »M. Alexius Bresnicerus Senior« bezeichnet.[59] Weiterhin erfahren wir über ihn, dass er am 8. Februar 1580 den am 30. Januar geborenen Gundaker von Liechtenstein getauft hat. Aus der Taufe hoben ihn der Onkel Georg Erasmus von Liechtenstein und dessen Tante Judith Jörger – unter allen Protestanten ein berühmter Name.[60] Christoph Jörger studierte in Wittenberg.

---

56 Der aus dem Schwäbischen stammende David Chytraeus, Schüler Melanchthons und einige Jahre in Wittenberg tätig, ging 1550 nach Rostock. Er hatte großen Einfluss und war – ähnlich Jakob Andreae – stets um die Einigung der Kirche bemüht. Er reiste mehrmals nach Österreich, um dort eine Kirchenordnung und Agende auszuarbeiten.
57 BACMEISTER (siehe Anm. 12), S. 21.
58 Vgl. HONORIUS BURGER: *Geschichtliche Darstellung der Gründung und Schicksale des Benediktinerstiftes S. Lambert zu Altenburg in Nieder-Oesterreich, dessen Pfarren und Besitzungen, und mehrere hiesige Gegend betreffende Ereignisse*. Wien 1862, S. 278. In Horn hielt sich auch Christoph Irinaeus auf, wo er jedoch 1584 entlassen wurde.
59 *Notizenblatt. Beilage zum Archiv für Kunde österreichischer Geschichtsquellen*. 3 (1853), S. 186.
60 THOMAS WINKELBAUER: *Fürst und Fürstendiener: Gundaker von Liechtenstein, ein österreichischer Aristokrat des konfessionellen Zeitalters*. Wien, München 1999 (*Mitteilungen des Instituts für Österreichische Geschichtsforschung. Ergänzungsband 34*), S. 54 Anm. 62.

Mit seinem Namen verbindet sich die Beziehung zu Martin Luther, die sich seit den 1520er Jahren entwickelte. Der Siegeszug des Protestantismus wurde ermöglicht durch den Verfall der katholischen Kirche in Österreich: Der hohe und niedere Adel in fast allen österreichischen Ländern bekannte sich zur neuen Lehre. 1555 wurde der erste evangelische Pfarrer berufen, doch erst 1571 lag die Sicherheit bietende Assekurationsurkunde vor, die das Recht auf evangelischen Gottesdienst festschrieb. Horn, das den Herren von Pucheim gehörte, wurde zu einem Zentrum des Protestantismus und das Land ob der Enns zu einem Refugium für Exulanten aus Deutschland.[61] Nikolaus Gallus, Superintendent in Regensburg – er wechselte Briefe mit Christoph Jörger –, hat zahlreiche Pfarrer für Österreich ordiniert. Einige seiner Schriften – auch mit Flacius Illyricus gemeinsam verfasste – finden wir in Bresnicers Bibliothek. Die Blütezeit des Protestantismus erlebte das Land unter Helmhard Jörger, dem Sohn Christophs. Bresnicers spätes Wirken fiel in jene Jahre, als für die Protestanten noch die besten Bedingungen bestanden, denn erst seit circa 1580 bildete sich eine katholische Adelspartei heraus, die die protestantischen Stände in Schwierigkeiten brachte, als diese durch Superintendenturen eine feste Organisation aufbauen wollten, – einer der Gründe, weshalb Lukas Bacmeister im Auftrag von D. Chytraeus die erwähnte Visitation durchführte. Die rückläufige Bewegung begann um 1590, doch diese Veränderungen hat der 1581 verstorbene Bresnicer nicht mehr erleben müssen.[62]

Alexius Bresnicer – bekennender und praktizierender Flacianer

Was lässt sich über Alexius Bresnicer als Anhänger des Flacius Illyricus sagen, der wegen seiner Überzeugung im Alter ein Leben im Exil führen musste? Flacius (1520–75) und Bresnicer waren Zeitgenossen, hatten sich aber nicht während des Studiums kennengelernt – Flacius ging 1541 nach Wittenberg –, sondern erst später. »In Flacius' Lebenswerk verbindet sich das theologische Vermächtnis Luthers mit der gestaltenden Kraft der humanistischen Bildung«,[63] was ihre gemeinsame Basis war. Flacius wählte den wissenschaftlichen Weg und ging »in die Kulturgeschichte Europas als einer der größten Theologen und Philosophen der Reformation ein. Aber seine Bedeutung ist noch weit größer. Er [war] Wissenschaftler und Systematiker, beharrlicher Forscher, der über die Theologie die Rolle und die Wichtigkeit der Natur für die menschliche Existenz offenbart[e]«.[64]

Wenn in der Fachliteratur zum Flaciuskreis zugehörige Namen zitiert werden, wird auf eine »stattliche Zahl von Männern« hingewiesen: Es werden jedoch immer nur einige bestimmte, sehr bekannte Namen genannt, meistens die Mitautoren seiner bedeutenden Werke. Bresnicers Name ist nicht darunter.[65] Wir finden ihn in Darstellungen, die die Biografie des Flacius einbeziehen und wo es um bestimmte Ereignisse und Abläufe, offizielle Anlässe, Dispute und Aktionen geht.[66] Es lässt sich aber nicht einschätzen, inwieweit Bresnicer persönlichen Kontakt zu Flacius hatte, und die wenigen dokumentierten Aussagen in den Protokollen zeigen das Verhalten eines Pfarrers, der die Lehre des Flacius vertrat und

61 Das Zentrum der streitbarsten und aufsehenerregenden Flacianer war Eferding. Vgl. dazu KARL EDER: Glaubensspaltung und Landstände in Österreich ob der Enns 1525–1602. Linz 1936 (*Studien zur Reformationsgeschichte Oberösterreichs*. 2), besonders S. 117–78.
62 Zur Geschichte des Protestantismus in Österreich vgl. u. a. PAUL DEDIC: Der Protestantismus in Steiermark im Zeitalter der Reformation und Gegenreformation. Leipzig 1930 (*Schriften des Vereins für Reformationsgeschichte*. 149). – GRETE MECCENSEFFY: *Geschichte des Protestantismus in Österreich*. Graz, Köln 1956.
63 SIEGFRIED RAEDER: Matthias Flacius als Bibelausleger. In: Matthias Flacius Illyricus – Leben & Werk. Internationales Symposium Mannheim, Februar 1991. München 1993 (*Südeuropa-Studien*. 53), S. 17. – Vgl. auch in diesem Tagungsband die Beiträge von ANTE BILOKAPIC: Die Erbsünde in der Lehre des Matthias Flacius Illyricus, S. 43–51; JURE ZOVKO: Zur Rezeption von M. Flacius in der philosophischen Hermeneutik, S. 177–97 und LUTZ GELDSETZER: Matthias Flacius Illyricus und die wissenschaftstheoretische Begründung der protestantischen Theologie, S. 199–223.
64 Vgl. die Einführung zur Tagung »Matthias Flacius Illyricus – Leben & Werk« (siehe Anm. 63), S. 12. – Vgl. auch die Beurteilung der Leistung in der TRE (siehe Anm. 19), Bd. 11, S. 206–14. Auf S. 208 heißt es: »Auf Grund von Bischof Michael Heldings Behauptung auf dem Reichstag 1547, daß die lateinische Liturgie unverändert von der Kirche der Apostel überkommen sei, begann Flacius' historisch-kritische und liturgiegeschichtliche Pionierforschung.« Es ist interessant, dass sich unter Bresnicers Büchern folgende 1550 bei Ivo Schöffer in Mainz erschienene Ausgabe befindet: MICHAEL, EPISC. SIDONIENSIS: *Brevis institutio ad christianam pietatem, secundum Doctrinam catholicam continens: Explicationem symboli Apostolici* ... (8° K 747 (1); VD 16 H 1580).
65 Vgl. u. a. JOACHIM MASSNER: Kirchliche Überlieferung und Autorität im Flaciuskreis: Studien zu den Magdeburger Zenturien. Berlin, Hamburg 1964 (*Arbeiten zur Geschichte und Theologie des Luthertums*. 14), S. 12/3 und Anm. 3.
66 Vgl. WILHELM PREGER: Matthias Flacius Illyricus und seine Zeit. 2 Bde. Erlangen 1859 und 1861. Nachdruck: Hildesheim 1964. Das beigegebene chronologisch geordnete Werkverzeichnis ist noch heute von Bedeutung.

in seinen Predigten vermittelte. In solchen detaillierten Fragen kann uns die überlieferte Bibliothek freilich nur begrenzt weiterhelfen.

Die großen wissenschaftlichen Werke des Flacius und gleichgesinnter Autoren gehörten nicht zum Bestand der Bibliothek, und doch konnte sie gewährleisten, dass Bresnicer zu allen wichtigen Themen der Zeit spezielle Schriften in seiner Bibliothek verfügbar hatte. Es dominieren die Streitschriften geringen Umfangs, die den praktizierenden Geistlichen richtungsweisend beeinflussten: die Adiaphora, der Streit mit Osiander, die Schriften gegen Calvin oder Schwenckfeld. Neben den Verfasserschriften existiert eine Fülle anonymer Texte, die sich Bekenntnis, Bericht, Concilium, Confessio, Dialog, Erklärung, Expositio, Gegenbericht, Klagrede, Pasquillus, Responsio, Scripta, Verantwortung, Verfälschung, Vermahnung und viele andere mehr nennen und deren Autoren zu den Gegnern gehörten. In diesen Schriften unterstrich Bresnicer oft Bibelzitate oder abwertende Begriffe, meist auch Schimpfwörter, die für die Flacianer von ihren Gegnern verwendet wurden; auch der Begriff »Flacianer« wurde damals negativ gebraucht.

Der früheste Druck einer Schrift von Flacius in Bresnicers Bibliothek ist eine Ausgabe aus dem Jahre 1549: *Liber de veris et falsis Adiaphoris, in quo integre propemodum Adiaphorica controversia explicatur* (8° K 519 (1); VD 16 F 1444). Sie erschien in Magdeburg, wo Flacius in den Jahren von 1549 bis 1557 tätig war. Inhaltlich handelt es sich um eines der zentralen Themen der Flacianer, das viele Autoren in ihren Schriften behandeln. Bresnicer stellte sich einen Sammelband zusammen, der weitere frühere Magdeburger Drucke – darunter drei aus dem Jahre 1550 – von Flacius enthält. Es ist einer der vielen thematisch geordneten Bände, wie sie für Bresnicers Aufbewahrung von Büchern so charakteristisch sind. Oft stellte er ihnen ein handschriftliches Inhaltsverzeichnis voran. Der zweite Titel des Sammelbandes ist eine Schrift des in Hamburg tätigen Joachim Westphal aus dem Jahre 1549 über Luthers Meinung zu den Adiaphora, die er in Form von *Sententiae* (8° K 519 (2); VD 16 L 3469) zusammenstellte. Weitere Autoren sind Nikolaus Gallus und Polydorus Vergilius. Am Schluss des Bandes sind zwei in Leipzig herausgegebene Schriften zu diesem Thema von Johann Pfeffinger beigebunden. Pfeffinger, der in Leipzig tätig war, wird zum Auslöser der synergistischen Streites über die Mitwirkung des Menschen an seiner Bekehrung und musste sich in der Folgezeit unter anderem mit Amsdorf und Flacius auseinandersetzen.

Dieser Band belegt, dass Alexius Bresnicer Ende der 1540er Jahre in Altenburg begann, sich den Flacianern anzuschließen. Von 1557 bis 1561 war Flacius in Jena tätig und prägte die Geschichte der dortigen Theologischen Fakultät. In diesem Zeitraum ist Bresnicer bereits bekennender Flacianer. Auch in Flacius' Regensburger Zeit 1562 bis 1566 dürfte der Kontakt zwischen beiden nicht abgebrochen sein, obwohl sie nicht direkt zusammengearbeitet haben. Der späteste erschienene Druck in seiner Sammlung stammt aus dem Jahre 1570, als Flacius in Straßburg lebte und gegen Verleumdungen zu kämpfen hatte: *Bericht und Verantwortung von seinem christlichen Schreiben ... wider etliche Mißgönner, ... Verleumdungen so neulich aufs unverschämtest ausgebreitet worden sein* (4° K 586 (5);

VD 16 F 1279). Zwei umfangreichere Werke, die er von Flacius besaß, sind die 1565 und 1566 in Basel erschienenen Schriften *De sectis dissentionibus, contradictionibus et contusionibus doctrinae, religionis, scriptorum et doctorum pontificiorum Liber ...* (4° K 523; VD 16 F 1496) und die *Refutatio invectiva Bruni contra Centurias Historiae Ecclesiasticae: ...* (Basel 1566; 4° K 140 (2); VD 16 F 1475).[67]

Die große Leistung von Flacius für die Reformationsbewegung und für Luthers Lehre ist heute unumstritten. Flacius stimmte mit vielen Vorstellungen Luthers überein und erhielt dadurch seine Anregungen zu seinen großen kirchengeschichtlichen und philosophischen Arbeiten. Darüber hinaus zeichnet die Flacianer ihre konsequente Haltung aus und dass sie sich nicht mit dem sich herausbildenden landesherrlichen Kirchenregiment abfinden konnten. Sie behielten Freiräume gegenüber der Obrigkeit und widersprachen auch den Landesfürsten.

Zudem waren es die Flacianer, die intensiv für die Pressefreiheit kämpften und gegen die Zensur auftraten. So schreibt Massner, dass neben der Einsetzung des Konsistoriums in Weimar ein Eingriff in die Freiheit, Bücher und Schriften im Druck zu veröffentlichen, erfolgen sollte. Die Gegenschrift verfasste Matthaeus Judex – zusammen mit Johannes Wigand Mitarbeiter an den Magdeburger Zenturien –, die 1566, zwei Jahre nach seinem Tode, in Kopenhagen erschien: *De typographiae inventione, et de praelorum legitima inspectione, libellus brevis et utilis*.[68] Bresnicer bewahrte ein Exemplar davon in seiner Bibliothek (8° K 1110 (6)).

Der Weg der Bibliothek
War es Bresnicer möglich, seine Bibliothek mit ins Exil zu nehmen? Abgesehen von den Kosten und Strapazen hat er das sicher nicht bewerkstelligen können, auch wenn das erste Exil in Öttingen nicht so weit entfernt lag wie das zweite in Österreich. Auch erhielt seine Sammlung in den 1560er Jahren noch beachtlichen Zuwachs, der mit dem Jahr 1570 endete, als Bresnicer wieder in Altenburg war. Was ist in den Jahren 1568 bis 1573, bevor er zum zweiten Mal ins Exil nach Österreich ging, geschehen? Es gibt zwei Möglichkeiten, die beide Vermutungen bleiben müssen.

Vielleicht wollte Bresnicer seine Bücher sichern und gab sie einem seiner Söhne in Obhut. Sein gleichnamiger Sohn Alexius hatte 1556 in Leipzig studiert[69] und war seit 1573 Probst in Mittenwalde, wo er 1575 – also vor seinem Vater – verstarb. Vor ihm war in Mittenwalde Petrus Gartz im Priesteramt, 1544 ordiniert und von 1551 bis 1573 als Propst tätig. Er stammte aus der Pritzwalker Linie der Garcaeus-Familie.[70] In Pritzwalk verbrachten auch der Vater des Joachim seine Jugend und von dort stammt auch sein Neffe Zacharias Garcaeus (1544–86), der berühmte Chronist der Mark Brandenburg, der seit 1575 Rektor der Lateinschule in der Altstadt Brandenburgs war.[71] Peter Garcaeus könnte der Vermittler der Bücher nach Brandenburg gewesen sein.

1574 studierte Johannes Bresnicer – wahrscheinlich ein jüngerer Sohn – an der Universität Frankfurt/Oder, wo Andreas Musculus (1514–81) bis zu seinem Tode der einzige Theologieprofessor und Superintendent der Kurmark war. Musculus war der Schwiegervater des Bücher-

[67] Zu den großen wissenschaftlichen Leistungen vgl. ARNO MENTZEL-REUTERS/MARTINA HARTMANN: Catalogus und Centurien. Interdisziplinäre Studien zu Matthias Flacius und den Magdeburger Centurien. Tübingen 2008 (*Spätmittelalter, Humanismus, Reformation*. 45).

[68] Vgl. MASSNER (siehe Anm. 65), S. 102 und S. 67 Anm. 49.

[69] Vgl. Die Matrikel der Universität Leipzig (siehe Anm. 7), S. 709.

[70] Vgl. OTTO FISCHER: Verzeichnis der Pfarrstellen und Pfarrer. Bd. 1. Berlin 1941 (*Evangelisches Pfarrerbuch für die Mark Brandenburg seit der Reformation*. 1.2), S. 187/8.

[71] Vgl. Brandenburg an der Havel. Lexikon zur Stadtgeschichte. Hrsg. UDO GEISELER und KLAUS HESS. Berlin 2008 (*Einzelveröffentlichungen der Brandenburgischen Historischen Kommission e.V.* XIII), S. 121.

und Bibliothekssammlers Joachim Garcaeus. Vielleicht sind die Entscheidungen in Cottbus gefallen; denn bevor Bresnicer nach Österreich ging, nahm er – wie erwähnt – einige Monate Zwischenaufenthalt in seiner Heimatstadt. Hier könnte er die entscheidenden Kontakte geknüpft haben.

Jedenfalls finden wir Bresnicers Bücher in Brandenburg als Teil der Bibliothek des Joachim Garcaeus wieder, der in den 1590er Jahren in Frankfurt/Oder und Sorau tätig war und ab 1618 in Brandenburg wirkte, wie zuvor bereits sein Vater Johannes. Dieser wurde 1561 zum Superintendenten in Brandenburg ernannt und starb im Jahre 1574, ein Jahr nach Bresnicers Auswanderung nach Österreich.

Die Familie Garcaeus

Johannes Garcaeus (1530–74), der Vater von Joachim, ist ein Zeitgenosse von Alexius Bresnicer, zuletzt tätig als Superintendent in Brandenburg an der Havel. Als Anhänger Luthers kommt bereits dem Großvater Joachims, Johannes Garcaeus d. Ä. (1502–58), Bedeutung zu. Alle waren sie publizistisch tätig und anerkannte Fachleute. Die Familie Garcaeus (Garz, Gartze u. a.) war weit verbreitet; bleibende Bedeutung erlangte der Historiker und Chronist Zacharias Garcaeus.

Der Großvater Johannes Garcaeus, 1502 in Spandau geboren, verbrachte seine Jugend in Pritzwalk, studierte 1521 in Wittenberg, wo 1530 sein gleichnamiger Sohn, der spätere Vater Joachims geboren wurde. Von 1534 bis 1543 wirkte er als angesehener Prediger in Hamburg und zog 1553 nach Brandenburg. Dort wirkte er in der Neustadt als Nachfolger des bekannten Erasmus Alberus bis zu seinem Tode, am 24. August 1558. Er gehörte zur ersten Generation um Luther und genoss die Wertschätzung Melanchthons. Er galt als ein sehr guter Mathematiker, hinterließ aber nur wenige Schriften. Von seinen sechs Söhnen trat Johannes, am 13. Dezember 1530 geboren und der Vater des Büchersammlers Joachim, nach seinem Theologiestudium an der dortigen Universität in die Fußstapfen des Vaters. Auch er stand Melanchthon nahe und hat als ein guter Mathematiker, der bei Kaspar Peucer studierte, einen Namen. Seinen Magistertitel und seine Professur der Philosophie erlangte er 1555 und 1556 in Greifswald. 1561 folgte er dem Ruf nach Brandenburg, wo er in der Katharinenkirche in der Neustadt Superintendent wurde. 1570 ernannte ihn die Wittenberger Universität zum Doktor der Theologie. Er publizierte viel, vor allem in den Fächern Mathematik, Astrologie und Meteorologie. Mit nur 43 Jahren starb er am 22. Januar 1574.

Sein 1567 geborener Sohn Joachim war sieben Jahre alt, als er und seine Geschwister ihren Vater verloren. Sein Stiefvater wurde der Brandenburger Ratsherr Nikolaus Buchholz, der mit ihm und seinem Bruder Johannes Bildungsreisen unternahm. Die Brüder studierten in Frankfurt/Oder; dort wurde der auffallend sprachbegabte Joachim – er beherrschte Hebräisch und orientalische Sprachen – 1591 Professor der griechischen Sprache und 1593 Doktor der Theologie. Seine Universitätslaufbahn setzte er jedoch nicht fort und ging 1597 als Superintendent nach Sorau. 1618 folgte er dem Ruf nach Brandenburg als Pfarrer und späterer Superintendent. Wie sein Großvater und Vater prägte er – stets den gelehrten Studien zugeneigt – wesentlich das kulturelle Leben in dieser Stadt, wo er am 2. Juni 1633 starb.

Die drei Generationen umspannenden Lebensläufe[72] sind durch die Lehre Luthers und die Ausbreitung und Wirkung der Reformation geprägt. Die hinterlassene Bibliothek dokumentiert als ein bleibendes Zeugnis diesen Epochenumbruch. Joachim hat in einer Zeit, in der im Zuge der Säkularisierung alte Bücherschätze verschleppt und teilweise vernichtet wurden, eine beachtenswerte Bibliothek zusammengetragen, die später auch die Wirren des dreißigjährigen Krieges, der die Mark Brandenburg stark verwüstete, überstanden hat.

Der derzeitige Forschungsstand erlaubt noch keine sichere Aussage, auf welchem Wege die Bibliothek Bresnicers sowie die Bücher anderer Zeitgenossen und Weggefährten in die bereits vorhandene Sammlung dieser bekannten Brandenburger Familie gelangten. Dennoch lässt sich bereits jetzt feststellen, dass die Büchersammlung für diese Region einzigartig und besonders wertvoll ist, dokumentiert sich doch hier ein Erbe der Reformationsbewegung, die Kultur und Wissenschaft in Mittel- und Ostdeutschland nachhaltig prägte.

72 LOTHAR NOACK/JÜRGEN SPLETT: Bio-Bibliographien. Brandenburgische Gelehrte der Frühen Neuzeit. Mark Brandenburg mit Berlin-Cöln. 1506–1640. Berlin 2009 (*Veröffentlichungen zur Brandenburgischen Kulturgeschichte der Frühen Neuzeit*). – Das Lexikon enthält auch einen Artikel über Andreas Musculus (Meusel).

17. & 18. Jahrhundert

DAPHNE M. HOOGENBOEZEM

Madame D'Aulnoy en Angleterre[1]: La réception des *Contes des fées*

DÈS LE DÉBUT DE LA VOGUE du conte de fées littéraire en France, au XVIIe siècle finissant, un débat intertextuel sur la définition du nouveau genre commence.[2] Les visions des auteurs se dessinent à travers un jeu de références dans lequel, outre le texte, les illustrations jouent un rôle important. Dans le célèbre recueil de Charles Perrault, *Histoires ou contes du temps passé*, le texte aussi bien que les images contribuent à la mise en scène d'une vision populaire du genre du conte de fées. Le style relativement simple du texte mime le langage de la conteuse populaire représentée dans le frontispice tandis que la composition délibérément naïve et la facture rustique des vignettes (visible notamment dans l'épaississement du trait) rappellent les gravures sur bois employées dans les éditions populaires de la bibliothèque bleue.[3] Ainsi, Perrault donne à son recueil le ton et l'apparence d'un livre ancien ou populaire.

Tandis que Perrault emploie le texte aussi bien que les illustrations afin d'associer son recueil de contes au folklore, la salonnière Marie-Catherine d'Aulnoy, souligne le caractère littéraire de ses contes de fées. Quelques mois seulement après la publication de la première édition imprimée des contes de Perrault, elle publie deux recueils de contes, *Les Contes des fées* (1697) et *Les Contes nouveaux ou les fées à la mode* (1698). Les contes dans ses deux collections sont plus longs et plus complexes. Dans le récit cadre de la première collection, dit le *Récit de Saint Cloud*, D'Aulnoy met en scène non pas une conteuse populaire comme Perrault, mais une dame aristocratique, Madame D***, une remplaçante de la conteuse elle-même. Au lieu de raconter des contes, cette dame lit des contes d'un manuscrit rédigé préalablement. D'Aulnoy propose ainsi un subtil changement de médium: au lieu de la transmission orale des contes, elle souligne la version écrite de ses contes de fées.[4] En outre, ses contes contiennent de multiples références intertextuelles à la mythologie antique et aux ouvrages littéraires de l'époque tels que les fables de Jean de la Fontaine et les romans de Madeleine de Scudéry. Si Perrault souligne les moralités dans sa préface, D'Aulnoy souligne la valeur esthétique et divertissantes des contes.[5] Les vignettes introduisant les contes de la salonnière sont moins naïves que celles dans le recueil de Perrault, bien qu'elles fussent gravées par le même graveur, Antoine Clouzier.

La mode du conte de fées ne reste pas limitée à la France. Bientôt après la publication des premières éditions françaises, les contes de Perrault et de D'Aulnoy sont publiés à l'étranger. Les éditions étrangères des contes de Perrault sont en général fidèles à l'original. On reprend le texte

1 Nous reprenons le titre de MELVIN D. PALMER, dont les études fondatrices ont permis de démontrer l'influence importante de l'œuvre de Marie-Catherine d'Aulnoy en Angleterre. La présente étude offre une analyse du texte et des illustrations des deux premières traductions anglaises des *Contes des fées*.

2 Cf. SOPHIE RAYNARD: Perrault et les conteuses précieuses de la génération 1690: Dialogue intertextuel ou querelle masquée. Dans: *The Romanic Review*. 3/4 (2008), pp. 317–31.

3 Pour une analyse des vignettes du manuscrit (1695) et de la première édition imprimée (Paris: A. Clouzier, 1697) des *Histoires ou contes du temps passé* de Charles Perrault voir DAPHNE M. HOOGENBOEZEM: Magie de l'image: Altérité, merveilleux et définition générique dans les contes en prose de Charles Perrault. Dans: *Relief*. 2 (2010), pp. 1–26 (www.revue-relief.org [13.12.2010]).

4 Cf. UTE HEIDMANN/JEAN-MICHEL ADAM: *Textualité et intertextualité des contes, Perrault, Apulée, La Fontaine, Lhéritier...* Paris 2010, p. 50.

5 Cf. CHRISTINE JONES: The Poetics of Enchantment (1690–1715). Dans: *Marvels & Tales: Journal of Fairy-Tale Studies*. 1 (2003), p. 55–74, ici p. 58.

[Fig. 1] Marie-Catherine d'Aulnoy: The Diverting Works of the Countess D'Anois (London: John Nicolson [sic], 1715), illustrations en regard de la page 369. Gravure sur cuivre anonyme. (BL C. 115. n. 12)

6 Une première traduction de quatre contes de D'Aulnoy est publiée en 1699. La préface de Nicholson montre que l'édition était déjà devenue rare au début du XVIIIe siècle et aucun exemplaire ne semble avoir été conservé. Cf. NANCY PALMER/MELVIN D. PALMER: English Editions of the French «Contes de fees» Attributed to Mme D'Aulnoy. Dans: Studies in Bibliography. 27 (1974), pp. 227–32. La mention "Newly done into English" sur la page de titre de l'édition Nicholson suggère cependant que l'anthologie contient une nouvelle traduction, différente de celle de l'édition 1699.

7 Outre les neufs contes, l'anthologie contient plusieurs nouvelles espagnoles de D'Aulnoy, The Mémoirs of the Countess D'Anois et onze contes du Chevalier de Mailly. Ces contes étaient inclus dans son recueil Les Illustres fées publié de manière anonyme en 1698. Ils étaient communément attribués à D'Aulnoy en France comme à l'étranger.

8 CHRISTINE JONES: Madame D'Aulnoy charms the British. Dans: The Romanic Review. 3/4 (2008), pp. 239–56, ici p. 245.

français ou bien on fait des traductions qui restent proches de l'original. Les illustrateurs s'inspirent presque toujours des gravures de l'édition princeps. Des copies remarquablement fidèles des cuivres de Clouzier ornent la première traduction anglaise de 1729, et continuent d'être employées dans les éditions anglaises jusqu'à la seconde moitié du siècle. L'édition de B. Collins, publiée en 1763, contient des copies des gravures originales. Les illustrations sont parfois inversées, souvent on traduit l'inscription sur le frontispice, mais il n'y a que très peu d'adaptations dans la composition des scènes.

La réception internationale des contes de D'Aulnoy est moins constante. Les éditeurs, traducteurs et illustrateurs successifs sont moins fidèles à l'original français. Aussi, leurs adaptations textuelles et visuelles, nous donnent-elles des informations précieuses sur l'image qu'ils ont cherché à créer de la conteuse et la façon dont ses ouvrages ont été offerts au public. Dans les deux premières éditions des Contes des fées de John Nicholson (1707) et Benjamin Harris et Ebenezer Tracy (1716), les traductions respectives ainsi que les illustrations laissent entrevoir deux types de réception: tantôt les contes de D'Aulnoy sont associés aux belles-lettres, tantôt au folklore anglais.

Les Contes des fées *et les «belles-lettres»*
Les Contes des fées de D'Aulnoy sont d'abord associés aux belles-lettres, tout comme ses nouvelles et ses mémoires pour lesquels elle était déjà célèbre outre-manche. La traduction la plus ancienne qui soit parvenue jusqu'à nous figure dans l'anthologie The Diverting Works of the Countess D'Anois, publiée par John Nicholson en 1707.[6] La collection contient une traduction anglaise des neuf contes inclus dans les deux premiers tomes des Contes des fées, mais également de plusieurs autres ouvrages de la conteuse ou attribués à elle.[7] L'anthologie volumineuse et par conséquent assez coûteuse de Nicholson est adressée à un lectorat adulte, lettré, et prospère. Les contes de fées n'y sont pas illustrés et ils y sont joints à ses nouvelles et mémoires, ouvrages plus prestigieux qui avaient, dans un premier temps, assuré le succès de l'auteur en Angleterre. En outre la réception du recueil de contes s'avère dans la nouvelle traduction. Le traducteur a rendu le français assez littéralement.[8] Or quelques petites adaptations semblent refléter l'intention du traducteur d'amplifier le raffinement stylistique des contes de D'Aulnoy dans le but d'affirmer leur appartenance aux belles-lettres. La version anglaise des contes de D'Aulnoy est moins ludique que l'original français.

Le caractère ludique du texte de D'Aulnoy paraît entre autres dans les multiples onomatopées et néologismes qu'elle emploie. Ces éléments textuels rappellent l'ambiance des salons parisiens, qui étaient de véritables laboratoires de littérature. Ces jeux de mots sont des aspects parfois difficiles à traduire, mais le traducteur de l'édition Nicholson les a omis surtout, semble-t-il, parce qu'il considérait ces jeux de mots comme puérils ou non littéraires. Il supprime les onomatopées et paraphrase les néologismes. Ainsi, dans le premier conte, Gracieuse et Percinet, la méchante duchesse Grognon fait visiter sa cave aux trésors au roi. Elle fait miroiter ses richesses en ouvrant les tonneaux à vin dans lesquels elles sont cachées avec un petit marteau. A chaque fois que Grognon perce une barrique, D'Aulnoy rend le bruit du marteau («toc toc»). Le traducteur anglais élimine ces onomatopées. Puis, dans le conte *L'oiseau bleu*, la princesse Florine, déguisée en pauvre paysanne, montre un carrosse miniature tiré par six souris vertes à sa rivale Truitonne. Cette dernière, voulant acheter cette curiosité, appelle Florine en disant: «Mie Souillon, Mie Souillon, veux-tu cinq sols du carrosse et de ton attelage souriquois».[9] Le traducteur omet le néologisme *souriquois* et rend le passage de la façon suivante: "D'ye hear, Gammar Souillon, Gammar Souillon, will you take a Piece of five Shillings for your coach and all that belongs to it".[10]

Deuxièmement, le traducteur enlève les formulettes récurrentes employées par D'Aulnoy. Ces formulettes faisaient partie du style d'écriture de D'Aulnoy, ainsi que du genre du conte de fées en général puisqu'elles évoquent les stratégies mnémotechniques de la transmission orale ou bien des formules magiques. Les deux aspects sont étroitement liés au genre du conte de fées. Or le traducteur les regardait sans doute comme des répétitions gênantes dans un texte littéraire. Dans le conte *La Belle aux cheveux d'or*, le héros, Avenant, sauve la vie de trois animaux, une carpe, un corbeau et une chouette. Ces animaux expriment leur reconnaissance et promettent une récompense à Avenant en utilisant la même phrase: «Je vous le revaudrai».[11] Cette formulette est rendue par trois phrases différentes dans la traduction anglaise: la carpe répond: "I will reward you", le corbeau: "I will do you as good a turn" et la chouette: "I will make ye amends".[12]

Un troisième type d'adaptation attestant de l'annexion des contes de D'Aulnoy aux belles-lettres est le fait que le traducteur ajoute une référence à la mythologie gréco-latine. Dans le conte *La Belle aux cheveux d'or*, l'une des tâches que la princesse impose à Avenant, est de tuer le géant Galifron. Le texte français mentionne seulement le succès du héros, qui rentre ensuite au palais en emportant avec lui la tête du géant. Le traducteur anglais, par contre, compare la laideur du géant avec celle des Gorgones de la mythologie antique en écrivant: "He mounted his courser, and rode away with the giant's head, no less dreadful than the Gorgon's."[13] Le traducteur élabore les références multiples à la mythologie employées par D'Aulnoy et en ce faisant il amplifie le caractère littéraire de ses contes.

Finalement, le traducteur garde les aspects français dans les contes de D'Aulnoy. Il conserve les noms français de la plupart des personnages et explique parfois leur signification. Le héros du conte *La Belle aux cheveux d'or*, par exemple, est décrit ainsi: "There was a young stripling at the court as lovely as the Sun and the best shap'd in all the kingdom, who because of his comely grace and wit, was call'd Avenant, or the Handsome".[14] D'autres aspects français sont les références à Paris. Ces références sont traduites littéralement en anglais. Sauf si la référence risque d'être complètement incompréhensible pour le lecteur anglais, alors le texte est adapté. Dans le conte *L'oiseau bleu*, le traducteur maintient les références aux foires parisiennes de Saint-Germain et de Saint-

[Fig. 2] Marie-Catherine d'Aulnoy: The History of the Tales of the Fairies (London: Eben. Tracy, 1716), Frontispice. Gravure sur bois anonyme. (Oxford, Bodleian L, Douce T 186)

9 MARIE-CATHERINE D'AULNOY (NADINE JASMIN ed.): *Contes des fées*. Paris 2008, p. 193.
10 *The Diverting Works of the Countess D'Anois*. London: John Nicholson [...], 1707, p. 437.
11 D'AULNOY (voir note 9), p. 145/6.
12 *Diverting Works* (voir note 10), p. 395/6.
13 Ibid., p. 401.
14 Ibid., p. 393.

Laurent, mais il supprime la référence à Léance. Ce nom de convention désignait peut-être une danseuse, mais la personne était inconnue du public anglais.

> Il y avait dans ce carrosse quatre marionnettes plus fringantes et plus spirituelles que toutes celles qui paraissent aux foires Saint-Germain et Saint-Laurent: elles faisaient des choses surprenantes, particulièrement deux petites Egyptiennes, qui pour danser la sarabande et les passe-pieds, ne l'auraient pas cédé à Léance.[15]
>
> There were beside the Coach four Puppets, much more spruce and pleasant than any you see at the Fairs of St. Germain's and St Laurence's; they play'd a thousand Tricks especially two little Gypsies, that for a Serraband and a Caper, surpass'd all the Masters about the Town.[16]

En 1715, une seconde édition de la compilation de Nicholson est publiée, contenant la même traduction mais également des illustrations nouvelles [fig. 1]. Il se peut que l'illustrateur se soit inspiré des cuivres de l'édition originale française. Le format réduit des vignettes dans l'édition anglaise rappelle celui des vignettes françaises et quelques images représentent des scènes presque identiques. Aucun frontispice n'a été ajouté à cette édition, mais la compilation volumineuse, la traduction et les cuivres raffinés attestent de l'association des contes de D'Aulnoy aux belles-lettres.

Contes de fées et contes populaires anglais

Cependant, en 1716, une année seulement après la publication de la seconde édition des *Diverting Works*, une traduction nouvelle est publiée par Benjamin Harris et Ebenezer Tracy. L'édition est intitulée *The History of the tales of the Fairies* et dédicacée aux "Ladies of Great-Britain", dans un but didactique. Melvin Palmer suggère que cette traduction nouvelle a été faite par Harris, comme les initiales B. H. paraissent en bas de la lettre de dédicace.[17] Dans cette lettre, le traducteur commente sa façon de traduire les contes français. La critique a surtout relevé le fait que dans cette nouvelle traduction, les contes ont été abrégés et les moralités soulignées.[18] Mais ce n'est pas tout.

Le traducteur-auteur a également rendu les contes plus anglais. Dans sa préface, il écrit: "I have indeed, in several places made use of some expressions to supply the Author's (D'Aulnoy's) because I would have them adapted more peculiarly to a *British* Genius; but omitted nothing that may justly render the work imperfect".[19] Ceci laisse à penser qu'il a seulement fait quelques petites adaptations. Or en fait le traducteur se fait auteur. Il réécrit le texte, élimine certains motifs et en ajoute d'autres. De plus, il commissionne un nouveau frontispice. Tout porte à croire qu'il adapte le texte et les images dans le but d'associer les contes de fées littéraires français au folklore anglais.

Tout d'abord, l'éditeur ajoute un nouveau frontispice : une gravure sur bois rustique accompagnée d'une légende [fig. 2]. D'après le poème qui constitue la légende, l'image représente un roi et une reine assis sur leur trône, qui observent un groupe de petites fées dansant la ronde.

---

15 D'AULNOY (voir note 9), p. 193.
16 *Diverting Works* (voir note 10), p. 436.
17 JONES (voir note 8), p. 245: "Palmer suggests that Harris may also have done the translation (diss. 147)."
18 PALMER et PALMER expliquent que dans l'édition de 1716, "(The) tales are drastically abridged-by about one half to two thirds-their morals are exaggerated, and many of their episodes sensationalized. PALMER / PALMER (voir note 6), p. 229. GABRIELLE VERDIER affirme que le traducteur B. H. souligne les moralités en ajoutant "des sous-titres qui insistent lourdement sur la leçon qu'il faut en tirer". De plus, il distingue d'emblée les bons et les méchants, éliminant ainsi les nuances qui risquent de faire perdre le fil. GABRIELLE VERDIER: De Ma Mère L'Oye à Mother Goose: La fortune des contes de fées littéraires français en Angleterre. Dans: *Contacts culturels et échanges linguistiques au XVIIe siècle en France: Actes du 3e colloque du Centre International de Rencontres sur le XVIIe siècle*. Éd. YVES GIRAUD. Paris etc. 1997, pp. 185–202, ici pp. 190/1. JONES (voir note 8), p. 247, remarque que dans la version anglaise "a certain prolixity and richness of detail is eliminated, (and the) translation has been embellished with a sort of blunt morality, which types characters in a more explicit way". Puis la traduction est plus attentive aux différences sociales.
19 *The History of the Tales of the Fairies*. London: Ebenezer Tracy, 1716, Epistle dedicatory, page non-numérotée.

> The Monarchy of FAIRIES once was great,
> As good old Wives, and Nurses do relate:
> Then was the golden Age, from whence did spring,
> A Race of Fairies, dancing round a Ring,
> Who in the Night-time did inform Mankind;
> Of what the following Tales will bring to mind.[20]

Comme l'affirme Gabrielle Verdier, le roi et la reine des fées rappellent Oberon et Titania, les protagonistes dans la célèbre pièce de William Shakespeare, *A Midsummernight's Dream* (1594).[21] Si cette pièce a certainement contribué à la célébrité des personnages folkloriques tels que Oberon et Robin Goodfellow,[22] la composition de la gravure suggère que l'illustrateur renvoie à une édition populaire et non pas à la pièce de Shakespeare. En effet, lorsque des illustrations paraissent dans les éditions des pièces de Shakespeare, ce sont en général des cuivres plus raffinés qui semblent inspirés par des représentations théâtrales. Ainsi, dans l'anthologie publiée par Nicholas Rowe en 1709, chaque pièce est illustrée d'une planche de cuivre gravée par Elisha Kirkall d'après les dessins de François Boitard. Si ces images ne représentent pas toutes des scènes telles qu'elles ont été jouées au théâtre à l'époque, Boitard s'inspire des conventions théâtrales pour la majorité d'entre elles.[23] Ces premières illustrations faites spécifiquement pour l'œuvre de Shakespeare ont eu une influence importante sur les éditions successives.[24]

Si Shakespeare s'inspire souvent de la culture populaire, il n'en est pas de même de l'iconographie qui se crée autour de ses pièces au début du XVIIIe siècle, qui emprunte avant tout des conventions théâtrales. Ceci vaut également pour l'illustration pour l'une des pièces les plus féériques de Shakespeare, *A Midsummernight's Dream*. Dans la gravure pour cette pièce [fig. 3], le roi et la reine ainsi que les fées sont de taille humaine et habillés à l'antique. Dans les éditions ultérieures de Shakespeare quelques planches ont été adaptées, mais l'illustration pour *A Midsummernight's Dream* est réemployée sans modifications significatives dans des éditions en 1714, 1728, 1734 et 1735.

Le frontispice des contes de D'Aulnoy ressemble plutôt aux illustrations employées communément dans les contes populaires anglais. Ces contes mettent en scène Oberon, Robin Goodfellow et des fées dansant au clair de la lune. Ils étaient publiés dans des éditions à bon marché tout le long du XVIIe siècle, mais les contes étaient sans doute beaucoup plus anciens. Le conte de Robin Goodfellow était connu d'un vaste public bien avant la publication de la pièce de Shakespeare. Ainsi Reginald Scot mentionne le conte de Robin Goodfellow à plusieurs reprises dans son livre *Discovery of Witchcraft* (1584), sans expliquer toutefois le contenu de cette histoire.[25] Ceci laisse à penser que c'était une histoire extrêmement connue. Le personnage de Robin Goodfellow parait également dans de nombreux autres livres de l'époque, dont *Tarlton's Newes out of Purgatory* (1590, 1593, 1630), *The Cobler of Caunterburrie* (1590, 1608, 1630) et *Tell-Trothes New Yeares Gift* (1593). Le personnage de Robin Goodfellow y est associé aux contes de vieille[26] et aux esprits du ménage qui aidaient parfois

---

20 *Tales of the Fairies* (voir note 19), frontispice.

21 VERDIER (voir note 18), pp. 191/2.

22 L'influence de la pièce de Shakespeare est décrite par Walter Scott, en 1802/3, dans *On the Fairies of Popular Superstition*: "Many poets of the sixteenth century and above all, our immortal Shakespeare, deserting hackneyed fictions of Greece and Rome sought for machinery in the superstitions of their native country. 'The Fays which nightly dance upon the Wold', were an interesting subject; and the creative imagination of the bard, improving upon the vulgar belief, assigned to them many of those fanciful attributes and occupations, which posterity have since associated with the name of fairy." Cité par MINOR WHITE LATHAM: *The Elizabethan Fairies: The fairies of Folklore and the fairies of Shakespeare*. New York 1930, p. 3.

23 STUART SILLARS: *The Illustrated Shakespeare 1709–1875*. Cambridge 2008, p. 38: "imaging of events in the theatre is in any case a complex matter, and simple visual records are rare. But key elements of Boitard's designs suggest that they take what they need from manuals of stage design, along with practices of costume and acting gesture, and ally them with painterly traditions of narrative and presentation."

24 Les éditions de Shakespeare du XVIIe siècle comportaient rarement des illustrations. Quelquefois un portrait de l'auteur est utilisé comme frontispice, parfois en combinaison avec une scène de l'une des pièces (*Rape of Lucrece* [...], London, Printed by J.G. for John Stafford [...] and Will. Gilbertson [...], 1655). Cf. T.S.R. BOASE: Illustrations of Shakespeare's Plays in the Seventeenth and Eighteenth Centuries. Dans: *Journal of the Warburg and Courtauld Institutes*. X (1947), pp. 83–108.

25 REGINALD SCOT: *The Discovery of Witchcraft, Being a reprint of the first edition published in 1584*. Wakefield 1973, pp. xx, xxii, 56, 67, 122.

26 "Hob Thrust, Robin Goodfellow and such like spirits (as they terme them of the buttry) famosed in every old wives chronicle for their mad merry prankes", *Tarlton's Newes out of Purgatory*, 1590, page non numérotée.

27 Le personage de Robin Goodfellow est associé aux tâches domestiques: "Indeede your granddames maides were woont to set a boll of milke before him and his cousine Robin good-fellow for grinding malt or mustard, and sweeping the house at midnight: and you have also heard that he would chase exceedingly, if the maid or good-wife of the house, having compassion of his nakedness, laid anie clothes for him besides his messe of white bread and milke, which was his standing fee. For in that case he saith; What have we here? Hemton, Hamten, here I will never more tread nor stampen". SCOT (voir note 25), p. 67. "Robin Goodfellow [...] who never did worse harm than correct manners and made diligent maides". *Tell-Trothes New Yeares Gift*, 1593, p. 1.

28 Malgré la date, JAMES ORCHARD HALLIWELL affirme dans *Illustrations of the Fairy Mythology of A Midsummer Night's Dream*, London, Printed for the Shakespeare Society, 1845, p. 120, que l'édition est sans doute plus ancienne: "The tract is dated 1628 but is in all a probability much earlier production, and although we have no proof of the fact, had most likely been seen by Shakespeare in some form or other". Lorsque le personnage est mentionné dans les livres antérieurs, les auteurs évoquent parfois des passages spécifiques décrits également dans l'édition du conte de 1628 (voir note précédente). De plus, le personnage y emploie les mêmes formulettes typiques (What himp and hamp, here will I never more grinde nor stamp / ho ho hoh) que dans l'édition de 1628. Ceci rend plausible qu'il y a eu des éditions plus anciennes contenant l'histoire complète de Robin Goodfellow.

29 *The Second Part of Robin Goodfellow, commonly called Hob-Goblin*. London: F. Grove, 1628, page non numérotée.

30 *The Mad Merry Pranks of Robin Good-Fellow, To the Tune of Dulcine &c.* London: Printed for F. Coles, T. Vere and J. Wright, [1663–74]. – *The English fortune-teller. Being a brief direction how to shun all strife, a brief instruction how to chuse a wife; whereby a man may lead a happy life: it shews difference in womens qualities, by colour of their hair, both face and eyes, the tune is, Ragged and torn. &c.* London: Printed for W. Thackerary [sic], T. Passenger, and W. Whitwood, [1670–79]. – *The Mad Merry Pranks of Robin Good-Fellow, To the Tune of Dulcine &c.* London: Printed for F. Coles, T. Vere and J. Clark, W. Thackeray and T. Passinger, [1680]. – *The Mad Merry Pranks of Robin Good-Fellow, To the Tune of Dulcine &c., Licens'd according to order.* [London]: Printed by and for W. O. and sold by C. Bates in Pye Corner, [1690 & 1709].

les bonnes femmes à effectuer leurs tâches domestiques,[27] mais aucune des éditions mentionnées ne raconte l'histoire de Robin Goodfellow. Il y apparaît plutôt comme un personnage type: le voyageur qui apporte des nouvelles des régions lointaines ou même de l'autre monde.

L'édition la plus ancienne du conte qui survit à ce jour est intitulée *Robin Goodfellow, His Mad Prankes and Merry Jests* et date de 1628.[28] L'auteur anonyme se présente lui-même comme un voyageur qui s'arrête pour la nuit dans une auberge (alehouse). L'hôtesse lui raconte "the long tale of Robin Goodfellow", fils du roi des fées Oberon et d'une jeune fille. L'histoire est composée de deux parties contenant plusieurs anecdotes racontant les aventures bizarres de Robin, un personnage curieux, insolent mais sympathique qui aide les bons et punit les méchants. Robin y est associé aux tâches domestiques, comme dans les textes antérieurs: "Robin Goodfellow oftentimes would in the night visit Farmers Houses, and helpe the Maydes to breake Hempe, to bowlt, to dresse flaxe, and to spin and do other workes, for he was excellent in every thing".[29] Il est en contact avec les humains mais également avec les êtres surnaturels, son père Oberon et les petites fées, avec qui il danse plusieurs fois au clair de la lune. L'histoire nous apprend également les exploits des petites fées et se termine par le départ de Robin au pays des fées. Cette édition contient un frontispice qui ressemble beaucoup à celui qui précède les contes de D'Aulnoy. Il représente Robin Goodfellow entouré d'un groupe de fées dansant la ronde [fig. 4]. Les lettres F. et G. paraissent de manière inverse dans les coins inférieurs de l'image. Ceci suggère que le libraire Francis Grove a également fait le frontispice pour l'édition. Cette image est réemployée dans d'autres éditions de ce livre (1639) ainsi que dans de multiples ballades publiées entre 1663 et 1709.[30]

L'illustrateur a probablement associé les contes de D'Aulnoy à ce conte populaire anglais à cause des multiples métamorphoses. Grâce au don de son père Oberon, Robin Goodfellow sait prendre différentes formes. Ainsi il prend l'apparence de plusieurs personnages dans l'histoire. Il paraît tantôt comme une jeune fille et tantôt comme un fantôme portant une torche. Robin assiste à un mariage en tant que violoniste et il traverse les villes sous l'apparence d'un mendiant ou d'un ramoneur portant son balai sur l'épaule. En outre, il se transforme en plusieurs types d'animaux dont un oiseau, un poisson, un cheval, un corbeau, un chien et un ours. Dans le frontispice on trouve des éléments évoquant les différents épisodes de l'histoire, dont les métamorphoses. Ainsi, Robin porte une torche et un balai. Les cornes qu'il porte sur la tête et au cou renvoient sans doute aux nombreux maris trompés dans l'histoire.[31] Le corbeau (ou l'oiseau) est représenté en haut à droite. L'animal à gauche pourrait être le chien ou l'ours. De plus, Tom Thumb, qui joue la cornemuse lorsque les fées dansent, est représenté à droite. Le pot et le verre sur le devant de la scène pourraient être des références à l'histoire cadre de l'hôtesse et du voyageur-auteur buvant de la bière au coin du feu pendant qu'elle lui raconte la vie de Robin.

La représentation de différents épisodes d'une histoire dans une seule image est fréquente, surtout lorsqu'il s'agit d'un frontispice, une image à but commercial et publicitaire évoquant en général les temps forts de la narration dans l'objectif d'influencer les lecteurs ou les acheteurs potentiels. Comme l'affirme Gilles Duval:

> l'ordre (des épisodes représentés) est en principe chronologique : l'action est rendue présente par une série de scènes accolées, «lues» de gauche à droite ou de haut en bas. [...] Cependant, il faut noter que les épisodes sont parfois livrés en vrac [...]. Il est probable que cette technique, attestée dès le Moyen Age, répondait au goût du public de l'époque.[32]

On trouve un exemple de la représentation «en vrac» de plusieurs épisodes dans *L'histoire de Tom Thumb* (1630). L'une des illustrations nous montre ses différentes mésaventures [fig. 5]. Le petit héros (fils miniature donné par l'enchanteur Merlin à ses parents, un laboureur et une fille de ferme) y est représenté assis sur le bord du bol de pudding dans lequel il tombera, il paraît attaché au chardon sur le point d'être mangé par une vache et on le voit dans le bec du corbeau. Les scènes successives du conte paraissent sur le même plan de l'image. La chronologie n'est suggérée ni par la perspective, ni par un sens de «lecture».

Or, dans le cas du frontispice de Robin Goodfellow, la représentation est plus fragmentaire encore. On n'y trouve point de scènes complètes, mais des figures (objets, animaux ou personnages) qui évoquent de manière emblématique les principales actions de l'histoire. Nous n'avons trouvé qu'un autre frontispice composé de cette façon. Il précède le conte *The Witch of the Woodlands. Or the Cobler's new Translation Written by L. P.* (Laurence Price) (London, Printed for John Stafford, 1655), une histoire dans laquelle les métamorphoses jouent également un rôle important. Le personnage principal de l'histoire, le cordonnier Robin (est-ce une coïncidence?), est transformé en différents animaux par quatre sorcières pour le punir pour ses méfaits passés. D'abord il devient une chouette. Obligée de voler le jour, elle est persécutée par tous les autres oiseaux. Puis, les sorcières le changent en cheval et se promènent sur son dos du matin au soir. Le frontispice [fig. 6] nous montre le personnage principal au centre. A gauche se trouve une des sorcières avec son chat. En haut on voit la chouette persécutée d'un corbeau et à droite Robin métamorphosé en cheval avec trois sorcières assis sur son dos.

Les métamorphoses sont également un motif central dans les contes de D'Aulnoy et l'illustrateur a employé la même stratégie emblématique pour les représenter dans le frontispice. Dans le conte *L'oranger et l'abeille*, une princesse est transformée en abeille. L'abeille est représentée en haut à droite. L'oiseau représenté en haut à gauche renvoie sans doute au conte *L'oiseau bleu*, dans lequel un prince est changé en oiseau d'un coup de baguette. Dans le conte *La princesse Rosette*, une jeune princesse jure de ne se marier jamais qu'avec le prince des paons. Il se peut que la décoration en forme de paon, placée de manière significative sur le trône, soit une référence à ce conte.

Le frontispice pour les contes de D'Aulnoy semble être inspiré par une image très répandue illustrant un conte populaire anglais. Réutilisées et copiées sur une période de plusieurs décennies voire plus d'un siècle, les gravures sur bois pouvaient devenir de véritables symboles évo-

31 Plusieurs passages du conte de Robin Goodfellow évoquent des maris cocus. Robin séduit la femme du tisserand pour qui il travaille et, transformé en ramoneur, il chante la chanson suivante: "Blacke I am from head to foote, And all doth come by chimney soote, Then Maydens come and cherish him, That makes your chimneys neate and trim. Hornes have I store, but all at my backe, My head no ornament doth lacke: I give my hornes to other men, And ne'er require them againe". *The Second Part of Robin Goodfellow* (voir note 29), page non numérotée.
32 GILLES DUVAL: *Littérature de colportage et imaginaire collectif en Angleterre à l'époque des Dicey (1720–v. 1800)*. Lille 1991, p. 474.

[Fig. 3] The Works of Mr. William Shakespeare; in six volumes. Adorn'd with cuts. Revis'd and corrected, with an account of the life and writings of the author. By N. Rowe (London: Jacob Tonson, MDCCIX), vol. 2, Frontispice for *A Midsummernight's Dream*. Gravure sur cuivre par Elisha Kirkall d'après le dessin de François Boitard.
(BL 2302. b. 14)

quant des contextes plus vastes que leurs significations visuelles inhérentes. Dans son étude sur l'illustration des ballades, Alexandra Franklin a montré de manière convaincante que les éditeurs jouaient parfois du pouvoir évocateur des bois et de la signification étendue des images en les plaçant dans des contextes nouveaux.[33] Contrairement à ce que la critique a longtemps supposé, l'emploi des gravures sur bois dans les éditions populaires se révèle parfois médité et significatif. Le fait qu'au moins deux copies du frontispice de Robin Goodfellow ont été fabriquées[34] atteste de la force évocatrice de cette image qui a dû rester dans la mémoire des lecteurs au début du XVIIIe siècle. L'élément des fées dansant la ronde était devenu également un signe visuel indépendant permettant d'évoquer le conte de Robin Goodfellow ou d'autres histoires merveilleuses. Après son apparence dans le frontispice de Robin Goodfellow, le signe a également été employé séparément. Ainsi une image représentant des fées presque identiques à celles de Robin Goodfellow assises à une table ronde, est employée pour illustrer la ballade *The Fairy Queen* (1648). On retrouve une image des fées dansant au clair de la lune en tête du dernier chapitre sur les fées dans *Round about our Coal Fire* (1730) ainsi que dans certaines éditions du livre *The Witch in the Woodlands* (1750).

Le frontispice de l'édition Tracy de 1716 a été fait exprès pour les contes de D'Aulnoy puisqu'elle contient des références à des contes multiples inclus dans le recueil. Cependant, grâce à sa facture rustique, sa composition emblématique et l'emploi du signe des fées dansant la ronde, l'image s'inscrit dans la tradition illustrative des éditions populaires anglaises. Le frontispice représente également un couple royal, le roi et la reine des fées selon le poème en dessous de l'image, et un groupe de petites fées. Ces personnages sont typiques du folklore anglais, mais ils ne paraissent pas dans les contes de D'Aulnoy. Souvent les bois naïfs (ré)employés dans différentes éditions populaires, au lieu d'ancrer une signification spécifique du texte en question, en brouillaient l'interprétation en créant des possibilités multiples et parfois contradictoires de lecture.[35] Ceci vaut également pour le frontispice de D'Aulnoy. En ajoutant cette référence visuelle aux éditions populaires, le traducteur fait une ouverture dans le recueil, il crée un lien au folklore anglais qui annonce et justifie les adaptations textuelles dans l'édition.

Adaptations textuelles dans l'édition 1716

Le texte de l'édition de 1716 comporte plusieurs types d'adaptations. D'abord certaines expressions ressenties comme typiquement françaises ont été remplacées par des expressions anglaises. Ainsi, dans le conte *Gracieuse et Percinet*, la méchante duchesse Grognon, assise sur le beau cheval de Gracieuse, a l'air d'un paquet de linge sale. La version anglaise la décrit de la façon suivante: "and so the Picture of ill Looks, rode like a Pedler's Bundle, till she came to Court."[36]

L'auteur ajoute également de nouvelles expressions. Ainsi il rend explicite la jalousie de Grognon lorsqu'elle s'aperçoit que Gracieuse est plus belle qu'elle en écrivant : "The eyes of all the court were only upon

---

33 ALEXANDRA FRANKLIN: The Art of Illustration In Bodleian Broadside Ballads Before 1820. Dans: *The Bodleian Library Record*. XVII (2000–02), p. 327–52.

34 Les copies du bois original paraissent dans les ballades *The Mad Merry Pranks of Robin Good-fellow to the Tune of Dulcina &c*. London: Printed for F. Coles, T. Vere and J. Wright, [1663–74], et *The English Fortune Teller*, London, Printed for W. Thackeray, T. Passinger, and W. Whitwood, [1670–79].

35 JAMES A. KNAPP: The Bastard Art: Woodcut Illustration in Sixteenth-Century England. Dans: *Printing and Parenting in Early Modern England*. Éd. DOUGLAS A. BROOK. Hampshire/Ashgate 2005, pp. 151–72, ici pp. 151/2.

36 *Tales of the Fairies* (voir note 19), p. 6.

the beautiful princess, and her pretty Page in Green: which made the ill-natur'd Grognon look as sowre as if she had eaten a Cart-Load of Crabs."[37] Dans l'original français, la duchesse, furieuse, « ne laissa pas de tempêter: voilà un tour de Gracieuse »[38] alors que dans la version anglaise Grognon "storm'd and rayl'd like a Billinsgate and swore 't was one of Graciosa's Tricks."[39] La référence au marché aux poissons à Londres est doublement significative. Elle permet de rendre à merveille le vilain langage de la Duchesse mais évoque également un lieu dans la ville associé à la populace et à ses histoires.[40]

Puis le traducteur se montre plus sensible à l'emploi ludique du langage de D'Aulnoy. S'il omet quelques jeux de mots pour lesquels il n'y a point d'équivalent en anglais, il en ajoute d'autres. Ainsi, dans le conte *The Bluebird* (L'Oiseau bleu), il omet la dispute entre Truitonne et le roi Charmant dans laquelle D'Aulnoy joue de la double signification du mot *roitelet*.[41] Or dans le conte *The Princess Rosetta* (La Princesse Rosette), il ajoute une nouvelle récompense pour le vieux pêcheur. Ayant sauvé la vie de la princesse, le pêcheur peut vivre au palais jusqu'à la fin de ses jours dans la version française, mais dans l'adaptation anglaise, la princesse le rend "Knight of the most noble Order of the *Dolphins*; and Vice-Admiral of the Seas."[42]

Enfin, l'auteur de l'édition Tracy supprime la plupart des références explicites à la France. Ainsi il remplace plusieurs noms par des équivalents anglais, dont le nom du petit chien d'Avenant, *Capriole*, appelé *Caper* dans la version anglaise du conte *La Belle aux cheveux d'or*. Puis, l'auteur omet les références explicites à la vie française, sauf si elles lui permettent de se moquer de manière subtile des Français. Ainsi, il omet les noms des boutiques parisiennes mentionnés dans *Le prince Lutin* mais dans le même passage il développe la référence aux singes français:

> Puis il (le prince Lutin) se souhaita à Paris, où il avait entendu dire que l'on trouvait tout ce qu'on voulait pour de l'argent. Il fut acheter chez Dautel, qui est un curieux, un petit carrosse tout d'or où il fit atteler six singes verts, avec de petits harnais de maroquin couleur de feu, garnis d'or; il alla ensuite chez Brioché, fameux joueur de Marionnettes, il y trouva deux singes de mérite: le plus spirituel s'appelait Briscambille et l'autre Perceforêt.[43] ¶ Then he [the Hobgoblin Prince] wish'd himself at *Paris*, where he bought a little Gold Chariot and two *French* Monkeys, (for you must know there are abundance of that passive breed in *France*) the one nam'd *Briscambril*, the other *Piercewood*.[44]

Outre ces adaptations textuelles somme toutes assez superficielles, le traducteur ajoute de nouveaux passages qui rappellent le folklore anglais. Ainsi, le traducteur insiste sur l'existence de la monarchie des fées annoncée dans le poème du frontispice. Dans plusieurs contes il mentionne une monarchie, un royaume ou un empire des fées. Une telle monarchie des fées est typique des contes anglais mettant en scène le roi des fées Oberon et la reine Mab, mais elle n'est pas évoquée dans les contes de D'Aulnoy. Le premier conte, *Gracieuse et Percinet*, commence ainsi dans la version anglaise: "The Empire of the fairies had not flourish'd many centuries, but there reigned in the Eastern countries, a King and Queen, with so much clemency and Justice, that they had gained the hearts of

[Fig. 4] Robin Goodfellow, His mad Prankes, and Merry Jests (London: F Grove, 1628), Frontispice. Gravure sur bois signée FG. (San Marino, The Huntington L, 137397)

37 Ibid., p. 6.
38 D'AULNOY (voir note 9), p. 119.
39 *Tales of the Fairies* (voir note 19), p. 7.
40 Dans "The Cobler's Epistle to the Gentlemen Readers", l'auteur explique: "Why were tavernes invented, but to ripen men's wits? And why were tales devised, but to make men pleasant? [...] my book, wherein are contained the tales that were tolde in the Barge betweene Billingsgate and Gravesend: imitating therein old father Chaucer, who with the like method set out his Caunterbury tales". *The Cobler of Caunterbury*. London: Printed for Robert Robinson, 1590.
41 NADINE JASMIN précise que ce mot désigne un « Roi ou seigneur d'un Petit pays (mais) aussi un oiseau fort petit, vif et plein de feu (Furetière) ». Dans D'AULNOY (voir note 9), p. 167. Le jeu de mots convient dans ce conte puisque le roi sera transformé en oiseau.
42 *Tales of the Fairies* (voir note 19), p. 117.
43 D'AULNOY (voir note 9), p.228.
44 *Tales of the Fairies* (voir note 19), pp. 77/8.

[Fig. 5] Tom Thumb his life and death. Wherein is declared many marvelous acts of manhood full of wonder and strange merriment, which little knight lived in King Arthurs time in the court of Great Britain (London: I. Wright, 1630), p. 5. (Oxford, Bodleian L, 8° L 79 (8) Art)

all their subjects."[45] La version anglaise du conte *La princesse Rosette* commence également par une référence à l'empire des fées, dont l'impératrice est Truffio, la fée aidant les amants dans le conte *The Orange Tree and its beloved Bee* (L'oranger et l'abeille). Puis, dans *The Golden Branch* (Le Rameau d'or), le roi Brun ne succède au trône qu'après la mort de la reine Gentilla, la fée qui offre le don de lutinerie à Léandre, dans le conte *The Fair Indifferent; or the Hobgoblin Prince and Furibon* (Le Prince Lutin). En ajoutant des références intertextuelles aux contes inclus dans le recueil, le traducteur semble esquisser toute une dynastie des fées. Les règnes des différents roi et reines des fées se succèdent et suggèrent une cohérence interne, comme si les contes dans le recueil faisaient tous partie des longues chroniques du monde des fées. Ces adaptations font écho au nouveau titre du recueil: *The History of the tales of the fairies*.

De plus, le traducteur ajoute plusieurs descriptions des fées à l'anglaise. Les fées sont alors des petites créatures éthérées alors que les fées de D'Aulnoy sont en général décrites comme des dames aristocratiques. Ainsi dans le premier conte, l'héroïne Gracieuse ouvre une boîte, de laquelle s'échappe une multitude de petits personnages. Dans la version française ce ne sont que des hommes et des femmes miniatures. Or dans la version anglaise, ils deviennent des fées.

> Elle l'ouvrit: et aussitôt il en sort tant de petits hommes et de petites femmes, de violons, d'instruments, de petites tables, petits cuisiniers, petits plats: enfin le géant de la troupe était haut comme le doigt: ils sautent dans le pré, ils se séparent en plusieurs bandes, et commencent le plus joli bal que l'on ait jamais vu.[46]

> Well, open'd it is, when, (O wounderful!) at that instant the meadow was fill'd with *Fairy* Men and Women of all Ranks and Qualities. There were among them, great Numbers of Musicians, Stage-Players, Fencers, Dancing-Masters, Cooks &c. and not a single melancholy Fairy among them all. The Fairies of Quality were drawn along the banks of small rivulets, in Chariots of Cockle shell by beautiful Humbirds, which made melodious harmony; whilst the rest Sung, danced, Play'd, Feasted and Revell'd wantonly about the Meadow, to the great Amusement of Graciosa.[47]

Dans le conte *L'oiseau bleu*, l'héroïne ouvre un œuf magique dont il sort des poupées en miniature qui dansent la Sarabande. Dans l'édition anglaise l'exotisme de D'Aulnoy est remplacé par un passage au goût plus folklorique: "They [the puppets] would dance upon a Spider's Web and throw themselves thro' the Eye of a Stocking-Needle."[48] Les quatre amours assistant à la noce des héros du conte *Le rameau d'or*, sont remplacés dans la version anglaise par une multitude de nymphes fées: "They were attended by the Graces and a Million of Fairy Nymphs supporting a rich Canopy over their Heads; the Zephirs and all the agreeable Deïties of the Woods and Plains made up the Company, with a Harmony equal to that of the Spheres."[49]

Ces fées miniatures si petites qu'un coquillage leur sert de carrosse et si légères qu'elles peuvent danser sur une toile d'araignée, rappellent celles des contes populaires anglais comme ceux de Robin Goodfellow et Tom Thumb. Les fées mentionnées à la fin du conte de Robin Goodfellow

---

45 Ibid., p. 1.
46 D'AULNOY (voir note 9), p. 136.
47 *Tales of the Fairies* (voir note 19), p. 19.
48 Ibid., p. 49.
49 Ibid., p. 140.

sont assez petites pour se laver dans un bol de potage, de lait ou de bière. Tom Thumb porte un chapeau fait d'une feuille de chêne et une chemise de toile d'araignée. Des petites fées paraissent également dans les adaptations littéraires de cette matière populaire, telles que les pièces de Shakespeare et le poème épique Nimphidea de Michael Drayton (1627). Ces deux derniers développent plus amplement les mondes miniatures.⁵⁰ Dans le dernier passage, évoquant les fées ainsi que le personnel mythologique, le traducteur-auteur de l'édition Tracy crée un curieux mélange de folklore et de mythologie antique, qui reste plus proche de l'original français.

En outre, le traducteur ajoute de nouvelles références à des superstitions anglaises. Dans le conte *Le rameau d'or*, une fée méchante essaye de séduire un prince, qui repousse ses avances en disant: "Madam, [...] I should not be such a fool as to place my Affections upon an Apparition that has influence over nothing but silly Glow-worms, Jack-a-Lantherns, and Will-in-the Whisps, Meteors, which serve only to deceive unthinking Travellers into endless wandrings."⁵¹

Ces lucioles, feux follets et météores sont tous des phénomènes naturels résultant dans des lumières mystérieuses ou des boules de feu dans le ciel. Cependant, ils engendraient également des superstitions et des croyances populaires très largement répandues. Les noms de "Jack-a Lantern" et "Will in the Whisp," par exemple, renvoient à un personnage très dangereux qui se plaisait à faire égarer les voyageurs, particulièrement lorsqu'il pouvait les envoyer se faire perdre dans des forêts boueuses.⁵² En fait, ces petites lumières étaient sans doute des flammes vacillant au dessus des terres marécageuses provoquées par du méthane (provenant de la putréfaction des plantes) qui avait pris feu. La légende de "Jack a Lantern" et "Will in the Whisp" remonte au moins jusqu'au début du XVIIᵉ siècle et elle figure également dans le conte de Robin Goodfellow. Dans l'un des épisodes, Robin s'amuse à dévier un groupe de jeunes hommes de leur chemin en paraissant devant eux comme une flamme mobile. L'histoire se termine par le poème suivant:

> Get you home, you merry lads,
> Tell your Mammies and your Dads,
> And all those that the newes desire,
> How you saw a walking fire.
> Wenches that doe smile and lispe,
> Use to call me Willy Wispe;
> If that you but weary be,
> It is sport alone for me,
> Away unto your houses goe,
> And I goe laughing ho, ho, hoh!⁵³

Chapbook ou imitation: le public de l'édition de 1716

Malgré le ton et l'apparence rustique et naïve, l'édition de 1716 ne visait sans doute pas un public exclusivement populaire. D'abord le livre est relativement long (plus de 160 pages) et son prix d'un shilling est assez élevé (plus que le double du prix courant des minces éditions popu-

[Fig. 6] The Witch of the Woodlands, Or, The Coblers New Translation, Written by L. P. (London 1655), Frontispice. (Oxford, Bodleian L, Wood 704 (2))

---

50 "In the beginning of the Jacobean times a little school of friends among the poets, Drayton, Brown, Herrick and the almost unknown Simon Steward, caught by the deliciousness of Shakespeare's fairies, and coming from counties where the small fairies belonged to the folk tradition, amused themselves and each other by writing fantasies on littleness." KATHARINE M. BRIGGS: *The Anatomy of Puck. An Examination of Fairy Beliefs Among Shakespeare's Contemporaries and Successors*. Londres 1959, p. 56.
51 *Tales of the Fairies* (voir note 19), p. 136.
52 Cf. D.L. ASHLIMAN: *Fairy Lore: A Handbook*. Westport etc. 2005, p. 203.
53 *Robin Goodfellow* (voir note 29), page non-numérotée.

laires).⁵⁴ Si des livres plus longs (plus de 70 pages) paraissaient sur la liste des chapbooks de l'un des principaux marchands, William Thackeray, le format et le prix de l'édition de 1716 suggèrent que le livre était sans doute assez cher pour les lecteurs les plus démunis. Cependant, comparée à l'anthologie luxueuse de Nicholson, le papier de l'édition de Tracy est de qualité médiocre et la mise en page est chargée. Le libraire semble avoir produit une édition sans prétentions destinée à un lectorat variant de la petite bourgeoisie aux classes plus aisées. Dans la lettre de dédicace adressée «aux dames» (The Ladies of Great-Britain), l'éditeur écrit: "The Works of the Original Author are too Voluminous and consequently of a large a Price".⁵⁵ Ceci montre que le libraire crée une édition moins volumineuse pour des raisons économiques, lisons: pour permettre aux lecteurs plus modestes de se procurer l'édition. Mais, en outre, l'éditeur précise que la petite édition de format duodécimo est facile à emporter pendant les promenades et que les contes offrent des lectures instructives de loisir. Comme l'affirme Jones, ceci suggère que le libraire visait également les dames des classes plus élevées.⁵⁶

Cette interprétation semble être confirmée par le fait que les noms de Tracy et Harris ne paraissent point parmi ceux des principaux marchands d'éditions populaires de l'époque, comme John Wright, John Clarke, Passinger and Thackeray, connus comme les "Ballad-partners."⁵⁷ Au lieu de se spécialiser entièrement dans la partie basse du marché, Tracy fournit des éditions appropriées pour des classes de lecteurs variées. La liste de livres vendus par Tracy, ajoutée dans un but publicitaire à la fin de la mince édition intitulée *The Life and Death of the English Rogue* (1700) souligne la variété de son assortiment: "Bibles in all volumes, All school books, all sorts of dictionaries and Spelling-books." L'énumération de livres religieux et didactiques est suivie d'une sélection de titres caractéristiques du fonds populaire. Marqués en caractères plus petites sur la liste, il y a entre autres *The History of Troy*, *The History of the Seven Champions*, and *Robin Hood's Garland*. Une autre liste, incluse à la fin d'un manuel de médecine, *Chirurgus Marinus: or The Sea-Chirurgion by John Moyle* (1693), comporte plusieurs livres de mathématiques et d'histoire ainsi que l'encyclopédie de médecine du Dr. Salomon en quatre tomes que Tracy propose à ses clients en différents formats (folio, quarto, octavo). Parmi les livres publiés par Tracy parvenus jusqu'à nous on trouve des titres classiques de l'édition populaire (*The Famous and Remarkable History of Sir Rich. Whittington, three times Lord Mayor of London*, 1678, 13 pages) et des romances plus longues telles que *Valentine and Orson* (1690, 1694 et 1700, plus de 90 pages) mais également des manuels scolaires et des livres plus savants et précieux (*The First Book of Architecture by Andrea Palladio*, 1693, 143 pages et illustré de nombreuses gravures sur cuivre très raffinées). Cette impression nécessairement rapide du fonds de Tracy, laisse entrevoir la politique commerciale du libraire. En variant les titres, les formats et les prix, Tracy constitue une collection convenant à des classes de lecteurs très disparates, ce qui lui permet sans doute de se distinguer de plusieurs de ses collègues-libraires.

Tracy tenait boutique aux "Three Bibles on London Bridge," comme

54 MARGARET SPUFFORD suggère que les chapbooks coûtent en général entre 2d et 6d (penny). Un shilling vaut douze penny. MARGARET SPUFFORD: *Small Books and Pleasant Histories. Popular Fiction and Its Readership in Seventeenth-century England.* Londres 1981, p. 131.
55 *Tales of the Fairies* (voir note 19), The Epistle Dedicatory, page non numérotée.
56 JONES (voir note 8), p. 244.
57 SPUFFORD (voir note 54), p. 83.

plusieurs marchands d'éditions populaires dont Josiah Blare, John Black, James Gilbertson, Charles Passinger et Thomas Passinger.[58] Ce dernier avait publié plusieurs ballades ornées de bois représentant Robin Goodfellow et les fées (*The English Fortune Teller*, 1675 et *Robin Goodfellow*, 1680). Tracy s'était probablement installé au pont avant 1678 (la date estimée de publication de l'édition la plus ancienne survivant aujourd'hui). Tracy avait repris le texte d'une édition de *Valentine and Orson* publiée par Passinger. Il connaissait forcément la marchandise des chapmen et s'en inspire pour l'édition de 1716.

Les stratégies éditoriales de Tracy et Harris montrent que l'édition n'est pas un véritable chapbook mais émule délibérément cet héritage culturel. L'édition n'était pas adressée à un public exclusivement populaire, elle visait, au contraire, un lectorat plus vaste. Sans doute, l'édition atteste d'un intérêt grandissant auprès du public cultivé pour la matière folklorique nationale. Dès le XVIe siècle finissant, le sentiment d'une nouvelle ère qui commence et d'un héritage culturel ancien sur le point de se perdre fait renaître auprès du public le goût pour cette matière. Ce sentiment d'un changement imminent est exprimé de manière éloquente par Scot, lorsqu'il associe la peur des apparitions aux contes de vieille que l'homme moderne ne peut prendre au sérieux:

> But in our childhood our mothers maids have so terrified us with [...] bull beggers, spirits, witches, urchens, elves, hags, fairies, satyrs, pans, faunes, sylens, kit in the cansticke, tritons, centaurs, dwarfes, giants, imps, calcars, conjurors, nymphes, changlings, Incubus, Robin good-fellowe, the spoorne, the mare, the man in the oke, the hell waine, the fierdrake, the puckle, Tom Thombe, hob gobblin, Tom Tumbler, Boneles, and such other bugs, that we are afraid of oure own shadowes [...]. Well, thanks be to God, this wretched and cowardly infidelitie, since the preaching of the gospell, is in part forgotten: and doubtles, the rest of those illusions will in short time (by Gods Grace) be detected and vanish awaie.[59]

Or, dans *The Cobler of Caunterbury*, les contes populaires sont associés à un passé mythique que l'auteur évoque avec nostalgie:

> It was not so when Robin Goodfellow was a Ruffler and helpt the country wenches to grinde their Mault: Then Gentlemen, the Ploughswaine meddled with his Teame; the Gentlemen with his Hound and his Hawke; the Artificer with his labour; & the Scholler with his booke, every degree contented him within his limits. But now the world has grown to that passe that Piere Plowman will prie into lawe, naie into divinity, and his duncerie must needs be doctrine: tush what of higher powers? what of Universities? the text to put downe them Babes and Sucklings and no more. This makes Robin Goodfellow, that was so merry a spirit of the Butterie, to leave all and keepe himselfe in Purgatorie, for Hospitality is so cleane run out of the Countrie, that he need not nowe help maids to grinde mault, for the drinke is so small it needes little corne, and if he should helpe, where he was woont to find a messe of Creame for his labour, he should scarse get a dish of floate Milke.[60]

Le goût pour la culture populaire est présent de manière allusive dès la fin du XVIe siècle dans les pièces de Shakespeare et les poèmes de Drayton, mais il se précise au XVIIIe siècle, comme en témoigne également la publication de la *Collection of Old Ballads* en trois volumes par Philips

---

58 Ibid., pp. 114/5.
59 SCOT (voir note 25), pp. 122/3.
60 *The Cobler of Caunterbury* (voir note 40), Robin Goodfellowes Epistle, page non numérotée.

Ambrose (1723–25). Dans cette compilation on trouve entre autres *The Seven Champions of Christendom*, *Robin Hood* et *The Children in the Wood*. Les références à la culture populaire anglaise dans l'édition Tracy ne servaient pas uniquement à rendre le livre attrayant pour un lectorat d'origine modeste, elles plaisaient également aux lectrices et aux lecteurs plus aisés, qui retrouvaient ainsi dans un contexte nouveau des éléments du folklore national.

Comme les auteurs des chapbooks, Harris et Tracy soulignent le caractère édifiant et moralement irréprochable des histoires contenues dans l'édition. Ainsi les lectrices sont invitées à mettre en pratique les moralités:

> She (D'Aulnoy) has given *Check* to the *Levity* of those Ladies who spend so much Time in Discourse *inconsistent* with their Duties and Characters; And yet, strange it is, many can commend her *instructive* TALES without imitation, and Read'em without putting in *practice* their Morals![61]

Ainsi les adaptations textuelles et visuelles du recueil de D'Aulnoy permettaient d'associer les contes de fées littéraires français au folklore anglais mais elles constituaient également un premier pas dans le processus de moralisation qui aboutira, dans la seconde moitié du XVIIIe siècle, à l'infantilisation du genre du conte de fées.

Conclusion

En France comme à l'étranger, les illustrations étaient employées comme un outil dans le processus de définition du conte de fées. Comme nous l'avons vu la réception internationale des *Contes des fées* de D'Aulnoy est moins constante que celle des contes de Perrault. En Angleterre ses contes sont d'abord offerts aux lecteurs comme un ouvrage appartenant aux belles-lettres. Le raffinement stylistique des contes est même amplifié dans la première traduction anglaise. Cependant, une réception parallèle apparaît à partir de 1716, qui associe les contes de fées français au folklore anglais. Le traducteur emploie plusieurs stratégies visuelles et textuelles pour créer un rapport entre les contes littéraires de D'Aulnoy et les contes populaires traditionnels anglais, tels que le conte de Robin Goodfellow. Le frontispice de cette édition relie le recueil de D'Aulnoy aux éditions populaires anglais. La méthode est comparable à celle de Perrault qui emploie le texte et les illustrations de ses *Histoires ou Contes du temps passé* pour créer l'impression d'un livre ancien ou populaire.[62]

Dès sa publication, l'adaptation de Harris et Tracy éclipse la traduction plus fidèle de Nicholson, dont plus aucune traduction ne paraît. Par contre, des rééditions de l'adaptation folklorique sont publiées tout le long du XVIIIe siècle. Or l'annexion des contes de fées de D'Aulnoy au folklore anglais et l'accent mis sur la moralité était sans doute contraire à l'idée de D'Aulnoy. En effet la salonnière avait une vision plus mondaine du genre du conte de fées et elle en soulignait la valeur esthétique et divertissante. Paradoxalement, c'est sous ce déguisement folklorique que les contes de D'Aulnoy ont survécu en Angleterre jusqu'au début du XIXe siècle.

---

61 *Tales of the Fairies* (voir note 19), The Epistle Dedicatory, page non numérotée.
62 Cf. HOOGENBOEZEM (voir note 3).

DENNIS E. RHODES

Bibliotheca Windhagiana.

Part II.

AFTER I HAD PUBLISHED my first account of the world-wide dispersal of the vast library which had been accumulated by Johann Joachim Entzmüller, Baron von und zu Windhag (1600–78) at his castle in Upper Austria, colleagues in several countries were kind enough to send me supplementary material, which now numbers eighteen more items in addition to the 54 which I originally listed.[1]

I have thought it interesting and useful to scholars to publish this second list, which now brings up to seventy-two the number of Windhag items which we can account for, even if the present location of a few of them remains unknown after a series of sales. No more books in Austria have hitherto been reported to me, but the best surprise is that one book recently located in Venice is the first example I have of a Windhag book ending up in Italy. The latest addenda are:

France
PETRUS HISPANUS (Pope John XXI): *Copulata omnium tractatuum et parvorum logicalium.* Cologne: [Heinrich Quentell] 7 and 8 April 1490. 4°. H 8703*. Voulliéme Köln 930.

Paris, B Victor-Cousin. Information from Paul Needham.

Great Britain
CLEMENT V, Pope: *Constitutiones.* Mainz: Peter Schoeffer, 8 October 1467. Fol. GW 7078.

On first leaf: Ex Bibliotheca Windhagiana. Chatsworth, Duke of Devonshire; Christie, 6 June 1974, lot 9; Wormsley Library of the late Sir Paul Getty. Information in a letter from Robert Harding, Maggs Bros., London, 6 July 2009. This is the oldest book known to have belonged to Windhag.

Italy
JOHANNES DAMASCENUS, St.: *Opera omnia.* Basle: Sebastian Henricpetri, 1575. Fol.

Now in Venice, Church of S. Francesco della Vigna.[2] With Windhag ex-libris of 1656. Bought in 1879 from a Milanese bookseller by Giacomo Perazzo, a priest at least nine of whose books are now at S. Francesco, this book eventually came into the hands of another Franciscan, Anacleto Sasso (1926–98), and so eventually was left to S. Francesco della Vigna. This proves that some Windhag books were on the market in the nineteenth century.

---

[1] D. E. RHODES: Bibliotheca Windhagiana. In: GJ 2009, pp. 307–12.
[2] Cf. *La Biblioteca di S. Francesco della Vigna e i suoi fondi antichi.* Venice 2009, pp. 31/2 and 108/9.

Germany

GIOVANNI ANTONIO MAGINI: *Ephemerides coelestium motuum.* [With Continuatio.] Francofurti: Typis Wolffgangi Richteri, sumptibus Ioan. Theobal. Schönwetteri, 1608. 4°.

UB Frankfurt J. C. Senckenberg. Information from Bernhard Wirth.

ARISTOTLE: *Opera.* Venice: Gregorius de Gregoriis for Benedictus Fontana, 13 July 1496. Fol. Goff A 966. GW 2341. Hummel 14. Schlägl StiftsB. Information from Paul Needham.

Türckische, tartarische, persische, griechische und venetianische Chronica. Frankfurt am Main: Wilhelm Serlin, 1665.

With coat of arms and bookplate dated 1651. UB Leipzig, Hist. Turc. 51-m. Information from Thomas Thibault Döring.

ANDREAS GRYPHIUS: *Teutsche Reimgedichte.* Frankfurt am Main: Johann Hüttner, 1650.

UB Leipzig, Lit. germ. E 4090. Information from T. T. Döring.

MARTIN PEREZ DE AYALA: *De divinis apostolicis, atque ecclesiasticis traditionibus.* Coloniae, excud. Iaspar Gennepeus, 1560. 8°.

Written on title page: Ex bibliotheca Windhagiana 1666. Binding dated 1561. UB Leipzig, Syst. Theol. 1760-C. Information from Thomas Thibault Döring.

MICHAEL DE CARCANO: *Sermonarium per quadragesimam de commendatione virtutum et reprobatione vitiorum.* Milan: Uldericus Scinzenzeler, for Raphael Peragallus, 11 July 1495. 4°.

BMC VI, 770. GW 6128. IGI 2517. It bears the owner's note: Ex Biblioth. Windhagiana. Leipzig, DNB. Information from Bettina Rüdiger.

Slovakia

ANSELMUS, St.: *Opera.* Nuremberg: Caspar Hochfeder, 27 March 1491. Fol. Goff A 759. GW 2032.

UL Brno. (Vladislav Dokoupil, Soupis prvotisku z fondu universitná v Brnê, 71.) Information from Paul Needham.

Slovenia

JOHANNES ROSINUS: *Romanarum antiquitatum libri decem. Secunda editio.* Lugduni: [for Sibille de la Porte], 1585. Fol.

Inscribed on title page: Ex Bibliotheca Windhagiana. Ljubljana, NL of Slovenia.

Switzerland

FRANCIS BACON: *Scripta in naturali et universali philosophia.* Amstelodami: apud Ludovicum Elzevirium, 1653. 12°.

Ex-libris of Windhag dated 1651. UB Bern. Information via IDS Basel Bern.

USA
Bible. Basle: Johann Froben, 27 June 1491. 8°.

Goff B 592. GW 4269. Tallahassee, Florida State UL. Information from Paul Needham.

FRANCESCO PETRARCA: *Opera*. Basle: Johann Amerbach, 1496. Fol.

Goff P 365. Washington/DC, LC. Information from Paul Needham.

OVIDIUS NASO: *Fasti. Tristia. De Ponto.* Basle: Heinrich Petri, March 1568. 8°.

Windhag bookplate of 1661. Bruce McKittrick Rare Books, Narberth, PA; Columbus/Ohio, Ohio State UL. Information from Andrew Gaub, Bruce McKittrick Rare Books, Inc.

Present location unknown

GIOVANNI FRANCESCO PICO DELLA MIRANDOLA: *De auro libri tres.* Oberursel: Cornelius Sutor, 1598. 8°.

Mirandola, Sgarbanti (bookseller), copy bound with another work on the title page of which is written: Ex Bibliotheca Windhagiana.[3]

GEORG RÜXNER: *Turnierbuch.* Siemern: Hieronymus Rodler, 3 August 1532. 536r 1486. Fol.

Goff J 529. Ludwig Rosenthal Cat. 169, nº 84 = L. H. P. Klotz sale, Christie's, London, 2 Nov. 1994, lot 96. Information from Paul Needham.

Seventy-two Windhag books have now been accounted for as follows: twenty-four in Austria, fifteen in USA, eleven in Great Britain, six in Germany, three in France, two in Belgium, and one each in Denmark, Italy, Czech Republic, Slovakia, Slovenia and Switzerland. Three also exist whose present location is unknown to me. The library as a whole was certainly not left to the University Library of Vienna; and even if the ***majority of its incunabula are now in the National Library of Austria (as the first volumes A and B, of that library's new incunable catalogue would suggest), there are still nine incunabula in Great Britain, five in USA, three in France, two in Germany, and one each in the Czech Republic, Denmark and Slovakia.

Even if more information reaches me (as it almost inevitably will), I shall probably not publish future lists. I have at least established that the magnificent seventeenth-century collection of books printed between 1467 and 1665, brought together by Baron von Windhag, must be one of the most widely dispersed of the major libraries of that century. It is usual for such accounts to conclude with the much-quoted motto »Habent sua fata libelli«.

---

[3] See LEONARDO QUAQUARELLI/ZITA ZANARDI: *Pichiana*. Firenze 2005, p. 252, nº 71.

WILLIAM A. KELLY

Survey of pre-1801 Low Countries Imprints in Scottish Research Libraries

Part Three

THE FOLLOWING DESCRIPTION is a supplement to my *Survey of pre-1801 Low Countries Imprints in Scottish Research Libraries*.[1] The University of Dundee Library could not be included there, as the early printed books were inaccessible because of building work. I am grateful to Mr. John Bagnall, the former Librarian, and especially to a continuing member of the staff, Mr. David Hart, for facilitating my visit to Dundee over several days.

15. University of Dundee

Address University Library, Small's Wynd, Dundee DD1 4HN
Telephone [+44 0] 1382 384087 *Fax* [+44 0] 1382 386228
E-mail library@dundee.ac.uk
Internet www.dundee.ac.uk/library
Governing body or responsible institution U of Dundee
Functions UL
Subjects Details of the categories of material held in Special Collections can be found at www.dundee.ac.uk/library/about/speccoll.html

15.1 Brief history of the institution

The origins of the University of Dundee go back to the general movement in the large industrial centers of Great Britain in the late nineteenth century for the extension of liberal and technological education. Through the generosity and foresight of two members of the wealthy local family of Baxter University College, Dundee was founded for "promoting the education of persons of both sexes and the study of Science, Literature and the Fine Arts". Despite its independent academic status, the College had no power to award degrees and for some years students were prepared for the external examinations of the University of London.

In 1897 University College became a part of the University of St Andrews and a medical school belonging to both institutions was set up in Dundee; "[t]his union served to give expression to local feeling that there should be a vital connection between the old and the new in academic affairs, and that a venerable institution in a small town and a modern establishment in a large city might well complement each other in a manner advantageous to both".[2]

This union, however, was dogged with tensions and a Royal Commission recommended the merger of University College and the Medical

---

[1] WILLAM A. KELLY: Survey of pre-1801 Low Countries Imprints in Scottish Research Libraries. Part one in: GJ 2007, pp. 278–337; Part two in: GJ 2008, pp. 165–232.

[2] University of Dundee Calendar, 2000–02, p. 44.

School into a new body, to be known as Queen's College, still within the University of St Andrews, which came into effect in 1954. Still an increasing pressure on expanding tertiary education in Scotland and the United Kingdom generally was felt in Dundee, where there was a long-standing feeling locally in favor of independence. This local feeling was encouraged by the comment in the Robbins Commission on Higher Education in October 1963 that "at least one, and perhaps two, of the new university foundations should be in Scotland". As a consequence of encouragement from central government plans were drawn up for the constitution of the new university, which came into effect on 1 August 1967.

Secondary literature MICHAEL SHAFE: *University education in Dundee 1881–1981. A Pictorial History*. Dundee 1982; DONALD SOUTHGATE: *University education in Dundee: a centenary history*. Edinburgh 1982.

15.2 *Brief history of the library*

The earliest accommodation for the College's library was a private house assigned by the College's Council for that purpose. The stock of books, naturally small, was dispersed through teaching departments to which they had been donated. A shortage of books was to be a continuing problem for academic staff and undergraduates throughout the life of University College and on into the 1950s. The economic conditions of the 1930s did not go unnoticed in the pressures exerted on the library and, had it not been for the bequests of two former professors, Stegall and Buist, and of several others, the library would have been in even greater straits. Indeed the thralldom of the College's library towards the considerably better facilities of that in St Andrews has been suggested as a powerful reason for ambitious members of the teaching staff of that period to live closer to the older institution. A plan in the early 1970s to erect a new library had to be abandoned when the University Grants Committee, at the government's behest, implemented a major cutback on all building projects. It was only indirectly as a result of the opening of the Medical Library at Ninewells and the relocation of the Law Library to the Scrymgeour Building that more space was freed in the main library building. Some additional easing in accommodation and book provision was made possible by collaboration in technical processes and in inter-library lending. It was not until 1988 that the library was built on the present site, with additions in 1997 and 2008.

The main collection likely to contain material of interest to a student of printing in the Low Countries prior to 1801 is:

15.3 *Brechin Diocesan Library*

This is the jewel in the crown of the Library's collections of early printed books. Its origins go back to a decision by those members of the Diocese of the Scottish Episcopal Church of Scotland present at a meeting in 1792 to found a library for their own needs. From its modest beginnings the library, which appears to have been housed in Laurencekirk, received a major addition of some seven hundred volumes in 1809 from the bequest of a former diocesan bishop, William Abernethy Drummond. Later in that century the library received two further donations, the first, consisting of over six hundred volumes, including many from the seventeenth and eighteenth centuries, from a clergyman in Glasgow, the Rev. Alexander Jamieson. While an indication of the growth of the library could have been seen in the printing of a catalogue in 1828, if only a copy had survived, another two decades had to pass before more concrete evidence became available in that of 1847. That the library continued to grow apace can be seen in the decision to print a third one in 1869, with an appendix printed ten years later. This appendix was made necessary by the library's third large donation in that century, which came from a later bishop, Alexander Penrose Forbes, who died in 1875. Forbes was a staunch protagonist of the Oxford Movement in Scotland, for which he has been dubbed the Scottish Pusey. He wrote extensively in defense of Catholic traditions of worship and church government, a stance which did not always endear him to his fellow bishops, who brought a charge of heresy against him, which resulted in an official censure. He left some two thousand volumes, rich in theological, liturgical and patristic studies, to the library. The present library consists of around ten thousand volumes and some manuscripts, which have been on permanent loan from the Diocese of Brechin since 1961. Some items are of great bibliographical interest.

Although it is surprising that there are no texts of Church Fathers, early Christian and medieval writers in the collection issued by printers in this area, especially in Flanders, given the generally high theological stamp of the Episcopal Church in Scotland, there is a small number of texts of the Bible issued by presses there, e.g..

Biblia ad vetustissima exemplaria nunc recens castigata (Antwerp 1570), *Biblia Hebraica.* Ed. X. PAGNINO & B. ARIAS MONTANO. Antwerp 1584; A. TOP: *The book of prayses, called the Psalmes*, etc. Amsterdam 1629; *Davids Psalmen, in't Nederduits berijmd.* Haarlem 1713, which is supported by a number of commentaries; B. ARIAS MONTANO: *Commentaria in Isaiae prophetae sermones.* Antwerp 1599; J. DRUSIUS: *Commentarius in prophetas minores* XII., etc. Amsterdam 1627; C. DE LAPIDE: *Commentaria in Salomonis proverbia.* Antwerp 1645; Ibid.: *Commentaria in qvatuor prophetas minores.* Antwerp 1654; Ibid.: *Commentaria in Pentateuchum Mosis.* Antwerp 1648; Ibid.: *Commentaria in Acta Apostolorum, Epistolas canonicas, et Apocalypsin.* Antwerp 1647; Ibid.: *Commentaria in Pentateuchum Mosis.* Antwerp 1648; Ibid.: *Commentarius in qvatuor Euangelia.* Antwerp 1640; and Ibid.: *Commentarii in Ecclesiasten.* Antwerp 1649.

However, what is noticeably in tune with the Episcopal Church in Scotland's theological stand is the number of devotional works by Roman Catholic writers, of whom Jeremias Drexel is an outstanding example. These include:

JEREMIAS DREXEL: *Deliciae gentis humanae Christus Iesus*, etc. Antwerp 1639; Ibid.: *David regius psaltes descriptus et morali doctrina illustratus.* Antwerp 1643; Ibid.: *Daniel prophetarum princeps descriptus, et morali doctrina illustratus.* Antwerp 1644; and Ibid.: *Caelum, beatorum civitas: aeternitatis pars* III. Antwerp 1635.

Secondary literature *The Brechin Diocesan Library, its origins and history.* [Typescript; based on notes by J. R. BARKER and A. N. CASS.][Dundee, c. 2000?]

15.4 *Collection H*

H is a collection on the history of medicine and kept at Ninewells Hospital. All enquiries about material with this pressmark should be directed to the head of library services there. The pre-1801 Low Countries imprints in this collection are not particularly noteworthy for their number or range of subject material, but do not deserve to be passed over in silence. They include:

J. FERNEL: *Universa medicina.* Leiden 1605; L. RIVIÈRE: *Praxis medica.* Leiden 1653; J. PRIMEROSE: *De vulgi erroribus in medicina, libri* IV. Rotterdam 1658; T. BARTHOLIN: *Anatomia.* The Hague 1666; *Antiquitatum veteris puerperii sinopsi.* Amsterdam 1676; ALBERTUS MAGNUS: *De secretis mulierum.* Amsterdam 1669; C. BARTHOLIN: *De inauribus veterum syntagma.* Amsterdam 1676; R. DESCARTES: *Tractatus de homine, et de formatione foetus.* Leiden 1677, J. B. V. LAMSWEERDE: *Historia naturalis molarum uteri: in qua de natura seminis, ejusque circulari in sanguinem regressu, accuratius disquiritur.* Leiden 1686; HIPPOCRATES: *Aphorismi.* Amsterdam 1685; G. BIDLOO: *Anatomia humani corporis.* Amsterdam 1685; A. M. VALSALVA: *De aure humana tractatus, in quo integra auris fabrica, multis novis inventis & iconismis illustrata, describitur,* etc. Utrecht 1707; H. BOERHAAVE: *Institutiones medicae in usus annuae exercitationis domesticos digestae.* Leiden 1713; and his *Libellus de materie medica et remediorum formulis, quae serviunt Aphorismis de cognoscendis et curandis morbis.* Leiden 1727; B. EUSTACHIUS: *Tabulae anatomicae.* Amsterdam 1722; J. LOMMIUS: *Commentarii de sanitate tuenda in primum librum De re medica A. C. Celsi.* Leiden 1724; H. V. DEVENTER: *Operationum chirurgicarum, novum lumen exhibentium obstetricantibus, pars prima.* Leiden 1725; D. LE CLERC: *Histoire de médicine ou l'on void l'origine & le progrès d cet art.* The Hague 1729; L. BELLINI: *De urinis et pulsibus, de missione sanguinis, de febribus, de morbis capitis, et pectoris.* Leiden 1730); W. HARVEY: *Exercitatio anatomica de motu cordis et sanguinis in animalibus.* Leiden 1737; and G. V. SWIETEN: *Commentaria in H. Boerhaave Aphorismos de cognoscendis et curandis morbis.* 3 vols. Leiden 1742.

Related to these strictly defined medical works in that the distinction which we place now between medicine and the natural sciences was not recognized and because many medical practitioners in earlier centuries were also keen students of such subjects as zoology and chemistry are the following:

THEOPHRASTUS: *De historia plantarum libri decem.* Amsterdam 1644; R. BOYLE: *Experimenta et considerationes de coloribus.* Rotterdam 1671; S. BASSO: *Philosophiae naturalis adversus Aristotelem libri* XII. Amsterdam 1649; F. BACON: *Novum organum scientiarum.* Leiden 1650; C. V. DIJK: *Osteologia, of, Naauwkeurige geraamt beschryving van verscheyde dieren,* enz. Amsterdam 1680; P. HERMAN: *Horti academici Lugduno-Batavi catalogus exhibens plantarum omnium nomina,* etc. Leiden 1687; I. NEWTON: *Philo-*

sophiae naturalis principia mathematica. Amsterdam 1723; N. BION: *Traité de la construction et des principaux usages des instrumens de mathématique.* The Hague 1723; A. SEBA: *Locupletissimi rerum naturalium thesauri accurata descriptio,* etc. 5ᵛ. Amsterdam 1734–65; and P.S. PALLAS: *Elenchus zoophytorum sistens generum adumbrationes generaliores etspecierum cognitarum succinctas descriptiones cum selectis auctorum synonymis.* The Hague 1766.

MARVIN J. HELLER

On the Identity of the First Printers in Slavuta

THERE IS A MYSTIQUE to books printed in Slavuta. They are especially valued in Hasidic circles, more so than other contemporaneous books. The attraction of Slavuta imprints can be attributed to their high quality, more so to the origin of the press, its Hasidic background, and most importantly to its tragic demise, beginning with a dispute with the Romm press in Vilna, and the denouement at the hands of the anti-Semitic Russian government.

Slavuta is today located in the Ukraine. Originally part of Poland, Slavuta was annexed by Russia after the second partition of Poland (1793), becoming part of the province of Volhynia. The publication of Hebrew books in Slavuta dates from 1791, when it was still part of Poland. Almost three hundred books, including Talmudic tractates numbered as individual titles, were printed in the four and a half decades that a Hebrew press was active in Slavuta.[1] The printer's name is absent from the title pages of the first Slavuta imprints, and afterwards, when names do appear on the title pages, confusion reigns as to the identity and number of printers active in that location. There is speculation that the names of the printers that do appear on many of the subsequent Slavuta imprints are meant to obfuscate rather than reveal their true identity. A number of suggestions have been made as to the identity of the unnamed printer or printers.

Despite, or perhaps due to the confusion as to the identity of the first printer(s), there have been several suggestions as to his (their) identity. Several bibliographers have determined, correctly, that the Slavuta press was in fact established by R. Moses Shapira (c. 1760–1839). What has not been done, however, is to critically review the history of the press, the various proposals, and, by analyzing their merits and demerits, clearly establish that Moses Shapira was indeed the founder of the Slavuta press. What follows then is not so much the unraveling of a bibliographic mystery as an attempt to make order out of the confusion, address in detail the early history of the Slavuta press, and conclusively prove that Moses Shapira was the first printer in Slavuta.

Twenty books, dated from 1791 through 1798, are recorded for Slavuta, all lacking the name of the printer. Printing began in 1791 with a Pentateuch, followed, in 1792, by *Reishit Hohkmah*, the kabbalistic ethical work of R. Elijah ben Moses de-Vidas (16th century), *Rav Yeivi*, the Hasidic homilies of R. Jacob Joseph ben Judah Leib of Ostrog (1738–91), and the testament of R. Naphtali ben Isaac Katz (1645–1719). The books printed in 1793 are the renowned anonymous ethical *Orkhot Zaddikim*, *Zohar Hadash*,

I would like to thank R. Jerry Schwarzbard, Henry R. and Miriam Ripps Schnitzer Librarian for Special Collections, The Library of the Jewish Theological Seminary for reading the article and for his comments.

[1] Cf. YESHAYAHU VINOGRAD: *Thesaurus of the Hebrew Book. Part I Indexes. Books and Authors, Bibles, Prayers and Talmud, Subjects and Printers, Chronology and Languages, Honorees and Institutes. Part II Places of print sorted by Hebrew names of places where printed including author, subject, place, and year printed, name of printer, number of pages and format, with annotations and bibliographical references.* Jerusalem 1993–95, Part II p. 490–6 [Hebrew].

Seder ha-Yom of R. Moses ben Judah ibn Makhir, *Oneg Shabbat* of R. Reuben Hoeshke ben Hoeshke Katz (d. 1673), *Shulhan Arukh Ha-Ari* of R. Isaac Luria (ha-Ari ha-Kodesh, 1534–72), *Tikkunei Zohar*, and *Tiferet Yisrael* of R. Judah ben Bezalel Loew (Maharal, c. 1525–1609).

The remainder of the titles, printed without the name of the printer, include important hasidic works, such the first part of the *Tanya* (*Likkutei Amarim*) of R. Shneur Zalman of Liady (Ba'al ha-Tanya, Alter Rebbe, 1745–1813), *Noam Elimelekh* of R. Elimelech of Lyzhansk (1717–87), *Yismah Lev* and *Me'or Einayim* of R. Menahem Nahum Twersky of Chernobyl (1730–98), *Kedushat Levi* of R. Levi Isaac of Berdichev (1740–1810), and halakhic works such as *Torat ha-Bayit* from R. Solomon ben Abraham Adret (Rashba, c. 1235–1310). The title pages of these first imprints give the place, date of publication, the latter in a chronogram, and the domain in Hebrew. In one case only, *Rav Yeivi* [fig. 1], a relatively large folio work (33 cm) printed on bluish paper, is the text of the title pages given in Polish as well as in Hebrew. All of these titles have approbations (*hascomas*) from prominent rabbis, which, as we shall see, are of considerable importance in resolving the identity of the printer(s).[2]

Although the name of the printer(s) is absent the title pages state clearly that they were printed in Slavuta, and identify the person(s) who brought the book to press, that is, the patron responsible for its publication. For example, *Reishit Hohkmah* was brought to press by R. Issachar Ber ben Zevi Hirsch of Korets; *Rav Yeivi* by R. Eliakim Gaetz, R. Judah Leib, and R. Pinhas; *Zohar Hadash* by R. Ezekiel ben Phinehas, Moses Shapira's half-brother; and *Noam Elimelekh* by R. Israel Abraham ben Meshullam Zussman, brother of the author, together with R. Samuel ben Nathan Nuta.

In 1799, the texts of the title pages begin to include the names of two printers. The *Zohar* and a Pentateuch printed that year are attributed to Dov Baer ben Israel Segal and Jacob ben Moses.[3] In 1801/2 a number of large and important works, such as the *Arba'ah Turim*, *ha-Maggid* (a Bible), *Shulhan Arukh*, and the tractates from the first Slavuta Talmud (1801–06) were printed. Here too the title pages identify the printers as Dov Baer ben Israel and Dov Baer ben Segal.

Based on the evidence of these early imprints, many bibliographers have attempted to determine the true identity of the printer of the first Slavuta titles. In the 1932 edition of *History of Hebrew Typography in Poland* Ch. Friedberg writes that "In 1792 [...] a Hebrew printing-press was established in Slavuta by, it would seem, the partners Dov Baer ben Israel Segal and Dov Baer ben Pesach."[4] Friedberg expresses some wonder at the omission of the partners' names from the title pages of these books, given the high quality of their work. This notwithstanding, Friedberg observes that after Moses Shapira began to print, and he dates the Shapira press from 1808, the press of Dov Baer ben Israel Segal and Dov Baer ben Pesach, whose books fared badly in comparison, was unable to compete with the Shapira press, and some time afterwards ceased to print.

Two important reviews of *History of Hebrew Typography in Poland* appeared shortly after the publication of that book, both in *Kiryat Sefer*,

---

2 In addition to the titles noted above several additional books are attributed to the Slavuta press in this period which are questionable, it being uncertain whether they were actually printed in Slavuta. We will not be concerned with those works.

3 One additional work, lacking the name of the printer, and uncertain, is another part of the *Tanya*. The title page, which lacks the name of the printer, gives the place of printing as Slavuta. The 1799 Slavuta edition of the *Tanya* is listed by CH. B. FRIEDBERG: *Bet Eked Sepharim*. Tel Aviv 1951, *tof* 565 [Hebrew]. This edition is noted as doubtful in VINOGRAD (see note 1), Part II p. 491 nº 23 and is recorded in JOSHUA MONDSHEIN: *Torat Habad. Bibliography of Habad Hasiduth Books I – Lekutei Amoraim, Sefer ha-Tanya, its editions, translations and commentaries (1796–1981)*. Brooklyn 1981, p. 36 [Hebrew], as a Zolkiew imprint. Concerning the confusion as to the place of printing ref. MONDSHEIN, p. 36 nº 2. The title page of the 1799 *Tanya* states that it contains the third part of that work, not previously printed in Slavuta, and, somewhat lower on the title page, in smaller letters, printed in Zolkiew.

4 CH. B. FRIEDBERG: *History of Hebrew Typography in Poland from its beginning in the year 1534 and its development to the present*. Antwerp 1932 [Hebrew], p. 77.

by the noted bibliographers Abraham Yaari and Isaac Rivkind. Yaari, in the first review, enumerates more than a hundred titles issued by small printing presses, omitted by Friedberg, noting that addressing the lacunae in major cities would require a separate work. Among the books listed by Yaari are twenty-three titles printed in Slavuta from 1806 to 1836. Rivkind, in a long, detailed, and critical review of Friedberg's book, discusses the chapter on Slavuta, remarking on what he considers to be the inadequate treatment of the controversy with the Vilna printers. Neither reviewer, however, challenges Friedberg's sequence of events concerning the establishment of the Slavuta press.[5]

A detailed review of the first books published in Slavuta was undertaken by Haim Liberman, who challenges the accepted order of events. Liberman, who is primarily interested in identifying the printer of the first edition of the *Tanya*, suggests that the printer of the first Slavuta imprints, that is, those books issued prior to 1798, intentionally omitted his name, in order to cloud his identity. Formal authorization to print had not yet been secured from the Russian government, and in the absence of such consent it was politic to be circumspect.

Nevertheless, there can be no question as to the identity of that printer, for a considerable body of evidence points to Moses Shapira as the one who established the first Hebrew print-shop in Slavuta. This evidence is comprised of Russian archival material, Hasidic tradition, approbations and other documents.[6] Liberman notes that Russian records, although of dubious reliability, date the opening of the Shapira press to 1790.

Hasidic tradition attributes the printing of the first edition of the *Tanya* to Moses Shapira. The Shapira press was selected by Shneur Zalman as an act of gratitude to Shapira's father, the *zaddik* R. Phinehas ben Abraham of Korets (1726–91), from whom the *Ba'al ha-Tanya* had benefited greatly. Another reason, given in an account of the family by a descendant, attributes the patronage of Shneur Zalman to the quality of the press work of the Shapira press, as well as the fact that no works of the *haskalah* (enlightment, or reform oriented books) were printed in Slavuta. Indeed, the first rebbe of Lubavitch reputedly traveled to Slavuta to meet with Moses Shapira a number of times, discouraging him from printing such works.[7]

Zikaron ha-Zaddikim informs us that Shapira became wealthy as a result of this patronage. Further evidence of a connection between Shapira and Shneur Zalman can be seen from the detour made by Shapira when he traveled to St. Petersburg to obtain a license to print, for Shapira is reputed to have stopped at Liady to meet with the *Ba'al ha-Tanya*, who counseled him on how to best proceed to obtain the desired permit.[8]

Evidence as to the identity of the anonymous printer can be found in the approbations in the Slavuta imprints from this period. Although the name of the printer is absent from the title pages, these approbations, which often mention different individuals, allude, in a number of instances, to the identity of the printer. Liberman informs us that the approbation of R. Jacob Samson of Shepetovka (d. 1801), *Av Beit Din* Slavuta, to *Noam Elimelekh* (1794) states that it is given to the distin-

[Fig. 1]

5 Cf. I. RIVKIND: Contributions to the History of Hebrew Printing in Poland. In: *Kiryat Sefer*. XI (1934), pp. 100/1 [Hebrew]. – Cf. also ABRAHAM YAARI: Review of History of Hebrew Printing in Poland. In: *Kiryat Sefer*. IX (1933), pp. 437/8 [Hebrew].
6 Cf. HAIM LIBERMAN: Hebrew Printing in Slavuta. In: *Kiryat Sefer*. XXVII (1951). Reprint: *Ohel* RHL. Brooklyn 1980, I, pp. 199–202 [Hebrew].
7 Cf. CHAVA SHAPIRA: The Brothers Slavuta. In: *ha-Shelo'ah*. XXX (1914), p. 542 [Hebrew].
8 Quoted in LIBERMAN (see note 6), pp. 199/200.

guished Moses, the son of the holy Phinehas. Jacob Samson continues "I have also seen books that were printed previously [by him] and all that he has done is very good."[9] Not all approbations are so explicit. In Abraham ben Mordecai's *Hesed le Avraham* (1794), the name of the printer is mentioned in a cryptic manner, that is, as "the son of Phinehas," leaving no doubt in the knowledgeable reader's mind that it is Moses Shapira, the son of Phinehas ben Abraham of Korets, who is the recipient of the approbation. No approbation makes mention of Dov Baer ben Israel Segal and Dov Baer ben Pesach.

Another conclusion as to the early printer in Slavuta was drawn by Gershom Scholem, who ascribes the Slavuta press to Phinehas [ben Abraham of Korets] Shapira, presumably also based on the approbations. Scholem describes the *Zohar Hadash* and *Tikkunei Zohar* as, "Slobuta ['Slawita'], Pinchas Shapira, 5593 [1793]. [1], 121 Bl. 4°. Slobuta ['Slawita'], Pinchas Shapira, 5553 [1793]."[10]

Clearly, Phinehas Shapira, who died in 1791, was not the printer of either the *Zohar Hadash* or *Tikkunei Zohar*. The approbations to other books, for example, Moses ben Judah ibn Makhir's *Seder ha-Yom* and to *Torat ha-Bayit*, do not comment on the identity of the printer. Nevertheless, the approbation to the latter work refers to the approbation to *Hesed le-Avraham*, thus inferring the same printer issued both works. It should also be noted that typographical material is shared by these works, further suggesting that they were issued by the same print-shop.

Despite the array of evidence marshaled by Liberman that the printer of the first edition of the *Tanya* was Moses Shapira he concludes with the caveat that it is also possible that the print-shop of Dov Baer ben Israel Segal and Dov Baer ben Pesach – initially the second partner was Jacob ben Moses – was also open at an early date, for when R. Shneur Zalman wanted to have the Talmud and the *Arba'ah Turim* published in 1801 the press he turned to was that of the two partners. They printed a number of important works, for example, *Zohar* (1798 and 1809), *Arba'ah Turim* (1801), *Ein Ya'akov* (1806 and 1812), and *Hilkhot Rav Alfas* (1807–10).[11]

This sequence of events was subsequently accepted by Friedberg, for in the second enlarged edition of his *History of Hebrew Typography in Poland* he begins the chapter on Slavuta by stating, "In the city of Slavuta in the province of Volhynia, which, at that time, was under the rule of Duke Hieronomous Yevstai Sangushka [...] a Hebrew press was established in 1791, with the permission of the aforementioned duke, by the rabbi of the community, Moses Shapira."[12]

Liberman suggests that the absence of the name of the printer on books printed before official authorization for a Hebrew press in Slavuta had been granted by the Russian government is not without difficulties. Slavuta did not, as noted earlier, become part of Russia until 1793. This is reflected on the title pages of the first books, where the authority acknowledged, and for some time afterwards as well, is that of the Polish duke Yevstai Sangushka, to whom the town of Slavuta belonged as part of his feudal estates. It would seem then, that prior to 1793 Russian authorization should not have been required. Moses Shapira opened his press

---

[9] Ibid.
[10] Cf. GERSHOM (GERHARD) SCHOLEM: *Bibliographia Kabbalistica; Verzeichnis der gedruckten* [...]. Leipzig 1927, pp. 176 nº 7 and 178 nº 12.
[11] For further discussion of the selection of Slavuta to print the *Tanya* ref. SHALOM DOV BER HA-LEVI WOLPE. In: *Kfar Habad*. 692 (1995), pp. 36/7.
[12] CH. B. FRIEDBERG: *History of Hebrew Typography in Poland from its beginning in the year 1534 and its development to the present.* [...] *Second Edition, Enlarged, improved and revised from the sources.* Tel Aviv 1950, p. 104 [Hebrew]. Unless otherwise noted all further references to the *History of Hebrew Typography in Poland* will be to this edition.

and issued titles prior to 1793, and his name is absent from those books as well. There is no evidence that acquiring authorization was an issue for the Slavuta printer in the dissolving Polish kingdom.

Furthermore, why, if the printer had to conceal his identity, is the place and date of printing stated on the title page, which would make identification of the press a simple matter? Also, as noted above, many title pages, while not mentioning Moses Shapira or any other printer, do identify the individuals who brought the work to press. For example, on the title pages of *Reishit Hohkmah* (1792) and *Zohar Hadash* (1793), respectively, the names of R. Issachar Ber ben Zevi Hirsch of Korets and R. Ezekiel ben Phinehas, the latter Moses Shapira's half-brother, appear prominently on the title pages. Why are their names, and especially that of a Shapira, mentioned on the title page of *Zohar Hadash* if the intent was obfuscation?

Indeed, a work based on Russian archives that discusses the first decade of printing in Slavuta in passing only, *The Drama of Slavuta*, by Saul Moiseyevich Ginsburg, provides another view of contemporary events that addresses our concerns, although it does not explain the absence of the printer's name from the title pages. Ginsburg writes that:

> Tsarina Catherine II, through a separate command of the year 1783 permitted the opening of printing presses without special permission. The Hasidism made broad use of Tsarist command that was valid for fifteen years. Many towns in Volhynia and Podolia, containing Jewish populations, belonging in those days to the feudal lords (Poritzim). The feudal lord (Poritz) would collect "tax" (rental fees) for the ground on which their houses stood. […] Many of the new Jewish printing houses were opened in that time with the permission of the feudal lords. […] In 1792 he [Moses Shapira] opened, with the permission of Count Sangushka, a Jewish printing press in Slavuta. Later, when the laws concerning printing establishments in Russia were changed, he also obtained special permission for his printing press from the Gubernator of Volhynia in December, 1819.[13]

Catherine II, Tsarina of Russia from 1762, daughter of Christian Augustus, prince of Anhalt-Zerbst and wife of Czar Peter III, succeeded her husband, who reigned a mere six months. His brutal and erratic manner, coupled with his unpopular policies, resulted in an army coup, perhaps organized by his wife, in which Peter was killed in 1762. A student of the French Enlightenment, Catherine supported liberal and book arts, although after the French Revolution she became increasingly conservative. She issued an *ukase* (decree), dated January 27, 1783, permitting the establishment of print-shops, without official license, a situation that lasted for about fifteen years. Catherine supported a system of local government which strengthened the authority of the local aristocracy, and, in the Charter to the Nobility of 1785, Catherine increased the control of landlords over peasants and serfs.

Catherine was succeeded by her son, Paul I (1754–1801), known as the Mad Czar, who reigned briefly, until he was assassinated in 1801. In the short time that he ruled Paul attempted to undo much of what his mother had instituted. Nevertheless, one of his first acts, on February 16, 1797, was to confirm one of Catherine's last *ukases*, that ordering unauthorized presses closed and establishing a bureau of censorship.[14]

13 Cf. SAUL MOISEYEVICH GINSBURG: *The Drama of Slavuta*. Tr. EPHRAIM H. PROMBAUM. Lanham 1991, pp. 28–30.
14 Cf. *Encyclopedia Britannica*. Eleventh Edition. New York 1910/1, V, pp. 526–8 and XXIII, pp. 901–3. – Cf. also K. WALISZEWSKI: *Paul the First of Russia, the Son of Catherine the Great*. 1913. Reprint: Hamden 1969, pp. 113/4.

[Fig. 2a]

Many Hasidic presses had opened in Volhynia and Podolia during the period when controls were relatively lax. Taxes and rental fees for the property where the press was located were paid to the local lord, Count Sangushka in Slavuta. Liberman, among others, informs us that a large number of Hebrew printing houses, beginning with Oleksinetz in 1767, existed in the region.[15] While the majority printed a very small number of works, were active for a brief period of time, and were not contemporaneous, their very existence attests to the relatively hospitable climate that allowed them to flourish.

It is during this period that the Slavuta press was established, presumably by Moses Shapira. When the laws concerning printing houses changed around 1798, Moses Shapira applied for permission for his press from the governor of Volhynia. When the laws were again revised in 1819, Moses Shapira requested and received special permission from the Gubernator of Volhynia to continue operating his press.[16] This political situation conforms with Ginsburg's account of events.

If Moses Shapira was the printer of the first books in Slavuta, and it appears that he was, there was no need for him to conceal his identity from the Russian authorities. Before we seek other reasons for the omission of his name from the title pages of the first Slavuta imprints there is the printing press attributed to the partners, Dov Baer ben Israel Segal and Dov Baer ben Pesach, to consider, as well as an additional and more recent suggestion concerning other proprietors of the Slavuta press in its first decade.[17]

The names of the printers appear, beginning in 1799, on the title pages of the books printed in Slavuta. In that year, as mentioned earlier, two titles, a *Zohar* and a Pentateuch, were published; the names of the printers are given as Dov Baer ben Israel Segal and Jacob ben Moses. Six titles are credited to the press in 1801, the *Arba'ah Turim*, *ha-Maggid* (a Bible), and four talmudic treatises (including an Order of Mishnayot). These tractates are part of the first Slavuta Talmud, completed in 1806. The printers names, as given on the title pages of these works, are Dov Baer ben Israel Segal and Dov Baer ben Pesach.

Printing the Talmud was the primary occupation of the Slavuta press during those years, although other, important works were also issued. For example, in 1802, in addition to nine tractates, a *Shulhan Arukh* and a prayer book, *Seder ha-Yom*, were published, and in the following year *Orkhot Zaddikim* and three tractates appeared. 1804 was an especially productive year, for, in addition to seven tractates, a *Zohar* and a large prayer book, *Siddur mi-ha-Ari Kol Ya'acov*, were printed. The prayer book was arranged by R. Jacob Koppel Lipshitz, the author of *Sha'arie Gan Eden*, and an important kabbalist. Thirteen tractates were printed in 1805, in addition to a Pentateuch, *selihot*, *Avodat ha-Kodesh* of the Rashba, *Porat Yosef*, the novellae of R. Joseph ben Benjamin Samegah (d. 1629).

In 1806, the year that this Talmud edition was completed, the press also issued an *Ein Ya'akov*. These titles indicate that the Slavuta press was not only able to undertake a major project such as an edition of the Talmud, but was able to simultaneously print other significant works.

---

15 Cf. HAIM LIBERMAN: Fabrication and Truth Concerning the Hasidic Pressses. In: *Ohel* RHL. III (1984), pp. 19/20 [Hebrew].

16 Cf. GINSBURG (see note 13), pp. 30/1. – *The Jewish Encyclopedia*. Ed. ISADORE SINGER. III. New York 1901–06, p. 650.

17 For an anecdotal account of the founding of the Slavuta press by Moses Shapira see B. FAIGON: Ha-Rav of Liady and the Printer from Slavuta. In: *Marbeh Seforim, Marbeh Hachmah*. Tel Aviv [n. d.], pp. 219–26.

The title pages of that Talmud, a large folio edition, inform that it was printed R. Dov Baer ben Israel Segal and Dov Baer ben Pesach. The monarch mentioned on the title page is Alexander I, who became czar after the assassination of his father, Paul I in 1801. Initially reform-minded, Alexander eventually became reactionary, and, after the Napoleonic wars, attempted to form a world order, the Holy Alliance (Grand Alliance) based on Christian principles.

This Talmud has seven approbations with twelve signatures (four rabbis at the *klaus* in Ostrog) prohibiting the printing of a rival edition for twenty five years. None of the approbations mention the printers, given on the title pages as Dov Baer ben Israel Segal and Dov Baer ben Pesach.[18]

The approbation of the *Kedushat Levi* is granted to Mordecai ben Baruch and Shalom Shakhna ben Noah, to bring "to the press in Slavuta, the most excellent and praiseworthy in the land, the Babylonian Talmud, based on the example of the Amsterdam and Vienna editions, and also the work of Rabbenu Ya'akov ba'al ha-Turim with the [commentaries of *Beit Yosef*, and *Darkhei Moshe* and the annotations of R. Leib Henlish]."

Liberman writes that R. Shneur Zalman of Liady was involved in the publication of this Talmud, although his name is not explicitly mentioned. He adduces this from the above statement in the approbation of the *Kedushat Levi*, that the work was brought to press by R. Mordecai ben Baruch and R. Shalom Shakhna ben Noah, the first the brother of Shneur Zalman of Liady and the second, Shalom Shakhna, Shneur Zalman's son-in-law and the father of R. Menahem Mendel Schneersohn, the third rebbe of Lubavitch (*Tzemah Tzedek* 1789–1866). Furthermore, in the printed version of his approbation to the second Slavuta Talmud (1808–13) the Ba'al ha-Tanya writes that the two had acted on his behalf as his representatives.[19] As we shall see there are difficulties with this approbation, not least the date of death of Shalom Shakhna, who, albeit mentioned in the past tense, appears to have died several years before the printing of this Talmud.[20]

The following year, 1807, the press turned its attention to another large work, *Hilkhot Rav Alfas*, completed in 1810, and also reissued *ha-Maggid*. Here too, the printers names on the title pages are Dov Baer ben Israel Segal and Dov Baer ben Pesach. In 1808 the testament of R. Shabbetai ben Isaiah Horowitz was published and work began on the second Slavuta Talmud, completed in 1813. In the first year of printing four tractates and *Seder Zera'im* were printed, followed, in 1809, by a *Zohar*, Pentateuch, the first two parts of *Lekutei ma-Haran* of Rav Nahum of Bratslav (1772–1810). In 1810 a Passover *Haggadah*, *Metzah Aaron*, and seven tractates were published, followed by, in 1811, four tractates and an *Ein Ya'akov*. In 1812 the *Ein Ya'akov* was completed and seven additional tractates and *Seder Tohorot* were printed.

The second Slavuta Talmud is generally attributed to Moses Shapira by Friedberg, Rabbinovicz, and Vinograd.[21] Nevertheless, it is Dov Baer ben Israel Segal and Dov Baer ben Pesach whose names appear on the title page of almost all the tractates in this Talmud [fig. 2a full page and 2b extract].

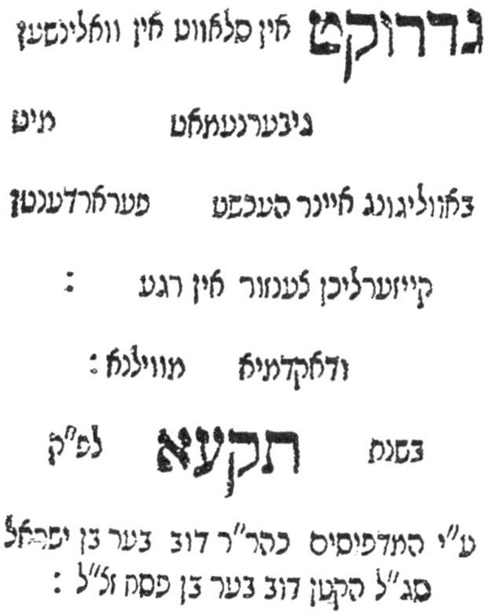

גדרוקט אין סלאוויט אין וואלינשען
מיט ניבערנעמאט
באוויליגונג איינער העכסט פערארדענטן
קייזערליכן צענזור אין ריגע :
ודאקדמיא מווילנא :
בשנת תקעא לפ״ק
ע״י המדפיסים כהר״ר דוב בער בן ישראל
סג״ל הקטן דוד בער בן פסח ז״ל :

[Fig. 2b]

18 Among the signatories are R. Aryeh Leib ben Shalom ha-Levi *Av Beit Din* (head of the rabbinical court) Voltschek, R. Benjamin ben Aaron Broda *Av Beit Din* Grodno (d. 1818), R. Jacob Samson of Shepetova, currently in Tiberias (d. 1801), who had been *Av Beit Din* Slavuta, R. Judah Leib Aeurbach, *Av Beit Din* Tarshin, R. Levi Isaac, *Av Beit Din* Berdichev, R. Bezalel ben Meir Margolius of Zwahil and Ostrog, R. Asher Zevi ben David of Ostrog, R. Judah ben Zevi Hirsch of Ostrog, R. Judah Leib ben Abrham Abele of Kormenetz, R. Joel ha-Kohen ben Nahmun Katz of Byehov, R. Israel Jacob ben Moses Judah, and R. Jacob ben Nathan.
19 Cf. LIBERMAN (see note 6), p. 201.
20 YITZHAK ALFASI: *Encyclopedia Li-Hassidut:Individuals*. Jerusalem 2004, pp. 894/5 [Hebrew] dates Shakhna's death as prior to 1800. HAYYIM MEIR HEILMAN: *Beit Rabbi*. Berdichev 1900. Reprint: Ashdod [n. d.], p. 117 [Hebrew], suggests 1800 or earlier but references the approbation in an accompanying footnote.
21 Cf. FRIEDBERG (see note 12), p. 77. – Cf. also RAPHAEL NATAN NUTA RABBINOVICZ: *Ma'amar al Hadpasat ha-Talmud with Additions*. Ed. A. M. HABERMANN. Jerusalem 1952, p. 129 and VINOGRAD (see note 1), Part II p. 492.

[Fig. 3]

הסכמה והרשאה מהרב המאור הגדול המפורסם החריף ובקי הגאון האמיתי איש אלהי קדוש יאמר לו מוהר"ר שניאור זלמן חונה פה ק"ק לאדי :

ה' חפץ למען צדקו יגדיל תורה והעיר רוח נדיבה בנדיבי עמו ה"ה המחזיק דק"ק סלאוויטא אשר נדב לבו לה' להדפיס הש"ס בבלי וד"ט בדפוסו המשובח שלו המעולה מכל הדפוסים שבמדינות אלו כתבנית אשר נדפסו שם מקרוב ע"י שלוחי מתאי"ע דידי ה"ה האחד המיוחד אחי הרבני המופלג הגאי' מוה' מרדכי נ"י וחד דעמיה הרבני המופלא המנוח מוה' שלום שכנא ז"ל כי ידוע ל. וכאשר יש בידי כתוב וחתום שהיו שלוחים. וכו'. ולזאת אמינא לפעולת טבא חילא לאורייתא והגני פותח פתח לרווחה למחזיק הדפוס הנ"ל הנד. בגדר סגדרו גאוני דורינו בהסכמותיהם על הדפסת הש"ס וד"ט הנ"ל שהדפסנו מקרוב בק"ק הנ"ל סגדרו וגזרו גזירת עירין של אחר כל המדפיסים ועל כללות עמנו י"ל לחזור ולהדפיס הש"ס או הד"ט עד תום משך כ"ה שנים מהתחלת הדפסת הנ"ל וזמנם הנה נל ופוי כח וכוח מהסכמות הגאונים הנ"ל נתובאים נתונים העומד למחזיק הדפוס הנ"ל וכו' כ"כ שחלילה חלילה לשום בר ישראל להשיג גבולו ח"ו לחזור ולהדפיס הש"ס או הד"ט בשום תחבולות וערמה בעולם הן בתבנית זה הן בתבנית אחר עד כלות חמשה ועשרים שנה מיום גלם הדפסת הנ"ל וכל המשיג גבולו ח"ו יהיה נידון בכלל ארור משגיב גבול דעתו וח"ו ארור בו וקללה בו וכו' ח"ו כנודע מנחא"רי ל ולשומעים יונעם ותחא ברכת טוב בכל מילי דמיטיב מוה' הטוב כ"ד המדבר לכבוד ה' ותורתו הקדושה הקטן שניאור זלמן במוה"ו מוה' ברוך ולה"ה

Among the seven approbations accompanying this Talmud are approbations from Shneur Zalman of Liady, Aryeh Leib ben Shalom ha-Levi, R. Benjamin ben Aaron Broda and the Kedushat Levi.[22] All of these rabbinic authorities, except for Shneur Zalman of Liady, who, as we have seen, was instrumental in the previous Talmud being brought to press, had granted approbations to the previous Slavuta Talmud, completed only two years earlier. The approbations given to the printers of the previous edition assigned them the exclusive rights to print the Talmud for a period of twenty five years. Furthermore, the approbations granted to this second Slavuta Talmud are not new approbations but rather are reprints of the approbations granted to the printers of the previous Talmud. If, as many bibliographers believe, the second Talmud was printed by Moses Shapira, an explanation for approving a second Talmud edition by another printer within such a short time frame, and in the same location, prior to the expiration of the first approbation is required.

The approbation granted by Shneur Zalman of Liady, as printed with tractate *Berakhot* includes the following paragraph [fig. 3]:

> the proprietor of the press in the holy congregation of Slavuta, who vowed in his heart to again print the Babylonian Talmud and *Arba'ah Turim* at his praiseworthy press, which is superior to all the presses in these lands, in the manner that it was printed there recently by my representatives, one is my brother, the distinguished, the noble, our teacher, Mordecai [may his light shine], and one of the people, and [...] the late [Shalom Shakhna], as is known to all, that I have written and sealed that they are my representatives. [...] to again print the Babylonian Talmud and *Arba'ah Turim* for a period of twenty five years from the beginning of the above printing [...].

This approbation does not mention the name of Moses Shapira. However, the same approbation, as printed in the collected letters of Shneur Zalman of Liady [fig. 4] specifically mentions Shapira by name and omits that of Shalom Shakhna, stating:

> The Lord desired for His righteousness sake, that the Torah be made great [Isaiah 42:21] and aroused a spirit of philanthropy in the princes of His people [Psalms 113:8], he is ha-Rav [...] the well known, the distinguished in Torah and fear of the Lord, His treasure, the son of the holy, the honorable [...] Moses, *Av Beit Din* of the Congregation Slavuta, who vowed in his heart to the Lord to again print the Babylonian Talmud and *Arba'ah Turim* at his praiseworthy press. [...] on all other printers and on all Israel, that they should not print the Talmud

---

22 The other approbations were from Aryeh Leib ben Shalom, *Av Beit Din* Voltschik, Judah Leib Aeurbach, *Av Beit Din* Vishnitz, and Joseph *Av Beit Din* Kosentin.

or the [*Arba'ah Turim*] for a period of twenty five years from the beginning of the above printing, and now all the rights and privileges from the approbations of the above geonim are assigned to the honorable rav, mentioned above [...]. This is the correct rendering of the text of the approbation, which, in the author's handwriting, mentions Moses Shapira's name rather than the reputed proprietors of the press.[23]

Until recently, bibliographers accepted the statements on the title pages of the first Talmud and other contemporary imprints that Dov Baer ben Israel Segal and Dov Baer ben Pesach were the printers of the books printed in Slavuta at this time. Samuel Weiner, in his catalogue of the Friedland collection, ascribes the 1804/5 *Zohar* to "(the partners: Dov Baer ben Israel Segal and Dov Baer ben Pesach)".[24] Similarly, Gershom Scholem, in *Bibliographia Kabbalistica*, attributes the 1804/5 and 1809/10 editions of the *Zohar* to the partners; the 1815 edition of that work is credited to Moses Shapira. More recently, the *Thesaurus*, which attributes the first imprints to [Moses Shapira] attributes the first two editions of the *Zohar*, and such other works as the *Siddur mi-ha-Ari Kol Ya'akov*, *selihot*, and *Ein Ya'akov*, to Dov Baer ben Israel Segal and Dov Baer ben Pesach.[25]

Liberman was not unaware of the confusion concerning the identity of the Slavuta printer. He arrives at different conclusions for two different works, *Hesed le-Avraham* (1794) and *Hilkhot Rav Alfas* (1807–10). He observes that *Hesed le-Avraham* has an approbation from R. [Jacob] Samson *Av Beit Din* Slavuta, unquestionably given to Moses Shapira, but printed without Shapira's name. He attributes this to the printers being circumspect. Liberman adduces that Moses Shapira was printing in Slavuta in 1800, for in that year a compromise was arrived at between Shapira and the printer in Minkovtsy, Ezekiel ben Shevach, over the right to publish the Prophets and Writings, printed in Minkovtsy in 1800 and in Slavuta in 1801 (*ha-Maggid*).[26] He writes concerning *Hilkhot Rav Alfas*, after noting that Moses Shapira was already printing in 1800, that the title pages mention the names of the two partners whereas the *approbation* from Judah Leib Aeurbach, printed with the second part of that work (1808), is given to Moses *Av Beit Din* of the Congregation Slavuta. Liberman concludes "What is Moses Shapira's name doing here. Wasn't it [*Hilkhot Rav Alfas*] printed at the press of the partners? This matter requires consideration."[27]

Friedberg, who initially suggested that the two print-shops were in competition, had modified his position by the time that the *History of Hebrew Typography in Poland* was reissued in 1950. In the enlarged and revised edition of that work Friedberg now suggests that there was a business relationship between Moses Shapira and Dov Baer ben Israel Segal and Dov Baer ben Pesach. He writes that in about 1801 new typographical material was acquired and that management of the press was handed over to the two partners, whose names subsequently appeared on the title pages as the printers. As before, Moses Shapira continued to conceal his participation in the partnership. Friedberg concludes that there can be no question, however, as to Shapira's involvement with the press. During the printing of the second Talmud, but prior to its completion, Dov Baer ben Israel Segal and Dov Baer ben Pesach withdrew from the press,

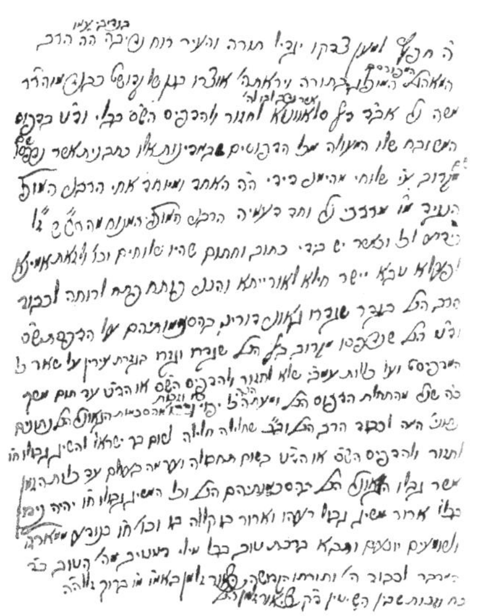

[Fig. 4]

23 *Igrois Koidesh Admur Hazoken, Admur Ha-Emtza'ee, Admur HaTzemach Tzedek* [sic!]. Brooklyn 1987, pp. 133/4 and, for a facsimile of the manuscript copy, p. 389.

24 SAMUEL WEINER: *Kehilat Moshe*. Jerusalem 1969, volume II p. 409 n° 3394A [Hebrew]. WEINER does not suggest a printer for works lacking the name of the printer, such as, *Yismah Lev* (1798) from Menahem Nahum Twersky of Chernobyl, II p. 625 n° 5085.

25 Cf. SCHOLEM (see note 10), p. 170, nos. 18, 21, and 25. – Cf. also VINOGRAD (see note 1), pp. 491/2 nos. 53, 75, and 76.

26 LIBERMAN (see note 6), pp. 201/2. The compromise is printed at the beginning of the book of *Joshua* in the Minkovtsy edition. Printing in Minkovtsy, Podolia, dates from 1796 when Ezekiel ben Shevach and two partners, Joseph ben Isaac and Moses ben Joseph printed Benjamin ben Aaron's *Amtachat Benjamin* on *Megillat Kohelet*. The Prophets and Writings were the last work printed by Ezekiel ben Shevach in Minkovtsy. Concerning this press ref. FRIEDBERG (see note 12), pp. 121/2.

27 LIBERMAN (see note 6), p. 202.

leaving Moses Shapira as the sole proprietor. From this time on Shapira's name appears on the title page of Slavuta imprints.²⁸ Whether Dov Baer ben Israel Segal and Dov Baer ben Pesach were proprietors or pseudonyms is not entirely resolved. What seems certain, however, whatever their true identity or role, they were not the primary proprietors of the press that bears their name.

In 1813, the last year of publication of the second Talmud edition, tractates *Hullin*, *Bekhorot*, *Arakhin*, *Keritot*, *Temurah*, and *Me'ilah* were printed. All of these treatises, as did the earlier tractates, name Dov Baer ben Israel Segal and Dov Baer ben Pesach as the printers, with the exception of *Bekhorot*, which names Moses Shapira as the printer of the tractate. Why Moses Shapira placed his name on one tractate only is not clear. Furthermore, it is Moses Shapira's name that appears on the title pages of subsequent works and on the title pages of the third Slavuta Talmud (1817–22) [fig. 5a full page and 5b extract]. On the title pages of the final and incomplete Talmud (1835), beyond the scope of this paper, the name of Moses Shapira's son appears as "printed by the son of the Rav of Slavuta, the honorable Samuel Abraham Shapira."

Perhaps the answer as to the identity of the proprietor of the Slavuta press is to be found in the approbation given by Shneur Zalman to Moses Shapira for the second Slavuta Talmud "to *again* [emphasis added] print the Babylonian Talmud," suggesting a continuity between the two Talmud editions. It informs us how the Talmud could be reprinted in spite of restrictive approbations within such a short time frame in the same location, and suggests that we have been dealing with a single press, despite the different names on the title pages of the Slavuta imprints.

The question has been raised, however, as to whether Moses Shapira was the sole proprietor of the Slavuta press. Writing on the bicentennial of the publication of the first edition of the *Tanya*, R. Shalom Ber Levin concludes that, based on a study of the approbations accompanying that work, in addition to Moses Shapira, there were silent partners in the press. After briefly reviewing the uncertainty surrounding the identity of the printer of the first Slavuta imprints, the solutions offered by Friedberg and Liberman, Levin writes that Moses Shapira, even in the first years of the press, that is, from 1791 to 1798: "did not direct the press by himself, for he was the rav of the community, but rather he had unnamed partners and directors."²⁹

Levin finds an allusion to these silent partners in the approbation given to the *Tanya* by Meshullam Zusal of Anapoli, where he states that "the Lord aroused the spirit of the partners [...] Shalom Shakhna and Mordecai ben Samuel ha-Levi [...] to bring this work to press," a phrase "customarily understood to refer to the printers rather than the representatives of the author."³⁰ Levin then comments that Shalom Shakhna "was not only a representative of *Rabbenu ha-Zaken* [Schneur Zalman] in printing the *Tanya*, but also a partner in its printing or in directing the press."³¹ He observes that Schneur Zalman used similar language in referring to Shalom Shakhna and Mordecai ben Samuel in the introduction to the *Tanya*. We have already observed a like reference to Shalom Shakhna (and Mordecai

[Fig. 5a]

28 Cf. FRIEDBERG (see note 12), pp. 104/5.
29 SHALOM DOV BER LEVIN: Two Hundred Years Since the First Printing of the Tanya in Slavuta. In: *Kfar Habad*. 693 (1996), p. 52.
30 LEVIN (see note 29), p. 52.
31 Ibid.

ben Baruch) in the approbation issued by the Kedushat Levi to the first Slavuta Talmud.

Levin finds further evidence, albeit circumstantial, in the fact that both men were occupied with printing for a considerable period of time, particularly in the publication of the works of Schneur Zalman. Mordecai ben Samuel was also involved in printing in a number of cities from 1806 to 1826, among them in Shklov, where he printed, perhaps intermittently, from about 1806 to 1814, Kopys, where he was partners with Israel Jaffe, and Sudilkov, where the *Rav Shulkan Arukh* was published in 1826.³² Shalom Shakhna was involved in the publication of the *Arba'ah Turim* and the Talmud in Slavuta, as noted above, as well as the *Tanya*.

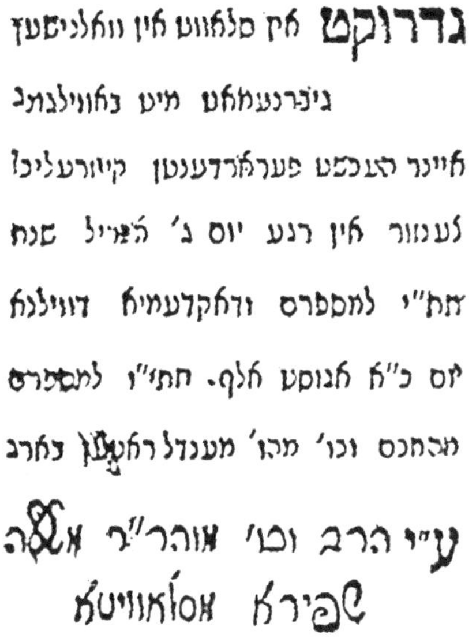

The involvement of Shalom Shakhna and Mordecai ben Samuel Horowitz with the Slavuta press can not be questioned. The arguments that they were silent partners, that is, proprietors in the press, is not compelling. Levin notes that Shakhna and Horowitz's primary purpose was the publication of the works of Schneur Zalman. As we have seen, Liberman determined that the printer of the first Slavuta imprints was Moses Shapira based on approbations granted to him for works in which there was no other reference to the printer. Furthermore, with the exception of the approbation of the Kedushat Levi to the first Talmud and the *Arba'ah Turim*, admittedly major works, the only books for which a relationship to these partners can be made are works written by the Ba'al ha-Tanya. In the case of the Kedushat Levi, the reference can also be understood, as Liberman does, to reflect the interest and approval of Schneur Zalman. We might inquire as to why their names are also absent from the books printed in Slavuta and when their involvement ceased.

As noted above, at least two early Slavuta imprints, *Reishit Hohkmah* (1792) and *Zohar Hadash* (1793), state on their title pages that they were brought to press, respectively, by Issachar Ber ben Zevi Hirsch of Korets and Ezekiel ben Phinehas, Moses Shapira's half-brother. On the title page of a slightly later work, *Siddur mi-ha-Ari Kol Ya'akov* (1804), the names of R. Aaron of Mezhirech and Issachar Ber ben Zevi Hirsch of Korets are mentioned as having brought the subject work to press, followed by a comment as to the expenditure of their money to publish the book, a phrase reserved for the sponsors of a work. Were Issachar Ber and Ezekiel ben Phinehas early partners in the press, or more likely, was their responsibility or participation limited to financing publications printed in Slavuta by Moses Shapira? Ezekiel ben Phinehas printed several kabbalistic books at presses owned by printers known for their piety. He was not, however, the proprietor of the press. Yet a cautionary note is in order. The sponsor of *Me'or Einayim* (1798) is referred to on the title page in a more customary manner, that is "at the command and expense" of Elijah ben Zev Wolf, that is, he was a sponsor only, likely without further involvement in the publication.

Shalom Shakhna and Mordecai ben Samuel, in contrast, were involved in the publication of the works of Schneur Zalman, taking great interest and care in their printing, reflecting their responsibility to the Ba'al ha-Tanya. This did not necessitate, however, their being proprietors. Never-

גדרוקט אץ סלאווט אין וואלינישען
גובערנעמטין מיט באוולנגתב
אייגר הגכמט פעראארדענטן קיוזרעליכן
לענזור אין רעג יוס ג' הציל שנת
תת"י למספרס ודהקדעמיח דווילגת
יום כ"א אנוסע אלף. תתי"ו למספרס
מהחכם וכו' מהו' מענדל רחאלן כארב
ע"י הרב ופו' אוהר"ר אלה
שפירא אסלאוויטא

[Fig. 5b]

32 FRIEDBERG (see note 12), pp. 135/6 writes that Mordecai ben Samuel Horowitz opened his press in Shkolov after printing in Kopys until 1810. LEVIN (see note 29), p. 52, however, based on MONDSHEIN (see note 3), p. 55, notes that Mordecai ben Samuel, together with Isaac ben Samuel, printed an edition of the *Tanya* in Shkolov in 1806 and that he was still active in Kopys as late as 1816 when the prayer-book of Schneur Zalman was printed.

theless, whatever the involvement of Shalom Shakhna and Mordecai ben Samuel in the Slavuta press, and Dov Baer ben Israel Segal and Dov Baer ben Pesach as well, it is evident that it was Moses Shapira managed and bore primary responsibility for that print-shop. He was the printer of the Slavuta books issued from 1791 to 1798 and managed the press later, giving it over to his sons when he retired.

Turning to Moses Shapira, we find that he was a scion of the Spira (Spiro, Shapira) family, whose members shared a reputation for piety, charity, and good works. He was the descendant of a long line of talmudic scholars, among them R. Nathan Nata ben Samson Spira (d. 1577), rabbi of Grodno and author of *Mebo Shearim*, on the classical work on shehitah, *Sha'arei Dura* (Cracow 1574) and *Imrei Shefer*, a super-commentary on the Torah commentary of Rashi (Cracow/Lublin 1597). R. Spira's grandson, R. Nathan Nata ben Solomon Spira (1585–1633), rabbi of Cracow, wrote both talmudic and cabalistic books, including two distinct works entitled *Megalleh Amukkot*, one containing 252 explanations of Moses' prayer in the verse in Deuteronomy 3:23 (Cracow 1637), and the other a Torah commentary (Lemberg 1795). Among this Spira's students was the famed R. Shabbetai b. Meir Kohen (*Shakh*, 1622–63).[33]

Moses Shapira's grandfather was R. Abraham Abba Shapira ben Phinehas of Shklov, a Lithuanian talmudic scholar. Forced to flee Lithuania as the result of a false accusation, Abraham Abba resettled in Miropol, Vohlynia. Although he came from a *mitnagid* (opponents of Hasidism) environment, Abraham Abba met the Ba'al Shem Tov and was sufficiently impressed to urge his son to join the new movement.[34]

Abraham Abba's son, Moses Shapira's father, was the *zaddik* R. Phinehas ben Abraham of Korets (1726–91).[35] Born in Shklov, Phinehas resided, at various times, in Korets, Ostrog, and Shepetovka, but is known as the Koretser from his long residence there.[36] He signature on his correspondence includes the family name Shapira, an unusual usage for the time, done because he cherished the name, tracing it back to Speyer in the middle ages.[37] Phinehas was, in addition to his talmudic scholarship, well versed in grammar and philosophy, and a student of the *Zohar*. Although deeply influenced by the Ba'al Shem Tov, whom he credited with changing his life, subsequently devoting himself to mystical studies, Phinehas did not regard himself as a student of the founder of the Hasidic movement.[38]

Moses Shapira was born about 1760/62 to Treina bat Jonah, the first wife of Phinehas, who died in the forest, where she had fled to escape from a plague ravaging the city.[39] From his youth Moses Shapira demonstrated a proficiency in graphic arts, so that his father, who believed that a person should be self-supporting and adhering to the injunction that a man should teach his son a craft (ref. *Kiddushin* 82a), had him instructed in – or Moses Shapira, sharing that belief, taught himself – the engravers craft. The letters that he engraved "excelled in their beauty and clarity. Jews used to say that 'the Holy Presence rested on them.'"[40]

Moses Shapira, and his sons after him, was the primary employer in Slavuta, engaging both Jewish and non-Jewish workers. It seems that

---

33 Yet another Spira (Shapira) of the same name, Nathan Nata ben Reuben David Tebele Spira (d. 1666), grandson of the second Nathan Nata, was a renowned kabbalist. He served as rabbi of a number of Polish communities before settling in the land of Israel, where he became rabbi of the Ashkenaz community. This Spira died in Italy, having gone there to raise funds for the community in Israel, which was in dire financial straits.

34 Cf. MILTON ARON: *Ideas and Ideals of the Hassidim*. New York 1969, p. 63.

35 Korets was not only a center of Hasidut, but was, perhaps for that reason, also home to four Hebrew print-shops, some associated with presses in Shklov, Nowy Dwor, and Ostraha. VINOGRAD (see note 1), pp. 599–602 records 135 titles attributed to Korets between the years 1776 to 1824. FRIEDBERG (see note 12), pp. 73–5 discusses Hebrew printing in Korets.

36 Korets, currently in the Ukraine, but previously part of Poland, was one of the oldest Jewish communities in that land, dating back to the 13th century. Between 1766 and 1819 four Hebrew presses in Korets, a number associated with presses in Shklov, Nowy Dwor, and Ostrog printed almost 100 books, primarily works of Kabbalah and Hasidus, which were an important factor in the spread of Hasidism. *Encyclopaedia Judaica*. Ed. MICHAEL BERENBAUM and FRED SKOLNIK. Vol. 12. 2nd ed. Detroit 2007, p. 308.

37 ISAAC RAFAEL: *On Hasidus and Hasidim*. Jerusalem 1991, p. 75 nº 23. Another distinguished family that traced its origins to Speyer is the Soncino family of printers, who traced their ancestry to the thirteenth-century Tosafist, R. Moses of Speyer.

38 Ibid., p. 76.

39 HAYYIM SHAPIRA: A Genealogical manuscript of the descendants of Rabbi Phinehas of Korets and Rabbi Zusha of Anapoli. In: *Siftei Zaddikim*. III (1991), pp. 89/90. SHAPIRA further informs us that Phinehas was earlier engaged to a Zlota, but broke that engagement. His first marriage to Hannah of Hemmelnick ended in divorce when her brothers attempted to trick Phinehas into violating the stringencies he observed in regard to Passover.

40 FRIEDBERG (see note 12), p. 104. – Cf. also GINSBURG (see note 13), pp. 29/30. – Cf. also SHAPIRA (see note 7), p. 542.

they were highly regarded by all, and when charges were later brought against the Shapiras they were neither initiated nor supported by their employees. The Shapiras printed works of an orthodox nature only, of Hasidic, ethical, or halakhic content, with the total and intentional exclusion of *haskalah* titles. His reputation for piety, humility, and charity, together with the quality of his press work, gained Moses Shapira's printshop a positive reputation in religious circles. This must certainly have been a factor in Shneur Zalman of Liady's selection of the Slavuta press, in addition to any sense of gratitude to Phinehas of Korets, as the printshop for the first edition of the *Tanya*. In addition, Moses Shapira was also the rav and *Av Beit Din* in Slavuta. There was, as noted above, a second rav in the community, R. Jacob Samson of Shepetovka, and it seems that Shapira served in that capacity infrequently. Friedberg suggests that it was because of his position as rav in Slavuta that Moses Shapira did not place his name on the title pages of the Slavuta imprints.[41]

In conclusion, Moses Shapira was a skilled craftsman and was, through that craft, self-supporting. He was known for his piety, integrity, and humility. Descended from a distinguished rabbinic family Shapira would not have done anything to sully his or his family's reputation. Given the responsibilities of his rabbinic position and the potential conflict, no matter how unlikely, between those duties and his chosen craft, it seems likely that Moses Shapira intentionally separated his professional activities and rabbinic duties to avoid any suggestion of impropriety. There is no reference in any source for the two partners whose names appear on the title pages of early Slavuta imprints, suggesting that they are pseudonyms. There are, however, allusions and references in the approbations to Moses Shapira. Together with what we know of his personality, we have credible support for the position that for the period under consideration Moses Shapira was not only the first printer in Slavuta but was the only printer in Slavuta.

---

41 Cf. FRIEDBERG (see note 12), p. 104.

STEVEN VAN IMPE

The Social and Geographical Repositioning of a Minor Printer in Eighteenth Century Antwerp

THE HISTORY OF THE BOOK in Antwerp is strongly associated with Christophe Plantin and the Officina Plantiniana which he founded in 1555 and which continued to exist under the Moretus family until the nineteenth century. The importance of the rich archives of the Officina is exemplified by their UNESCO recognition as part of the "Memory of the World".[1] This situation has, however, drawn attention away from other printing firms in Antwerp. More importantly, the exceptional position of the Officina Plantiniana means that it is dangerous to draw general conclusions based upon its unique status. The ongoing research by Stijn van Rossem on the Verdussen firm is a first important step to begin readjusting the image we have of printing in Antwerp after the sixteenth century.[2]

In the present article I will be looking at another Antwerp printer, Jan Baptist Carstiaenssens. Carstiaenssens' name can be found on publications from 1772 to 1810, proving that his career spanned almost four decades.[3] Like Plantin, he lived in a difficult and confusing time with political instability and economic hardship. But where Plantin printed for kings, Carstiaenssens printed for the lower classes. It may be a sign of the existing differences between the two that we know what Plantin looked like because Rubens painted his portrait, whereas for Carstiaenssens all we have is a description from an arrest warrant. In this article, I will describe how Carstiaenssens gradually came to print almost exclusively the cheapest publications.

An unhappy life

When Cristiaenssens started his career, the city of Antwerp was part of the Austrian Netherlands, and firmly Catholic. The river Scheldt had been closed since 1585. In that year, the Protestant insurgents were driven from Antwerp by the troops of the Spanish king. The rebellious provinces in the North would form the independent, Protestant United Provinces. They blocked all direct traffic over the river Scheldt, holding Antwerp in an economical stranglehold. The Golden Age came to an end when Spanish troops reconquered the city on the Protestant United Provinces. The Golden Age was a distant memory, but that does not mean that this was an age of extreme poverty. There was political stability, which also benefited the economy. The Plantin firm still sent its liturgical books worldwide, but this was an exception. Most printers catered to a regional market. There was a small top layer of publishers who formed a modest part of the "Catholic enlightenment", like the well-known publisher

---

This article is based on a lecture given on 17. 8. 2010 at the 18th SHARP Conference in Helsinki, where I received valuable input. I thank Dr. Annika Bautz and Dr. Goran Proot for their helpful comments on an earlier version of this paper.

1 Cf. www.unesco.org [13. 12. 2010].

2 Cf. for example STIJN VAN ROSSEM: The Bookshop of the Counter-Reformation Revisited. The Verdussen Company and the Trade in Catholic Publications, Antwerp, 1585–1648. In: *Quaerendo*. 38 (2008), pp. 306–21.

3 A detailed biographical account of Carstiaenssens' life may be found in STEVEN VAN IMPE: Verloren illusies of bijgestelde ambities? Leven en loopbaan van Jan Baptist Carstiaenssens. In: *De Gulden Passer*. 87.2 (2009), pp. 69–91. This is the first study in any detail since FLORIS PRIMS: Het drukkersproces Carstiaenssens. In: *Antverpiensia*. IX (1935), pp. 241–7 (which does not cite its sources). Overview articles mention his name in passing, and some details can be found in HENRY DE GROOTE: *Vijftig jaar boekdrukkunst te Antwerpen 1764–1841*. Antwerpen 1961.

Joannes Petrus Josephus Grangé, but most of their colleagues printed chapbooks, prayer books, songbooks, almanacs and the like.[4] The leading cultural center in the Low Countries was now the capital Brussels. In this respect, Antwerp had become a second-rate city like so many others.[5]

Carstiaenssens became a master printer in 1772. A few years earlier, he had associated himself with bookseller and publisher Michael Bruers and his wife Catharina Everaerts. It was Catharina Everaerts who formed the link to an old printing family through her father Alexander Everaerts (active 1722–67). With a loan from his former boss, Carstiaenssens bought a house and printing equipment, and after a period of "job printing", started a firm of his own. The beginning of his career coincides almost exactly with the first signs that the tranquil period described above was coming to an end. In 1773, by papal decree, the Jesuit order was disbanded, and this was a major blow to the printing industry. Not only were the Jesuits avid students, readers and buyers of books, they were also prolific writers.[6] In the decades to come, the Emperor Joseph II would drastically reform both the political and religious infrastructure in the countries under his dominion, leading to a pamphlet war unheard of in the history of the Southern Netherlands and, eventually, to the Brabant Revolution of 1789/90. After the death of Joseph II, his brother Leopold managed to restore order to the Austrian Netherlands, only to be driven out eventually by the French revolutionary army (1792–94). The Catholic church, already under pressure in Emperor Joseph II's time, was now oppressed even further.[7]

Meanwhile, Carstiaenssens' personal life was also in crisis. After losing his first wife Cornelia Jacobs (died 1774), who was very probably also his shopkeeper, he remarried in 1776. Shortly after that, he had to declare bankruptcy; his new wife Isabella de Gorter filed for a divorce before the marriage was a year old. She managed to convince her husband's creditors to reimburse her dowry and thus became a creditor herself.[8] However, when Carstiaenssens obtained "letters of cession", protecting him from further creditors, the couple was reunited and Carstiaenssens used his wife's money to begin anew. This was not to the liking of his largest creditor and former boss Michael Bruers and his wife Catharina Everaerts, who suspected a scam.

Up to this point, Jan Baptist Carstiaenssens seems to have enjoyed some repute as a publisher. One of his very first books, published in 1773 in association with Michael Bruers, contained a set of engravings of snow statues, and was edited by the Count de Robiano. Copies of this book are to be found in art collections and libraries worldwide. Carstiaenssens also continued the publication project of a Dutch Bible translation with extensive commentaries (in Latin and including Greek and Hebrew citations) by the Franciscan friars, and became the designated printer for doctoral theses defended by the Franciscans in their Antwerp school for theology and linguistics.[9] He published some literature in the vernacular, two medical manuals for which he advertised in several weekly newspapers not only in Antwerp but also in Louvain and Mechelen, and, like most printers, prayer books and other devotional works.[10]

4 Cf. HELMA HOUTMAN-DE SMET: «Le gros libraire» Joannes Petrus Josephus Grangé. Beknopte geschiedenis van de Antwerpse drukkerij en boekhandel Grangé (18de en 19de eeuw). In: *Cultuurgeschiedenis in de Nederlanden van de Renaissance naar de Romantiek. Liber amicorum J. Andriessen s. j., A. Keersmakers, P. Lenders s. j.* Leuven 1986, pp. 179–202.
5 Cf. ALFONS K. L. THIJS: *Van geuzenstad tot katholiek bolwerk. Maatschappelijke betekenis van de Kerk in contrareformatorisch Antwerpen.* Turnhout 1990. – Antwerpen in de XVIIIde eeuw. Instellingen, economie, cultuur. Antwerpen 1952 (Uitgaven van het Genootschap voor Antwerpse Geschiedenis. 3).
6 Cf. Jesuit books in the Low Countries, 1540–1773. Ed. PAUL BEGHEYN et al. Leuven 2009 (Documenta Libraria. 38).
7 Cf. *La Belgique autrichienne, 1713–1794: les Pays-Bas méridionaux sous les Habsbourgs d'Autriche.* Ed. HERVÉ HASQUIN. Brussels 1987.
8 According to the Antwerp customary law, the personal properties a woman had acquired before marriage could not be seized to pay off debts incurred by her husband: BART WILLEMS: *Leven op de pof. Krediet bij de Antwerpse middenstand in de achttiende eeuw.* Amsterdam 2009, pp. 83–5.
9 Cf. STEPHANUS SCHOUTENS: *Geschiedenis van het voormalig minderbroedersklooster te Antwerpen (1446–1797).* Antwerpen 1894, p. 158–82. – Cf. also C. DE CLERCQ: La »versio Belgica« de la Bible du franciscain Guillaume Smits. In: *De Gulden Passer.* 33 (1955), pp. 48–91.
10 Many thanks to Dr. Goran Proot and Dr. Godelieve Spiessens for alerting me to several advertisements by Carstiaenssens in the *Wekelyks bericht uit Mechelen* and the *Gazette van Antwerpen*. For more context cf. CLAUDE BRUNEEL: Les annonces littéraires dans le Wekelyks Nieuws uyt Loven. In: *Het oude en het nieuwe boek. De oude en de nieuwe bibliotheek. Liber amicorum H. D. L. Vervliet.* Ed. JULIEN VAN BORM and LUDO SIMONS. Kapellen 1988, pp. 271–83.

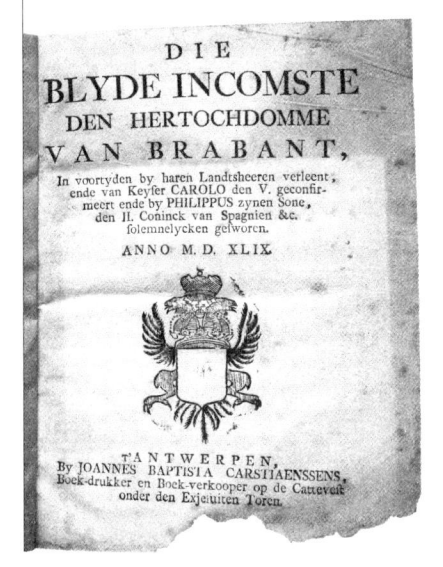

[Fig. 1] Title page of Carstiaenssens' reissue of *Die blyde incomste den hertochdomme van Brabant*, one of the old constitutional texts that was used to justify the Brabant Revolution (Stadsarchief Mechelen, A.10761/A)

11 Cf. JAN ROEGIERS: At the origin of revolution: printing in exile. In: *Quaerendo*. 38 (2008), pp. 322–32. – Cf. also GEERT VAN DEN BOSSCHE: *Enlightened innovation and the ancient constitution. The intellectual justification of Revolution in Brabant (1787–1790)*. Brussels 2001.
12 Cf. JAN FRANS VAN DER STRAELEN/JAN BAPTIST VAN DER STRAELEN: *De kronijk van Antwerpen*. Ed. A. VAN BERENDONCKS and J. RYLANT. Antwerpen 1929–35 (8 vols.), vol. VI, p. 221. – PRIMS (see note 3), pp. 241–7. – DE GROOTE (see note 3), passim.
13 As of 30 September, 2010 the database contains 316 records of different editions in 612 copies, 196 of which have so far been catalogued based on autopsy of a copy.
14 Editions which cannot be assigned to an address were excluded from the data sets used for this analysis. Data harvested from online library catalogues is not always sufficient to place an edition with a certain address, and the criteria used for determining the format or the number of pages (including or excluding blank or unnumbered pages) differ widely.

[Table 1]

STREET	SHOP SIGN	TIME PERIOD	EDITIONS
Blauwhandse rui	In de Zwarte adelaar	02.1772 – 03.1773	15
Klapdorp	In het Wit kruis	06.1773 – 1778	44
Sint-Kathelijnevest	In het Wit kruis	1778 – 04.1789	85
Steenhouwersvest		04.1789 – 04.1810	134

As a printer of theological and devotional books, and as a religious person himself, Carstiaenssens was directly affected by the dramatic measures taken by Emperor Joseph II. The publication of the Bible translation by the Franciscans was halted. Little wonder that Carstiaenssens ended up in the revolutionary camp. He supported the case by reprinting old constitutional texts that demonstrated that the Provincial States had primacy over the emperor, and when revolution finally did break out he printed declarations of the United Belgian States.[11]

He would continue this pro-Catholic stance during the French revolutionary period, with severe consequences: he was imprisoned for a year for printing pamphlets against the republic, and his house was raided when it was suspected that he hid a priest and held secret masses. In the end, the French authorities denied him a printing license. Carstiaenssens died in 1812, 79 years old, after a printing career of 38 years. In the last 20 years of his life, apart from anti-French pamphlets, his production consisted almost exclusively of devotional texts, most of them smaller than a single sheet of paper. For a man who had started his career with a book of engravings edited by a count, this was clearly a downfall.[12]

The output

This qualitative appreciation of Carstiaenssens' output can be confirmed by a chronological analysis of the size of his publications. To this end I created a bibliographical database that I filled with information taken from various sources, mostly library catalogs. To complete the data, I examined as many copies as possible.[13] Many editions were printed without a date, but because most of them have an address in the imprint or colophon I was able to at least file them under the correct period in Carstiaenssens' life, represented by the letters A to D [see table 1]. We should keep in mind that not all addresses were used for an equal amount of time, and that printing many smaller publications may take the same amount of time as one larger book.

The specific nature of Carstiaenssens' publications poses another problem. In the eighteenth century, the price of paper was one of the most important factors in the production of a book. In book historical research, the accepted unit of measurement is therefore the sheet of paper. However, many of Carstiaenssens' publications are smaller than a single sheet of paper, and we have no way of knowing whether he printed several editions of the same text, or several different texts on the same sheet. We will have to work with less reliable data such as pagecounts and bibliographical format. Fortunately, both show a clear pattern that leaves no doubts regarding its interpretation.[14]

[Table 2] Size ratio per address

ADDRESS / FORMAT	1°	4°	8°	12°	16°	24°
Blauwhandse rui	–	1	6	8	–	–
Klapdorp	–	1	16	9	–	–
Sint-Kathelijnevest	1	12	16	34	–	–
Steenhouwersvest	2	17	19	58	2	1

[Table 3] Pagecount per address

ADDRESS / PAGECOUNT	1–4 pp.	5–32 pp.	33–96 pp.	> 96 pp.
Blauwhandse rui	7	6	2	2
Klapdorp	7	17	5	6
Sint-Kathelijnevest	24	34	6	10
Steenhouwersvest	63	34	12	5

The graphs show that Carstiaenssens' output shifted throughout time. The number of editions in 12° increased significantly during the second half of his career, as did the number of editions with a short text. Note that the increase in the number of editions runs parallel to the number of years Carstiaenssens lived at these addresses. The typical product of Carstiaenssens' press is indeed the four page duodecimo containing a prayer, most often a litany. These are found by the dozen in pamphlet volumes, typically including a few dozen litanies by different printers. Many more that remained unbound have probably not survived.

Geographical repositioning

We can follow Carstiaenssens' decline on the social ladder not just in his production, but also in the consecutive residences he took up in Antwerp. Whereas most publishing firms remained in the same building for generations, Carstiaenssens had no less than four different addresses throughout his career [fig. 3].[15]

His first domicile, *De Zwarte adelaar* (the Black Eagle), which he bought in 1770 with a loan from Michael Bruers, was situated on the Blauwhandse Rui in the northern district of the city, in a neighborhood with many warehouses and proto-industrial activity, for example brewing and cloth dying. This may have been a fine location for printing and storing books, but not so much for bookselling. The idea was probably that Carstiaenssens would act as a semi-independent printer, selling his books through the shop of Bruers, which was situated closer to the city center and near many other bookshops.[16]

But after a year, Carstiaenssens started renting his own shop a few hundred meters closer to the shopping district, at Klapdorp. This was the street of the popular bookshop *in de Vyf Ringen* (in the Five Rings), where generations of booksellers sold chapbooks and other cheap works.[17] Carstiaenssens never printed chapbooks himself, although advertisements indicate that he did sell them. It is very probable that he printed his theological, medical and literary publications at the Black Eagle on the Blauwhandse Rui, but sold them at Klapdorp. It is at this point in his career that Carstiaenssens went bankrupt, possibly because he was living

15 The study of the locations of printing offices is a difficult but exciting research topic; changes in address are obscured by catalogs or bibliographies citing only the city where a certain edition was printed, but the imprint on the book often mentions the street address and shop sign as well. Inheritance through the female line, or an assistant taking over his master's shop, should also be taken in consideration. Many workshops remained on the same location for generations, as documented for the case of Leuven by PIERRE DELSAERDT: *Suam quisque bibliothecam: boekhandel en particulier boekenbezit aan de oude Leuvense universiteit, 16de–18de eeuw.* Leuven 2001, pp. 73–118. It is difficult to assess how extraordinary Carstiaenssens was in this respect; for anecdotal evidence of a printer relocating throughout his career, cf. JUDITH GROOTENDORST: "Broer Jansz" omzwervingen door zeventiende-eeuws Amsterdam. In: *Janboel. Opstellen aangeboden aan Jan Bos bij de afronding van de Short-Title Catalogue, Netherlands.* Den Haag 2009, pp. 11–6.

16 I found but few editions with Bruers' name in the imprint. Further bibliographical analysis is needed to establish whether these publications were actually printed by Carstiaenssens.

17 Notably members of the family Willemsens (relations of Catharina Everaert) until 1767 and then Franciscus Ignatius Vinck (active 1768–84) and possibly his sons. Cf. FRANS OLTHOFF: *De boekdrukkers, boekverkoopers en uitgevers in Antwerpen sedert de uitvinding van de boekdrukkunst tot op onze dagen.* Antwerpen 1891, p. 131.

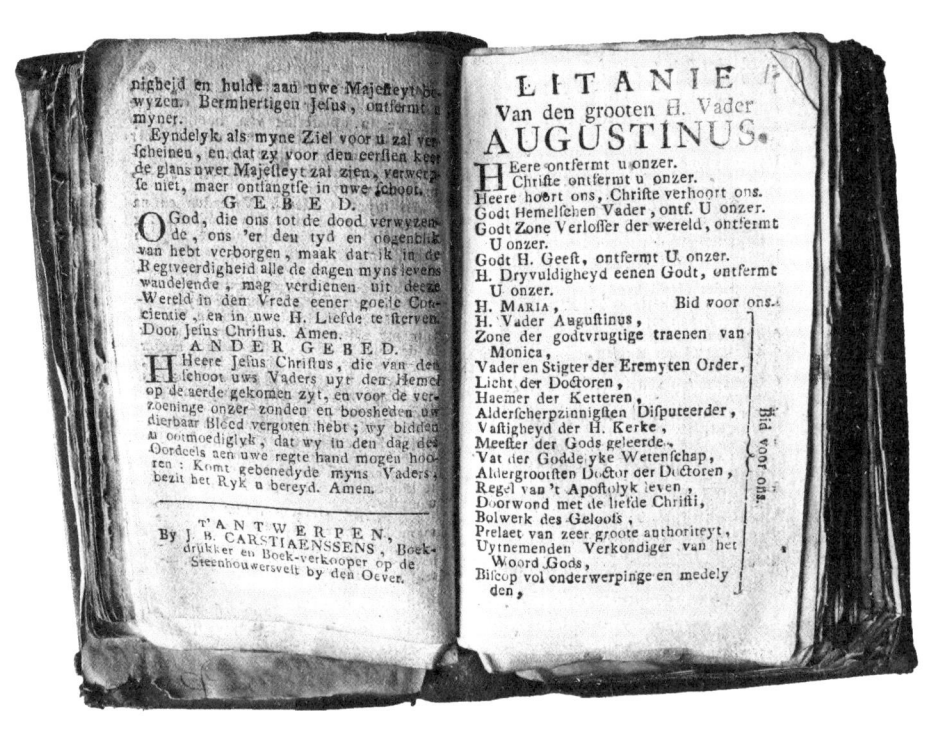

[Fig. 2] Two litanies printed by Carstiaenssens, later bound in a pamphlet volume: on the left fol. [A]2 verso, with the colophon, of *Litanie om een goede dood te verkrygen*, on the right fol. [A]1 recto of *Litanie van den grooten H. vader Augustinus*. (Antwerp, Ruusbroec-genootschap, RG 3096 E 1)

beyond his means, having bought one house and renting another, and having invested in printing material: presses, letters, ink and paper.[18]

A year after his bankruptcy, Carstiaenssens moved again, setting up shop at the Katelijnevest, in the heart of the printing district. Among his neighbors were not only his former boss and creditor Michael Bruers but also the successful publisher Hubert Bincken. Several other booksellers lived nearby. Carstiaenssens remained here for ten years, printing mostly devotional books, prayers and anti-reform pamphlets.[19]

In the days leading up to the Brabant Revolution Carstiaenssens moved again, this time to the Steenhouwersvest. Although located just around the corner of the famous Officina Plantiniana, this was definitely not the hub of the Antwerp's book industry. The Friday Market, where all kinds of goods had been sold publicly since the fifteenth century, had a rather bad name. The Steenhouwersvest was taken up mostly by second-hand shops catering to the poorer citizens of Antwerp, hence the popular name "Rag Street". The Oever, on the corner of which Carstiaenssens rented his shop, was a permanent flea market. These streets formed the transition between the city center and the St. Andries-quarter, one of the poorest parts of town known in the nineteenth century as the "parish of misery". It seems that regarding the location of his business, Carstiaenssens had reached rock bottom.[20]

But is this really true? So far, it seems that I have chronicled the downfall of an unhappy printer, a story that might remind us of a novel in the tradition of Dostoyevsky. But there is another way of looking at the data. After all, Carstiaenssens managed to remain in business for 20 more years at the Steenhouwersvest. Having focused on the consecutive geographical locations of Carstiaenssens' printshop, let us now take the position of eighteenth century printers in society into account.

18 Although the dossier of Carstiaenssens' bankrupcy, kept in the Antwerp City Archives, is fragmentary and vague, I have been able to reconstruct at least a part of the economical network. I hope to be able to publish more details at a later stage.
19 LEON VOET: Boeken en drukkers. In: *Antwerpen in de* XVIIIde *eeuw* (see note 5), pp. 314–47, here p. 317.
20 ILJA VAN DAMME: *Verleiden en verkopen: Antwerpse kleinhandelaars en hun klanten in tijden van crisis (ca. 1648–ca. 1748)*. Amsterdam 2007, pp. 84/5.

Social repositioning

Henri-Jean Martin described the bookshop as a «lieu de sociabilité», a social meeting point, with the bookseller as a mediator, the hub in a micro-environment.[21] It seems that Carstiaenssens played this role quite well in the second half of his career. His opposition to the Josephine reforms must have generated some notoriety in the days leading up to the Brabant revolution, as proven by the fact that his shop was raided by the police.[22]

Especially during the French period (1794–1814) Carstiaenssens became a local celebrity. He is mentioned from time to time in the detailed chronicle of historian and bibliophile Jean-Baptiste Van der Straelen (1761–1847), a well-to-do Catholic citizen who may have been a part of the social circle of the printer.[23] During the time when church services were suspended, Carstiaenssens arranged readings of the rosary in his bookshop. When the authorities raided one of those prayer meetings, suspecting to find a forbidden mass and a priest in hiding, they found a large group of attendants. Half a year later, another raid revealed anti-revolutionary pamphlets being printed, and Carstiaenssens was taken into custody and tried. According to Van der Straelen, the proceedings were followed by "thousands" of people. When the verdict came around two o'clock at night the crowd sighed with relief: the printer had only received a sentence of one year of imprisonment, where many had feared that he would be guillotined.[24] Even if we take this eye-witness account with a pinch of salt, it is clear that Carstiaenssens' trial was anxiously followed by a large group of people. A few years after being released, Carstiaenssens was again accused of printing anti-revolutionary tracts, proving how important the production of these texts must have been to him. So far, I have not been able to determine the outcome of this second trial.[25]

The model developed by Henri-Jean Martin for upper class printers can be applied to printers and booksellers in the lower regions of society as well. Carstiaenssens was not able to work his way into the higher echelons, where it seems that he was always an outsider. By taking a step down and moving his shop to the Steenhouwersvest, he almost literally placed himself in the center of the poorer part of Antwerp, where he became a man of repute. In the absence of egodocuments, it is impossible to determine whether this was a conscious decision or not. It is tempting to see a link to one of the many prayers Carstiaenssens printed (and reprinted a couple of times). It is a prayer of submission to the will of God:

> Blind, crazy and miserable am I, I presume to know what I need. [...] Without thee, I go as a blindman, I conduct myself as a madman, I let myself be brought down by the least misfortune, like a man without courage. [...] And yet I think greatly of myself. [...] Thou changeth all my mysery into good; the loss, the tortures, the misadventures that befall me, become under Thy hands the sources of graces and gifts. [...] And Thou leadst me often into my happiness, by the same road that I take to be my doom.[26]

It is very well possible that Carstiaenssens was forced by economical circumstances to limit his printing to the four-page duodecimo litanies and prayers that make up the bulk of his production at the Steenhouwersvest. They require little investment in paper, labor and storage; because

21 HENRI-JEAN MARTIN: Les espaces de la vente à Paris à l'époque artisanale. In: *Le livre français sous l'Ancien Régime*. Revised and ed. HENRI-JEAN MARTIN. Paris 1987, pp. 89–111.
22 Cf. VAN DER STRAELEN (see note 12), vol. 3, p. 91.
23 Cf. H. VANDER LINDEN: Straelen (Jean-Baptiste vander). In: *Biographie nationale*. Brussels 1926–29, vol. 24, col. 107/8. – Cf. also ALPHONSE GOOVAERTS: [Introduction]. In: *Les collections Van der Straelen-Moons-van Lerius à Anvers. Catalogue raisonné*. Anvers [1884], vol. 1, pp. I–XIX.
24 Cf. VAN DER STRAELEN (see note 12), vol. 6, p. 234.
25 Cf. VAN IMPE (see note 3), p. 86/7.
26 *Gebed van overgevinge in de gelykvormigheyd aen den wille van Godt*. Antwerpen: J. B. Carstiaenssens, s. d. Quotation translated by the author.

[Fig. 3] Map of Antwerp. A. COQUART: Plan de la ville et citadelle d'Anvers, renomee tant pour la bonté de son port que pour le grand commerce qui se faisait autre fois. Paris 1708. (BN de Portugal). Locations of Carstiaenssens' shops: A Blauwhandse rui; B Klapdorp; C Sint-Kathelijnevest and D Steenhouwersvest

the selling price was low there was a large target audience.[27] However, the existence of longer works published at the Steenhouwersvest indicates that he was able to undertake larger-scale projects as well. In any case, the business model seems to have been strong enough to support Carstiaenssens and his family for nearly two decades. Further comparative research into the strategies of other Antwerp booksellers in the eighteenth century will be necessary to appreciate how exceptional Carstiaenssens' career was.

27 RUWET and WELLEMANS estimate the literacy rate of the population in cities in the Flemish speaking parts of the Austrian Netherlands in 1779 at 57% for men, and 45% for women. Antwerp was not included in the study, but it is safe to assume that in such an important commercial city, where advanced schooling was both available and useful for many professions, the number was at least the same if not higher: JOSEPH RUWET/YVES WELLEMANS: *L'analphabetisme en Belgique* (XVIIIème–XIXème *siècles*). Louvain 1978.

21. Jahrhundert

KATHARINA EBENAU

»Als die Bücher laufen lernten ...« Buchtrailer als Marketinginstrument in der Verlagsbranche

IN DEN LETZTEN JAHREN veröffentlichen immer mehr Verlage im Internet kurze Filme zu ihren Büchern. Diese Buchtrailer sollen Bücher schnell, witzig und spannend bewerben und dabei vor allem jüngere Leser ansprechen, die einen großen Teil ihrer Freizeit im Internet verbringen. Buchtrailer können den ganzen Produktzyklus des Buchs online begleiten: Vom Erstkontakt mit dem Leser in einem Buch-Blog, über die Kaufentscheidung in einer Online-Buchhandlung, während des Lesens in einem enhanced E-Book bis zur nachträglichen Zusatzinformation auf der Autorenwebsite.[1] Obwohl sie ein interessantes Forschungsfeld zwischen Buch-, Filmwissenschaft und Medienkonvergenz bieten, wurden die Produktion, Rezeption und Ästhetik von Buchtrailern bisher noch nicht eingehend untersucht. Daher soll dieser Beitrag die Entstehung, Erscheinungsformen und die Rezeption von Buchtrailern analysieren und die Entwicklung von 2008 bis heute nachzeichnen.[2]

Dass bisher für Bücher kaum mit bewegten Bildern geworben wurde, liegt nicht daran, dass sich das Medium Film nicht dafür eignen würde. Es liegt vielmehr am hohen Kostenaufwand für Produktion und Fernsehausstrahlung solcher Werbespots.

Einzelne Verlage wagten in den letzten Jahren dennoch den Sprung auf den Bildschirm. So bewarb der Suhrkamp Verlag im Juli 2005 den Roman *Zorro*[3] von Isabel Allende mit einem vier Sekunden langen Fernsehspot, den die ARD 41 Mal ausstrahlte und der das Marketing-Budget enorm belastete: Allein die Ausstrahlung der 13 Spots, die direkt vor der Tagesschau platziert waren, kostete pro Spot € 4056.[4] Der Kostenaufwand erbrachte allerdings nicht den erhofften Erfolg: Als sich der Geschäftsführer für Marketing und Vertrieb, Georg Rieppel, nach nur anderthalb Jahren vom Suhrkamp Verlag trennte, schob die Presse dies auch auf das »Desaster«[5] mit Isabel Allendes *Zorro*. Der Titel sei zu teuer eingekauft und zu teuer beworben worden, man sah deshalb sogar die »ökonomische Gesundheit«[6] des Verlags in Gefahr.

Ein Jahr später machte die Verlagsgruppe Lübbe mit ihrer Fernsehwerbung zum Titel *Das Magdalena-Evangelium*[7] der amerikanischen Autorin Kathleen McGowan dagegen gute Erfahrungen:[8] Das Buch befand sich sechs Wochen lang in den Top 10 der Spiegel-Bestsellerliste und konnte sich danach weitere siebzehn Wochen in den Top 50 halten.[9]

Die Beispiele zeigen, dass Fernsehwerbung für Buchverlage sehr riskant ist, da die Wirkung nicht kalkuliert werden kann. Verlage mit ihrem eher kleinen Werbeetat setzten daher in der Vergangenheit eher

---

1 Vgl. BETTINA FÜHRER: Mehrverkauf dank Buchtrailer. In: *Anzeiger. Das Magazin für die österreichische Buchbranche* vom 15.11.2010. Online abrufbar (siehe Verzeichnis der Webseiten auf S. 374).
2 Als Grundlage diente meine Magisterarbeit *Buchtrailer – aktuelle Konzepte des Buchmarketings im Internet*, die von Stephan Füssel betreut und 2009 am Institut für Buchwissenschaft der Johannes Gutenberg-Universität Mainz eingereicht wurde, wobei die Beispiele ergänzt und auf den Stand von Januar 2011 aktualisiert wurden. Dennoch kann bei Informationen, die sich auf das schnelllebige Medium Internet beziehen, immer nur von Momentaufnahmen gesprochen werden.
3 ISABEL ALLENDE: *Zorro*. Frankfurt a. M. 2005.
4 HOLGER HEIMANN: Zur besten Sendezeit. In: *Börsenblatt für den deutschen Buchhandel*. 26 (2005), S. 29.
5 IJOMA MANGOLD: Heroischer Wahnsinn. In: *Süddeutsche Zeitung* vom 14./15.1.2006, S. 15.
6 Ebd., S. 15.
7 KATHLEEN MCGOWAN: *Das Magdalena Evangelium*. Bergisch Gladbach 2006.
8 [O. A.]: (K)ein Fall für die Inquisition. In: *Buchreport Express*. 33 (2006), S. 12.
9 Eigene Auswertung der Spiegel-Bestsellerlisten, die wöchentlich im Magazin *Buchreport Express* abgedruckt werden. Untersucht wurde der Zeitraum Juli 2006 bis Februar 2007.

auf traditionelle Marketinginstrumente wie Printanzeigen, Plakate, Displays oder Lesezeichen, statt sich auf das Wagnis Werbespot einzulassen. Anders sieht es bei der Veröffentlichung von kurzen Filmen im Internet aus: Das Einstellen von Filmen im Internet ist bei Videoplattformen kostenlos möglich, hier fallen nur noch die Produktionskosten an. Zudem haben Online-Videos bei einer geschickten Platzierung weniger Streuverlust als Fernsehwerbung. Sie können sich durch virales Marketing verbreiten und direkt in Online-Buchhandlungen eingesetzt werden.

Als Erfinder des Buchtrailers bezeichnen sich Kam Wai Yu und Derek Armstrong, die Armstrongs Buch *Song of Montségur*[10] mit einem kurzen Film bewerben wollten.[11] Sie gründeten 1988 in Kanada die Werbeagentur *Persona Corp.*, in der sie nach eigener Aussage den ersten Buchtrailer produzierten und 2001 ins Internet stellten. Das führte schnell zu hohen Klickzahlen und überzeugte die beiden Erfinder, ein funktionierendes Instrument für virales Marketing im Internet gefunden zu haben.[12]

2002 hatte Sheila English[13] in den USA die gleiche Idee: "[I]f music videos sell CDs, and movie trailers convince people to go to the theater, perhaps book videos […] would encourage readers to buy a book."[14] Sie überzeugte die Autorin Christine Feehan von ihrer Idee und produzierte mit Hilfe eines Videofilmers einen Buchtrailer[15] für Feehans Buch *Dark Symphony*.[16] Als sich herausstellte, dass sich das Buch auf diese Weise gut vermarkten ließ, gründete sie die Agentur *Circle of Seven Productions* und ließ sich die Begriffe *book trailer* und *book teaser* rechtlich schützen.[17] Zunächst wurden die Buchtrailer im Fernsehen und Kino ausgestrahlt, 2006 in insgesamt 2996 Kinos in den USA. Seit 2006 sind Buchtrailer vor allem im Internet abrufbar.[18] Die von *Circle of Seven Productions* produzierten Buchtrailer "allow consumers to get a feel for what the book is about through a visual synopsis, rather than just looking at the book cover."[19]

Die Buchtrailer zogen schnell Aufmerksamkeit auf sich. 2005 bekamen mehrere Buchtrailer von *Circle of Seven Productions* den amerikanischen *Telly Award*,[20] der Fernsehproduktionen und Werbespots prämiert. 2006 veranstaltete das Magazin *The Book Standard* in Zusammenarbeit mit Random House (USA) den ersten *Book Video Award*, der ausschließlich Buchtrailer prämierte. Der Wettbewerb erweckte ein großes Medieninteresse und wurde noch im gleichen Jahr ein zweites Mal für den Bereich Kinder- und Bilderbücher veranstaltet.[21]

Nachdem der Bertelsmann-Konzern mit seiner Verlagsgruppe Random House (USA) gute Erfahrungen mit Buchtrailern gemacht hatte, schrieb der Club Bertelsmann auch in Deutschland einen solchen Wettbewerb aus. Der Wettbewerb *Der Buchtrailer* beruht auf dem Konzept, Filmstudenten bei der Umsetzung von Buchtrailern zu fördern. Die zehn Bücher, die dafür zur Auswahl stehen, verlegt der Club als sogenannte »Club Premieren« selbst. Die Themen der Bücher sind sehr unterschiedlich, sie reichen vom Kochbuch über Thriller bis zum Gedichtband. Solche Wettbewerbe führen nicht nur zu einem großen Medieninteresse, das dem Buch und dem Verlag nutzt, sondern bringen auch kreative und – gegenüber den Kosten für eine Werbeagentur – günstige Buchtrailer hervor. Auch der aufwendige Buchtrailer zum Roman *Ich werde hier sein im*

10 Erschienen als: DEREK ARMSTRONG: *The Last Troubadour – Song of Montségur*. Ontario 2007.
11 Vgl. [o. A.]: *Persona Invention: The animated trailer*. Online abrufbar (siehe Verzeichnis der Webseiten).
12 Vgl. KIMBERLEY MAUL: Book Videos: Where Did They Come From? In: *allbusiness.com* vom 9. 10. 2006. Online abrufbar (siehe Verzeichnis der Webseiten).
13 Heute: Sheila Clover oder Sheila Clover-English.
14 DONNA SIMPSON: *Circle of Seven Book Videos. Revolutionizing Book Promotion with Video, Music & Special Effects*. Online abrufbar (siehe Verzeichnis der Webseiten).
15 SHEILA CLOVER-ENGLISH: *The Book Trailer Revolution. Book Marketing and Promotion Through Digital Videos*, S. 12/3. Online abrufbar (siehe Verzeichnis der Webseiten).
16 CHRISTINE FEEHAN: *Dark Symphony*. New York 2003.
17 Vgl. SIMPSON (siehe Anm. 14).
18 Vgl. CLOVER-ENGLISH (siehe Anm. 15), S. 13
19 MAUL (siehe Anm. 12).
20 Vgl. Homepage der *Telly Awards* (siehe Verzeichnis der Webseiten).
21 Vgl. North Carolina School of the Arts: NCSA *Film Students Take Two of Three 2006 Book Video Awards*. Online abrufbar (siehe Verzeichnis der Webseiten). – Vgl. ebenso: JOEL RICKETT: Film "trailers" for books. In: *The Bookseller*. 5309 (2007), S. 8.

Sonnenschein und im Schatten[22] des Kiepenheuer & Witsch Verlags entstand in Zusammenarbeit mit Studenten der Filmakademie Baden-Württemberg.

Welcher Verlag nach dem Wettbewerb des Club Bertelsmann den ersten Buchtrailer in Deutschland in Auftrag gab, ist unklar. Die erste auf Buchtrailer spezialisierte Agentur in Deutschland, *Litvideo*, gibt an, 2006 den ersten Buchtrailer produziert zu haben,[23] also etwa gleichzeitig zur ersten Preisverleihung von *Der Buchtrailer*. Seit 2008 werden Buchtrailer von großen Verlagen vermehrt eingesetzt. Vor allem Belletristik-Verlage wie S. Fischer, Kiepenheuer & Witsch, Droemer Knaur, Ullstein und Rowohlt verwenden sie in zunehmendem Maße, aber auch der Campus Verlag, der Sachbücher und Ratgeber herausgibt, setzt sie ein. In der Entwicklung der Buchtrailer zwischen 2008 und 2010 ist vor allem eine gesteigerte Professionalisierung zu bemerken. 2008 wurden noch viele Videos online gestellt, in denen Praktikanten, Volontäre oder andere Verlagsmitarbeiter schauspielern, in denen wackelige Kamerafahrten verrieten, dass kein professioneller Kameramann am Werk war, oder in denen einzelne Motive amateurhaft animiert wurden. Seit 2010 sind nahezu alle Buchtrailer von Werbeagenturen gestaltet.

Die Buchtrailer werden nicht nur professioneller, sie werden auch häufiger eingesetzt: Der Verlag Kiepenheuer & Witsch bewirbt inzwischen fast jeden Spitzentitel mit einem Buchtrailer, manche Bücher sogar mit mehreren verschiedenen. So finden sich zu *Tiere essen*,[24] dem 2010 erschienenen Sachbuch von Jonathan Safran Foer, auf der Website des Verlags vier unterschiedliche Buchtrailer, die je eine knappe Minute dauern.

Buchtrailer haben sich zu einer eigenen Werbeform entwickelt. Um sie von anderen (Werbe-)Kurzfilmen abzugrenzen, soll im Folgenden eine Definition entwickelt werden. Dafür muss zunächst geklärt werden, was im Mutterland des Buchtrailers unter dieser Bezeichnung verstanden wird: In den USA bezeichnet *trailer* eine Programmform, die Filmproduktionen in Fernsehen und Kino bewirbt: "short videos that are used to promote a film or program [...] are called trailers."[25] Im Gegensatz dazu steht der Werbespot (*promo*), der Produkte außerhalb des Mediums Film bewirbt. Buchtrailer bilden also eine Mischform zwischen klassischen Werbespots und Kinotrailern; sie wechseln das Medium, um die narrativen Inhalte eines Buchs zu bewerben.

Während sich in Deutschland das deutsch-amerikanische Mischwort Buchtrailer manifestiert hat, wird im US-amerikanischen Raum sowohl die Bezeichnung *book trailer* als auch *book video* verwendet. Nach der Definition von Sheila English ist *book video* der Überbegriff zu visualisierten Büchern: "This is the most generic term for a book shown in a visual manner [...]. The term 'book video' can be used to describe any type of visual synopsis for a book".[26] Darunter fallen neben Buchtrailern auch Autoreninterviews und Lesungen. *Book trailer* definiert sie dagegen so: "Booktrailers use scenes from the book with live actors."[27] Der Eintrag *book trailer* in der englischen Version von Wikipedia wurde von der Agentur Vidlit[28] initiiert. Deren Definition lautet: "A book trailer is a video advertisement for a book which employs techniques similar to those of movie trailers. They are circulated on television and online in most common digital video formats."[29]

---

22 CHRISTIAN KRACHT: *Ich werde hier sein im Sonnenschein und im Schatten*. Köln 2008.

23 Vgl. FÜHRER (siehe Anm. 1).

24 JONATHAN SAFRAN FOER: *Tiere essen*. Köln 2010.

25 ROBERT REED/MAXINE REED: *The Encyclopedia of Television, Cable and Video*. New York 1992, S. 549.

26 CLOVER-ENGLISH (siehe Anm. 15), S. 16.

27 Ebd., S. 16.

28 Gegründet 2004 von Liz Dubelman (siehe Verzeichnis der Webseiten).

29 [o. A.]: Trailer (book). In: *Wikipedia, the free encyclopedia*. Online abrufbar (siehe Verzeichnis der Webseiten). Da es sich bei Buchtrailern um ein Internet-Phänomen handelt, ist die *Wikipedia*-Definition als relevant zu betrachten.

Dies erklärt auch den Unterschied, der zwischen der Bildsprache von amerikanischen und deutschen Buchtrailern herrscht: Während amerikanische *book trailer* eher an Hollywood-Filme erinnern, experimentieren deutsche Buchtrailer mit verschiedenen Darstellungs- und Visualisierungsformen. Dabei können drei Formen unterschieden werden: a) Buchtrailer, die animierte Schrift verwenden; b) Buchtrailer, die mit animierten Bildern gestaltet sind und c) Buchtrailer, bei denen Spielszenen mit Schauspielern verwendet werden, die also am meisten an einen Kinotrailer – und damit auch an amerikanische *book trailer* – erinnern.

Die Entscheidung, welche Umsetzung für einen Buchtrailer gewählt wird, beeinflusst die Kosten enorm. Ein Buchtrailer mit professionellen Schauspielern kann sehr kostspielig sein. Bei einem Trailer mit animierten Inhalten hängen die Kosten von der Qualität der Grafik ab. Im Folgenden werden Beispiele für diese drei Trailer-Arten vorgestellt.

Buchtrailer mit animierter Schrift
Bei den Buchtrailern, die animierte Typografie benutzen, ist der Bezug zum Medium Buch am deutlichsten. Ein Beispiel dafür ist der Buchtrailer zum Titel *Dinge geregelt kriegen*[30] von Kathrin Passig und Sascha Lobo. Dieser unterhaltsame Buchtrailer verbreitete sich – sicherlich auch wegen der Bloggertätigkeit der beiden Autoren – rasend schnell im Internet. Weitere Beispiele sind die Buchtrailer zu den Romanen *Dear American Airlines*[31] und *Ein König für Deutschland*.[32] Bei allen drei Trailern wird Text aus dem Off gesprochen, gleichzeitig kann man den Text dazu mitlesen. Die Wörter erscheinen aber nicht in der gewohnten Leserichtung von links nach rechts und von oben nach unten, sondern nehmen Formen an, die das Gesagte und Geschriebene nachahmen. Der Buchtrailer zu *Ein König für Deutschland* [Abb. 1] reiht Politikerzitate, die sich in der Vergangenheit als unwahr herausstellten, aneinander. Darunter sind auch die berühmten Zitate von Norbert Blüm »Die Rente ist sicher« oder von Walter Ulbricht, dass »niemand die Absicht hat, eine Mauer zu errichten«. Dabei werden im Buchtrailer die Worte wie Steine einer Mauer aufeinandergeschichtet und am Schluss mit einem Stacheldraht bekrönt. Auch einzelne Worte verdeutlichen ihre Aussage durch Farbe, Form und Größe.

Im Trailer zu *Dear American Airlines* [Abb. 2] werden »blutunterlaufene Augen« in blutroter Schrift und »Schaum vor dem Mund« in weißer Schrift, von der Schaum herabtropft, dargestellt. Der gesprochene und geschriebene Text wird selten durch andere Bilder ergänzt, wie im Trailer zu dem Buch *Dinge geregelt kriegen* [Abb. 3], das das Phänomen des Aufschiebens von zu erledigender Arbeit beschreibt. Der Buchtrailer spielt mit der Idee, was aus der biblischen Schöpfungsgeschichte geworden wäre, wenn Gott sie »auf den letzten Drücker« erledigt hätte. Hier wird das Ergebnis der Schöpfung als Polaroid neben die Schrift gelegt und ergänzt so die Aussage des Textes. Die Form des typografischen Buchtrailers wird vor allem für Bücher benutzt, deren Themen und Aussagen kurz zusammengefasst werden können. Ziel ist, die Zuschauer zu erheitern, indem absurde Situationen generiert werden. Die animierten Buchstaben, die zum gesprochenen Text erscheinen, verdeutlichen diese Situation.

30 KATHRIN PASSIG / SASHA LOBO: *Dinge geregelt kriegen – ohne einen Funken Selbstdisziplin*. Berlin: Rowohlt, 2008.
31 JONATHAN MILES: *Dear American Airlines*. Bergisch Gladbach 2009.
32 ANDREAS ESCHBACH: *Ein König für Deutschland*. Bergisch Gladbach 2009.

[Abb. 1 bis 3]

Buchtrailer mit animierten Bildern

Buchtrailer, die mit animierten Bildern arbeiten, abstrahieren zwar deutlicher vom Text als jene, die animierte Schrift benutzen. Trotzdem wirken sie nicht so real wie Trailer mit Schauspielern und überlassen die Leser somit weitgehend ihrer Fantasie. Beispiele für diese Trailer sind die zu den Romanen *Ich werde hier sein im Sonnenschein und im Schatten* [Abb. 4] von Christian Kracht und *Slam*[33] von Nick Hornby sowie einer der Trailer zum Sachbuch *Tiere essen* [Abb. 5] von Jonathan Safran Foer.

Ich werde hier sein im Sonnenschein und im Schatten zeigt eine animierte Welt, die sehr idyllisch wirkt: Wald, Wolken, Berge, Vögel, Schmetterlinge. Das alles kommt ohne Musik aus, es wird nur von der Stimme des Sprechers und den Geräuschen der Vögel etc. begleitet. Die Idylle wird am Ende des Trailers jäh unterbrochen, wenn ein Soldatenstiefel die Blume und den daraufsitzenden Schmetterling zertritt, gleichzeitig sind Schüsse zu hören. Der Schreibstil des Autors wird deutlich, da Textteile vorgelesen werden. Insgesamt fängt der Trailer die Stimmung des Buchs gut ein, indem der Inhalt in assoziative Bilder umgesetzt wird. Allerdings sagt der Trailer recht wenig über den Inhalt des Romans aus.

Die Buchtrailer zu *Slam* und *Tiere essen* sind nicht mit aufwendiger Trickfilmtechnik hergestellt, sondern verwenden collagenartig Bilder, die sich zum Text bewegen. In beiden Trailern werden die Bilder durch gesprochenen und/oder eingeblendeten Text ergänzt und geben so bessere Informationen über die Handlung des Buchs. Durch diese Herangehensweise wirken die Trailer zwar weniger kunstvoll, sagen aber mehr über die Handlung des Buchs aus.

Trailer mit animierten Bildern werden vor allem für Bücher benutzt, bei denen sich die Handlung nicht in kurzen (und möglichst treffsicheren) Schlagworten zusammenfassen lässt. Sie sind für Romane oder Sachbücher geeignet, es gibt jedoch auch Trailer mit animierten Bildern, die für Spannungsliteratur werben. Diese Trailerform wird häufiger verwendet als die beiden anderen, denn sie transportiert den Inhalt eines Buchs, ohne ihn zu sehr zu verkürzen. Gleichzeitig ist die Collagentechnik, die die Trailer zu *Tiere essen* und *Slam* auszeichnet, weniger aufwendig als Schrift zu animieren oder ein Filmteam und Schauspieler zu engagieren.

Buchtrailer mit Schauspielern

Bei der dritten Umsetzungsform werden Schauspieler und reale Drehorte verwendet. Diese Trailer zeigen die Verwandtschaft zum Kinotrailer am deutlichsten. An ihnen wird jedoch auch häufig kritisiert, dass den Zuschauern etwas von ihrem Lesevergnügen, sich die Figuren des Romans selbst vorzustellen, genommen wird, wenn diese durch Schauspieler verkörpert werden. Ein Gegenargument lautet, dass auch die Abbildungen auf den Buchcovern nicht dazu führen, dass sich Leser in ihrer Fantasie beeinträchtigt fühlen. Ein weiteres Gegenargument besagt, dass sich kein Leser die Bilder des Buchtrailers, die er nur wenige Minuten sieht, so detailliert merken könne, dass sie später sein Lesevergnügen schmälern würden.[34] Dennoch sieht man in diesen Buchtrailern

---

[33] NICK HORNBY: *Slam*. Köln 2008.
[34] Vgl. ANTONIA BERNEIKE: Buchtrailer-Trend: Angucken, kaufen! In: *Spiegel Online* vom 1.11.2008. Online abrufbar (siehe Verzeichnis der Webseiten).

die Gesichter der Schauspieler nur kurz und ausschnittsweise. Beispiele für den Buchtrailer mit Schauspielern sind die Trailer zu dem Kriminalroman *Nacht unter Tag*,[35] zu *Die Tribute von Panem – Flammender Zorn*,[36] dem dritten Band einer Fantasy-Trilogie, und zum Thriller *Erbarmen*.[37]

Die Buchtrailer mit Schauspielern zeichnen sich durch eine Montagetechnik aus, die auch bei Musikvideos und Kinotrailern verwendet wird. In kurzen Abständen werden verschiedene Szenen gezeigt, die mit Musik hinterlegt sind. Beim Fantasyroman *Die Tribute von Panem – Flammender Zorn* [Abb. 6] sieht man zum Beispiel einen Wald, Flammen und eine Gestalt im Umhang, die einen Bogen spannt. Dadurch wird weniger die Handlung des Buchs, sondern vielmehr die Atmosphäre eines spannenden Fantasyromans vermittelt. Alle drei Trailer verwenden kurze Textzitate, die eingeblendet und teilweise aus dem Off mitgesprochen werden. Bei *Nacht unter Tag* lautet der eingeblendete Text: »Ein vermisster Vater [...] schlägt ein dunkles Kapitel auf [...] Eine Mauer des Schweigens [...] Dunkle Geheimnisse« um dann mit den in schneller Folge eingeblendeten Worten »Mord [...] Habgier [...] Verrat« zu enden. Diese Schlüsselworte bauen Spannung auf, sagen aber nicht viel über die Handlung des Buchs aus.

Wie man an den Beispielen sehen kann, werden Trailer mit Schauspielern vor allem für Spannungsliteratur – Kriminalromane, Thriller oder Fantasy – hergestellt. Es werden stereotype Motive verwendet, die den Zuschauern aus Krimi- und Fantasy-Serien in Fernsehen und Kino geläufig sind. Deswegen ist der Medienwechsel zwischen Buch und Film, der häufig bei dieser Form von Buchtrailern als Kritik genannt wird, irrelevant für Leser und Zuschauer, die sich mit diesen Genres beschäftigen.

Die Beispiele zeigen, wie unterschiedlich die Stilmittel von Buchtrailern sein können. Im Gegensatz zur Definition von Sheila English setzen sie keineswegs immer die Handlung des Buchs in Bilder um, sondern transportieren Schlagworte, Assoziationen und Atmosphäre. Eine mögliche Definition, die dieser Formenvielfalt gerecht wird, wäre:

> Buchtrailer sind Werbevideos für Bücher, die im Auftrag von Verlagen entstehen und im Internet (seltener im Fernsehen, Kino oder am Point of Sale) zirkulieren. Die Visualisierung des Buchinhaltes wird durch Musik, gesprochenen oder eingeblendeten Text unterstützt. Es unterscheiden sich grob drei Arten Buchtrailer: Solche, die mit animierter Typografie arbeiten, solche, die animierte Bilder benutzen und solche, in denen Spielszenen mit Schauspielern eingesetzt werden. Häufig werden für Buchtrailer die Montage-Techniken von Kinotrailern genutzt.

Diese Definition schließt allerdings einige Filme aus, die in der Praxis ebenfalls als Buchtrailer bezeichnet werden. Das sind zum einen die Buchtrailer »ohne Handlung«. In diesen Filmen wird lediglich der Buchumschlag abgefilmt oder es werden wechselnde unbewegte Abbildungen gezeigt. Dazu kommt ein Sprechtext, der die Handlung des Buchs erläutert oder die Vita des Autors vorstellt. Bei diesen Trailern steht die Information im Vordergrund, sie sprechen kaum die Gefühle der Zuschauer an. Man kann sie daher auch als »digitales Plakat« bezeichnen. Sie werden eher selten für Endkunden verwendet; meistens sollen sie mit ihrem hohen Informationswert den Buchhandel direkt ansprechen.

[Abb. 4 bis 6]

35 VAL MCDERMID: *Nacht unter Tag.* München 2009.
36 SUZANNE COLLINS: *Die Tribute von Panem – Flammender Zorn.* Hamburg 2011.
37 JUSSI ADLER-OLSEN: *Erbarmen.* München 2009.

Beispielsweise ließ die Branchenzeitschrift *Buchreport* 2009 solche Buchtrailer für die Online-Ausgabe seiner Bestsellerlisten produzieren;[38] da die Verlage inzwischen deutlich häufiger eigene Buchtrailer produzieren, verwendet der *Buchreport* diese Info-Filme mittlerweile nicht mehr.

Zum anderen werden Filme ausgeschlossen, die Hintergrundmaterial zu Autoren und Büchern zeigen, wie Mitschnitte von Fernsehsendungen, Interviews oder kurze Biografien. Hier wird nicht die Handlung des betreffenden Buchs in Bilder umgesetzt, sondern nur darüber gesprochen.

Für die Veröffentlichung von Buchtrailern im Internet gibt es verschiedene Möglichkeiten. Das Einstellen bei einer Videoplattform eignet sich, um das Phänomen des viralen Marketings zu nutzen. Die Videos können von den Nutzern kommentiert, bewertet und weiterempfohlen werden. Zusätzlich können andere Websites (Blogs, Zeitschriften, etc.) den Film auf ihrer Seite einbinden. Videoplattformen können grundsätzlich kostenlos genutzt werden, wenn der eingestellte Film unter zehn Minuten bleibt. Einige Verlage lassen die Videos über den Account ihrer Werbeagentur einstellen, andere haben ihren eigenen Account. Letzteres ist als günstiger zu bewerten, da dem Nutzer so weitere Videos des eigenen Verlags vorgeschlagen werden und der Verlagsname im Bewusstsein der Nutzer gestärkt wird. Buchverlage, die einen Auftritt in Social Media-Portalen wie Facebook haben, verlinken die Buchtrailer, die sie auf einer Videoplattform hochgeladen haben, auch dort. Dadurch bietet sich für die Verlage wieder die Gelegenheit, direkt in Kontakt mit den Lesern zu treten, die das Video kommentieren und weiterempfehlen können.

Das Einbinden von Buchtrailern auf der Angebotsseite für das Buch in Online-Buchhandlungen wie beispielsweise amazon.de, buch.de oder bol.de ist für Verlage besonders vorteilhaft. Hier geht nichts von der Werbewirkung des Buchtrailers verloren, Kunden können das Buch sofort nach Ansehen des Videos erwerben. Das Einstellen von Buchtrailern bei Online-Shops ist für Verlage aber nicht kostenlos möglich, die Kosten werden individuell vom Vertrieb mit der Buchhandlung verhandelt.[39]

Werden die Buchtrailer auf den Verlagswebsites vorgestellt, findet man sie auf den Informationsseiten zu den einzelnen Büchern oder in einer eigenen Rubrik, die »Multimedia« oder »Buchtrailer« genannt wird. Um Videos in eine Website einbinden zu können, muss die Technik der Website auf dem neuesten Stand sein, was nicht bei allen Verlagswebsites der Fall ist. Diese Verlage verlinken meist das Video auf den Videoplattformen. Eine andere Lösung hat der Verlag Droemer Knaur gefunden. Die Buchvideos wurden ganz ausgelagert und sind seit Oktober 2007 auf dem Web TV-Portal lesungen.tv zu finden.[40] Hier sind nicht nur Buchtrailer, sondern auch Interviews und Hintergrundinformationen zu den Büchern als Video abrufbar.

Buchtrailer haben sich aus Sicht der Verlage in den letzten fünf Jahren etabliert. Ihre Herstellung hat sich professionalisiert und die Verbreitung durch verschiedene neue Kanäle vergrößert. Über die Akzeptanz und Bekanntheit auf der Seite der Rezipienten – der Buchkäufer – sagt dies allerdings nur wenig aus. Deswegen wurde 2009 eine empirische Untersuchung unter Studierenden der Johannes Gutenberg-Universität

---

38 Vgl. [o. A.]: Bestseller im Bild. In: *Buchreport Online* vom 5. 5. 2009. Online abrufbar (siehe Verzeichnis der Webseiten).

39 Vgl. Interview mit Marco Verhülsdonk, Tina Pfeifer und Laura Bastian (Verlag Kiepenheuer & Witsch) vom 11. 8. 2009. In: KATHARINA EBENAU: Buchtrailer – aktuelle Konzepte des Buchmarketings im Internet. Magisterarbeit Johannes Gutenberg-Universität Mainz 2009, Anhang II.2.c.

40 Vgl. Homepage (siehe Verzeichnis der Webseiten). – Vgl. außerdem: NICOLE BACH: Die Offensive. In: *BuchMarkt*. 10 (2007), S. 62/3.

Mainz durchgeführt.[41] Der Schwerpunkt der Untersuchung wurde auf die Akzeptanz und die unterschiedliche Beurteilung der drei Trailer-Formen gelegt. Dabei stellte sich heraus, dass nur etwas mehr als ein Fünftel der Befragten bereits einen Buchtrailer gesehen hatte. Dieser Wert steigt jedoch erheblich, wenn man nur Personen betrachtet, die sich häufig im Internet über Bücher informieren und dort Buchkäufe tätigen. Die Buchtrailer wurden größtenteils »durch Zufall« gesehen, am häufigsten in Online-Buchhandlungen und auf Videoportalen.

Schließlich wurden den Studierenden drei Buchtrailer gezeigt, die jeweils eine der oben definierten Typen vertreten. Dabei wurde das Beispiel eines Buchtrailers mit animierter Schrift, *Dear American Airlines*, als nicht besonders informativ bezeichnet, erzielte aber unter den drei Beispielen die besten Werte bei der Unterhaltung und der Kaufbereitschaft der Befragten. Der Buchtrailer mit animierten Bildern zum Roman *Ich werde hier sein im Sonnenschein und im Schatten* wurde als nicht informativ und nicht unterhaltsam angesehen, machte jedoch knapp ein Fünftel der Befragten auf das Buch neugierig. Die Kaufbereitschaft war mit einem Sechstel der Befragten die Niedrigste unter allen drei Buchtrailern. Der dritte Buchtrailer war der zum Kriminalroman *Nacht unter Tag*, bei dem Schauspieler Romancharaktere darstellen. Beim Informationswert schnitt dieser Trailer besser ab als die beiden anderen Beispiele. Obwohl die Befragten sowohl bei der Unterhaltsamkeit als auch bei der Frage nach dem geweckten Interesse eher mittlere Werte angaben, überlegte sich fast ein Viertel, das Buch zu kaufen.

Offenbar ist es wichtig, dass Buchtrailer nicht nur die Stimmung des Romans wiedergeben, sondern auch Informationen über die Handlung enthalten, beziehungsweise die Neugierde und das Intresse an der Handlung wecken. Die beiden Buchtrailer, die durch Spannung und Witz verstärkt Emotionen ansprachen, führten zu einer höheren Kaufbereitschaft. Dies ist auch den Genres der Bücher geschuldet: Während bei einem Kriminalroman die Grundzüge der Handlung bekannt sind und Andeutungen genügen, um Spannung aufzubauen, muss bei einem Roman wie *Ich werde hier sein im Sonnenschein und im Schatten* die Handlung in Gänze erklärt werden. Die Handlung des Romans bleibt im Buchtrailer allerdings recht vage. Die Tatsache dass er viel künstlerischer gestaltet ist als die beiden anderen gezeigten Trailer konnte die Befragten nicht überzeugen. Damit ein Buchtrailer die gewollte Wirkung entfaltet, muss er also nicht nur künstlerisch perfekt ausgearbeitet sein, sondern auch eine Geschichte erzählen, die die Zuschauer selbst in einen Kontext setzen können. Dazu können Stereotype aus Film und Fernsehen verwendet werden. Gleichzeitig sollten Emotionen geweckt werden, die der Zuschauer einem Genre zuordnen kann. Buchtrailer eignen sich also vor allem für Spannungs- und Unterhaltungsliteratur, weniger für Belletristik, deren komplexe Handlung und Schreibstil besser in einem Text – beispielsweise in einem Klappentext – dargestellt werden kann.

Auf die Frage nach der grundsätzlichen Akzeptanz der Werbeform bewerteten fast 56% Buchtrailer positiv, während etwa 44% Buchtrailer ablehnten. Diese Ablehnung wurde zum einen dadurch begründet, dass

41 Vgl. EBENAU (siehe Anm. 39), Anhang II.1.

das Zeigen von Buchcharakteren die eigene Vorstellung beeinträchtigen könnte (wobei der typografische Trailer regelmäßig ausgenommen wurde). Zum anderen hatten die Befragten Probleme mit dem Medienwechsel zwischen Buch und Film.

In den letzten Jahren hat sich die Werbeform Buchtrailer weiterentwickelt. Sie ist aus dem Stadium des Experiments heraus getreten und hat sich bei Verlagen etabliert. Es haben sich unterschiedliche Buchtrailer-Formen entwickelt, die je nach Buchgenre benutzt und von Agenturen professionell umgesetzt werden. Dass Buchtrailer auch vom Publikum angenommen werden, wird unter anderem durch die Studie von 2009 belegt. Auch das *Börsenblatt des deutschen Buchhandels* hat festgestellt, dass Buchtrailer inzwischen längst in der Verlagsbranche angekommen sind und veröffentlichte deshalb in der Ausgabe von August 2010 eine Checkliste »Buchtrailer konzipieren und produzieren« und einen Kommentar, der die Vorteile von Buchtrailern für Verlage anpreist: »Ein Buchtrailer kann in kürzester Zeit die Stimmung eines Buchs vermitteln – schneller, als es jeder Text schafft. Mit einem Helden, der als echte Person im Video auftaucht, identifiziert sich ein Leser leichter als mit der Romanfigur, deren Aussehen und Charakter sich erst nach einigen Buchseiten erschließt«.[42]

Im wissenschaftlichen Diskurs wurden Buchtrailer jedoch bisher noch nicht beachtet. Dabei enthält das Thema Buchtrailer zahlreiche Teilaspekte, die sich zur wissenschaftlichen Untersuchung anbieten: Die Abgrenzung von Buchtrailern zu Kinotrailern und Werbespots kann medienwissenschaftlich untersucht werden. Auch die Ästhetik, Produktion und Rezeption von Buchtrailern im Vergleich zu anderen Werbefilmen kann analysiert werden. Um die Wirkung der Trailer zu untersuchen, fehlt eine aktuelle und repräsentative Studie. Die Einsatzmöglichkeiten von Buchtrailern, die durch E-Books und Tablet-Computer ganz neue Dimensionen bekommen sowie die Beziehungen zu anderen Werbemitteln im Web 2.0 bieten ebenfalls ein interessantes Forschungsfeld.

Gerade im Kontext der E-Books darf auf die Weiterentwicklung der Werbeform Buchtrailer gespannt gewartet werden. Die Börsenblatt-Redakteurin Sandra Schüssel verweist ebenfalls auf diesen Zusammenhang: »Verlage, die heute Erfahrungen mit Videos sammeln, rüsten sich für multimediale E-Books von morgen«.[43]

---

[42] SANDRA SCHÜSSEL: Buchtrailer: Das Gefühl im Bauch. In: *Börsenblatt für den deutschen Buchhandel*. 34 (2010), S. 20.
[43] Ebd., S. 20.

CHRISTOPH KOCHHAN
Kinder- und Jugendliteratur

Chancen des E-Books im Markt für junge Leser

DAS THEMA E-BOOKS ist seit einigen Jahren in aller Munde. Immer wieder hört oder liest man Prognosen, wie sich der Markt für die elektronische Variante des Buches entwickeln wird. Dabei gehen die Annahmen über die zu erwartenden Marktanteile in den kommenden fünf Jahren von fünf bis 15% weit auseinander. Dies kommt einer inhaltlichen Spanne gleich von »die Akzeptanz von E-Books ist gering« bis hin zu »die Rezeption von Inhalten in elektronischer Form wird zunehmend alltäglich«.

Doch wer sind die Nutzer des E-Books? Beleuchtet man diese Frage unter dem demografischen Aspekt des Alters, so kann man – plakativ gesprochen – annehmen, dass insbesondere Menschen jüngerer Generationen für diese Editionsform aufgeschlossen sind. Sie sind in der Regel technikaffiner als ältere Menschen und oftmals, auch über ihre berufliche Biografie, mit neuen Medien vertraut. Noch einen Schritt weiter gedacht ist in dieser Hinsicht zu erwarten, dass das E-Book gerade auch für Kinder beziehungsweise Jugendliche eine interessante Möglichkeit darstellt, Literatur zu »konsumieren«: Schüler werden mit den neuen Medien sozialisiert, so dass der Umgang mit Medien gleich welcher Art für sie alltäglich und selbstverständlich ist. Vor diesem Hintergrund dürfte man davon ausgehen können, dass das Genre des Kinder- und Jugendbuchs schon heute eine Chance hat, in Form von E-Books bei den Heranwachsenden und deren Eltern Vertrauen und Akzeptanz zu finden.

Dieser – als einer von vielen – Fragen ging die Studie *Kinder- und Jugendbücher. Einblicke in die Lebens- und Lesewelten relevanter Zielgruppen* nach, die von der Gesellschaft für Konsumforschung (GfK) und dem Institut Sinus im Auftrag des Börsenvereins des Deutschen Buchhandels und der Arbeitsgemeinschaft von Jugendbuchverlagen (AVJ) im Sommer 2010 durchgeführt wurde. Im Rahmen der Studie wurden 1875 Käufer von Kinder- und Jugendbüchern ab zehn Jahren befragt, die 2009 mindestens ein Kinder- oder Jugendbuch gekauft hatten. Neben dieser Ad-hoc-Befragung wurden im Rahmen der Auswertung die Daten aus dem repräsentativen GfK Buchmarktpanel mit 20 000 Befragten integriert. Darüber hinaus wurden zwölf ethnografische Interviews geführt, jeweils mit Kindern beziehungsweise Jugendlichen im Alter zwischen zehn und 14 Jahren und deren Eltern, die die quantitativen Umfrageergebnisse in ihren Aussagen unterstützten. Bei der Auswahl der Interviewpartner wurde deren Lebenswelt Beachtung geschenkt. Grundlage bildeten hier die sogenannten Sinus-Milieus, die die Gesellschaft nach sozialer Lage und Wertorientierungen in verschiedene Segmente differenzieren.

[Abb. 1] 77% der Befragten gaben an, das Buch für andere Personen gekauft zu haben; 23% für sich selbst. Diese 23% wurden befragt, ob sie sich vorstellen könnten, das Buch als E-Book zu lesen [Basis: Käufer von Kinder- und Jugendbüchern 2010]:

Auf alle Fälle	4%
Wahrscheinlich	12%
Wahrscheinlich nicht	32%
Auf keinen Fall	52%

Auf die Frage, ob sie sich vorstellen könnten, das Buch als E-Book zu kaufen antworteten:

Auf alle Fälle	2%
Wahrscheinlich	6%
Wahrscheinlich nicht	28%
Auf keinen Fall	64%

Unabhängig von den Lebenswelten der Kinder und Jugendlichen beziehungsweise ihrer Eltern zeigt ein Blick auf die Medienausstattung der Heranwachsenden, gegenüber welcher medialen Konkurrenz sich Kinder- und Jugendbücher behaupten müssen. Denn in Deutschland beschäftigen sich Kinder und Jugendliche täglich durchschnittlich 5½ Stunden mit digitalen Medien wie etwa Computer oder Smartphones – eine Dauer, die länger ist als der Schulunterricht. Dieser nimmt – bezogen auf eine gesamte Woche – im Durchschnitt knapp vier Stunden pro Tag in Anspruch.[1]

Bücher im Kontext der Medienausstattung von Kindern und Jugendlichen
Kinder und Jugendliche wachsen mit technischen Geräten auf. In nahezu jedem deutschen Haushalt sind ein Handy sowie ein Computer vorhanden. In den meisten Fällen geht damit die Möglichkeit einher, ins Internet zu gehen. Aber nicht nur im Haushalt verfügen die Heranwachsenden über den Zugriff auf technische Geräte. Im Rahmen der JIM-Studie 2010[2] wurden Jugendliche im Alter zwischen 12 und 19 Jahren nach ihrer eigenen Medienausstattung gefragt: Allen voran steht wiederum das Handy. 98% der Mädchen und 96% der Jungen besitzen ein eigenes Handy. Auf den weiteren Plätzen folgen mp3-Player sowie Computer beziehungsweise Laptops. Während in Bezug auf mp3-Player 88% der Mädchen und 80% der Jungen ein eigenes Gerät besitzen, verhält es sich hinsichtlich des Besitzes eines Computers oder Laptops umgekehrt: 77% der Mädchen nennen einen Computer ihr Eigen, aber 80% der Jungen können über einen eigenen PC verfügen.

Unabhängig vom Geschlecht des Medien-Besitzers spiegeln die Daten der JIM-Studie die Selbstverständlichkeit wider, die Medien allgemein und der Umgang mit ihnen für Heranwachsende besitzen. Dabei zeigt sich, dass Medien umso bedeutsamer werden, je älter die Kinder beziehungsweise Jugendlichen sind: Haben beispielsweise »lediglich« 65% der 12- bis 13-Jährigen einen eigenen Computer, so sind es bei den 18- bis 19-Jährigen mehr als 86%.[3]

Mit diesen Bestandsaufnahmen zur Medienausstattung korrespondieren die Umfrageergebnisse zum Thema Medienbeschäftigungen. Diese können – sicherlich etwas überspitzt – zusammengefasst werden mit einem Zitat aus einer Studie, in der eine Mutter das Bild ihres 15 Jahre alten Sohnes bei den Vorbereitungen zu einer Klassenarbeit beschreibt: »Die Lehrbücher lagen ungeöffnet in seiner Tasche, wohingegen der Laptop auf seinem Schreibtisch immer aufgeklappt war. Auf dem Bildschirm waren irgendwelche Geschichte/Englisch/Physik-Dokumente geöffnet, aber gleichzeitig auch seine Facebook- und iTunes-Seiten. In seinen Ohren spielten die iPod-Ohrhörer einen Podcast, und manchmal, nur um seine Konzentration noch weiter zu unterbrechen, lief auch noch ein Video auf Youtube.«[4]

Entsprechend diesem Szenario kann nachvollzogen werden, dass das Internet im Beliebtheitsranking der Medienbeschäftigungen bei den Heranwachsenden weit vorne steht. Mit diesem Medium beschäftigen sich 63% der Jugendlichen täglich und 27% mehrmals in der Woche. Noch beliebter ist lediglich der Umgang mit dem Handy (80% nutzen es täglich,

---

1 Vgl. MANFRED SPITZER: Im Netz. In: *Frankfurter Allgemeine Zeitung* vom 22. 9. 2010, S. 8.
2 Vgl. JIM-Studie. Jugend – Information – (Multi-)Media. Basisuntersuchung zum Medienumgang 12- bis 19-Jähriger. Hrsg. vom MEDIENPÄDAGOGISCHEN FORSCHUNGSVERBUND SÜDWEST. Stuttgart 2010. (Online verfügbar unter www.mpfs.de [13. 12. 2010]).
3 Neben dem Alter spielt auch hier wieder die Bildung eine Rolle: Während knapp 70% der Hauptschüler einen eigenen Computer besitzen, liegt der Wert bei den Gymnasiasten bei 80%.
4 SPITZER (siehe Anm. 1), S. 8.

11% mehrmals in der Woche). Nach Handy und Internet folgen Fernseher, mp3, Radio, Musik-CDs/Kassetten. Auf Rang sieben im Ranking der Medienbeschäftigungen findet sich als erstes Printmedium die Tageszeitung. Auf Platz acht schließt sich die Lektüre von Büchern an: 22% der Befragten geben zu Protokoll, dass sie sich täglich, 16%, dass sie sich mehrmals pro Woche mit Büchern beschäftigen.

Allerdings zeigt sich hier wiederum das aus Umfragen zum Leseverhalten[5] bekannte Bild, wenn man die Nutzer nach ihrem Geschlecht differenziert: 48% der Mädchen greifen täglich oder mehrmals pro Woche zum Buch, bei Jungen liegt der entsprechende Wert bei 28%. Genau umgekehrt verhält es sich bei Computer- bzw. Konsolenspielen. Hier sind es vor allem männliche Jugendliche, die täglich oder mehrmals pro Woche mit diesen Medien umgehen.

Die unterschiedlich starke Bedeutung des Mediums Buch für Jungen und Mädchen zeigt sich auch, wenn man Kinder und Jugendliche nach der Wichtigkeit einzelner Medien befragt: Während 62% der Mädchen die Lektüre von Büchern als wichtig oder sogar sehr wichtig erachten, sind es bei Jungen 39%. Anführer der Aufzählung der wichtigsten Medien beziehungsweise Medienbeschäftigungen sind allerdings, sowohl bei Mädchen als auch bei Jungen, Musik und Internet – für je mehr als 85% der Befragten sind das Hören von Musik und die Nutzung des Internets wichtig oder sehr wichtig. Dabei gewinnt das Internet zunehmend an Bedeutung als eine Option, mit der Musik gehört werden kann. Es bleibt zu fragen, inwieweit neben einer Verknüpfung von »Internet« und »Musik« auch die Kombination von »Internet« und »Buch« auf das Interesse der Kinder und Jugendlichen stößt: Wie stehen die Käufer von Kinder- und Jugendbüchern dieser Möglichkeit zur Zeit gegenüber und wie sehen sie die zukünftigen Chancen dieses Genres in Form elektronischer Angebote?

Kinder- und Jugendbücher in elektronischer Form

Überblick zum Kaufverhalten
Kinder- und Jugendbücher erfreuen sich einer zunehmenden Beliebtheit. 2009 haben 14,1 Millionen Deutsche mindestens ein Kinder- und Jugendbuch gekauft – ein leichter Anstieg gegenüber dem Vorjahr (2008: 13,9 Millionen Käufer). Im Durchschnitt erwirbt ein Käufer von Kinder- und Jugendbüchern pro Jahr fünf Bücher. 2009 gab er hierfür € 42 aus, 2008 waren es € 39, so dass nicht nur mehr Kinder- und Jugendbücher gekauft wurden, sondern auch mehr Geld dafür im Budget vorhanden ist.[6]

Doch wie sieht es mit der bevorzugten Editionsform aus? Kauft man Kinder- und Jugendbücher lieber in gedruckter oder digitaler Form? Um im Hinblick auf die bevorzugte Publikationsvariante erste Informationen zu erhalten, wurden im Rahmen der Studie *Kinder- und Jugendbücher. Einblicke in die Lebens- und Lesewelten relevanter Zielgruppen* (2010) diejenigen, die ein Kinder- und Jugendbuch für sich selbst gekauft haben, gefragt, ob sie sich vorstellen könnten, das erworbene Buch auch in elektronischer Form zu lesen: Lediglich 16% derjenigen, die ein Buch für sich

[Abb. 2] Die bis 19-Jährigen können sich eine Nutzung des E-Books am stärksten vorstellen. Gefragt wurde: Könntest du dir bzw. könnten Sie sich vorstellen, dieses Buch als E-Book zu lesen? [Basis: Personen, die für sich selbst gekauft haben; Käufer von Kinder- und Jugendbüchern 2010]

	Auf alle Fälle	Wahrscheinlich	Wahrscheinlich nicht	Auf keinen Fall
Gesamt	4	12	32	52
10 – 12 Jahre	5	17	36	42
13 – 14 Jahre	4	14	42	40
15 – 19 Jahre	4	16	40	40
20 – 29 Jahre	2	7	21	69
30 – 49 Jahre	5	9	24	63
50 Jahre +	0	3	28	69

[5] Vgl. beispielsweise CHRISTOPH KOCHHAN/KRISTIANE SCHENGBIER: Bücher und Lesen im Kontext unterschiedlicher Lebenswelten. Nutzung und Bedeutung von Büchern im Medienvergleich unter Berücksichtigung webbasierter Alternativen. In: *Media Perspektiven*. 12 (2007), S. 622–33 oder ANNETTE KLIEWER: Risikogruppe Jungen. Einige Konsequenzen für den geschlechter-differenzierenden Deutschunterricht. In: *Lesen in Deutschland 2008*. Hrsg. von STIFTUNG LESEN. Mainz 2008, S. 46–51.

[6] Käufer von Kinder- und Jugendbüchern sind vor allem Frauen. Sie machen zwei Drittel der Käuferschaft aus – ein Wert, der über die vergangenen drei Jahre konstant blieb. Zudem sind die Käufer in der Regel älter als 20 Jahre (über 90%). Das Kinder- und Jugendbuch hat also zwei Zielgruppen: Zum einen Erwachsene als Filter, in der Regel Eltern und Großeltern, die Bücher für Kinder und Enkelkinder erwerben. Zum anderen Kinder und Jugendliche, die Bücher für sich selbst kaufen (ein kleinerer Teil wird vom Taschengeld gekauft) oder die Kaufentscheidungen der Erwachsenen beeinflussen.

[Abb. 3] Beim zukünftigen E-Book-Kauf ist die Zielgruppe (noch) überschaubar. Gefragt wurde: Könntest du dir bzw. könnten Sie sich vorstellen, dieses Buch als E-Book zu kaufen? [Basis: Personen, die für sich selbst gekauft haben; Käufer von Kinder- und Jugendbüchern 2010]

	Auf alle Fälle	Wahrscheinlich	Wahrscheinlich nicht	Auf keinen Fall
Gesamt	2	6	28	64
10 – 12 Jahre	1	9	32	58
13 – 14 Jahre	2	6	34	59
15 – 19 Jahre	3	7	37	53
20 – 29 Jahre	0	4	15	81
30 – 49 Jahre	3	6	25	66
50 Jahre +	0	3	25	72

selbst gekauft haben, gaben diesbezüglich zu Protokoll, dass sie es für möglich hielten, das gekaufte Kinder- beziehungsweise Jugendbuch als E-Book zu lesen. Die Hälfte dieser Gruppe (8% der Personen, die sich vorstellen könnten, das gekaufte Buch als E-Book zu lesen) wäre auch bereit, dieses zu kaufen.

E-Book-Fans sind also im Bereich des Kinder- und Jugendbuchs noch eher die Minderheit. Dabei sind es vor allem die Jüngsten, die Freude an E-Books hätten. 5% der befragten Käufer im Alter zwischen zehn und zwölf Jahren könnten sich auf jeden Fall vorstellen, das gekaufte Buch auch als E-Book zu lesen. Immerhin 17% sagen, dass sie es als wahrscheinliche Option erachten. In der jüngsten Altersgruppe findet sich damit ein Marktpotenzial von 22% – sicherlich der Tatsache Tribut zollend, dass Medien zunehmend den Alltag der Kinder und Jugendlichen mitbestimmen und die Lesesozialisation noch in vollem Gange ist. Zudem ist auch die Gruppe der 13- bis 19-Jährigen gegenüber E-Books relativ offen.

Ältere Altersgruppen, die ein Kinder- und Jugendbuch gekauft haben, möchten es hingegen nur in geringem Maße in elektronischer Form lesen. Ab 20 Jahren können sich nur etwa 10% der Befragten vorstellen, ein Kinder- und Jugendbuch als E-Book zu lesen, etwa 4% würden eventuell auch die elektronische Variante käuflich erwerben wollen. Werden Kinder- und Jugendbücher als Geschenk gekauft (77%), ist die Haltung gegenüber der elektronischen Variante noch zurückhaltender: Unter den Geschenkkäufern erwarten nur etwa 10%, dass der Empfänger das gekaufte Buch auch als E-Book lesen würde. Gleichzeitig äußern 59%, dass sie sich dies auf gar keinen Fall und 30% wahrscheinlich nicht vorstellen können.

Interessant ist – bezogen auf unterschiedliche Altersgruppen –, dass sich die 20- bis 29-Jährigen deutlich skeptischer äußern als die anderen Altersgruppen: 84% dieser Altersgruppe können sich auf keinen Fall vorstellen, dass die Beschenkten das Buch auch in elektronischer Form lesen würden – eventuell, da gerade die 20- bis 29-Jährigen insbesondere Kinderbücher für jüngere Personen kaufen, die noch nicht in der Lage sind, Computer oder elektronische Lesegeräte zu bedienen. Deutlich aufgeschlossener hingegen sind die über 50-Jährigen. Offensichtlich attestieren sie den (Kinder- und Jugendbuch-)Beschenkten am ehesten eine Affinität zu digitaler Technik.

Festzuhalten bleibt, dass insbesondere diejenigen Kinder und Jugendlichen, die selbst Bücher kaufen, das E-Book als alternative Editionsform für möglich halten – also junge Menschen, die mit den neuen Medien aufwachsen und diese als selbstverständlich erachten. Ältere Befragte, und damit zumeist die Eltern der Kinder, stehen dem Kinder- und Jugendbuch in elektronischer Form – ähnlich dem Bild zu E-Books in der Gesamtgesellschaft – noch zurückhaltender gegenüber. Im Hinblick auf die (zu erwartende) Akzeptanz des elektronischen Kinder- und Jugendbuchs scheint jedoch ein Blick auf die Lebenswelten mit ihren unterschiedlichen Einstellungen und Werteorientierungen lohnenswert, in denen die Kinder und Eltern zu Hause sind, und inwiefern sich hier unterschiedliche Einstellungen zum E-Book finden lassen.

Akzeptanz in unterschiedlichen Lebenswelten

Die von Sinus Sociovision entwickelten Lebenswelten, die sogenannten Sinus-Milieus,[7] bieten eine Möglichkeit, soziale Gruppen differenziert zu erfassen: Die Gesellschaft wird hierfür in zehn Milieus gegliedert, als Abgrenzungskriterien der einzelnen »Gruppen« dienen einerseits die soziale Lage und andererseits die Werteorientierungen.

Innerhalb der Milieus sind nicht nur Unterschiede in Bezug auf die übergeordneten Unterscheidungskriterien zu beobachten, sondern – hieraus resultierend – auch bezüglich ihrer Affinität zu Büchern. Betrachtet man das Leseverhalten[8] und das Kaufverhalten[9] einzelner Milieus – und damit die Bereitschaft, für Bücher auch Geld auszugeben – zeigt sich, dass sich insbesondere diejenigen Lebenswelten, die sich durch eine hohe soziale Lage sowie eine moderne Werteorientierung (mit Ausnahme der Gruppe der Konservativen) auszeichnen, mit Büchern wohlfühlen. In Bezug auf Kinderbücher sind es insbesondere Postmaterielle, Moderne Performer sowie das Milieu der Bürgerlichen Mitte, die zentrale Käufer dieses Genres darstellen. Betrachtet man deren grundsätzliche Einstellung zu Inhalten auf elektronischen Medien, so zeigen die Ergebnisse der Studie *Buchkäufer und Leser 2008*, dass von diesen drei Milieus insbesondere die technikaffinen Modernen Performer das E-Book als sympathisch einstufen.[10] Postmaterielle und die Bürgerliche Mitte äußern sich eher zurückhaltend, wenngleich nicht ablehnend, zu E-Books. In Bezug auf die Frage, ob man sich in diesen Milieus vorstellen könne, das gekaufte Kinder- und Jugendbuch als E-Book zu lesen, zeigt sich durchgängig eine eher ablehnende Haltung.

Selbst die Modernen Performer, die multimediale Avantgarde, sind in Bezug auf das Genre Kinder- und Jugendbuch nur durchschnittlich offen. Technischen Optionen stehen sie hier – noch – eher im Bereich der Musik als der Literatur aufgeschlossen gegenüber. Für sie ist es wichtig, Kinder und Jugendliche in dieser Lebensphase nicht zu überfrachten. Sie sehen das Buch bewusst als Möglichkeit, sich aus der digitalen Medienwelt einmal »auszuklinken«. Allerdings vermutet ein im Rahmen der ethnografischen Interviews befragter Vater, der dem Milieu der Modernen Performer zuzuordnen ist, dass E-Books das Lesen für die Heranwachsenden eventuell interessanter machen könnte: »Wenn man was in der Hand hat, mit dem man noch ins Internet geht und, äh, die Seiten hin und her blättert, mit dem Finger, das könnte es interessanter machen, glaube ich, ja.«

Auch andere Milieus, die in ihrem Arbeitsumfeld häufig mit dem Computer umgehen, lehnen Kinder- und Jugendbücher in Form von E-Books ab (99 bis 100% Ablehnung).[11] Dies spiegelt sich etwa in der Äußerung einer bibliophilen Postmateriellen-Mutter wider: »[...] dass ich mir niemals ein E-Book kaufen werde, weil ich muss auch ein Buch in der Hand halten. Ich gehöre auch zu denen, die früher immer Randbemerkungen rangeschrieben haben.«

In der Regel spiegeln diese qualitativen Ergebnisse jedoch folgende Situation wider: Eltern schließen das Lesen von E-Books für sich selbst aus, sehen es aber für ihre Kinder als Zukunftsoption.

[Abb. 4] Bei den 20- bis 29-Jährigen polarisiert das E-Book. Gefragt wurde: Könntest du dir bzw. könnten Sie sich vorstellen, dass die Person, für die du bzw. Sie dieses Buch gekauft hast bzw. gekauft haben, dieses Buch auch als E-Book liest? [Basis: Personen, die für eine andere Person gekauft haben; Käufer von Kinder- und Jugendbüchern 2010

	Auf alle Fälle	Wahrscheinlich	Wahrscheinlich nicht	Auf keinen Fall
Gesamt	1	10	30	59
10 – Jahre	0	11	48	41
13 – 14 Jahre	0	9	36	55
15 – 19 Jahre	0	4	56	50
20 – 29 Jahre	0	11	5	84
30 – 49 Jahre	0	7	33	59
50 Jahre +	2	15	32	51

7 Die vorliegenden Untersuchungen folgen dem Milieu-Modell aus dem Jahr 2008, da dies noch während der Durchführung der Befragung im Frühjahr 2010 Gültigkeit hatte; das im August 2010 veröffentlichte, neuere Strömungen in der Gesellschaft aufgreifende Milieu-Modell bleibt im Folgenden unberücksichtigt. Zu den Milieus im Überblick vgl. die Homepage der SINUS Markt- und Sozialforschung GmbH (www.sinus-institut.de [15. 3. 2011]).
8 Insgesamt finden sich in der Gesellschaft Nichtleser (10%), Wenigleser (43%), Durchschnittsleser (23%) und Vielleser (25%). Vgl. *Buchkäufer und Leser. Profile, Motive, Wünsche*. Hrsg. vom BÖRSENVEREIN DES DEUTSCHEN BUCHHANDELS. Frankfurt a. M. 2008, S. 19.
9 Dieses ergibt 43% Nichtkäufer, 38% Wenigkäufer, 10% Durchschnittskäufer sowie 9% Vielkäufer. *Buchkäufer und Leser* (siehe Anm. 8), S. 15.
10 Vgl. ebd., S. 160.
11 Da die Anzahl der gegebenen Antworten bei der Frage, ob das Kinder- und Jugendbuch für sich selbst gekauft wurde, gering war (204 Personen), sind die Ergebnisse vorsichtig zu bewerten. Eine repräsentative Übertragbarkeit auf die Bevölkerung kann nicht gewährleistet werden, so dass man hier von Trendaussagen sprechen muss.

Haben die Befragten das Kinder- und Jugendbuch nicht für sich selbst, sondern als Geschenk gekauft, sind keine Milieuschwerpunkte zu identifizieren, wohl aber leichte Tendenzen: Unter Postmateriellen und Experimentalisten bezweifeln 92%, dass der Empfänger das Buch auch als E-Book lesen würde, innerhalb der Konservativen und Etablierten liegt der Wert mit 85% etwas niedriger. Generell ist also auch in Bezug auf den Geschenkkauf ebenso wie hinsichtlich des Kaufes für den Eigenbedarf (bislang noch) nur eine geringe Akzeptanz des E-Books im Genre Kinder- und Jugendbuch vorhanden.

Fazit

E-Books verankern sich zunehmend im Bewusstsein der Bevölkerung und werden als Alternative zu gedruckten Inhalten wahrgenommen. Gleichwohl zeigt sich, dass die elektronische Option noch nicht zu einem allgemein akzeptierten Standard unter den angebotenen Editionsformen avanciert ist. Die im Rahmen der Studie erhaltenen Befunde signalisieren im Hinblick auf Kinder- und Jugendbücher noch eine Zurückhaltung der Käufer und Leser – und dies über alle Lebenswelten hinweg. Auch die qualitativen Interviews, die mit den Eltern aus denjenigen Lebenswelten geführt wurden, die vor allem im Hinblick auf Kinder- und Jugendbücher eine kaufintensive Gruppe darstellen – also Postmaterielle, Bürgerliche Mitte und Moderne Performer – untermauern insgesamt noch die vorhandene Zurückhaltung gegenüber E-Books. Jedoch darf nicht übersehen werden, dass es bereits vereinzelte Akzeptanz gibt. Einer der befragten Jungen hat zum Beispiel einen Buch-Editor auf seinem Handy installiert, ein Mädchen hat auf ihrem iPod Touch einen Add-on, mit dem sie Bücher kaufen und lesen kann. Es bleibt abzuwarten, inwieweit aus diesen aktuell noch eher »Ausnahmefällen« in Zukunft ein Standard wird. Dies wird sicherlich auch abhängig sein von den Marktangeboten, die entwickelt und vom Leser akzeptiert werden – mögliche Zusatzelemente wie etwa Spiele oder Hintergrundinformationen zum Thema können beispielsweise das Lesen ergänzen.

Es ist möglich, dass sich die Akzeptanz im Hinblick auf Kinderbücher und Bücher für Jugendliche unterscheidet. Vor kurzem ging man noch davon aus, dass gerade Kinderbücher in Form von Bilderbüchern in der gewohnten Printform Bestand haben werden – die Jüngsten würden kaum mit Hilfe elektronischer Geräte an Lese- beziehungsweise Bilderinhalte herangeführt. Inzwischen hat sich der Markt weiterentwickelt und Eltern und Kindern stehen animierte Bilderbücher zur Verfügung. Das heißt, auch in Bezug auf Inhalte für die 3- bis 6-jährigen Kinder können die Eltern bereits auf sogenannte *enhanced E-Books* (erweiterte E-Books) zurückgreifen und deren Vorteile, zum Beispiel Interaktivität, nutzen. Inwieweit sich diese Applikationen durchsetzen werden, hängt sicherlich auch in entscheidendem Maße von der Verbreitung der Endgeräte ab. Hier bleibt letztlich zu fragen, ob animierte Bilderbücher Eltern dazu veranlassen können, ein entsprechendes Lesegerät zu erwerben oder ob das Vorhandensein eines Endgerätes im Haushalt die Voraussetzung dafür ist, sich ein Bilderbuch in elektronischer Form anzuschaffen.

Animierte Bilderbücher für die 3- bis 6-Jährigen stellen eine neue Option dar. Dennoch bleibt offen, ob sich diese Entwicklung altersmäßig nach unten fortsetzt und auch die Eltern der sogenannten 0- bis 2-jährigen Kinder, für die der Markt Papp- und Fühlbilderbücher produziert, demnächst auf interessante elektronische Varianten zurückgreifen können. Zur Zeit ist dies eher unvorstellbar, jedoch längerfristig eine Möglichkeit, die man nicht aus dem Auge verlieren darf. Gleichwohl muss hier gefragt werden, ob Kinder in diesem Alter von »Bildschirmen« lernen können. Manfred Spitzer weist auf Studien hin, nach denen Kleinkinder von Bildschirmen und Lautsprechern nichts lernen: »In Kalifornien konnten neun bis elf Monate alte Säuglinge chinesische Laute von einer Chinesin lernen, die ihnen vorlas. Wenn sie dieselbe Chinesin auf CD oder Video hörten oder sahen, lernten sie jedoch nichts. Säuglinge brauchen den sozialen Kontakt und eine Stimulation über alle Sinne [...]. Kleine Kinder lernen – das abgedroschene Wort muss hier genannt werden, weil kein anderes so gut passt – ganzheitlich.«[12]

Anders dürfte es sich mit Jugendbüchern verhalten. Computernutzung oder PC-Spiele haben ihren festen Platz als Freizeitaktivität Jugendlicher. Vor diesem Hintergrund ist es gut möglich, dass Jugendliche auch die digitale Nutzung von Buchinhalten zunehmend in ihren Alltag integrieren wollen beziehungsweise werden. Es lohnt sich also, E-Books auch für Jugendliche aufzubereiten, da junge Generationen mit digitalen Formen der Wissensvermittlung und des Entertainments aufwachsen. Generell sollte der Zugriff auf Buchinhalte über unterschiedliche Wege möglich sein, so dass Jugendliche sich dem Buch nicht aufgrund seiner Editionsform verschließen. Jedoch werden es auch hier – ähnlich dem Kinderbuch – sicherlich die Eltern sein, die aufgrund ihrer Sozialisation und entsprechend präferierten Editionsformen die Akzeptanz des E-Books bei den Nachwuchslesern zumindest mitbestimmen.

12 SPITZER (siehe Anm. 1), S. 8.

ELMAR MITTLER / CHRISTINA SCHMITZ
Digitale Edition und Forschungsbibliothek

Ein Tagungsbericht

DIE KOMPLEXEN ASPEKTE der Medienkonvergenz durch den zunehmenden Einfluss der Digitalisierung sind das Thema des gleichnamigen Forschungsschwerpunktes der Universität Mainz. Im Bereich des wissenschaftlichen Publizierens in den Geisteswissenschaften ist der Prozess digitaler Erfassung, Bearbeitung und Bereitstellung in gedruckter und digitaler Form im letzten Jahrzehnt teilweise in internationaler Kooperation bei den Editionen besonders weit vorangeschritten. Was lag näher, als den Stand der Entwicklung zum Gegenstand einer Tagung im Rahmen des Fellowships beim Gutenberg-Forschungskolleg von Prof. Elmar Mittler zu machen. Gemeinsam mit Dr. Malte Rehbein vom Fachbereich Computerphilologie der Universität Würzburg hatte er für den 13. und 14. Januar 2011 zur Fachtagung »Digitale Edition und Forschungsbibliothek« eingeladen. Veranstalter waren der Forschungsschwerpunkt Medienkonvergenz der Johannes Gutenberg-Universität Mainz (JGU) gemeinsam mit dem Zentrum für digitale Edition der Universität Würzburg und dem Institut für Dokumentologie und Editorik (IDE) sowie der Zeitschrift *Bibliothek und Wissenschaft*. Ziel war es dabei auch, das Wechselspiel zwischen Bibliotheken und den Erstellern und Nutzern digitaler Editionen in einer sich wandelnden medialen Landschaft zu verbessern. Mit über 90 Teilnehmern – Wissenschaftlern, Editoren, Bibliothekaren und Studierenden aus ganz Europa – kam eine optimal zusammengesetzte Gruppe nach Mainz, um die Chancen und Herausforderungen digitaler Editionen kennenzulernen, interdisziplinär zu diskutieren und zukunftsfähige Szenarien der Zusammenarbeit zu entwickeln.

Elmar Mittler wies einleitend auf die großen Anstrengungen der Bibliotheken hin, insbesondere auch durch große Digitalisierungsprojekte, den Zugang zum schriftlichen Kulturerbe zu verbessern. Sie haben digitale Fachbibliotheken aufgebaut und begonnen, sich aktiv an der Entwicklung von virtuellen Forschungsumgebungen zu beteiligen, um den Nutzern zukunftsorientierte Arbeitsmöglichkeiten anzubieten. Auf der anderen Seite haben die Editoren in vielfältigen Projekten unterschiedliche Formen digitaler Bereitstellung und Publikation erprobt, ohne dass es schon zu einer Standardisierung gekommen ist. Möglichkeiten der Zusammenarbeit zwischen beiden Gruppen werden aber noch zu wenig genutzt, weil die Bibliotheken weitgehend nur als Content-, nicht auch als Service-Anbieter wahrgenommen werden. Chance dieser Tagung, ebenso wie der im Anschluss geplanten Veröffentlichung der Beiträge in einem Schwerpunktheft von *Bibliothek und Wissenschaft* als »Publikationsorgan für beide Welten«, ist – neben der Darstellung des Status quo – die Verbesserung des Dialogs von Bibliothekaren und Editoren unterschiedlicher Disziplinen, wie dies ähnlich 1996 mit der Thematik »Forschung in der Bibliothek« bei einer Wolfenbütteler Tagung gelungen ist, bei der erstmals das Konzept digitaler Forschungscluster – heute würde man Plattform sagen – entwickelt wurde.[1] Dabei zeigt das beeindruckende fächerübergreifende Interesse die Aktualität der Thematik und das Bedürfnis nach einer interdisziplinären und internationalen Zusammenarbeit. Indem er die Frage nach den Ansprüchen der Nutzer und den Wünschen der Editoren an die Bibliotheken aufwarf, machte Mittler auch darauf aufmerksam, dass sich die Bibliotheken in der Forschungslandschaft neu positionieren müssen, um den veränderten Anforderungen gerecht zu werden.

Sektion 1, »Digitale Edition und Bibliothek«, wurde von Prof. Ulrich Johannes Schneider, Direktor der Universitätsbibliothek Leipzig, eingeleitet. »Digitalisierung, virtuelle Zusammenführung und digitale Bereitstellung des *Codex Sinaiticus* in Zusammenarbeit mit einem internationalen Konsortium sowie wissenschaftliche Erschließung des Leipziger Teils des *Codex Sinaiticus*« war ein erfolgreiches DFG-Projekt, das die Vorteile digitaler Editionen deutlich werden lässt, mit denen »die Ketten der Buchform gesprengt« würden und die Texte eine neue Freiheit bekämen. Digitale Texte sind in unbegrenztem Maße recherchierbar, so dass man beispielsweise die ersten Sätze aller digitalisierten Exemplare eines Werkes unmittelbar vergleichen kann. Durch die weltweite Erreichbarkeit digital edierter Werke fällt nach Schneider auch die Trennung zwischen den schwer zugänglichen kostbaren Handschriften und den »immer« erreichbaren Drucken weg. Übersetzer, Forscher, Restauratoren und viele weitere Personen können gemeinsam an einer digitalen Edition arbeiten, seien sie räumlich auch noch so weit voneinander entfernt. So entgrenzten sich in einer digitalen Bibliothek die Einheiten, um zu einem vielstimmigen Dialog zu werden. Die 2008 online gestellte, virtuelle Gesamtedition des *Codex Sinaiticus*[2] stellte Mustafa Dogan (jetzt Staats- und Universitätsbibliothek Göttingen), der technische Koordinator des Projekts, als Fallstudie vor. Die Ziele des Projekts sind die virtuelle Wiedervereinigung des Codex, von dem sich Fragmente in der Universitätsbibliothek Leipzig, der British Library, der Russischen Nationalbibliothek und dem Katharinen-Kloster auf dem Sinai erhalten haben, zudem die Einrichtung eines globalen Zugangs, die digitale Archivierung und erweiterte Nutzungsmöglichkeiten, die zugleich inhaltliche, historische und konservatorische Studien erlauben. Der Erfolg des Projekts und damit der Bedarf und das Interesse an digitalen Editionen wurde bereits bei der Veröffentlichung der Website deutlich, die nach drei Stunden sechs Millionen Zugriffe und 70 000 Nutzer verzeichnete. Abschließend gab Dogan zu bedenken, dass bei der Erarbeitung einer virtuellen Edition, die immer international ist, verschiedene Kulturen und Sichtweisen berücksichtigt werden können. So steht, je nach Nutzer, eine faksimileartige wie auch eine besonders leserfreundliche Ansicht mit vielen Zusatzinformationen bereit.

---

[1] Vgl. *Bibliothek und Wissenschaft*. 30 (1997), vor allem S. 141–9.
[2] www.codexsinaiticus.org/de [11. 2. 2011].

Eine grundlegende Aufarbeitung des Verhältnisses Bibliothek – Editionswissenschaftler bot Prof. Bodo Plachta von der Vrije Universität Amsterdam, der darauf hinwies, dass Bibliotheken es in früheren Jahrhunderten teilweise abgelehnt haben, Material zu erwerben, mit dem Varianten auch gedruckten Materials untersucht werden konnten, um dann für die Gegenwart ein Plädoyer für die Digitalisierung und Online-Bereitstellung von möglichst vielen Exemplaren eines (oft nur scheinbar identischen) Druckwerks zu halten. Er bedauert, dass nur wenige Bibliotheken noch eine führende Rolle bei Editionen haben, die heute eher bei Archiven und Akademien angesiedelt sind. Die ideale Edition der Zukunft sieht er in der Verknüpfung von Textphilologie und Dokumentendatenbank wie beispielsweise im Heine-Portal[3] oder in elektronischen Forschungsplattformen aus Dokumenten und Editionen wie der Neuen Mozart-Ausgabe.[4] Doch indem die Schnittstellen von Bibliotheken und editorischer Arbeit gesucht und genutzt würden, könnten die Bibliotheken beweisen, dass sie den Nutzern nicht nur Service, sondern als neue »Gedächtnisagenturen« auch optimale Forschungsmöglichkeiten bieten. Dem erhöhten Erklärungsbedarf, den wir haben, sobald wir uns im oft kontextneutralen Internet bewegen, könne man begegnen, indem man die Methoden der Editionswissenschaft mit dem Wissen der Bibliotheken (zum Beispiel bei den Standarddateien für Namen) vereint, um gemeinsam eines zu sichern: die Qualität der Edition auch im Zeitalter der Digitalisierung.

Wie die Bibliotheken ihre neue Aufgabe der Bereitstellung von Editionen wahrnehmen können, um vorliegende Editionsansätze der wissenschaftlichen Öffentlichkeit im Internet zu präsentieren, zeigte Stefan Cramme an einigen Beispielen aus der Bibliothek für Bildungsgeschichtliche Forschung (BBF) des Deutschen Instituts für Internationale Pädagogische Forschung. Durch die Konzentration auf ein Forschungsfeld kann die 1876 gegründete Bibliothek mit ihren 700 000 Bänden, darunter mehrere Spezialsammlungen, von einer engen Verbindung mit der Fachcommunity profitieren. Neben der Digitalisierung von ausgewählten Werken (Scripta Paedagogica Online[5]), Bildern (Pictura Paedagogica Online[6]) und Tondaten (Vox Paedagogica Online[7]) dient die BBF als Servicecenter für computergestützte Aufbereitung von Editionen. Anhand von Erfahrungsberichten zu den aktuellen Projekten der BBF wie der Briefausgabe Friedrich Fröbels oder der Edition der pädagogischen Schriften Adolf Reichweins machte Cramme deutlich, dass die Nutzung standardisierter *Mark up*-Sprachen trotz nicht auszuschließender Modifikationen notwendig ist. Die für die bildungsgeschichtliche Forschung besonders bedeutende Identifizierung von Personen wurde durch die Online-Bereitstellung von biografischen Datenbanken und die Verknüpfung von PND-Nummern qualitativ wesentlich verbessert, ist aber trotzdem noch sehr aufwendig. Bei der bibliothekarischen Arbeit liegt das Hauptaugenmerk auf Normdaten, Metadaten, persistenter Adressierung, der Einbindung in weitere Angebote und der langfristigen Verfügbarkeit.

In dem didaktisch sehr geschickten Beitrag von Prof. Mats Dahlström (Bibliothekshögskolan, Borås) – "Editing Libraries" – wurde das Spektrum der Editionsmöglichkeiten in der Bibliothek von der einfachen Massen-

---

[3] Hier werden die beiden großen Heine-Editionen mit Faksimiles von Handschriften, Drucken und weiteren Originalmaterialien gemeinsam zugänglich gemacht (http://urts55.uni-trier.de:8080/Projekte/HHP [11.2.2011]).

[4] http://dme.mozarteum.at/nma [11.2.2011].

[5] http://bbf.dipf.de/retro-digit0.htm [11.2.2011].

[6] http://bbf.dipf.de/VirtuellesBildarchiv/ [11.2.2011].

[7] http://bbf.dipf.de/vpo/ [11.2.2011].

digitalisierung bis zur wissenschaftlichen Edition vorgestellt, in der er das Feld enger Zusammenarbeit zwischen Bibliothekaren und Editoren sieht. Die Bibliotheken könnten dabei an ihre editorische Rolle anknüpfen, wie sie in Alexandria über Jahrhunderte gepflegt wurde.

Sektion 2, »Nutzer und Nutzung digitaler Editionen«, brachte mit dem Beitrag von Prof. Michael Stolz (Universität Bern) – »Benutzerführung in digitalen Editionen. Erfahrungen aus dem Parzivalprojekt« zunächst eine praxisnahe Darstellung der ausgefeilten Palette an Zugriffsmöglichkeiten der Berner Parzivaledition, die leider nur als CD-ROM vorliegt. Diese aber bietet beispielhaft den Beginn einer vollständigen Neuedition des *Parzival*, die in ihrer gesamten Fülle der Überlieferung derzeit bloß in größeren Teilabschnitten vollständig präsentiert werden kann. Man kann sich bloß wünschen, dass diese immense Arbeit vollendet und viele der realisierten Darstellungs-, Kombinations- und Zugriffsmöglichkeiten bei zukünftigen Editionen vergleichbarer mittelalterlicher Texte aufgegriffen werden.

Andrea Rapp (Universität Trier) konnte in ihrem Beitrag »TextGrid als virtuelle Infrastruktur für digitale Editionen«, zeigen, wie die Werkbank des zukünftigen Texteditors aussehen könnte, dem schon jetzt ein Fülle von Tools für die Bild/Textverknüpfung oder die Wörterbuchrecherche bis hin zum XML-Editor im »TextGridLab« angeboten werden, denen in den nächsten Monaten ein Noten- und ein Glossen-Editor folgen sollen. Das »TextGridRep« bietet Speicherungsmöglichkeiten für Forschungsdaten und Texte. Es wird um Komponenten für die Langzeitarchivierung ergänzt. TextGrid dient vor allem auch der kollaborativen Edition über Institutionen- und Ländergrenzen hinweg.

Patrick Sahle (Universität Köln), einer der besten Spezialisten für das digitale Editieren, der schon 1997 seine epochemachenden Thesen zur Edition historischer Quellen vorgelegt hat,[8] bot mit seinem Beitrag »Funktionalität und Formensprache von Oberflächen digitaler Editionen: Grundsätzliche Probleme und gegenwärtige Lösungen« im Ansatz nach eine umfassende Darstellung der digitalen Edition, in der die Repräsentation von Daten durch Präsentation auf einer Oberfläche geschieht. Aus Zeitgründen wurde diese aber nur ausschnittweise vorgetragen.

Sektion 3, »Chancen und Herausforderungen der Bibliotheken im digitalen Zeitalter«, begann mit dem Beitrag von Thomas Stäcker (HAB Wolfenbüttel) – »Creating the knowledge site – Herausforderungen an die Edition der Zukunft«, der aus seinem breiten Erfahrungsschatz mit Editionen im eigenen Hause berichten konnte. Für ihn ist das Ende des experimentierenden elektronischen Inkunabelzeitalters erkennbar. Auch er betonte die Bedeutung der Anwendung von Standards, um die Interoperabilität aber auch die dauerhafte Zugänglichkeit der Ergebnisse zu gewährleisten. Die Rolle der Bibliotheken liegt nicht nur in der Einrichtung und dauerhaften Bereitstellung der "knowledge sites", die moderne Editionen darstellen; sie sollen auch editorisch weniger erfahrenen Wissenschaftlern Hilfestellung zum Beispiel bei der TEI-Anwendung geben.

Die großen Aufgaben, die auf eine zur Langzeitarchivierung verpflichtete Einrichtung zukommen, machte Reinhard Altenhöner (Deutsche

[8] PATRICK SAHLE: Digitale Edition (Historischer Quellen) – Einige Thesen. Stand: 20.7.1997. Online verfügbar über: www.uni-koeln.de.

Nationalbibliothek, Frankfurt am Main) in »Trau, schau, wem – Zur Authentizität und Langzeitverfügbarkeit digitaler Objekte« deutlich. Die DNB baut ihr Langzeitarchivierungssystem systematisch auf, entwickelt die notwendigen Workflows und weitet das angeforderte Material schrittweise aus – ist aber von einer vollständigen Erfassung des Aufkommens digitaler Veröffentlichungen noch weit entfernt.

Joris van Zundert und Peter Boot (Koninklijke Nederlandse Akademie van Wetenschappen, Huygens Institute Den Haag) rundeten im abschließenden Beitrag "Services not Resources" das Bild der modernen Edition ab, wie sie in der vorbildlichen Edition der Briefe Van Goghs vom Huygens Institute realisiert worden ist.[9] Sie legen Wert darauf, Editionen für die aktive Mitarbeit und Weiterentwicklung auch Außenstehender zu öffnen. Auch sie sehen die Zukunft in der Entwicklung virtueller Forschungsumgebungen nicht nur für das Edieren von Texten, die das weltweite gemeinsame Arbeiten von Wissenschaftlern ermöglichen.

In der Abschlussdiskussion wurde die Zukunft der Buchedition trotz der vielen Vorzüge der interaktiven Datenbanken nicht grundsätzlich in Frage gestellt – auch von der Van Gogh Briefedition ist eine gedruckte Fassung erschienen. Ob das allerdings noch bei neuen vielbändigen Gesamtwerkeditionen möglich sein wird, ist sicher fraglich. Damit stellt sich auch die Frage nach der Rolle der Verleger in der sich abzeichnenden Entwicklung hin zu digitalen Editionen und virtuellen Forschungsumgebungen, die Dauerhaftigkeit und Neutralität des Angebotes erfordern, die – wie die Langzeitarchivierung – eher in neutralen Institutionen wie Bibliotheken, Akademien und Archiven gesichert zu sein scheint. Zweifellos gibt es aber auch weiterhin Chancen für verlegerische Arbeit und Absatzmöglichkeiten für innovative Produkte.

Unterschiedlich wurden die Chancen des offenen Zugangs zu Editionen beurteilt, deren Integrität auf jeden Fall gesichert bleiben muss. Eine Versionskontrolle wie bei Wikipedia wird als nicht ausreichend angesehen. Der Einsatz von *crowdsourcing* im editorischen Bereich ist derzeit eher noch im experimentellen Stadium.

Als beste Strategie zur Durchsetzung von Standards wird das Angebot zum Beispiel von XML-Editoren und Schulungen nach dem Vorbild Wolfenbüttels und nachträgliches Verbessern von Editionen gesehen. Von großer Wichtigkeit ist dafür aber auch die Ausweitung der Ausbildung in *Digital Humanities* wie sie zum Beispiel in Darmstadt, Köln und Würzburg bereits besteht. Unter Federführung des Cologne Center for eHumanities der Universität Köln wird derzeit ein Curriculum für *Digital Humanities* in interdisziplinärer Zusammenarbeit entwickelt, für das ein breiter Bedarf gesehen wird.

Insgesamt hat die Mainzer Tagung einen umfassenden Einblick in die Werkstatt digitaler Editionen, ihren Wert und ihre Zukunftsperspektiven gegeben. Es ist erfreulich, dass man in wenigen Monaten mit der Publikation der Vorträge, die um einige zusätzliche Beiträge ergänzt werden, in der Zeitschrift *Bibliothek und Wissenschaft* rechnen kann.

---

[9] Vincent van Gogh: The Letters. Hrsg. von LEO JANSEN, HANS LUIJTEN u. NIENKE BAKKER. Van Gogh Museum Amsterdam. Online verfügbar unter www.vangoghletters.org [11. 2. 2011].

Zur Diskussion gestellt

ANNIKA ROCKENBERGER

Albrecht Dürer, Sebastian Brant und die Holzschnitte des *Narrenschiff*-Erstdrucks (Basel 1494)

Ein forschungskritischer Einspruch

IM 1494 IN BASEL PUBLIZIERTEN, vermutlich von Michael Furter mit finanzieller Unterstützung Johann Bergmanns von Olpe gedruckten *Narrenschiff*-Erstdruck[1] gibt es 114 bildliche, den Text illustrierende Darstellungen in Form einfarbiger Abzüge von unsignierten Holzschnitten. Da diese Abzüge zugleich mit dem Textabdruck im Hochdruckverfahren erzeugt wurden, müssen die zugrunde liegenden Holzschnitte (d. h. die geschnittenen Holzstöcke), in der prä-typografischen Phase des arbeitsteiligen Produktionsprozesses, jedoch (für den vorliegenden Fall) chronologisch auf die (handschriftliche) Abfassung des Textes folgend, hergestellt worden sein.[2]

Im folgenden Aufsatz diskutiere ich Versuche, die (anteilige) Urheberschaft für besagte Holzschnitte dem Autor Sebastian Brant und/oder dem jungen Albrecht Dürer zuzuschreiben. Ehe ich alle hierfür angeführten Argumente und Quellenbelege[3] einer eingehenden Überprüfung unterziehe, seien einige dem besseren Verständnis der Problemerörterung dienliche medientechnikhistorische Hinweise vorausgeschickt.

Die Herstellung der text-illustrierenden Holzschnitte erfolgte in der Regel in einem arbeitsteiligen Prozess, an dem verschiedene Akteure in verschiedenen Funktionen beteiligt waren. Über die Arbeitsteilung bei der Herstellung xylografischer Illustrationen gegen Ende des 15. Jahrhunderts ist man aus verschiedenen Quellen informiert.[4] Konventionell sah ein Herstellungsablauf so aus: Ein Maler – in der Funktion des Entwerfers – erstellte einen Entwurf der Illustration, indem er die Informationen über Bildinhalt und -komposition direkt aus dem zum Druck vorgesehenen Text beziehungsweise aus Textteilen entnahm. Dieser oder ein anderer Maler – in der Funktion des Reißers – übertrug den

---

1 Dieser Aufsatz entstand als Nebenprodukt einer medienhistorisch-druckanalytischen Untersuchung zu Produktion und Überlieferung des *Narrenschiff*-Erstdrucks: ANNIKA ROCKENBERGER: Produktion und Drucküberlieferung der editio princeps von Sebastian Brants Narrenschiff (Basel 1494). Eine medienhistorisch-druckanalytische Untersuchung. Frankfurt a. M. 2011 (*Europäische Hochschulschriften: Reihe 1, Deutsche Sprache und Literatur*. 2009). – Für eine Reihe kritischer Einwände und weiterführender Hinweise danke ich herzlich Per Röcken (Berlin).
2 In der Frühzeit der kunst- und literaturwissenschaftlichen Forschung zu den Illustrationen des *Narrenschiffs* wurde auch die Auffassung vertreten, dass vom Text vorerst nur eine grobe Konzeption vorgelegen habe, nach der die Holzschnitte von einem autonomen Künstler gearbeitet wurden, die ihrerseits dann die inhaltliche Vorlage für den ausformulierten Text abgegeben haben sollen. Meines Wissens wird diese Thesen nicht mehr ernsthaft vertreten. Vgl. aber CHARLES SCHMIDT: *Histoire littéraire de l'Alsace à la fin du XVᵉ et au commencement du XVIᵉ siècle*. Paris 1879. 2 Bde. Reprografischer Nachdruck der Erstausgabe: Hildesheim 1966. Bd. 1, S. 323–9. Eine schwächere Variante geht dahin, dass nur die Motti zeitlich nach den fertig gestellten Holzrissen entstanden sind. Diese Auffassung kann heute als *communis opinio* gelten; vgl. dagegen jedoch vor allem HELMUT ROSENFELD: Sebastian Brant und Albrecht Dürer. Zum Verhältnis von Bild und Text im Narrenschiff. In: GJ 1972, S. 328–36 und DERS.: Brants »Narrenschiff« und seine Stellung in der Publizistik und zur Gesellschaft. In: *Beiträge zur Geschichte des Buches und seiner Funktion in der Gesellschaft*. Hrsg. von ALFRED GERARD SWIERK u. HANS WIDMANN. Stuttgart 1974, S. 230–45.
3 Einen guten Überblick zu den

Entwurf auf den vorbereiteten Holzstock, den Holzriss. Ein Formschneider fertigte daraus einen druckfähigen Holzschnitt an.[5]

Eine Abwandlung dieses dreistufigen Modells eines Arbeitsablaufs geht dahin, dass der Entwerfer nicht der Maler, sondern der Verfasser oder Editor des Textes oder der Drucker war. »Entwerfen« heißt in diesem Zusammenhang, dass mehr oder weniger detailliert ausgearbeitete Konzepte für Bildinhalt und -komposition – das können knappe oder ausführliche schriftliche Erläuterungen und/oder bildliche Skizzen auf Papier (oder einem ähnlichen Beschreibstoff) oder bereits auf den für die Holzschnitte vorgesehenen Holzstöcken gewesen sein.[6] Ein – oder bei umfangreichen Illustrationsarbeiten auch mehrere – handwerklich-künstlerisch ausgebildete Reißer arbeiteten auf Grundlage dieser »Visierungen« die Risse aus. Die Vorstellung eines am Bildentwurf maßgeblich beteiligten Visierers, der kein ausgebildeter Künstler-Handwerker war, ist nur für sehr wenige Fälle frühneuzeitlicher Drucküberlieferung dokumentiert, wird aber für eine Vielzahl der gelehrten Dichter der Renaissance respektive der Frühneuzeit postuliert.

Eine dritte Variante des arbeitsteiligen Herstellungsvorgangs ist das Nachschneiden von Bildvorlagen anderer Drucke oder Handschriften – als Verfahren häufig beim Kopieren beziehungsweise Nach- oder »Raubdrucken« angewandt. Die Funktion des Entwerfers oder Visierers war hier nicht nötig, die möglichen Funktionsträger reduzierten sich entsprechend auf Reißer und Formschneider.

Eine vierte Variante ist die Wiederverwendung bereits für andere Drucke in den oben genannten Verfahren hergestellter Holzschnitte, die durch den Drucker erworben wurden oder sich bereits als Resultat vorhergehender Druckprojekte in dessen Besitz befanden. Hierbei veränderte sich zwar der Verwendungszusammenhang, jedoch nicht die Herstellungsweise.

Für den *Narrenschiff*-Druck Basel 1494 können die beiden letztgenannten Herstellungsverfahren ausgeschlossen werden: Weder ist eine Wiederverwendung bereits in anderem Zusammenhang hergestellter Holzschnitte nachweisbar, noch handelt es sich bei dieser Ausgabe um Nachschnitte bereits gedruckter Vorlagen. Für die Rekonstruktion des Produktionsprozesses muss demnach geklärt werden, ob es Indizien gibt, die für die konventionelle Herstellungsvariante oder die Visierer-Variante

---

einbezogenen Materialien und einen Eindruck von den aus diesen üblicherweise gezogenen Schlussfolgerungen bieten (zuweilen forschungsskeptisch und im Ergebnis inkonsequent) CORNELIA SCHNEIDER: *Das Narrenschiff*. Ausst.-Kat. Mainz 1994, S. 47–58 sowie (affirmativ) WOLFGANG SCHMID: *Dürer als Unternehmer. Kunst, Humanismus und Ökonomie in Nürnberg um 1500*. Trier 2003, S. 64–70 (»Das Narrenschiff und weitere Arbeiten in Basel«).

4 Zum (druck-)technischen Aspekt des Holzschnitts vgl. nur die entsprechenden Abschnitte bei CLAUS W. GERHARDT: *Geschichte der Druckverfahren*. Bd. 2: Der Buchdruck. Stuttgart 1975 sowie FONS VAN DER LINDEN: *DuMonts Handbuch der grafischen Techniken. Manuelle und maschinelle Druckverfahren*. 3. Aufl. Köln 1990, S. 27–94.

5 Vgl. hierzu neuerdings CHRISTOPH RESKE: Der Holzschnitt bzw. Holzstock am Ende des 15. Jahrhunderts. In: GJ 2009, S. 71–8.

6 Ein Beispiel solcher elaborierten Visierungen liegt im Überlieferungsfall der handschriftlichen Vorarbeiten zur lateinischen Druckausgabe der *Schedelschen Weltchronik* vor. Vgl. hierzu die mustergültige Untersuchung von CHRISTOPH RESKE: *Die Produktion der Schedelschen Weltchronik in Nürnberg. The Production of Schedel's Nuremberg Chronicle*. Wiesbaden 2000; vgl. auch DERS.: Albrecht Dürers Beziehung zur »Schedelschen Weltchronik« unter besonderer Berücksichtigung des »Berliner Stockes«. In: GJ 2003, S. 45–66. – Da der Druck der *Weltchronik* in vielerlei Hinsicht von dem des *Narrenschiffs* verschieden ist, sind Analogieschlüsse äußerst problematisch. Zur Frage, ob bei der Druckkonzeption des *Narrenschiffs* Visierungen vom Autor vorgelegen haben, vgl. unten den Abschnitt zur »Brant-Visierer-These«.

sprechen und daraus folgend, welche Funktionsträger – Entwerfer oder Visierer, Reißer, Formschneider – in welchem Maße an der Herstellung der Illustrationen beteiligt gewesen sind.

Bei einem flüchtigen Blick in die ungewöhnlich umfangreiche multidisziplinäre Forschungsliteratur zu diesem Aspekt der Produktion des *Narrenschiff*-Druckes scheint es, als seien sowohl die Frage nach dem Herstellungsvorgang als auch die nach der Identität und dem jeweiligen Urheberanteil der verschiedenen Funktionsträger an den Holzschnitten geklärt. Dabei erweisen sich die jeweils zur Untermauerung der vertretenen Thesen angeführten Argumente als hochkomplex und äußerst voraussetzungsreich, so dass ich es als sinnvoll erachte, die jeweiligen Argumentationsstrategien hier einmal *en detail* zu rekonstruieren. Dies erscheint mir auch deshalb angezeigt, weil der Erstdruck des *Narrenschiffs* auch in dieser Hinsicht als Sonderfall dargestellt wird, wobei die Maxime gilt, dass diejenige argumentative Strategie zu bevorzugen ist, die dem Gegenstand ein Maximum an (ästhetischem, geistigem etc.) Wert und ein Maximum an »Bedeutung« zuschreibt und zugleich bestimmten Autor- und Künstlerbildern den Vorzug gibt.

Ich erhebe – dies sei noch vorausgeschickt – nicht den Anspruch, die aufgestellten Thesen widerlegen zu können oder meinerseits neue Thesen zu formulieren, sondern möchte darauf aufmerksam machen, dass eine These (a) nicht dadurch bestätigt wird, dass sie nicht widerlegt werden kann[7] und (b) die schiere Möglichkeit, dass ein Sachverhalt zutreffen kann, noch nichts über die Wahrscheinlichkeit seines Zutreffens aussagt (hier gilt bekanntlich als allgemeine Regel für Modalitätsschlüsse: *a posse ad oportere non valet consequentia*).

Anders als Klaus Manger bin ich nicht der Auffassung, dass der inzwischen erreichte Diskussionsstand »allein durch gesicherte Zeugnisse voranzubringen«[8] wäre, sondern meine, dass vor allem eine nüchterne Einschätzung der seit langem vorliegenden gesicherten Informationen

---

[7] Dieser argumentative Fehlschluss firmiert gemeinhin unter dem Namen *argumentum ad ignorantiam*. Vgl. dazu nur DOUGLAS WALTON: The Appeal to Ignorance, or Argumentum Ad Ignorantiam. In: *Argumentation*. 13 (1999), S. 367–77. Die Beweislast liegt in jedem Fall bei demjenigen, der diese These vertritt, nicht bei demjenigen, der ihre Gültigkeit bestreitet.

[8] KLAUS MANGER: *Das »Narrenschiff«. Entstehung, Wirkung und Deutung*. Darmstadt 1983, S. 62.

[9] Die sich mit diesem Thema befassenden Aufsätze und Monografien sind Legion und geben vor allem Aufschluss über die Mechanismen affirmativer Bezugnahme auf einen extrem wirkmächtigen Behauptungsdiskurs. – Die im Folgenden ausgewerteten Forschungsbeiträge stammen jeweils von den Hauptvertretern der einen oder anderen Argumentationsstrategie, sind oder waren in ihrem jeweiligen Fach etabliert und haben zur Bildung der heutigen *communis opinio* maßgeblich beigetragen; ihnen sind alle wesentlichen Argumente zu entnehmen. Die prominentesten Vertreter der »Dürer-Reißer-These« sind: CARL FRIEDRICH VON RUMOHR: *Zur Geschichte und Theorie der Formschneidekunst*. Leipzig 1837, S. 8 und S. 81; DANIEL BURCKHARDT: *Albrecht Dürer's Aufenthalt in Basel. 1492–1494. Mit 15 Text-Illustrationen und 50 Tafeln in Lichtdruck*. München, Leipzig 1892; DERS.: Dürer und der Meister der Bergmannschen Offizin. Mit zwanzig Textabbildungen. In: *Jahrbuch der Preußischen Kunstsammlungen*. 28.3 (1907), S. 168–80; HEINRICH WÖLFLIN: *Die Kunst Albrecht Dürers* (EA 1905). Bearb. von KURT GERSTENBERG. 6. Aufl. München 1943, S. 48–51; FRIEDRICH WINKLER: *Dürer und die Illustrationen zum Narrenschiff. Die Basler und Straßburger Arbeiten des Künstlers und der altdeutsche Holzschnitt*. Berlin 1951; ERWIN PANOFSKY: *Das Leben und die Kunst Albrecht Dürers* (EA 1943). München 1977, S. 31–40; MANFRED LEMMER: *Die Holzschnitte zu Sebastian Brants »Narrenschiff«*. 2. Aufl. Leipzig 1979; WALTER L. STRAUSS: *Albrecht Dürer. Woodcuts and Woodblocks*. New York 1980, S. 64/5 sowie ERNST REBEL: *Albrecht Dürer. Maler und Humanist*. München 1996, S. 51–3. – Die überwiegende Mehrheit der neueren und neuesten Beiträge, die die Holzschnitte zum Gegenstand haben, beziehen sich zustimmend auf diese Gewährsleute. Nicht oder nicht zustimmend rezipiert sind dagegen die der These eher ablehnend gegenüberstehenden Kunsthistoriker, namentlich WERNER WEISBACH: *Der Meister der Bergmannschen Officin und Albrecht Dürers Beziehungen zur Basler Buchillustration. Ein Beitrag zur Geschichte des deutschen Holzschnittes*. Strassburg 1896; DERS.: *Der junge Dürer. Drei Studien*. Leipzig 1907, S. 22–7; HANS TIETZE / ERIKA TIETZE-CONRAT: *Kritisches Verzeichnis der Werke Albrecht Dürers*. 2 Bde. Augsburg 1928. Bd. 1, S. 302–4 sowie EDUARD FLECHSIG: *Albrecht*

angezeigt ist. Dort, wo ausreichend validierbares Quellenmaterial fehlt, ist ohnehin Zurückhaltung geboten und das Eingeständnis des Nicht-Wissens jedenfalls redlicher als die fortwährende Tradierung für selbstevident und höchstwahrscheinlich ausgegebener Spekulationen und hausgemachter Gewissheiten.

Die Dürer-Reißer-These
Die Frage nach der Urheberschaft der *Narrenschiff*-Illustrationen wird in der kunst- wie literaturhistorischen Forschung seit dessen »Wiederentdeckung« in der ersten Hälfte des 19. Jahrhunderts heftig diskutiert.[9] Heute gilt folgende These in der Kunst- und Literaturgeschichte als *communis opinio*:[10] Albrecht Dürer hat die meisten (oder alle) Holzschnitte des *Narrenschiffs* gemacht – genauer: Er hat die Holzrisse für die Illustrationen angefertigt. Obwohl keinerlei direkte Belege für eine wie auch immer geartete Beteiligung Dürers an der Illustration des Druckes bekannt sind und eine solche nur mehr oder weniger wahrscheinlich gemacht werden kann, wird suggeriert, dass die Dürer-These belegt, wenn nicht bewiesen sei. Die verschiedenen zu diesem Zweck in Anschlag gebrachten Argumentationsstrategien zeichnen sich in kunst- wie literaturhistorischer Forschung als mehrschichtig und voraussetzungsreich aus. Ich werde im Folgenden den Versuch unternehmen, die zentralen Argumente zu rekonstruieren und zu überprüfen, um so der Frage nach einer Beteiligung Dürers – und zwar in der Funktion des beziehungsweise eines Reißers – in der prä-typografischen Produktionsphase des *Narrenschiff*-Erstdrucks nachzugehen.

Drei Argumente werden für die Zuweisung der (mehrerer, der meisten, aller) *Narrenschiff*-Holzschnitte an Albrecht Dürer angeführt:

1. Chronologische, genauer: biografische Gründe sprächen für eine Urheberschaft Dürers. Hierbei wird davon ausgegangen, dass sich der junge Albrecht Dürer während seiner Gesellenwanderung lange genug

Dürer. Sein Leben und seine künstlerische Entwickelung. 2 Bde. Berlin 1928–31. Bd. 1, S. 3–10, S. 129–39 und S. 304–9. – Inkonsequenterweise wird in der neuesten Werkzusammenstellung (2004) trotz der geäußerten Zweifel an der Zuschreibung dieser und weiterer unsicherer Holzschnitte an Dürer festgehalten; vgl. RAINER SCHOCH: Albrecht Dürer und der Buchholzschnitt in Basel und Straßburg 1492–1494. In: *Albrecht Dürer. Das druckgraphische Werk. Bd. III. Buchillustrationen (Werkkatalog)*. Hrsg. von DEMS., MATTHIAS MENDE u. ANNE SCHERBAUM. München u. a. 2004, S. 23–32.

10 Seit dem »Machtwort« FRIEDRICH WINKLERS (siehe Anm. 9) hat es meines Wissens weder in der kunsthistorischen (die einzige mir bekannte Ausnahme ist jetzt ANJA GREBE: *Albrecht Dürer. Künstler, Werk und Zeit.* Darmstadt 2006, S. 31–3), noch in der literaturwissenschaftlichen Debatte einen Beitrag gegeben, der in dieser Frage wesentlich von der *communis opinio* abweicht. In den gängigsten fachspezifischen Nachschlagewerken neuesten Datums spiegelt sich dies wider. Zwei Beispiele sollen hier genügen: Bei HERBERT JAUMANN: *Handbuch Gelehrtenkultur der Frühen Neuzeit. Bd. 1. Bio-bibliographisches Repertorium.* Berlin, New York 2004 findet sich unter dem Stichwort »Brant, Sebastian« der Hinweis (S. 129): »Das wirkungsvollste Hauptwerk ist die Satire in Versen *Das Narrenschiff* (zuerst 1494, mit Holzschnitten des jungen Albrecht Dürer)«; in der revidierten Ausgabe des Verfasserlexikons (JOACHIM KNAPE: Artikel zu Brant (Titio), Sebastian. In: *Deutscher Humanismus 1480–1520. Verfasserlexikon.* 2 Bde. Hrsg. von FRANZ JOSEF WORSTBROCK. Berlin 2008. Bd. 1, Sp. 247–83, hier Sp. 253) ist zu lesen: »Bergmann von Olpe und B[rant] gaben Aufträge zur Herstellung der Holzschnitte an mindestens vier Reißer; unter ihnen gilt der junge Albrecht Dürer mit etwa zwei Dritteln der Entwürfe als Hauptmeister«. Vgl. als neuere literaturgeschichtliche Beiträge noch ROMY GÜNTHART: *Deutschsprachige Literatur im frühen Basler Buchdruck (ca. 1470–1510).* Münster u. a. 2007, S. 225, Anm. 246: »Die Zuweisung an Dürer ist mittlerweile unbestritten« und SERAINA PLOTKE: Emblematik vor der Emblematik? Der frühe Buchdruck als Experimentierfeld der Text-Bild-Beziehungen. In: *Zeitschrift für deutsche Philologie.* 129.1 (2010), S. 127–42, hier S. 129, Anm. 12: »Die Erstausgabe von Brants ›Narrenschiff‹ war mit über 100 Holzschnitten versehen, die zum Großen Teil von Albrecht Dürer stammen«.

in Basel (und der näheren Umgebung) aufgehalten habe, um alle (oder einige) der ihm zugeschriebenen Holzschnitte anzufertigen.

2. Die Zusammenarbeit zwischen Dürer und anderen an der Herstellung des *Narrenschiff*-Drucks beteiligten Akteuren bei anderen lokalen Druckprojekten lasse den Analogieschluss zu, dass eine solche Zusammenarbeit auch im Fall des *Narrenschiff*-Erstdrucks vorgelegen habe.

Konfundiert werden diese Argumente durchweg mit dem Postulat einer Wertmaximierung[11] des *Narrenschiffs* und/oder der Präferenz bestimmter Autor- und Künstlerbilder. Dieses Postulat leitet vor allem die stilkritischen Argumente an und erklärt gleichzeitig (wenigstens zum Teil) die Persistenz der Dürer-These.

3. Eine Reihe stilkritischer Belege wiesen eindeutig auf Dürer hin.

Zu 1.: Für die Zuweisung der oder einiger Holzschnitte des *Narrenschiff*-Druckes an Albrecht Dürer (also für das Beweisziel: Dürer ist Urheber der/einiger *Narrenschiff*-Holzschnitte) ist es zunächst eine notwendige Bedingung, dass sich dieser für eine bestimmte Zeitdauer vor der Fertigstellung des Erstdruckes am 11. Februar 1494 am Ort der Drucklegung, Basel, aufgehalten haben muss.[12] Wie verhält es sich mit Belegen für diese Bedingung? Zunächst zu den quellenkundlichen Kriterien. Es gibt für den in Frage kommenden Zeitraum schriftliche Quellen mit biografischen Informationen zu Dürers Aufenthaltsort (a–d).

a. Die *Familienchronik* Albrecht Dürers von 1524,[13] in der es heißt: »Und da ich außgedient hat, schickt mich mein vatter hinwegg, und bliebe vier jahr außen, biß daß mich mein vater wider fordert. Und alß ich im 1490 jahr hinwegg zug, nach Ostern (= 11. April 1490), darnach kam ich wider, alß man zehlt 1494 nach Pfingsten (= 18. Mai 1494)«.

Was wird in der Chronik berichtet? Nach der Beendigung der Lehrzeit (»da ich außgedient hat«) ist Dürer als Geselle für eine Dauer von vier Jahren auf Wanderschaft; er hat sich vom 11. April 1490 bis zum 18. Mai 1494 nicht in Nürnberg aufgehalten (»bliebe vier jahr außen«). Die Quelle gibt über den oder die Aufenthaltsorte der Wanderzeit nur im Hinblick darauf, wo er nicht war, Auskunft; das Ziel beziehungsweise die Stationen seiner Gesellenfahrt bleiben offen.

b. Zu diesen Zielen beziehungsweise Stationen gibt eine andere

---

[11] Um zwei illustrative Beispiele zu nennen: THOMAS CRAMER: »Der bildniss ich hab har gemacht« – Noch einmal: zu Text und Bild im »Narrenschiff«. In: *Beiträge zur Geschichte der deutschen Sprache und Literatur.* 111.2 (1989), S. 314–35; JÜRGEN SCHULZ-GROBERT: Das Straßburger Eulenspiegelbuch. Studien zu entstehungsgeschichtlichen Voraussetzungen der ältesten Drucküberlieferung. Tübingen 1999 (*Hermaea* NF. 83), S. 38–42 und S. 96–9.

[12] Es ist meines Wissens kein Fall aus der späteren Inkunabelzeit respektive Frühdruckzeit bekannt, der belegt, dass die Herstellung der Holzschnitte o. ä. an einem anderen als dem Druckort erfolgt ist.

[13] Die sogenannte *Familienchronik* Albrecht Dürers ist nicht als Autograf überliefert; es existieren noch vier 4 bis 6 Blätter umfassende Abschriften sowie ein Abdruck (der möglicherweise auf eine weitere ältere Abschrift zurückgeht) aus dem 17. Jahrhundert, die im Textbestand »im wesentlichen« miteinander übereinstimmen; keines der Dokumente geht direkt auf Dürers Autografen zurück. Vgl. dazu ausführlicher: Albrecht Dürer. Schriftlicher Nachlaß. Bd. 1: Autobiographische Schriften, Briefwechsel, Dichtungen, Beischriften, Notizen und Gutachten, Zeugnisse zum persönlichen Leben. Hrsg. von HANS RUPPRICH. Berlin 1956, S. 27–34, hier S. 31, Z. 205–10. Ich zitiere hier und im Folgenden nach dieser Ausgabe durch Angabe von Seiten- und Zeilenzahl.

[14] Christoph II. Scheurl (1481–1542), Rechtsgelehrter, ab 1512 Rechtskonsulent (im diplomatischen Dienst) der Stadt Nürnberg. Vgl. NDB. Bd. 22, S. 715/6, unter dem Stichwort.

[15] CHRISTOPH SCHEURL: *Vita reverendi patris domini Anthonii Kressen.* Nürnberg 24. 07. 1515. Abgefasst 1513. Scheurl fertigte auch eine handschriftliche Übersetzung der *Vita* ins Deutsche an; aus dieser wird im Folgenden nach RUPPRICH (siehe Anm. 13) zitiert. Der Passus über Albrecht Dürer ist eine Richtigstellung eines Abschnitts in Jakob Wimpfelings Geschichtsschrift *Epithoma rerum Germanicarum usque ad nostra tempora*, § 68: De pictura et plastice (1502, gedruckt in Straßburg 1505), in dem über Dürer berichtet wird, er sei Schüler

schriftliche Quelle, die von Dürers Zeitgenossen und Freund Christoph Scheurl[14] verfasste *Vita Antonii Kressen*,[15] Auskunft. Es heißt hier über den fraglichen Zeitraum: »Nachfolgent, als er [Albrecht Dürer] in Teütschland hin vnd wieder gezogen, vnd in dem 92. jar gen Colmar komen werr, do hetten jhm Caspar vnd Paulus, goltschmid, vnd Ludwig, maler, der gleichen zu Basel Georg, goltschmid, all deß Schon Merten gebrüdere, gute gesellschaft gelaist.«[16]

Dürers eigene unspezifische Angaben werden hier zum Teil spezifiziert: (I) Die Wanderschaft habe ihn durch Deutschland (i. e. die Territorien des Heiligen Römischen Reichs deutscher Nation) geführt. (II) Stationen waren u. a. die oberrheinischen Städte Colmar und Basel, wobei die Aufzählung erst Colmar, dann Basel im Bericht nicht zwingend auch die Chronologie des Besuchs wiedergibt. (III) Diese Orte soll er im Jahr 1492 erreicht haben beziehungsweise dort eingetroffen sein. (IV) Er hat sowohl in Colmar als auch in Basel die Brüder des (bereits verstorbenen) Malers und Kupferstechers Martin Schongauer, »Schon Merten«, aufgesucht. Trotz einer Unstimmigkeit im Bericht Scheurls, die Eduard Flechsig im Zuge seiner quellenkritischen Auseinandersetzung aufgelöst hat, ist diese sekundäre biografische Quelle mit der *Familienchronik* in jedem Punkt vereinbar. Sie zeigen – zumindest für das Jahr 1492 –, dass sich Albrecht Dürer lange genug in Basel aufgehalten haben kann, um einige oder alle der ihm für die »Basler Zeit« zugeschriebenen Holzschnitte anzufertigen.

c. Eine weitere Quelle, die Aufschluss über Stationen beziehungsweise Ziele der Wanderschaft gibt, ist das *Imhoffsche Inventar* (1573), in welchem unter vielen anderen zwei – nicht überlieferte – Gemälde Dürers aufgelistet sind, die einen (längeren) Aufenthalt desselben in Straßburg um 1494 nahe legen. So heißt es im Inventar: »no. 26 ein alter man in ein tefelein, ist zu Straspurg sein meister gewest – auf pergamen fl. 4[.] no. 27 ein weibspild auch in ein tefelein, olifarb, so darzu gehoert, gemalt von im zu Straspurg 1494 fl. 3«.[17]

Diese Quelle wird in der Forschung so gedeutet, dass Dürer (I) während der Wanderschaft in Straßburg gewesen sei und darüber hinaus (II) dort bei einem Meister gearbeitet habe (»ein alter man […] ist […] sein

(»discipulus«) Martin Schongauers gewesen. Scheurl berichtet am Anfang des Dürer-Passus, er habe Dürer hierzu befragt und dieser habe ihm geschrieben und oft mündlich berichtet, wie es sich zugetragen habe (RUPPRICH [siehe Anm. 13], S. 294, Z. 24/5: »Aber Durer, als jch ihm daß eröffnet, schreibt, vnd sagt mir auch offt mündlich […]«). Quellenkritisch ist der Bericht Scheurls dem des Jakob Wimpfeling vorzuziehen, da er erstens vereinbar ist mit den Informationen aus der Familienchronik und sich zweitens direkt auf das schriftliche und mündliche Zeugnis Dürers selbst bezieht. Zur ausführlichen quellenkritischen Bewertung des Dürer-Passus in der *Vita Antonii Kressen* vgl. FLECHSIG (siehe Anm. 9), Bd. 1, S. 6–8.

16 Zitiert nach RUPPRICH (siehe Anm. 13), S. 295, Z. 35–40. In der lateinischen Druckausgabe heißt es: »tandem peragrata Germania, quum anno nonagesimo secundo Colmariam venisset a Caspare et Paulo aurifabris et Ludovico pictore, item etiam Basileae, a Georgio aurifabro, Martini fratribus, susceptus quidem sit benigne atque humane tractatus.« Zitiert nach RUPPRICH, S. 294, Z. 28–33.

17 Das sog. *Imhoffsche Inventar* ist das Inventar der Kunstgegenstände aus dem Nachlass des Willibald Imhoff (1519–80), eines Enkels des Nürnberger Patriziers, Zeitgenossen und Freundes Albrecht Dürers Willibald Pirckheimer (1470–1530). Das Inventar ist 1573 handschriftlich erstellt worden und listet allerlei Kunstgegenstände, darunter viele aus dem Besitz Albrecht Dürers, mit Verkaufspreisen versehen, auf. Die Einträge des Inventars sind im Folgenden zitiert nach der Quellenedition von HORST POHL: *Willibald Imhoff, Enkel und Erbe Willibald Pirckheimers. (Edition der Imhoffschen Inventare).* Nürnberg 1992, hier S. 82.

meister gewest«), das heißt eine bestimmte, längere Zeitdauer vor dem 18. Mai 1494, dem Datum seiner Heimkunft in Nürnberg, in der Stadt zugebracht hat. Was ist vom Aussagewert dieser Quelle im Hinblick auf eine Aufenthaltszeit Dürers im Basler Raum im entsprechenden Zeitabschnitt zu halten? Zunächst einmal geht aus der Notiz im Inventar nicht hervor, woher die mitgeteilten Informationen stammen. Entnimmt Imhoff diese etwaigen Aufschriften auf Vorder- oder Rückseite der »tefelein«? Oder identifiziert Imhoff das Dargestellte aus dem Gedächtnis, möglicherweise nach mündlicher Information Dürers? Oder stammen die Informationen über das Dargestellte und die Entstehungszeit von Dritten? Da weder die Tafeln noch irgendeine andere von Dürer stammende Information über einen Straßburger Meister, bei dem er im Jahr 1494 gewesen sei, überliefert sind, sollte der Quelle ein nicht zu hoher Wert im Hinblick auf die Frage nach Dürers Wanderschaft und einer längeren Verweildauer in Straßburg zugemessen werden. Selbst wenn diese Einträge im *Imhoffschen Inventar* eindeutig belegen würden, dass Dürer 1494 in Straßburg war, kann daraus weder geschlussfolgert werden, dass er auch in Basel war, noch, wann und für wie lange er in Basel gewesen ist.

d. Neben den schriftlichen Quellen liefert ein Artefakt einen weiteren Beleg, der für einen Aufenthalt Dürers in Basel im entsprechenden Zeitraum spricht. Es handelt sich um einen bereits geschnittenen Holzstock, der den Hl. Hieronymus mit dem Löwen zeigt. Auf der Rückseite des Holzstocks befindet sich die Aufschrift »Albrecht Dürer von nörmergk«.[18] Ein Abzug desselben Holzstocks ist erstmals als Titelholzschnitt der zweiten Ausgabe des Drucks der *Epistolae*[19] des Hieronymus von Nikolaus Kessler vom 8. August 1492 nachweisbar. Das Artefakt beziehungsweise die von diesem abgeleiteten Informationen stehen nicht im Widerspruch mit den Angaben der schriftlichen Quellen, sondern belegen Dürers Aufenthalt in Basel für einen zunächst unbestimmten Zeitraum vor dem 8. August 1492.

Eduard Flechsig[20] hat den Versuch unternommen, ausgehend von einer Rekonstruktion des Produktionsprozesses des Kesslerschen *Epistolae*-Drucks, diesen Zeitraum einzugrenzen. Wenn Dürer für den Holzschnitt verantwortlicher Handwerker-Künstler war, dann müsse er spätestens

18 In Basel aufgefunden und publiziert wurde der Holzstock von Daniel Burckhardt; zu finden ist er heute in der Öffentlichen Kunstsammlung Basel, Kupferstichkabinett, Inv.-Nr. 1662.169; Abbildung und Beschreibung bei SCHOCH (siehe Anm. 9), S. 35/6; Abbildungen des rückseitigen Namenszugs bei BURCKHARDT 1892 (siehe Anm. 9), S. 4/5. Neuerdings liegen beide Seiten des Holzstocks in Originalgröße vollständig reproduziert vor bei RAMONA BRAUN / ANJA GREBE: »Albrecht Dürer von nörmergk«. Zur Frage von Dürers Basler Buchholzschnitten. In: *Das Dürer-Haus. Neue Ergebnisse der Forschung.* Hrsg. von G. ULRICH GROSSMANN u. FRANZ SONNENBERGER. Nürnberg 2007, S. 193–226, hier S. 198/9.

19 *Epistolare beati Hieronymi.* Bd. 1. Basel: Nicolaus Kessler, 1492.
20 Vgl. FLECHSIG (siehe Anm. 9), Bd. 1, S. 132–5.
21 Obwohl die Argumente FLECHSIGS (siehe Anm. 9), die den Zeitpunkt der Herstellung des Holzstocks einigermaßen eng eingrenzen, nachvollziehbar und gut begründet scheinen, müssen einige Einschränkungen gemacht werden: Zunächst hat er keine druckanalytische Untersuchung vorgenommen, aus der er die Druckchronologie rekonstruiert, sondern geht von der Prämisse aus, dass die sequentielle Anordnung des Textes der Druckfolge entspricht; dies wäre zu überprüfen. Darüber hinaus handelt es sich bei dem Druck nicht um einen Erstdruck, sondern eine Neuausgabe

eines bereits von Kessler 1489 gedruckten Textes; statt eines zeitaufwendigen Neusatzes kann es sich um seitengetreuen Nachsatz handeln – die Herstellungsdauer verringert sich hierdurch erheblich und infolgedessen auch der Zeitpunkt der Anfertigung des Holzschnitts.
22 Die Zuschreibung der Signatur an Dürer wurde bereits (ohne Resonanz in der Forschung) angezweifelt bei TIETZE / TIETZE-CONRAT (siehe Anm. 9), Bd. 1, S. 4 (ad Nr. 17) und besonders vehement von FRIEDRICH HAACK: *Funde und Vermutungen zu Dürer und zur Plastik seiner Zeit.* Erlangen 1916, S. 73–6.
23 Anders als SCHOCH (siehe Anm. 9; ad Nr. 261, S. 36 und dort Anm. 4) meint, ergibt ein solcher Vergleich – wenngleich dies ohnehin schwer zu objektivieren ist

im Frühjahr 1492 in Basel eingetroffen sein, denn da es sich um einen Titelholzschnitt handle, der druckchronologisch am Anfang eines circa halbjährigen Setz- und Druckvorgangs liege, müsse mit dessen Fertigstellung durch den Reißer um den Monat Februar gerechnet werden.[21] Dies sagt zunächst einmal nichts über die Dauer seines Aufenthalts aus, noch darüber, dass er schon vorher eingetroffen oder über die Fertigstellung des Holzschnittes hinaus in Basel geblieben sein kann. Ein Aufenthalt Dürers in Basel ist somit für 1492 möglich und für die erste Jahreshälfte 1492 wahrscheinlich. Zur Einschränkung der Beweiskraft dieses Quellenartefakts ist jedoch Folgendes anzumerken:[22] (I) Es ist auf dem gegenwärtigen Stand der Forschung nicht abschließend geklärt, ob der Namenszug von Dürer selbst stammt und (II) wann dieser auf den Holzstock geschrieben worden ist. An der »Echtheit« respektive Authentizität des Namenszugs wird in den mir bekannten kunsthistorischen Publikationen kaum gezweifelt. Abgesehen davon, dass eine solche Signierung eines Holzblocks durch den Reißer zeitgenössisch äußerst ungewöhnlich ist, bleiben diejenigen, die die Behauptung aufstellen, es handle sich hier um den autografen Namenszug Dürers, entweder schuldig, entsprechende beispielsweise paläografisch-graphematische Belege beizubringen oder aber führen die Vergleichung auf intersubjektiv nicht nachvollziehbare Weise aus. Es ist festzuhalten, dass Handschriftliches von Dürer, mit dem man den Schriftzug vergleichen könnte, erst für die Zeit ab 1500 überliefert ist, also mindestens acht Jahre zwischen möglichen vergleichbaren Handschriften liegen.[23] Darüber hinaus ist deren Vergleichbarkeit mit anderen Schriftproben durch den Beschreibstoff (Birnbaumholz vs. Schreibpapier, Pergament) und das Schreibwerkzeug (Breitfeder vs. Spitzfeder bei brieflicher Korrespondenz) beeinträchtigt. Eine Vergleichung erschwert auch die Beschädigung des Artefakts durch Wurmfraß. Dies war auch schon 1892 der Fall, als Daniel Burckhardt in seiner Studie zu Dürers Basler Aufenthalt einen Ausschnitt der Rückseite mit der Aufschrift fotografierte und reproduzierte.

Vor diesem Hintergrund ist es nicht auszuschließen, dass es sich bei dem Schriftzug um eine (irrtümlich oder absichtlich) falsche fremde Zuschreibung des Stocks an Albrecht Dürer[24] oder um eine Fälschung

– auf der Ebene einzelner Grapheme signifikante Unterschiede; überdies sprechen sprachwissenschaftliche Erwägungen gegen eine Zuschreibung an Dürer, bei dem sich die Schreibung »nörmergk« nicht nachweisen lässt; so auch GREBE (siehe Anm. 10), S. 32/3; Neuerdings liegt mit dem hervorragenden Aufsatz von BAUER, GREBE (siehe Anm. 18), bes. S. 210–8 eine linguistische Analyse des Namenszugs vor, in der die Autorinnen belegen können, dass im überlieferten handschriftlichen Werk Dürers niemals die Schreibung »nörmergk«, noch ähnliche Schreibungen wie »nörmerk«, »nörmerck« noch auch »nörmerg«, sondern nur die Schreibungen »nörnberg«, »nornberg«, seltener »nörnbergk« und »nochnberg«

vorkommen. Ich teile die Einschätzung, dass es »damit äußerst wahrscheinlich ist, dass die Signatur auf dem Basler Hieronymus-Holzstock nicht von Albrecht Dürer geschrieben [...] wurde« (S. 213). Auch konnte in dieser Studie gezeigt werden, dass die in aller Regel als zeitnahes, »autografes« Vergleichsmaterial herangezogenen Schriftzeilen auf den so genannten Kostümbildern mit Nürnberger Trachten (vier Federzeichnungen aus dem Jahr 1500), nicht von Dürer selbst, sondern von zwei unterscheidbaren, späteren Händen hinzugefügt worden sind. – SCHOCH (siehe Anm. 9, S. 36, dort Anm. 4) dagegen bezeichnet (ohne Belege anzugeben) »nörmergk« als »die bei Dürer übliche Schreibweise«.

24 Dies erwägt bereits BURCKHARDT

1892 (siehe Anm. 9), S. 5; vgl. hierzu auch GREBE (siehe Anm. 10), S. 32: »Die nahe liegendste Erklärung für die höchst ungewöhnliche Aufschrift ist ihre spätere Hinzufügung. Die Schrift ähnelt zwar Dürers Handschrift, ist jedoch nicht identisch. Sie wurde sehr wahrscheinlich von einem späteren Besitzer, vielleicht Amerbach selbst [in dessen Sammlung sich der Holzstock, inventarisiert unter dem Namen Dürers, ja auch befand; AR], angebracht, um den Wert des Holzblocks zu steigern«. Hierfür spricht auch, dass sich der Zusatz »aus Nürnberg« funktional eher wie eine nachträgliche Zuschreibung ausnimmt. Mir ist kein Fall bekannt, in dem Dürer bei der Signatur einer Arbeit seinen vollen Namen und zusätzlich noch seinen Herkunftsort angegeben hätte.

(das heißt eine falsche Zuschreibung mit Täuschungsabsicht) späterer Jahrhunderte handelt.[25]

(III) Die von Kunsthistorikern angeführten stilkritischen Argumente den Holzriss und -schnitt betreffend sprechen nicht für eine Urheberschaft Dürers.[26]

(IV) Nach den Ergebnissen der linguistischen Analysen des Namenszugs und der Ortsbezeichnung ist es sehr unwahrscheinlich, wenn auch nicht auszuschließen, dass Dürer Urheber desselben ist.[27]

(V) Selbst wenn es sich um den authentischen Namenszug von Albrecht Dürers Hand handelt, ist damit nicht geklärt, in welcher Funktion er bei der Bearbeitung des Holzstockes tätig war: als selbständiger Reißer, als Reißergehilfe oder als Formschneider.

(VI) Es fehlt an einer Erklärung für diese nicht zeitgenössischen Konventionen entsprechende Praxis: Warum signierte Dürer den Holzstock? Üblich – und dies gilt auch für Dürers spätere Holzschnitte – war, dass der Formschneider seine Arbeit (vor allem zu Abrechnungszwecken) mit einem Kürzel abzeichnete.

Solange diese Einschränkungen nicht ausgeräumt sind, kann das Artefakt des *Hieronymus*-Holzstocks zwar ein Indiz für Dürers Aufenthalt in Basel um 1492 sein, ist jedoch kein zwingender Beweis.

In summa: Aus den angeführten Quellen zum biografischen Kontext lässt sich für die notwendige Bedingung eines Basel-Aufenthalts Dürers vor dem 11. Februar 1494 schließen, dass es zumindest möglich ist, dass sich dieser (lange genug) dort aufgehalten hat, um einige oder alle der ihm für diese Zeit zugeschriebenen Holzschnitte anzufertigen.

Zu 2.: Der Basel-Aufenthalt ist auch die notwendige Bedingung für das zweite, die Dürer-These für den *Narrenschiff*-Druck stützende Hauptargument der Forschung, nämlich folgenden Analogieschluss: Da es auch sonst eine Zusammenarbeit zwischen Albrecht Dürer als Illustrator und einem oder mehreren der am *Narrenschiff*-Erstdruck beteiligten Akteure gegeben hat, hat eine solche auch für das *Narrenschiff* bestanden.

Die Forschung stützt sich für dieses Zusammenarbeits-Argument auf mehrere Indizien. So wird behauptet, Dürer habe an mehreren Basler Druckprojekten als Illustrator mitgearbeitet, an denen auch der Autor Sebastian Brant, der Verleger Johann Bergmann von Olpe und der Drucker Michael Furter beteiligt gewesen sind:

a. Dürer habe die 45 Holzschnitte des *Ritters vom Thurn* (1493)[28] – gedruckt von Michael Furter, verlegt von Bergmann von Olpe – gerissen;

---

[25] In der kunsthistorischen Echtheitskritik spricht man in diesem Fall von »Teilveränderungen mit dem Ziel der Täuschung« – einschließlich Signaturfälschungen –, die seit der Renaissance immer wieder auftauchen. Als beispielgebend für diese Praxis wird bezeichnenderweise darauf hingewiesen, dass »schon im 16. Jahrhundert [...] Einsetzungen des Dürermonogramms in Druckstöcke (erfolgten), die nicht von diesem selbst stammten«. (HERMANN BAUER: Kunsthistorik. Eine kritische Einführung in das Studium der Kunstgeschichte. 3., durchges. u. erg. Aufl. München 1989, S. 115) – Dass es sich um eine nicht-zeitgenössische falsche Zuschreibung oder Täuschung handelt, ließe sich heute mittels berührungsfreier naturwissenschaftlicher Materialanalysemethoden (bspw. der Röntgenfluoreszenz-Analyse) leicht ermitteln, dies ist meines Wissens bisher jedoch nicht vorgenommen worden.

[26] Vgl. FLECHSIG (siehe Anm. 9), Bd. 1, S. 304/5: »Seiner Formensprache und Zeichenweise nach erinnert der Holzschnitt weder an frühere noch an spätere Arbeiten Dürers, ja nicht einmal an die Art bekannter Nürnberger Künstler, wie Michel Wolgemuts. Nirgends kann man anknüpfen. Also auf Grund von stilistischen Kennzeichen, die doch sonst bei solchen Fragen unbedingt den Ausschlag zu geben pflegen, läßt sich Dürers Urheberschaft nicht beweisen, ja nicht einmal ahnen«.

[27] BAUER, GREBE (siehe Anm. 18) kommen in ihrer Studie zu der Konklusion: »die Beschriftung auf dem Holz-

b. Dürer habe die 132 Holzrisse einer 1492/93 geplanten Druckausgabe der *Komödien des Terenz* – angeblich ediert von Sebastian Brant, verlegt von Johann Amerbach – angefertigt. Daraus wird geschlussfolgert, die 105 (oder 73) Holzschnitte des *Narrenschiff*-Drucks – verfasst von Brant, verlegt von Bergmann von Olpe, gedruckt von Furter – stammen ebenfalls von Dürer.

Problematisch bei dieser Argumentation sind die folgenden Punkte: (I) In keinem der genannten Fälle gibt es irgendeinen Beleg (außer dem Vorhandensein von unsignierten Illustrationen) für Dürers Mitwirken. Die Mitwirkung Dürers an diesen Projekten stützt sich (II) entweder ebenfalls auf Analogieschlüsse oder (III) auf höchst umstrittene stilkritische Argumente.[29] (IV) In jedem Fall handelt es sich zudem um Zirkelschlussargumente: Es wird gefolgert, dass Dürer am *Narrenschiff* beteiligt war, weil er an anderen Projekten der Herausgeber beteiligt war; diese Beteiligung wird ihrerseits daraus geschlossen, dass er die *Narrenschiff*-Illustrationen kunsthandwerklich ausgeführt hat.

Bevor ich auf die stilkritischen Argumente – die sowohl einen Teil der »Belege« für das Zusammenarbeits-Argument ausmachen als auch ihrerseits für die Hauptthese herangezogen werden – zu sprechen komme, werde ich die Belege für die Analogieschlüsse prüfen.

Der am häufigsten angeführte »eindeutige Beleg« für eine Zusammenarbeit des Illustrators Dürer und des Autors beziehungsweise Editors Brant sind die 132 Holzstöcke der sogenannten *Terenz*-Ausgabe. Es wird behauptet, Brant habe gemeinsam mit dem Basler Drucker Johann Amerbach um 1492/93 eine illustrierte Druckausgabe der *Komödien des Terenz* geplant und vorbereitet, zu deren Drucklegung es wegen der Veröffentlichung einer Lyoneser *Terenz*-Ausgabe 1493 jedoch nicht gekommen sei; die bereits vorangeschrittenen Arbeiten seien abgebrochen worden. Kenntnis von einem solchen Projekt hat man ausschließlich aufgrund der überlieferten, teilweise bereits geschnittenen Holzstöcke, die Szenen aus *Terenz*-Komödien zeigen und auf deren Holzstockrückseiten sich unter anderem handschriftliche Szenenangaben befinden. Woraus zieht die Forschung den Schluss, dass es sich bei den »Beteiligten« um das Trio Brant-Dürer-Amerbach gehandelt habe?

Auf den Drucker Amerbach wird aufgrund zweier Überlieferungsumstände geschlossen: Erstens, die Holzstöcke haben sich im Bestand des Amerbach-Kabinetts befunden und seien mit diesem 1661 durch Verkauf in die öffentliche Basler Kunstsammlung gelangt.[30] Zweitens, auf den Holzstöcken befinden sich handschriftliche Aufschriften und »Kritzeleien«,

---

stock [kann] nicht von Dürer stammen« (S. 219). Hiergegen ist jedoch einzuwenden, dass sich auf Basis des überlieferten autografen Schriftmaterials nur schließen lässt, dass es für die fragliche Schreibung »nörmergk« keinen weiteren Beleg in Dürers Œuvre gibt und die Möglichkeit besteht, dass es sich um ein *Hapax legomenon* handelt. Dies ist zwar sehr unwahrscheinlich, aber dennoch möglich.

28 GEOFFROY DE LA TOUR LANDRY: Livre pour l'enseignement de ses filles. (Der Ritter vom Turn). Deutsch von

Marquart vom Stein. Basel: Michael Furter (für Johann Bergmann von Olpe), 1493; vgl. für die vollständige Titelangabe GW online Nr. M 17154.

29 Zur Methode der Stilkritik und deren Kritik vgl. weiter unten.

30 Vgl. THOMAS WILHELMI: Zur Entstehung des »Narrenschiffs« und der illustrierten Terenz-Ausgabe. Beschreibung der Rückseiten der Terenz-Druckstöcke. In: *Sebastian Brant. Forschungsbeiträge zu seinem Leben, zum »Narrenschiff« und zum übrigen Werk*. Hrsg. von DEMS.

Basel 2002, S. 103–24, hier S. 106, Anm. 16 und BURCKHARDT 1892 (siehe Anm. 9), S. 19: Hier heißt es zunächst relativierend über die Provenienz der Holzstöcke: »Die durch Basilius Amerbach gegen Ende des 16. Jahrhunderts [1585–87] angelegten Inventare, die doch sonst mit aller nur wünschbaren Ausführlichkeit über die Kunst Holbeins und der spätern Schweizer Meister handeln, wissen nichts von den Holzstöcken, welche doch schon allein durch die Thatsache, dass sie sich auf der Basler Kunstsammlung befinden,

die vom Enkel Johann Amerbachs, Basilius Amerbach im Kindesalter, stammen sollen.[31] Auf die Beteiligung Brants wird aufgrund fragwürdiger Schriftvergleiche der rückseitigen Szenenbeschriftungen mit Brantschen Autografen (u. a. in der Basler Universitätsmatrikel) auf Grundlage der Prämisse, dass Brant nachweislich[32] für andere von ihm als Editor betreute Projekte (unter anderem den postumen Druck der deutschen Übersetzung von Petrarcas *De Remediis*, 1532) dem Illustrator skizzenhafte Angaben für Bildkomposition und -inhalte gegeben habe, geschlossen.[33] Auf Dürers Beteiligung nun wird zum einen aufgrund stilkritischer Untersuchungen der Risse geschlossen, zum anderen wird als »Beleg« für gute Bekanntschaft, die eine Zusammenarbeit einschließe, ein Brief Dürers an Amerbach herangezogen.[34] Die Datierung der Holzstöcke auf 1492/93 leitet sich unmittelbar aus dem oben genannten ab: Das Erscheinen der Lyoneser Ausgabe 1493 ist der *terminus ante quem*, Dürers mögliche Ankunft in Basel 1492 der *terminus post quem*, die den zeitlichen Rahmen der Herstellung der Risse abstecken. Die Zuweisung der Holzstöcke an jeden der angeblich Beteiligten ist äußerst unsicher und mitunter rein spekulativ. Auf dieser dürftigen Basis ist ein Analogieschluss auf die Zusammenarbeit Dürer-Brant beim *Narrenschiff*-Druck nicht überzeugend.

Zu 3.: Stilkritische Argumente. Da die quellenkundlichen Kriterien als Belege für eine Urheberschaft Dürers nicht ausreichen, werden sowohl zu deren Bekräftigung als auch zur Stützung der übergeordneten Dürer-These stilkritische Argumente angeführt. Die Stilkritik als kunsthistorische Methode der Händescheidung und Firmierung von bildnerischen Kunstwerken ist umstritten; entsprechend kommen die verschiedenen Untersuchungen mit derselben Methode zu stark voneinander abweichenden und mitunter unvereinbaren Ergebnissen im Hinblick auf die »eindeutig von Dürer stammenden« Holzschnitte. Dies spricht meines Erachtens weder für die Stilkritik, noch macht es die Beteiligung des Künstlers Dürer irgendwie wahrscheinlicher. Verfahren wird in den stilkritischen Argumentationsstrategien wie folgt:

a. Zunächst wird postuliert, es habe einen abrupten Wandel in der »Formensprache« des Basler (Buch-)Holzschnitts gegeben – dieser sei plötzlich »lebendig«, »ausdrucksstark«, »realistisch«. Dieser Wandel falle

---

ihre Provenienz aus dem ehemaligen Amerbach'schen Cabinet und somit wohl auch aus dem Besitze des Buchdruckers Hans Amerbach bekunden.« Über die tatsächliche Herkunft der *Terenz*-Holzschnitte ist nichts bekannt. Weder findet sich ein Eintrag in den Amerbachschen Inventaren, noch sind sie anlässlich der Übergabe der Amerbachschen Sammlung in den Besitz der Stadt Basel (1661) inventarisiert worden. Eine erste Erwähnung der Holzstöcke liegt in der 1852-56 vorgenommenen beschreibenden Inventarisierung der Basler Öffentlichen Kunstsammlung vor. Vgl. hierzu: *Dürer, Holbein, Grünewald. Meisterzeichnungen der Deutschen Renaissance aus Berlin und Basel.* Hrsg. von GERHARD BRUNNER. Ausst.-Kat. Ostfildern-Ruit 1997, S. 99.

31 Der zehnjährige Basilius habe diese »als eine Art von Schreibübung in Ermangelung geeigneteren Materials« auf die »werthvollen Reliquien« (die Holzstöcke) gemacht, welche sich in der Offizin des Großvaters Johann befunden haben sollen. Dass Basilius der Verfasser einiger Aufschriften ist, leitet BURCKHARDT 1892 (siehe Anm. 9) aus den in »Kinderschrift« ausgeführten Rufnamen, die er als Namen von Familienmitgliedern identifiziert, und Schriftvergleichen mit Autografen des Basilius (von 1544) ab. Welche Autografen das sind, wo sie aufbewahrt werden oder wie der Schriftvergleich anhand welcher paläografischen Kriterien durchgeführt worden ist, hält Burckhardt nicht für mitteilenswert; vgl. ebd., S. 18–20.

32 Dies wird zwar postuliert, den Nachweis bleiben bisher alle Vertreter der Prämisse schuldig.

33 Vgl. ALFRED WOLTMANN: *Geschichte der deutschen Kunst im Elsaß. Mit 74 Illustrationen in Holzschnitt.* Leipzig 1876. WOLTMANN hat als Erster die Hypothese aufgestellt, Brant habe Skizzen zu den *Terenz*-Holzschnitten angefertigt, popularisiert wurde sie vor allem von WILHELM FRAENGER: *Hans Weiditz und Sebastian Brant.* Leipzig 1930.

34 Es wird von den Verfechtern dieser These behauptet, aus einem Brief, den Albrecht Dürer 1507 an Johann Amerbach schickt, gehe eindeutig hervor, dass sich diese persönlich bekannt sein müssen. Da Dürer Basel, den Wohn- und Wirkort Amerbachs, nur während seiner Wander-

zusammen mit dem (möglichen) vorübergehenden Aufenthalt Dürers in Basel irgendwann zwischen 1490 und 1494.

b. Die mit dem Postulat einhergehende Bewertung dieser Holzschnitte als »herausragend«, »hochwertig« etc. gilt dann als Indiz für eine Beteiligung Dürers als Reißer. Hierbei gilt die Prämisse, alle von Dürer im Laufe seines Lebens geschaffenen Kunstwerke seien im Vergleich mit dem zeitgenössisch Üblichen höherwertig. Ergo müsse alles, was als »höherwertig« erkannt worden ist, von Dürer stammen. Dabei erfährt diese Regel in den Argumentationen der Kunsthistorik noch folgende Einschränkungen: (I) Alles das, was an den als höherwertig charakterisierten Holzschnitten »misslungen« sei, gehe nicht auf Dürer sondern auf Dritte zurück (hierin der Prämisse folgend, dass Formschneider immer die Vorzeichnungen beziehungsweise Holzrisse verschlechtern). (II) Holzschnitte, die hochwertig, aber für als von Dürer stammende nicht hochwertig genug erachtet werden, seien zumindest von diesem »beeinflusst« (es gilt die Prämisse, dass unabhängig vom sozialen Status Dürers dessen »hochwertiger« kunsthandwerklicher »Stil« immer Einfluss auf andere hat, nicht umgekehrt).

c. Die so als von Dürer stammend identifizierten Holzschnitte werden in einigen wenigen technischen Details (Faltenwurf von Gewändern oder Draperien; Haarlocken; Kniescheiben etc.) oder indirekten Signaturen (ein springendes Hündchen, Narrenkappenschellen etc.) als stilkritische Vergleichsfälle herangezogen nach dem Argumentationsmuster: Ein Holzschnitt (A) ist im stilkritischen Vergleich mit anderen als »höherwertig« evaluiert. Auf diesem gibt es ein oder mehrere als nicht bildinhaltlich wesentlich identifizierte Elemente (beispielsweise ein springendes Hündchen, ein runder Busch, eine Schellenreihe an der Narrenkappe etc.). Diese seien »indirekte Signaturen«[35] des Reißers. Ergo stammen andere Holzschnitte (B), die ebenfalls eines oder mehrere dieser Elemente aufweisen, von demselben Künstler.

d. Oder aber: Solche Details oder »Stilzüge« werden aus anderen (z. T. firmierten) bildnerischen Arbeiten Dürers verschiedener Zeiten, Materialien, Entstehungs- und Verwendungszusammenhänge mit den Abzügen nicht erhaltener Holzschnitte verglichen.[36] Intersubjektiv nicht nach-

jahre 1490–94 besucht habe, müsse auch die Bekanntschaft beider aus dieser Zeit und einer unterstellten Zusammenarbeit an gemeinsamen Projekten herrühren. Im Brief Dürers an Amerbach vom 20. 10. 1507 aus Nürnberg heißt es: »Dem erberdenn weisen meister Hannsen puchtrucker in der kleinen stadt zw Pasell, meinem lieben herren. Mein willigen dinst zw vor, lieber meister Hans! Ewer glücklichs tzw stan ist mir ein sundre frewd, des halb ich ewch gluck vnd heill gün vnd allen, den jr woll wölt, vnd sunderlich ewrer erberen hawsfrawen, der ich aws ganczen herczen gutz gön. – Vnd pit vch, wolt mir schreiben, was jr gutz jcz macht, vnd verczeicht mir, daz ich ewch mach lesen mein einfaltig schreiben. – Hie mit vill guter nacht.

Tatum Nörnberg 1502/20. Octobris. Albrecht Dürer.« (S. 61, Z. 1–12, zitiert nach RUPPRICH [siehe Anm. 13]). – Ein Antwortbrief Amerbachs hat sich nicht erhalten. Der Passus »vnd sunderlich ewrer erberen hawsfrawen, der ich aus ganczen herczen gutz gön« wird dahingehend gedeutet, dass Dürer während seines Basel-Aufenthalts als junger Mann in Amerbachs Haus untergekommen sei und/oder dort besonders freundlich von dessen Frau aufgenommen oder behandelt worden sei. Diese Deutung scheint mir weder in dem kurzen Brief angedeutet zu sein, noch darauf hinzuweisen, dass Dürer sich längere Zeit bei Amerbachs aufgehalten habe oder aber hier eine berufliche Zusammenarbeit beider zwischen den Zeilen angedeutet sei. Diese Briefstelle

ist als Beleg für o. g. Argument äußerst dürftig, wenn nicht völlig wertlos.

35 WINKLER (siehe Anm. 9), S. 12/3.

36 Ich schließe mich uneingeschränkt RESKES kritischen Einwänden (siehe Anm. 6), S. 61 in Bezug auf die Methode der Stilkritik an: »Bei der Stilkritik handelt es sich somit um eine höchst schwierige Methode, die immer das Kunstwerk als Ganzes betrachten muß. Die Beschränkung auf einzelne ausgewählte Phänomene ist unzureichend. [...] Desweiteren muß der Vergleich auf der Grundlage vieler weiterer der Gattung entsprechender Kunstwerke beruhen. [...] Ein Vergleich verschiedener Gattungen wie Gemälde und Graphik oder Zeichnung und Graphik ist dagegen äußerst heikel.«

vollziehbare Übereinstimmungen in Details werden dann als die Urheberschaft bestätigende Belege bemüht.

Ich fasse zusammen: Die Rekonstruktion der Argumentationsstrategien hat gezeigt, dass die Dürer-These – auf dem derzeitigen Stand der Forschung – nicht zu bestätigen ist. Die angeführten Argumente sind entweder unzulässige Analogie- oder Zirkelschlüsse oder haben eine so schmale empirische Basis, dass eine Beteiligung Dürers an irgend einem der ihm zugeschriebenen Holzschnitte zwar möglich oder denkbar wäre, jedoch kaum wahrscheinlich zu machen ist. Ich halte deshalb im Rahmen meiner Rekonstruktion des Produktionsprozesses des *Narrenschiff*-Erstdrucks bis auf weiteres fest, dass ein Reißer oder Reißerkollektiv (eine Werkstatt) mit der Herstellung der Holzrisse beauftragt worden ist.

Es ist möglich, dass Albrecht Dürer in irgendeiner Funktion an dieser prä-typografischen Phase beteiligt gewesen ist: als Entwerfer und/oder Reißer der Bilder auf Papier und/oder die Holzstöcke; als Mit- oder Zuarbeiter, Gehilfe eines Basler Reißers oder einer Malerwerkstatt, die Risse angefertigt hat; als Formschneider oder Gehilfe eines solchen beziehungsweise einer Werkstatt. Genauso ist es möglich, dass Dürer in keiner Weise an der Herstellung der Illustrationen beteiligt gewesen ist. Wir wissen es nicht. Solange keine weiteren Belege für eine Beteiligung Dürers beigebracht werden, sollte davon Abstand genommen werden, diesen Künstler-Handwerker mit dem *Narrenschiff*-Druck in Verbindung zu bringen.[37] Bis auf weiteres bleibt der künstlerisch-handwerkliche Urheber der Illustrationen anonym.[38]

Die Brant-Visierer-These

In einer ähnlich komplexen, mit Werturteilen und Bedeutungszuschreibungen konfundierten Argumentationsweise wird versucht, die These zu stützen, dass es in der prä-typografischen Phase des Produktionsprozesses einen weiteren einflussreichen Bildurheber – nämlich den Entwerfer beziehungsweise Visierer – gegeben habe: den Autor des Textes, Sebastian Brant. Die *Visierer-These* besagt, dass es vom Autor Sebastian Brant eigens entworfene Visierungen für die *Narrenschiff*-Illustrationen gegeben habe. Deren Vertreter[39] argumentieren so: Brant habe nachweislich für andere von ihm betreute illustrierte Druckwerke (die illustrierte *Petrarca*-Ausgabe von 1532[40] und das nie realisierte Projekt einer illustrierten *Terenz*-Druckausgabe[41]) »visierliche Anweisungen« gegeben. Also war Brant auch für den *Narrenschiff*-Druck als Visierer tätig. Dieser einfache Analogismus allein wird als hinreichender Beleg für die Brant-Visierer-These in der neueren und neuesten Forschung vertreten. Darüber hinaus wird zusätzlich eine Belegstelle aus dem *Narrenschiff*-Text in Anschlag gebracht: »Vil narren / doren kumen dryn | Der bildniß jch hab har gemacht | Wer yeman der die gschrifft veracht | Oder villicht die nit künd lesen | Der siecht jm molen wol syn wesen | Vnd fyndet dar jnn / wer er ist | Wem er glich sy / was jm gebrist / | Den narren spiegel ich diß nenn | Jn dem ein yeder narr sich kenn«.[42] Diese wird als Aussage des *empirischen Autors* dahingehend gedeutet, dass Brant selbst die – bildlichen – Visierungen beziehungsweise Bildentwürfe (»bildniß«) für die Illustrationen des *Nar-*

---

37 Welche forschungspraktischen Konsequenzen aus der Zuschreibung der *Narrenschiff*-Holzschnitte an Dürer erwachsen können, zeigt z. B. GOTTFRIED SEEBASS: Dürers Stellung in der reformatorischen Bewegung. In: DERS.: *Die Reformation und ihre Außenseiter. Gesammelte Aufsätze und Vorträge.* Göttingen 1997, S. 79–112, der mit Hinweis darauf, dass Dürer »Illustrationen zu Brants ›Narrenschiff‹ [...] während seines Basler Aufenthalts lieferte« (S. 91), Schlussfolgerungen hinsichtlich der weltanschaulichen (hier kirchenkritischen) Überzeugungen Dürers plausibilisieren möchte.

38 Durch die Dominanz der Dürer-These sind quellenbasierte Forschungen zu möglichen oder wahrscheinlichen anderen für die Basler Druckereien arbeitenden Reißern und Formschneidern der 1490er Jahre nicht systematisch unternommen worden. Da entsprechende Archivalien in Basel verhältnismäßig gut überliefert und dokumentiert sind, könnten eingehende buch- und druck- oder kunsthistorische Untersuchungen hier anknüpfen, möglicherweise diese und ähnliche Fragekomplexe erhellen. Zu einem alternativen Vorschlag die *Narrenschiff*-Illustrationen einem Basler Reißer respektive einer Malerwerkstatt zuzuschreiben vgl. WEISBACH 1896 (siehe Anm. 9), der jedoch keinen nachhaltigen Einfluss auf die Forschung genommen hat.

39 Zuletzt wurde diese These von WILHELMI (siehe Anm. 30) vertreten. Vgl. auch EVA MARIA MARXER: Text und Illustration bei Sebastian Brant und Konrad Celtis. Diss. Wien 1961; JOACHIM KNAPE: *Dichtung, Recht und Freiheit. Studien zu Leben und Werk Sebastian Brants 1457–1521.* Baden-Baden 1992, S. 271/2 sowie SCHNEIDER (siehe Anm. 3), S. 47–49.

40 FRANCESCO PETRARCA: *Von der Artzney bayder Glück, des guten vnd widerwertigen.* Augsburg 1532.

41 Zur *Terenz*-Ausgabe vgl. zuletzt WILHELMI (siehe Anm. 30).

42 SEBASTIAN BRANT: *Das Narrenschyff.* Basel 1494, S. A2b, Z. 8–16. Zitiert nach dem Exemplar der *editio princeps* im Besitz der SBB-PK, Signatur: Inc. 604.8° an Inc. 607.8°.

renschiffs angefertigt (»gemacht«) habe. Was ist von diesen Argumenten zu halten?

1. Der empirische Gehalt des innertextuellen Belegs, der für die Beteiligung Brants an der Herstellung der Illustrationen bemüht wird, ist in seiner Reichweite über die Fiktion hinaus gering. Hierzu wäre zunächst zu klären, ob die Äußerung in paratextueller oder innertextueller Umgebung steht. Genauer: ist sie Teil einer paratextuellen Vorrede oder Teil eines innertextuellen Vorspanns resp. ersten Kapitels? Dann wäre zu klären, wen »jch« an dieser Stelle bezeichnet: (a) den empirischen Autor, der sich an den impliziten Leser in einer paratextuellen Vorrede wendet oder (b) die Herausgeberfiktion oder (c) die auktoriale Erzählerinstanz im Text des *Narrenschiffs*.[43] Danach wäre zu klären, wie die Lexeme »bildniß« und »gemacht« im Sprachgebrauch der Zeit und der oberelsässischen Region verwendet worden sind. Ein Beleg für die Beteiligung Brants an der Produktion der Illustrationen wäre mit dem Verweis auf diese Textstelle nur dann gegeben, wenn (a) zutrifft und gleichzeitig die Lexeme «bildniß» und «gemacht» in der Wortbedeutung »bildliche Darstellungen« und «herstellen/anfertigen/zeichnen/entwerfen« nachweisbar im regionalen historischen Sprachgebrauch verwendet worden sind. Dies ist nicht der Fall.[44]

2. Die Belege für eine Identifizierung der Visierungen beziehungsweise Entwürfe für die projektierte *Terenz*-Ausgabe als Autografe Brants sind nicht stichhaltig. Auf den 132 überlieferten – teilweise federgezeichneten, teilweise schon geschnittenen – *Terenz*-Druckstöcken sind unterschiedliche handschriftliche Notizen und/oder Skizzen mehrerer Hände enthalten.[45] Wilhelmi – sich hierbei Burckhardt, Winkler und Knape anschließend[46] – schreibt diese als Visierungen Brant zu: »Auf den Rückseiten der Druckstöcke finden sich [...] auch Angaben von Brants Hand: Brant bezeichnete stets den Akt und die Szene und gab dazu den Textanfang. In einem Fall ist uns eine Szenenskizze von Brants Hand überliefert: zu Andria V.4, ein eindeutiger [!] Beleg für Brants Beteiligung an der Gestaltung der Illustration«.[47] Es wird nicht deutlich, anhand welcher Kriterien die Zuweisung der (skizzierenden und schreibenden) Hand an Brant vollzogen worden ist; überprüfbare Belegstellen werden nicht gegeben. Außerdem ist »*eine* (Hervorhebung durch die Autorin) Szenenskizze« kein »eindeutiger Beleg« für eine »Beteiligung an der Gestaltung der Illustration« – sie mag, wenn überhaupt, Beleg für die Gestaltung dieser einen Illustration sein, das würde aber ebenfalls die Nachvollziehbarkeit und Überprüfbarkeit der Zuweisung der Skizze als »von Brants Hand« voraussetzen! Auf keinem der Druckstöcke finden sich Brants Name oder Signatur. Die von Wilhelmi als analogieschlussfähige Belegstelle bemühten Brantschen »visierlichen Angebungen« zur Ausgabe von Petrarcas *Glücksbuch* bleiben ohne Nachweis als sei deren Vorliegen bereits zur *communis opinio* geronnen.

Als einer der Ersten hat Woltmann 1876 die Brant-Visierer-These aufgestellt. In der mittlerweile kaum noch zugänglichen Abhandlung über Sebastian Brant und Hans Weiditz »argumentiert« er positiv für die entwerfende Tätigkeit Brants bei den Illustrationen, zunächst wie oben

[43] Erste Ansätze hierzu finden sich bei JOACHIM KNAPE: Wer spricht? Rhetorische Stimmen, Poetologie und anthropologische Modelle in Sebastian Brants Narrenschiff. In: Sebastian Brant (1457–1521). Hrsg. von HANS-GERT ROLOFF, JEAN-MARIE VALENTIN u. VOLKHARD WELS. Berlin 2008 (*Memoria*. 9), S. 268–97; vgl. weiterführend auch ROCKENBERGER (siehe Anm. 1), S. 38–41.

[44] Vgl. hierzu die Lemmata in: *Mittelhochdeutsches Wörterbuch*. Hrsg. VON WILHELM MÜLLER u. FRIEDRICH ZARNCKE. Leipzig 1854–66. Bd. 1, S. 120–2 und Bd. 2, S. 15/6 sowie *Frühneuhochdeutsches Wörterbuch*. Hrsg. von ULRICH GOEBEL u. OSKAR REICHMANN in Verbindung mit dem Institut für deutsche Sprache. Bd. 4. Berlin 2001, Sp. 392–5. Die Wendung »bildniß ... gemacht« ist hier auffallend häufig als Vulgata-Paraphrase von Gen. 9,6 dokumentiert; womit auch für o. g. Vers eine plausiblere Deutung möglich wird. Regionalsprachliche Abweichungen von der Bedeutung der Lexeme habe ich nicht ermitteln können.

[45] WILHELMI (siehe Anm. 30) identifiziert auf den Druckstockrückseiten neben Brants Handschrift »Kritzeleien von Kinderhand (wohl von Basilius Amerbach und seinen Geschwistern) und Notizen des späteren Besitzers Basilius Amerbach« (S. 107). Er weist nicht nach, wie bzw. anhand welcher (paläografischen) Methoden die Unterscheidung und die Identifizierung vorgenommen worden sind.

[46] Vgl. BURCKHARDT (1892, siehe Anm. 9), WINKLER (siehe Anm. 9), KNAPE (siehe Anm. 39): Hier heißt es, Brant habe »in einem Fall (dem besagten *Terenz*-Holzstock) nachweislich [!] selbst zum Zeichenstift gegriffen«, dies sei »Zeugnis eigener zeichnerischer Entwurfstätigkeit« (S. 272).

[47] WILHELMI (siehe Anm. 30), S. 107.

bereits skizziert ausgehend von innertextuellen Belegstellen in von ihm verfassten beziehungsweise edierten Druckausgaben: »wiederholt gewähren seine eigenen Worte in Werken, die er herausgegeben [sic!]; hiefür Belege. [...] [N]ach einigen Stellen ließe sich vermuthen, daß er selbst die Skizzen zu vielen Illustrationen gemacht [hat]«.[48]

Die »Stellen«, von denen die Rede ist, sind zum einen der bereits oben wiedergegebene Passus aus dem Vorspann des *Narrenschiffs*, zum anderen die Verse in Brants Widmungsgedicht zu Grüningers Straßburger *Vergil*-Ausgabe von 1502, wo es heißt:

> Lectori loquitur liber hic: pictasque tabellas – Commendat quales Virgilio addiderit. – [...] Hic lege historias commentaque plurima doctus – Nec minus indoctus perlegere illa potest. – Dardanium Aeneam doctum non legimus usquam, – Picturam potuit perlegere illa tamen.
>
> Sed quorsum, o lector, nos haec meminisse putabis – Picturae laudem quam damus eximiam? – Quam nisi, ut has nostras quas pinximus ecce tabellas – Virgilio, charas tu quoque habere velis.[49]

Hieraus zieht Woltmann den Schluss: »Auf alle Fälle legte er [Brant] auf die Illustrationen das größte Gewicht, er wendete ihnen unausgesetzte Aufmerksamkeit zu«, es »kommt doch kein Bild in seinen Büchern vor, das nicht der Ausdruck seiner Intentionen wäre, er hat Alles angegeben und überwacht«.[50]

Eine »Mitwirkung Sebastian Brant's« bei den »vorbereiteten Holzstöcken zum Terenz« sei ebenfalls »anzunehmen«.[51] Dass Brant irgendetwas mit der Herausgabe der *Komödien des Terenz* zu tun gehabt habe, führt er darauf zurück, dass sich in der Grüningerschen *Terenz*-Ausgabe von 1502 ein Gedicht Brants finde – obwohl er sogleich einschränkt, dass »von den Abbildungen [...] in den Versen nicht die Rede [ist]«.[52]

Ausgangspunkt seiner Überlegungen ist die Zuschreibung »visierlicher Angebungen« Dritter an Sebastian Brant. Ich habe ermittelt, dass der Ausdruck »visierliche angebung«, welcher sich immer wieder ohne den entsprechenden bibliografischen Nachweis in den Beiträgen der neueren und älteren Literatur zum Thema findet, ein Zitat aus dem Vorwort des Druckers Heinrich Steiner zur zweibändigen deutschen Übersetzung von Petrarcas *De Remediis* (das sog. *Glücksbuch*) ist. In der 1532 in Augsburg erschienenen Druckausgabe heißt es dort in einem für den Kauf des – scheinbar teuren – Buches werbenden Vorwort an den Leser: »An gesehen dz | diser aller werdest schatz den Teütschen / wie oben gedacht / lange zeyt vnbekant | geweßt / hab ich mich kosten vnd müsamkait / vmb des gemainen hayls willen / nit thauren noch hindern lassen / sunder das erst buoch (so mit etwas hochbräch | tigen gehaymnussen / subtyler vnd verplümpter worten / also kluog vnd werck⸗ | lich gezieret ist / das es schier allain ainem künstlichen wol belesnen / vnd versten | digen leser gezimmen wil) mit vil zierlichen vnd wunder lustparlichen figurenn / | so nach visierlicher angebung des Hochgelerten Doctors Sebastiani Brandt | seligen / auf jeglichs Capitel gestellet sind / nit vmm ain klein gelt erkauft / vnd in an | schawung sölchen lust empfangen [...]«.[53]

Anzumerken ist hier: Es ist nicht Brant, der von sich sagt, er habe »visierliche angebungen« gemacht. Noch dazu bezieht sich diese Aus-

---

[48] WOLTMANN (siehe Anm. 33), S. 268.
[49] Zitiert nach WOLTMANN (siehe Anm. 33), S. 268.
[50] Ebd., S. 268.
[51] Alles ebd., S. 269.
[52] Ebd., S. 270.
[53] A3a. Zitiert mit Bogensignatur nach der Reprintausgabe FRANCESCO PETRARCA: *Von der Artzney bayder Glück, des guten vnd widerwertigen.* Hrsg. und kommentiert von MANFRED LEMMER. Leipzig 1983.

sage Steiners auf eine Ausgabe, die 1532, also posthum gedruckt worden ist. Die konzeptionellen Arbeiten an der Übersetzung datieren zwar in die Jahre 1518–22, doch auch hier ist eine Beteiligung Brants als Mitwirkender zumindest problematisch. Brant stirbt am 11. Mai 1521 in Straßburg. Das Buchprojekt der Verleger Grimm und Wirsing wird in Augsburg konzipiert, die deutsche Übersetzung von *De Remediis* in Nürnberg und Logau 1520 bis zum 21. September 1521 angefertigt. Ein (Augsburger) Reißer soll die circa 200 Holzschnitte entwerfen, reißen und an einen Formschneider geben, der diese druckfertig ausarbeitet.

Das heißt, wenn Brant hier als Bildkonzeptor oder Visierer tätig gewesen sein soll, dann muss er dies (I) über eine große räumliche Distanz (Straßburg–Nürnberg–Augsburg) gewesen sein, (II) weit vor dessen Fertigstellung an dem Projekt mitgearbeitet haben, es müssen (III) Informationen über diese Mitarbeit dem Drucker Steiner 1532 noch vorgelegen haben, so dass dieser seine Aussage auf unmittelbare Belege stützen konnte. Es gibt jedoch, von der Steinerschen Aussage in besagtem Vorwort abgesehen, keinen einzigen Beleg für eine Zusammenarbeit Brants mit den Verlegern Grimm und Wirsing, noch auch Belege dafür, dass Brant in irgendeiner Form mit dem – anonymen – Nürnberger Reißer korrespondiert hat.[54] Das Vorhandensein einer Widmungsvorrede Brants in dieser Druckausgabe kann – den zeitgenössischen Konventionen entsprechend – rein werbende Funktion haben und bereits vor der Fertigstellung des Projekts vorgelegen haben. Außerdem ist nicht gesichert, ob es sich bei den Versen um Brants Text oder um den Text eines anderen handelt, der als der Brants ausgegeben werden sollte (im Sinne einer wert- und bedeutungssteigernden Zutat).

Das heißt, mit der gebotenen Zurückhaltung wäre dieser Analogismus nur dann argumentationsstützend einbeziehbar, wenn nachgewiesen würde, dass Brant tatsächlich selbst an den Visierungen der Illustrationen anderer von ihm betreuter Druckausgaben beteiligt gewesen ist. Dieser Nachweis muss von denjenigen geführt werden, welche die Brant-Visierer-These aufstellen; sie ist nicht damit bestätigt, dass sie – aufgrund fehlender oder nicht aussagekräftiger Belege – nicht widerlegbar ist. Alles Übrige ist Spekulation.

Ich halte fest: Es ist möglich, dass der Autor Sebastian Brant Visierungen der (oder einiger) *Narrenschiff*-Holzschnitte angefertigt hat oder in einer ähnlichen Funktion am Herstellungsprozess der Holzschnittillustrationen beteiligt gewesen ist. Berücksichtigt man hier weiterhin die Möglichkeit, dass Brant diese oder eine ähnliche Funktion im Rahmen anderer von ihm editorisch und/oder redaktionell betreuter Drucke übernommen haben könnte, wäre ein hierauf gründender Analogieschluss unter bestimmten Voraussetzungen als Argument akzeptabel. Solange es keine stichhaltigen positiven Belege für eine solche Funktion Brants – das Argument wäre im Fall von Belegen im Zusammenhang mit dem *Narrenschiff*-Druck am stärksten – gibt, ist meines Erachtens davon abzusehen, Brant diese zuzuschreiben. Die dekontextualisierte Kumulation unspezifischer Aussagen Brants oder Dritter zum Text-Bild-Verhältnis im Rahmen seiner (fiktionalen) Texte, wie sie in allen mir bekannten

54 Vehement wird dagegen in der Forschung der berechtigte Einwand bei RAINER WOHLFEIL / TRUDL WOHLFEIL: Verbildlichung ständischer Gesellschaft. Bartholomäus Bruyn d. Ä. – Petrarcameister (mit Exkursen von Marlies Minuth und Heike Talkenberger). In: Ständische Gesellschaft und soziale Mobilität. Hrsg. von WINFRIED SCHULZE. München 1988 (*Schriften des Historischen Kollegs: Kolloquien.* 12), S. 269–331, hier S. 314 zurückgewiesen. So hat KNAPE (siehe Anm. 39) eine Auseinandersetzung mit den kritischen Einwänden nicht einmal mehr nötig, wenn er schreibt: »die bei Wohlfeil deutlich werdende Zurückhaltung hinsichtlich der Frage nach Brants Anteil am ›Glücksbuch‹-Bildprogramm [ist] unbegründet« (S. 272, Anm. 119).

Beiträgen der älteren und neueren Forschung gang und gäbe ist, kann als Beleg nicht taugen. In meiner Rekonstruktion des Produktionsprozesses sehe ich daher bis auf weiteres keine Veranlassung, von der zeitgenössischen Konvention in Bezug auf diesen Aspekt der prä-typografischen Phase abzuweichen und einen zusätzlichen Funktionsträger anzunehmen respektive diese Funktion dem Autor des Textes zuzuschreiben.

Erwartungsgemäß zurückhaltend – dies der Vollständigkeit halber – äußert sich die kunsthistorische wie literaturwissenschaftliche Forschung im Hinblick auf den letzten Funktionsträger dieser Produktionsphase, den oder auch die Formschneider. In aller Regel wird dieser Herstellungsinstanz nur marginaler Einfluss auf die Bildgestaltung zugebilligt; allenfalls »verschlechternd« wirke sich die Beteiligung des handwerklich-technischen Formschneidens auf den Holzschnitt aus.

Diese anachronistische Rückprojektion widerspricht jedoch den Konventionen der Frühdruck- und Handpressenzeit. Zwar sind Formschneider – wie das Gros der an einem Druckwerk beteiligten Akteure des Literatursystems – in den primären und sekundären Quellen zum Buchdruck weitgehend anonym geblieben (das Anbringen von Signaturen jedweder Art ist für das ausgehende 15. Jahrhundert in diesem Handwerk noch unüblich), die materielle Bewertung ihres Anteils an der Herstellung der Holzschnitte zeigt indes, dass die vor dem Hintergrund eines bestimmten ahistorischen Kunst- und Künstlerbildes marginalisierte, als qualitativ minderwertig charakterisierte Handwerksarbeit des Formschneidens im Verhältnis zu den übrigen Arbeiten hoch vergütet wurde.

Einige zeitgenössische Quellen belegen, dass die Entlohnung für das Formschneiden zwölf Mal so hoch wie die für das Entwerfen und immerhin vier Mal so hoch wie die für das Reißen war.[55] Über den oder die Formschneider der *Narrenschiff*-Illustrationen ist allerdings nichts bekannt, und es gibt meines Wissens keine direkten oder indirekten Quellenbelege, die diesen Aspekt der prä-typografischen Phase erhellen könnten.

Fazit

Ausgehend vom einfachen Normalfall arbeitsteiligen Herstellens von Holzschnitten für Buchillustrationen am Ausgang des 15. Jahrhunderts kann für den *Narrenschiff*-Erstdruck in Ermangelung entsprechender Belege und aufgrund einiger weniger Indizien Folgendes festgehalten werden:

1. Es ist möglich, wenn auch nicht wahrscheinlich, dass der Autor des *Narrenschiffs*, Sebastian Brant, als Entwerfer respektive Visierer für die Illustrationen tätig war. Wenn Brant in dieser Funktion tätig war, bleibt dennoch offen, in wie weit dies das materiell-mediale Resultat – die Abzüge der Holzschnitte im Druck – beeinflusst hat.

2a. Es ist möglich, dass die Risse von einer einzigen Person angefertigt worden sind.[56] Darüber hinaus ist es möglich, dass diese Person Albrecht Dürer war, das heißt, dass dieser an allen Holzschnitten (oder dem Großteil dieser) beteiligt gewesen ist. Es gibt aber keinen Beleg dafür, dass dies (auch nur wahrscheinlich) der Fall war.

2b. Es ist wahrscheinlich, dass die Risse für sich in einem arbeitsteil-

---

55 Vgl. RESKE (siehe Anm. 5), S. 74 u. ö.
56 Ein häufig vorgebrachter Einwand gegen die Annahme, es könne sich um nur einen einzigen Reißer handeln, lautet dahingehend, dass die stilistische Ausführung der Holzschnitte zu verschieden sei, um nur von einer einzigen Person herrühren zu können. Hierzu nur soviel: Es ist nicht auszuschließen, dass alle Holzschnitte von nur einem Reißer stammen und die jeweils exponierten Differenzmerkmale (a) durch Schwankungen in der Arbeitsweise dieses einen Reißers und/oder (b) durch die mehr oder weniger saubere Arbeit der beteiligten Formschneider zu erklären sind.

igen Produktionsgang in einer entsprechenden Malerwerkstatt von mehreren Personen gemeinsam hergestellt worden sind. Hierfür sprechen die große Anzahl (105 Stück) und das mittelgroße Format (ca. 11,5 × 8 cm bzw. 16 × 10,5 cm) der Holzschnitte.

2c. Es ist ebenfalls möglich, wenn auch nicht wahrscheinlich, dass mehrere Reißer unabhängig voneinander – in unterschiedlichen Werkstätten – einzelne Holzschnitte angefertigt haben.

3. Es ist in diesem Zusammenhang ebenfalls – auf Basis zeitgenössischer Konventionen – wahrscheinlich, dass der Formschnitt arbeitsteilig unter mehreren Handwerkern aufgeteilt worden ist. Möglich ist auch, dass der Formschnitt auf mehrere unabhängige Werkstätten aufgeteilt worden ist.

4. Da außer den überlieferten Exemplaren des *Narrenschiff*-Erstdrucks mit den Abzügen der Holzschnitte keine weiteren für den Produktionsvorgang und/oder die an ihm beteiligten Funktionsträger auswertbaren Informationen überliefert und bekannt sind, kann bis auf weiteres nicht mehr über diese Phase der Druckherstellung ausgesagt werden.

FRIEDER SCHMIDT

Überlegungen zu einer Klassifikation der Aufzeichnungs-, Speicher-, Kopier- und Vervielfältigungssysteme aus fertigungstechnischer Sicht

*Aber es geht alles auf und unter in der Welt,
und es hält der Mensch mit aller seiner Riesenkraft nichts fest.*
FRIEDRICH HÖLDERLIN[1]

KANN ES EINEN ANALYTISCHEN ANSATZ GEBEN, der es erlaubt, in körperlicher Form vorliegende menschliche Aufzeichnungen – seien es Felszeichnungen australischer Aborigines, seien es mittelalterliche Buchmalereien oder Siebdrucke aus der Factory von Andy Warhol – in überschaubarer und einheitlicher Weise zu klassifizieren? Kann eine solche Klassifikation gleichzeitig auch der Speicherung – also der Aufbewahrung und der Bereitstellung zum »wieder abrufbar Machen« über den Tag hinaus –, der Kopier- und Vervielfältigungsfähigkeit Rechnung tragen? Im Rahmen eines musealen Ausstellungsprojekts ist diese Frage aufgeworfen und auch verworfen worden, weil sie im wissenschaftlichen Mainstream bisher keine Verankerung hat. Dies kann nicht verwundern, weil bereits durch die genannten Beispiele die Vielzahl der berührten Disziplinen deutlich wird: Es sind Materialien angesprochen, die zum Gegenstandsbereich der Ethnologie, der Handschriftenkunde und der Schriftgeschichte, der Kunstwissenschaft und der Druckgeschichte gehören. Leicht ließen sich weitere Beispiele nennen, die auch die Buchgeschichte, die Geschichte der Fotografie etc. berühren. Offenkundig handelt es sich um eine Fragestellung, die interdisziplinären Charakter hat und deshalb dem kritischen Blick von Vertretern unterschiedlicher Fachrichtungen vorzulegen ist. Kurzum: Die nachfolgenden Ausführungen skizzieren ein analytisches und terminologisches Verfahren, das nicht ausgereift und in langjähriger Praxis erprobt ist, wohl aber zur Diskussion gestellt sein will.

Klassifikationen sind mentale Konstrukte, die an die Welt herangetragen werden, um Sinneseindrücke und Gegenstandsbereiche systematisch abzugrenzen und zu ordnen.[2] Klassifikationssysteme sind umso mächtiger, je weltgesättigter sie sind, das heißt, je intensiver sie auf große, ja sehr große Mengen von Fällen angewendet wurden und werden. Ausgereifte Klassifikationssysteme sind deshalb tragfähig und nützlich, weil sie Gleichartiges gleich behandeln und im Sinne von Ockhams Rasiermesser sparsamsten Gebrauch von klar und präzise unterschiedenen Kategorien machen. Ein Klassifikationssystem erfüllt seinen Zweck besonders gut, wenn es nach Möglichkeit das ganze Universum des in Frage stehenden Gebiets und der zu taxierenden Gegebenheiten abdeckt und

[1] FRIEDRICH HÖLDERLIN: *Hyperion oder der Eremit in Griechenland.* Bd. 1. 2. Aufl. Stuttgart, Tübingen 1822, S. 50.

[2] Die Klassifizierung der Wolken erfolgte beispielsweise 1802 durch Luke Howard (1772–1864), der in einem Vortrag (*On the Modification of Clouds*) ein System veröffentlichte, dessen Wolkenklassen Cirrus, Stratus, Cumulus und Nimbus immer noch geläufig sind. Vgl. die Darstellung von RICHARD HAMBLYN: *Die Erfindung der Wolken. Wie ein unbekannter Meteereologe die Sprache des Himmels erforschte.* Frankfurt a. M. 2003 (*st.* 3527).

[3] Vgl. HARALD HAARMANN: *Universalgeschichte der Schrift.* Frankfurt a. M. 1990. – ANDREW ROBINSON: *Die Geschichte der Schrift.* Düsseldorf 2004.

[4] Vgl. *Geschichte der Druckverfahren.* 4 Bde. Stuttgart, 1973–93 (*Bibliothek des Buchwesens*). – HEIJO KLEIN: *DuMont's kleines Sachwörterbuch der Drucktechnik und grafischen Kunst. Von Abdruck bis Zylinderpresse.* 2., erw. Aufl. Köln 1976 (*DuMont-Kunst-Taschenbücher.* 15). – FONS VAN DER LINDEN: *DuMont's Handbuch der grafischen Techniken. Manuelle und maschinelle Druckverfahren; Hochdruck, Tiefdruck, Flachdruck, Durchdruck; Reproduktionstechniken; Mehrfarbendruck.* 3. Aufl. Köln 1990.

[5] Vgl. ANTONELLA FUGA: *Techniken und Materialien der Kunst.* Berlin 2005 (*Bildlexikon der Kunst.* 10).

[6] Um Missverständnissen vorzubeugen, seien vorab mehrere Klarstellungen getroffen. Es geht in den nachfolgenden Ausführungen um die materiale Seite der Aufzeichnungs-, Speicher-, Kopier- und Vervielfältigungssysteme. Schriftsysteme, Zeichenkodierungssysteme etc. werden nur insofern berücksichtigt, wie sie sich in unmittelbarer Wechselwirkung mit der Realisierung in einem Aufzeichnungsmedium entwickelt haben – man denke an das Lochkartensystem, mit dem Joseph-Marie Jacquard (1752–1834) die Informationen über das zu webende Muster aufzeichnete, oder an

keine »weiße Flecke« auf dessen mentaler Landkarte lässt bzw. diese nicht mit unklaren Signaturen versieht. Dies bedeutet, dass Klassifikation auf Vollständigkeit ohne unbehandelten Rest zielt. Gleichzeitig soll ein Klassifikationssystem überschaubar bleiben, weshalb es in der Regel hierarchisch aufgebaut ist und die Klassen der übergeordneten Stufen jeweils in Teilklassen aufteilt.

Auf welche Vorarbeiten kann man aufsetzen, um eine solche Klassifikation für Aufzeichnungs-, Speicher-, Kopier- und Vervielfältigungssysteme zu entwickeln? Standardwerke zur Schriftgeschichte,[3] zur Geschichte der Druckverfahren[4] oder der Techniken und Materialien der Kunst[5] bieten hierzu keine generalisierbaren Ansatzpunkte. Jedes dieser Werke hilft beim Verständnis einzelner Teilaspekte, gibt aber keinen Ansatzpunkt, wie alle Teilaspekte in ein durchgängiges Klassifikationssystem integriert werden könnten.[6]

Aufzeichnungsverfahren als Fertigungsverfahren
Der im Folgenden unterbreitete Ansatz schlägt vor, alle für das Aufzeichnen, Speichern, Kopieren und Vervielfältigen von Texten, Ornamenten[7] oder Bildern verwendeten Techniken oder Methoden als Verfahren zu betrachten, bei denen etwas verfertigt wird. Wenn man ein Holzstück mit Schneidemessern so bearbeitet, dass ein Holzstock entsteht, von dem ein Abdruck erzeugt werden kann, so haben wir es am Ende mit zwei Erzeugnissen zu tun: Erstens mit einem Holzstock mit erhabenen und vertieften Bereichen, die zusammen einen bestimmten Bildeindruck wiedergeben, und zweitens einem Blatt Papier, auf dem der mit Druckerschwärze eingefärbte Holzstock ein Abbild hinterlassen hat, wobei entweder der Druck eines Reibers oder der einer Druckerpresse für den Transfer der Farbe vom Holz zum Papier gesorgt hat. Wenn man mit dem Füllfederhalter auf einem Briefbogen einen Text verfasst, dann fertigt man ein partiell mit Tinte beschichtetes Stück Papier an. Zum Aufbringen eines Logos auf einen Überseecontainer kann man eine Schablone verwenden, die zuvor in der Weise angefertigt wurde, dass man mit einem geeigneten Werkzeug – einem Messer oder einem Laserstrahl – formgerechte Aussparungen in das Schablonenmaterial (ein Blech, eine Folie oder ähnliches) geschnitten hat, durch die hindurch nun die Farbe durch Auftupfen, Aufsprühen etc. konturgenau aufgebracht wird; diese Technik ist die dem Patronieren der Spielkartenmacher des 18. Jahrhunderts sehr ähnlich.[8] Bei der Straminstickerei werden Buchstaben per Kreuzstich appliziert und fügen sich – wie dies auf einem Handarbeitsmustertuch aus dem Jahr 1918 im Ebersdorfer Schulmuseum Chemnitz zu sehen ist – zu einem Alphabet.[9] Solche Beispiele ließen sich in beliebiger Fülle ergänzen.[10]

In einem zweiten Schritt wird der Vorschlag gemacht, diese verfertigten Aufzeichnungen im Sinne der Fertigungstechnik, einer ingenieurwissenschaftlichen Teildisziplin, zu klassifizieren.[11] Fertigungstechnik (engl. *manufacturing engineering*) befasst sich im Rahmen der Produktionstechnik und des Maschinenbaus mit der Herstellung von Werkstücken aus einem gegebenen Ausgangsmaterial und deren Zusammenbau. Da-

die von Louis Braille (1809–52) entwickelte Schrift erhabener Punkte (Blindenschrift). Die Unterscheidung zwischen Kopiersystemen und Vervielfältigungssystemen mag spitzfindig erscheinen, denn im Zeitalter moderner Bürotechnik macht es keinen großen Unterschied, ob man das Kopiergerät auf 1 oder auf 99 Exemplare stellt. Im angelsächsischen Sprachgebrauch wird zudem die Auflagenhöhe eines Drucks mittels der Bezeichnung *copies* angegeben. In den nachfolgenden Ausführungen wird zwischen Kopieren und Vervielfältigen unterschieden. Als Kopie wird in vorliegendem Zusammenhang eine Zweitschrift verstanden, die aufgrund bestimmter Merkmale in der Lage ist, in formaler und inhaltlicher Hinsicht an die Stelle des Originals zu treten. Die Vervielfältigung eines Textes oder Bildes hingegen kann von der ursprünglichen Form in formaler und auch in inhaltlicher Hinsicht erheblich abweichen – man denke an einen handschriftlichen Leserbrief, der in einer Zeitung ohne Anschrift und Datum sowie in gekürzter Form abgedruckt wird, oder man denke an ein Farbfoto, von dem ein Ausschnitt als Graustufenbild vervielfältigt wird.

7 Ornamente sind im Westen im Verlauf des 20. Jahrhunderts stark in den Hintergrund getreten, aus einer globalen Sicht menschlicher Aktivitäten bilden sie jedoch seit dem Paläolithikum bis in unsere Gegenwart hinein ein kontinuierliches Element gestaltender Tätigkeit, das schriftlosen und über Schriftkultur verfügenden Gesellschaften gemeinsam ist und deshalb hier besondere Beachtung verdient. Vgl. JAMES TRILLING: The Language of Ornament. London 2001 (*World of Art*).
8 Vgl. DETLEF HOFFMANN: *Die Welt der Spielkarte. Eine Kulturgeschichte.* 2. Aufl. Leipzig 1983, S. 8.
9 Ebersdorfer SchulM Chemnitz, Inv.-Nr. 7.01.21, siehe auch Verzeichnis der Webseiten auf S. 374.
10 Diese Beispiele machen aber auch deutlich, dass bestimmte vergängliche künstlerische Leistungen, die den Charakter einer Performance haben, nur dann berücksichtigt werden können, wenn es aus diesem Kontext heraus dauerhafte Hervorbringungen gibt, die gespeichert werden und aus diesem Speicher heraus wieder reaktivierbar sind.
11 Vgl. *Grundlagen der Fertigungstechnik.* Hrsg. von BIRGIT AWISZUS, JÜRGEN BAST u. HOLGER DÜRR. 4., aktualisierte Aufl. München 2009.

bei können Halbfabrikate und Endprodukte entstehen. Im Fertigungsverfahren werden geometrisch bestimmte feste Körper produziert, wobei Werkzeuge und Wirkmedien zum Einsatz kommen. Ein vom Deutschen Institut für Normung erarbeiteter Standard, die DIN Norm 8580, legt die Begriffe und die Einteilung der Fertigungsverfahren fest. Im Einzelnen werden dabei sechs Hauptgruppen unterschieden, wobei vor allem die Frage nach dem Zusammenhalt von Stoffteilchen und von den Einzelteilen eines zusammengesetzten Körpers interessiert. Diese Hauptgruppen sind:

1. das Urformen (Zusammenhalt schaffen),
2. das Umformen (Zusammenhalt beibehalten),
3. das Trennen (Zusammenhalt vermindern),
4. das Fügen (Zusammenhalt vermehren),
5. das Beschichten (Zusammenhalt vermehren),
6. das Stoffeigenschaften Ändern.

Eine deutliche Vorstellung der gemeinten Verfahren vermittelt beispielsweise die Fertigung eines Verbrennungsmotors für ein Automobil. Da werden per Urformen ein Motorblock, ein Zylinderkopf oder einzelne Kolben gegossen, per Umformen eine Kurbelwelle geschmiedet, per Trennen Zylinder ausgedreht und Flächen geschliffen, per Fügen Kurbelwelle, Pleuelstangen und Kolben montiert, per Beschichten Oberflächen veredelt und beim Härten von Bauteilen Stoffeigenschaften verändert.

Aus dieser Welt des industriellen Fahrzeug- und Maschinenbaus stammen eigentlich die Kernbegriffe dieser Systematik der Fertigungsverfahren. Untersucht man Schritt für Schritt die Welt der Aufzeichnungsverfahren und die damit in Verbindung stehenden Speicherungs-, Kopier- und Vervielfältigungstechniken, wie sie seit vorgeschichtlichen Zeiten bis in unsere aktuelle Gegenwart hinein zum Einsatz kommen, so zeigt sich rasch, wie sinnvoll auch in diesem Bereich mit diesen Kategorien systematische Klarheit geschaffen werden kann. In der Folge erlaubt dies, auch ziemlich komplexe Prozesse als eindeutig und konsequent strukturierte Fertigungsabläufe zu beschreiben, die auf einem überschaubaren Repertoire von Grundverfahren aufsetzen.

Die sechs Hauptgruppen der Fertigungstechnik als Klassen des Aufzeichnens

1. Urformen

Die Hauptgruppe des Urformens (engl. *creative forming*[12]) befasst sich mit dem Schaffen von Zusammenhalt. Dabei wird aus einem formlosen Stoff – es kann sich dabei um ein Gas, eine Flüssigkeit, ein plastisches, körniges oder pulverförmiges Material handeln – die Erstform eines geometrisch bestimmten Körpers hervorgebracht. Eine klassische Technik des Urformens ist das Gießen, aber auch das Sintern oder das Galvanoformen aus dem ionisierten Zustand, wobei aus einem wässrigen Salzbad ein Metall elektrolytisch ausgeschieden wird, gehören hierzu. Beim Urformen werden also Materialien in sehr unterschiedlichem Zustand als Ausgangs-

---

12 Vgl. KLAUS LOCHMANN / KATRIN HÄDRICH: PONS *Fachwörterbuch Fertigungstechnik*. Stuttgart u. a. 2009.

stoff genommen. Durch Urformen können geeignete Trägermaterialien für die Aufzeichnung von Ornamenten, Schriftzeichen und Bildern hervorgebracht werden.¹³ Hierbei ist zunächst an das Formen von tafelförmigen, prismatischen oder tonnenförmigen Tonkörpern zu denken, wie sie vor allem im Zweistromland zwischen Euphrat und Tigris für Keilschriftaufzeichnungen genutzt wurden.¹⁴ Im Bronzeguss wurden metallene Tafeln, Kirchentüren und Glocken, aber auch Kanonen hergestellt, wobei Schrift und Bild schon vorab geformt sein mussten, denn beim Urformen sind geeignete Formen oder Gefäße erforderlich, die dem zu fertigenden Gegenstand die Gestalt geben. Diese selbst waren wiederum in einem oder mehreren Schritten unter Einsatz der genannten grundsätzlichen Fertigungstechniken erarbeitet worden und konnten dann entweder einmal (verlorene Form) oder mehrfach eingesetzt werden. Bereits in der Antike nutzte man Gussverfahren, um durch Urformen das nachzubilden, was beim Münzprägen mit Stempeln durch Umformen gestaltet worden war.¹⁵ Aus Quarzsand und sodahaltiger Pflanzenasche wurde Glas erschmolzen, das zu Gefäßen (Hohlglas) oder als Scheiben (Flachglas) geformt als Schrift- und Bildträger taugte. Ein Urformen aus einem faserförmigen Zustand fand und findet seit zweitausend Jahren beim Papiermachen statt, wenn ein schwimmendes Sieb, eine Schöpfform oder ein endloses Maschinensieb einem sich aus wässriger Suspension bildenden Faservlies Gestalt gibt. Ein Urformen findet aber auch bei der Anfertigung von Schreib- und Zeichenstiften statt, wenn pulverförmige Pigmente zusammen mit einem Bindemittel in die entsprechende Form gebracht werden. Pastellfarben erlangten ihre Stiftform, indem man Azurit oder Hämatit mit »Wasser und Bindemitteln wie Gummiarabicum, Feigenbaummilch, Fischleim oder Kandiszucker«¹⁶ vermengte und austrocknen ließ. Ohne Urformen ist die Welt Gutenbergs und des Buchdrucks nicht denkbar. Das Schriftgießen war ein elementarer Verfahrensschritt, damit zentnerweise gleichartige Typen für den Satz ganzer Druckbogen zur Verfügung standen. Im 19. Jahrhundert eröffnete das neu entdeckte elektrochemische Verfahren der Galvanoplastik die Abformung ganzer Druckstöcke und komplett ausgeschlossener Seiten, wodurch Auflagenhöhen in bisher nicht gekanntem Maße erzielt werden konnten. Erfolgte das Gießen der individuellen Typen zunächst einzeln und mit dem Handgießinstrument, so wurden im 19. Jahrhundert Schriftgießmaschinen erfunden, mit denen man gleichartige Typen in großen Mengen fertigen konnte. Die Linotype-Setzmaschinen von Ottmar Mergenthaler (1854–99) erlaubten das Gießen einer kompletten, ausgeschlossenen Zeile, während das von Tolbert Lanston (1844–1913) erfundene Monotype-Verfahren das Setzen und das Gießen auf zwei Maschinen, den Taster und die Gießmaschine, aufteilte. Bei dem Verfahren der Stereotypie schließlich – eine fertig gesetzte Druckseite wird abgeformt, die Form mit Letternmetall ausgegossen – kommt beim Stanhope'schen oder Gips-Verfahren das Urformen zweimal zum Einsatz: Zunächst wird ein Gipsabguss angefertigt, dann dieser nach entsprechender Präparierung mit Letternmetall ausgegossen. Wenn man für die Abformung kein Urform-Verfahren, sondern ein Umform-Verfahren wählte, konnte man

13 Wenn als Schriftträger Schildkrötenpanzer (vgl. ANDREW ROBINSON: *Die Geschichte der Schrift*. Düsseldorf 2004, S. 183) oder Palmblätter verwendet werden, so hat man hier das Urformen der Natur überlassen, die allerdings nicht geometrisch definierte, sondern genetisch festgelegte Formen hervorgebracht hat.
14 Sehr anschaulich dargestellt bei EDWARD CHIERA: *Sie schrieben auf Ton. Was die babylonischen Schrifttafeln erzählen*. Hrsg. von GEORGE G. CAMERON. 3. Aufl., Zürich 1953, insbesondere Abb. 23 (Tonprisma von Sanherib und Tonnen von Sargon und Nebukadnezar).
15 CHRISTOPHER HOWGEGO: *Geld in der antiken Welt. Was Münzen über Geschichte verraten*. Darmstadt 2000, S. 29: »Auch einige Fälscher bedienten sich des Gussverfahrens, weil es der einfachste Weg war, um offizielle Münzen nachzuahmen.«
16 FUGA (siehe Anm. 5), S. 39.

das Satzbild in eine Matrizenpappe einprägen und diese ausgießen. Bog man diese Mater in geeigneter Weise, so ließen sich Rundstereos erzeugen, mit denen man auf der Rotationsdruckmaschine Papier von der Rolle verdrucken konnte – damit war der Weg frei für auflagenstarke Zeitungen.

2. Umformen

Die Hauptgruppe des Umformens (engl. *conversion, transformation*) befasst sich mit Fertigungsmethoden, bei denen der Stoffzusammenhang erhalten bleibt. Werkstoffe werden dabei gezielt plastisch verformt. Ohne hier auf all die Möglichkeiten der Umformtechnik einzugehen, die in modernen industriell eingesetzten Produktionsprozessen zum Zuge kommen, sei hier direkt auf Beispiele aus dem Bereich des Aufzeichnens eingegangen. Verformende Eindrücke, zum Beispiel Ornamente, in getöpferten Gefäßen sind hier als sehr frühe Beispiele zu nennen.[17] Alteuropäische Funde lassen bereits an eine frühe Schrift denken.[18] Siegel beziehungsweise Rollsiegel sind zu nennen, die in Verschlussmarken eingedrückt wurden und so den Inhalt von Tonkrügen, aber auch von Urkunden sicherten.[19] In den altkretischen Diskos von Phaistos (18./17. Jh. v. Chr.) sind in den formbaren Ton der etwa 16 cm Durchmesser aufweisenden Scheibe auf beiden Seiten sich mehrfach wiederholende Zeichen (45 verschiedene Motive menschlicher, tierischer, pflanzlicher oder gegenständlicher Art) in einer spiralförmigen Anordnung mittels Stempeln eingedrückt. Interessante Beispiele sind die 1964 von Massimo Pallottino (1909–95) in Pyrgi ausgegrabenen, sehr dünnen Goldbleche, die als Eindrücke Inschriften in etruskischer und punischer (bzw. phönizischer) Sprache aufweisen.[20] Besondere Bedeutung erlangte das Umformen mit dem Aufkommen geprägter Münzen: »Prägen ist für die Massenproduktion viel effizienter als Gießen.«[21] Für das Prägen sind geeignete Stempel erforderlich, in die das Gegenstück zum Münzbild eingearbeitet ist – was auf der Münze erhaben erscheinen soll, muss beim Stempel seitenverkehrt und vertieft gearbeitet sein. Der Vorderseitenstempel wird in einen Amboss eingesetzt, der Rückseitenstempel ist der obere Stempel. Die Siegelabdrücke und die Münzprägungen bilden zwei sehr umfangreiche Gruppen der kulturellen Überlieferung. Siegel, Münzen und Medaillen zeigen schriftliche, bildliche und ornamentale Aufzeichnungen und sind uns in ganz erheblicher Zahl erhalten geblieben.[22] Es gibt aber auch ein Aufzeichnen durch Umformen, das nicht auf die lange Überlieferung berechnet ist. Bei Wachstafeln waren Holztafeln ein- oder beidseitig mit Wachs beschichtet (entsprechend gearbeitete Vertiefungen waren mit Wachs ausgegossen), mehrere Tafeln konnten zu einem zwei- oder mehrteiligen Wachstafelbuch zusammengebunden werden; in diese Wachsschichten ließen sich nun mit einem Stylus Notizen eindrücken, hatten diese ihren Zweck erfüllt, wurde mit dem abgeflachten Ende des Schreibstifts das Wachs wieder glatt gezogen.[23] Das plastische Umformen konnte also sowohl dem Aufzeichnen, als auch dem Löschen der Aufzeichnungen dienen. Zum Umformen gehört auch das Herstellen von Draht, zunächst durch Schmieden, dann durch Ziehen. Drähte aus Metallen beziehungsweise Legierungen eignen sich insbesondere zur Schmuckanfertigung

---

17 Vgl. die Zusammenstellung jungsteinzeitlicher Keramikgefäße mit ihren vielfältigen Formen und Verzierungen in: SIEGMAR VON SCHNURBEIN/BERNHARD HÄNSEL: *Atlas der Vorgeschichte. Europa von den ersten Menschen bis Christi Geburt.* 2., korr. Aufl. Stuttgart 2010, S. 65.

18 Vgl. HARALD HAARMANN: Der alteuropäisch-altmediterrane Schriftenkreis. In: Schrift und Schriftlichkeit. Ein interdisziplinäres Handbuch internationaler Forschung. 1. Halbbd. Berlin, New York 1994 (*Handbücher zur Sprach- und Kommunikationswissenschaft.* 10.1), S. 268–74.

19 Vgl. *Mit sieben Siegeln versehen. Das Siegel in Wirtschaft und Kultur des Alten Orients.* Hrsg. von EVELYN KLENGEL-BRANDT. Ausstellungskatalog Vorderasiatisches Museum Berlin. Mainz 1997.

20 Vgl. TIM CORNELL/JOHN MATTHEWS: Rom. Kunst, Geschichte und Lebensformen. Augsburg 1998 (*Bildatlas der Weltkulturen*), S. 28. – ROBINSON (siehe Anm. 13), S. 152/3.

21 HOWGEGO (siehe Anm. 15), S. 29.

22 Metallobjekte sind stets der Gefahr des Einschmelzens ausgesetzt. Bei Brandkatastrophen lässt es sich nicht vermeiden, bei Metallgeld ist der Reiz zum Einschmelzen dann gegeben, wenn der Metallwert den Münzwert überschreitet.

23 Vgl. WILHELM SCHUBART: *Das Buch bei den Griechen und Römern.* Hrsg. von EBERHARD PAUL. 3. Aufl. Heidelberg 1962, S. 28–32. – HARALD FROSCHAUER: Antike Schreibgeräte von Ägypten bis Rom. In: Vom Griffel zum Kultobjekt. 3000 Jahre Geschichte des Schreibgerätes. Hrsg. von CHRISTIAN GASTGEBER u. HERMANN HARRAUER. Wien 2001 (*Nilus.* 6), S. 1–14. – Gutenberg – Aventur und Kunst. Vom Geheimunternehmen zur ersten Medienrevolution. Anlässlich des 600. Geburtstages von Johannes Gutenberg hrsg. von der Stadt Mainz. Mainz 2000, S. 285 (Wachstafeln des 14. Jahrhunderts aus dem Lübecker Schulgerätefund).

(Biegen von Ornamenten), aber auch zur Herstellung von Sieben. Seit dem 13. Jahrhundert wurden ausgehend von Italien Papierschöpfformen mit starrem Holzrahmen und einer Bespannung aus Metalldraht hergestellt (Rippdrähte und Kettdrähte). Gebogene, auf der Schöpfform angebrachte Drahtfiguren, nachweisbar seit spätestens 1282, gegebenenfalls auch schon seit 1271, hinterlassen im Papier sogenannte Wasserzeichen.[24] Durch Umformen entstandene Gebilde erzeugen so innerhalb des Papierbogens während der Blattbildung dünnere Bereiche, die im Durchlicht heller erscheinen. Dieser Bildeindruck kann mit dem Schöpfen jedes weiteren Papierbogens übertragen und während der Lebensdauer der Schöpfform hunderttausendfach vervielfältigt werden.

3. Trennen

Wenden wir uns dem Trennen (engl. *separation*) zu, also dem Vermindern des Zusammenhalts, ein Verfahren, das in vielfältigster Weise durch Ritzen, Schaben, Kratzen, Schleifen, Schneiden, Ätzen seine spezifischen Ausprägungen erhält. Beim Trennen werden von dem Werkstück größere oder kleinere Materialmengen entfernt. Die ältesten uns überlieferten Felsritzungen wurden mittels härterer Steine in weichere Steine eingraviert. Zum Teil wurden dabei nur oberflächlich entstandene Verwitterungsschichten entfernt, und es kam dann das darunter liegende Gestein zum Vorschein, zum Teil handelte es sich aber um Absplitterungen, die vor allem durch die Wirkung von Licht und Schatten wahrgenommen werden konnten. Mit wachsender Erfahrung und zunehmender Materialkenntnis wurden im Lauf der Zeit die härtesten Mineralien entdeckt: Topas ist härter als Quarz, Korund härter als Topas, Diamant härter als Korund – in der Härteskala des Mineralogen Friedrich Mohs (1773–1839) bilden die vier genannten Beispiele die Härtestufen 7 bis 10. In der Altsteinzeit dienten gezielt als Abschläge von Feuersteinknollen hergestellte Klingen als Schneid- und Schabwerkzeuge. Sie erlaubten das Abtrennen von tierischem und pflanzlichem Material, Hölzer konnten mit Kerbungen versehen werden. Aus dem Aurignacien sind uns verzierte kleine Tierplastiken und Flöten überliefert, deren Ornamente mit Feuersteinklingen in das Mammutelfenbein geschnitten bzw. geritzt wurden.[25] Stein war das gängigste Material bei der Siegelherstellung, wobei neben weichen Steinen auch härtere Halbedelsteine zum Einsatz kamen.[26] Sobald man die Verhüttung von Erzen beherrschen lernte, standen zunächst Kupferwerkzeuge, dann solche aus Bronze (einer Legierung von Kupfer und Zinn), schließlich aus Eisen und Stahl zur Verfügung. Daraus konnten Meißel hergestellt werden, mit denen sich Inschriften auf immer härteren Gesteinen anbringen ließen. Auch in Holz konnte man mit metallenen Klingen immer besser arbeiten. Es entwickelte sich zunächst der mit der pflanzlichen Faser verlaufende Holzschnitt, dann der Holzstich, bei dem die Vertiefungen mit Stahlsticheln in das wesentlich härtere Hirnholz eingebracht werden.[27] Ziel ist jeweils ein Druckstock, der an den erhabenen Stellen so eingefärbt werden kann, dass die gezielte Beschichtung eines Druckträgers möglich wird (Hochdruck). Farbe, die sich in Vertiefungen einer Druckplatte

24 Vgl. CARMEN KÄMMERER / PETER RÜCKERT: Die Welt im Wasserzeichen. In: *Ochsenkopf und Meerjungfrau. Papiergeschichte und Wasserzeichen vom Mittelalter bis zur Neuzeit*. Ausstellungskatalog. Stuttgart und Wien 2009, S. 29.
25 Vgl. *Eiszeit. Kunst und Kultur*. Hrsg. von SUSANNE RAU, DANIELA NAUMANN u. MARTINA BARTH. Ausstellungskatalog Archäologisches LandesM Baden-Württemberg. Ostfildern 2009, S. 249 und 320.
26 Vgl. RALF-BERNHARD WARTKE: Materialien der Siegel und ihre Herstellung. In: KLENGEL-BRANDT (siehe Anm. 19), S. 41–61.
27 Zum Holzschnitt und den weiteren grafischen Techniken vgl. die sehr anschaulichen Darstellungen der Werkzeuge und ihrer Handhabung bei VAN DER LINDEN (siehe Anm. 4).

befand, ließ sich unter hohem Druck ebenfalls übertragen (Tiefdruck). Beim Kupferstich werden Gravuren mit stählernen Grabsticheln in polierte, mit abgerundeten Ecken und facettierten Kanten versehene Kupferplatten gestochen. Etwas komplexer sind die Verhältnisse beim Stahlstich. Hier werden zuerst die Materialeigenschaften der Platte verändert – Glühen setzt die Härte so weit herab, dass der Stahl gravierbar wird. Nach Vollendung der Darstellung wird der Stahl wieder gehärtet und erlaubt eine Auflage, die zehnmal höher war als die des Kupferstichs. Nicht alle Tiefdruckverfahren arbeiten mit dem Prinzip der Trennung. Beim Punzenstich werden durch Umformen kleine Gruben in das Metall getrieben, die dann die Farbe aufnehmen. Beim um 1730 von John Walsh (1665–1736) erfundenen Notenstich erfolgt nur ein Teil des Aufzeichnens durch Gravieren – die Notenlinien, die Taktstriche, Hälse, Balken und Bögen –, während die Notenschlüssel, die Notenköpfe und Text mit Punzen in die Pewter genannte Legierung aus Blei, Zinn und Antimon getrieben werden.[28] Mit wachsenden chemischen Kenntnissen nahm die Fertigkeit zu, Material auf nasschemischem Wege abzutrennen und wegzuätzen. Das Ätzen musste gezielt und selektiv erfolgen, was nur durch indirekte Verfahren erreicht werden konnte. Säuren wirken bei diesen Verfahren nur an solchen Stellen auf die Metallplatte, wo eine bearbeitete Schutzschicht freien Zugang lässt. Diese Methoden hatten zunächst Waffenschmiede als Dekortechnik für Harnische und anderes Kriegsgerät aus Eisen entwickelt, seit dem frühen 16. Jahrhundert entwickelte sich das Verfahren zur grafischen Drucktechnik. Metallplatten wurden mit einem Firnis aus Harz und Terpentin abgedeckt, dann die Zeichnung in diese Schicht eingraviert und anschließend in das Metall geätzt. Eisen, mit dem Albrecht Dürer seit 1515 experimentierte (u. a. *Der Verzweifelnde*[29] und *Gebet am Ölberg*), stellte nicht richtig zufrieden.[30] Der Übergang zu Kupferätzungen lieferte dann bessere Ergebnisse. Es handelt sich also um ein Verfahren, bei dem sich an ein erstes Beschichten ein dreistufiges Trennen anschließt – mechanisches Gravieren, chemisches Vertiefen, schließlich Abnahme der Firnisschicht mittels eines Lösungsmittels. Es folgt die Beschichtung der Druckplatte mit Farbe, das Sauberreiben derselben und schließlich der Abdruck auf Papier. Die chemische Wirkung der Säure konnte aber auch zur Herstellung von Hochätzungen verwendet werden. Der Däne Christian Piil (1804–84) entwickelte 1843 ein Verfahren namens Chemitypie, bei dem eine Zinkplatte zweimal geätzt wurde.[31] Auch die Zinkografie ist in diesem Kontext zu nennen.[32] Eine spezielle Form des Trennens stellt das Verdrängen dar, wie es bei der Herstellung von Kleisterpapieren vorkommt. Bei der Produktion solcher Buntpapiere werden weiße Papierbogen mit einer Schicht von gefärbtem Kleister überzogen, anschließend wird ein Teil desselben mit kleinen Werkzeugen, Stempeln oder anderen Hilfsmitteln verdrängt, so dass an den bearbeiteten Stellen wieder das Weiß des Rohpapiers durchscheint und entsprechende Dekorationsformen zeigt.[33] Unter das Trennen fallen schließlich Aufzeichnungen, die durch Perforieren geschehen. In die Dokumente werden kleine Lochungen gestanzt, die zu Zeichen, Buchstaben und Ziffern angeordnet sind. Auf diese Weise lassen sich recht fäl-

---

28 Vgl. MARTIN GIESEKING: *Code-basierte Generierung interaktiver Notengraphik. Zur Entwicklung einer dynamischen Notendarstellung in interaktiven Lernprogrammen und musikspezifischen Multimedia-Applikationen.* Osnabrück 2001, S. 21. – DERS.: Zur Geschichte des Notendrucks – ein Überblick. In: Musik im Spektrum von Kultur und Gesellschaft. Hrsg. von BERNHARD MÜSSGENS, MARTIN GIESEKING u. OLIVER KAUTNY. Osnabrück 2001 (Osnabrücker Beiträge zur Musik und Musikerziehung. 1), S. 339–53, hier S. 347.
29 Vgl. *Dürer, Himmel und Erde. Gottes- und Menschenbild in Dürers druckgraphischem Werk. Holzschnitte, Kupferstiche und Radierungen aus der Sammlung Otto Schäfer II.* Schweinfurt 1999, S. 150/1.
30 Vgl. ERWIN PANOFSKY: *Das Leben und die Kunst Albrecht Dürers.* München 1977, S. 259–63.
31 Vgl. *Deutsches polygraphisches Kompendium. Encyklopädisches Hand- und Lehrbuch für Buchdruck, Schriftgiesserei, Buchhandel und die verwandten Fächer: Lithographie, Photochemie, Xylographie.* Hrsg. von PAUL HEICHEN. Leipzig 1883, Bd. 1, S. 207.
32 Vgl. EVA HANEBUTT-BENZ/ KRISTIN WIEDAU: Die drucktechnische Revolution im 19. Jahrhundert. In: *Bilderlust und Lesefrüchte. Das illustrierte Kunstbuch von 1750 bis 1920.* Hrsg. von EVA HANEBUTT-BENZ u. KATHARINA KRAUSE. Ausstellungskatalog Gutenberg-M Mainz. Leipzig 2005, S. 43–58, hier S. 52.
33 Vgl. ALBERT HAEMMERLE: *Buntpapier. Herkommen, Geschichte, Techniken, Beziehungen zur Kunst.* 2. Aufl. München 1977, S. 137–9.

schungssicher Nummern in Sparbüchern, Datumsangaben in Wertpapieren, Kennzeichnungen in Filmmaterial oder Entwertungsvermerke in abgelaufenen Reisepässen anbringen. Datum- und Textperforiermaschinen sowie Lochentwertungsgeräte übernehmen diese Aufgaben.

4. *Fügen*

Unter Fügen (engl. *joining*, *assembly*) sind alle die Operationen zu verstehen, durch die ein Zusammenhalt vermehrt wird. Das Auffädeln verschiedener Perlen zu einer Kette ist ein solcher Vorgang, und wenn Größe und Farbe der Perlen eine Bedeutung haben beziehungsweise deren Abfolge eine charakteristische Form annimmt, so liegt bereits hier eine bestimmte Form der Aufzeichnung vor. Ethnologische Sammlungen enthalten eine Vielzahl solcher Objekte aus den unterschiedlichsten Ländern und Kulturen. Knotenschnüre (*Quipus*) der Inka bestehen aus einem langen Hauptfaden, an die Nebenfäden geknüpft sind, die sich durch farbliche Abstufungen voneinander unterscheiden. Verschiedenartige Knoten an unterschiedlichen Positionen dieser Nebenfäden dienten zur Aufzeichnung quantitativer Daten, die für Verwaltungszwecke wichtig waren.[34] Beim Teppichknüpfen werden einzelne Knoten reihenweise auf Kettfäden geknüpft. Feinste persische Knüpfteppiche erreichen eine Knotendichte von mehr als einer Million Knoten pro Quadratmeter, wobei zur Darstellung von Mustern Wollfäden in mehreren Dutzend verschiedenen Farben verwendet werden können, so dass eine hochauflösende Darstellung mit feinen Farbabstufungen produziert werden kann. Des Weiteren ist die musivische Kunst zu nennen, deren Ursprünge in Mesopotamien bis in sumerische Zeit zurück reichte. Einzelne Mosaiksteinchen werden zu einem Bild oder zu einem Ornament zusammengefügt, auch die Wiedergabe von Buchstaben kann so erfolgen. Die klassische Antike kennt Bodenmosaiken, in denen gleichzeitig alle drei Elemente vertreten sind. In Griechenland wurden zunächst Kieselmosaiken aus hellen und dunklen Steinen angefertigt (*Opus-lapilli*-Technik), in hellenistischer Zeit ging man dazu über, zurechtgeschnittene Mosaiksteine zu verwenden, das Würfelmosaik (*Opus-tesselatum*-Technik). Diese sind bei der *Opus-vermiculatum*-Technik so winzig, dass bis zu 68 Würfelchen pro Quadratzentimeter verarbeitet wurden.[35] Vor das Fügen kam also zunächst ein Trennen. Entsprechende Plättchen müssen nicht aus Stein sein, auch Glas, Metall, Perlmutt und andere Werkstoffe kommen in Frage. Bei der *Opus-sectile*-Technik handelt es sich nicht mehr um Mosaiken, sondern um den Intarsien vergleichbare Arbeiten.[36] Bei letzteren werden dünne Teile aus verschiedenen Holzarten zusammengefügt. Auf menschlicher Haut Stich für Stich aneinandergereiht entstehen Tätowierungen, nachweisbar bereits bei der Gletschermumie vom Hauslabjoch (volkstümlich als »Ötzi« bekannt), dem bereits vor mehr als 5000 Jahren Kohlenstaub in feine Schnittwunden gerieben wurde.[37] Blumenteppiche, wie sie an Fronleichnam oder beim Erntedankfest ausgelegt werden, sind solche aus Blumen, Blüten oder Blumenteilen zusammengefügte Bilder oder Ornamente, denen nur eine sehr kurze Dauer beschieden ist. Dies ist auch bei den Sandmandalas des tibetischen Buddhismus der Fall –

34 Vgl. das Khipu Database Project (siehe Verzeichnis der Webseiten auf S. 374). – GARY URTON: The Inca Khipu. Knotted-Cord Record Keeping in the Andes. In: *The Handbook of South American Archaeology.* New York 2008, S. 831–43.
35 Vgl. FUGA (siehe Anm. 5), S. 176–80.
36 Vgl. ebd., S. 181/2.
37 Vgl. Ötzi – der Mann aus dem Eis. Die Tätowierungen. Homepage des Südtiroler ArchäologieM Bozen (siehe Verzeichnis der Webseiten auf S. 374).

Mönche stellen diese in tage- und wochenlanger meditativer Tätigkeit her, um sie anschließend in einer rituellen Handlung wegzukehren (der gesammelte Sand wird anschließend nach Möglichkeit einem fließenden Gewässer übergeben und nie ein zweites Mal verwendet).[38] Das Zusammenfügen von einzelnen Elementen zu einem Ganzen ist natürlich auch das Grundprinzip Gutenberg'scher Satzarbeit. Individuelle Zeilen werden aus Einzeltypen gesetzt und ausgeschlossen, absatzweise zu ganzen Seiten gruppiert, schließlich werden diese Seiten so zusammen montiert (ausgeschossen), dass nach erfolgtem Schön- und Widerdruck der gefaltete Bogen die richtige Seitenabfolge aufweist. Ein oder mehrere Bogen bilden eine Lage, die Lagen werden zusammengetragen und bilden einen kompletten Buchblock. Das ganze Buchdruckverfahren ist eine Summe von Teilschritten, die am Ende ein Ganzes ergeben. Mehrere Bände passen in einen Schuber und bilden eine Werkausgabe, viele Bücher, die geordnet zusammengefügt werden, bilden eine Bibliothek. Beim Buchdruck erlaubt es spezielles Typenmaterial, ganze Ornamentleisten und Rahmen zusammenzufügen. Zum Fügen gehört auch das Füllen, das seit der Antike eine große Rolle spielt: Niello ist eine schwarze Masse aus Kupfer, Blei und Schwefel, die bei Gold- und Silberschmiedearbeiten zum Ausgießen der eingravierten Zeichnungen dient. Die Masse wird nach dem Einschmelzen in das Metall poliert, wodurch sich die Zeichnung schwarz vom Edelmetall abhebt.[39] Schon in Altägypten bekannt, erlangte das Verfahren im europäischen Mittelalter seinen Höhepunkt.[40] Zum Fügen gehört das bereits erwähnte Aufnähen oder Auflöten gebogener Drahtfiguren – seien es bildhafte Elemente, seien es Buchstaben oder Zahlen – auf die Rippung von Papierschöpfformen, die im damit per Urformen gebildeten Papierblatt dünnere Stellen erzeugen, die im Durchlicht hell erscheinen (Wasserzeichen).[41]

5. Beschichten

Als fünftes Fertigungsverfahren ist das Beschichten (engl. *coating*) zu nennen. Auf einen Träger wird eine fest haftende Schicht aus einer formlosen Substanz aufgebracht. Hierunter fallen das Bemalen, Lackieren oder Emaillieren, aber auch das Beschriften mit einer Tinte oder mit Tusche. Der schematische Aufbau eines Leinwandbilds zeigt, dass es sich um eine ganze Abfolge von Schichten handeln kann – auf dem Bildträger finden sich Vorleimung, Grundierung, Unterzeichnung, Imprimitur, Untermalung, Hauptmalschicht, Lasurschicht und Abschlussfirnis.[42] Für die Beschichtung werden häufig Pigmente verwendet, die mit einem Bindemittel vermischt sind. Letzteres sorgt sowohl für den Zusammenhalt der einzelnen Pigmentteilchen, als auch dafür, dass diese nach Abtrocknen oder Abbinden dauerhaft auf dem Träger haften bleiben. Als organische Bindemittel kommen folgende Naturstoffe in Frage: Wachse, trocknende Öle, Harze, tierische Leime (Proteine) und pflanzliche Leime (Kohlehydrate). Anorganische Bindemittel können Kalk, Gips und Wasserglas sein.[43] Ergänzend kommen heute eine Vielzahl synthetischer Bindemittel hinzu (z. B. Acrylharzdispersionen). Das Auftragen einer Beschichtung kann auf sehr unterschiedliche Weise passieren: mit einem

---

38 Vgl. BARRY BRYANT: *The Wheel of Time Sand Mandala. Visual Scripture of Tibetan Buddhism.* San Francisco 1995, S. 27–37, 168–75 und 228–31.

39 Vgl. HEINRICH LÜTZELER: Bildwörterbuch der Kunst. 4., durchges. Aufl. Bonn 1989 (Dümmlerbuch. 8501), S. 279/80.

40 Vgl. HELGA GIERSIEPEN / CLEMENS BAYER: Inschriften, Schriftdenkmäler. Techniken, Geschichte, Anlässe. Niedernhausen 1995, S. 37.

41 Vgl. ROBERT GROSSE-STOLTENBERG: Beiträge zur Wasserzeichenforschung, technische Varianten bei der Fertigung der Drahtform. In: *Papiergeschichte.* 15.5/6 (1965), S. 73–9. – EDO G. LOEBER: *Paper Mould and Mouldmaker.* Amsterdam 1982.

42 Vgl. HANS PETER SCHRAMM / BERND HERING: Historische Malmaterialien und ihre Identifizierung. Berlin 1988. Reprint Ravensburg 2000 (Bücherei des Restaurators. 1), S. 9.

43 Vgl. ebd., S. 79–81.

Pinsel oder einer Feder, durch Aufsprühen – Sprühtechniken gab es vermutlich schon in der steinzeitlichen Höhlenmalerei,[44] gibt es immer noch in der modernen Lackiertechnik, aber auch bei bürotauglichen Tintenstrahldruckern – oder durch Aufstempeln oder Aufdrucken. Bis auf den trockenen Prägedruck, der mit der Technik der Umformung arbeitet, sind die anderen wichtigen Druckverfahren – Hochdruck, Flachdruck, Tiefdruck und Siebdruck – Beschichtungsverfahren, bei denen entsprechende Druckfarben auf geeignete Träger aufgetragen werden, wo sie dauerhaft verbleiben sollen. Eine Ausnahme sind Abziehbilder, bei diesen wird das gedruckte Bild auf ein anderes Material übertragen (Porzellan, Nähmaschinen oder andere zu beschriftende oder zu schmückende Gerätschaften). Eine besondere Rolle spielen seit dem späten 19. Jahrhundert beschichtete Papiere. Ein Rohpapier (»Streichpapier«[45]), das stark holzschliffhaltig, aber auch völlig holzfrei sein konnte, wurde – sehr gleichmäßig mit einer Streichmasse bestrichen – zu Chromopapier (einseitig gestrichen) oder Kunstdruckpapier (zweiseitig gestrichen) veredelt.[46] Moderne gestrichene Papiere lassen mit ihren sehr feinen Beschichtungen gar nicht mehr erkennen, dass sich im Innern ein Faservlies befindet. Mit lichtempfindlichen Emulsionen der unterschiedlichsten Art wurden und werden diverse Materialien wie Glasplatten, Filme, Papiere, Druckplatten und Siebe beschichtet.

6. Stoffeigenschaften Ändern

Die letzte Hauptgruppe der Fertigungstechniken wird als Stoffeigenschaften Ändern (engl. *alteration in material characteristics*) bezeichnet. Hierzu gehören Verfahren wie das Brennen, Sintern und Glasieren – man denke an das Anfertigen von Keramiken in Form von Gefäßen oder Fließen sowie an das Emaillieren mit transparenten oder opaken Schmelzgemischen –, hierzu gehören Wärmebehandlungen wie Glühen und Härten, die bei der Arbeit der Schriftschneider beim Verfertigen der stählernen Stempel von großer Bedeutung waren. Weitere Prozesse dieser Art sind Magnetisieren, Bestrahlen und fotografische Verfahren, die mit Belichtung arbeiten. Es wird unmittelbar deutlich, welche große Bedeutung gerade solche Verfahren beim Aufzeichnen seit dem Jahr 1839 erlangt haben, als Louis Daguerre seine Versuche in der französischen Akademie der Wissenschaften vorgestellt und Frankreich dessen Erfindung aufgekauft hatte, um sie der ganzen Welt zum Geschenk zu machen. Fotografische Verfahren veränderten in der Folge viele Bereiche des Aufzeichnens, Kopierens und Vervielfältigens, konventionelle Filmbelichtungsverfahren waren unverzichtbar beim Siegeszug des Offsetdrucks und müssen heute der digitalen Druckplattenbelichtung Platz machen, bei denen unterschiedliche Lichtquellen und Plattenbeschichtungen zum Zuge kommen. Der Künstler Sigmar Polcke (1941–2010) machte von Materialien Gebrauch, deren Farbton sich bei Lichteinfall änderte und auf Temperaturwechsel reagierte. Mittels TSP (engl. *temperature sensitive paint*) können in technischen Versuchen Oberflächentemperaturen angezeigt werden, doch handelt es sich dabei um eine Anzeigetechnik, nicht aber um eine Aufzeichnungstechnik, denn der Vorgang ist reversibel.

44 Vgl. MICHEL LORBLANCHET: Höhlenmalerei. Ein Handbuch. 2., aktualisierte Aufl. Sigmaringen 2000 (Thorbecke-Speläothek. 1), S. 240/1.
45 FRITZ HOYER: *Papiersorten-Lexikon. Ein Nachschlagewerk für die tägliche Praxis*. Stuttgart 1929, S. 193.
46 In Deutschland gehörte Adolph Scheufelen zu den Pionieren, vgl. *100 Jahre Phoenix Kunstdruckpapier. Von der hohen Kunst des Kunstdruckpapiers – 100 Jahre im Zeichen des Phoenix*. Hrsg. von der PAPIERFABRIK SCHEUFELEN. Lenningen 1992.

Schlussfolgerungen

Die vorgehenden Ausführungen suchten zu belegen, dass mit den sechs Hauptgruppen der Fertigungstechnik ein Klassifizieren der von der Menschheit seit Zehntausenden von Jahren bis hin zur aktuellen Gegenwart benutzten Aufzeichnungstechniken, die zur Speicherung, aber auch zum Kopieren und Vervielfältigen von ornamentalen, bildlichen und zeichenhaften Darstellungen dienen, möglich ist.

Es stellt sich dabei heraus, dass die beim Verfertigen gezielt zur Erzeugung einer geometrisch definierten Form eingesetzten Prozesse des Urformens, Umformens, Trennens, Fügens, Beschichtens und Stoffeigenschaften Änderns letztendlich identisch sind mit jenen Prozessen, die bei der Verfertigung und Vervielfältigung körperlicher Medien zum Zuge kommen. Die Begriffsbildung der Fertigungstechnik taugt keineswegs nur für fabrikmäßige Produktion des Industriezeitalters, sondern sie erlaubt eine Sicht, die den gesamten Zeitraum seit der Eiszeit bis in unsere Gegenwart hinein abzudecken vermag, um kulturelle Hervorbringungen vielfältigster Art in ihrem Entstehungsprozess zu charakterisieren und zu klassifizieren.

In den Ingenieurwissenschaften sind die sechs Hauptgruppen der Fertigungstechnik in differenzierter Weise weiter untergliedert. So unterteilt zum Beispiel die DIN 8593 das Fügen in neun Gruppen. Als Fügeverfahren werden benannt: Zusammensetzen, Füllen, An- und Einpressen, Fügen durch Urformen, Fügen durch Umformen, Fügen durch Schweißen, Fügen durch Löten, Kleben und Textiles Fügen. Es ist zu fragen, ob eine solche Verfeinerung des Klassifikationssystems auch bei den Aufzeichnungssystemen und den damit verbundenen Techniken des Speicherns, Kopierens und Vervielfältigens in analytischer und in handlungsorientierender Weise einen positiven Beitrag leisten kann.

Vieles spricht dafür, dass es lohnenswert ist, das Klassifikationssystem in einer solch differenzierten Weise auszubauen. Der detaillierte Beleg hierfür muss jedoch weiteren Untersuchungen vorbehalten bleiben.[47]

47 Viele Beispiele deuten auch darauf hin, dass eine Anwendung der vorgestellten Klassifikation wesentlich zum Verständnis von Alterung und Zerstörung von Aufzeichnungen beitragen kann, gleichzeitig auch die Ansatzpunkte für Maßnahmen der Konservierung und Restaurierung genauer benennen lässt, eine Überlegung, die hier nur angedeutet, aber nicht ausgeführt werden kann.

Nachruf

WOLFGANG SCHMITZ

Der Bucharchivar. Nachruf auf Ludwig Delp

(1921–2010)

LUDWIG DELPS UNVERÖFFENTLICHTE autobiografische Skizzen tragen den Titel *Buch und Leben*.¹ Das Buch war das zentrale Objekt seines geistigen und beruflichen Lebens, als Informationsträger, als Objekt der Wirtschaft und des Rechts. Darum drehen sich seine zahlreichen Publikationen und sein berufliches Engagement.

Geboren wurde er am 25. November 1921 in Darmstadt als Sohn eines Rechnungsprüfers. Dort und in Leipzig, der Bücherstadt Deutschlands, verbrachte er eine unbeschwerte Jugend, in der schon das Buch eine bedeutende Rolle spielte. Dann aber musste er als Angehöriger seiner Generation nach dem Abitur 1940 und kurzer Möglichkeit zum Studium der Wirtschafts- und Rechtswissenschaften in Leipzig den Kriegsdienst absolvieren, der durch eine schwere Verwundung 1943 in Rußland ein jähes Ende fand.

Nach längeren Lazarettaufenthalten konnte er erst ab 1946 das Studium in München wieder aufnehmen, sein Hauptinteresse galt den Wirtschafts- und Rechtsfragen des Buch- und Zeitschriftenwesens. Glückliche Umstände führten ihn mit wegweisenden Leuten des Münchner Buch- und Verlagswesens zusammen wie Horst Kliemann: »Plötzlich war ich mitten im Geschehen des sich gerade aus den Ruinen aufraffenden Buchhandels und Verlagswesens.«² 1947 legte er die Dipl.-Volkswirt-Prüfung mit der Arbeit *Der Außenhandel mit Büchern und seine Bedeutung für die deutsche Nachkriegswirtschaft* ab, deren Veröffentlichung großes Interesse fand. 1948 folgte die erste juristische Staatsprüfung und 1950 das zweite juristische Staatsexamen mit hervorragender Note. 1949 erhielt er die Bestallung als Sachverständiger für Rechts- und Wirtschaftsfragen des Buch- und Zeitschriftenwesens in München (später als vereidigter Sachverständiger vor Gericht), die er bis zum gesetzlichen Höchstalter von 73 Jahren (1994) wahrnahm.

Die Dissertation zum Dr. Juris 1951 folgte mit dem Thema *Die Mikrokopie* über das Kopieren urheberrechtlich geschützter Werke zum eigenen beziehungsweise persönlichen Gebrauch diesem Pfad. Im selben Jahr ließ er sich als selbstständiger Anwalt nieder, wirkte in der Wirtschaft als Justitiar und Geschäftsführer, u. a. fungierte er als Rechtsberater des Bayerischen Verleger- und Buchhändlerverbandes. Erst Ende 2006 gab er seine Anwaltskanzlei weitgehend auf. Diese erfolgreiche Tätigkeit brachte ihm angemessenen Wohlstand und Ansehen; sie war aber nur das Fundament für seine besondere Lebensleistung, die Gründung des Deutschen Bucharchivs und die wissenschaftliche Beschäftigung mit dem Buch.

---

1 LUDWIG DELP: Buch und Leben. Autobiographische Notizen. Zum 60. Gründungstag des Bucharchivs München. Ungedr. Typoskript. München 2007.
2 DELP (siehe Anm. 1), S. 9.

Als Student machte er im zerstörten Nachkriegs-München seine eigenen Erfahrungen mit der Materialbeschaffung bei der Anfertigung wissenschaftlicher Arbeiten. Gerne erzählte er die Geschichte, wie es zur Gründung des Bucharchivs kam: »Es gab in der unmittelbaren Nachkriegszeit kaum umfassendes Quellenmaterial. Ich besprach das mit Horst Kliemann auf einem Spaziergang, die Ludwigsstrasse entlang und in der Nähe der Ecke Schellingstrasse. Das war im Sommer 1947. Kliemann kam auf das Archiv des Börsenvereins in Leipzig zu sprechen und erklärte mir, dieses Archiv sei im Bombenkrieg untergegangen und wäre auch jetzt vom Westen aus nicht zugänglich. Ich erwiderte, so sehr dies zu bedauern sei, aber ein solches Archiv sei ja erneut machbar. Wie wäre es denn, wenn man in München, der neuen Nachkriegsstadt des Buchhandels, ein solches Archiv für das Buchwesen ins Leben riefe? Horst Kliemann blieb wie angewurzelt stehen und schaute mich gross an. Dann sagte er, das sei zwar eine grossartige Tat, aber ein ausserordentlich schwieriges Unterfangen.«³

Und so schuf er mit einem »Überschuss an idealistischem Drang« (so seine eigene Aussage) 1947 noch als Student im Elternhaus im Zusammenwirken mit den bayerischen Buchhändler- und Verlegerverbänden die Grundlagen des Bucharchivs. »Es sollte vom Autor bis zum Leser alles erfassen, was Kulturgeschichte, Wirtschaftswissenschaften, Jurisprudenz und Technik in Bezug auf das Verfassen, Abbilden, Zeichnen, Gestalten, Verbreiten, Bereithalten, Lesen und Thesaurieren betrifft.« Die Anfänge kann man sich gar nicht einfach genug vorstellen: »Am 1. Januar 1948 fingen wir einfach an. Ein handgemaltes Pappschild an der Wohnungstür im Münchner Stadtteil Sendling, Cimbernstraße, etablierte das Bucharchiv nach außen. Natürlich war die Wohnung überbelegt; aber es fand sich doch der eine oder andere Platz zu systematischer Ablage und Ordnung. Befreundete Nachbarn gestatteten nachsichtig die Benutzung ihres Telefonapparates. Briefbogen entwarf, druckte und stiftete die Münchner Meisterschule für Deutschlands Buchdrucker, die meinem Vorhaben freundlich gesinnt war. Eine Mitarbeiterin [...] fand sich und machte mit, buchstäblich ›für ein Butterbrot‹«.⁴

Fortan entwickelte sich aus kleinsten Anfängen eine der heute bedeutendsten Dokumentations- und Informationsstellen für das weite Gebiet des Buchwesens mit dem Ziel, eine Infrastruktur zur wissenschaftlichen Beschäftigung mit dem Buch technisch, kulturell, rechtlich, wirtschaftlich, aber nicht isoliert, sondern verzahnt zu schaffen. Zielgruppe waren Buchwissenschaftler, Praktiker aus dem Buch- und Verlagswesen, Studenten, Interessenten, denen dort eine exzellente Spezialbibliothek (die Fachsystematik mit einem ausgeklügelten Facettensystem von Abzissen und Ordinaten, von potentiellen Unterthemenfeldern mit dem Feinheitsgrad bis zu 10 000 hatte er selbst entwickelt) mit einer außergewöhnlich dichten Dokumentation geboten wurde, gleichzeitig Fortbildungsstätte für den Nachwuchs und Zentrum für Veröffentlichungen.

Hier konnten die Buchwissenschaften betrieben werden, wie er sie verstand, nämlich »dass der Fachgenosse einer mit dem Buch- und Zeitschriftenwesen befassten Wissenschaften in dieser seiner angestammten wissenschaftlichen Disziplin Buchforschung betreibt, und dass, andere-

Ludwig Delp
(1921–2010)

3 Ebd., S. 5. – LUDWIG DELP: Das Deutsche Bucharchiv München 1947–1967. München 1967 (*Buchwissenschaftliche Beiträge.* 2), S. 13–30.
4 LUDWIG DELP: Buchwissenschaften – Dokumentation und Information. Fünfzig Jahre Deutsches Bucharchiv München. Eine zeitdokumentarische Bestandsaufnahme. Wiesbaden 1997 (*Buchwissenschaftliche Beiträge.* 57), S. 17.

seits, kompetente Buchforschung nur durch Vertreter der einzelnen in Betrachtung kommenden Wissenschaften betrieben werden kann, deren Lehren das Buch unter anderem jeweils als geistige Aussage, als gewerbliches Erzeugnis, als Gegenstand des Handels- und Rechtsverkehrs sowie der Vermarktung, als Objekt des Sammelns und Erschließens, als Partner des Lesers, aber auch als Quelle weiterer Nutzungen in Presse, Film, Video, Rundfunk und Fernsehen betrachten« und er folgerte: »Buchwissenschaftliche Forschungstätigkeit muss deshalb interdisziplinär entwickelt und kooperativ abgestimmt, aber monodisziplinär durchgeführt und als Beitrag zu einem Gesamtprogramm mit buchwissenschaftlicher Zielsetzung verstanden werden.«[5]

Immer wieder suchte er die Arbeitsfähigkeit seines Bucharchivs zu erhöhen und finanziell abzusichern. Zur Mittelbeschaffung nach der Währungsreform entwickelte er eine Verlagsproduktion des Bucharchivs mit den Schriftenreihen *Hilfsmittel für das Buchwesen* (ab 1948) und *Buchwissenschaftliche Beiträge* (ab 1950, wieder aufgenommen 1983) und gab 1967 bis 1972 die Branchenkorrespondenz *Buchinformation* heraus. Ab 1956 veröffentlichte er den rechtswissenschaftlichen Teil des Bucharchiv-Fachkatalogs als angesehene *Bibliographie des gesamten Rechts der Presse, des Buchhandels, des Rundfunks und des Fernsehens*. Er organisierte Veranstaltungen zum Betriebsvergleich im westdeutschen Verlagswesen und seit 1985 Management-Seminare für Verlage im Deutschen Bucharchiv.

Intensiv betrieb er den organisatorischen Ausbau durch Gründung eines Kuratoriums, das im November 1965 wegen der überregionalen Bedeutung die Namensgebung »Deutsches Bucharchiv München« beschloss. Daneben initiierte er eine Fördervereinigung und einen Wissenschaftlichen Beirat. Ein wichtiger Schritt der Konsolidierung war 1977 die von ihm mit angestoßene Waldemar-Bonsels-Stiftung durch die Witwe des Schriftstellers zur Förderung der buchwissenschaftlichen Forschung und damit auch des Bucharchivs. Ihr folgte 1985 mit gleicher Zielsetzung die Ludwig-Delp-Stiftung aus seinem Privatvermögen.

Die endgültige Sicherung der Existenz des Bucharchivs erreichte er 2006 durch Gründung der Stiftung »St. Galler Zentrum für das Buch« zusammen mit den kooperierenden Münchner Stiftungen, der Universität St. Gallen und dem Kanton St. Gallen. Er macht deutlich, worin der besondere Vorteil dieser speziellen Lösung lag: »Mein fortschreitendes Lebensalter war Anlass, für die Buchwissenschaften und für das Bucharchiv, eine universitäre Verankerung zu finden. Ein bedeutendes akademisches Zentrum musste gewonnen werden, das die Buchwissenschaften als Forschungs- und Lehrfach auf seine Fahnen schreibt. Eine wirtschaftswissenschaftlich und juristisch orientierte ehemalige Handelshochschule mit internationaler Anerkennung schien hierfür aufgeschlossen. Die Pflege kommunikationswissenschaftlicher Lehren war eine geeignete Brücke, dort Buchwissenschaften anzusiedeln.«[6] Die Kantonsbibliothek Vadiana übernahm als Dauerleihgabe die Bibliothek des Bucharchivs (60 000 Bände) und führt sie fort. Das St. Galler Zentrum für das Buch ist als eines der wichtigsten buchwissenschaftlichen Kompetenz-Zentren Europas ohne Zweifel die Krönung von Delps Lebenswerk.

---

[5] LUDWIG DELP: Buch und Wissenschaften. Ein Beitrag zur Wissenschaftstheorie. In: *Das Buch in Praxis und Wissenschaft. 40 Jahre Deutsches Bucharchiv München*. Hrsg. von PETER VODOSEK. Wiesbaden 1989, S. 768–93, hier S. 773.

[6] DELP (siehe Anm. 1), S. 6/7.

Aber Delp war nicht nur Organisator, er selbst hat zur Entwicklung der Buchwissenschaft Namhaftes beigetragen. Meisterhaft verstand er es, schwierige rechtliche Zusammenhänge übersichtlich darzustellen. Aus dem schlichten Hilfsmittel mit dem Titel *Der Verlagsvertrag* unmittelbar nach der Währungsreform entwickelte sich in späteren Auflagen ein Handbuch für das gesamte Urhebervertragsrecht mit Vertragsmustern und Erläuterungen (8. Auflage 2008). 1953 bis 2006 gab er (später gemeinsam mit Anwaltsozius Dr. Peter Lutz) eine fünfbändige Loseblatt-Sammlung, *Sammlung Delp – Das gesamte Recht der Publizistik*, heraus. Auf Anregung seines Mentors Horst Kliemann verfasste er 1958 eine besonders bei Buchhändlern beliebte, volkstümliche Schrift *Kleines Praktikum für Urheber- und Verlagsrecht* (5. Auflage 2005). Sein Ansehen als Fachmann für Rechtsfragen des Buchwesens zeigt sich auch in der Beauftragung für die juristischen Stichwörter bei der zweiten Auflage des Lexikons für das Gesamte Buchwesen (LGB²) ab 1982.

Sein wichtigstes Werk, wie er es auch selbst sah, war *Das Recht des geistigen Schaffens in der Informationsgesellschaft. Medienrecht, Urheberrecht, Urhebervertragsrecht* (2. Auflage 2003). Darin behandelt er kompetent sämtliche rechtlichen und faktischen Tendenzen und Kräfte des Kultursektors, bringt sie in einen Zusammenhang und erörtert die relevanten praktischen Fragen, für die er sich das Ansehen eines unangefochtenen Fachmanns erworben hatte.

Nicht zu vergessen ist seine jahrzehntelange Herausgebertätigkeit der renommierten *Buchwissenschaftlichen Beiträge* aus dem Deutschen Bucharchiv im Harrassowitz-Verlag, bei der ihn viele Jahre Ursula Neumann unterstützte: 74 Bände waren es bis zu seinem Ausscheiden 2007. In manchen Bänden hat er selbst mitgewirkt, vielfach auch mit theoretischen Betrachtungen zum Verständnis des Buches im digitalen Zeitalter.[7]

1999 gründete er die Deutsche (seit 2007: Internationale) Buchwissenschaftliche Gesellschaft, in der sich Buch- und Medienwissenschaftler, aber auch Praktiker (Verleger, Buchhändler, Buchgestalter, Illustratoren, Schriftkünstler) zusammenfinden, um im interdisziplinären Gespräch buchwissenschaftliche Forschung, Lehre, Dokumentation, Information und Nutzanwendung zu fördern.

Ein Wort muss noch dem Menschen Ludwig Delp gelten. Wer ihm begegnete, traf auf einen anregenden, kreativen und durchsetzungsfähigen Menschen, der viel erreicht hatte und sich seines Wertes durchaus bewusst war. Er konnte mit Überzeugungskraft und Beharrlichkeit Leute für sich und seine Ziele gewinnen, war ein ebenso zäher Verhandler wie kompetenter Autor mit klaren Vorstellungen, kantig und streitbar, aber eben auch konziliant und kultiviert, wie ihn der Lektor des Beck-Verlages Bernhard von Becker erlebte.[8] Was man vielleicht nicht unbedingt erwartete: Er verfasste Gedichte mit durchaus ernstem, tiefen Hintergrund und andere zu heiterem Anlass in Beruf und Familie.

Seine Energie, die er sich trotz der Kriegsverletzung abrang, zeigte sich in seinen weiten, alle Kontinente umspannenden Reisen mit dem »Drang, aus der eigenen engen Welt auszubrechen, fremde Menschen und fremde Kulturen kennenzulernen, deren Sehenswürdigkeiten zu

7 LUDWIG DELP: Reflexionen aus fünfzig Jahren Deutsches Bucharchiv, aus zwanzig Jahren Waldemar Bonsels-Stiftung und über das digitale Medienzeitalter. In: *Fünfzig Jahre Deutsches Bucharchiv München und sein Einzug in das Literaturhaus*. Wiesbaden 1997 (Separatdruck zu Buchwissenschaftliche Beiträge. 57), S. 16–26, hier S. 24.
8 BERNHARD VON BECKER: Festrede auf Prof. Dr. Ludwig Delp. In: *Festakt zum Abschied Ludwig Delps von der Führung seiner Stiftungen: Stiftung Deutsches Bucharchiv München, Stiftung St. Galler Zentrum für das Buch. Festakt am 19. Januar 2007 im Literaturhaus München*. München 2007, S. 23–9.

bestaunen und damit die bunte, weite Welt kennenzulernen.«[9] Darunter waren viele strapaziöse und viele Bergsteigertouren bis hin zur Teilnahme an der Nanga Parbat-Expedition zur Diamir-Flanke 1961 mit Karl Herrligkoffer. Anstrengende Kulturreisen unternahm er mit der ihm eigenen Disziplin bis ins hohe Alter. Gerne berichtete er darüber in Vorträgen vor einem größeren Freundeskreis.

Dennoch war er hinter aller Distanz in mancher Beziehung verletzlicher und sensibler, als es auf den ersten Blick scheinen mochte. Wenn er Vertrauen fasste, öffnete er sich. So habe ich es als besondere Auszeichnung empfunden, dass er, dem das Herz nicht auf der Zunge lag, vom Tod seines ältesten Sohnes berichtete, der mit 26 Jahren 1981 im Karwendel tödlich abgestürzt war. Das hat er nie verwunden. Auch ließ er durchblicken, wie sehr ihn die lange und schwere Erkrankung seiner Frau bedrückte, einer Diplombibliothekarin, die er 1954 heiratete, mit der er drei Kinder hatte und die ihn überlebte.

So mischen sich Licht und Schatten. Sein Leben war an Ehren und Anerkennung nicht arm:[10] 1988 erhielt er das Bundesverdienstkreuz am Band, seit demselben Jahr war er Lehrbeauftragter für Rechtsfragen im Buchwesen an der Universität Erlangen, die ihn 1993 zum Honorarprofessor am Institut für Buchwissenschaft ernannte. Wie alle starken Charaktere konnte er auch im Alter nur schwer loslassen. 2007 bestellte er sein Haus und nahm Abschied von den Stiftungen und Ämtern, im Münchner Literaturhaus festlich begangen. Die letzte Wegstrecke war nicht leicht. Nach längerer Krankheit ist er, geborgen in seiner Familie, am 2. Februar 2010 gestorben.

9 DELP (siehe Anm. 1), S. 29.
10 Vgl. die Reden zum 80. Geburtstag von Professor Dr. Ludwig Delp am 1. Dezember 2001 im Bayerischen Hof, München. Privatdruck München o. J. und die Reden in der in Anm. 8 genannten Broschüre.

ABKÜRZUNGSVERZEICHNIS
FÜR ARCHIVE, BIBLIOTHEKEN, MUSEEN
UND UNIVERSITÄTEN

Arch. Archiv
B Biblioteca, Bibliothek, Bibliothèque, Bücherei
BC Biblioteca centrale, Bibliothèque centrale
BL British Library London (früher British Museum Library)
BM British Museum London
B mun. Biblioteca, Bibliothèque municipale
BN Biblioteca nacional, Biblioteca nazionale, Bibliothèque nationale
BNC Biblioteca Nazionale Centrale
BR Bibliothèque royale
BSB Bayerische Staatsbibliothek München
Coll. College, Collège
DB Die Deutsche Bibliothek (bis 2007) (Deutsche Bücherei Leipzig, Deutsche Bibliothek Frankfurt a. M.)
DNB Deutsche Nationalbibliothek (ab 2008)
DSB Deutsche Staatsbibliothek Berlin (bis 1991)
FB Fachbibliothek, Fachbücherei
FHSB Fachhochschulbibliothek
FLB Forschungs- und Landesbibliothek
GHB Gesamthochschulbibliothek
GNM Germanisches Nationalmuseum Nürnberg
HAB Herzog August Bibliothek Wolfenbüttel
HSB Hochschulbibliothek
Kgl. B Königliche Bibliothek
L Library
LB Landesbibliothek
LC Library of Congress Washington
LuHSB Landes- und Hochschulbibliothek
LuStB Landes- und Stadtbibliothek
M Museum, Museo
NB Nationalbibliothek
NL National Library

NSuUB Niedersächsische Staats- und Universitätsbibliothek Göttingen
ÖB Öffentliche Bibliothek, Öffentliche Bücherei
ÖNB Österreichische Nationalbibliothek Wien
PL Public Library
SArch. Staatsarchiv
SB Staatsbibliothek
SB PK Staatsbibliothek zu Berlin – Preußischer Kulturbesitz – (bis 1991)
SBB-PK Staatsbibliothek zu Berlin – Preußischer Kulturbesitz – (seit 1992)
Staatl. B Staatliche Bibliothek, Staatliche Bücherei
StArch. Stadtarchiv
StB Stadtbibliothek
StM Stadtmuseum
StuLB Stadt- und Landesbibliothek
StuUB Stadt- und Universitätsbibliothek
SuStB Staats- und Stadtbibliothek
SuUB Staats- und Universitätsbibliothek
TH Technische Hochschule
THB Bibliothek der Technischen Hochschule
TU Technische Universität
TUB Bibliothek der Technischen Universität
U Universität, University usw.
UB Universitätsbibliothek
UL University Library
UuLB Universitäts- und Landesbibliothek
UuStB Universitäts- und Stadtbibliothek
Wiss. StB Wissenschaftliche Stadtbibliothek
ZArch. Zentralarchiv
ZB Zentralbibliothek, Zentralbücherei

ABKÜRZUNGSVERZEICHNIS
VON HÄUFIG ZITIERTEN BIBLIOGRAFIEN, NACHSCHLAGEWERKEN UND ZEITSCHRIFTEN

Bei Inkunabelbibliografien richtet sich die Zitierweise im Allgemeinen nach dem Verzeichnis: Abkürzungen für angeführte Quellen. In: Gesamtkatalog der Wiegendrucke. Neuausgabe. Bd. 8. Stuttgart, Berlin, New York 1978, S. *14–*38.

Adams Herbert Mayow Adams: Catalogue of books printed on the continent of Europe, 1501–1600 in Cambridge libraries. Vol. 1. 2. Cambridge 1967.

ADB Allgemeine Deutsche Biographie. Hrsg. durch die Historische Commission bei der Königl. Akademie der Wissenschaften (München). Bd. 1–56. Leipzig 1875 bis 1912. (Repr. Berlin 1967–71.) Online-Version, URL: http://www.deutsche-biographie.de

AGB Archiv für Geschichte des Buchwesens. Hrsg. von der Historischen Kommission des Börsenvereins des Deutschen Buchhandels. Bd. 1. Frankfurt a. M. 1956ff.

Baudrier Henri Louis Baudrier: Bibliographie lyonnaise. Vol. 1–12. Lyon 1895–1921. [Nebst] Tables. Genève 1950 (Travaux d'humanisme et renaissance. 1). (Repr. Sér. 1–13. Paris 1964/5.)

Benzing Josef Benzing: Die Buchdrucker des 16. und 17. Jahrhunderts im deutschen Sprachgebiet. 2., verb. und erg. Aufl. Wiesbaden 1982 (Beiträge zum Buch- und Bibliothekswesen. 12).

BL The British Library. General Catalogue of printed books to 1975. Vol. 1–360; Suppl. 1–6. London, München, New York, Paris 1979–87; 1987/8. – ... 1976 to 1982. Vol. 1–50. London 1983. ... 1982 to 1985. Vol. 1–26. London 1986 [...]

BMC Catalogue of books printed in the 15th century now in the British Museum. P. 1–10 und P. 12. London 1908–71 und 1985. (Repr. P. 1–6, Facs. P. 1/3, 4/7. London 1963.)

Borchling/Claussen Conrad Borchling und Bruno Claussen: Niederdeutsche Bibliographie. Gesamtverzeichnis der niederdeutschen Drucke bis zum Jahre 1800. Bd. 1. 2. 3, Lfg. 1. Neumünster 1931–57.

Brunet Jacques Charles Brunet: Manuel du libraire et de l'amateur de livres. 5. éd. T. 1–6 [Nebst] Suppl. T. 1. 2. Paris 1860–80. (Repr. Berlin 1921; New York 1923; Paris 1923 und 1928.)

BSB-Ink. Bayerische Staatsbibliothek München. Inkunabelkatalog. Wiesbaden 1988ff. Online-Version, URL: http://www.inkunabeln.digitale-sammlungen.de

C/HC Walter A. Copinger: Supplement to Hain's Repertorium bibliographicum. P. 1. 2, vol. 1. 2. [Nebst] Index. London 1895–1902. (Repr. Berlin 1926; Milano 1950.)

CA Marinus Frederick Andries Gerardus Campbell: Annales de la typographie néerlandaise au 15e siècle. [Nebst] Suppl. 1–4. Le Haye 1874–90.

Cat. Gen. Catalogue général des livres imprimés de la Bibliothèque nationale. T. 1. Paris 1897ff.

CIBN Bibliothèque nationale. Catalogue des Incunables. Paris 1981–96.

Claudin Anatole Claudin: L'histoire de l'imprimerie en France au 15e et au 16e siècle. T. 1–4. Paris 1900–14. T. 5: Tables alphabétiques. Red. sous la dir. de L. Delisle par Paul Lacombe. Paris 1917. (Repr. Nendeln/Liechtenstein und Wiesbaden 1971 bis 1976.)

EDBD Online-Datenverbund der Sammlungen von Einband-Durchreibungen der Württembergischen LB Stuttgart (Sammlung Kyriss), der HAB Wolfenbüttel (Sammlung Wolfenbüttel), der BSB München (Sammlung München), der SBB-PK (Sammlung Schunke und Sammlung Paul Schenke), der UuLB Darmstadt (Sammlung

Darmstadt) und der UB Rostock (Sammlung Floerke). Online: www.hist-einband.de

Einbl. Einblattdrucke des 15. Jahrhunderts. Ein bibliographisches Verzeichnis. Hrsg. von der Kommission für den Gesamtkatalog der Wiegendrucke. Halle/S. 1914 (Sammlung bibliothekswissenschaftlicher Arbeiten. 35/36). (Repr. Nendeln/Liechtenstein und Wiesbaden 1968.)

Essling Victor Prince d'Essling Duc de Rivoli: Les livres à figures vénetiens de la fin du XVe siècle et du commencement du XVIe. 6 Vols. Florence, Paris 1907–14.

Geldner Ferdinand Geldner: Die deutschen Inkunabeldrucker: Ein Handbuch der deutschen Buchdrucker des 15. Jahrhunderts nach Druckorten. Bd. 1. 2. Stuttgart 1968–70.

GJ Gutenberg-Jahrbuch. Begründet von Aloys Ruppel. Jg. 1ff. Mainz 1926ff.

GK Gesamtkatalog der Preußischen Bibliotheken mit Nachweis des identischen Besitzers der Bayerischen Staatsbibliothek in München und der Nationalbibliothek in Wien. Hrsg. von der Preußischen Staatsbibliothek. Bd. 1–8 [Buchst. A.]. Berlin 1931–35. [Forts.:] Deutscher Gesamtkatalog. Hrsg. von der Preußischen Staatsbibliothek. Bd. 9–14 [bis Beethordnung]. Berlin 1936–39.

Goff Frederick Richmond Goff: Incunabula in American libraries. A third census of fifteenth-century books recorded in North American collections. 1. 2 (Suppl.). New York 1964–72.

Graesse Jean George Théodore Graesse: Trésor de livres rares et précieux ou nouveau dictionnaire bibliographique. T. 1–7. Dresde 1859–69. (Repr. Paris 1900/01; Berlin 1922; Milano 1950; New York 1950/51.)

GW Gesamtkatalog der Wiegendrucke. Hrsg. von der Kommission für den Gesamtkatalog der Wiegendrucke. Bd. 1–8, Lfg. 1. Leipzig 1925–40. – 2. Aufl. (Durchgesehener Neudruck der 1. Aufl.) Bd. 1–7. Stuttgart 1968. – Neuausgabe Bd. 8. Stuttgart 1978ff. Online-Version, URL: http://www.gesamtkatalogderwiegendrucke.de

H Ludwig Hain: Repertorium bibliographicum, in quo libri omnes ab arte typographica inventa usque ad annum MD. typis expressi ... recensentur. Vol. 1, P. 1. 2; Vol. 2, P. 1. 2. Stuttgar-tiae & Lutetiae Par. 1826–38. (Repr. Frankfurt a. M. 1920; Berlin 1925; Milano 1948 und 1964.) [Nebst] Register von Konrad Burger. Leipzig 1891 (Zentralblatt f. Bibliothekswesen [ZfB]. Beih. 8).

Haebler Konrad Haebler: Typenrepertorium der Wiegendrucke. Halle/S. 1905. (Repr. Nendeln/Liechtenstein, Wiesbaden 1968.)

Haebler/Schunke Konrad Haebler: Rollen- und Plattenstempel des 16. Jahrhunderts. Unter Mitwirkung von Ilse Schunke. Bd. 1. 2. Leipzig 1928/29 (Sammlung bibliothekswissenschaftlicher Arbeiten. 41. 42). (Repr. Wiesbaden 1968.)

HHBD Handbuch der historischen Buchbestände in Deutschland. Hrsg. von Bernhard Fabian et. al. 30 Bde. Hildesheim 1992–2000.

Helwig Hellmuth Helwig: Handbuch der Einbandkunde. Bd. 1–3. Hamburg 1953–55.

IBE Catálogo general de incunables en bibliotecas españolas. Coordinado y dirigido por Francisco García Craviotto. 2 Bde. Madrid 1989ff.

IGI Indice generale degli incunaboli delle biblioteche d'Italia. Comp. da Teresa Maria Guarnaschelli. Vol. 1–6. Roma 1942–81 (Ministero dell'educazione nazionale. Indice et cataloghi. N. S. I, 1–6).

IISTC Illustrated Incunabula Short Title Catalogue on CD-ROM (IISTC). In association with the British Library. CD-ROM. 2nd ed. Reading 1998

Isaac Franc Isaac: An index to the early printed books in the British Museum. P. 2: 1501 to 1520, Section 2/3: Italy, Switzerland and Eastern Europe. London 1938.

ISTC The British Library. Incunabula Short Title Catalogue. London 1980ff.

STC (Johnson/Scholderer) Alfred Forbes Johnson – Victor Scholderer: Short title catalogue of books printed in the German-speaking countries and German books printed in other countries from 1455 to 1600 now in the British Museum. London 1962.

STC (Johnson/Scholderer/Clarke) Alfred Forbes Johnson – Victor Scholderer – Derek Ashdown Clarke: Short-title catalogue of books printed in Italy and of Italian books printed in other countries from 1465 to 1600 now in the British Museum. London 1958 [1959].

Kyriss Ernst Kyriß: Verzierte gotische Einbände im alten deutschen Sprachgebiet. Text- [nebst] Tafel-Bd. 1–3. Stuttgart 1951–58.

LGB² Lexikon des gesamten Buchwesens (LGB²). 2., völlig neubearb. und erw. Aufl. Hrsg. v. Severin Corsten †, Stephan Füssel, Günther Pflug † und Friedrich-A. Schmidt-Künsemüller †. Bd. 1ff. Stuttgart 1987ff.

NDB Neue deutsche Biographie. Hrsg. von der Historischen Kommission bei der Bayerischen Akademie der Wissenschaften. Bd. 1ff. Berlin 1953ff.

Nijhoff/Kronenberg Wouter Nijhoff en Maria Elizabeth Kronenberg: Niederlandsche Bibliographie van 1500 tot 1540. Deel 1–3, 3. [Nebst] Suppl. 1–3. 's-Gravenhage 1923–1971.

NUC The National Union Catalog. A cumulative author list represented by Library of Congress printed cards and titles reported by other American libraries. Vol. 1ff. Washington 1956ff. ... 1952–55 imprints. Vol. 1–30, Ann Arbor, Mich. 1961; ... 1982. Vol. 1–21. Washington 1983.

Oates John Claud Trewinard Oates: Catalogue of the fifteenth-century printed books in the University Library Cambridge. Cambridge 1954.

PA Georg Wolfgang Panzer: Annales typographici ab artis inventae origine ad annum MD. Vol. 1–11. Norimbergae 1793–1803. (Repr. Hildesheim 1963.)

PDA Georg Wolfgang Panzer: Annalen der älteren deutschen Literatur ... welche von Erfindung der Buchdruckerkunst bis 1526 in deutscher Sprache gedruckt worden sind. Bd. 1. 2[und] Zusätze. Nürnberg (& Leipzig) 1788–1802. (Repr. Hildesheim 1961/62.)

Pellechet/Polain Marie Pellechet: Catalogue général des incunables des bibliothèques publiques de France. T. 1. 2 et 3 cont. par Marie-Louis Polain. Paris 1897–1909. (Repr. Nendeln/Liechtenstein 1970.)

Polain Marie-Louis Polain: Catalogue des livres imprimés au 15e siècle des bibliothèques de Belgique, 1932–78. T. 1–4. [Nebst] Suppl. Bruxelles 1932–79.

RSTC (Pollard/Redgrave) Alfred William Pollard – Gilbert Richard Redgrave: A short-title catalogue of books printed in England, Scotland and Ireland and of English books printed abroad 1475–1640. (First print 1926, repr. 1946, 1948, 1950.) London 1950. – 2nd ed., revised and enlarged by W. A. Jackson and F. S. Ferguson, completed by Katharine F. Pantzer. Vol. 1: A – H. London 1986. Vol. 2: I – Z. London 1976.

Pr Robert Proctor: An index to the early printed books in the British Museum ... to the year 1520. With notes of those in the Bodleian Library. P. 1. 2. Suppl. 1–4. London 1898–1903. (Repr. in 1 Bd.: London 1960.)

R/HCR Dietrich Reichling: Appendices ad Hainii-Copingeri Repertorium bibliographicum. Additiones et emendationes. Fasc. 1–6 [Nebst] Indices and Suppl. Monachii (Suppl.: Monasterii Guestph.) 1905–14. (Repr. Milano 1953.)

Renouard Philippe Renouard: Répertoire des imprimeurs parisiens jusqu'à la fin du seizième siècle. Paris 1898. (Repr. 1965.)

Reske Christoph Reske: Die Buchdrucker des 16. und 17. Jahrhunderts im deutschen Sprachgebiet. Auf Grundlage des gleichnamigen Werkes von Josef Benzing. Wiesbaden 2007.

Ritter Incun./15e et 16e siècle. François Ritter: Répertoire bibliographique des livres imprimés en Alsace aux 15e et 16e siècles. Fasc. hors Sér. I – V (Partie prélim.): Les incunables. P. 1. 2, vol. 1–4. P. 3. 4. Strasbourg 1932–60.

Rouzet Anne Rouzet: Dictionnaire des imprimeurs, librairies et éditeurs de 15e et 16e siècles dans les limites géographiques de la Belgique actuelle. Nieuwkoop 1975 (Collection du Centre-national de l'archéologie et de l'histoire du livre. Publ. 3).

Sander Max Sander: Le livre à figures italien depuis 1467 jusqu'à 1530. Essai de sa bibliographie et de son histoire. Vol. 1–6. Milan 1942 (Repr. Nendeln/Liechtenstein 1969).

Schr Wilhelm Ludwig Schreiber: Manuel de l'amateur de la gravure sur bois et sur métal au 15e siècle. T. 1–8. Berlin (4–8: Leipzig) 1891–1910.

Schramm Albert Schramm: Der Bilderschmuck der Frühdrucke. Bd. 1–23. Leipzig 1920–43.

Schreiber HANDBUCH Wilhelm Ludwig Schreiber: Handbuch der Holz- und Metallschnitte des 15. Jahrhunderts. Stark vermehrte und bis zu den neuesten Funden ergänzte Umarbeitung des Manuel de l'amateur de la gravure sur bois et sur métal au 15e siècle. Bd. 1–8. Leipzig 1926–30. – 3. Aufl. (Vollst. Neudruck des Gesamtwerkes.) Bd. 1–10. Stuttgart 1969; Bd. 11 [Abbildungsband zum Gesamtwerk]: Heinrich Theodor Musper: Der Einblattholzschnitt und die Blockbücher des 15. Jahrhunderts. Stuttgart 1976.

Stevenson Enrico Stevenson: Inventario dei libri stampati Palatino-Vaticani. Vol. 1, 1. 2; 2, 1. 2. Roma 1886–89.

Thomas STC Henry Thomas: Short-title Catalogue of books printed in France and of French books printed in other countries from 1470 to 1600 now in the British Museum. London 1924. (Repr. London 1966.)

VD 16 Verzeichnis der im deutschen Sprachbereich erschienenen Drucke des 16. Jahrhunderts. Hrsg. von der BSB in München in Verb. mit der HAB in Wolfenbüttel. Redaktion Irmgard Bezzel. I. Abt.: Autoren – Körperschaften – Anonyma. Bd. 1 (1993) – 22 (1995). – II. Abt.: Register der Herausgeber, Kommentatoren, Übersetzer und literarischen Beiträger. Bd. 23–24 (1997) – III. Abt.: Register der Druckorte, Drucker, Verleger und Erscheinungsjahre. Bd. 25 (2000). Stuttgart 1983–2000. Online-Version, URL: http://www.vd16.de

VD 17 Verzeichnis der im deutschen Sprachraum erschienenen Drucke des 17. Jahrhunderts. Online-Bibliographie, URL: http:/www.vd17.de

VE 15 Falk Eisermann: Verzeichnis der typographischen Einblattdrucke des 15. Jahrhunderts im Heiligen Römischen Reich Deutscher Nation. 3 Bde. Wiesbaden 2004.

VGT Veröffentlichungen der Gesellschaft für Typenkunde des 15. Jahrhunderts. Jg. 1–33 (2 460 Tafeln). Halle/S. und Berlin & Leipzig 1907–39. (Repr. Osnabrück 1966.) Typenregister zu Tafel 1–2460 von Rudolf Juchhoff und E. von Kathen. Osnabrück 1966.

Weale/Bohatta W. H. Jacobus Weale – Hanns Bohatta: Catalogus Missalium ritus Latini ab anno MCCCCLXXIV impressorum. London & Leipzig 1928. (Repr. Stuttgart 1990.)

Weller Emil Weller: Repertorium typographicum. Die deutsche Literatur im ersten Viertel des 16. Jahrhunderts. [Nebst] Suppl. [1.] 2. Nördlingen 1864–85. (Repr. Hildesheim 1961.)

Wing STC Donald Wing: Short-title catalogue of books printed in England, Scotland, Ireland, Wales and British America and of English books printed in other countries 1641 to 1700. Vol. 1–3. New York 1945–51. – 2nd rev. and enlarged ed. Vol. 1. New York 1972.

AUTORENANSCHRIFTEN

Hermann Baumeister MA
Höllentalstraße 68
D 79199 Kirchzarten
baumeisterh@t-online.de

Prof. Dr. Francisco J. Cornejo Vega
Facultad de Bellas Artes
Universidad de Sevilla
C / Laraña nº 3, E 41003 Sevilla

Katharina Ebenau MA
Schleusenstr. 17 D 60327 Frankfurt
kebenau@students.uni-mainz.de

Federica Fabbri
Facoltà di Conservazione dei Beni Culturali
Università degli Studi di Bologna
Via Mariani 5, I 48121 Ravenna
rike1@libero.it

H. George Fletcher
300 Central Park West, Apt. 2F2
USA New York / NY 10024-1576
h.georgefletcher@yahoo.com

Marvin J. Heller
1028 East 28th Street
USA Brooklyn / NY 11210
mjh1mjh@yahoo.com

Dr. Randall Eugene Herz
Äußere Brucker Straße 43
Apartment D 101, D 91052 Erlangen
rlherz@gmx.de

Daphne M. Hoogenboezem
University of Groningen
Romance Languages and Cultures
PO Box 716, NL 9700 AS Groningen
d.m.hoogenboezem@rug.nl

Dr. William A. Kelly
Scottish Centre for the Book
Edinburgh Napier University
Craighouse Campus
GB Edinburgh EH10 5LG
william@kelly65.plus.com

Prof. Dr. Christoph Kochhan
Marketing, Markt und Werbepsychologie
SRH FernHochschule Riedlingen
Lange Straße 19 D 88499 Riedlingen
christoph.kochhan@fh-riedlingen.srh.de

Dr. Anette Löffler
Pappelweg 2, D 04683 Belgershain
Anette.Loeffler@gmx.de

Prof. Dr. Dr. h. c. mult. Elmar Mittler
Fellow des Gutenberg-Forschungskollegs, Forschungsschwerpunkt Medienkonvergenz, Johannes Gutenberg-Universität, D 50099 Mainz
emittle@gwdg.de

Dr. Gisela Möncke
Bayerische Staatsbibliothek
Ludwigstraße 16, D 80539 München
moencke@bsb-muenchen.de

Dr. András Németh
Research Fellow,
Manuscript Collection,
Hungarian National Library
Budavári Palota F épület
HU 1827 Budapest
anemeth@oszk.hu

Mahendra Patel
19/437, Satyagraha, Satellite Road
IN Ahmedabad 380 015
mcpatel@theleafdesign.com

Bruno Pfäffli
11bis, rue Guynemer
F 92330 Sceaux
bruno.pfaffli391@dbmail.com

Dr. Dennis E. Rhodes
Early Printing Collection
The British Library
96 Euston Road, GB London NW 12 DB

Dr. Siegfried Risse †

Annika Rockenberger MA
Bergaustraße 24, D 12437 Berlin
annika@rockenberger.com

Dr. Frieder Schmidt
Deutsche Nationalbibliothek
Deutsches Buch- und Schriftmuseum / Kultur- und Papierhistorische Sammlungen
Deutscher Platz 1, D 04103 Leipzig
f.schmidt@d-nb.de

Dr. Anneliese Schmitt
Mellenseestraße 16, D 10319 Berlin
wolfliese@web.de

Christina Schmitz MA
Forschungsschwerpunkt
Medienkonvergenz
Johannes Gutenberg-Universität
D 55099 Mainz
christina.schmitz@uni-mainz.de

Prof. Dr. Wolfgang Schmitz
Universität zu Köln
Universitäts- und Stadtbibliothek
Universitätsstraße 33, D 50931 Köln
schmitz@ub.uni-koeln.de

Dr. Hans-Walter Stork
Staats- und Universitätsbibliothek Hamburg, Abendländische und außereuropäische Handschriften
Von-Melle-Park 3, D 20146 Hamburg
stork@sub.uni-hamburg.de

Dr. Adolfo Tura
Viale Principe Amedeo 26
I 47921 Rimini
tura@happyfew.it

Steven Van Impe
Erfgoedbibliotheek
Hendrik Conscience
Hendrik Conscienceplein 4
B 2000 Antwerpen
Steven.VanImpe@stad.antwerpen.be

EHRENTAFEL
DER INTERNATIONALEN GUTENBERG-
GESELLSCHAFT

Gutenberg-Preisträger

1968 Giovanni Mardersteig † 1977
1971 Henri Friedlaender † 1996
1974 Hermann Zapf Darmstadt
1977 Rudolf Hell † 2002
1980 Hellmut Lehmann-Haupt † 1992
1983 Gerrit Willem Ovink † 1984
1986 Adrian Frutiger Bremgarten-Bern/CH
1989 Lotte Hellinga London/GB
1992 Ricardo J. Vicent Museros Valencia/E
1994 Paul Brainerd Seattle, WA/USA
1996 John G. Dreyfus † 2002
1998 Henri-Jean Martin † 2007
2000 Joseph M. Jacobson Cambridge, MA/USA
2002 Otto Rohse Hamburg
2004 Robert Darnton Princeton, NJ/USA
2006 Hubert Wolf Münster
2008 Michael Knoche Weimar
2010 Mahendra Patel Ahmedabad/INDIEN

Ehrenmitglieder
der Internationalen Gutenberg-Gesellschaft

John F. Fontana Huntington, NY/USA
Hans Hermann Schmidt Mainz
Franz Leschinkohl Mainz

Träger des Ehrenringes
der Internationalen Gutenberg-Gesellschaft

Dr. Helmut Beichert Mainz
Fritz Kind Gütersloh
Hans Klenk † 1983
Prof. Dr. Aloys Ruppel † 1977
Dr. Ludwig Strecker † 1978

Senatorenrat
der Internationalen Gutenberg-Gesellschaft

Dr. Peter Hanser-Strecker Mainz
Wolfgang A. Hartmann Barcelona/E
Jost Hochuli St. Gallen/CH
Heinz Knauer Tarasp/CH
Dipl. Kfm. Dr. Ernst-Erich Marhencke Molfsee
Hans-Otto Reppekus Gelsenkirchen
Hon. Gen.-Konsul Hannetraud
Schultheiss Mainz (Vorsitzende) † 2011
Emil van der Vekene Niederanven/LUX
Ricardo J. Vicent Museros Valencia/E

VORSTAND DER
INTERNATIONALEN GUTENBERG-
GESELLSCHAFT 2010

PRÄSIDENT Jens Beutel Oberbürgermeister der Stadt Mainz
EHRENPRÄSIDENT Herman-Hartmut Weyel Mainz
VIZEPRÄSIDENT Günther Knödler Mainz
SCHATZMEISTER Hans-Günter Mann Mainz
SCHRIFTFÜHRER Univ.-Prof. Dr. Stephan Füssel Mainz

Dr. Annette Ludwig Mainz
Walter Schumacher Mainz
Univ.-Prof. Dr. Georg Krausch Mainz
Marianne Grosse Mainz
Hon. Gen.-Konsul Hannetraud Schultheiss † 2011

Werner von Bergen Mainz
Prof. Johannes Bergerhausen Mainz/Köln
Rudolf Bödige Mainz
Prof. Dr. Heinz Finger Neuss
Hartmut Flothmann Idstein
Dr. Anton M. Keim Mainz
Günter Lindner Mainz
Dr. Simone Sanftenberg Mainz
Bertram Schmidt-Friderichs Mainz
Hans-Georg Schnücker Mainz
Hans-Joachim Schulze Mainz
Dr. Bettina Wagner München

Geschäftsführerin der
Gutenberg-Gesellschaft
Christina Schmitz Mainz

Geschäftsstelle
Liebfrauenplatz 5, D 55116 Mainz
Telefon 06131.22 64 20, *Telefax* 06131.23 35 30
www.gutenberg-gesellschaft.de
info@gutenberg-gesellschaft.de

JAHRESBERICHT

DER GUTENBERG-GESELLSCHAFT

FÜR 2010

Personelle Veränderungen
Seit dem 15. April 2010 hat die Gutenberg-Gesellschaft eine neue Geschäftsführerin. Als Nachfolgerin für Sabine Idstein wurde die Buchwissenschaftlerin Christina Schmitz eingestellt, die sich auf der Mitgliederversammlung im Juni den Mitgliedern vorstellte. Das Vorzimmer der Geschäftsstelle ist seit Mai 2010 regelmäßig mit Praktikanten besetzt. Bisher konnten fünf Studierende für jeweils drei Monate Berufserfahrung sammeln und die Geschäftsführung unterstützen.

Auch im Gutenberg-Museum fand in diesem Frühjahr ein Personalwechsel statt: Dr. Eva Hanebutt-Benz ist Ende März 2010 nach 22 Dienstjahren als Direktorin des Gutenberg-Museums und damit auch als Präsidiumsmitglied der Gutenberg-Gesellschaft ausgeschieden. Als neue Museumsdirektorin hat Dr. Annette Ludwig am 15. Mai 2010 ihre Arbeit im Museum und im Präsidium der Gutenberg-Gesellschaft aufgenommen.

*Trauer um Generalkonsulin
Hannetraud Schultheiß*
Am 31. Januar 2011 verstarb unsere langjährige Senatorenratsvorsitzende Generalkonsulin Hannetraud Schultheiß, die sich trotz ihres hohen Alters von 91 Jahren bis zuletzt aktiv für die Gutenberg-Gesellschaft einsetzte. Mit Hannetraud Schultheiß verliert die Gutenberg-Gesellschaft eines ihrer engagiertesten Vorstandsmitglieder. Mehr als drei Jahrzehnte lang hat sie sich in den Dienst der Erforschung der Geschichte und Entwicklung der Drucktechnik und der schriftorientierten Medien gestellt. Selbstbewusst und großzügig hat sie die Gesellschaft mitgeprägt und trug daher zu Recht seit 1981 den Ehrentitel der Senatorin. Von 1993 bis 2007 war sie Vizepräsidentin der Gutenberg-Gesellschaft.

Mit unermüdlichem Elan setzte sie sich als Vorsitzende des Senatorenrates und der Stiftung Moses für die Gutenberg-Gesellschaft ein. Als Schatzmeisterin hat sie zwei Jahrzehnte lang leidenschaftlich die finanziellen Herausforderungen der Gutenberg-Gesellschaft bewältigt.

Ihr unvergleichlicher persönlicher Einsatz für Gesellschaft und Kultur fand unter anderem 1999 mit der Gutenberg-Plakette der Stadt Mainz und zuletzt 2007 mit der Ehrennadel der Stadt Mainz seine hochverdiente Anerkennung. Wir verabschieden uns von ihr in Dankbarkeit und Hochachtung.

Förderung
Dem Vereinszweck gemäß förderte die Internationale Gutenberg-Gesellschaft in Mainz e. V. auch im Jahr 2010 die wissenschaftliche Beschäftigung mit Geschichte und Gegenwart des Buches durch Publikationen, Vorträge und eine Exkursion. Bedingt durch einen beträchtlichen Rückgang an Spenden und die hohe Anzahl an säumigen Mitgliedern konnte das Gutenberg-Museum im Jahr 2010 zunächst noch nicht finanziell unterstützt werden (Stand: 31. Januar 2011).

Entwicklung der Mitgliederzahl
Die Zahl der Austritte ließ sich 2010 nicht durch Neueintritte ausgleichen. Neben Kündigungen sorgten allerdings auch einige Todesfälle, Insolvenzen und nicht mehr ermittelbare Mitglieder für eine Reduzierung der Mitgliederzahl. So wurden im Jahr 2010 44 Austritte, acht Todesfälle und zwei Insolvenzen verzeichnet. Zudem mussten drei Mitgliedschaften gelöscht werden, weil die Mitglieder nicht mehr ermittelbar waren. Dem stehen 22 Neueintritte gegenüber. Der Mitgliederbestand reduzierte sich zum 31. Dezember 2010

auf 1170 Mitglieder. Wir betrauern den Tod der Mitglieder Jacques Bollens, Erwin Britt, Helmut Höhler, Gustav Jaeger, Wolfgang Mellert, Karl Heinz Wedekind, Otmar Weis und Helmut Zöllner. Als Neumitglieder aus dem Ausland begrüßen wir Ines Jerele (Slowenien), Prof. Mercedes Fernández Valladares (Spanien), Florian Graefe Aguado (Spanien), und Dr. Roland Folter (USA).

Wirtschaftlicher Lagebericht

Trotz einer relativ guten wirtschaftlichen Ausgangslage zu Beginn des Jahres 2010 stellten ein erheblicher Spendenrückgang und beträchtliche Zahlungsrückstände bei den Mitgliedsbeiträgen die Gutenberg-Gesellschaft vor eine schwierige Aufgabe. Auch das Mahnverfahren Anfang November 2010 brachte nicht die erhofften Summen. Erfreulicherweise konnte unser Schatzmeister Hans-Günter Mann durch Spendenaufrufe aber noch € 7870 einwerben. Im Jahr 2010 standen den Einnahmen von insgesamt € 93707 Ausgaben in Höhe von € 98161 gegenüber.

Mitgliederversammlung und Gutenberg-Preis 2010

Die 109. Mitgliederversammlung fand wegen der nachfolgenden Verleihung des Gutenberg-Preises im Mainzer Rathaus statt. Den 86 anwesenden Mitgliedern im Valencia-Zimmer stellten sich Christina Schmitz als neue Geschäftsführerin und Dr. Annette Ludwig als neue Museumsdirektorin vor. Auch ihre Vorgängerin Dr. Eva Hanebutt-Benz nahm an der Veranstaltung teil, um sich mit einem kurzen Rückblick auf ihre lange Dienstzeit und guten Wünschen für ihre Nachfolgerin von den Mitgliedern zu verabschieden. Die Mitglieder billigten den Haushaltsbericht von 2009 und den Haushaltsplan für 2010 und erteilten dem Vorstand und der Geschäftsführung der Gesellschaft einstimmig Entlastung für das Jahr 2009 und abschließend auch für das Krisenjahr 2007. Nachdem die ehrenamtlichen Rechnungsprüfer Dr. Wilhelm Mettner und Bernd Rehling erneut bestellt worden waren, beschloss der Präsident die Mitgliederversammlung, um alle zur Verleihung des Gutenberg-Preises in den Ratssaal einzuladen.

Zu Beginn der Festveranstaltung stellte der Herausgeber Prof. Dr. Stephan Füssel das frischgedruckte Gutenberg-Jahrbuch 2010 vor. Das erste Buch überreichte er diesmal nicht wie üblich dem Präsidenten der Gutenberg-Gesellschaft, sondern dem Gutenberg-Preisträger Mahendra Patel. Denn in diesem Jahr erschien das Jahrbuch mit einer neuen Schrift, der LT Malabar. Ihr Schöpfer, Dan Reynolds, gestaltete diese Schrift für zwei Zeichensysteme: Devanagari für den Satz in Hindi und das lateinische Alphabet. Das zweite Exemplar des neuen Jahrgangs überreichte Prof. Füssel dem Designstudenten Marcus Blättermann von der Hochschule für Kunst und Design Halle, der mit seinem künstlerischen Schutzumschlagentwurf den diesjährigen Wettbewerb gewann. Sein Entwurf, auf dem die verschiedenen Stationen in der Entwicklung der Drucktechnik dargestellt sind, ziert das Gutenberg-Jahrbuch 2010. Prof. Ralf de Jong von der Folkwang Universität der Künste Essen lobte den Entwurf und beglückwünschte den Preisträger zu seiner gelungenen Arbeit.

Höhepunkt der Veranstaltung war die Verleihung des Gutenberg-Preises 2010 an den indischen Schriftdesigner Prof. Mahendra Patel. Oberbürgermeister Jens Beutel überreichte dem Preisträger im gut gefüllten Ratssaal eine Urkunde und das Preisgeld in Höhe von € 10 000. Zuvor hatte er Patel als indischen Johannes Gutenberg des 20. und 21. Jahrhunderts bezeichnet, da er mit seinen modernen Entwürfen für verschiedene indische Schriften die Typografie seines Landes wesentlich geprägt habe.

In seiner Laudatio zeichnete der Schweizer Typograf und Buchgestalter Bruno Pfäffli aus Paris den Werdegang von Mahendra Patel nach. Als besonders prägend schilderte er Patels einjährigen Aufenthalt in Paris bei Adrian Frutiger, einem der bedeutendsten Schriftgestalter der Gegenwart und selbst Gutenberg-Preisträger, bei dem auch er selbst Patel kennenlernte. Gemeinsam mit Frutiger arbeitete Patel an verschiedenen Schriftentwürfen. Nach der Laudatio bedankte sich Patel für die große Ehre, dass er als erster Inder zum Gutenberg-Preisträger gewählt wurde. Das Preisgeld möchte er für die Arbeiten seiner Studenten verwenden, denn in der Rolle des Lehrers sieht er seine besonderen Fähigkeiten.

Fachexkursion nach Brüssel und Antwerpen
Im September 2010 wandelten 34 Mitglieder der Gutenberg-Gesellschaft zwei Tage lang in der belgischen Hafenstadt auf den Spuren Christoph Plantins, der zu den produktivsten und einflussreichsten Buchdruckern und Verlegern des 16. Jahrhunderts zählt. Bereits auf der Hinreise tauchten wir in die belgische Buch- und Druckgeschichte ein: Unser erstes Ziel war die Königliche Bibliothek in Brüssel. Dort stimmten uns die Altbestands-Spezialisten Op de Beeck und Renaud Adam bei einer Führung durch das integrierte Druckmuseum und die Abteilung für Alte Drucke ein. Dabei konnten wir sogar ein paar ausgewählte Schätze der Druckkunst selbst durchblättern, die sonst der Öffentlichkeit verborgen bleiben.

Danach ging es weiter nach Antwerpen zur geschichtsträchtigen Hendrik Conscience-Bibliothek, deren Auftrag es ist, das flämische Kulturerbe zu bewahren. Im prächtigen Nottebohmzaal gab uns zunächst Steven Van Impe, Kurator der Historischen Sammlungen, einen Einblick in die Geschichte und den Auftrag des Hauses.

Anschließend durften wir uns auf einen hochinteressanten Vortrag zur flämischen Druckerfamilie Verdussen freuen. Stijn van Rossem, Präsident der Flemish Society of Book History, berichtete unter anderem darüber, wie die Druckerfamilie im 16. und 17. Jahrhundert geschickt die städtischen Strukturen Antwerpens nutzte, um sich im Druckgewerbe zu etablieren. Hauptziel unserer Reise war das berühmte Plantin-Moretus-Museum am zweiten Tag der Exkursion. Der Stadtpalast der Familie Plantin-Moretus zählt zu den eindrucksvollsten Häusern des 16. Jahrhunderts in Antwerpen. Das Museum verschafft einen einzigartigen Überblick über die Buchdruckkunst und besitzt die zwei ältesten Druckerpressen der Welt (um 1600). Davon konnten wir uns in einer exklusiven Führung selbst überzeugen, bei der uns auch die Direktorin des Museums, Iris Kockelbergh, herzlich begrüßte.

Nach einer frühen Mittagspause hatten wir dann noch Gelegenheit, wahlweise bei einer Stadtführung oder einem Besuch des Rubenshauses tiefer in die Geschichte der Stadt einzudringen.

Veranstaltungen der Gutenberg-Gesellschaft
Im Jahr 2010 organisierte die Gutenberg-Gesellschaft für ihre Mitglieder und alle Interessierten mit großem Erfolg verschiedene Veranstaltungen. Den Anfang machte Mahendra Patel, der Gutenberg-Preisträger 2010, bei einer Veranstaltung, die die Gutenberg-Gesellschaft gemeinsam mit Prof. Bergerhausen von der FH Mainz und Uta Schneider von der Stiftung Buchkunst organisierte. Bereits am Vorabend der Preisverleihung entführte Patel gut 70 gespannte Gäste im Vortragssaal des Gutenberg-Museums in die »fremde« Welt des indischen Schriftsystems und gewährte Einblicke in sein Lebenswerk. Unter dem Titel *Letter Design to Logotype – A Visual Presentation* stellte er seine Schriftentwürfe vor, die in verschiedensten Bereichen Anwendung finden, beispielsweise auf Straßenverkehrsschildern, Landkarten oder Handydisplays. Dabei ging Patel auf die Schwierigkeiten des komplizierten Schrift- und Sprachsystems seines Heimatlandes Indien ein. Seine Entwürfe haben die indische Schriftgestaltung wesentlich geprägt und den Weg zu einem modernen Schrift- und Druckwesen in Indien geebnet.

Im Oktober führte Dr. Annette Ludwig für die Mitglieder der Gutenberg-Gesellschaft und des Fördervereins ein gut besuchtes Künstlergespräch mit dem aktuellen Stadtdrucker Philipp Hennevogl, der sich gerne den zahlreichen Fragen der Gäste stellte. Schließlich zog es wieder gut 70 interessierte Besucher in den Vortragssaal des Gutenberg-Museums, wo unser Präsidiumsmitglied Prof. Dr. Stephan Füssel das neue Faksimile von Bodonis *Manuale Tipografico* (1818) anschaulich vorstellte. Bei einem gemütlichen Glas Wein im Foyer des Museums nutzten viele Gäste im Anschluss die schöne Gelegenheit lebhaft das Gehörte zu diskutieren und die gewonnenen Eindrücke beim Blättern im Faksimile zu vertiefen.

Das monatliche Gesprächsforum der Freunde Gutenbergs im Museumscafé Codex, veranstaltet von unseren Vorstandsmitgliedern Hartmut Flothmann und Günter Lindner, erfreute sich auch im Jahr 2010 wieder großer Beliebtheit. Höhepunkte waren die Veranstaltung vom 25. Februar, in der sich Frau Dr. Eva Hanebutt-Benz als Direktorin des Gutenberg-Museums verabschiedete, und die Veranstaltung vom 27. Mai, in der sich Frau Dr. Ludwig als neue Museumsdirektorin vorstellte. Auf dem gut besuchten 35. Jour Fixe wurde zudem die zweite erweiterte Auflage des Jour Fixe Büchleins vorgestellt, herausgegeben von Hartmut Flothmann und Günter Lindner, den Initiatoren des Jour Fixe der Freunde Gutenbergs. Der neu vorliegende Band enthält 64 ausgewählte Kurzreferate und einige Grußworte von mehr als 60 Autoren. Zu den Extras gehören Auszüge aus dem Gästebuch, Bildgalerie, Pressespiegel und Stimmen zum Jour Fixe Büchlein.

Messebeteiligungen

Wie schon in den Jahren zuvor präsentierte sich die Gutenberg-Gesellschaft auch 2010 wieder auf Messen. Im Oktober war die Geschäftsführerin im Wechsel mit den zwei Praktikantinnen Nina Geise und Ines Leising am Stand der Mainzer Buchwissenschaft vertreten, die sich an dem Gemeinschaftsstand »Studium rund ums Buch« präsentierte. Hier nutzte die Gesellschaft jede Gelegenheit Interessierte anzusprechen und Neugier für die Gesellschaft zu wecken. Auch auf der gut besuchten Mainzer Büchermesse im Rathausfoyer fehlte die Gutenberg-Gesellschaft nicht. Zum Motto der Messe »Mainz und seine Partnerstädte« hatte sich die Gesellschaft etwas ganz Besonderes ausgedacht: In einer Hochvitrine präsentierten wir einige ausgewählte, kostbare Faksimiles aus dem Verlag unseres Senators und Gutenberg-Preisträgers Ricardo Vicent Museros in Valencia, beispielsweise das Burgos-Exemplar der 42-zeiligen Gutenberg-Bibel oder Bernhard von Breydenbachs *Reise nach Jerusalem*. Dazu verkauften wir thematisch passende Titel aus unserer Reihe »Kleine Drucke«. Besonders gut kamen bei den Besuchern unsere Handzettel zum Mitnehmen an, auf denen wir in kurzer Form Informationen rund ums Buch über die Partnerstädte zusammengestellt hatten. Gemeinsam mit der tatkräftigen Unterstützung des Vizepräsidenten Günther Knödler, der Vorstandsmitglieder Hartmut Flothmann und Günter Lindner und der Praktikantinnen Ines Leising und Theresa Müller konnte die Geschäftsführerin zahlreiche E-Mail-Adressen von Interessierten sammeln, die gerne über die Aktivitäten der Gesellschaft informiert werden möchten.

Öffentlichkeitsarbeit

Seit August 2010 finden regelmäßige Treffen der AG Mitgliederwerbung statt, die es sich zum Ziel gesetzt hat, Maßnahmen zur Mitgliedergewinnung zu konzeptionieren und umzusetzen sowie mit der Organisation von interessanten Veranstaltungen neue Mitglieder zu werben und die bestehenden zu binden. Als erstes großes Projekt konnte in diesem Rahmen erstmalig ein Jahresprogramm erstellt werden, mit Veranstaltungen der Gutenberg-Gesellschaft und Terminhinweisen für 2011. Zudem konnte pünktlich zum Jahresende die neue, benutzerfreundliche Website der Gutenberg-Gesellschaft (www.gutenberg-gesellschaft.de) online gestellt werden. So werden die Mitglieder ganz aktuell über Neuigkeiten und Veranstaltungen informiert; Bildergalerien illustrieren das rege Vereinsleben und die Suchfunktion ermöglicht das schnelle Finden eines gewünschten Themas.

Fördermitglieder und Sponsoren

Zum Schluss des Berichts danken wir allen Mitgliedern für die ideelle Unterstützung und den finanziellen Beitrag, besonders denjenigen Mitgliedern, die freiwillig einen erhöhten Beitrag zahlen. Allen Spendern und Fördermitgliedern, die unsere Arbeit 2010 mit größeren Beiträgen unterstützt haben, danken wir besonders herzlich:
– Sparkasse Mainz
– Mainzer Volksbank
– VR-Bank Mainz
– LBS Rheinland-Pfalz

Christina Schmitz
Geschäftsführerin

JAHRESBERICHT DES GUTENBERG-MUSEUMS FÜR 2010

Im Jahr 2010 konnten insgesamt 109 483 Museumsbesucher im Gutenberg-Museum gezählt werden, darunter über 23 500 Kinder und Jugendliche. Der Druckladen wurde von etwa 11 500 Personen aufgesucht. Wie im Vorjahr verringerte sich allerdings vor allem die Zahl der amerikanischen Touristen.

Ausstellungen
- 31. 1. – 14. 3. Mario Derra: *Ein Gesicht für Peter Schöffer. Die Historie der Druckkunst in der Interpretation eines heutigen Künstlers. Farbholzschnitt, -radierung und -lithographie.*
- 25. 3. – 8. 8. *Felix Martin Furtwängler. Printing into Thinking. Folgen-Suiten-Zyklen.* Mit Katalog (Harrassowitz Verlag).
- 3. 9. – 28. 11. *Philipp Hennevogl – Mainzer Stadtdrucker 2010/2011. Ein Meister des Linolschnitts.*
- 4. 12. – 27. 2. 2011 *Otto Rohse – Das Werkarchiv. Kupferstiche, Holzstiche, Pressendrucke.*

Kleine Ausstellungen
- 14. 1. – 21. 3. *Papierballett. Eine Installation von Cäcilie Davidis.*
- 11. 6. – 17. 6. *Beispiele aus der Bucheinband-Mustersammlung von Heinz Petersen* anlässlich der Schenkung an das Gutenberg-Museum.
- 21. 8. – 14. 11. *Boek bindt Kunst. Buch bindet Kunst – Bucheinbände der Künstlergruppe* MET6. Ausstellung von handgefertigten Bucheinbänden aus Belgien und den Niederlanden.
- 28. 10. – 30. 10. 2011 *Lost Gutenbergs. Die Verlorenen Gutenbergs. Die Entdeckung von 128 ungebundenen original Cooper Square-Gutenberg-Bibeln in den* USA.
- 15. 12. – 19. 12. *Kommunikations- und Mediendesign im Gutenberg-Museum Mainz. Diplomanden der Fachhochschule Mainz präsentieren ihre Abschlussarbeiten.*

Präsentationen
Die schönsten deutschen Bücher 2007, Stiftung Buchkunst.

Neue Reihe *Exlibris des Monats*
Oktober: *Gianfranco Schialvino für Giorgio Armani* (1982); November: *Joseph Sattler für Victoria Kaiserin Friedrich* (1840 – 1901); Dezember: *Konstantin Kalinovich für Isolde Kern* (2000).

Ausstellungen im Druckladen
- 6. 11. 2009 – 31. 5. 2010 *Arbeitsprobe. Typografische Arbeiten von Studierenden der Buchwissenschaft der Johannes Gutenberg-Universität Mainz.*
- 18. 5. – 30. 9. *Letterbugs und anderes Geziefer.* »Typografische Insekten« und »Tragbare Kleinplastiken« von Bill Moran und Anja Germann.
- 2. 10. – 29. 4. 2011 *Balanziergang … durch die Stadt.* Eine Ausstellung des Literaturmagazin Wortschau und des Leistungskurses Bildende Kunst am Gymnasium zu St. Katharinen, Oppenheim.

Besondere Veranstaltungen im Museum
Neben zahlreichen Ausstellungsführungen fanden folgende Veranstaltungen statt:
- 31. 1., 28. 2., 21. 3. und 18. 4. Sonntagsmatinee, Vortragsreihe »Bibel und Literatur«: Lesungen mit Iris Melamed: *Mein Gott! Warum hast Du mich verlassen!*, Helga Bender und Dr. Anton Maria Keim: *Eher geht ein Kamel durch ein Nadelöhr*, Gaby Reichardt: *Der Tod des Mose*, Arno Hermer: *Willst Du gesund werden?*
- 26. 3. Übergabe von Büchern und Werken von Gunter Böhmer als Schenkung an das Gutenberg-Museum.
- 16. 5. Internationaler Museumstag: Tag der offenen Tür.

- 29.5. Lange Nacht der Mainzer Museen zum Thema »Illumination«: Beleuchtungskonzept, Führung Illumination von Inkunabeln, Miniaturmalerei, Drucken von Ablassbriefen, Informationsstand der Restaurierungswerkstatt »Schäden durch Licht«.
- 11.6. Übergabe der Bucheinband-Mustersammlung von Heinz Petersen als Schenkung an das Gutenberg-Museum.
- 25.6. Vortrag von Prof. Mahendra Patel, Gutenberg-Preisträger der Stadt Mainz: Letter Design to Logotype – A Visual Presentation (in Zusammenarbeit mit der Internationalen Gutenberg-Gesellschaft und der Stiftung Lesen).
- 25./26.6. Johannisfest; Drucken von Ablassbriefen.
- 1.10. Autorenlesungen im Rahmen der Ausstellungseröffnung *Balanziergang ... durch die Stadt* im Vortragssaal.
- 12.10. Übergabe des Kinderführers »Gutenberg für Kinder« mit Doris Ahnen, Ministerin für Bildung, Frauen und Jugend und dem Förderverein Gutenberg e. V.
- 12.–16.10. Woche des Stadtdruckers: Einblicke in die Arbeit Philipp Hennevogls, Druck von Linolschnitten, Führungen, Künstlergespräch, Workshops.
- 15.10. Künstlergespräch mit Philipp Hennevogl und Dr. Annette Ludwig.
- 21.10. Künstlergespräch mit Philipp Hennevogl und Dr. Annette Ludwig für die Mitglieder der Internationalen Gutenberg-Gesellschaft.
- 23.10. Kinderfest mit den »Poppets« Gunzi Heil und Marcus Dürr zum Thema »Druck«.
- 18.11. Vortrag Prof. Dr. Stephan Füssel, Johannes Gutenberg-Universität Mainz: Der König der Drucker und der Drucker der Könige. Über das *Manuale Typografico* Bodonis (in Zusammenarbeit mit der Internationalen Gutenberg-Gesellschaft).
- 22.11. Mitgliederversammlung und Tagung des Museumsverbands Rheinland-Pfalz.
- 26.11. Bundesweiter Vorlesetag: MitarbeiterInnen des Gutenberg-Museums lesen Geschichten rund um Buch, Druck und Schrift.
- 26.11. Vortrag Dr. Anton Maria Keim: Ein Gutenberg-Krimi. Gutenberg kehrt heim aus New York (mit Filmpräsentation).
- 14.12. Vorführung »Gestochen scharf – die Technik des Kupferstichs« mit Michael Rausch.

Besondere Veranstaltungen im Druckladen
Veranstaltungen und Kurse im Rahmen der Ausstellung *Philipp Hennevogl – Mainzer Stadtdrucker 2010/2011*:
- 14.10. Eintägiger Ferienworkshop für Kinder ab 10 Jahren.
- 28.10. und 18.11. Linolschnitt und Druck für Erwachsene.
- Wöchentlich samstags: »Ich druck mir meinen Hennevogl«. Künstlerische Interpretation eines Druckstocks von Philipp Hennevogl.
- Jeden ersten Donnerstag im Monat »Offene Werkstatt« (bis 20 Uhr).
- Ab Juni Kombiführung für Schüler in Museum und Druckladen: »Kommt mit! Wir treten in Gutenbergs Fußstapfen«. Neues Angebot des Gutenbergs-Museums in Zusammenarbeit mit der Touristik Centrale Mainz.
- 26.6. Preisverleihung zum Wettbewerb der Johannisnacht 2010.
- 23.11., 2.12. Schüler lesen Zeitung (in Kooperation mit der Allgemeinen Zeitung); Besuch in einer Grundschule, Schülerreporter drucken im Druckladen.
- Nov. und Dez.: Weihnachtskartendruck

Wochenendworkshops:
- 20./21.2. Textura – Gundela Kleinholdermann.
- 6./7.3. Klassischer Bleisatz – Rainhard Matfeld.
- 20./21.3. Paper Art – Elli Weishaupt.
- 17./18.4. Buchbinden Grundkurs – Ludger Maria Kochinke.
- 12.5. Notenstich – Peter Gass-Domes.
- 12./13.6. Kaltnadel – Gunter Staschik.
- 28./29.8. Grüsse aus ... – Tanja Labs.
- 18./19.9. Buchbinden: Steifbroschur und Schachtel – Ludger Maria Kochinke.
- 20./21.11. Paper Art – Elli Weishaupt.

Die mobile Druckwerkstatt wurde an 32 Schulen und andere Institutionen ausgeliehen. Die rekonstruierte Gutenberg-Presse wurde gezeigt:
- 15.3.–22.3. Leipziger Buchmesse.
- 29.3.–7.4. Bibliotheekhuis Limburg.
- 16.6.–21.6. Bayerisch-Oberösterreichischer Klostermarkt Schweiklberg.
- 1.10.–31.10. Frankfurter Buchmesse.

Museumspädagogik

Aktion »Lebendiges Museum« (jeweils vor den Oster-, Sommer-, Herbst- und Winterferien) im Ausstellungsgebäude. Es fanden an 32 Tagen Vorführungen in den verschiedenen Abteilungen des Museums statt. Die Vorführungen umfassten folgende Themen: Letterngießen und Druck an der Gutenberg-Presse, Buchbindetechniken, Notenstich, Arbeiten an der Linotype, Handsatz, Ebru-Marmorpapier, Kupferstich, Papierschöpfen, Islamische Schrift und Buch, Sütterlin-Schreiben, Keilschrift-Schreiben, Koreanische Schrift und Buchkultur, Bleisatz mit der Linotypesetzmaschine und anschließendem Druck auf dem Heidelberger Tiegel.

Monatliche Kinderführungen mit Druckvorführung, Gießen von Bleilettern und Rundgang durch das Museum.

Monatliche Familiensamstage mit Workshops und Führungen zu den Themen Buchdruck, Papierherstellung, Buchbinden, Schriftgeschichte, Hieroglyphen, Faltbücher, Wasserzeichen.

Gutenberg-AG des Maria Ward-Gymnasiums zu den Themen Buchdruck, Papierherstellung, Buchbinden, Schriftgeschichte.

Projekttage des Maria Ward-Gymnasiums vor den Sommerferien 2010 zum Thema Schriftgeschichte – Englische Schreibschrift.

Publikationen

Dr. EVA HANEBUTT-BENZ
- Buchdruck im alten China. In: *Impuls. Jahrespublikation der Johannes-Gutenberg-Schule Stuttgart*. Stuttgart 2010, S. 26–31.
- Persönliche und museale Höhepunkte. 22 Jahre im Gutenberg-Museum. In: *Mainz. Vierteljahreshefte für Kultur, Politik, Wirtschaft, Geschichte*. 2 (2010), S. 26–31.
- Museen erleben, Museen gestalten. In: *Aus dem Antiquariat. Zeitschrift für Antiquare und Büchersammler*. NF 8 (2010), S. 148–57.
- Die Sammlung Schrift und Druck in Korea im Gutenberg-Museum Mainz. In: *Entdeckung Korea! Schätze aus deutschen Museen*. Ausstellungskatalog der Wanderausstellung, organisiert durch die Korea Foundation Berlin 2011, S. 177–80.

Dr. ANNETTE LUDWIG
Das Gutenberg-Museum Mainz: Museum, Lernort, Werkstatt und Laboratorium der Druckkunst. In: *Land der Möglichkeiten. Kunst, Kultur und Kreativwirtschaft in Rheinland-Pfalz*. Hrsg. von KARIN DRDA-KÜHN und JOE WEINGARTEN. Idar-Oberstein 2010, S. 136/7.

Dr. CLAUS MAYWALD
- *Buchverschlüsse, Buchbeschläge und sonstige Metallteile am Buch*. Rossdorf 2010.
- *Schreibtinten, Einführung und Übersicht*. Rossdorf 2010.
- Informationsblätter: The Reproduction of Words and Pictures before Gutenberg; Historische Bucheinbände (engl. Version: Historic Book Covers); Making a Modern Hand Binding; Coloured Paper; Books and Script in the World of Islam; Druck in arabischen Lettern (engl. Version: Printing with Arabic Letters). Mainz 2010.

Dr. ELKE SCHUTT-KEHM
- Klein, kleiner, am kleinsten: Miniatur-Exlibris. In: *Miniaturbuch Journal*. 1 (2010), S. 4–7.
- Von Kaiser Wilhelm II. bis Giorgio Armani, von Dürer bis Janosch. Verborgene Schätze in Mainzer Museen: die Exlibris-Sammlung des Gutenberg-Museums. In: *Mainz. Vierteljahreshefte für Kultur, Politik, Wirtschaft, Geschichte*. 3 (2010), S. 98–101.
- Il Museo Gutenberg (Magonza/Germania). La casa dell'arte della stampa e sede di una straordinaria collezione di ex libris. In: *Inpressioni. Colloquia graphica et exlibristica*. 2 (2010), S. 29–32.
- Michelle Hothum (ehemals Beberashvili). In: *Mitteilungen der Deutschen Exlibris-Gesellschaft*. 3 (2010), S. 75.
- Zu gut, um vergessen zu werden: Hans Schmandt (1920–1993). In: *Mitteilungen der Deutschen Exlibris-Gesellschaft*. 3 (2010), S. 65/6.
- Armani im Gutenberg-Museum. Auftakt einer neuen Präsentationsreihe: Das Gutenberg-Museum zeigt monatlich Highlights seiner bedeutenden Sammlung. In: *Mitteilungen der Deutschen Exlibris-Gesellschaft*. 3 (2010), S. 67.

ANNETTE LANG-EDWARDS
Kluge Konservierung für Mainzer Inkunabeln (Beschreibung des »Boxing-Projektes« der vorangegangenen Jahre auf der Website des Produzenten Klug-Conservation mit Fotos). www.klug-conservation.com.

Dr. MARTIN WELKE, Stiftung Deutsches Zeitungsmuseum im Gutenberg-Museum
Die Zeitung – eine elsässische Erfindung. In: *Annuaire de la Société d'Histoire du Val et de la Ville de Munster*. LXIV (2010), S. 57–86.

Jurys, Vorträge und Seminare
Dr. ANNETTE LUDWIG
WS 2010/11 Übung und Jurytätigkeit: »On type. Texte zur Typografie«, Fachhochschule Mainz, Kommunikationsdesign (mit Prof. Dr. Isabel Nägele und Prof. Dr. Petra Eisele).
22.11. Kuratoriumssitzung Gutenberg-Preis Leipzig.

Dr. CLAUS MAYWALD
6.5. Kommunikation im 15. Jahrhundert. Gutenberg und seine Zeitgenossen. Vortrag im Rahmen des Symposions »Von Gutenberg bis zur Globalisierung. Zukunft der Druckgestaltung in der Zeit der Digitalisierung« der Kroatisch-Deutschen Gesellschaft Split.

Dr. CORNELIA SCHNEIDER
SS 2010 Übung: »Der Holzschnitt als illustrative Druckgrafik in Inkunabeln«, Kunsthistorisches Seminar der Johannes Gutenberg-Universität.
20.10. Vortrag anlässlich der Eröffnung des Kongresses »Ultraschall 2010. Ultraschall in der digitalen Welt«, Mainz.

Dr. INGE DOMES
21.9. Lehrerfortbildung: Schüler lesen Zeitung.

Interne Aktivitäten
– Zweisprachige Neubeschriftung der Abteilung Buchdruck im 15. und 16. Jahrhundert.
– Acht englische und deutsche Informationsblätter.
– Umbau der ostasiatischen Abteilung.
– Neugestaltung Kinder-Kino.

Bibliothek, wissenschaftliche Bearbeitung und Konservierung
– Restaurierung von Inkunabeln, einer Chronik von 1745 und einiger grafischer Blätter.
– Konservatorische Arbeiten am Bestand der Graphischen Sammlung.
– Bibliothekarische Inventarisierung von 875 Bänden.
– Apparat zur Ausstellung *Philipp Hennevogl – Mainzer Stadtdrucker 2010/11* sowie Dokumentation mit Literatur zu allen Mainzer Stadtdruckern bis 2010, zu Druckgrafik und Linolschnitt.
– Bibliothekarische Erschließung des Werkarchivs von Otto Rohse.
– Vorakzession, formale und sachliche Erschließung von Nachlässen, u. a. Nachlass Dr. Helmut und Helga Häuser, Nachlass Philipp Bertheau, Nachlass Gunter Böhmer.
– Es wurden ca. 900 Exlibris neu katalogisiert und eingescannt. Die endgültige Ordnung der alten Exlibris (16. Jh. bis 1850) und die Vorordnung der Neuzugänge wurde fortgeführt. Es konnten 85 Anfragen zur Exlibris-Sammlung beantwortet werden.

Sonstiges
Der antiquarische Büchermarkt zur Mainzer Johannisnacht umfasste über 50 Aussteller.
Der monatliche Antiquariatsmarkt vor dem Hof des Gutenberg-Museums freute sich über ein stabiles Aussteller- und Publikumsinteresse. 2010 erfolgten Vorarbeiten für den V. O. Stomps-Preis, Webauftritt unter www.stomps-preis.de.

Schenkungen und Stiftungen (Auswahl)
– Faksimile Cooper-Square-Gutenberg-Bibel von Michael Chrisman (New York).
– Bücher und Werke von Gunter Böhmer.
– Bucheinband-Mustersammlung von Heinz Petersen an das Deutsche Buchbinder-Museum im Gutenberg-Museum.
– Zwei Lithografien und Publikationen von Mario Derra.
– Kupferstich Otto Rohse: »Schloss Waldthausen« von Anton Issel (Mainz).

- 166 Exlibris, vor allem durch Schenkungen von Erhard Beitz (Oranienburg), Mario De Filippis (Arezzo/I), Dr. Uwe Eckardt (Wuppertal), Weronika Podstawka (Lublin/P), Reglinde Lattermann (Hamburg) und Hofrat Karl F. Stock (Graz/A).
- Bibliothek des Typografen Philipp Bertheau.
- *A Catalogue of Books Printed in the Fifteenth Century Now in the Bodleian Library.* Hrsg. von ALAN COATES. 6 Bde. Corby 2005.

Besondere Erwerbungen
Die Internationale Gutenberg-Gesellschaft förderte u. a. den Ankauf mehrerer Künstlerbücher (z. B. *Lehnwörter [für ein Leben aus Eigensinn]* mit fünf Federzeichnungen und einer Gouache von Friedrich Danielis), eines Spruchkartenspiels sowie wichtiger Publikationen für die Bibliothek, darunter das seltene Werk *Klimschs Druckereianzeiger* (1927–43) und Carl Theodor Löwstädt: *Porte-feuille för historiska a teckningar* (ca. 1827).

Der Förderverein Gutenberg e. V. finanzierte u. a. den Ankauf des Holzschnittzyklus *Peter Schöffer und die Entwicklung der beweglichen Lettern* von Mario Derra (Kassette mit 22 Einzelblättern) sowie den Erwerb der Arbeit *An Angel told me. Hommage à Ian Hamilton Finlay* (2004/05) von Felix M. Furtwängler.

Die Stiftung Moses besorgte die Renovierung des Gästezimmers des Gutenberg-Museums und stellte großzügig Mittel zur Neumöblierung bereit.

Der Internationalen Gutenberg-Gesellschaft, dem Förderverein und der Stiftung Moses sei herzlich für die Unterstützung der Sonderausstellungen gedankt. Darüber hinaus danken wir allen Förderern und Stiftern, auch den hier nicht genannten, herzlich für die Unterstützung des Museums.

Besondere Gäste im Gutenberg-Museum
- 18. 5.–29. 5. Bill Moran, Gründer von Blinc Publishing, St. Paul, MN/USA.
- 29. 5. Rainer Brüderle, Bundesminister für Wirtschaft und Technologie, mit Amtskollegen aus der Schweiz und Österreich.
- 9. 7. Swiss Graphic Designer.
- 23. 7. Mainzer Musiksommer.
- 1. 10. Ministerpräsident Kurt Beck anlässlich der Ausstellungseröffnung *Balanziergang ... durch die Stadt* im Druckladen des Gutenberg-Museums.
- 13. 10. Arbeitskreis »Innere Sicherheit« der Ständigen Konferenz der Innenminister und -senatoren der Länder.
- 22. 10. Prof. Dr. Jean-Christophe Ammann und das kunstpädagogische Seminar der Johann Wolfgang Goethe-Universität Frankfurt a. M.
- 28. 10. AG »Internationale Polizeimissionen«.

Personalangelegenheiten
Ihre Arbeit im Gutenberg-Museum nahmen auf:
- 1. 4. Jael Dörfer MA (wiss. Volontärin).
- 15. 5. Dr. Annette Ludwig (Direktorin).
- 6. 9. Dr. Astrid Blome (Kuratorin Zeitungssammlung und Allgemeine Museumsangelegenheiten).
- 1. 10. Dana Wipfler (Bibliothekarin).

In der zweiten Jahreshälfte konnten Werkverträge für den Aufbau von Adressverteilern (Dr. Juliane Schwoch) und für die Pflege des Hausarchivs (Wolfgang Steen) abgeschlossen werden.

Ausgeschieden sind:
- 31. 3. Dr. Eva-Maria Hanebutt-Benz (Direktorin).
- 30. 6. Christian Richter (Bibliothekar).
- 15. 8. Natasa Babic (Verwaltung).
- 30. 11. Zeynep Yildiz (Bibliothek).

Zahlreiche Praktikantinnen und Praktikanten konnten in mehrwöchiger Mitarbeit Berufserfahrung sammeln: zwei im Museum, zwei in der Gutenberg-Bibliothek, 17 im Druckladen. Im Gutenberg-Shop waren 32 ehrenamtliche Mitarbeiterinnen und Mitarbeiter tätig; im Druckladen arbeiteten 31 Mitarbeiterinnen und Mitarbeiter auf ehrenamtlicher Basis.

Herzlichen Dank für die produktive Zusammenarbeit und die tatkräftige Unterstützung!

Dr. Eva-Maria Hanebutt-Benz
Dr. Annette Ludwig

JAHRESBERICHT DES INSTITUTS FÜR BUCHWISSENSCHAFT DER JOHANNES GUTENBERG-UNIVERSITÄT MAINZ

Das Jahr 2010 stellte das Mainzer Institut für Buchwissenschaft in der Lehre und in der Forschung vor besondere Herausforderungen: Nach 104 Kommilitonen im Sommersemester schrieben sich zum Wintersemester 2010/11 sogar 254 Studierende für den Bachelor Buchwissenschaft ein. Es erforderte einen hohen logistischen Aufwand, eine ausreichende Zahl an Lehrveranstaltungen so kurzfristig zu organisieren. Die Universitätsleitung unterstützte dieses Vorhaben durch die Bereitstellung (im Rahmen des Hochschulpaktes) von einer Lehrkraft für besondere Aufgaben und einer Juniorprofessur. Die Juniorprofessur wurde inzwischen ausgeschrieben und wird zum Sommersemester 2011 besetzt werden können. Parallel dazu hat das Institut einen Numerus clausus beantragt, der ab dem Sommersemester 2011 ebenfalls greift.

Da im Sommersemester 2011 die ersten Bachelor-Studierenden ihr Examen ablegen, wird zum Wintersemester 2011/12 der Masterstudiengang »Buchwissenschaft« aufgenommen werden.

Als Lehrbeauftragte wirkten im vergangenen Jahr u. a. mit: die Doktorandinnen Elke Flatau, Jasmin Marschall und Sandra Oster, Maria Scholz (Govi), Mario Früh (Büchergilde Gutenberg), Dr. Christoph Kochhan (Börsenverein), Dominique Pleimling (Eichborn), Hon.-Prof. W. Robert Müller, Dr. David Oels (Humboldt-Universität Berlin), Wolfgang Schneider, Dr. Rainer Weiss (weissbooks.w).

Neu eingestellt wurden die Doktorandin Christina Schmitz und Ines Kolbe (Deutsche Nationalbibliothek Frankfurt). Die Lehre wurde ferner bereichert durch Prof. Dr. Elmar Mittler, der 2010/11 als Fellow des Gutenberg-Forschungskollegs die Arbeit der Mainzer Buchwissenschaft aktiv unterstützt.

Aber auch die Forschungsaktivitäten verstärkten sich nachdrücklich: Dr. Stephan Pelgen erhielt ein zweijähriges Forschungsstipendium der DFG (s. u.), Dr. Axel Kuhn wurde in der Förderlinie 1 der Universität Mainz und vom Forschungsschwerpunkt Medienkonvergenz unterstützt (s. u.). Als Sprecher des Forschungsschwerpunkts Medienkonvergenz erstellte Prof. Füssel einen Antrag zum Thema *Media Convergence* im Rahmen der Exzellenzinitiative des Bundes und der Länder, an dem 34 Professorinnen und Professoren der Universität Mainz beteiligt sind und die eine Brücke zwischen Geistes- und Sozialwissenschaft unter Einschluss von Medienrecht, Medienökonomie und Neurolinguistik schlägt.

Als Beauftragter des Präsidenten der Universität für die Errichtung des »Mainz Media Labs«, einem 14-geschossigen Medienhaus auf dem Campus mit 6-stöckigem Studiogebäude, das bei einer Pressekonferenz im Mai 2010 von der Ministerin Doris Ahnen vorgestellt wurde, stellte Herr Füssel einen ergänzenden Antrag auf Errichtung eines Forschungsbaus an den Wissenschaftsrat.

Der Forschungsschwerpunkt stellte einen Antrag auf unterstützende Fellows an das Gutenberg-Forschungskolleg der Universität. Auf Empfehlung von Prof. Bläsi wurde Dr. Axel Ngonga Ngomo von der Leipzig School of Media, auf Empfehlung von Prof. Füssel Prof. Dr. Elmar Mittler (Göttingen) für jeweils ein Jahr zur Unterstützung des Forschungsschwerpunktes aufgenommen. Beide Fellows haben sich mit einem Vortrag bei der Tagung »Medienkonvergenz – transdisziplinär« am 9. November 2010 vorgestellt.

Die klassischen Arbeitsbereiche des Instituts

werden darüber nicht vernachlässigt, im Gegenteil: die weitere Erarbeitung und Erschließung des Mainzer Verlagsarchivs macht erhebliche Fortschritte. Besonders das Schenker-Ehepaar Dr. Sabine und Kurt Groenewold haben sich durch die Bereitstellung weiterer, wichtiger Archivalien im Herbst 2011 erneut beteiligt. Beide nahmen im Sommersemester 2010 am Hauptseminar »Rotbuch-Verlag« von Prof. Füssel und Herr Groenewold mit einem Beitrag über »1968 und die Folgen für den Verlagsmarkt« im Rahmen von Herrn Füssels Vorlesung »Der Buchmarkt in der Bundesrepublik Deutschland« aktiv teil. Darüber hinaus stehen sie Studierenden für Auskünfte zur weiteren Erschließung der Materialien immer wieder gerne zur Verfügung.

XVI. Mainzer Kolloquium
Dem Erschließen der Verlagsarchivalien war auch das XVI. Mainzer Kolloquium mit dem Titel »›Ungeöffnete Königsgräber‹. Chancen und Nutzen von Verlagsarchiven für die Branche, die Wissenschaft und die Öffentlichkeit« am 28. Januar 2011 unter Leitung von Prof. Dr. Stephan Füssel gewidmet. Es referierten:
- RA Kurt Groenewold, Verleger: Verlagsarchive und Zeitgeschichtsforschung nach 1968.
- PD Dr. Gabriele Dietze, Amerikanistin und Lektorin: Doppelblind. Die Arbeit an der Literatur zwischen Lektorat und Wissenschaft.
- Dr. Michael Knoche, Bibliotheksdirektor HAAB: Die Bedeutung von Verlagsarchiven für die Wissenschaftsgeschichte. Beispiel Springer.
- Dr. Jan Bürger, Leiter des S. Unseld Archivs im Deutschen Literaturarchiv Marbach: Verlagsarchive und Autorennachlässe – eine kreative Symbiose.
- Dr. Christoph Links, Verleger: Die Bedeutung von Verlagsarchiven für die Kulturgeschichtsschreibung. Beispiel DDR-Verlage.
- Prof. Dr. Siegfried Lokatis, Buchwissenschaftler: Das Verlagsarchiv als buchwissenschaftliches Forschungslabor am Beispiel Reclam Leipzig und »Buchverlag der Morgen«.
- Hermann Staub, Leiter des Archivs und der Bibliothek des Börsenvereins in der DNB: Verlagsarchive und Branchenarchiv – ein Problemaufriss.
- Dr. Helen Müller, Leitung Corporate History, Bertelsmann: Der Beitrag der Verlagsarchive für die Unternehmenskommunikation.

Dissertationen
- Brünle, Elke Bibliotheken von Arbeiterbildungsvereinen im Königreich Württemberg 1848–1918. Wiesbaden 2010 (*Mainzer Studien zur Buchwissenschaft*. 20).
- Lange, Jasmin Der deutsche Buchhandel und der Siegeszug der Kinematographie 1895–1933. Wiesbaden 2010 (*Mainzer Studien zur Buchwissenschaft*. 21).
Betreuer jeweils Univ.-Prof. Dr. Stephan Füssel

Magisterarbeiten in Auswahl
- Dauber, Andrea Digitale Piraterie in der Buchbranche – moderne Urheberrechtsproblematik und Lösungsansätze.
- Wankerl, Katharina Die Wahrnehmung und Relevanz von belletristischen Imprints als Medienmarken. Eine empirische Analyse der Erfolgsfaktoren.
Betreuer jeweils Univ.-Prof. Dr. Christoph Bläsi

- Buch, Julia Die Bücher des Abtes Johannes Trithemius. Die Sponheimer Bibliothek im Spiegel des rheinischen Klosterhumanismus.
- Bußmann, Carla Deutschsprachige Erfolgsautoren – ein aktueller Trend auf dem Buchmarkt? Eine Analyse der belletristischen Bestsellerlisten der Jahre 1987–2008.
- Engelhardt, Ilka Marketing in Kalenderverlagen.
- Pflüger, Felizia Herausforderung E-Book – Aktuelle Strategien im Preismanagement von Fachverlagen.
- Rave, Barbara Mainzer Kalender in der Franzosenzeit.
- Ries, Regine Die wirtschaftliche Situation des Sortimentsbuchhandels im Nationalsozialismus.
- Schedy, Stefanie Im Wettbewerb mit den Branchenriesen – Konzepte und Strategien für das unabhängige Sortiment.
- Tavares, Filipe Der Buchhandel und der »Siegeszug« des Fernsehens in der Bundesrepublik Deutschland (1953–63). Reaktionen und Strategien im medialen Wettbewerb.
- Wesenberg, Katrin Die ausgegrabenen Bücher.

Carl Maria Seyppels *Ägyptische Trilogie* unter Berücksichtigung der Editionsgeschichte.
– Wielan, Stephanie Die Espresso Book Machine – Dezentrales Drucken als Chance für das Printmedium Buch.
Betreuer jeweils Univ.-Prof. Dr. Ernst Fischer

– Bottlinger, Andrea Der Fantasy-Boom im deutschen Buchmarkt.
– Duster, Monika Werbung *im* Buch.
– Riedl, Claudia Der Literaturpreis Ruhr – Ein Steuerinstrument des regionalen Marktes?
– Sawatzki, Wibke Bookcrossing.
Betreuer jeweils Univ.-Prof. Dr. Stephan Füssel

– Brack, Karola Zwischen Lokalpatriotismus und Weltruhm – Heinrich Hoffmann und Friedrich Stoltze im Gedächtnis ihrer Heimatstadt Frankfurt am Main.
– Dahmke, Julika Der Briefwechsel Eugen Diederichs' mit seinen Buchgestaltern um 1900.
– Hammann, Julia Einen Mausklick vom Kunden entfernt – Status Quo und Perspektiven von Download-Portalen auf dem deutschen Hörbuchmarkt.
– Jarr, Anneke Hype-Kommunikation im Buchhandel am Beispiel aktueller Bestseller.
– Jensen, Linn Alternative buchhändlerische Zusammenschlüsse bis zur Reorganisation des Börsenvereins der deutschen Buchhändler 1928.
– König, Sarah E-Commerce im Antiquariatsbuchhandel – Analyse aktueller Tendenzen.
– Krysciak, Silvia Konsens und Kontroversen – Karl Gutzkows Autor-Verleger-Beziehungen im Vergleich.
– Masky, Petra Camões, Pessoa, Saramago – und mehr? Portugiesische Literatur auf dem deutschsprachigen Buchmarkt seit 1997 bis heute.
– Neunzerling, Lisa Die Auswirkungen der Italiensehnsucht auf den deutschen Buchmarkt der 1950er Jahre.
– Seymer, Franziska Literatur-Communities im Web – Eine Untersuchung aus verlagsstrategischer Sicht.
– Wolf, Katja Wie werden kulturelle Strömungen von Verlagen umgesetzt? Eine Analyse des italienischen Programms bei Klaus Wagenbach.
Betreuerin jeweils Prof. Dr. Ute Schneider

Besondere Aktivitäten der Institutsmitglieder

Univ.-Prof. Dr. CHRISTOPH BLÄSI
Vorträge / Tagungen
– 6. 5. »Medienautomation« – ein neues Forschungsthema in Mainz. Vortrag im Rahmen des Leipziger Semantic Web Tags 2010, Leipzig.
– 19. 5. Aktuelle mediale Entwicklungen und ihre Relevanz für Fachverlage. Vortrag im Rahmen des Kongresses Deutsche Fachpresse 2010, Wiesbaden.
– 25./26. 8. Who is in charge to finance and approve learning material in Germany? Vortrag im Rahmen des International Symposium on Schoolbooks, Ljubljana (SLO).
– 15. 9. Für mehr Produktivität und Innovationskraft in Verlagen – Der Einsatz von Smartphones bei der Leistungserstellung. Vortrag bei der Akademie des Deutschen Buchhandels, München.
– 27. 9. Chancen für das Unerwartete: Bringt die überbordende Digitalisierung der Kommunikation Verlagen und Bibliotheken wichtige Aufgaben zurück? Vortrag bei der AG med. Bibliothekswesen, Mainz.
– 6. 10. eReader – Herausforderung Design. Moderation im Forum Herstellung der Frankfurter Buchmesse 2010, Frankfurt.
– 14. 10. Der deutsche Buchmarkt auf dem Weg in die Digitalisierung? Vortrag im Rahmen eines vom Goethe Institut organisierten Besuchs einer chinesischen Verlegerdelegation, Mainz.
– 4. 11. Buch 2020. Nutzungsverhalten der Leser im sich wandelnden Markt – prognostische Überlegungen. Vortrag beim Landesverband BV Berlin-Brandenburg, Berlin.
– 6. 11. Workshop zur Bedeutung des Familienbesitzes für die Reaktionen von Verlagsunternehmen gegenüber disruptiven Innovationen, Mainz.
– 15. 11. An 'inverted' case study: What can you do with smartphone applications in a publishing house? Vortrag an der City University London, London (UK).

Interviews
– 13. 1. Wikipedia / Enzyklopädien. BR.
– 21. 9. Professorenweiterbildung an der JGU. Deutschlandradio Kultur.

– 30. 9.: Buchmesse / Zukunft des Buches / E-Book. ZDF.
– 8. 10.: Zukunft des Buches / E-Book. Radio DRS (CH).

Sonstiges / Persönliches
Gutachtertätigkeit für den High-Tech Gründerfond, Bonn im Zusammenhang mit einer Investitionsentscheidung in ein Buchtechnologie-Start-up-Unternehmen.

Gutachter für die EU-Kommission beim *Call for Proposal* im Programm ICT PSP (information and Communication Technologies / Policy Support Program), Thema 2 "Digital Libraries" in Luxemburg (L).

Jury-Mitglied bei den von der Frankfurter Buchmesse, IARTEM (International Association for Research on Textbooks and Educational Media) und EEPG (European Educational Publishers' Group) vergebenen *Best European Schoolbook Awards* vom 16. bis 20. August in Rønde (DK).

Einrichtung der Doktorandengruppe »Lesen im Kontext digitaler und Printmedien« mit Prof. Dr. Stefan Aufenanger und Prof. Dr. Gregor Daschmann, FB 02.

Christoph Bläsi hat für das Projekt »Kulturzeitschriften – Medien zwischen Buch und Zeitschrift« (zur Vorbereitung eines mittlerweile gestellten DFG-Antrages von Dr. Axel Kuhn; bearbeitet mit diesem 2010) Mittel von der inneruniversitären Forschungsförderung der Förderstufe I sowie für das Projekt »BLS / Book and Library Statistics [Arbeitstitel]« (zur Vorbereitung der Beantragung eines umfangreicheren Projektes zum Thema wahrscheinlich bei der DFG, ebenfalls bearbeitet mit Dr. Axel Kuhn 2010/11) Mittel des FSP Medienkonvergenz bewilligt bekommen.

Christoph Bläsi nahm mit Dr. Axel Kuhn und drei seiner Doktorandinnen am 10./11. 6. am vom Hochschulverband Informationswissenschaft veranstalteten Doktorandentreffen der Informationswissenschaft (institutions- und fächerübergreifendes Doktorandenseminar) in Berlin teil.

Dr. ALBERT ERNST, Dipl.-Des. / Lehrdruckerei
In Kooperation mit dem Fachbereich Gestaltung der FH Mainz, dem Fach Medienmanagement der Universität und der Ströer Deutsche Städte Medien GmbH fand eine Lehrveranstaltung statt, die die Planung und Realisation einer Plakatkampagne zur »Stadt der Wissenschaft 2011« zum Inhalt hatte. Aus der Reihe der Buchwissenschaftler gehörten Hanne Mandik und Matea Prgomet zu der Gruppe, deren Plakatentwurf ausgezeichnet wurde.

Rege Teilnahme von Kommilitonen bei der Präsentation der Buchwissenschaft auf dem Wissenschaftsmarkt im September 2010; »rund ums Buch« wurden in Kooperation fast aller Kolleginnen und Kollegen mehrere Stationen eingerichtet, an denen Besucher die verschiedenen Erscheinungsformen des Mediums »Buch« erleben konnten; das »Marktblatt« erschien mit Zeitungsköpfen in acht verschiedenen Sprachen (mit Unterstützung des Fachbereichs Translations-, Sprach- und Kulturwissenschaft in Germersheim).

Exkursion ins Klingspor-Museum, Offenbach.

Die guten Kontakte zum Druckladen des Gutenberg-Museums führten dazu, dass Studierende aus dem Bachelor-Studiengang dort Praktika aufnehmen konnten.

Eigene Ausstellungsbeteiligung, Wiesbaden: »Der Blaue Salon trifft seine Künstlerinnen und Künstler«.

Univ.-Prof. Dr. ERNST FISCHER
Publikationen
– Buchmarkt. In: *Europäische Geschichte Online* (EGO). Hrsg. vom Institut für Europäische Geschichte (IEG). Mainz 3.12.2010. www.ieg-ego.eu/fischere-2010-de
– Übersetzungen auf dem Markt: Institutionen und Steuerungsfaktoren. In: *Streifzüge im translatorischen Feld. Zur Soziologie der literarischen Übersetzung im deutschsprachigen Raum.* Hrsg. von NORBERT BACHLEITNER und MICHAELA WOLF. Münster 2010, S. 33–64.
– Buchwissenschaft im 21. Jahrhundert. Probleme und Perspektiven. In: *Neues vom Buch.* Hrsg. von DORIS MOSER, ARNO RUSSEGGER und CONSTANZE DRUMM. Innsbruck 2010, S. 26–38.

Vorträge / Tagungen
- 12. 5. Book Economy in Transition: The German Publishing Industry and its Current Challenges. Vortrag, gehalten auf der "Book Business Conference 2010" im Rahmen der Internationalen Buchmesse Seoul, Südkorea.
- 16. 7. Schriftsteller als Hüter der Meinungsfreiheit. Zensurdiskurse in der Bundesrepublik Deutschland und in Österreich. Vortrag im Rahmen der Tagung »Kunstfreiheit und Zensur in der Bundesrepublik (1949–2009)«, Deutsches Literaturarchiv Marbach a. N.

Persönliches
Ernennung zum ordentlichen Mitglied der Historischen Kommission des Börsenvereins des Deutschen Buchhandels.

Univ.-Prof. Dr. STEPHAN FÜSSEL
Publikationen
- (Hrsg.) *Giambattista Bodoni: Handbuch der Typografie.* Parma 1818. Vollständiger Reprint mit Kommentar. Köln u. a. 2010 (parallele Ausgaben in englischer, spanischer, italienischer und französischer Sprache). Darin: Schriftgeschichtliche Einführung, S. 5–33.
- Die Bertelsmann Buchverlage 1945–2010. In: *175 Jahre Bertelsmann. Eine Zukunftsgeschichte.* Gütersloh 2010, S. 86–130.
- (Hrsg.) GJ 2010.
- (Mithrsg.) LGB². Bd. 8, Lieferung 59 (Voß – Werkform) [Ende der Mitherausgeberschaft].

Vorträge / Tagungen
- 15. 1. Die Welt im Buch. Kartografie der frühen Neuzeit. Vortrag im Rahmen des Festkolloquiums zum 80. Geburtstag von Prof. Dr. Dieter Wuttke, Universität Bamberg.
- 29. 4. Das Mainzer Verlagsarchiv. Vortrag im Rahmen des »Jour fixe der Freunde Gutenbergs«, Gutenberg Museum Mainz.
- 17. 9. 175 Jahre Bertelsmann. Vorstellung der Festschrift. Berlin, Konzerthaus, Gendarmenmarkt.
- 6. 11. Willibald Pirckheimer und der europäische Humanismus. Vortrag vor dem Verein der Bibliophilen, Pirckheimer, Magdeburg.
- 9. 11. Eröffnungsvortrag zur Tagung »Medienkonvergenz transdisziplinär«. Vorstellung der fünf Fellows des Gutenberg-Forschungskollegs am Forschungsschwerpunkt Medienkonvergenz der Johannes Gutenberg-Universität Mainz, Mainz.
- 12. / 13. 11. Naturwissenschaft und Humanismus um 1500. Sektionsleitung der Tagung der Willibald Pirckheimer-Gesellschaft für Renaissance- und Humanismusforschung, Nürnberg.
- 18. 11. Giambattista Bodoni. König der Drucker – Drucker der Könige. Buchvorstellung des Reprints des *Manuale Tipografico* (1818), Gutenberg Museum Mainz.
- 2. 12. Die Zukunft der Medien. Perspektiven und Erwartungen. Vortrag an der Georg August Universität Göttingen.
- 13. 12. Die Herausforderung der Medienkonvergenz und die Antwort der Johannes Gutenberg-Universität. Vortrag am Tag der Technologie und der Forschung des Landes Rheinland-Pfalz, FH Mainz.

Persönliches
Sprecher des Forschungsschwerpunktes Medienkonvergenz der Johannes Gutenberg-Universität Mainz.

Antragsteller *Cluster Media Convergence* im Rahmen der Exzellenzinitiative des Bundes und der Länder.

Beauftragter der Universität Mainz für den Bau des »Medienhauses Campus«.

Senator der Johannes Gutenberg-Universität, wiedergewählt 2011–14.

Mitglied des Fachbereichsrates des Fachbereichs 05, Philosophie und Philologie, wiedergewählt 2011–14.

Mitglied der Enquête-Kommission des rheinland-pfälzischen Landtags »Verantwortung in der medialen Welt« 2010/11.

Vizepräsident der Willibald Pirckheimer-Gesellschaft zur Erforschung von Renaissance und Humanismus e. V. Nürnberg (wiedergewählt 2010–13).

Dr. AXEL KUHN

Publikationen

– Der virtuelle Sozialraum digitaler Spielewelten am Beispiel von World of Warcraft. Struktur und Auswirkungen auf das Spielerleben. In: *Clash of Realities 2010. Computerspiele: Medien und mehr…* Hrsg. von WINFRIED KAMINSKI und MARTIN LORBER. München 2010, S. 129–46.
– (zus. mit ELKE GREIFENEDER und SANDRA RÜHR) Aufbau und Entwicklung einer digitalen Buchgeschichte. Zielgruppenanalyse und Anforderungen (*Alles Buch. Studien der Erlanger Buchwissenschaft*. XXXIV). Erlangen 2010, S. 45–59.
– Einfluss sozialer Interaktion auf Flow-Erleben in virtuellen Wirklichkeiten. In: *Medien Journal, Zeitschrift für Kommunikationskultur. Vierteljahreszeitschrift der Österreichischen Gesellschaft für Kommunikationswissenschaft*. 2 (2010).
– (zus. mit SANDRA RÜHR) Stand der Lese- und Leserforschung. Eine kritische Analyse. In: *Buchwissenschaft in Deutschland. Ein Handbuch*. Hrsg. von URSULA RAUTENBERG. Berlin 2010, S. 585–654.

Vorträge / Tagungen

– 7. / 8. 1. Hörbuch-Download auf mobile Hightech-Geräte. Analyse im Rahmen des Erlanger Vier-Kanal-Modells zur Betrachtung von elektronischen Handelsformen. Vortrag im Rahmen der Tagung »Verliert das Hörbuch seinen Körper? Die Auswirkungen des Downloads auf Bibliotheken, Buchbranche und Nutzer« der Buchwissenschaft an der FAU Erlangen-Nürnberg.
– 21.–23. 4. Der virtuelle Sozialraum digitaler Spielwelten am Beispiel von World of Warcraft: Struktur und Auswirkungen auf das Spielerleben. Vortrag im Rahmen der Tagung "3rd International Computer Game Conference Cologne 'Clash of Realities'".

Sonstige Aktivitäten

Antragstellung DFG »Bedeutung und Veränderung des Mediensystems Kulturzeitschrift in Deutschland nach 1945«.

(Zus. mit Anke Vogel) Vereinbarung einer Kooperation mit dem Börsenverein des Deutschen Buchhandels zur Durchführung einer Studie »Electronic Commerce im Bucheinzelhandel«.

CORINNA NORRICK MA

Publikationen

– Young Adult Fiction in 1980s (West) Germany: The Paperback Series "Rororo Panther" (Rowohlt)
– "Problem-oriented Novels" for Young Adult Readers. In: *The International Journal of the Book*. 2 (2010), S. 23–30.

Redaktion

GJ 2010

Vorträge / Tagungen

– 18. 8. rororo rotfuchs – A Children's Paperback Series with Literature "from below", Published "from above". Vortrag im Rahmen der Konferenz "Book Culture from Below – SHARP 2010" in Helsinki / FIN.
– 7. 11. "Reader, I married him". 19th Century Reading Practices, Reading, and Readers in Charlotte Brontë's *Jane Eyre*. Vortrag im Rahmen der "8th International Conference on the Book" in St. Gallen / CH.

Exkursionen

– 26. 1. Organisation und Durchführung einer eintägigen Exkursion zur Müller Martini GmbH (Bad Mergentheim).
– 8. 7. Organisation und Durchführung einer Exkursion ins Deutsche Zeitungsmuseum (Wadgassen / Saar) mit dem Fachschaftsrat Buchwissenschaft.

Persönliches

Ausgezeichnet mit dem "Graduate Scholar Award" der "8th International Conference on the Book", St. Gallen / CH, 6.–8. 11. 2010.

Aufnahme als Junior Fellow in die Gutenberg-Akademie (Auswahl der besten Doktoranden der Universität Mainz).

Hochschuldidaktische Weiterbildungen zu den Themen »Lehren & Lernen in Theorie und Praxis«, »Grundlagen des Präsentierens in Theorie und Praxis«, »Gruppenarbeit in der Hochschullehre erfolgreich einsetzen« und »Studierende motivieren«.

BEATRIX OBAL MA

Im Rahmen einer Übung zur Geschichte des Kirchenliedes kam es zur Zusammenarbeit mit dem Interdisziplinären Arbeitskreis Gesangbuchforschung (JGU). In Vorträgen von Prof. Dr. Hermann Kurzke und Dr. Christiane Schäfer sowie einer Führung durch die eindrucksvolle Gesangbuch-Sammlung wurde den Teilnehmern die Vielfalt dieses Forschungsgebietes nahegebracht.

Mit der Bearbeitung der Reihen *sachbuch film* und *sachbuch sport* trugen die Teilnehmer der Archivkunde-Übungen 2010 weiter zur Erfassung des Rowohlt Verlagsarchivs bei. Zum Abschluss entstand jeweils auch eine kleine Ausstellung in den Räumen des Mainzer Verlagsarchivs.

Dr. STEPHAN PELGEN MA
Publikationen
– Aus der Geschichte der Gemeinde und Kirche Mariä Opferung in Sörgenloch. »In der hiesigen Gegend wirklich unter allen die schönste…«. Sörgenloch 2010.
– Ein Geheimdossier des Großhofmeisters Friedrich Graf von Stadion über den Zustand des Mainzer Domkapitels zu Jahresbeginn 1753. In: *Mainzer Zeitschrift*. 105 (2010), S. 169–78.
– Ein Neufund zu Burkhard Zamels und der Grabplatte für Christoph Rudolph von Stadion im Mainzer Dom. In: Ebd., S. 223–5.
– Neue Quellen zu Johann Adam Ignaz Hutter (1768–1794) sowie zur »Löhrischen Daktyliothek«. In: Ebd., S. 227–38.
– Wiederaufgefundenes Empfehlungsschreiben des Fürsten Kaunitz vom 13. Dezember 1790 für Joseph Haydns erste Reise nach London. In: *Haydn-Studien*. 10.1 (2010), S. 71–3.

Vorträge
– 1.3. *Der Spiegel* – Eine ganz besondere Mainzer Zeitschrift für Kunst und Literatur der Jahre 1823–1824. Vortrag vor dem Mainzer Altertumsverein, Mainz.
– 24.9. Johann Friedrich Schiller in Mainz. Eine bemerkenswerte Bücher-Biographie. Vortrag bei der VHS Mainz.
– 21.10. Briefwechsel Stephan Alexander Würdtweins. Vortrag beim Workshop »Digitale Briefeditionen«, Berlin.

Drittmittelprojekt
Pränumerationen und Briefwechsel als Prinzipien wissenschaftlichen Publizierens im 18. Jh. (am Beispiel von Stephan Alexander Würdtwein). DFG-Einzelförderung (seit August 2010).

Dr. Dipl.-Ing. CHRISTOPH RESKE
Publikationen
– Das VD 17 als Quelle für die Buchwissenschaft. In: Schmelze des barocken Eisbergs? Das VD 17. – Bilanz und Ausblick. Beiträge des Symposions in der Bayerischen Staatsbibliothek München am 27./28.10.2009. Hrsg. von CLAUDIA FABIAN. *Bibliothek und Wissenschaft*. 43 (2010), S. 121–38.
– Johannes Gutenberg. In: Mainz. Menschen – Bauten – Ereignisse. Eine Stadtgeschichte. Hrsg. von FRANZ DUMONT und FERDINAND SCHERF. Mainz 2010, S. 74–8.
– Lemmata: Hieronymus Andreae; Birckmann family; Christian Egenolff the Elder; Endter family; Homann family; Melchior Lotter the Elder; Hans Lufft; Carl Ernst Poeschel; Alois Senefelder. In: The Oxford Companion to the Book. Hrsg. von MICHAEL F. SUAREZ und H. R. WOUDHUYSEN. 2 Bde. Oxford [u. a.] 2010.

Vortrag
23.10. Die drucktechnischen Möglichkeiten zur Zeit Stefan Georges. Vortrag im Rahmen der Jahrestagung »Buchkunst und Buchkultur um 1900« der Stefan-George-Gesellschaft e. V. am 23./24.10.2010, Bingen.

Persönliches
Lehrpreis der Johannes Gutenberg-Universität Mainz 2010.

Prof. Dr. UTE SCHNEIDER
Publikationen
– (zus. mit Volker Remmert) *Eine Disziplin und ihre Verleger. Disziplinenkultur und Publikationswesen der Mathematik in Deutschland, 1871–1949*. Bielefeld 2010.
– Springer, Verleger. In: NDB, Bd. 24, S. 755–7.
– Lemmata: Albatross Verlag; Andere Bibliothek; Aufbau Verlag; Baedeker, Karl; Baer; Beck, C. H.; Bertelsmann; Braun + Schneider; Bremer Presse; Brockhaus, F. A.; Bronke, Wilhelm; Campe,

Julius; Cassirer, Paul and Bruno; Cornelsen; Cotta, Johann Friedrich; Cranach-Presse; de Gruyter; Deutsche Verlagsanstalt; Deutscher Taschenbuchverlag (dtv); Diederichs; F. Eher Nachf.; Fischer, S.; Fock; Göschen; Gutenberg-Jahrbuch; Gutenberg-Preis; Hanser; Harrassowitz; Haufe; Herder; Holtzbrinck; Hugenberg; Insel; Imprimatur; Klett; Langen; Langenscheidt; Lorck; Malik Verlag; Mathematical tables; Metzler; Meyer / Bibliogr. Institut; Müller, Georg; Nicolai, Friedrich; Oldenbourg; Perthes; Reclam; Reclams Universalbibliothek; Rowohlt, Ernst; Sammlung Göschen; Saur, K. G.; Schocken Books; Schott (Music); Scientific books and journals; Seven Seas Books; Springer; Suhrkamp, Peter; Taschen; Tauchnitz; Teubner; Thieme, Georg; Ullstein; Vandenhoeck; Volk und Welt; Weidmann and Reich; Wolff, Kurt. In: The Oxford Companion to the Book. Hrsg. von MICHAEL F. SUAREZ und H. R. WOUDHUYSEN. 2 Bde. Oxford [u. a.] 2010.
– Winter, C. Universitätsverlag. In: LGB². Lieferung 60 (2010), S. 292.
– Wissenschaftliches Verlagswesen. In: LGB². Lieferung 60 (2010), S. 299

Tagungen
29. 1. Planung und Durchführung des XV. Mainzer Kolloquiums: »Das Sachbuch – ein erfolgreiches Marktsegment«. Es diskutierten Wissenschaftler und Praktiker sowie ein Bestsellerautor über die aktuellen Tendenzen auf dem Sachbuchmarkt. Referenten: Dr. David Oels, Humboldt-Universität Berlin; Michael Schikowski, Köln; Dr. Stefan Klein, Berlin; Jens Dehning, Rowohlt Verlag Berlin; Sabine Cramer, Verlagsgruppe Lübbe.

ANKE VOGEL MA
Publikation
Verlags-PR. Social Web: Foren, Trailer und virtuelle Lesereise im Internet. In: *Bücher kommunizieren*. Hrsg. von RALF LAUMER. 2. überarb. und aktualisierte Aufl. Bremen 2010, S. 105–12.

Vorträge
– 14. April: Leitung einer Fortbildungsveranstaltung »Aktuelle Entwicklungen im Bereich der Kinder- und Jugendliteratur und ihre Auswirkungen auf die Literaturvermittlung« beim Deutschen Bibliotheksverband e. V., Landesverband Thüringen.
– 26. 4. Der Medienklassiker Buch in einer konvergierenden Medienumwelt. Vortrag im Rahmen der Vortragsreihe »›Revolution in der Medienwelt‹ – Neue Formen von Konvergenz und Crossmedia« des Fachschaftsrates Publizistik, Johannes Gutenberg-Universität Mainz.

Buchmessen
Am Gemeinschaftsstand »Studium rund ums Buch« haben die Teilnehmer der Übungen »Präsentation und Veranstaltungsmanagement Buchmesse« auch in diesem Jahr wieder das Institut bei den Buchmessen in Leipzig und Frankfurt vertreten. Unter anderem diskutierten Studierende mit Alumni des Instituts über Berufseinstieg und -perspektiven. Der passionierte Büchersammler Hans Eckert (UB Frankfurt) ließ sich von stud. phil. Florian Tukker zum Thema »Bibliophilie – ist das ansteckend?« interviewen. Außerdem stellte die Autorin Vanessa Fogel ihr bei weissbooks.w erschienenes Buch *Sag es mir* vor und sprach mit stud. phil. Andreas Fenz über dessen Entstehungsprozess.

Persönliches
Seit Juni 2010 Sprecherin des Nachwuchsforums der Internationalen Buchwissenschaftlichen Gesellschaft; in Zusammenarbeit mit Prof. Dr. Christine Haug (München) Organisation der Kick-Off-Veranstaltung des Forums am 27. 10., an der Nachwuchswissenschaftler von verschiedenen buchwissenschaftlichen und benachbarten Instituten teilnahmen.

Hochschuldidaktische Weiterbildungen zu den Themen »Lehren im interkulturellen Kontext« und »Heterogenität in der Lehre«.

Aktuelle Informationen zum Institut findet man stets unter:
www.buchwissenschaft.uni-mainz.de.

Stephan Füssel, Institutsleiter

FRANCISCO CORNEJO VEGA
12 http://expobus.us.es [29. 7. 2010]
50 Ejemplares consultados en línea
   [en caso no especificado, último acceso 15. 11. 2010]
   – 1 www.ub.uni-bielefeld.de/diglib
   – 2 http://inkunabeln.ub.uni-koeln.de
   – 3 http://inkunabeln.ub.uni-koeln.de
   – 4 http://inkunabeln.ub.uni-koeln.de
   – 5 http://daten.digitale-sammlungen.de
   – 6 http://mdz1.bib-bvb.de
   – 7 http://daten.digitale-sammlungen.de
   – 9 http://daten.digitale-sammlungen.de
   – 10 http://daten.digitale-sammlungen.de
   – 11 http://daten.digitale-sammlungen.de
   – 12 http://fondotesis.us.es
   – 13 http://daten.digitale-sammlungen.de
   – 14 http://daten.digitale-sammlungen.de
   – 15 http://daten.digitale-sammlungen.de
   – 16 http://gallica.bnf.fr
   – 17 http://daten.digitale-sammlungen.de
   – 18 http://www.juntadeandalucia.es
   – 19 http://daten.digitale-sammlungen.de
   – 20 http://daten.digitale-sammlungen.de
   – 21 http://daten.digitale-sammlungen.de
   – 23 http://daten.digitale-sammlungen.de
   – 24 http://daten.digitale-sammlungen.de
   – 25 http://www.mediatheque-agglo-troyes.fr
     [último acceso 25. 6. 2009]
   – 26 http://diglib.hab.de
   – 27 http://daten.digitale-sammlungen.de
   – 28 http://diglib.hab.de
   – 29 http://daten.digitale-sammlungen.de
   – 30 http://diglib.hab.de
   – 32 http://daten.digitale-sammlungen.de
   – 33 http://daten.digitale-sammlungen.de
   – 34 http://gallica.bnf.fr

KATHARINA EBENAU
 1 http://www.buecher.at/show_content.php?sid=122&
   detail_id=3431 [30. 1. 2011].
11 http://personaco.com/trailers [29. 1. 2011].
12 http://www.allbusiness.com/retail-trade/miscellaneous-
   retail-miscellaneous/4404531-1.html [29. 1. 2011].
14 http://www.suite101.com/content/circle-of-seven-book-
   videos-a35720 [30. 1. 2011].
15 http://www.cosproductions.com/pdf/BookTrailerRevo-
   lution_DigitalVideoMarketing.pdf [29. 1. 2011].
20 http://www.tellyawards.com/ [29. 1. 2011].
21 http://www.uncsa.edu/pressreleases/Releases2006/
   March2006/bookvideoawards.htm [29. 1. 2011].
28 http://www.vidlit.com/ [30. 1. 2011].
29 http://en.wikipedia.org/wiki/Book_video [zuletzt
   verändert am 23.10.2010, zuletzt geprüft am 30. 1. 2011].
34 http://www.spiegel.de/kultur/litera-
   tur/0,1518,584090,00.html [30. 1. 2011].
38 http://www.buchreport.de/nachrichten/in_eigener_
   sache/in_eigener_sache_nachricht/datum/2009/05/05/
   bestseller-im-bild.htm [30. 1. 2011].
20 http://www.lesungen.tv [30. 1. 2011].

FEDERICA FABBRI
 8 http://digilib.ub.uni-freiburg.de [2. 12. 2010]
 9 http://daten.digitale-sammlungen.de [2. 12. 2010]
11 http://aleph.onb.ac.at [2. 12. 2010]
16 http://thesaurus.cerl.org [2. 12. 2010]
17 http://thesaurus.cerl.org [2. 12. 2010]
18 http://134.76.163.162/fabian?Oesterreich [2. 12. 2010]
27 http://www.cbt.trentinocultura.net [2. 12. 2010]
28 http://www.esterbib.it [2. 12. 2010]
37 http://cataloghistorici.bdi.sbn.it [2. 12. 2010]

ANDRÁS NÉMETH
33 http://pinakes.irht.cnrs.fr [28. 12. 2010]
53 http://archive.thulb.uni-jena.de/hisbest/receive/
   HisBest_cbu_00006127 [28. 12. 2010]
88 http://www.corvina.oszk.hu/studies/corvo_it.pdf
   [28. 12. 2010]

FRIEDER SCHMIDT
 9 http://www.bam-portal.de [22. 12. 2010]
34 http://khipukamayuq.fas.harvard.edu [22. 12. 2010]
37 http://www.iceman.it [22. 12. 2010]

IMPRESSUM

Gutenberg-Jahrbuch 2011, 86. Jahrgang.
Im Harrassowitz Verlag, Wiesbaden.
ISSN 0072-9094
ISBN 978-3-447-06487-3

Die für den Buchhandel bestimmten Exemplare vertreibt der Harrassowitz Verlag, Wiesbaden.

Anschrift des Verlages
Harrassowitz Verlag
D 65174 Wiesbaden
Telefon (+49) 611.53 09 05
Telefax (+49) 611.53 09 99
verlag@harrassowitz.de
www.harrassowitz-verlag.de

Herausgeber Univ.-Prof. Dr. Stephan Füssel
Redaktion Corinna Norrick MA
Korrektorat (deutsche Texte)
Christiane Lawall
Anschrift des Herausgebers
Institut für Buchwissenschaft
Johannes Gutenberg-Universität
D 55099 Mainz
Telefon (+49) 61 31.3 92 25 80
Telefax (+49) 61 31.3 92 54 87
fuessel@uni-mainz.de

Internationale Gutenberg-Gesellschaft in Mainz e.V.
Liebfrauenplatz 5
D 55116 Mainz
Telefon (+49) 61 31.22 64 20
Telefax (+49) 61 31.23 35 30
info@gutenberg-gesellschaft.de

Das Gutenberg-Jahrbuch veröffentlicht Beiträge in deutscher, englischer, französischer, italienischer, spanischer und lateinischer Sprache.
Die Autorinnen und Autoren werden gebeten, ihre Manuskripte auf digitalen Datenträgern in druckreifer Form dem Herausgeber vorzulegen. Merkblätter über die Manuskriptgestaltung können angefordert werden. Der Einsendetermin für die Manuskripte ist jeweils der 30. September des Vorjahres.

Nachdruck und Wiedergabe, auch in elektronischen Medien (auch auszugsweise), sowie fotomechanische Reproduktion einzelner Beiträge nur mit ausdrücklicher Genehmigung durch die Gutenberg-Gesellschaft.

Typografische Konzeption, Layout
Prof. Ralf de Jong, Essen.
Textschrift LT Malabar (Linotype GmbH)
Lithos Reinhold Amann
Druck Memminger MedienCentrum AG, Memmingen
Bindearbeiten Real Lachenmaier, Reutlingen
Einbandmaterial Canoso von Kaliko
Textpapier geglättet holzfrei säurefrei bläulichweiß »Alster« 1,3fach, 110 g/qm
Vorsatzpapier matt holzfrei gerippt bläulichweiß Vorsatzpapier »Passat«, 120 g/qm; beide geliefert von Geese Papier GmbH und produziert von Salzer Papier GmbH

Wappen der Gutenberg-Gesellschaft auf dem Einband nach einem Entwurf von Jost Hochuli, St. Gallen.

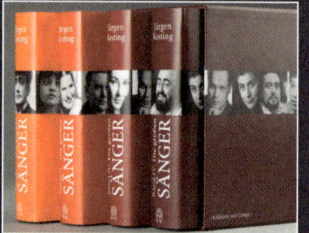

Wir verarbeiten Ihre Printmedien zu anspruchsvollen Vorzeigeprodukten.

Gerne entwickeln wir für Sie kreative, maßgeschneiderte Lösungen zur Umsetzung Ihrer Ideen.

Lachenmaier – der Qualitätsbuchbinder.

Unsere Spezialitäten:

- Formate, die aus dem Rahmen fallen
- Buchblockstärken bis 76 mm
- Bindung – mit bestem Aufschlagverhalten
- Schnittveredelung – Silber, Gold und Farbe
- Deckenfertigung – individuell und flexibel
- Prägen – vielfältig und präzise
- Leder und Dünndruckverarbeitung

Lachenmaier
Buch.kreativ

In Laisen 34 | 72766 Reutlingen | Tel. +49 (0) 71 21/14 96-0 | Fax +49 (0) 71 21/14 96-33

[www.lachenmaier.de]

Bücher für die Ewigkeit.

» Einer schnellen Zeit widersteht das Gedruckte wie ein Kleinod aus vergangener Zeit. Wir nehmen es aus dem Regal und sind mitten in der Zeit, in der wir seinen Deckel zum ersten Mal aufschlugen. «

Memminger MedienCentrum
Druckerei und Verlags-AG

Fraunhoferstraße 19   Tel. 0 83 31/92 77-0   info@mm-mediencentrum.de
87700 Memmingen   Fax 0 83 31/92 77-133   www.mm-mediencentrum.de

HEI SCHOOL

Wissen ist Fortschritt und wesentlich für Unternehmensentwicklung. Machen Sie sich und Ihre Mitarbeiter fit und gestalten Sie die Zukunft der Branche. Erweitern Sie Ihre Fähigkeiten und Kompetenzen mit Trainings, Seminaren und dem Knowhow unserer Print Media Academy. Bei uns lernen Profis von Profis.
www.heidelberg.com

HEIDELBERG

Akko &
Akko rounded
cozy and tender but definite

Thin
Thin Italic
Light
Light Italic
Regular
Italic

Medium
Medium Italic
Bold
Bold Italic
Black
Black Italic

Thin
Thin Italic
Light
Light Italic
Regular
Italic

Medium
Medium Italic
Bold
Bold Italic
Black
Black Italic

New

A new typeface *by Akira Kobayashi*

12 weights between Thin and **Black**

New *adjustable levels* of *spherical* abberations

THE PRINCIPLE OF BLURRING THE EDGES

The Source of the Originals
www.linotype.com

LinotYPE
by Monotype Imaging

Jill Bepler, Helga Meise (Hg.)
Sammeln, Lesen, Übersetzen als höfische Praxis der Frühen Neuzeit
Die böhmische Bibliothek der Fürsten Eggenberg im Kontext der Fürsten- und Fürstinnenbibliotheken der Zeit
Wolfenbütteler Forschungen 126
2010. 412 Seiten, 72 Abb., gb
ISBN 978-3-447-06399-9
€ 89,– (D) / sFr 150,–

Monika E. Müller (Hg.)
Schätze im Himmel – Bücher auf Erden
Mittelalterliche Handschriften aus Hildesheim
Ausstellungskataloge der Herzog August Bibliothek Wolfenbüttel 93
2010. 472 Seiten, 280 Abb., gb
ISBN 978-3-447-06381-4
€ 49,80 (D) / sFr 86,–

Im Jahre 1010 legte Bischof Bernward von Hildesheim den Grundstein für die Errichtung der Michaeliskirche, einer der bedeutendsten Kirchenbauten des Frühmittelalters. Das zugehörige Kloster stattete er reich mit Gütern und überaus wertvollen Büchern für Liturgie und Gebet aus. Einen Schatz im Himmel und das Seelenheil wollte er sich damit erwerben, wie auch viele andere Hildesheimer Bischöfe und Kanoniker nach ihm. Bernwards persönlichen Psalter konnte die Herzog August Bibliothek im Jahre 2007 erwerben. Dies und das tausendjährige Jubiläum der Hildesheimer Michaeliskirche geben den Anlass für die Ausstellung „Schätze im Himmel – Bücher auf Erden. Mittelalterliche Handschriften aus Hildesheim". Die Bandbreite der vorgestellten Handschriften aus der mittelalterlichen Dombibliothek St. Michael reicht von der Gründungsphase bis zur Blüte der Buchproduktion und zum Beitritt des Michaelisklosters zur Reformbewegung der Bursfelder Kongregation im 15. Jahrhundert. Es werden nicht nur alle bernwardinischen Prachthandschriften, sondern auch weitere Glanzpunkte wie die berühmten Schwesterhandschriften des Ratmann-Sakramentars und des Stammheimer Missale (um 1170) präsentiert.

Der reich bebilderte Ausstellungskatalog beschreibt ausführlich die Exponate. Die zahlreichen Essays behandeln wichtige Aspekte der mittelalterlichen Buchkultur und zentrale geistesgeschichtliche Entwicklungen wie das Bildungssystem der Klöster im Gegensatz zu Studium und Wissenschaft des Klerus an den berühmten Schulen Frankreichs. Erstmals überhaupt wird hier ein Überblick über die Geschichte der Bibliothek von St. Michael gegeben.

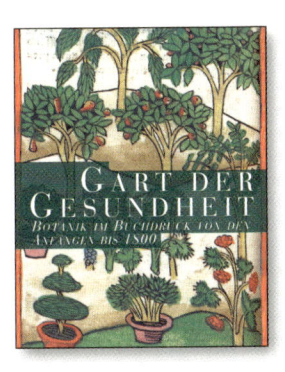

Irmgard Müller, Werner Dressendörfer (Hg.)
Gart der Gesundheit
Botanik im Buchdruck von den Anfängen bis 1800
Kataloge der Franckeschen Stiftungen 26
2011. 208 Seiten, 128 Abb., br
ISBN 978-3-447-06464-4
€ 19,– (D) / sFr 33,60

Kräuterbücher, Herbarien, Floren und andere botanische Werke des Mittelalters und der Frühen Neuzeit gewähren einen faszinierenden Einblick in die Geschichte der Naturwissenschaften. In der vom Museum Otto Schäfer in Zusammenarbeit mit dem Stadtarchiv Schweinfurt, den Franckeschen Stiftungen und der Bibliothek der Leopoldina – Nationale Akademie der Wissenschaften in Halle veranstalteten Ausstellung zum Thema werden anhand repräsentativer Ausschnitte aus den reichen Beständen der Leihgeber Werke der Botanik vom Mittelalter bis ins 18. Jahrhundert unter verschiedenen Aspekten vorgestellt. Dazu zählen der Wandel der Natur- und Pflanzenbetrachtung durch die zunehmende Einfuhr außereuropäischer Pflanzenarten, die Organisation des botanischen Wissens durch Forscher wie Carl von Linné, der Wandel in der Pharmazie und schließlich auch die Funktion von Pflanzen als Symbolträger. Der reich bebilderte Begleitkatalog enthält darüber hinaus Beiträge zur Geschichte der Pflanzendarstellungen und der Visualisierung botanischer Ordnungen. Die Bestände an botanischer Literatur in den Bibliotheken der vier Leihgeber werden sachkundig aufbereitet.

Christine Haug, Vincent Kaufmann (Hg.)
Kodex.
Jahrbuch der Internationalen Buchwissenschaftlichen Gesellschaft 1 (2011)
Die digitale Bibliothek
2011. Ca. 240 Seiten, br
ISBN 978-3-447-06485-9
Ca. € 39,80 (D) / sFr 69,–

Leipziger Jahrbuch zur Buchgeschichte 19 (2010)
2011. 420 Seiten, 49 Abb., 2 Tabellen, gb
ISBN 978-3-447-06486-6
€ 59,– (D) / sFr 101,–

Melanie Grimm, Claudia Kleine-Tebbe, Ad Stijnman
Lichtspiel und Farbenpracht
Entwicklungen des Farbdrucks 1500–1800
Aus den Beständen der Herzog August Bibliothek
Wolfenbütteler Hefte 29
2011. 108 Seiten, 62 Abb., br
ISBN 978-3-447-06457-6
€ 14,80 (D) / sFr 26,70

Christine Haug, Winfried Schröder, Franziska Mayer (Hg.)
Geheimliteratur und Geheimbuchhandel in Europa im 18. Jahrhundert
Wolfenbütteler Schriften zur Geschichte des Buchhandels 47
2011. Ca. 292 Seiten, 11 Abb., gb
ISBN 978-3-447-06478-1
Ca. € 79,– (D) / sFr 134,–

Carsten Wurm (Hg.)
Neue Jubelrufe aus Bücherstapeln
Widmungsexemplare aus dem Besitz von Sammlern
Ein Almanach
Herausgegeben im Auftrag der Pirckheimer Gesellschaft
2011. 172 Seiten, 63 Abb., gb
ISBN 978-3-447-06207-7
€ 58,– (D) / sFr 99,–

HARRASSOWITZ VERLAG · WIESBADEN
www.harrassowitz-verlag.de · verlag@harrassowitz.de

Orient · Slavistik · Osteuropa · Bibliothek · Buch · Kultur

Handbuch Buchverschluss und Buchbeschlag

Terminologie und Geschichte im deutschsprachigen Raum, in den Niederlanden und Italien vom Frühen Mittelalter bis in die Gegenwart

Von Georg Adler mit Zeichnungen von Joachim Krauskopf

2010. 4°. 256 S., 923 farbige Abb., 169 techn. Zeichnungen, geb., 98,– EUR (978-3-89500-752-1)

Der vorliegende Band schafft eine notwendige standardisierte Terminologie für Buchverschlüsse und Buchbeschläge, die eine eindeutige Kommunikation zwischen Einbandforschern, Bibliothekaren, Restauratoren, Sammlern und Antiquaren auf Grundlage exakt definierter Begriffe – auch im internationalen Rahmen – ermöglicht. Im ersten Teil des Buches entwickelt Georg Adler eine Terminologie, die auf Konstruktion und Funktion des Buchverschlusses/Buchbeschlages beruht. Über 140 technische Zeichnungen stellen die verschiedenen Verschluss- und Beschlagtypen vor.

Der zweite Teil präsentiert Buchverschlüsse und Buchbeschläge in über 750 Fotos, beschreibt sie ausführlich und ordnet sie den verschiedenen Epochen vom 8. bis zum 20. Jahrhundert zu.

Für die Praxis unerlässlich sind die detaillierten Anhänge des Bandes. Übersichten über die Verschlusstypen und die Beschlagformen erlauben deren schnelle Zuordnung. Weitere Listen stellen die neu definierten Begriffe den bereits aus der Literatur bekannten gegenüber und nennen ihre niederländischen, englischen, französischen und italienischen Äquivalente.

Reichert Verlag Wiesbaden
www.reichert-verlag.de

Venator & Hanstein
Buch- und Graphikauktionen

Bücher · Autographen · Manuskripte · Zeichnungen · Alte, Moderne und Zeitgenössische Graphik

Auktionen im Frühjahr und im Herbst. Einlieferungen sind jederzeit willkommen

Neunte deutsche Bibel. Nürnberg bei Anton Koberger, 1483. Verkauft für € 74.000,-

Cäcilienstraße 48 · 50667 Köln · Tel. 0221–257 54 19 · Fax 257 55 26 · www.venator-hanstein.de

Einbandmaterial
CANOSO 0262
in frechen Farben.

buchleinen up to date

Bamberger Kaliko

Ein Buchleinen aus hochwertiger, feinfädiger Baumwolle, das durch eine besondere Beschichtung seine charakterstarke Oberfläche erhält. Canoso wirkt in traditionellen und leuchtend modischen Tönen gleichermaßen ausdrucksstark.

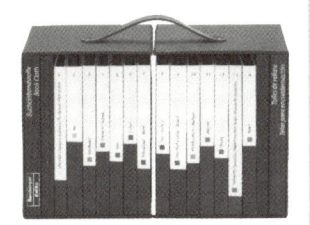

Bamberger Kaliko GmbH
Kronacher Straße 59
96052 Bamberg
Telefon +49 (0)951 4099-165
Fax +49 (0)951 4099-176
info@bamberger-kaliko.de
www.bamberger-kaliko.de

Ein Statement für Erfolg:
Weltweit mehr als 130.000 Schnellschneider

Als selbständiges Familienunternehmen hat sich POLAR in den letzten 100 Jahren zum Weltmarktführer für Schnellschneider und Schneidsysteme entwickelt.

Erfahren Sie mehr über POLAR unter
www.polar-mohr.com

distributed by
HEIDELBERG

POLAR
...EINFACH NÄHER DRAN.

REISS & SOHN
Godebert M. Reiss · Clemens Reiss
Buch- und Kunstantiquariat · Auktionen

Adelheidstr. 2, 61462 Königstein/Taunus
Tel. 06174 / 92 72 0 · Fax 06174 / 92 72 49
reiss@reiss-sohn.de · www.reiss-sohn.de

Auktionen im Frühjahr und im Herbst

Kataloge auf Anfrage oder im Internet

unter www.reiss-sohn.de

Einlieferungen jederzeit erbeten

Hieronymus, Epistolae. Mainz, Peter Schöffer, 7. September 1470
Auf Pergament gedruckt. In einem Einband von Derome le Jeune

Landeshauptstadt München
Referat für Bildung und Sport

Ausbildung

- einjährige Vollzeitausbildung
- Prüfung in allen vier Teilen der Meisterprüfung Handwerk

Besondere Highlights

- professionelles und zeitgemäßes Unterrichtsangebot
- Workshops unter der Leitung internationaler Experten

Workshopreihe „Buchbindermeister auf Europa vorbereiten 2011"

Francois Brindeau, Ana Ruiz-Larrea, Paris: Französischer Lederband
Edgard Claes, Brüssel: Stilkunde moderner Einbandkünstler
Markus Janssens, Neuss: Reparaturtechniken
Claude Ribal, Paris: Techniken des Handvergoldens
Christiane Kubias, München: Buntpapiertechniken
Olav Nie, Inning a. A.: Einbandtechniken Pergamentband

- Kurs Maschinentechnik mit praxisorientierten Exkursionen zu Maschinenherstellern ins In- und Ausland
- kaufmännische Grundlagen in Kalkulation, Buchführung und Rechnungswesen

Weitere Informationen unter www.senefelder.musin.de

Städtische Meisterschule für das Buchbindehandwerk

Berufliches Schulzentrum Alois Senefelder
Pranckhstraße 2, 80335 München

Böttcher Systems

» Bewahre das Gute aus der Tradition und schaffe das Neue aus der eigenen Stärke «

Mit diesem Leitmotiv hat sich Böttcher über mehr als 285 Jahre entwickelt. Mit Druckwalzen, Drucktüchern und Druckchemikalien sorgen wir für ein brilliantes Druckbild.

Mit schnellen Lieferungen oder mit all unserem Sachverstand sind wir für Sie da. Das wissen bereits 80.000 Kunden weltweit und verlassen sich auf unser Team.

Unsere Größten. Unsere Zeitung.

www.allgemeine-zeitung.de

Allgemeine Zeitung
Unsere Zeitung!

PROFITABEL **UND** PERSÖNLICH

EFFIZIENT **UND** VERLOCKEND

ZIELGERICHTET **UND** RELEVANT

EINFACH **UND** LEICHT ZUGÄNGLICH

WENDIG **UND** FESSELND

EINE PERFEKTE VERBINDUNG ERFORDERT MEHR ALS TECHNOLOGIE. SIE ERFORDERT EINEN PARTNER.

Es ist Zeit für Lösungen, die den Ansprüchen von Menschen und den Zielen Ihres Unternehmens gerecht werden. Für Ideen, die Sie profitabler und effizienter machen. Für Innovationen, die Ihnen mehr Möglichkeiten bieten, ohne dass Sie Zugeständnisse machen müssen. Und für integrierte Workflow-Lösungen, die insgesamt für reibungslosere betriebliche Abläufe sorgen. Ob Sie im Verpackungs-, Akzidenz- oder Verlags- und Illustrationsdruck, in der datengesteuerten Kommunikation oder im Document Imaging tätig sind, wenn Sie die Verbindung mit Kodak suchen, erhalten Sie mehr als nur Spitzentechnologie. Sie gewinnen einen Partner, der Ihnen helfen kann, mehr und neues Geschäft zu generieren.

Es ist Zeit für Sie **UND** Kodak

kodak.com/go/connect

Kodak

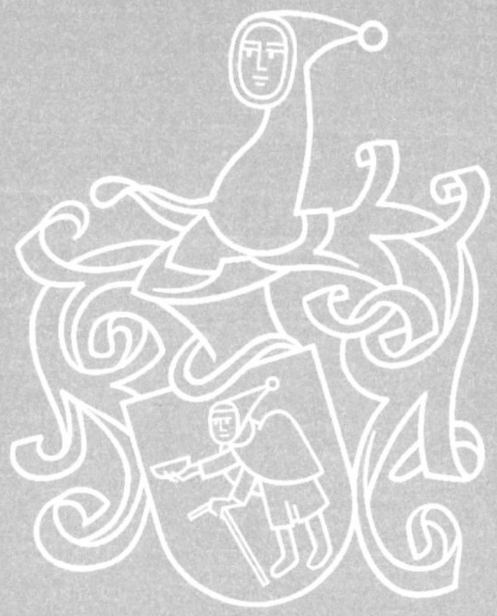